THE CAMBRIDGE HANDBOOK OF LABOR AND DEMOCRACY

We are currently witnessing some of the greatest challenges to democratic regimes since the 1930s, with democratic institutions losing ground in numerous countries throughout the world. At the same time, organized labor has been under assault worldwide, with steep declines in union density rates. In this timely handbook, scholars in law, political science, history, and sociology explore the role of organized labor and the working class in the historical construction of democracy. They analyze recent patterns of democratic erosion, examining its relationship to the political weakening of organized labor and, in several cases, the political alliances forged by workers in contexts of nationalist or populist political mobilization. The volume breaks new ground in providing cross-regional perspectives on labor and democracy in the United States, Europe, Latin America, Africa, and Asia. Beyond academia, this volume is essential reading for policymakers and practitioners concerned with the relationship between labor and democracy.

ANGELA B. CORNELL is a Clinical Professor at Cornell Law School and founding director of the Labor Law Clinic. Her teaching, practice, and scholarship focus on domestic and international labor law, business and human rights. Her research has been published in a number of journals, and her analysis has appeared in *The New York Times*, *The Economist*, and *The Washington Post*, as well as heard on BBC and NPR.

MARK BARENBERG is the Isador and Seville Sulzbacher Professor of Law at Columbia University and Director of the Columbia Program on Labor Law and Political Economy. He has taught at the universities of Yale, Harvard, Tokyo, Beijing, Rome, Cologne, and the European University Institute.

T0384870

The Cambridge Handbook of Labor and Democracy

Edited by

ANGELA B. CORNELL

Cornell University

MARK BARENBERG

Columbia University

CAMBRIDGE
UNIVERSITY PRESS

Shaftesbury Road, Cambridge CB2 8EA, United Kingdom

One Liberty Plaza, 20th Floor, New York, NY 10006, USA

477 Williamstown Road, Port Melbourne, VIC 3207, Australia

314–321, 3rd Floor, Plot 3, Splendor Forum, Jasola District Centre, New Delhi – 110025, India

103 Penang Road, #05–06/07, Visioncrest Commercial, Singapore 238467

Cambridge University Press is part of Cambridge University Press & Assessment,
a department of the University of Cambridge.

We share the University's mission to contribute to society through the pursuit of
education, learning and research at the highest international levels of excellence.

www.cambridge.org
Information on this title: www.cambridge.org/9781009374705

DOI: 10.1017/9781108885362

First published 2022
First paperback edition 2023

A catalogue record for this publication is available from the British Library

Library of Congress Cataloging-in-Publication data
NAMES: Cornell, Angela B., 1961- editor. Barenberg, Mark, editor.
TITLE: The Cambridge handbook of labor and democracy edited by Angela B. Cornell, Cornell University, New York;
   Mark Barenberg, Columbia University, New York.
DESCRIPTION: Cambridge, United Kingdom ; New York, NY Cambridge University Press, 2022. Series Cambridge law
   handbooks Includes bibliographical references.
IDENTIFIERS: LCCN 2021024732 (print) LCCN 202102473 (ebook) ISBN 9781108839884 (hardback) ISBN 9781108885362
   (epub)
SUBJECTS: LCSH Labor laws and legislation–United States. Industrial relations–Political aspects–United States. Labor
   laws and legislation–United States. Industrial relations–Political aspects–United States.
CLASSIFICATION: LCC KF3319.A2 C36 2022 (print) LCC KF3319.A2 (ebook) DDC 344.7301–dc23
LC record available at https://lccn.loc.gov/2021024732
LC ebook record available at https://lccn.loc.gov/2021024733

ISBN   978-1-108-83988-4   Hardback
ISBN   978-1-009-37470-5   Paperback

Contents

Contributors

Mark Anner is a professor of labor and employment relations at the Pennsylvania State University. He holds a PhD in Government from Cornell University and a master's degree in Latin American Studies from Stanford University. He has written on international labor solidarity, labor law reform in Latin America, and workers' rights in global supply chains. He is the recipient of the 2019 Labor and Employment Relations Association (LERA) Susan C. Eaton Outstanding Scholar-Practitioner Award. Before becoming an academic, he lived for over a decade in Nicaragua, El Salvador, and Brazil, where he conducted research and worked with labor rights organizations.

Mark Barenberg is Isador and Seville Sulzbacher Professor of Law at Columbia University, and Director of the Columbia Program on Labor Law and Political Economy. His research and teaching are in the fields of US and international labor law, constitutional law, legal theory, democratic theory, and political economy. He has published in many law reviews and anthologies, and taught at the universities of Yale, Harvard, Tokyo, Beijing, Rome, and Cologne, and the European University Institute. He earned his AB at Harvard College, his MSc at the London School of Economics, and his JD at Harvard Law School, where he was editor of the *Harvard Law Review*.

Chanda Chungu is a lecturer at the University of Zambia. He obtained both his Bachelor of Laws (LLB) and Master of Laws (LLM) degrees in Commercial and Labor Law from the University of Cape Town, as well as a second master's degree from the University of Oxford. His research interests are in labor law, industrial relations, and administrative and constitutional law. He has published several books and peer-reviewed articles in these areas. He was previously a teaching assistant and junior lecturer at the University of Cape Town as well as a researcher for the International Labor Organisation and the World Bank.

Angela B. Cornell is a clinical professor at Cornell Law School and founding director of the Labor Law Clinic, which is committed to providing legal representation that advances freedom of association. Her teaching, practice, and scholarship focus on domestic and international labor law and business and human rights. Before joining faculty in 2005, she was a partner in a union-side labor and employment law firm and served as labor commissioner in the state of New Mexico. Her research has been published in a number of outlets and her opinions referenced by the media, including *The New York Times, Economist, BBC, Ms. Magazine, Washington Post,* and *NPR*.

Deborah Dinner is a professor at Cornell Law School and previously held positions at Washington University in St. Louis School of Law and Emory University School of Law. She is a legal historian of work and labor, gender and sexuality, and capitalism and the welfare state in the twentieth-century United States. Her scholarship analyzes the interaction between social movements, political culture, and legal change. She is the author of *The Sex Equality Dilemma: Work, Family, and Legal Change in Neoliberal America* (forthcoming, Cambridge University Press).

Cynthia Estlund is the Catherine A. Rein Professor at the New York University School of Law. Her new book is *Automating the Future: Why and How to Save and Spread Work in a World with Less of It* (forthcoming, Oxford University Press). She has published widely on the law and regulation of work, including three earlier books – *A New Deal for China's Workers?* (Harvard University Press, 2017); *Regoverning the Workplace: From Self-Regulation to Co-Regulation* (Yale University Press, 2010); and *Working Together: How Workplace Bonds Strengthen a Diverse Democracy* (Oxford University Press, 2003) – and more than sixty articles, book chapters, reviews, and essays, and two coedited volumes.

Keith D. Ewing has been professor of public law at King's College London since 1989, and before then held positions at the Universities of Edinburgh (1978–1983) and Cambridge (1983–1989). He has had visiting appointments in Australia, Canada, and Spain. Professor Ewing is president of the Institute of Employment Rights, and vice president of the International Centre for Trade Union Rights, both of which are UK-based trade union–funded think tanks. He is also president of the Campaign for Trade Union Freedom, and writes widely on labor law and related issues. Other roles include legal editor of *International Union Rights*.

Anibel Ferus-Comelo teaches and directs the Labor Studies program at the University of California, Berkeley. Her research interests focus on labor standards, gender, migration, international political economy, and worker power in global supply chains. She has supported the rights of low-paid, migrant workers through unions and workers' centers for twenty-five years in the USA, the UK, and India. Before coming to Berkeley, she worked in the Indian labor movement as an educator, researcher, and policy analyst for over ten years. Her expertise lies in building effective research and service-learning partnerships that inspire and connect students from diverse backgrounds to the labor movement.

Paul Frymer is a professor of politics at Princeton University. He is the author of three books, including *Black and Blue: African Americans, the Labor Movement, and the Decline of the Democratic Party* (Princeton University Press, 2008).

Charlotte Garden is a professor at Seattle University School of Law. Her teaching and scholarship focus on the intersection of labor unions, labor law, and the Constitution, with an emphasis on how US constitutional law stymies unions' and workers' participation in electoral politics. Her articles have appeared in the *University of Pennsylvania Law Review*, the *Emory Law Journal*, and the *Boston University Law Review*, among others. She is also a co-author of two of the leading casebooks in labor and employment law, and her analysis for practitioners and non-academic audiences has appeared in outlets such as *SCOTUSblog*, *The Atlantic*, and *NBCThink*.

Jacob M. Grumbach is an assistant professor of political science at the University of Washington and a faculty associate with the Harry Bridges Center for Labor Studies. Grumbach's research focuses broadly on the political economy of the United States, with an emphasis on public policy, racial and economic inequality, American federalism, and statistical methods.

Sarita Gupta is the director of the Future of Work(ers) Program at the Ford Foundation, which is focused on increasing the voice and influence of all workers, particularly those with the least power historically, in reimagining labor and social policies. Sarita joined the foundation with more than twenty years of experience working to expand people's ability to come together to improve their workplaces, their communities, and their lives. She has expertise in policy advocacy, organizing, and building partnerships, having served as the executive director of Jobs with Justice and co-director of Caring Across Generations.

Bill Ong Hing is a professor of law and migration studies at the University of San Francisco. He is the founder and general counsel of the Immigrant Legal Resource Center and directs the USF Immigration & Deportation Defense Clinic. Professor Hing teaches immigration law & policy, migration studies, and rebellious lawyering. His books include *American Presidents, Deportations, and Human Rights Violations* (2019); *Immigration Law and Social Justice* (2021); *Ethical Borders – NAFTA, Globalization and Mexican Migration* (2010); and *Deporting Our Souls – Values, Morality, and Immigration Policy* (2006). He was co-counsel in the Supreme Court asylum precedent-setting case INS v. *Cardoza-Fonseca* (1987).

Lauren Jacobs is the executive director of PowerSwitch Action (formerly Partnership for Working Families) a national network of local power building organizations that bring together community, labor, faith, racial justice, and environmental justice movements into powerful coalitions. Originally born and raised in New York City, Lauren has lived in cities across the USA, where she has organized textile, janitorial, security, and restaurant workers into powerful multi-racial formations. For twenty-five years she has developed and executed effective strategies to build long-term power with working people via local and national campaigns. A believer in the transformational possibilities of multi-racial, feminist democracy, Lauren has shared her dreams and analysis in *Boston Review* and *Next City*.

Evance Kalula is chairperson of the ILO Committee on Freedom of Association (CFA), a position to which he was appointed in June 2018. He is also Emeritus Professor of Law at the University of Cape Town, Honorary Professor of Law at the University of Rwanda and Fellow of Stellenbosch Institute for Advanced Study. He holds a number of degrees in law, including a PhD. He was educated at the University of Zambia School of Law; King's College, London; Balliol College, Oxford (where he was a Rhodes Scholar); and the University of Warwick School of Law. His areas of teaching and research interests are international and comparative labor law, international trade, regional integration, and social protection.

Jaok Kwon is assistant professor at the Center for East Asian Studies at Heidelberg University, Germany. Her research interests include the sociology of development, labor and gender, economic elites in East Asia, and transnational labor migration. She teaches courses on Asian capitalism, labor and gender, labor market and industrial relations, civil society, and social movements in East Asia. Currently, she is working on a project examining the transnational labor migration of highly skilled workers in information technology industry from East Asia to Europe. Her work on socioeconomic issues in East Asia has appeared in *Gender Studies*, *Labor History*, *International Journal of Japanese Sociology*, and *Korea Observer*, among other publications.

Stephen Lerner is a labor and community organizer and architect of the groundbreaking Justice for Janitors campaign and served for many years on the Service Employees International Union's executive board. He is a leading critic of Wall Street and the increased financialization of the US economy. Lerner argues the growing power and influence of the finance sector has led to record wealth inequality. He is a senior fellow at the Kalmanovitz Initiative for Labor and the Working Poor at Georgetown University.

Nelson Lichtenstein, research professor at the University of California, Santa Barbara, is the author or editor of sixteen books, including a biography of the labor leader Walter Reuther and *State of the Union: A Century of American Labor*. With Roman Huret and Jean-Christian Vinel, he is the editor of *Capitalism Contested: The New Deal and Its Legacies* (2020). Other publications include *Achieving Workers' Rights in the Global Economy*, edited with Richard Appelbaum, and *The Retail Revolution: How Wal-Mart Created a Brave New World of Business*. Lichtenstein is currently writing a history of economic policymaking in the administration of Bill Clinton. He writes for *Dissent*, *Jacobin*, *New Labor Forum*, and *American Prospect*.

Risa L. Lieberwitz is a professor of labor and employment law in the Cornell University School of Industrial and Labor Relations (ILR School), where she has been on the faculty since 1982. Since July 2014, she has also held an appointment as General Counsel of the American Association of University Professors (AAUP), and serves as a member of AAUP Committee A on Academic Freedom and Tenure. From 1979 to 1982, she was a field attorney in Region 10 of the National Labor Relations Board.

Wilma B. Liebman was designated by President Obama as chairman of the National Labor Relations Board on January 20, 2009. She served as chairperson until August 2011, when her third term expired. Since then, she has served in various consulting roles and on several boards and has taught at several universities. Ms. Liebman was first appointed to be a member of the NLRB by President Clinton and was twice reappointed by President Bush. Earlier, Ms. Liebman served as deputy director of the Federal Mediation and Conciliation Service and as counsel with the Bricklayers and Allied Craftsmen and the International Brotherhood of Teamsters.

Julia López López is a professor of labor law and social security law at the Pompeu Fabra University in Barcelona and senior researcher in the Research Group for Labor and Social Security Law, GREDTISS. She is the author of books and articles on comparative, European Union, and Spanish labor law. Much of her work deals with multilevel legal dynamics and with interactions between protest, democratic governance, and legal institutions. Among her most recent publications are *Collective Bargaining and Collective Action: Labor Agency and Governance in the Twenty-First Century?* and, with Alexandre de le Court, *When the Corporate Veil is Lifted: Synergies of Public Labor Institutions and Platform Workers* in *King's Law Journal*.

Joseph A. McCartin is professor of history and founding executive director of the Kalmanovitz Initiative for Labor & the Working Poor (KI) at Georgetown University. He works at the intersection of labor, politics, and public policy. He has written prize-winning books, including *Labor's Great War: The Struggle for Industrial Democracy and the Origins of Modern American Labor Relations* and *Collision Course: Ronald Reagan, the Air Traffic Controllers, and the Strike that Changed America*; edited several volumes on labor and social history; authored dozens of articles and book chapters; and held numerous fellowships, including two from the National Endowment for Humanities.

Timothy J. Minchin is a professor of North American history at La Trobe University in Melbourne, Australia. He received his PhD from the University of Cambridge and previously taught in the UK. He has published widely on the post-1945 United States, particularly in the fields of civil rights history, labor history, and industrial history. His books include *Labor Under Fire: A History of the AFL-CIO Since 1979* and *Empty Mills: The Fight Against Imports and the Decline of the US Textile Industry*. His most recent book is *America's Other Automakers: A History of the Foreign-Owned Automotive Sector in the United States* (Athens: University of Georgia Press, 2021).

Thomas Ogorzalek is the author of *The Cities on the Hill: How Urban Institutions Transformed American Politics* (Oxford University Press 2018), and co-director of the Chicago Democracy Project.

David Ost is professor of political science at Hobart and William Smith Colleges in Geneva, New York. He has written widely on east European and particularly Polish politics and society, with a focus on labor, class, democracy, and the new right. His books include *Solidarity and the Politics of Anti-Politics*, *Workers After Workers' States*, *The Defeat of Solidarity: Anger and Politics in Postcommunist Europe*, and the edited collection *Class After Communism*, which appeared as a special issue of the journal *East European Politics and Societies*. He is currently working on a project about workers and fascism, past and present.

Kenneth M. Roberts is the Richard J. Schwartz Professor of Government at Cornell University. His research is focused on party systems, populism, social movements, and the politics of inequality in Latin America and beyond. He is the author of *Changing Course in Latin America: Party Systems in the Neoliberal Era* (Cambridge University Press) and *Deepening Democracy? The Modern Left and Social Movements in Chile and Peru* (Stanford University Press). He is also the co-editor of *The Resurgence of the Latin American Left*, *The Diffusion of Social Movements*, and *Democratic Resilience: Can the United States Withstand Rising Polarization?*

Gabriel Winant is assistant professor of history at the University of Chicago. His first book, *The Next Shift: The Fall of Manufacturing and the Rise of Health Care in Rust Belt America*, was recently published by Harvard University Press.

Acknowledgments

We wish to thank Cornell Law School and University for their support, which was instrumental to this book project. This volume is the outgrowth of a workshop at Cornell University Law School in May 2019 that explored broadly the topic of labor and challenges to democracy. The workshop was co-sponsored by the Cornell Law School Labor Law Clinic and Cornell University's Government Department, Latin American Studies Program, Institute for African Development, and School of Industrial and Labor Relations. The workshop received additional support from Cornell's Berger International Legal Studies Program and Law and Society Minor. We appreciate the meaningful contributions of the workshop participants to this project and their enthusiastic support when it was at a nascent stage.

It has been a privilege to work with the accomplished scholars who contributed chapters to this volume. Their insightful contributions push the discourse about labor and democracy forward at a particularly critical time.

Thanks also go to Cornell Law student Kaitlyn Marasi for her assistance on many of the chapters in this volume, particularly on citation uniformity. At Cambridge University Press, much appreciation goes to the senior editor, Matt Gallaway, for his confidence in the merits of the proposal, and to the wonderful staff who moved our work along so helpfully. Angela also wishes to express appreciation to the Institute for Advanced Study for the opportunity to do work related to this book project.

Angela extends a special dedication to her partner, Ken, for his substantial support for this project from the very beginning, and their three children, Natalia, Alejandra, and Tristan, for their tolerance during the project's demanding periods, and for their uplifting presence in her life.

Mark expresses boundless gratitude to his wife, Laura, and children, Otto and Evie, for the gift of their love and support, and for the sparkling sunlight they shone throughout the difficult and busy year of the pandemic, when work on this book was most intensive.

Introduction

Angela B. Cornell

We've learned from labor the meaning of power.
Dr. Martin Luther King, Jr.

This volume comes together at a time when democracy on a global scale is facing its greatest challenges in eighty years and is under siege in every region of the world by autocratic leaders and parties. After thirty years of steady democratic advances in much of the world during the latter decades of the twentieth century (Huntington 1991; O'Donnell & Schmitter 1986; Roberts 2016), Freedom House has documented a decline in civil and political rights in both newly established and long-standing democratic regimes since the early 2000s, characterizing this trend as "democracy in retreat" on the global stage (Freedom House 2019: 1). This downward spiral continued and intensified over the second decade of the twenty-first century, with autocratic leaders pursuing unchecked power and demonizing political and cultural minorities, producing destabilizing effects around the globe (V-Dem Institute 2021).

The revival of authoritarian and even fascist political currents, including in some of the world's most advanced, long-standing democracies, helped to motivate this project's focus on labor rights and the prospects for democracy. Democracy's global retreat has coincided with an erosion of the organizational and political strength of labor unions in much of the world, but the relationship between these two empirical trends has yet to receive systematic scholarly attention. Scholars have extensively explored how democratic erosion or "backsliding" is related to growing political polarization (Haggard & Kaufman 2021; Levitsky & Ziblatt 2018; Lieberman et al. 2021); the rise of "illiberal" populist, nationalist, and religious currents (Mudde & Rovira Kaltwasser 2012; Müller 2016; Zakaria 2007); racial and ethnic antagonisms (Bartels 2020; Parker & Barreto 2013); and the erosion of Western liberal hegemony on the global stage (Diamond 2019; Levitsky & Way 2020). To date, however, scholars have largely neglected to examine how democratic regress has been fostered or conditioned by the synchronous weakening of organized labor as a political force, particularly in an era of unfettered global markets, highly concentrated wealth, and politically empowered private capital.

This relative neglect is especially striking given the long tradition of scholarship exploring the role of organized labor and the working class in the historical construction of democracy (Collier 1999; Rueschemeyer et al. 1992; Seidman 1994). Likewise, there is an extensive literature on the efforts of labor unions to deepen or extend democratic practices to broader spheres of social and economic relationships (Castles 1978; Huber & Stephens 2001).

Democracy's retreat in recent times thus calls for a reexamination of labor's role in historical and contemporary democratization struggles, as well as its role in processes of democratic erosion or backsliding. If labor has been – and often remains – a central figure in struggles for democracy around the world, has it also been a stalwart defender of democracy against autocratic challengers? Is democratic erosion tied to the political weakening of organized labor, and is it associated with the emasculation of labor rights? Or are there conditions under which labor's political alliances and its intersection with racial, ethnic, or nationalist politics undercut its democratizing potential?

Perhaps most important, what are the prospects for labor to play a constructive role in securing both political democracy and social and economic citizenship rights in the contemporary global arena? Democratic erosion is not a one-way street, and it is hardly an uncontested process. Efforts to restrict or dismantle democratic practices are invariably met with countervailing pressures to protect or even expand democratic rights and social inclusion, as contemporary US politics vividly demonstrate. So conceived, crises of democracy can also be seen as singular opportunities to extend its reach, incorporating new actors into the democratic arena or expanding the range of citizenship rights.

This volume addresses these questions from a range of disciplinary perspectives. Its interdisciplinary focus brings together a rich and varied collection of contributions from scholars in the fields of law, political science, history, and sociology. It also includes international and cross-regional comparative perspectives in order to highlight the global character of challenges to labor rights and democracy. It examines these questions not only in advanced industrial societies that are historic – if increasingly contested – bastions of democracy, but also in developing regions where democratic institutions are more recently and tenuously established, or still in gestation.

The chapters are complementary in their exploration of these challenges, but they offer different perspectives as well as critical insights into what can sometimes be a complex relationship between labor and democracy. Underlying themes throughout the chapters include class and economic inequality; capitalism and its turn toward neoliberalism; the implications of industrial democracy for workers' economic and political rights; systemic racism and the intersection between class, racial, ethnic, and gender inequalities; the destabilizing impact of the Covid-19 pandemic on the working class; and the complex relationship between the erosion of labor rights and democratic institutions. The book is divided into five parts: (I) Labor and Democracy: Theory and Practice; (II) History, Politics, and Law; (III) Labor, Diversity, and Democracy; (IV) Country and Regional Perspectives; and (V) Labor and Democracy Sectoral Case Studies: Platform Workers, Higher Education, and the Care Industry.

LABOR AND DEMOCRACY: THEORY AND PRACTICE

Part I of the book provides a theoretical grounding for the thematic parts that follow. This part maps out the most important analytical dimensions along which labor's relationship to democracy are dissected in this book, moving from the workplace to broader spheres of social and economic relationships, national political regimes, and international law. Together, the chapters in Part I illustrate the multifaceted character of labor's role in the struggle to democratize political as well as economic institutions.

Mark Barenberg tackles a new labor vision in Chapter 1. His chapter reinforces many of the arguments made in subsequent chapters, but it also stands in some tension with others. He argues that labor's power to strengthen both industrial democracy and political democracy depends on the structure of much more than the field of workplace law as conventionally defined. While most analyses of the legal construction of worker power – and proposals for legal reform – focus on the law of collective bargaining, employment conditions, and social insurance, Barenberg looks not only to those but also to components of the law of domestic and international finance, national security, the Constitution, communication, advertising, zoning, education, and others. His broad "new labor law" would bring all those components within its scope and generate radical proposals for legal reconstruction to promote worker empowerment in democratic capitalist and democratic socialist regimes.

In Chapter 2, Kenneth Roberts provides additional theoretical grounding through a multidimensional approach to labor's relationship to democracy. Scholars have long debated whether and how labor contributes to the construction of democratic regimes and the expansion of social citizenship rights, but recent patterns of democratic backsliding make it abundantly clear that democratic advances are subject to reversal. As such, it is imperative to interrogate labor's role in the defense of democratic rights and liberties, and not merely the introduction or expansion of those rights. Roberts calls for a view that explores labor's role in (1) constructing democratic regimes, (2) deepening democracy by expanding social citizenship rights, and (3) defending democracy against its adversaries and authoritarian currents in society. This framework facilitates analysis of democratic struggles around the world, and provides leverage to examine potential linkages between backsliding and the generalized weakening of organized labor.

In Chapter 3, Angela Cornell focuses on the juxtaposition of labor's exalted place in international human rights law with its subordinate position in domestic law, particularly in the USA, which fails to comply with widely accepted freedom of association norms. In international human rights instruments and jurisprudence, labor unions hold a special position, and freedom of association is the critical foundational right upon which other rights and interests are advanced. Furthermore, in social science literature, labor unions are generally recognized to have pro-democracy attributes. The chapter reviews labor containment under authoritarian regimes and finds parallels with the treatment of labor in the USA, and questions why labor policy is not used to strengthen democratic institutions when they are at their weakest point since the 1930s.

In Chapter 4, Keith Ewing focuses on the characteristics of new forms of populist government and the emergence of illiberal types of democracy that violate conventional democratic norms, such as civil rights and liberties or the rights of political opposition. Ewing examines the consequences of "illiberal democracy" for trade unions both politically and industrially. He uses the example of the United Kingdom to dig deeper into the consequences of illiberal democracy and economic liberalism.

HISTORY, POLITICS, AND LAW

Threads that run through the chapters in Part II are the linkages between industrial democracy and political democracy, labor's diminishing bargaining power, and the capacity and implications of expanded collective bargaining. These US-focused chapters describe the unraveling of the social compact, disturbing levels of inequality, and the new Gilded Age. They also suggest some tangible ways to recalibrate the balance between capital and labor in order to advance social solidarity and a more progressive vision of what constitutes a good society. A dramatic and creative expansion of collective bargaining to substantially advance the interests of working people is part of the solution, one aided by Charlotte Garden's proposal to expand the interpretation of the First Amendment to better protect the collective rights of workers.

We begin Part II with Chapter 5, by Nelson Lichtenstein, which discusses new forms of sectoral bargaining that have their origins in the wage determinations of the Progressive Era. Lichtenstein provides useful examples from the past and present as he develops a persuasive argument for bolstering working-class institutions. It is difficult to imagine a truly revitalized labor movement without some sectoral bargaining, which makes the topic critical for wider consideration. He emphasizes that the far-reaching impact of sectoral bargaining across an occupation or industry can distribute higher working standards regardless of the attitude of workers or employers. The chapter offers a practical path forward to lift the dismal working conditions of wide swaths of working people while advancing social solidarity.

The broader potential of collective bargaining is also contemplated in Chapter 6, where Stephen Lerner, Joseph McCartin, Sarita Gupta, and Lauren Jacobs discuss a bargaining approach to strengthen communities. Like Lichtenstein's proposal, this chapter contemplates bargaining with an impact that is much broader than a particular worksite. This creative bargaining strategy can help address some of the festering problems that have been building for decades, including the fraying of the social fabric affecting working people particularly in communities of color, which they frame as an existential threat to democracy. Their broader vision is to help build a twenty-first-century economy.

Collective bargaining as a mechanism for industrial democracy is explored historically in Chapter 7, by Wilma Liebman. She reminds us that 100 years ago leaders considered labor rights to be the "constitutive moral, political, and social dilemma of the new industrial order." Over a century later we revisit the same issues and dramatic parallels with a return to the Gilded Age of wealth and power. The New Deal labor reforms delivered a measure of industrial and economic democracy for working people, creating a broad middle class and widely expanded political participation. However, these early gains have receded over time, particularly over the last forty years, with the law's ossification and the corrosive impact of corporate dominance in the workplace and public life. Liebman reminds us that no other major American legal regime has been so paralyzed in the past without being updated to more effectively deal with decades of changes in the nature of work. But, she sees reason for optimism in the momentum of recent collective activity and the courageous labor struggles, including the wave of recent worker protests of public sector teachers and tech workers, and the many examples of essential workers facing the Covid-19 risks who have contributed to a quarter-century high mark for work stoppages.

Tim Minchin documents the role of organized labor in the USA as an important force for democracy, providing a voice for and fighting for the interests of working people in Chapter 8. Rejecting attacks against organized labor that characterize unions as a "special interest," Minchin documents unions' role in consistently fighting for workplace health and safety, higher pay, and workplace democracy, as well as their role in advancing the political interests of working people beyond the workplace.

In Chapter 9, Charlotte Garden argues for a First Amendment interpretation that advances democratic deliberation and participation, considering the important contributions that unions make toward strengthening democratic institutions. Instead of treating unions with suspicion and disdain, she asserts that the US Supreme Court, when interpreting the First Amendment, should recognize labor unions' role in making democracy stronger and more representative. While there is a legal foundation that acknowledges and values political advocacy by labor unions on behalf of workers' interests, the judiciary, especially through recent decisions such as *Janus* v. *AFSCME*, has undermined unions' capacity, weakened freedom of association, and villainized unions.

LABOR, DIVERSITY, AND DEMOCRACY

The four chapters in Part III cover the intersection of labor with race, immigration status, and gender, and explore the broader implications for democracy. Labor unions play an important role in influencing the attitudes of their members toward diversity. As the largest mass membership organization of people of color, unions can play a critical role in advancing civil rights and racial justice, and they have the potential to bridge racial and ethnic divisions in their pursuit of economic and political interests that workers share in common. However, significant divisions along racial lines continue to persist in US society, and the labor movement has not been immune from these tensions, historically or in present times. These chapters thus tackle the critical importance of social inclusion and the relationships between class inequality, labor organization, and other forms of inequality based on race, ethnicity, and gender. They cover labor's role in bridging the divides over race, gender, and ethnicity, but also the historical exclusions by labor tied to race and immigration status.

Chapter 10, by Cynthia Estlund, lays a foundation for understanding the important contributions labor unions make toward bridging racial, ethnic, and ideological divisions within the working class. Estlund identifies the critical role unions have played in bringing heterogeneous groups of workers together to identify their common interests. She describes the density of workplace ties, which serve as a powerful unifying force that can help counter exclusionary ethno-nationalist politics and right-wing populism. Unions contribute to greater equality, but Estlund argues powerfully that they also serve as a distinctive force for an inclusive and sustainable economy. In so doing, they help strengthen political democracy.

In Chapter 11, Paul Frymer, Jacob M. Grumbach, and Thomas Ogorzalek further support the argument that unions are critically important for the advancement of civil rights and greater racial tolerance in the USA. They conclude, however, that this dynamic must be actively nurtured and advanced by labor leaders. They look at historical cases and survey data to underscore their position that union members are less likely to have racist attitudes. However, they also share the historical context of racial exclusion and white privilege that undermined class solidarity between white and black workers, particularly in the south during the Jim Crow era, and the exclusionary aspects of the National Labor Relations Act (NLRA), which does not extend legal protection to agricultural and domestic workers.

In Chapter 12, Bill Ong Hing poignantly describes the horrors of workplace raids by the US Immigration and Customs Enforcement (ICE) and the way immigrant workers are demonized and commodified. The racial implications of these raids are not given enough attention, he argues. Indeed, immigration law institutionalizes values that dehumanize, demonize, and criminalize immigrants of color, according to Hing. He goes on to connect immigration enforcement with workers' unionization efforts, examining how enforcement not only impacts undocumented workers but also undermines all workers' freedom of association – and ultimately democracy.

In Chapter 13, Deborah Dinner powerfully underscores how the failure to support care providers has undermined democratic vitality and deepened gender, race, and class inequalities, rendering the social and political fabric even more fragile. The last half a century of neoliberal policies rendered the nation ill-prepared to tackle the demands of the pandemic. She connects the exacerbation of class inequalities to populist enthusiasm for authoritarian government. Apart from threatening to devastate the nation's already fragile care infrastructure, the impact on women – particularly women of color – has been enormous, upending women's work in the home and pushing women out of the workforce and imperiling the health of essential workers and their families.

COUNTRY AND REGIONAL PERSPECTIVES

The chapters in Part IV provide comparative perspectives on labor and democracy covering Latin America, Africa, Europe, and Asia. In these countries and regions, independent labor movements were often instrumental in democratic transitions, but they continue to face an array of challenges, including the repression of trade unionists, the spread of informal and precarious forms of employment, and the expansion of platform work. Furthermore, examples of state- and employer-created organizations or coopted unions that undermine freedom of association and supplant the ability of independent unions to form and thrive exist in many areas. More recently, the harsh impact of neoliberalism on workers and the expansion of precarious work has helped to elect right-wing populists who undermine workers' freedom of association and the strength of democracies.

Latin America's tumultuous struggles with democracy cannot be analyzed well without referencing its labor movements. In Chapter 14, Mark Anner traces labor's lengthy struggle in Latin America for workers' rights, equity, and democracy through periods of corporatism, authoritarian rule, neoliberalism, and contemporary left- and right-wing populist governments. Trade unionists have suffered tremendously over the decades for their role in these struggles, and Latin America continues to be one of the most dangerous places in the world for the labor movement. Anner finds that the labor movement has had a positive impact on democracy in the region, including what he refers to as the indirect impact on reducing inequality, but he cautions that there are examples of labor being co-opted by autocratic states and political elites. However, labor's commitment to principles of liberal democracy has served to strengthen democratic institutions in the region and support national struggles for democratization.

Latin America and Africa share a number of similarities, including challenges to democratic institutions, labor market features (such as high levels of informality), and examples of labor being co-opted by autocratic states and ruling elites. The independence of labor unions is critically important for freedom of association to be realized, and it also impacts the capacity of unions to support democratic institutions. Evance Kalula and Chanda Chungu describe the ability of some African states to weaken independent unions perceived as being hostile to government by controlling and manipulating union leadership in Chapter 15. They describe the link between freedom of association and democracy as unassailable, but remind us that the independence of trade unions from both state and employer control is at the core of freedom of association. According to Kalula and Chungu, freedom of association and democracy share the same roots: liberty, independence, pluralism, and a voice in decision-making. They draw our attention to the important work of the ILO in supporting freedom of association in Africa and both industrial and political democracy, citing the ILO for the conclusion that without workers' freedom of association, "the foundations of the democratic political system will be shaken" (Curtis 2004: 89). Their chapter on labor's role as an enhancer of democratic governance in Africa places labor at the center of the struggle for democracy for decades since the movements for decolonization and political emancipation. Kalula and Chungu describe labor as being instrumental in supporting nationalist campaigns. Labor's role in deepening democracy in Africa, they note, has often been tied to social movement unionism.

In Chapter 16, David Ost looks at the relationship between workers and democracy in Poland's labor movement and analyzes how this relationship can shift over time. He begins by recounting the union movements that were leading the democratization struggles in the 1980s in Brazil, South Africa, and Poland. Tracking the shifting position of Poland's solidarity union, which started as a broad proponent of democratization during state socialism, he analyzes the shift under neoliberalism to support for the current right-wing efforts to undermine aspects of democracy. Ost develops three concepts of democracy: political, egalitarian, and formal-institutional, or Democracy I, II, and III, which he uses to analyze the shift in workers' orientation in capitalist societies, in some cases to oppose rather than support egalitarianism. Workers are increasingly being blamed for the rise of right-wing populist administrations around the globe, but Ost identifies neoliberalism and the exclusion of workers from decision-making and wealth-sharing as the root of the crisis of democracy today, primarily by generalizing a fear of insecurity, immigrants, and ethnic minorities. As Ost suggests, labor's democratic potential often hinges on its political alliances, and unions may cease to advance the democratic cause if they become politically aligned with the forces of exclusionary ethno-nationalism.

Asia is the focus of Chapters 17 and 18, the last chapters in Part IV, which cover issues of labor and democracy in India and Korea. The threat to democracy in India posed by the 2019 re-election of Narendra Modi and his hard-line Hindu supremacist and anti-labor policies is the topic of Chapter 17. India, like the USA since 2016, has been ranked as a "flawed democracy" in The Economist Intelligence Unit's Democracy Index (PTI 2020b). Chapter 17 focuses on the tremendous challenges faced by the Indian labor movement to reclaim democracy and advance the interests of the working class. India has been categorized as the "worst in the world for working people" in the ITUC Global Rights Index, and Anibel Ferus-Comelo highlights the country's brutal repression of strikes, mass dismissals, and regressive labor laws. She goes on to describe the high unemployment, precarious work, and grinding poverty, where 90 percent of workers are in the informal sector, and 18.4 million toil as bonded laborers in indentured servitude with conditions of quasi-slavery, raising issues of caste, class, gender, and religion. Nevertheless, labor pulled together what has been referred to as the largest general strike in the world in January 2020, with 250 million workers demanding improvements in labor law and enforcement. There have also been examples of success to applaud, such as the sanitation workers in Mumbai and the national domestic workers campaign. With India's unprecedented authoritarian backsliding under Modi, Ferus-Comelo sees independent unions as the antidote at the national level across industries, sectors, and companies, while social movement unionism that brings in the informal sector can help strengthen labor's defense of democracy.

Chapter 18 focuses on South Korea. Although the labor movement was the strongest driving force in the 1987 transition to democracy after more than two decades of oppressive authoritarian rule, Jaok Kwon provides a critical feminist perspective on the state of democratic unionism today and questions its representative character. The social movement unionism that was instrumental in ending authoritarian rule was a feat of class consciousness and solidarity recounted in the chapter. This independent trade union movement, according to Kwon, was a key factor in the struggle for democracy and a complete departure from the pro-government trade union federation created by the authoritarian state as a tool to obstruct the formation of an independent movement. Despite the "moral force" the independent trade union movement played in the democratic transition, Kwon describes the ways in which it has lost sight of the growing diversity of the Korean labor force, and undervalued women and marginalized workers. The Candlelight protest movement was important in the toppling of a corrupt administration in 2017, and it has been much more diverse and representative of Korean work life, incorporating those who have been most seriously impacted by neoliberalism and the fraying employment relationship between workers and Korean companies. Kwon describes how the movement has been influential in creating change using non-violent means without the more militant tactics and male-dominated culture of Korean unionism. Perhaps the movement is a model for a more inclusive and responsive labor movement that can help expand union density.

LABOR AND DEMOCRACY SECTORAL CASE STUDIES: PLATFORM WORKERS,
HIGHER EDUCATION, AND THE CARE INDUSTRY

The sectoral studies in Part V link significant labor issues in particular sectors of the economy to the corrosion of democratic institutions, providing another contextual lens for the exploration of contemporary challenges to democracy. The critical threshold question of who meets the definition of an employee for coverage of legal protections, including the right to organize collectively in many countries, surfaces in Part V. Also addressed is the expansion of the misclassification of workers as independent contractors and the challenges of identifying what entity is the employer. The plight and precariousness of platform workers is the emblematic global struggle over how to define employees in an environment dominated by technological changes and transnational capital and influence, but these issues also surface in the care industry in the USA. Both areas are occupied by low-wage and precarious workers, who are also a growing part of the labor market in higher education, which relies heavily on adjunct and temporary faculty, challenging models of shared governance and workplace democracy.

In Chapter 19, López López describes the institutional erosion of labor organizations and workers' interests, and how collective labor law as a core of social democracy has been questioned in recent decades. Labor law as a democratic institution has been transformed by an industrial relations ecosystem in which transnational firms function as more than just employers, as they are also significant political actors challenging domestic laws and the power of nation states, according to López. For platform workers often excluded from the legal infrastructure and the safety net, workers and unions have redirected their efforts using a multilevel and multimodality strategy of mobilization at the local, national, and supranational levels of protest. This mobilization includes demonstrations, negotiations, and judicial action, which have greatly improved workers' circumstances in terms of labor conditions as well as healthcare and social security.

The democratic public mission of universities is interdependent on a labor model for faculty that is based on democratic professional norms of academic freedom, tenure, due process, and collective shared governance. As Risa Lieberwitz demonstrates in Chapter 20, however, these institutional goals and structures are increasingly contested and in tension with the corporatization of universities and their use to serve the private interests of industry. Lieberwitz surveys the interconnections among democracy in the wider culture and polity, labor regimes within universities, and concentrated economic powers, and she describes the changing historical forces that tilted universities toward either public democratic or private corporate interests.

Expanding significantly in the USA, the care economy is critically important, but perpetuates inexcusably poor working conditions mainly affecting women, immigrants, and workers of color. In Chapter 21, Gabe Winant describes the unregulated and nonunion workplaces where workers have faced considerable occupational health and safety issues. Although these workers provide a vital social service for children, the elderly, the disabled, and the sick, these destabilized work settings are rife with myriad problems, not the least of which are tied to subcontracting, franchising, and misclassification. Winant describes these workplaces as being produced by the state and franchised to the private sector to carry out state functions, separating the purpose of the work from its control and administration.

CONCLUSION

At a time when democracy is threatened in every region of the globe, this volume explores the important nexus between labor and democracy from wide and varied perspectives, across different academic disciplines, geographic regions, and socioeconomic sectors. Different types of workers and workers' organizations are covered in this volume, and the intersectionality of labor movements with those based on race, gender, ethnicity, and immigration status is thoroughly examined. Historical patterns are compared and contrasted with contemporary manifestations of globalized, neoliberal capitalism and its transformative effects on labor markets, workers' movements, social inequality, and democratic institutions.

Recent events demonstrate the fragility of democracy even in countries that have had long-standing democratic traditions. The refusal of a sitting US president to accept the outcome of a legitimate election with the support of his party followed by the violent assault on the Capitol in early 2020 are jarring examples of a corroded democracy. There remains a critical need to strengthen democracy-supporting institutions, including the labor movement, which the scholarship in this volume demonstrates has enormous capacity as a force for democratization, deepening democracy, and defending democracy against authoritarian tendencies. Labor unions expand political participation, enhance the interests of working people in the political realm, lessen economic polarization, and help to build solidarity among the working class in ways that reduce support for authoritarian or ethno-nationalists parties. Also relevant to the analysis is the relationship between disempowerment in the workplace and the weakening of political democracy. Given the challenges faced by both labor and democracy in the current era, the contributions to this volume are often sobering but never despairing, and they offer grounds for hope tempered by a healthy dose of realism. Taken together, they leave little doubt that labor's historical struggles for democracy – political, social, and economic – will remain vibrant in the twenty-first century, even if they take different forms than those seen in the past. How much more the labor movement can deliver to the cause of democracy may depend on whether workers are able to fully exercise their fundamental right of freedom of association.

REFERENCES

Bartels, Larry M. 2020. "Ethnic Antagonism Erodes Republicans' Commitment to Democracy," *Proceedings of the National Academy of Sciences of the United States of America* 37, 117: 22752–22759.
Castles, Francis. 1978. *The Social-Democratic Image of Society*. London: Routledge and Kegan Paul.
Collier, Ruth Berins. 1999. *Paths toward Democracy: The Working Class and Elites in Western Europe and South America*. New York: Cambridge University Press.
Diamond, Larry. 2019. *Ill Winds: Saving Democracy from Russian Rage, Chinese Ambitions, and American Complacency*. New York: Penguin Books.
Freedom House. 2019. *Freedom in the World 2019*. Washington, DC: Freedom House. https://freedomhouse.org/sites/default/files/Feb2019_FH_FITW_2019_Report_ForWeb-compressed.pdf
Haggard, Stephan, and Robert Kaufman. 2021. *Backsliding: Democratic Regress in the Contemporary World*. New York: Cambridge University Press.
Huber, Evelyne, and John D. Stephens. 2001. *Development and the Crisis of the Welfare State: Parties and Policies in Global Markets*. Chicago: University of Chicago Press.
Huntington, Samuel P. 1991. *The Third Wave: Democratization in the Late Twentieth Century*. Norman: University of Oklahoma Press.
Levitsky, Steven, and Daniel Ziblatt. 2018. *How Democracies Die*. New York: Broadway Books.
Levitsky, Steven, and Lucan Way. 2020. "The New Competitive Authoritarianism," *Journal of Democracy* 31, 1: 51–65.
Lieberman, Robert, Suzanne Mettler, and Kenneth M. Roberts, eds. 2021. *Democratic Resilience: Can the United States Withstand Rising Polarization?* New York: Cambridge University Press.
Mudde, Cas, and Cristóbal Rovira Kaltwasser, eds. 2012. *Populism in Europe and the Americas: Threat or Corrective to Democracy?* Cambridge: Cambridge University Press.

Müller, Jan-Werner. 2016. *What Is Populism?* Philadelphia: University of Pennsylvania Press.

O'Donnell, Guillermo, and Philippe C. Schmitter. 1986. *Transitions from Authoritarian Rule: Tentative Conclusions about Uncertain Democracies.* Baltimore: Johns Hopkins University Press.

Parker, Christopher S., and Matt Barreto. 2013. "Change They Can't Believe." In: *The Tea Party and Reactionary Politics in America.* Princeton: Princeton University Press.

Roberts, Kenneth. 2016. "Democracy in the Developing World: Challenges of Survival and Significance," *Studies in Comparative International Development* 51, 1: 32–49.

Rueschemeyer, Dietrich, Evelyne Huber Stephens, and John D. Stephens. 1992. *Capitalist Development and Democracy.* Chicago: University of Chicago Press.

Seidman, Gay W. 1994. *Manufacturing Militance: Workers' Movements in Brazil and South Africa, 1970-1985.* Berkeley: University of California Press.

V-Dem Institute. 2021. *Autocratization Turns Viral: Democracy Report 2021.* Gothenburg: University of Gothenburg.

Zakaria, Fareed. 2007. *The Future of Freedom: Illiberal Democracy at Home and Abroad.* New York: W. W. Norton.

PART I

Labor and Democracy: Theory and Practice

1

A New Labor Law for Deep Democracy

From Social Democracy to Democratic Socialism

Mark Barenberg

INTRODUCTION

If our goal is to construct workplace relations that maximally empower workers and best sustain ideal forms of industrial democracy and worker-centered political democracy, how should we remake labor law? This chapter argues that the academic field of labor law, if it is to further that goal, must expand far beyond its conventional scope of studying the law of collective bargaining, the employment contract, and workplace standards.[1] And, correlatively, the political work of legal-institutional reconstruction must reach beyond the domain of the legal rules and institutions that directly shape unionization, contracting, and employment standard-setting into other legal-institutional domains not presently constructed with the goal of worker empowerment and democratic deepening in mind. The chapter applies this "new labor law" to two types of regimes: first, the US variant of social democracy – that is, the current incarnation of the New Deal regime that promotes unionization within a capitalist economic system; and second, a democratic socialist regime for a post-capitalist economy centered on fully worker-controlled enterprises.

The argument of this chapter proceeds in four sections. The first sets out the basic problem of sustaining industrial and political democracy in a capitalist economy. In order to flesh out that problem, the second offers a conceptualization of capitalist *political and economic* institutions – and of the disempowerment of workers in both the workplace and politics – that is more multi-faceted than New Deal labor law's sole focus on the institution of wage labor. The second then argues that mapping the essential *legal* infrastructure of this panoply of capitalist institutions has been undervalued by leftist labor lawyers and political economists. The purpose of expanding the scope of labor law as a field of legal *study* is, precisely, to examine how legal *rules and institutions* presently construct workplaces in ways that both promote and undermine worker power and democracy and how those rules and institutions could be reconstructed to better realize those values.

---

[1] For ease of exposition, this chapter uses the term "labor law" to denote what, in the United States, is conventionally divided into two sub-fields: "labor law," which covers the law of collective organizing, bargaining, and striking, and "employment law," which covers regulation of the terms of individual employment contracts, other working conditions, and worker benefits. In Europe and elsewhere, those two sub-fields, plus the law of social insurance, conventionally comprise the field of "social law." This chapter argues that "labor law" as a field must be enlarged well beyond even the scope of "social law."

The third section therefore applies the new labor law to critique the current version of the New Deal labor policy and many other fields of law and to propose their renovation to support a deepened, worker-centered form of social democracy suited to post-mass-production finance capitalism. The fourth argues that, perhaps unexpectedly, many of the reforms that would strengthen worker power and democracy within contemporary capitalism would also be essential for realizing the same goal within post-capitalist democratic market socialism. That section, again applying the new labor law, then discusses some key additional legal questions that would need to be answered to construct and sustain the worker-controlled enterprises at the heart of the latter regime.

Within the scope of this chapter, all four sections of the argument must necessarily be highly compressed and schematic. The chapter maps in a skeletal and merely illustrative fashion some of the specific elements in just a few of the legal domains outside of conventional labor law that structure contemporary capitalism and that could structure an imagined democratic socialism. The chapter is therefore intended only as a prolegomenon to a more comprehensive treatment of the new labor law, as applied to varieties of both existing capitalism and alternative capitalist and post-capitalist possibilities.[2] The goal here is to persuade the reader that expanding labor law's scope will advance the project of conceiving legal reforms to strengthen worker power and democracy across a range of political economies.

Three prefatory notes, the first substantive, the second and third terminological: First, although this chapter points to certain possible reforms in existing law within capitalism and discusses general problems of legal design raised by democratic socialism, in both cases real reconstruction cannot and should not be specified in an analyst's blueprint but, rather, would be shaped by participants in the political movements and struggles that might bring about the reconstructed institutions.

Second, when this chapter refers to the legal "construction" of political and economic institutions, that word is used in a special and expansive sense. It denotes that a law or legal institution strongly influences the political or economic institutions in question. The means of such influence may be either coercive legal sanctions or the law's non-coercive ideological effects; may be implemented through legislative, judicial, or administrative rules, principles, and processes; and may be either a prohibition or permission of economic or political action. And, reference to legal construction of political and economic institutions does not mean that law and legal institutions are not reciprocally influenced by those institutions and by political and ideological contestation among social actors. This chapter assumes just the contrary: the legal infrastructure of particular political economies must be mapped and analyzed, in order to conceive both radical legal reform to strengthen worker power and democracy *and* the political action to achieve it.

Third, the term "strengthening worker power and democracy" should be read as a shorthand, denoting the individual and collective empowerment of workers in the workplace, and the deepening of industrial democracy and worker-centered political democracy.

THE INHERENT TENSION BETWEEN CAPITALISM AND DEMOCRACY

An unassailable proposition advanced by progressive and socialist theorists and actors at least since Karl Marx is that capitalist economies pose a systematic threat to both industrial and political democracy. In 1936, a year after enactment of the National Labor Relations Act

---

[2] A book-in-progress by this author undertakes such a treatment.

(NLRA or Wagner Act), Franklin Roosevelt echoed Marx's diagnosis: "Here in America we are waging a ... war for the survival of democracy" against the "economic royalists" whose "[n]ew kingdoms were built upon the concentration of control over materials things," who "reached out for control of Government itself," and who took "[t]he hours of men and women worked, the wages they received, [and] the conditions of their labor ... beyond the control of the people ..." (Roosevelt 1936).

To understand the tension between capitalism and democracy with enough specificity to criticize and reconstruct labor law, we must ask: what are the core institutions that define capitalism and that determine the degree of worker power and depth of democracy? In many standard Marxist accounts – far more simplified than Marx himself assayed – the defining institution of capitalism is wage labor (just as the defining institution of feudalism is serf labor, and the defining institution of a slavocracy is slave labor): to survive, property-less workers must sell their labor power to the property-owning class of capitalists, and the same necessity disempowers workers within workplace and political hierarchies dominated by the propertied class.

This account of worker disempowerment and domination is also at the center of the decidedly non-Marxist labor policy of the New Deal, which sought to reconstruct, rather than overthrow, capitalist work. Senator Wagner, the architect of that policy, often stated that it was a response to one fundamental injustice – the coercive denial of individual freedom and collective democracy – flowing from the wage-laborer's need to enter employment to survive (Barenberg 1993: 1422–1427). And Section 1 of the NLRA states that legally protected unionization, in and of itself, creates "equality of bargaining power,"[3] with no regard to reconstructing legal institutions outside the Act's narrow field of vision.

THE PANOPLY OF ECONOMIC AND POLITICAL INSTITUTIONS NECESSARY TO SUSTAIN WAGE-LABOR MARKETS AND WORKPLACE HIERARCHIES

The New Deal labor policy thus delimited the scope of the law necessary to solve the problem of worker disempowerment – and the coterminous scope of the conventional study of labor law ever since. That limited scope was not a creature of normative thought but rather of the ideology corresponding to a contingent truce line in the political struggles of the 1930s and 1940s. However, Marx's work, and subsequent writing by Weber, Schumpeter, Keynes, and many other political economists, reveal a complex of additional political and economic institutions that sustain the institution of wage labor. The particular contours of these additional institutions empower or disempower workers, just as does the particular structure of wage labor itself.

What are these additional institutions? In order to realize profit, the capitalist enterprise must sell the goods or services made by the wage-laborer into the product market. This fact alone entails that mass wage labor requires the institution of a monetary system to enable the purchase of both labor power and products (think of the Marxist term "cash nexus" [Marx 1990]). The institutions of property, contract, and corporations[4] are also essential to competition among private profit-taking employers, for obvious reasons (Polanyi 1944; Weber 2003 [1927]). And since continuous capital accumulation and investment are entailed by product-market competition among profit-taking owners, financial institutions and capital markets are also inherent features

---

[3] 29 USC Section 151.
[4] This chapter uses the terms "employers," "private enterprises," and "corporations" synonymously. All are short-hand for the many different types of private profit-taking enterprises that employ wage-laborers, not including worker-controlled enterprises which are the basis of the form of post-capitalist regime discussed in the fourth section.

of capitalism (Schumpeter 1994 [1954]: 78). In addition, all contractual transactions require methods of communication; and the intrinsic capitalist drive to secure and expand markets – as individual capitalist enterprises compete for survival and enrichment – spawns the institutions of marketing and advertising, forms of communication more specific yet more culture-shaping than those required for generic contractual transacting. And the institutions of taxation and of state structures are essential to provide the monetary, financial, corporate, and other apparatus just described (Miliband 1973), as well as the legal system itself. Even further, as Max Weber argued, capitalism is fostered by an international order of multiple competing nation-states, as opposed to a single global state or empire: when independent states must compete for cross-border investment, capitalist private enterprises are, to a substantial degree, protected against comprehensive state discipline (Ingham 2008: 176) or state confiscation. Hence, the institutions of international trade, capital flows, and monetary transactions, and of national security are stanchions of domestic as well as global capitalist institutions, and therefore of capitalist wage labor and workplace hierarchies.

Needless to say, comprehensive mapping of the variety of capitalist economic and political institutions, historical and today's, calls for vastly extended analysis, and the literature on the subject is rich and ranges across many disciplines. Institutions may look quite different but carry out similar functions in each of the "necessary" domains catalogued above (Hyman 2009: 17), and successful reconstruction of one capitalist institution may not require concurrent reconstruction of another (Unger 2009: 14). The new labor law's proposals for institutional reconstruction must be responsive to the highly specific forms of capitalist production systems, enterprise organizations, markets, communication systems, political structures, and international orders that obtain, or might obtain, in various political economies.

Since all the (highly generalized) *economic* and *political* institutions just discussed are, for the reasons sketched, necessary simply to sustain the two (also highly generalized) institutions of central concern to labor lawyers – that is, wage-labor markets and workplace hierarchies – it follows that the *legal* underpinnings of *all* those economic and political institutions are as essential to the disempowerment and domination of workers as are the law of labor-management relations and working conditions within the workplace hierarchy, and the law of employment contracts, whether individual or collective. Hence, if we seek to answer the fundamental question that concerns many progressive and socialist labor lawyers – "What are the legal institutions that determine both worker power and labor's capacity to deepen industrial and political democracy?" – we must look not only to the field of labor law as conventionally defined, as important as that law is to the question of worker power and democracy.[5] We must look also to the laws of property, contract, money, corporations, communication, domestic and international capital markets, taxation, state administration, and so on. Whether these other legal fields are more or less important than conventionally defined labor law in answering the question just asked demands extensive empirical research.

Having said this, the new labor law will not bring together the *entirety* of each of the conventionally defined fields that in some way influence worker power and democracy. That would aggregate nearly all law. Rather, the new labor law will include and examine the particular *elements* or *components* of each conventionally defined legal field that most significantly reach – like tentacles – into the shaping of the relative power of workers and owners and into the determination of workers' capacity to achieve industrial and political democracy.

---

[5] Forerunners and inspirations for this approach include the legal realist Robert Hale (1923, 1943) and the critical legal theorist Duncan Kennedy (1991), although my conceptual strategy differs from theirs in significant ways.

APPLYING THE "NEW LABOR LAW" TO EMPOWER WORKERS AND DEEPEN
DEMOCRACY IN THE CONTEMPORARY CAPITALIST ECONOMY

This section offers illustrations of several elements of multiple fields of law that construct worker power and democracy – including conventional labor law and domestic finance law and their interaction with constitutional law; the law of international trade, global capital markets, and national security; the law of the "social wage;" and various fields that comprise the law of consumption. The illustrations are drawn exclusively from contemporary United States law and political economy.

Conventional Labor Law, and Its Interaction with Constitutional Law

Although a key theme of this chapter is that conventional labor law studies only one field of law that constructs worker power and democracy, it is, needless to say, an important – and possibly the most important – field. This sub-section gives a synoptic picture of the conventional US labor laws and legal institutions most vital to that construction. The sub-section also gives illustrations of how those laws and institutions interact with constitutional law in ways that significantly construct worker power and democracy.

US law constructs great impediments to union organizing. By requiring majority-rule elections to achieve unionization, granting employers the right to run anti-union campaigns in the extended election campaign, and imposing minimal sanctions against employers that coerce workers during the campaign, the law constructs both the opportunity and incentive for employers to engage in such coercion. The startling rate of firings of union supporters in the run-up to the election – between one out of seven and one out of twenty, depending on the study – is an artifact of those legal components.

Union density is also diminished by the law's construction of decentralized bargaining units[6] and, at best, partial or "non-encompassing" unionization of the many employers across product markets or enterprise networks (Rogers 1990). Multi-employer bargaining is permitted only when a union is able to organize multiple individual employers and then win the voluntary consent of each to multi-employer units (Barenberg 2015). This legal construct is the critical foundation for the weakening of worker power via the conversion of vertically integrated enterprises to contractually interconnected supply chains and networks. What was once a permissible primary strike against all phases of production in the integrated corporation becomes an impermissible secondary strike against the very same multiple phases of production now lodged in multiple enterprises within separate bargaining units (Barenberg 2015). In other words, the most basic components of US labor law conspire with, and indeed accelerate, the disintegration of enterprises that is a hallmark of contemporary capitalism, by discouraging the enlargement of worker organizing in fluid, multi-employer bargaining units that match the equally fluid boundaries – in the political economy of post-mass-production finance capitalism – of production-and-distribution networks, geographic clusters, and sectors (Barenberg 1994: 881–884, 977–983; Barenberg 2015). (Recent proposals to mandate rigid sectoral bargaining in the USA do not take account of this fluidity in contemporary capitalism, although a sectoral scope may be the most desirable multi-employer unit in certain quarters of the economy – desirable, because most worker-empowering in context.)

---

[6] A "bargaining unit" is the group of employees who may, by majority choice, designate a particular union as their collective representative.

Those basic legal components also construct the very geography of the US economy and society. The legal construction of decentralized and non-encompassing units greatly incentivizes individual employers not only to fight unionization to avoid competition with non-union employers in the same product market, but also to break or escape a union that has successfully organized the employer (Kochan et al. 1994). Other components of conventional labor law construct smooth escape routes for the employer. First, employers are not punished for closing a union facility and opening a non-union facility elsewhere, so long as the employer is not foolish enough to reveal anti-union emotion. Second, the law of successorship permits de-unionization by means of selling a going business, so long as the purchaser follows its lawyer's advice not to recruit the majority of the new workforce from the old.[7] Third, a 1947 Amendment of the NLRA authorizes state laws against compulsory dues payments, generating less unionized states and regions that attract capital from the more unionized.

These escape routes – and others constructed by bankruptcy law, corporate law, constitutional law, and the law of taxation and subsidies discussed below – may be just as important as the legal construction of coercive anti-union campaigns in diminishing union density in the USA (Kochan et al. 1994). The result: employers hopscotch from unionized to non-unionized regions, from urban areas to suburban or rural "industrial parks" where inter-union solidarity is relatively incapacitated, and from less to more racist regions to capitalize on racial divide-and-conquer strategies against worker solidarity (Davis 2018).

These clusters of law – constructing non-union or anti-union regions (the Southern, Mountain, and Plains states) and areas (suburban and rural) – also indirectly weaken worker power and democracy by entrenching right-wing, anti-union blocs in the federal legislative process by reason of peculiarities of US constitutional law, including the electoral college method of electing the President, the constitutional authorization of states to draw congressional district lines, and the Supreme Court's refusal to review state governments' partisan "gerrymandering" of those districts.[8] In a vicious cycle, constitutional law's undemocratic empowerment of regions to which non-union capital has already moved enables federal policy-making that turns those non-union regions into even stronger magnets for the mobile capital that conventional labor law, in the ways just explained, permits and encourages (Hertel-Fernandez 2018). Without understanding this – and many other – interlocks of conventional labor law and constitutional law, the legal system's full force in disempowering workers by encouraging capital mobility cannot be critically analyzed and leftists' political energies cannot be well-directed.

The same goes for the US law of political spending. Conventional labor law permits political spending by unions, although yet another interaction of constitutional and conventional labor law now bars unions and employers from agreeing to require non-consenting bargaining-unit members to pay an increment of dues to fund that spending; each worker must consent to pay that increment.[9] But, compared to revision of those rules, imaginable constitutional and legislative rules of political spending – beyond the scope of conventional labor law – could be just as or more important in building workers' power to democratize a capitalist polity in the interest of working people, and to win substantive policies that would, reciprocally, strengthen unions and their political power, in a virtuous cycle.

The discussion above has focused on the law that constructs union organizing, capital's escape from unions, differentiation among pro- and anti-union regions, and political spending –

---

[7] *Fall River Dyeing & Finishing Corp. v. NLRB*, 482 US 27 (1987).

[8] *Rucho v. Common Cause*, 588 US —, 139 S. Ct. 2484 (2019).

[9] *Communication Workers v. Beck*, 487 US 735 (1988); *Janus v. AFSCME*, 585 US —, 138 S. Ct. 2448 (2018).

a network of law that interlaces strands of conventional labor law, constitutional law, and election law. Internal to conventional labor law, rules governing strikes, obviously, are also a key component in determining the relative degree of worker empowerment. Startlingly, US law permits employers to fire workers for all forms of slowdowns and work stoppages, other than full primary strikes and only when no contract is in effect. Even in the latter instance, employers may permanently replace strikers, who retain the right only to return to a job if a position reopens.

Finally, the exclusion of large swaths of workers from even the limited federal legal protections discussed above constructs worker disempowerment in two key ways. First, by excluding managers and supervisors from protections against employer retaliation, employers can effectively conscript those workers into participating in the employer's anti-union-organizing campaign and strike-breaking efforts. That is, the employer starts a union election campaign with a large campaign organization in place, one that – unlike the union's campaign organization – reaches every voter in the electorate for forty hours per week and that may lawfully require workers, on pain of discharge, to attend anti-union speeches during work time, an infrastructure that candidates running for political office could only dream of. And the employer has a large corps of conscripted strike-breakers – every manager and supervisor – at the ready in the event of a strike.

Second, workers excluded from protections under federal labor law are placed at the tender mercies of state governments, reinforcing and reinforced by the legal construction of regional variation in pro- and anti-union politics in the US federal system discussed above. Here again, conventional labor law intermeshes with constitutional law, in this instance the constitutional jurisprudence on "preemption." The predictable and well-documented result is yet another vicious cycle, this time at the level of state rather than federal policy-making – a cycle of right-wing state governments enacting laws that weaken or repress unions, and of weakened unions lacking the power to prevent the enactment of further such laws or to gain their repeal (Hertel-Fernandez 2018).

Laws of International Trade, Global Capital Markets, and National Security

The relevant components of the law of international trade, global capital markets, and national security must also be folded into the "new labor law," if capital mobility and product-market competition and their damaging consequences for worker power and democracy are to be fully analyzed and resisted.

The international dimension of conventional labor law does address trade legislation and trade agreements, along with the core "International Labor Code" of the International Labor Organization. But the study of these bodies of law must be redirected, in quite specific ways, if they are to be radically reformed to genuinely empower workers in the USA and globally. Surprisingly perhaps, US trade legislation is the most pro-labor in the world. One provision of the Trade Act of 1974 as amended – Section 301(b)[10] – requires the President to impose remedies to ensure that every government that trades with the USA enforces internationally recognized labor rights. Another set of provisions – the Generalized System of Preferences (GSP)[11] – authorizes the President to withdraw trade benefits from certain developing countries if they fail to take steps to enforce the same rights. Any "interested party" can file a petition; there is

---

[10] 19 USC Section 2411(b).
[11] 19 USC Sections 2461–66 (2000). The European Union also has a GSP program, but has not deployed or threatened to deploy the program with nearly the vigor and sanctions of the US GSP program.

neither a standing nor a case-or-controversy requirement. The potential remedy includes the exercise of any or all Executive powers. And, of greatest note, the petition may demand inquiry into conditions across entire labor markets and into a multiplicity of legal institutions in the foreign country. This process and inquiry are wholly unlike other forms of US litigation, which invoke narrowly bounded judicial or administrative processes to determine whether remedies should be granted to redress violations of rights of particular parties to a factually focused dispute.

If the President systematically enforced these US trade statutes as constitutionally required, we would see the kind of floor placed under global worker rights and standards that multilateral institutions have neither the authority nor political will to impose. Indeed, as erratic and hesitant as it has been, the President's use of these statutory powers has been the most powerful state tool for enforcing transnational labor rights. (The International Labor Organization promulgates but, unlike the US government, does not deploy sanctions to enforce international labor rights.) Even the mere filing of a GSP petition by a worker organization can cause a trading partner to improve its labor rights record in order to avoid a potential collapse in its exports to the enormous US consumer market (Douglas et al. 2004).

It behooves labor law scholars to formulate detailed proposals for radically strengthened enforcement of these statutes, akin to the insistence on stronger enforcement of domestic worker rights. By way of example, here are two: although any interested party can file a Section 301 or GSP petition demanding a Presidential inquiry, the courts have ruled that that party cannot obtain judicial intervention when the President fails to carry out his or her constitutional duty to enforce internationally recognized labor rights under those statutes.[12] Congress could straight-forwardly mandate judicial enforcement of the President's obligation (Barenberg 2009).

A second, more far-reaching proposal: Congress could create an International Labor Rights Commission that would, instead of the President, enforce the trade statutes. The Commission might be composed of worker representatives and jurists, charged with developing specific, revisable indicators of compliance with internationally recognized labor rights, well-adapted to countries' variegated economic conditions; applying those indicators to trading partners' worker-rights enforcement records; and ordering calibrated sanctions for non-compliance with bench-marks of improvement (Barenberg 2009: 23–28). Most boldly, the Commission members might include worker representatives of all trading partners, not just domestic worker representatives, to mitigate the imperialist nature of unilateral US enforcement of global labor rights and, from an international standpoint, to democratize the Commission's decisions.

The weak worker rights provisions in US trade agreements could be strengthened by incorpor-ating analogous enforcement mechanisms. The reforms would respond to the question that leftists who are all-out opponents of trade agreements have not fully put their minds to: can we imagine reforms of trade agreements that would actually succeed in enforcing global worker rights and standards? Until that question is deeply explored and answered in the negative, there is no justification for ruling out trade agreements altogether. After all, US leftists did not turn their backs on federal unionization rights in the 1930s on the ground that such rights would inevitably fail if lodged in the competitive multi-state market constructed by US constitutional law; nor did they press for the US common market to be fragmented into separate state markets in order to better enforce worker rights.

The law of global capital markets is, for purposes of the new labor law, a confederate of the law of international trade. It is the combination of liberalized trade flows and liberalized capital flows that has constructed global labor markets, which often intensify the downward pressure on

---

[12] *International Labor Rights and Education Fund* v. *Bush*, 752 F. Supp. 495 (DDC 1990).

workplace standards and worker power in the current era of globalized capitalism.[13] Workers in other countries produce goods that are exported to the USA, taking advantage of liberalized trade rules; thanks to capital-market liberalization, the USA sends capital overseas to build the factories (so-called export platforms) that produce goods for shipment back to the US, European, or other consumer markets; and US owners rely on cross-border allocation of their enterprise investments and profits for tax arbitrage or repatriation, thanks again to capital-market liberalization. One critical function of free trade and free investment agreements is assuring US capitalists that they can continue to reap and relocate overseas profits and continue to export from overseas platforms. These legal constructs are therefore foundations of product-market and labor-market competition on a global scale and, like domestic laws constructing product and labor markets, encourage capital mobility that often flows from unionized to non-unionized production.

The law of global capital flows constructs US workers' empowerment (or disempowerment) in yet another critical way – demonstrated vividly in the financial crisis of 2008. One source of that crisis was the sequence of explosive growth in (and implosion of) toxic assets held by US financial institutions and investors and traded in Wall Street's casino capital markets. That process was fueled, in part, by a bountiful inflow of foreign investment, including from China, with whom the USA had effectively swapped the transfer of US manufacturing facilities in return for such capital exports to the USA.

But the much-criticized China-USA trade imbalance was only part of the story. In fact, the global financial system is not coterminous with trade imbalances; the 2008 financial crisis was in significant part driven by the entanglement of US and European financial institutions and capital markets (Tooze 2018). This is another reason why it is critical for analysts of law's disempowerment of workers to focus not just on the usual suspect – international trade agreements – but also on the law that constructs global finance.

How do these sorts of capital flows – and the crises that are likely to continue punctuating our age of financial disequilibrium – disempower workers? The 2008 crisis is exemplary. First, the crisis transferred income and savings from working people to bailed-out financial institutions (Hockett 2009). Second, the shock led ultimately to a politics of austerity that diminished the social wage and, hence, worker power. But third, and less visibly, global imbalances were a means of transferring wealth extracted from exploited workers in countries like China – which, like the United States, fails to enforce and actively suppresses worker rights – to sustain debt-fueled consumption of US households whose income was abated by the corrosion of worker rights. As discussed below, this mode of consumption in turn weakens worker power and democracy.

Yet another sprawling body of law constructs global capital markets and their potentially worker-disempowering effects: the US and international law of national security. Three illustrations must suffice here. First, many components of national security law construct the global military power of the United States, which provides insurance that US parties' foreign investments will not be confiscated by host governments. Here, one of countless legal instruments is the International Emergency Economic Powers Act, the progeny of legislation invoked to

---

[13] Depending on the circumstances, liberalization of trade and capital flows may also boost workers' power and conditions, through technology and capital transfers, transmission of organizational practices across borders, and other mechanisms.

impose an embargo – cautionary to all governments – against the country (Cuba) that effected the first large-scale confiscation of overseas property of US businesses.[14]

Second, the same legally constructed global power makes US assets comparatively safe investments, underwriting the inflow of capital to the USA of the sort that fueled Wall Street's creation of toxic assets. Third, that geopolitical power also enables the USA to negotiate trade and investment agreements on terms favorable to the USA, requiring signatories to meet US metrics on pain of withdrawal of US trade or other benefits.

These are necessarily spare illustrations of the main point: to call the domestic law of collective bargaining and international trade agreements "labor law," but not so label the law of global finance and national security, is not just artificial; it also diverts left legal scholars' analysis away from many significant mechanisms through which law constructs worker power and democracy.[15]

Laws of Domestic Financial Institutions, Capital Markets, and the Constitution

The domestic law of financial institutions and capital markets constructs worker power and democracy in ways that parallel the international laws just discussed. Rather than repeating the domestic analogues of those international laws, I will offer additional relevant components of domestic law, again merely illustrative of the chapter's main thesis.

First, the basic role of financial institutions and capital markets, in theory, is to aggregate the savings of individuals and enterprises and channel those resources to individuals and enterprises that will use them most productively. In practice, our financial institutions and capital markets do not play that role well. They are instead often devoted to creating and trading complex assets at several removes from production in the real economy (Admati & Hellwig 2013: 162; Lothian 2017). This detachment of finance from production – driven in part by the last forty years of legally encouraged consolidation of big banks and hypertrophic growth of the financial sector – weaken community-based finance of local and worker-centered production systems (Krippner 2011; Wilmarth 2013). Proposals for radical legal reform that would reconstruct financial markets to foster worker-empowering enterprises therefore include laws that promote community banks, cooperative banks, union-owned banks, non-profit banks, and localized, government-subsidized variants of venture-capital funds that would direct capital to unionized and worker-controlled firms (Block 2014; Unger 2001: 149–150). We see experimental legal institutions of this sort in regional "social economies" or "cooperative economies" around the world (e.g. Bourgue et al. 2013).

Second, when the law constructs private banks', corporations', and institutional investors' control over investment decisions, there is an anti-democratic, systemic bias against law reforms designed to strengthen unions and other worker-empowering, social democratic programs. This bias, theorized by Michał Kalecki, rests on the fact that, when investment decisions are under the control of private profit-seeking actors, the level of investment in an economy depends on the degree of those actors' confidence that government policy will be business-friendly in the

---

[14] 50 USC Sections 1701–1707.

[15] Of course, leftist political economists and scholars from other disciplines have produced an enormous body of literature on these questions (e.g., Shefner & Fernandez-Kelly 2011), but that makes all the more striking the paucity of scholarship that, in depth and detail, connects their research with questions of specifically *legal* infrastructure of worker power.

near future (Kalecki 1943). Leftist parties will therefore hesitate to enact labor-empowering policies, since their reelection will be put at risk by the expected decrease in investment – "capital strikes," in effect – that would diminish economic growth, employment, and wages.

Note that, by contrast, most political strikes by unions are both illegal under the NLRA[16] and "unprotected" – that is, the employer may fire workers for engaging in them. Yet, capitalists' power to engage in political strikes – just described – is fully constructed by law; and, unlike labor strikes that require solidaristic co-action among workers, capital strikes require no coordination among enterprises, which reduce investment when they separately but simultaneously lose business confidence.

If legal reform placed limitations on private control over investment decisions, this intrinsic constraint on worker-empowering democracy would be loosened. Indeed, historically, social democratic legal reforms have occurred precisely when that constraint has been relaxed, as during the Great Depression, when business confidence and investment were already so low that the threat of an additional capital strike to block such reforms was weak (Barenberg 1993: 1397).

Third, the existing law of finance constructs "short-termism" among institutional investors and executives whose compensation or continued employment depend on the price of their corporations' shares. To inflate share prices by "pleasing the markets," executives implement mass layoffs or finance-driven restructurings that undermine worker power, not just through the direct effect of job loss but also by disrupting hard-won workplace communities of solidarity and labor-centric collaboration with local production managers (e.g. Kristensen & Zeitlin 2005).

In a final illustration, constitutional jurisprudence propels capital movement. The "dormant commerce clause" fashioned by the Supreme Court prohibits state laws that discriminate against out-of-state economic actors on behalf of in-state interests. The Court has, however, carved out a wholly unprincipled exception to that rule.[17] A state is permitted to engage in open discrimination if it uses as its means the granting of subsidies paid out of the state's general revenue to particular in-state businesses or sectors, and states in practice grant tax rebates and credits as well.[18] The practical consequence of this exception is predictable. States compete with one another to attract or retain footloose capital by granting subsidies and tax incentives, in a race to the bottom that disempowers workers in at least three ways: the incentives redistribute resources from workers and other ordinary taxpayers; the systematic bite from the state treasury requires cuts in the state's social wage; and capital's hop-scotching batters communities of solidarity in and out of workplaces.

Through these three labor-disempowering mechanisms, the particular federalist structure of US constitutionalism again amplifies the incentives created by conventional labor law for regions and states to adopt anti-union policies and cultivate political cultures designed to attract capital from unionized areas. The new labor law's proposed reform is simple: the Supreme Court, or Congress, should overturn the exception for competitive subsidies and tax breaks.

---

[16] Political strikes generally violate Section 8(b)(3) of the NLRA on the grounds that the subject of the strike is a "permissive" rather than "mandatory" subject of bargaining. *NLRB v. Wooster Division of Borg-Warner Corp.*, 356 US 342 (1958).

[17] *New Energy Company of Indiana v. Limbach*, 486 US 269, 273–274 (1988).

[18] As distinct from imposing penalties or regulations on out-of-state actors, which remain barred by the dormant commerce clause, even though such state laws have the same discriminatory effect as subsidies and tax reductions for in-state businesses.

The Law of the "Social Wage"

When workers decide whether to organize a union or to strike, they fear that they face the risk of retaliatory discharge – and that fear is justified, as the data mentioned above show. Workers' willingness to empower themselves therefore turns in significant part on the personal cost they face should they lose their job. For that reason, workers' bargaining power is constructed in part by the law of the social wage – that is, the panoply of social insurance and other government-provided "public goods" that soften the blow for workers who lose their jobs: unemployment insurance, welfare benefits, healthcare, childcare, higher education, subsidized housing and food, worker retraining, pensions, low-cost public transportation in working-class neighborhoods, and many more.

Other legal programs can empower workers in a manner similar to the way that public goods reduce the cost of discharge. An increase in the minimum wage pushes up wages of all low-wage jobs and therefore generates more living-wage jobs that a worker, if discharged, could expect to find. A law mandating government provision of jobs when the private sector fails to achieve full employment would greatly empower workers. For decades, winning such a full employment mandate was a high political priority of the AFL-CIO,[19] and proposals for a jobs guarantee have been renewed with the recent resurgence in the progressive movement (Sanders 2020). A universal basic wage, also on the progressive-labor agenda, would have analogous empowering effects.

Since lower rates of unemployment empower workers and higher rates disempower, macro-economic policy (both monetary and fiscal) has a critical effect on workers' willingness to organize and strike – as both unions and employers well know. As for monetary policy, an effective (rather than just paper) legal mandate that the Federal Reserve give higher priority to lowering the rate of unemployment than to protecting against inflation would inflect the law of macro-economic policy-making in a worker-empowering direction. Episodes of expansionary fiscal policies have done and would continue to do likewise, but labor law researchers should systematically formulate proposals to construct automatic counter-cyclical increases in spending across all legal domains.

The law of the social wage, if reconstructed in the ways just mentioned, may have greater labor-empowering and democracy-fortifying impact than many of the standard proposals for reforming elements of conventional labor law.

The Law of Consumption: Communication, Household Finance, Education, Zoning, Discrimination, and Taxation

Consumption and work are not often studied in conjunction, including in legal scholarship. But the relationship between the two is a critical determinant of worker power; therefore, the "law of consumption" is yet another field that constructs the strength of worker power and democracy. The relevant law is often studied in sub-categories such as the law of telecommunications, the internet, advertising, the new media, legacy media, household finance, taxation, and education, among others.

---

[19] In fact, when the Democratic Party failed to win union-strengthening labor law reform in 1977–78, the party gave the labor movement the second best piece of legislation, a full employment law – second rather than first best, only because the full employment program was precatory, not mandatory. Full Employment and Balanced Growth Act of 1978. 15 USC Sections 3101–3152.

Before turning to the legal infrastructure of consumption, the antecedent socioeconomic question is: how does consumption affect worker empowerment? A key mechanism is illustrated by late nineteenth-century industrialists' practice of hiring so-called family men rather than single men or women. Employers preferred to hire workers with greater obligations to support household consumption, since they were less likely to risk discharge by supporting unions and strikes and, in individual negotiations, less able to hold out for better terms. The general phenomenon illustrated by that one historical practice is this: the more urgent a worker's felt need to consume – or, put more starkly, the greater the desperation for wage income – the weaker the worker's bargaining power. Consider the following: if one had no need to consume, one would have no material need to work and would have maximum bargaining power relative to the employer.

The importance of the law that constructs the urgency of workers' private consumption is a close cousin of the importance of the social wage. One can view the social wage as the public payment for consumption needs, reducing the urgency of the workers' felt need to earn through market employment (depending, of course, on the distribution of tax burdens to fund those goods, pointing to yet another legal domain that the new labor law must encompass). In part for this reason, it is misguided for analysts to "blame" low-wage workers for "undisciplined" private consumption, which, in the USA, is rooted not so much in personal indulgence as in the burden workers have increasingly borne for spending on needs previously met by public-goods provision; on basics such as education, healthcare, and housing, the prices of which have increased relative to median wages in recent years (Nutting 2018); and on new socially constructed labor-market necessities such as laptops, smart phones, and associated service-provider contracts.

But worker power and democracy are constructed by the entire body of law, not just the law of the social wage, that calibrates the urgency of household expenditure. The background to that law is the political drive for ever-increasing consumption, which is, nearly universally across the political spectrum, pronounced the core of the "American Dream" (Sanders 2019; Tankersley 2016). Even when commentators and politicians claim to define the "dream" as equality of opportunity rather than raw consumption, they measure opportunity by upward mobility, comparing children's material consumption to their parents' (e.g. Kristof 2014).

The felt need for constant growth in purchasing power of course has psychological propulsions. One is the continuous conversion of discretionary consumption into necessary consumption. That is, worker-consumers initially experience desires for certain goods and services as less urgent, but over time experience those goods as more urgent or even as absolute needs. Another is the free-floating nature of desire; that is, once one object of desire is obtained, desire is only temporarily satiated, resurging and attaching to new objects (Zizek 2009).

But, clearly, there are important legal mechanisms at work too, tied to the institutions of contemporary capitalism that so dramatically unleash the desire to consume. I have already discussed many domestic and international legal institutions that construct the product-market competition that is a key driving force behind the ever-increasing production and consumption inherent in a capitalist economy. Here are just a few more examples of laws and legal institutions – outside the bounds of conventional labor law – that drive the cult of consumption and weaken worker power in the contemporary period:

Consider, first, the law that constructs our advertising-driven culture. In the USA, before the recent rise of commercial-free streaming services, the average person watched four hours per day of network and cable television commercials – nearly equivalent to an astounding eight weeks of eight-hour workdays per year. The advent of streaming services has cut that by more than half – but the total time spent viewing advertisements is still remarkable, especially when taking account of large concurrent increases in time viewing online websites populated with advertisements (Nielsen 2018; Staff 2020). The average person sees at least two million advertisements in their lifetime.

Most of us take for granted that the predominant business model of both old and new media is profit earned by advertising. But the law deeply constructs this world of continuous commercial inflaming of desires attached helter-skelter to commodity after commodity. Most deeply, when each major medium was aborning – radio, television, the internet – there were very real political debates about whether advertising would be permitted (Briggs & Burke 2020). Alternative models, including local and national community funding, were proposed and actually put into practice, briefly in the United States (in community radio stations, and in the early non-commercialized years of the internet), longer-term in other countries (think of the BBC in the UK) (Briggs 1986; Wu 2016). If these alternatives or if novel legal constructions of social ownership and funding of media now seem distant or aberrant, consider that there are traces of such "aberrations" in several areas of existing law: the law that provides some, if minimal, community funding of public broadcasters; the law that allocates the broadcast spectrum; the law that delegates to corporate owners of private media the general power to choose and censor the advertising and other messages they display (Zuboff 2019: 191); laws that regulate specific forms of advertising, such as false advertising, certain advertising directed toward children, certain types of obscene or pornographic advertising, and other categories; laws that authorize and regulate subscription-funded rather than advertising-funded broadcasting, such as certain types of cable television networks and streaming services; and many others.

Does all of that law matter for worker empowerment? It certainly does: the authorization of commercial advertising and delegation of power to private profit-making enterprises to choose its content and frequency – a legal construct – has had radical consequences. From the standpoint of inflating material consumption and therefore deflating worker bargaining power, the broad difference between a profit-driven culture and a hypothetical non-profit-based culture is obvious enough. Not only does each advertisement encourage heightened or wholly new desires, but it also anthropomorphizes the corporate producer as a caring friend with only the consumer's and society's best interests at heart. There is no "equal time" given to messages about the advertiser's exploitation of workers, environmental depredations, fraud, and other legal wrongdoings that are pervasive among capitalist corporations. In this respect, advertisements, individually and in the aggregate, present a relentless picture of capitalist enterprise as the best of vehicles, as the natural and inevitable means, for meeting our needs and our wants. Advertising sells capitalism itself.

This legal construct, then, has a triple impact on worker power. First, the ratcheting of desire and ever-greater urgency of private consumption reduces worker bargaining power in the way described above. Second, nearly all media are owned by capitalist corporations. It would be astounding if their shows, texts, and images did not, overall, convey negative images of unions or other organizations that challenge the profitability of capitalist enterprise, and there is ample evidence that their messaging does just that, when it does not exclude text and images about worker organizations or other opponents of corporate capitalism altogether, turning unions into an "absence" or an alien presence in the culture (Martin 2003; Puette 1992). Third, when workers seek to organize a union, they face a steep burden of persuasion, in light of co-workers' lifetime of viewing commercial advertising – which, as just argued, is a lifetime of messaging about the immutability and virtue of capitalist enterprise, of which their employer is an emblem.

Of course, workers, unlike viewers of their employer's advertising, have seen behind the employer's door and know, by hard experience, at least patches of their employer's darker side – hence, the activation of change agents within the workplace and the reality of union organizing and of powerful labor movements in certain times and places. Still, the cultural and psycho-logical burden of persuasion facing the union activist is heavy, and it is not coincidental that the decline in union density and worker bargaining power followed a cultural shift in the balance between people's identity as workers and as consumers.

Numerous other legal fields intermesh with communication law to construct people's felt imperative to consume. Just two examples: first, a high, but progressive, tax on consumption would dampen that imperative, in contrast to our present reliance on taxation of income. Second, changes in zoning, education, and anti-discrimination law would abate the arms race among families in bidding up the prices of housing, which leaves households struggling to meet their monthly mortgage payments. Today, out of love for their children, many parents over-stretch their budget on housing, as they compete to live in more affluent neighborhoods with better schools – a competition caused by zoning laws that generate residential segregation based on home valuations; by weak legal remedies for racial segregation in schools, which propelled suburbanization and residential wealth segregation when racist white families fled cities; by public education and property tax laws that create wide disparities in the quality of schools in wealthier and poorer neighborhoods; and by constitutional law that permits such disparities (Warren & Tyagi 2016).

So far, I have mentioned the general law that constructs profit-driven means of mass communication, and particularities of tax, zoning, anti-discrimination, and education law that further enlarge personal spending needs. The new labor law must also attend to the complex legal rules and institutions that regulate each medium of communication (print, radio, televi-sion, internet) in labor-disempowering ways that are specific to each and that evolve over time. In our time, the baleful consequences for labor politics of the more particular nature of the various legally constructed media – especially new media – have become stark.

Social media and other forms of online communication have fragmented and polluted the sphere of public discourse in profoundly anti-democratic ways (Sunstein 2017). The more specific effect on labor politics has been equally corrosive. One of the deepest challenges for a renewal of labor-centered democracy is the substantial number of largely non-unionized workers who have been drawn into right-wing, ethno-nationalist, populist movements (Isser 2020). The convergence of *disorganized* capitalism (Offe 1985) and the new media has mani-festly propelled this phenomenon. When large segments of the working classes are disorganized (non-unionized), and when they experience the fear and anxiety rooted in a half-century of persistent crises in capitalist labor markets, they are more receptive to the demagoguery that social media greatly enables.

Social media, although relatively new, has the core characteristic of past means of authoritar-ian leaders' communication to atomized citizenries: it enables direct communication from the demagogue to the individual without intermediation by independent media organizations, by civic organizations and, especially, by worker organizations. Those organizations encourage workers to deliberate in public settings in which hateful communication is discouraged, to participate together in political education programs, and to engage with electoral and coalitional politics across ethnic and racial differences. Donald Trump decisively lost the votes of members of union households by a margin of 16 percent, showing the continuing importance of unionization for left-leaning political forces (Isser 2020).

The upsurge in right-wing populism has shaken labor politics not only in the wider democ-racy. It has also impeded organizing, and attendant democratization, at the workplace level; in order to achieve collective solidarity, unions in many sectors and workplaces must now navigate the caustic divide in political allegiances within the relevant workforces.

Elaborating the new labor law and applying it in the service of worker power and democracy therefore calls for mapping, and proposing deep reform of, the existing legal rules and institutions (a) that enable direct, unmediated communication from the demagogue to the individual, non-unionized worker, and (b) that encourage the metastasis of online sites and networks of rage-filled, unreasoned responses to workers' plights.

Again, let me offer mere illustrations of the rules that call for radical reform. First, consider again the rules that authorize advertising-driven business models. To maximize profits, social media companies entice advertisers by attracting the greatest number of users or "eyeballs" (Wu 2016). One now-familiar technique for keeping users' attention is feeding them extremist variants of messages to which they have shown a predisposition (Zuboff 2019). These techniques encourage "horizontal" communication among disorganized workers that, subsequent to the demagogic leader's "vertical" messaging to them, amplifies that message through online person-to-person networks – amplification that is, again, unmediated by unions or other intermediary organizations.

These techniques point to a second well-known, pertinent cluster of legal rules – namely, the body of rules that authorize social media and other online sites to collect, bundle, and sell personal data from which the social-media companies and would-be advertisers can determine users' predispositions, and the rules that shield the companies against liability for the content they publish (Sunstein 2017; Zuboff 2019). If this cluster of laws of privacy, data-collection, data-usage, third-party tracking, liability protections, and so on, were overturned or significantly modified, the horizontal amplification of the demagogue's messages, and the social media companies' stoking of those messages, would be, at least to some substantial degree, diminished.

Imagine a world in which our culture were shaped by exchange of meaningful, other-regarding words and images in public arenas that discourage hateful appeals, and not by expansion of material desire and ethno-nationalist rage. Such a world – constructed, in part, by a renovated law of consumption – would give significantly greater support to worker bargaining power, worker organizing, and worker-centered democracy. The law of consumption therefore falls within the ken of the new labor law.

* * *

Obviously, the new labor law must include elements of many other fields: corporate law, antitrust law, criminal law, property law, contract law, immigration law, administrative law, family law, and others. In light of space limits here, it must be left to future publications to comprehensively map and apply the new labor law by examining the full body of particular elements of those fields that strengthen or weaken worker power and democracy in the contemporary capitalist political economy.

THE LEGAL INFRASTRUCTURE OF WORKER POWER UNDER DEMOCRATIC SOCIALISM

From Social Democracy Underpinned by Collective Bargaining to Democratic Socialism Underpinned by Worker Cooperatives

The previous section suggests radical reforms of several fields of law in the service of a form of social democracy suited to contemporary economic organization, but it assumes the continuation of the defining capitalist institutions of wage labor, capital-controlled enterprises, and relatively competitive product markets, together with the multiple economic and political institutions without which those defining institutions could not function. In such a regime, worker power and democracy are strengthened through legal construction of (a) the institutions of unionization, collective bargaining, and channels of political action by worker organizations, and (b) worker-empowering variants of the many political and economic institutions that sustain wage labor.

In the shift from a capitalist social-democratic to a post-capitalist democratic-socialist political economy, the central institutional transformation is the end of wage labor in enterprises controlled by their capital suppliers. What replaces that central institution of capitalism? Louis Brandeis answered the question simply, though he did not use the term "socialism." He wrote that the ultimate aim of industrial democracy was workers' assumption of "full responsibility for business, as in cooperative enterprises" (Strum 1984: 192, quoting Brandeis' letter to Henry Bruère). In US history, Brandeis' conception of a non-capitalist, worker-controlled enterprise is traceable to the post-Civil War decades, when the Knights of Labor led the opposition to what appeared then as a strange new social order based on an economy of mass wage labor.

The Normative Argument for the Replacement of Collective Bargaining with Full Workers' Control

For the Knights of Labor and for labor-progressives like Brandeis, wage labor was incompatible with political democracy – at least if the wage-laborers were employed by capital suppliers and not by worker-owned enterprises. Indeed, the Knights of Labor argued that the subordination inherent in wage labor violates the Constitution's vision of independent citizens unbeholden to others (Forbath 1985).

While that normative argument rests on the commitment to political democracy, a second argument for full workers' control rests on the commitment to workplace democracy, reflected in Brandeis' proposition quoted above. The latter argument begins, as does the argument for unionization in a social-democratic capitalist economy, with the understanding that workplaces have the key feature that defines a political system. The enterprise makes workplace rules (analogous to the legal rules of a political regime) and enforces those rules under the coercive penalty of discharge (analogous to the coercive legal sanctions imposed by a political regime).

Proponents of collective bargaining in capitalist enterprises argue that unionization achieves industrial democracy by giving workers a collective voice in negotiations with managers, who are the collective representatives of the enterprise's second stakeholder: the capital suppliers. Democratic socialists riposte that, while collective bargaining represents a step toward democracy in a capitalist economy, it fails to achieve the deepest democracy in either the workplace or the polity. As for deepening industrial democracy, workers are the *only* "citizens" of the workplace political system, since they alone live day to day under the enterprise's coercively enforced rules. External capital suppliers – shareholders or other owners – do not. Yet collective bargaining enables workers – the workplace citizenry – to participate in making and enforcing workplace rules only by means of exerting the coercive power of the strike against the putative capitalist stakeholder, not by means of one-citizen-one-vote rule-making. The unionized enterprise is analogous to a political system in which the citizenry influences legal rule-making only through tax strikes or other modes of inflicting economic harm against an authoritarian government. The workplace must instead be governed entirely by workers, to fulfill the principle of industrial democracy, while concurrently deepening political democracy in the manner articulated by the Knights of Labor, Karl Marx, and many others.

Legal Construction of Worker-Controlled Enterprises

An enterprise fully controlled by workers can be governed either by directly deliberative meetings of the entire workforce, or by managers elected by the entire workforce (Wolff 2012). At first glance, therefore, it appears that corporate law and the law of finance are the decisive fields in the legal construction of worker power and democracy in a democratic socialist regime. Under existing law, capital-suppliers – that is, shareholders, in the types of corporations that employ most of the workforce, and the institutional investors, private equity firms, and other entities that own or invest in corporations – either themselves act as managers or elect and control managers, whose fiduciary legal obligations run predominantly to the shareholders and other investors alone and not to other stakeholders, including non-shareholding workers.

These legal obligations presume that the overweening goal of natural persons is to maximize their monetary benefit and that the legally created "persons" in which natural persons invest – that is, corporations and institutional investors – should also act immoderately toward that goal. The law therefore constructs millions of artificial actors that are required to act as sociopaths (Bakan 2005), in the sense that no psychologically and morally healthy person would make every plan and take every action to maximize monetary interests with minimal regard to the well-being of others (unless the other's well-being is a precondition or by-product of fulfilling the monetary interests of the actor) and to humans' full range of other ethical considerations, such as not exploiting or manipulating others, caring selflessly for those we love, giving due regard to the rights of others (including future generations), fulfilling civic and communitarian values, avoiding harms to the natural environment, and so on. The legal system constructs millions of entities that not only behave that way, but are legally required to, and that exert overwhelming power in politics, notwithstanding that they are not only sociopaths but are not even citizen-voters (that is, not members of the "demos"). This legal and social analysis augments Marx's and Roosevelt's normative arguments against capital suppliers' domination of the political system by virtue of their concentrated economic power.

For democratic socialists, then, the shift from workplace control by suppliers of capital to workplace control by suppliers of labor brings democracy to fruition not only in the workplace but also in the polity, for one and the same reason: the power of concentrated capital, embodied in a political army of artificial behemoths, is neutralized by eliminating capitalist enterprise itself.

If these simple syllogisms are correct, then it might seem, from the point of view of radical legal reform, that the master key to unlocking industrial and political democracy is simply to reconstruct the law of corporations and finance to prohibit control of management by capital and to mandate instead that that control be vested in those who work in the enterprise.

But things are not as simple as this legal silver bullet, as economic and political analysts of market socialism have known and debated for a long time (e.g. Bardhan & Roemer 1993). The success of industrial and political democracy in a democratic socialist regime would depend on many other institutions, even if enterprises were cooperatively controlled by workers. Therefore, applying the new labor law to democratic socialist institutions requires attention not just to the law of corporate ownership and of investment in the enterprise, but to many other legal fields.

Legal Reconstruction of Other Institutions in Support of Worker Cooperatives

The assumption of many proponents of democratic socialism, including myself, is that the worker-controlled enterprise would, like the unionized capitalist enterprise, earn profit by selling goods and services into a relatively competitive product market, even though that profit flows to workers and not capital suppliers (see, e.g. Dreze 1993; Fleurbaey 1993; Ranis 2016). This is, then, a form of market socialism. The continuing commitment to the market mechanism, even in a post-capitalist regime, is based in part on the failed historical experiments in centralized coordination of economic activity – failures that, in some instances, came at incalculable human cost. It is true that those experiments were undertaken by authoritarian, not democratic, political regimes. But there is little reason to believe that democratic governance of a centralized coordination mechanism would solve the fundamental problem of a central actor's incapacity to aggregate and process local information about vast numbers and varieties of ever-changing work arrangements, product selection and design, production methods, technologies, interactions among enterprises, and other basic processes of a complex, large-scale, densely networked, locally diverse, and socially embedded economy.

This is not to say that greater – sometimes centralized – social regulation and redistribution than at present is unwarranted, either in our existing economy centered around capitalist wage-labor enterprises or in an imagined future economy centered around worker-controlled enterprises. Quite the contrary. The preceding section of this chapter offers many illustrations of new legal regulations and institutions – whether public or public-private hybrids, whether centralized or decentralized – that respond to the worker-disempowering pressures generated by private profit-seeking enterprise, by product-market competition, and by the many collateral institutions that sustain them. Market socialism, because it retains the basic institutions of profit-seeking enterprise and product-market competition, will generate many of the same worker-disempowering and democracy-threatening pressures – as confirmed by the experience of even the most successful cooperatives, both contemporary and historical, such as the well-documented struggles of the Mondragon complex of Spanish cooperatives which, while maintaining much of their original structure and ethos, have turned to two-tier employment and increasingly technocratic management in order to succeed in the marketplace (Duncan & Raymond 2018). These pressures must therefore be countered by legal infrastructure resembling the legal proposals in the preceding section, albeit adapted to the new core institution, the worker-controlled enterprise.

For example, interaction between consumption and worker empowerment will still characterize democratic socialism, since workers in a worker-controlled enterprise will seek to ensure the survival of their jobs and their accumulated savings (held as shares in the enterprise they own, in the simplest model of finance in a cooperative economy), both of which depend on the success of their enterprise in competition with other worker-controlled enterprises. Worker-controlled businesses, just like unionized capitalist firms, will therefore seek to maintain or expand their market share and profitability. Hence, worker-empowering legal reconstruction of marketing, advertising, media ownership, public education, taxation, anti-discrimination law, and zoning, such as the reforms discussed in the previous section, will be just as warranted as in an economy of capital-controlled firms.

Likewise, the legal construction of the international movement of capital, goods, and services will strengthen or weaken worker empowerment and democracy in a democratic socialist economy much the same as in a unionized capitalist economy – since, again, that body of international law constructs the larger product, capital, and labor market to which the worker-controlled enterprise must respond.

Indeed, even though worker-controlled enterprises in themselves mark a leap forward in industrial and political democracy, a market socialist economy contains new, potentially worker-disempowering features, well-known to political economists. One of these was just alluded to. The members of a worker cooperative face severe undiversified risk, compared to the workers in a unionized wage-labor economy. The former's two most valuable assets – their employment and their savings – are dependent on the firm's success, so long as they must hold an equity stake in their cooperative or their share of profits must be reinvested in it. For the unionized (or non-unionized) workers in the capitalist economy, their employment is vested in their workplace, but they can diversify their savings across an array of assets other than shares in their own enterprise.

Political economists and policy-makers have discussed a variety of mechanisms for mitigating this problem of a democratic socialist economy. But the full extent of the possible mitigation must rest on experimentation of the sort that awaits a deeper transition from wage labor to workers' control than we have yet seen, though there is already much to be learned in regions that have adopted collaborative forms of production short of full-fledged market socialism. The point here is that the various mitigation strategies must be addressed by legal scholars, not just by political economists, through rigorous legal design of various proposed means of financial pooling across a diverse range of worker-controlled enterprises (e.g. Bardhan & Roemer 1993). As shown by the erratic experience of many "solidarity" banks in regional social or collaborative economies, we cannot expect legally well-designed financial institutions in support of worker power and democracy to spring forth by simply mandating that enterprises be controlled by workers instead of capital suppliers.

In addition, whether the worker's savings are vested in their own cooperative or diversified across a local or regional network of cooperatives, the design of social wage programs in a democratic socialist regime may be as important as in a capitalist political economy. If the economic security of workers' co-workers and community are tied to the success of workers' own cooperative or a local or regional network of cooperatives, they may feel inhibited from engaging in acts of militancy against worker-disempowering decisions that expert managers claim are dictated by technological and market imperatives, notwithstanding that workers have elected those managers or perhaps even *because* workers have elected the managers, whose decisions therefore wear a halo of democratic legitimacy. To challenge the manager is, in effect, to challenge one's co-workers in the cooperative or, assuming diversification of ownership, one's "co-workers" across the network of local or regional cooperatives in which all workers are invested. It is therefore important that workers who are wondering whether or not to make trouble by acting individually or collectively against entrenched or imperious managers, or against the complicity of a majority of co-workers with such managers, have a cushion outside the cooperative or network of cooperatives.

The flip side of this problem is similar to a familiar problem in political economies that have decentralized systems of unionization. In the latter regime type, unions face incentives to protect the jobs in the particular enterprise-level bargaining unit represented by the union, even when the welfare of the broader community, and the bargaining-unit members themselves, might be better served by greater fluidity of work processes and greater worker mobility. Note that this problem is not inherent in unionism; it is an artifact of laws, like those in the USA, that excessively decentralize worker organization and that provide a weak social wage that does not give workers adequate financial support and retraining to enable them to move across enterprises without significant personal spending. Similar, if not even more pressing, problems of legal construction arise in the democratic socialist economy, in the absence of a well-designed solution to the problems generated by both the jobs and savings of workers being vested in their own enterprise or network of enterprises. Hence, the importance for legal scholars to design a social wage that supports, and is reciprocally supported by, the particular legal infrastructure of the financial pooling mechanisms mentioned above.

* * *

Again, these are mere illustrations of the wide scope of legal fields and of questions of legal-institutional design that must be brought within the new labor law, to develop proposals for a legal infrastructure to strengthen worker power and democracy by building a democratic socialist regime. If a post-capitalist political economy seems utopian, the sketch of legal questions in this section is intended as a "real utopia," in the sense that it points toward a span along the political and legal horizon toward which pragmatic legal reforms, small or big, might be directed.

CONCLUSION

Empowering workers serves the goal of enlarging worker freedom – that is, enabling each worker to choose which capacities to develop, to select a life path that exercises those capacities, to continuously enlarge and reimagine the self, and to engage in risky but mutually empowering, transformative engagements with others (Unger 2001). It also serves the goals of deepening collective democracy at work and in politics. In a capitalist economy, those goals are served by worker organizations, typically unions, that strengthen workers' voice in the workplace and in the polity and, correspondingly, weaken capital-suppliers' and corporations' domination of daily life at work and of political processes and outcomes. The ambition of a democratic socialist economy – so far, only a dream – is to give workers more comprehensive control over making and enforcing workplace rules and sovereign law.

This chapter launches the project of, first, mapping a "new labor law" that encompasses the full range of legal domains – in and out of the scope of conventional labor law – that construct the strength or weakness of worker power, industrial democracy, and political democracy; and, second, developing legal proposals for reconstruction in the service of empowerment and democratic deepening, both in (capitalist) social democratic and in (post-capitalist) democratic socialist political economies. Given limits of space, the chapter is only that – a start to the project, offering only illustrations of legal fields outside of conventional labor law that are critical to the construction of worker power and democracy, and illustrations of proposed renovations of certain elements in each of those fields. The ambition of the chapter is to persuade the reader, through these illustrations, that the new labor law is worthy of comprehensive development.

REFERENCES

Admati, Anat, and Martin Hellwig. 2013. *The Bankers' New Clothes: What's Wrong With Banking and What to Do About It?* Princeton, NJ: Princeton University Press.

Bakan, Joel. 2005. *The Corporation: The Pathological Pursuit of Profit and Power.* New York: Free Press.

Barden, Pranab, and John Roemer, eds. 1993. *Market Socialism: The Current Debate.* New York: Oxford University Press.

Barenberg, Mark. 1993. "The Political Economy of the Wagner Act: Power, Symbol, and Workplace Cooperation," *Harvard Law Review* 106, 7: 1379–1496.

1994. "Democracy and Domination in the Law of Workplace Cooperation," *Columbia Law Review* 94, 3: 743–983.

2009. "Sustaining Workers' Bargaining Power in an Age of Globalization: Institutions for the Meaningful Enforcement of International Labor Rights," *Economic Policy Institute*, Briefing Paper #246 (October 9, 2009).

2015. "Widening the Scope of Worker Organizing: Legal Reforms to Facilitate Multi-Employer Organizing, Bargaining, and Striking," *The Roosevelt Institute* (October 7, 2015).

Block, Fred. 2014. "Democratizing Finance," *Politics & Society* 42, 1: 3–28.

Bourgue, Gilles, Margie Mendell, and Ralph Rouzier. 2013. "Solidarity Finance: History of an Emerging Practice," in Marie Bouchard, ed. *Innovation and the Social Economy: The Quebec Experience.* Toronto: University of Toronto Press, pp. 180–205.

Briggs, Asa. 1986. *The BBC: The First Fifty Years.* Oxford: Oxford University Press.

Briggs, Asa, and Peter Burke. 2020. *A Social History of the Media.* 4th ed. London: Polity.

Davis, Mike. 2018. *Prisoners of the American Dream: Politics and Economy in the History of the US Working Class.* Brooklyn, NY: Verso.

Dewey, John. 1939. *Theory of Valuation.* Chicago: Chicago University Press.

Douglas, William, John-Paul Ferguson, and Erin Klett. 2004. "An Effective Confluence of Forces in Support of Workers' Rights: ILO Standards, US Trade Laws, Unions, and NGOs," *Human Rights Quarterly* 26, 2: 273–299.

Dreze, Jacques. 1993. "Self-Management and Economic Theory: Efficiency, Funding, and Employment," in Pranab Barden and John Roemer, eds. *Market Socialism: The Current Debate.* New York: Oxford University Press.

Duncan, Della, and Robert Raymond. 2018. "Worker Cooperatives: Widening Spheres of Democracy," *Upstream, Podcast Transcript: Episode 8.1, Pt. 2.*

Fleurbaey, Marc. 1993. "Economic Democracy and Equality: A Proposal," in Pranab Barden and John Roemer, eds. *Market Socialism: The Current Debate.* New York: Oxford University Press.

Forbath, William. 1985. "The Ambiguities of Free Labor: Labor and Law in the Gilded Age," *Wisconsin Law Review* 1985: 767–817.

Hale, Robert. 1923. "Coercion and Distribution in a Supposedly Non-Coercive State," *Political Science Quarterly* 38, 3: 470–494.

  1943. "Bargaining, Duress, and Economic Liberty," *Columbia Law Review* 43, 5: 603–628.

Hertel-Fernandez, Alexander. 2018. "Policy Feedback as Political Weapon: Conservative Advocacy and the Demobilization of the Public Sector Labor Movement," *Perspectives on Politics* 16, 2: 362–379.

Hockett, Robert. 2009. "Bringing It All Back Home: How to Save Main Street, Ignore K Street, and Thereby Save Main Street," *Fordham Urban Law Journal* 36, 3: 427–445.

Hyman, Richard. 2009. "How Can We Study Industrial Relations Comparatively?", in Roger Blanpain, ed. *The Modernization of Labor Law and Industrial Relations in Comparative Perspective.* The Hague: Kluwer.

Ingham, Geoffrey. 2008. *Capitalism.* Cambridge: Polity.

Isser, Mindy. 2020. "The Union Members Who Voted for Trump Have to Be Organized – Not Ignored," *In These Times* (December 28, 2020).

Kalecki, Michał. 1943. "Political Aspects of Full Employment," *Political Quarterly* 14, 4: 322–330.

Katznelson, Ira. 2013. *Fear Itself: The New Deal and the Origins of Our Time.* New York: W. W. Norton & Co.

Kennedy, Duncan. 1991. "The Stakes of Law, or Hale and Foucault!," *Legal Studies Forum* 15, 4: 327–361.

Kochan, Thomas, Harry Katz, and Robert McKersie. 1994. *The Transformation of American Industrial Relations.* Ithaca, NY: Cornell University Press.

Krippner, Greta. 2011. *Capitalizing on Crisis: The Political Origins of the Rise of Finance.* Cambridge, MA: Harvard University Press.

Kristensen, Peer, and Jonathan Zeitlin. 2005. *Local Players in Global Games: The Strategic Constitution of a Multinational Corporation.* Oxford: Oxford University Press.

Kristof, Nicholas. 2014. "It's Now the Canadian Dream," *The New York Times* (May 15, 2014).

Lothian, Tamara. 2017. *Law and the Wealth of Nations: Finance, Prosperity, and Democracy.* New York: Columbia University Press.

Martin, Christopher. 2003. *Framed!: Labor and the Corporate Media.* Ithaca, NY: Cornell University Press.

Marx, Karl. 1990. *Capital, Vol. 1* [1st German ed., 1867]. Ben Fowkes, trans. London: Penguin Books.

Miliband, Ralph. 1973. *The State in Capitalist Society: The Analysis of the Western System of Power.* London: Quartet Books.

Nielsen. 2018. "Americans Today Spend Nearly Half a Day Interacting with Media," *Nielsen Insights* (July 18, 2018).

Nutting, Rex. 2018. "America's Inflation Problem Isn't High Wages, It's High Rent." *MarketWatch* (March 13, 2018).

Offe, Claus. 1985. *Disorganized Capitalism: Contemporary Transformations of Work and Politics.* Cambridge, MA: MIT Press.

Padget, Stephen, and William Peterson. 1991. *A History of Social Democracy in Post-war Europe.* London: Longman.

Pilling, David. 2018. *The Growth Delusion: Wealth, Poverty, and the Well-Being of Nations.* New York: Tim Duggan Books.

Polanyi, Karl. 1944. *The Great Transformation: The Political and Economic Origins of Our Time.* 1st ed. New York: Farrar & Rinehardt.

Polaski, Sandra. 2009. "Harnessing Global Forces to Create Decent Work in Cambodia," *International Institute for Labour Studies* 119. Geneva: International Labor Office.

Puette, William. 1992. *Through Jaundiced Eyes: How the Media View Organized Labor.* Ithaca, NY: Cornell University Press.

Ranis, Peter. 2016. *Cooperatives Confront Capitalism: Challenging the Neoliberal Economy.* London: Zed Books.

Rogers, Joel. 1990. "Further 'Reflections on the Distinctive Character of American Labor Laws'," *Wisconsin Law Review* 1990, 1: 1–147.

Roosevelt, Franklin D. "Acceptance Speech, Democratic National Convention" (June 27, 1936). http://millercenter.org/president/speeches/speech-3305

Sanders, Bernie. 2019. "Speech from Senate Floor: The Promise of the American Dream," *Facebook* (October 14, 2019) (last visited December 27, 2020). www.facebook.com/watch/?v=10158295736002908

2020. "Issues: Jobs and an Economy For All," *"Bernie's" Website* (last visited December 27, 2020). https://berniesanders.com/issues/jobs-for-all

Schumpeter, Joseph. 1994. *A History of Economic Analysis* [1st ed. 1954]. London: Routledge.

Shefner, Jon, and Patricia Fernandez-Kelly, eds. 2011. *Globalization and Beyond.* University Park, PA: Penn State University Press.

Staff. 2020. "Netflix Saved its Average Viewer From 9.1 Days of Commercials in 2019," *Review.com* (November 6, 2020).

Streeck, Wolfgang. 2014. *Buying Time: The Delayed Crisis of Democratic Capitalism.* Patrick Camiller, trans. New York: Verso.

Strum, Phillipa. 1984. *Louis D. Brandeis: Justice for the People.* Cambridge, MA: Harvard University Press.

Sunstein, Cass. 2017. *#Republic: Divided Democracy in the Age of Social Media.* Princeton, NJ: Princeton University Press.

Tankersley, Jim. 2016. "American Dream Collapsing for Young Adults, Study Says, As Odds Plunge that Children Will Earn More than Their Parents," *The Washington Post* (December 8, 2016)

Tooze, Adam. 2018. *Crashed: How a Decade of Financial Crises Changed the World.* New York: Viking Press.

Unger, Roberto Mangabeira. 2001. *Democracy Realized: The Progressive Alternative.* New York: Verso. 2009. *The Left Alternative.* New York: Verso.

Warren, Elizabeth, and Amelia Warren Tyagi. 2016. *The Two-Income Trap: Why Middle-Class Families Are (Still) Going Broke.* New York: Basic Books.

Weber, Max. 2003. *A General Economic History* [1st German ed., 1927]. Frank Knight, trans. Mineola, New York: Dover Publications.

Wilmarth, Arthur. 2013. "Turning a Blind Eye: Why Washington Keeps Giving in to Wall Street," *University of Cincinnati Law Review* 81: 1283–1446.

Wolff, Richard. 2012. *Democracy at Work: A Cure for Capitalism.* Chicago: Haymarket Books.

Wu, Tim. 2016. *The Attention Merchants: The Epic Scramble to Get Inside Our Heads.* New York: Knopf.

Zizek, Slavoj. 2009. *A Plague of Fantasies.* New York: Verso.

Zuboff, Shoshana. 2019. *The Age of Surveillance Capitalism: The Fight for a Human Future at the New Frontier of Power.* New York: PublicAffairs.

2

Labor and Democracy

Constructing, Deepening, and Defending Citizenship Rights

Kenneth M. Roberts

The working class and organized labor have a long, storied relationship to democratic struggles, one that has spawned a venerable tradition of social science scholarship. Although classic works in the field continue to provide essential insights for understanding labor and democracy in the world today, much of the theoretical edifice built around this topic is in need of an update at a time when democracy itself is facing formidable challenges, even in some of its historical bastions (Diamond 2019; Freedom House 2019; Levitsky & Ziblatt 2018). The fact that recent patterns of democratic "backsliding" around the world have followed in the wake of a generalized weakening of organized labor under the modern, globalized variant of capitalism raises a number of new and provocative questions about labor's relationship to democracy. Scholars have long debated whether and how labor contributes to the construction of democratic regimes and the expansion of social citizenship rights, but the current period makes it abundantly clear that democratic advances are always contingent and subject to reversal. As such, it is imperative to interrogate labor's role in the *defense* of democratic rights and liberties, and not merely the introduction or expansion of those rights. Is a weakening of organized labor a contributing factor in democratic backsliding, or even constitutive of the latter process itself?

These questions call for a multi-dimensional approach to the study of labor's relationship to democracy, one that explores labor's role in (1) constructing democratic regimes, (2) "deepening" democracy by expanding social citizenship rights, and (3) defending democracy against its adversaries and authoritarian currents in society. This chapter develops a framework to analyze these three different dimensions of labor's relationship to democracy, all of which are in need of new theoretical reflection and empirical analysis in light of recent trends in global political affairs. Classic studies of labor's role in the construction of democracy, for example, centered largely on industrial capitalist societies, but the spread of liberal democracy in the late twentieth century to much of the developing world and post-communist societies makes it imperative to consider a broader range of social alignments and political pathways that are potentially associated with democratic outcomes. Similarly, labor's role in the construction of democratic welfare states with extensive social citizenship rights in the twentieth century has been transformed – and put on the defensive – in the contemporary era of globalized market liberalism and welfare state retrenchment. Finally, democracy's global retreat during the first two decades of the twenty-first century places in stark relief labor's role in the defense of democracy itself, as well as the extent to which efforts to roll back labor rights are integral to processes of democratic backsliding.

LABOR AND THE CONSTRUCTION OF DEMOCRACY

Neither the working class nor organized labor is a uniformly democratic political actor. Indeed, influential early works in political sociology tended to overlook labor's role in democratization struggles, if they weren't skeptical of it altogether. Seymour Martin Lipset (1960: 97–130), for example, saw the working class as being predisposed toward authoritarian cultural and political values, and like most modernization theorists of his era, he considered the middle class to be the principal bearer of democratic norms like tolerance and respect for civil liberties. Drawing from different theoretical underpinnings, Barrington Moore – like Karl Marx before him – famously declared a strong, independent bourgeoisie to be the essential social foundation for a liberal democratic political order. As Moore (1966: 418) pithily stated, "No bourgeois, no democracy."

Subsequent scholarship, however, significantly shifted the intellectual debate regarding the social bases of democracy and the political orientation of the working class and its organizational expressions in trade unions and labor-based political parties. This scholarship also backed away from essentialist characterizations of class interests and preferences in order to understand more historically grounded and politically contingent struggles to construct democratic political orders as alternatives to monarchic and feudalistic *ancien régimes*, as well as more modern forms of personalistic or military dictatorship. With democracy conceived as a historical political construct, rather than a natural expression of a specific class project, the varied and contingent roles of national bourgeoisies and middle classes was better understood, and the centrality of the organized working class in most democratic struggles became readily apparent.

As Rueschemeyer et al. (1992) demonstrate, although traditional landed elites relying on labor-repressive agricultural practices were routinely opposed to the cluster of political reforms associated with democratization, the capitalist bourgeoisie and heterogeneous middle classes often played important, if highly conditional, roles in historical struggles for political democracy in industrializing societies. For these social classes, the introduction of parliaments offered a range of civil and political liberties, along with institutional channels to represent their interests and shape state policies toward capitalist development. Democratization, therefore, was integral to their efforts to balance the power of autocrats and agrarian elites under the *ancien régime*. It also, however, proved to be a dual-edged sword, as the logic of democratization was not easily capped at the extension of political rights to middle and upper classes; democracy's egalitarian ethos and universalizing thrust inevitably allowed for the working and lower classes to claim and exercise political rights as well. Indeed, it created the potential for these latter groups to wield their strength in numbers as a counterweight to the intrinsic political advantages of wealth and privilege.

The specter of subaltern empowerment, therefore, was integral to the qualified and conditional character of middle- and upper-class support for democracy in much of Europe and Latin America. It accounted for elite efforts to strictly limit the suffrage through property, tax, and literacy requirements, thereby excluding working classes from democratic participation, and guarding against efforts to translate parliamentary reforms into genuine mass democracy. It also magnified the importance of conservative parties to provide representation for elites and protect their interests as the democratic arena expanded (Ziblatt 2017). When such protection faltered, elites and middle classes often sought to roll back democratic gains and resort to authoritarian means of political exclusion. As stated by Rueschemeyer et al. (1992: 58), "for every case in which the bourgeoisie included the working class in the political system (sometimes with apparent willingness, in most cases only in response to actual or anticipated pressure) there is at least one other in which the bourgeoisie participated in rollbacks of democracy in order to defend economic interests" against perceived threats to the status quo. Indeed, the control or repression of organized labor was a prominent feature of the authoritarian waves that reversed early processes of democratization in inter-war Europe and Latin America in the 1960s and 1970s. As O'Donnell (1973) explained, the political mobilization and incorporation of the working class under democratic regimes in Latin America in the middle of the twentieth century accentuated distributive conflicts, producing an authoritarian backlash among business and technocratic elites who supported military interventions to repress labor unions and their partisan allies.

Given the highly conditional, context-dependent character of elite and middle-class support for democracy, scholars like Collier (1999), Rueschemeyer et al. (1992), and Therborn (1977) emphasized the centrality of working-class struggles for political and economic rights in the historical construction of democratic regimes. These authors were sensitive to historical contingencies and the multiple pathways toward democratic governance that they created, recognizing that labor was not always a central player in the democratization process, nor a uniformly democratic political actor. In a small number of countries, for example – in particular Switzerland, Norway, and the northern half of the United States – small-holder agriculture provided a social foundation for inclusionary democracy prior to widespread industrialization and the formation of an industrial proletariat. In other countries intra-elite competition sometimes induced conservative forces to support an extension of the suffrage in an effort to gain working-class support (see Therborn 1977: 25–27). And in some countries, such as Argentina and Mexico, labor unions became staunch allies of populist parties and leaders who supported workers' material interests – including collective bargaining rights, higher wages, and social security benefits – in exchange for institutionalized forms of political control under regimes that were manifestly authoritarian (Collier & Collier 1979, 1991; Middlebrook 1995).

In general, however, the working class and its organizational referents were heavily involved in historical struggles to build democracy and extend citizenship rights to mass publics, beyond the class-restricted suffrage regimes of early democratic experiments. Although full universal suffrage did not arrive until women also received the right to vote in the twentieth century – making women's movements, as well as labor movements, critical architects of modern democracy – organized labor consistently created pressure "from below" to open up democratic competition to mass participation. In many countries, the demand for basic citizenship rights was intimately tied to labor mobilization in the workplace, as workers' demands for the rights to unionize and engage in collective bargaining over wages, hours, and benefits rang hollow when they were excluded from broader forms of political participation.

Democracy, to be sure, was not a panacea for workers; regime institutions offered a plethora of opportunities for elite actors to protect their interests, and they hardly guaranteed policy responsiveness to working- and lower-class constituencies. Nevertheless, democracy offered a more tolerant and inclusive institutional foundation for labor-based collective action, claims-making, and political representation. As such, it encouraged workers to weld together struggles for economic rights on the factory floor with broader struggles for citizenship and political rights, including freedom of speech, press, and assembly, as well as the right to vote. Not surprisingly, then, during Europe's critical transition from restricted to mass democracy in the late nineteenth and early twentieth centuries, the organized working class was "the most consistently prodemocratic force," as European labor movements "converged on an ideology which placed the achievement of universal suffrage and parliamentary government at the center of their immediate program" (Rueschemeyer et al. 1992: 97–98). In advanced capitalist societies, according to Therborn (1977: 5), even labor movements with revolutionary origins came to view liberal democracy "as an important popular conquest, which lays the basis for further advance."

Clearly, labor struggles for democracy were more likely to bear fruit when political alliances could be forged with other class actors, in particular sectors of the middle class or small independent farmers (see Luebbert 1991; Rueschemeyer et al. 1992; Therborn 1977). If this was true in advanced capitalist societies, where industrialization created a large (but not typically majoritarian) working class, it was even more the case in developing regions where delayed industrialization and uneven development left behind a formal sector proletariat that was, comparatively speaking, numerically small, less densely organized, and politically weak or fragmented. With few exceptions – most notably Argentina, where Peronism built the developing world's most powerful labor movement – capitalist development in the Global South created formidable structural impediments to the political empowerment of organized labor. The industrial working class in many countries has long been outnumbered by the rural peasantry and urban informal sectors, while the structural heterogeneity, dispersion, and precariousness of these subaltern groups often make them difficult to organize on the basis of class interests or identities. In part for this reason, popular mobilization in developing countries has increasingly occurred along ethnic or territorial lines rather than those of social class, with peasants organizing through local indigenous communities (Yashar 2005), and informal sector or unemployed workers mobilizing through community-based organizations in low-income urban neighborhoods (Rossi 2017).

Nevertheless, organized labor has often been a major actor in democratization struggles in developing countries, typically within broad, multi-class democratic alliances. As democratization spread across the Global South and post-communist Central and Eastern Europe in the 1980s and 1990s, scholars debated the relative importance of elite strategic behavior and bottom-up popular mobilization in processes of regime transition. In the influential model developed by O'Donnell and Schmitter (1986) – one based heavily on experiences in Southern Europe and Latin America – democratic transitions were understood to be triggered by divisions within incumbent authoritarian regimes, pushed forward by civic activism, and then secured by intra-elite political bargaining or "pacts." Specialists on East European and African politics often dissented, placing greater emphasis on the role of social mobilization and protest "from below" in pushing autocrats from power (see, for example, Bratton & van de Walle 1994: 460–466; Bunce 2003: 171–174). Systematic cross-regional comparative work by Haggard and Kaufman (2012) offered qualified support for both lines of argument by demonstrating that multiple pathways to democracy exist: whereas some transitions were the product of intra-elite rivalries or conflicts with little in the way of pressure from below, others were heavily conditioned by distributive conflicts and the patterns of social mobilization and protest they elicited.

Organized labor was typically on the front lines in the latter mode of democratization across the developing world in the waning decades of the twentieth century, the height of what came to be known as the "Third Wave" of democratization (Huntington 1991). Although labor unions were heavily repressed or coopted by authoritarian states under various forms of corporatist control, workers often remained the best organized sector of civil society, as well as a sector that occupied strategic positions in national economies. The capacity of workers to engage in collective action and disrupt the economy provided unions with valuable forms of political leverage. Where the ability of workers to collectively articulate and advance their economic interests was severely restricted by authoritarian coercion or state corporatist control, unions had incentives to embed their economic claims within broader claims for citizenship rights and democratic representation – that is, for regime change. Consequently, in countries like Brazil and South Korea, where military regimes had long controlled weak and compliant labor unions, new independent unions led massive strike waves that helped to spearhead broader democratic protest movements and set the stage for regime transitions in the 1980s (Buchanan & Nichollos 2003: 212–216; Keck 1992; Seidman 1994). As Seidman (1994: 31) notes, industrial workers in Brazil and South Africa began to organize "outside the legal framework of labor relations" in the 1970s under regimes that severely restricted labor and citizenship rights, and they forged strong ties to broader activist networks in the communities where they lived. In so doing, they created forms of "social movement unionism" that shifted "away from their initial factory-based perspective," appealed to broader constituencies, and redefined their goals "to include democratization of the state" (Seidman 1994: 196).

Similar patterns played out in a number of other "third wave" democratic transitions in developing countries with strong labor movements. In Latin America, the Chilean copper miners' federation convoked the first mass protest against the brutal military dictatorship of Augusto Pinochet in 1983, launching a protracted cycle of social and political protest that culminated in the electoral defeat of the dictator in a popular referendum (Roberts 1998: 121–127). Likewise, after a decade of military rule, Uruguayan labor unions founded a new national confederation in 1983, led the first mass protest against the regime on May Day that year, and followed up with a general strike in early 1984 as the military negotiated with opposition parties over the terms of a democratic transition (Drake 1996:102–109). In Mexico, dissident teachers' unions independent of the state's corporatist union monopoly played a major role in the construction of a more autonomous civil society that challenged the electoral stranglehold of a dominant authoritarian party in the 1980s and 1990 (Cook 1996).

In Africa's transitions to democracy in the early 1990s, the role of organized labor was especially prominent in Zambia, where wildcat strikes by rank-and-file miners and public sector workers progressively eroded the corporatist bonds between the national labor confederation and the ruling party. When protests and strikes against economic austerity and liberalization measures spread over the second half of the 1980s, the labor confederation took the lead in founding a new opposition party to push for competitive elections, defeating the long-ruling incumbent party in 1991 (LeBas 2011: 81–98, 147–162). As stated by Riedl (2016: 156), a diverse array of student, business, religious, and civic groups were "united by the infrastructure and resources of the national trade union," which "provided an institutional basis to mobilize opposition" and establish "a broad-based alternative ruling coalition." In Eastern Europe, the Solidarity labor movement spawned by a series of shipyard strikes in Gdansk, Poland, played a critical role in challenging Communist single-party rule throughout the 1980s. Solidarity became the first independent labor union to obtain state recognition in the Communist bloc, and after surviving the imposition of martial law in 1981, it led diverse opposition forces in roundtable talks with the government that culminated in competitive elections and the region's first post-Communist democratic transition in the summer of 1989 (Ost 1990). More recently, the "Arab Spring" protest movement that toppled the Mubarak dictatorship in Egypt was preceded by five years of unprecedented labor unrest and the rise of independent labor unions that challenged the state's corporatist control of workers (Bishara 2018).

These cases provide ample evidence that political and organizational autonomy are critical for labor unions to advance the cause of democracy in a consistent manner. Political alliances with parties or states may help unions obtain some material gains for workers, but where such alliances entail a substantial loss of autonomy, democracy is likely to suffer. Indeed, unions – or union leaderships – that are coopted and controlled by dominant parties and coercive states are less likely to represent workers' interests effectively over the long term, and they may even become part of the authoritarian institutional edifice itself. Such patterns of corporatist state control are a major reason why scholars like Bellin (2000) and Levitsky and Mainwaring (2006) have argued that labor's contributions to democratic struggles are varied and contingent. Dissident unions that battle authoritarian states and their "official" union structures for associational freedom in the workplace often begin with claims related to wages, benefits, and the representation of rank-and-file workers; repeatedly, however, such narrow economistic claims become broadened to include more far-reaching demands for citizenship rights and regime change. Such demands, in turn, connect union struggles to those of students, community organizations, and other civic actors who contest authoritarian rule. For this reason, associational freedom in the workplace is surely a cornerstone of a democratic civil society, and of democratic political regimes across all the major world regions.

DEEPENING DEMOCRACY: THE CONSTRUCTION OF SOCIAL CITIZENSHIP

If labor has been a major actor in the construction of liberal democracy as a political regime, it has arguably been even more central to efforts to extend democratic citizenship rights to the broader sphere of social and economic relationships. The middle class and propertied groups that often joined labor in securing democratic political rights were not always supportive of efforts to push for broader forms of social citizenship. The latter, therefore, were indelibly marked by historical struggles by unions and union-allied parties to endow democratic citizenship with social content, including a robust set of social and economic rights aimed at reducing inequalities and market insecurities.

In T. H. Marshall's (1950) classic trilogy of citizenship rights, based on the British experience, different types of rights – civil, political, and social – were progressively extended to citizens as full and equal members of the national political community. Marshall recognized, however, that these rights could be either fused or separated in different historical contexts, and that class inequalities called into question the full and equal exercise of political rights. Civil rights – referring to the rule of law and the protection of individual liberties – preceded and provided a foundation for political rights, or "the right to participate in the exercise of power," either "as a member of a body invested with political authority," or as "an elector of the members of such a body" (1950: 8). Taken together, civil and political rights comprise the "procedural minimum" that Robert Dahl (1971) established for democratic governance, or what he labeled "polyarchy." They are the bedrock of democracy in the liberal tradition, one that is beholden to a procedurally minimalist conceptualization of the regime type.

What Marshall characterized as social citizenship – most basically "the right to a modicum of economic welfare and security," and more expansively "the right to share to the full in the social heritage and to live the life of a civilized being according to the standards prevailing in the society" (Marshall 1950: 8) – is more an appendage than a constitutive element of democratic citizenship in the liberal tradition. In practice, however, liberal democracy provided an institutional foundation to secure associational freedoms and channels of representation, allowing labor unions and their partisan allies to place social citizenship rights on the democratic agenda. As Marshall (1950: 16–17) recognized, the notion of social citizenship could be traced back to the adoption of universal public education in the nineteenth century, well before unions or social democratic parties had acquired access to state power. Other forms of social citizenship, such as retirement pensions and national health insurance plans, were sometimes introduced by conservative leaders – such as Germany's Otto von Bismarck – to preempt emerging socialist parties as they mobilized working-class support in the late nineteenth century. The most consistent champions of expansive social citizenship rights, however, were labor unions and their partisan allies, in particular the socialist and social democratic parties that came to power in many northern and central European countries in the middle of the twentieth century (Bartolini 2000).

Indeed, social citizenship rights were integral to the "democratic class compromise" that undergirded European social democracy in the Nordic region (Castles 1978; Korpi 1983). Under this class compromise, labor unions and socialist parties accepted private property and competitive markets, while capital and conservative parties agreed to levels of market regulation and taxation that would allow for sufficient transfer of wealth to construct generous welfare states. These social democratic welfare states differed in important ways from those constructed in other advanced industrial democracies, where social protection programs were built along more liberal or corporatist/Christian Democratic principles (the former predominating in Anglo-Saxon countries, and the latter in continental Europe). Largely in response to pressures from organized labor, these latter types of welfare states also recognized important social citizenship rights, even if they were less extensive or universal than those found under the social democratic model.

As Esping-Andersen (1990: 19–21) emphasizes, the differences between liberal, corporatist, and social democratic welfare states were categorical in nature, and not merely differences of degree, as in levels of spending or the generosity of social protection programs. Social democratic welfare states were qualitatively different, as they were grounded in universalistic principles of social citizenship and substantial (though never complete) decommodification of labor. In contrast to liberal or "residual" welfare states, which provided means-tested social assistance to the needy "when the family or the market fails," or corporatist welfare states that made benefits dependent on employment status and individual contributions, the universalistic logic of social democratic welfare states promoted "equality of status," as all citizens were "endowed with similar rights, irrespective of class or market position" (1990: 20, 25). Citizens not only had rights to universal public education, but also to health, accident, and unemployment insurance, old age pensions, and a range of allowances related to housing, parenting, day care, and job training. These expansive citizenship rights induced both working- and middle-class support for state social programs, and they provided forms of income security that at least partially decommodified labor by reducing individuals' dependence on labor market earnings.

Labor unions were staunch supporters of these social programs and the models of social citizenship they embodied, and labor-based socialist and social democratic parties were typically at the forefront of national governments that implemented the most expansive and redistributive welfare states. Indeed, these welfare states have been associated historically with high levels of trade union density, centrally organized labor movements, electorally powerful parties of the left, and strong organic linkages between unions and leftist parties – patterns of political organization that enhanced the class-based "power resources" of left-labor blocs in competitive democratic arenas (Huber & Stephens 2001). Neither labor nor the partisan left, however, expanded social citizenship on their own, as they needed political allies to achieve a solid governing majority (see Przeworski 1985). In the gestation of the Nordic social democratic models, small farmers and the centrist agrarian parties they supported were critical coalition partners of the left-labor bloc (the so-called Red-Green alliance), and the middle class became an increasingly vital source of support for social democratic welfare states over time. As Esping-Andersen (1990: 30) stated, "One of history's many paradoxes is that the rural classes were decisive for the future of socialism" in Europe, and the "structure of class coalitions is much more decisive than are the power resources of any single class."

Labor unions and labor-based populist or leftist parties have also been central players in the development of welfare states in Latin America, generally along the lines of the corporatist models found in continental Europe. The extension of social citizenship rights in the region, however, has been far less universal than that seen in the archetypal cases of European social democracy, and also more narrow or "segmented" than that seen under the corporatist models in continental Europe. The relative narrowness of social citizenship reflects, in part, underlying sociological differences in class formation in Latin America (and other developing regions), where the number of peasants and informal sector workers was comparable to, and sometimes larger than, the number of workers in the formal sector of the economy. The rise of populist governments with strong corporatist ties to organized labor in the middle of the twentieth century led to the adoption of pension plans, healthcare, and other forms of social assistance, but these programs were predominantly contributory in nature, concentrating their benefits on the middle class and the most heavily unionized workers in the formal sector of the economy (see Huber & Stephens 2012). The peasantry and urban informal sectors were typically excluded from these contributory social protection programs, creating welfare states – and social citizenship regimes – that were highly segmented or truncated rather than universalistic.

In recent decades some Latin American states have made concerted efforts to reduce this segmentation by incorporating labor market "outsiders" – the urban and rural poor – into public healthcare and pension plans, as well as family assistance and targeted cash transfer programs. As Garay (2016) demonstrates, this expansion of social citizenship rights was most likely to occur in countries with vigorous competition between political parties for the electoral support of outsider groups, and where coalitions of labor unions and social movements mobilized pressure on governments "from below" to address urgent social needs (see also Pribble 2013). Labor unions, therefore, played a significant role in this expansion of social citizenship rights in Latin America, even if union members were not the primary beneficiaries of that expansion. As Murillo and Schrank (2005) demonstrate, Latin America has a long history of both labor-mobilizing and labor-repressive regime types, and there is significant cross-national variation in the extent to which labor unions have strong partisan allies. Such variation continues to create very different political environments for labor activism across the region.

If organized labor has consistently pushed liberal democracy toward a broader conception of social citizenship rights, so also has it advocated for more expansive forms of democratic participation outside the electoral arena. Especially in the "coordinated" market economies of northern and central Europe (Hall & Soskice 1991), national labor confederations have joined business associations and state agencies in centralized, tripartite bargaining forums that shape national policies on wages, investment, and social programs (Lehmbruch & Schmitter 1982). At the firm level, works councils provide input on training programs, benefits, and the organization of the workplace, as well as representation on corporate governing boards (or "co-determination"). In the socialist tradition, experiments with worker self-management of socialized firms occurred in Yugoslavia under Tito and Allende's Chile, and more recently workers in Argentina responded to a severe financial crisis in 2001–2002 by taking over hundreds of failed firms and transforming them into self-managing worker cooperatives (Vieta 2020).

These varied experiences demonstrate that organized labor has long been at the forefront of efforts not only to create liberal democracy, but to extend democratic principles of participation and representation to a wide range of decision-making spheres in the domain of social and economic relationships. Not surprisingly, empirical research has found a strong positive relationship between union membership and political participation in the USA, as union members are more likely to vote, sign petitions, donate and volunteer for political campaigns, join civic associations, and engage in protest activities. These effects are magnified among low income and less educated individuals who are otherwise less likely to participate in democratic politics

(Kerrissey & Schofer 2013). As such, unions do not simply provide a form of collective voice or representation for underprivileged sectors in the democratic arena; they provide a stimulus to broader forms of political engagement and mobilization that help level the playing field and make democracy more inclusive and responsive to popular constituencies. In the absence of political organization and collective action, suffrage rights alone do not ensure that democratic institutions will be responsive to popular constituencies, rather than the interests of a narrow elite with concentrated political resources and privileged access to the halls of power (Gilens 2012; Winters 2011). Historically, then, labor unions and their partisan allies have been instrumental to the forms of collective action that have empowered popular constituencies and provided a counterweight to democracy's oligarchic tendencies.

DEFENDING DEMOCRACY

In contrast to the 1980s and 1990s, when over sixty countries across the world transitioned from authoritarian rule to democracy, the political momentum has shifted against democracy since the first decade of the twenty-first century. Confirming that "[d]emocracy is in retreat," Freedom House reported in 2019 that its global index of civil rights and political liberties had declined for thirteen consecutive years (Freedom House 2019). In many cases, this democratic retreat was not attributable to a regime collapse from a military coup or political revolution; instead, it reflected the progressive erosion of democratic checks and balances and a concentration of powers in the hands of elected autocrats who used democratic institutions to undermine democracy itself. Such patterns of democratic "backsliding" often culminated in hybrid regime forms, or "competitive authoritarian" regimes that held elections but so tilted the playing field as to nullify meaningful democratic contestation (Levitsky & Way 2010).

Given the centrality of labor struggles in historical processes of democratization, it is only natural to ask whether democracy's recent global retreat is related to the generalized weakening of organized labor across much of the world during the modern era of market globalization or "neoliberalism." Outside the Nordic bastions of social democracy – where unionization rates remain above 50 percent of the labor force, and above 65 percent in Sweden, Finland, Denmark, and Iceland – trade union density has steadily declined across most of the OECD, as well as Latin America, since the mid-1980s. Average levels of unionization across the OECD fell from around 30 percent in 1985 to 17 percent in 2015, with especially steep declines in the English-speaking countries and Central and Eastern Europe (OECD 2017: 134). In Latin America, unionization fell from an average of 22.9 percent to 13 percent during this period (Roberts 2014: 100), with the steepest declines occurring in countries that previously boasted relatively robust labor movements.

This organizational decline was part of a larger weakening of labor's political project in an era of neoliberal capitalism. For a generation after World War II, democratic competition in most advanced industrial democracies was structured and stabilized by well-organized class cleavages, a product of the socio-political conflicts spawned by the rise of labor movements and labor-based parties of the left during the era of industrial capitalism (Bartolini 2000; Bartolini & Mair 1990; Lipset & Rokkan 1967). As Duverger (1954) recognized, mass party organizations – those built around local party branches, rather than elite parliamentary cliques – were largely a socialist invention, and these parties played a critical role in integrating the working class into democratic institutions and civic life more broadly. As agents of social and political integration, leftist parties penetrated and organized civil society, and they performed a wide range of functional roles. In so doing they embedded labor unions within a larger web of civic associationism that included women's and youth organizations, sports and cultural groups, educational programs, and press and radio communications channels. They also offered workers an ideological identity and a programmatic platform – one centered on redistributive policies and universal social citizenship rights – that clearly differentiated the left from conservative, liberal, and Christian Democratic parties.

Along multiple dimensions, these labor-based, party-mediated, and highly participatory forms of social and political integration have withered in an era of globalized markets, mass media communications, and technocratic neoliberal policymaking. As Schmitter (2001) pithily stated, "Parties are not what they once were," an observation that holds especially true for the labor-based partisan left. Parties became increasingly multi-class, "catch-all" organizations, softening class cleavages (Kirchheimer 1966); they professionalized their organizations, electoral campaigns, communications outlets, and fund-raising activities, allowing their participatory local branches and membership rolls to atrophy (Dalton & Wattenberg 2000; Panebianco 1988); they concentrated their work on electoral activities while privileging their relations with the state, reducing their extra-electoral civic roles and their roots in civil society (Katz & Mair 1995); and under the constraints of global markets, they largely converged on pro-business neoliberal platforms that accelerated international economic integration while exposing domestic workers to a wide range of market insecurities (Berman 2019; Mair 2013).

Taken together, these trend lines uprooted and detached parties from their social bases, undermining the integration of the working class into democratic politics by traditional socialist and leftist parties. Where the left falters in performing this historical integrative role, and fails to mobilize workers around a progressive platform that responds to their material interests and political identities, it opens the door for right-wing alternatives to appeal to workers on the basis of cultural and national identities that often assume an ethno-nationalist bent. Indeed, in contexts where low income and less educated individuals perceive themselves to have been marginalized or left behind by the structural and political changes associated with globalization (Gidron & Hall 2020; Kriesi 2008), ethno-nationalist identities can easily be harnessed to workers' material interests through appeals to trade protectionism and anti-immigrant "welfare chauvinist" stands – demagogic appeals that are all the more effective when transmitted through new social media that bypass intermediary organizations and speak directly to ordinary, atomized individuals. It is hardly surprising, then, that workers have become a core constituency of far-right nationalist parties (Harteveld 2016; Oesch & Rennwald 2018) that adopt highly exclusionary stands on citizenship rights (Mudde & Kaltwasser 2013) and often manifest authoritarian tendencies (Kitschelt & McGann 1995).

Unions, however, often act as a counterweight to the working-class penetration of far-right ethno-nationalist parties. As Mosimann et al. (2019) suggest, the political projects of the labor movement and the far right are radically at odds and very much in competition with one another. Whereas organized labor advocates transnational and multi-racial forms of class solidarity, the class appeal of the far right is ethno-nationally exclusive. Consequently, like the fascist right of the 1930s, the contemporary far right is typically hostile to labor unions, and it draws its blue collar support primarily from unorganized sectors of the working class (2019: 68–69). Frymer and Grumbach (2021) demonstrate that union membership conditions racial attitudes in the USA, as white workers who join unions are less likely to harbor racial resentments and more receptive to affirmative action and other policies that benefit African Americans. As such, vibrant labor movements may well be one of the best lines of defense against the advance of far-right nationalisms: they can offer civic resistance to exclusionary ideologies and practices; defend democratic norms of tolerance, solidarity, and social inclusion; and provide associational intermediaries as a counterweight to the direct appeals of conspiratorial social media to disconnected individuals. Seen in this light, the long-term political and economic changes that have weakened labor unions in much of the world not only undermine workers' rights and exacerbate inequalities; more fundamentally, they may also pose a threat to democracy itself.

CONCLUSION

Labor unions have been central actors in democratic movements around the world since the latter part of the nineteenth century, and they remain deeply engaged in contemporary efforts to construct democratic regimes, deepen and extend citizenship rights to new spheres of social and economic relationships, and defend democratic norms and practices in the face of authoritarian challenges. The liberalization and globalization of capitalist relations of production in the late twentieth and early twenty-first centuries, however, weakened labor movements organizationally and politically in much of the world. With organized labor a diminished actor on the democratic landscape, democracy itself has become less robust, and the political incorporation of working classes around a platform of expansive and inclusive citizenship rights has been challenged by new exclusionary movements with markedly authoritarian tendencies. The resiliency of democratic institutions may well rest on the ability of labor and other civic actors to reinvigorate democracy's participatory and egalitarian ethos, crafting more inclusive democratic futures that harness workers' material interests to an expanded notion of citizenship rights.

REFERENCES

Bartolini, Stefano. 2000. *The Political Mobilization of the European Left, 1860–1980: The Class Cleavage*. Cambridge: Cambridge University Press.
Bartolini, Stefano, and Peter Mair. 1990. *Identity, Competition, and Electoral Availability: The Stabilization of European Electorates 1885–1985*. Cambridge, MA: Cambridge University Press.
Bellin, Eva. 2000. "Contingent Democrats: Industrialists, Labor, and Democratization in Late-Developing Countries," *World Politics* 52, 2: 175–2005.
Berman, Sheri. 2019. "Populism Is a Symptom Rather than a Cause: Democratic Disconnect, the Decline of the Center-Left, and the Rise of Populism in Western Europe," *Polity* 51, 4: 654–667.
Bishara, Dina. 2018. *Contesting Authoritarianism: Labor Challenges to the State in Egypt*. New York: Cambridge University Press.
Bratton, Michael, and Nicolas Van de Walle. 1994. "Neopatrimonial Regimes and Political Transitions in Africa," *World Politics* 46, 4 (July): 453–489.
Buchanan, Paul G., and Kate Nicollos. 2003. "Labour Politics and Democratic Transition in South Korea and Taiwan," *Government and Opposition* 38, 2: 203–237.
Bunce, Valerie. 2003. "Rethinking Democratization: Lessons from the Postcommunist Experience," *World Politics* 55, 2: 167–192.
Castles, Francis. 1978. *The Social-Democratic Image of Society*. London: Routledge and Kegan Paul.
Collier, Ruth Berins. 1999. *Paths toward Democracy: The Working Class and Elites in Western Europe and South America*. New York: Cambridge University Press.
Collier, Ruth Berins, and David Collier. 1979. "Inducements versus Constraints: Disaggregating Corporatism," *American Political Science Review* 73, 4 (December): 967–986.
   1991. *Shaping the Political Arena: Critical Junctures, the Labor Movement, and Regime Dynamics in Latin America*. Princeton, NJ: Princeton University Press.
Cook, María Lorena. 1996. *Organizing Dissent: Unions, the State, and the Democratic Teachers' Movement in Mexico*. University Park: Pennsylvania State University Press.
Dahl, Robert A. 1971. *Polyarchy: Participation and Opposition*. New Haven, CT: Yale University Press.
Dalton, Russell J., and Martin P. Wattenberg, eds. 2000. *Parties without Partisans: Political Change in Advanced Industrial Democracies*. Oxford: Oxford University Press.

Diamond, Larry. 2019. *Ill Winds: Saving Democracy from Russian Rage, Chinese Ambition, and American Complacency*. New York: Penguin Press.

Drake, Paul W. 1996. *Labor Movements and Dictatorships: The Southern Cone in Comparative Perspective*. Baltimore: Johns Hopkins University Press.

Duverger, Maurice. 1954. *Political Parties: Their Organization and Activity in the Modern State*. New York: John Wiley and Sons.

Esping-Andersen, Gøsta. 1990. *The Three Worlds of Welfare Capitalism*. Princeton, NJ: Princeton University Press.

Freedom House. 2019. *Democracy in Retreat: Freedom in the World 2019*. New York.

Frymer, Paul, and Jacob M. Grumbach. 2021. "Labor Unions and White Racial Politics," *American Journal of Political Science* 65, 1: 225–240.

Garay, Candelaria. 2016. *Social Policy Expansion in Latin America*. New York: Cambridge University Press.

Gidron, Noam, and Peter A. Hall.2019. 2020. "Populism as a Problem of Social Integration," *Comparative Political Studies* 53, 7 (June): 1027–1059.

Gilens, Martin. 2012. *Affluence and Influence: Economic Inequality and Political Power in America*. Princeton, NJ: Princeton University Press.

Haggard, Stephan, and Robert R. Kaufman. 2012. "Inequality and Regime Change: Democratic Transitions and the Stability of Democratic Rule," *American Political Science Review* 106, 3 (August): 495–516.

Hall, Peter A., and David Soskice, eds. 1991. *Varieties of Capitalism: The Institutional Foundations of Comparative Advantage*. Oxford: Oxford University Press.

Harteveld, Eelco. 2016. "Winning the 'Losers' but Losing the 'Winners'? The Electoral Consequences of the Radical Right Moving to the Economic Left," *Electoral Studies* 44: 225–234.

Houtman, Dick. 2003. "Lipset and 'Working-Class' Authoritarianism," *The American Sociologist* 34, 1: 85–103.

Huber, Evelyne, and John D. Stephens. 2001. *Development and the Crisis of the Welfare State: Parties and Policies in Global Markets*. Chicago: University of Chicago Press.

2012. *Democracy and the Left: Social Policy and Inequality in Latin America*. Chicago: University of Chicago Press.

Huntington, Samuel P. 1991. *The Third Wave: Democratization in the Late Twentieth Century*. Norman: University of Oklahoma Press.

Katz, Richard S., and Peter Mair. 1995. "Changing Models of Party Organization and Party Democracy: The Emergence of the Cartel Party," *Party Politics* 1, 1: 5–31.

Keck, Margaret. 1992. *The Workers' Party and Democratization in Brazil*. New Haven, CT: Yale University Press.

Kerrissey, Jasmine, and Evan Schofer. 2013. "Union Membership and Political Participation in the United States," *Social Forces* 91, 3: 895–928.

Kirchheimer, Otto. 1966. "The Transformation of the Western European Party Systems," in Joseph LaPalombara and Myron Weiner, eds. *Political Parties and Political Development*. Princeton, NJ: Princeton University Press, pp. 177–200.

Kitschelt, Herbert, and Anthony J. McGann. 1995. *The Radical Right in Western Europe: A Comparative Analysis*. Ann Arbor: University of Michigan Press.

Korpi, Walter. 1983. *The Democratic Class Struggle*. London: Routledge and Kegan Paul.

Kriesi, Hanspeter. 2008. "Contexts of Party Mobilization," in Hanspeter Kriesi, Edgar Grande, Romain Lachat, Martin Dolezal, Simon Bornschier, and Timotheos Frey, eds. *West European Politics in the Age of Globalization*. New York: Cambridge University Press, pp. 23–52.

LeBas, Adrienne. 2011. *From Protest to Parties: Party-Building and Democratization in Africa*. Oxford: Oxford University Press.

Lehmbruch, Gehard, and Philippe C. Schmitter, eds. 1982. *Patterns of Corporatist Policy-Making*. Thousand Oaks, CA: Sage.

Levitsky, Steven, and Scott Mainwaring. 2006. "Organized Labor and Democracy in Latin America," *Comparative Politics* 39, 1: 21–42.

Levitsky, Steven, and Lucan Way. 2010. *Competitive Authoritarianism: Hybrid Regimes after the Cold War*. New York: Cambridge University Press.

Levitsky, Steven, and Daniel Ziblatt. 2018. *How Democracies Die*. New York: Crown Publishers.

Lipset, Seymour Martin. 1960. *Political Man: The Social Bases of Politics*. New York: Doubleday.

Lipset, Seymour Martin, and Stein Rokkan. 1967. "Cleavage Structures, Party Systems, and Voter Alignments: An Introduction," in Seymour Martin Lipset and Stein Rokkan, eds. *Party Systems and Voter Alignments: Cross-National Perspectives*. New York: Free Press, pp. 1–64.

Luebbert, Gregory M. 1991. *Liberalism, Fascism, or Social Democracy: Social Classes and the Political Origins of Regimes in Interwar Europe*. Oxford: Oxford University Press.

Mair, Peter. 2013. *Ruling the Void: The Hollowing of Western Democracy*. London: Verso.

Marshall, T. H. 1950. *Citizenship and Social Class*, republished in T. H. Marshall and Tom Bottomore, *Citizenship and Social Class*. London: Pluto 1992.

Mudde, Cas, and Cristóbal Rovira Kaltwasser. 2013. "Exclusionary vs. Inclusionary Populism: Comparing Contemporary Europe and Latin America," *Government and Opposition* 48, 2: 147–174.

Murillo, M. Victoria, and Andrew Schrank. 2005. "With a Little Help from My Friends: Partisan Politics, Transnational Alliances, and Labor Rights in Latin America," *Comparative Political Studies* 38, 8: 971–999.

Middlebrook, Kevin. 1995. *The Paradox of Revolution: Labor, the State, and Authoritarianism in Mexico*. Baltimore: Johns Hopkins University Press.

Moore, Barrington. 1966. *Social Origins of Dictatorship and Democracy: Lord and Peasant in the Making of the Modern World*. Boston: Beacon Press.

Mosimann, Nadja, Line Rennwald, and Adrian Zimmermann. 2019. "The Radical Right, the Labor Movement, and the Competition for the Workers' Vote," *Economic and Industrial Democracy* 40, 1: 65–90.

O'Donnell, Guillermo. 1973. *Modernization and Bureaucratic-Authoritarianism: Studies in South American Politics*. Berkeley, CA: Institute of International Studies.

O'Donnell, Guillermo, and Philippe C. Schmitter. 1986. *Transitions from Authoritarian Rule: Tentative Conclusions about Uncertain Democracies*. Baltimore: Johns Hopkins University Press.

OECD. 2017. *OECD Employment Outlook 2017*. Paris: OECD Publishing.

Oesch, Daniel, and Line Rennwald. 2018. "Electoral Competition in Europe's New Tripolar Political Space: Class Voting for the Left, Center-Right, and Radical Right," *European Journal of Political Research* 57, 4: 783–807.

Ost, David. 1990. *Solidarity and the Politics of Anti-Politics: Opposition and Reform in Poland Since 1968*. Philadelphia: Temple University Press.

Panebianco, Angelo. 1988. *Political Parties: Organization and Power*. Cambridge, MA: Cambridge University Press.

Pribble, Jennifer. 2013. *Welfare and Party Politics in Latin America*. New York: Cambridge University Press.

Przeworski, Adam. 1985. *Capitalism and Social Democracy*. New York: Cambridge University Press.

Riedl, Rachel Beatty. 2016. *Authoritarian Origins of Democratic Party Systems in Africa*. New York: Cambridge University Press.

Roberts, Kenneth M. 1998. *Deepening Democracy? The Modern Left and Social Movements in Chile and Peru*. Stanford, CA: Stanford University Press.

2014. *Changing Course in Latin America: Party Systems in the Neoliberal Era*. New York: Cambridge University Press.

Rossi, Federico M. 2017. *The Poor's Struggle for Political Incorporation: The Piquetero Movement in Argentina*. New York: Cambridge University Press.

Rueschemeyer, Dietrich, Evelyne Huber Stephens, and John D. Stephens. 1992. *Capitalist Development and Democracy*. Chicago: University of Chicago Press.

Schmitter, Philippe C. 2001. "Parties Are Not What They Once Were," in Larry Diamond and Richard Gunther, eds. *Political Parties and Democracy*. Baltimore: Johns Hopkins University Press, pp. 67–89.

Seidman, Gay W. 1994. *Manufacturing Militance: Workers' Movements in Brazil and South America, 1970–1985*. Berkeley: University of California Press.

Therborn, Göran. 1977. "The Rule of Capital and the Rise of Democracy," 103 (May–June): 71–109.

Vieta, Marcelo. 2020. *Workers' Self-Management in Argentina: Contesting Neo-Liberalism by Occupying Companies, Creating Cooperatives, and Recuperating Autogestión*. Leiden, The Netherlands: Brill.

Winters, Jeffrey. 2011. *Oligarchy*. New York: Cambridge University Press.

Yashar, Deborah. 2005. *Contesting Citizenship in Latin America: The Rise of Indigenous Movements and the Postliberal Challenge*. New York: Cambridge University Press.

Ziblatt, Daniel. 2017. *Conservative Parties and the Birth of Democracy*. New York: Cambridge University Press.

3

Labor's Obstacles and Democracy's Demise

*Angela B. Cornell**

The struggle for a voice in industry through the process of collective bargaining is at the heart of the struggle for the preservation of political as well as economic democracy in America.

Senator Robert Wagner (*New York Times Magazine*, 1937)

We are witnessing some of the greatest challenges to democratic regimes since the 1930s, with democratic institutions losing ground in numerous countries throughout the world. Freedom House documents a decline in civil and political rights in both long-standing democracies and consolidated authoritarian regimes in 2018, characterizing these dual trends as "democracy in retreat" (Freedom House 2019: 1). At the same time that we celebrate the International Labor Organization's 2019 Centennial and the international consensus that fundamental labor rights are essential to social justice and political stability, we also see organized labor under assault worldwide with steep declines in levels of unionization. This confluence of events makes this an important time to consider labor's role in democracy and how that should impact public policy.

Like several other countries, the USA has experienced significant challenges that undermine the strength of its democracy, culminating with the unprecedented effort of an incumbent president to overturn the 2020 election results. Even before the destabilizing challenges to the election results, Freedom House documented the decline in the US ranking on political rights and civil liberties in recent years, asserting "its democratic institutions have suffered erosion, as reflected in partisan manipulation of the electoral process, bias and dysfunction in the criminal justice system, flawed new policies on immigration and asylum seekers, and growing disparities in wealth, economic opportunity, and political influence" (Freedom House 2020). Political parties, legislative performance, and a sense of social cohesion "are all in serious and accelerating decline" (Ginsburg et al. 2018: 246). The World Justice Project Rule of Law Index likewise shows a decline in the United States (WJP Rule of Law Index 2020). Furthermore, the extreme and rising inequality in the USA is among the very worst of wealthy industrialized countries, and returning to the levels witnessed in the Gilded Age with the Gini index moving in the wrong direction. This level of inequality erodes social cohesion and undermines democratic institutions. The American wealth gap has gotten so dramatic that in 2020 we saw the rise of centibillionaires – people worth more than $100 billion. Not only has the weakening of labor since the 1970s coincided with increasing inequality, it is also a period where we see growing

* I want to express my appreciation to Mary Fainsod Katzenstein and Aziz Rana for their comments on this chapter. Additionally, my thanks to the Clinical Law Review Writers' Workshop for feedback from participants on an earlier draft.

concern about the erosion of the quality of democracy and the distortions of the democratic process by concentrated wealth.

Strengthening labor rights in the USA is one path to shoring up our democracy. This chapter discusses relevant social science literature on labor's role in forging and sustaining democracy as well as labor's critical place in international human rights law, and questions why domestic labor law, particularly in the USA, does not do more to advance freedom of association. This chapter discusses the legal framework governing collective rights and unions in the USA and questions whether the constraints on freedom of association are more similar to those denounced in authoritarian regimes than with international labor standards most often identified in advanced industrialized democracies. It will also explore the juxtaposition of labor's place in international law with its subordinate position in domestic law. In international human rights instruments and jurisprudence, labor unions hold a special position, and freedom of association is the critical foundational right upon which other rights and interests are advanced. Labor unions are unique among civil society organizations because of their pro-democracy attributes. Despite their elevated place in the international human rights framework, labor unions have suffered disfavor and disadvantage in domestic courts, particularly in the USA.

Labor has long occupied a very important place in international human rights law, and its role in helping to forge and sustain democracies is documented extensively in social science literature. Nevertheless, union rights and union density are declining in much of the world, with unfavorable domestic law jurisprudence aiding the downward spiral of collective rights. Union density in OECD countries has fallen on average from 30 percent to 17 percent from 1985 to 2016 (OECD 2017). The share of employees covered by collective bargaining agreements also declined by a quarter in the past three decades, from 45 percent to 33 percent. Although the decline in union density is a worldwide phenomenon tied in part to geopolitical and techno-logical changes as well as neoliberal economic restructuring, these factors alone cannot account for the dramatic decline in union density in the USA, which has slipped to 10.8 percent, about half of what it was in the 1980s (US Bureau of Labor Statistics 2021).[1] Political and legal actors have played important roles in suppressing organized labor, which has intensified since the 1980s. Government deregulatory policies and judicial disfavor of collective labor rights help explain the exceptionally low union density rate or the "slow strangulation" of unions in the USA, which now has one of the very lowest rates of OECD countries – an outlier in advanced industrial nations (Freeman & Medoff 1984: 221–224).

LABOR UNIONS AND THEIR ROLE

International human rights instruments, as well as the relevant social science literature, use the term "labor" to refer to "organized labor" (i.e. unions). Labor rights have an important collective dimension that encompasses the right to organize, bargain collectively, and strike; these rights are interdependent and mutually reinforcing. Freedom of association in this context likewise contemplates the role of labor unions. Labor unions are voluntary associations of workers. Unions are perhaps best known for their organizing activities and for negotiating collective bargaining agreements that improve the terms and conditions of employment of their bargaining unit members, as well as thousands of other workers covered by the collective bargaining

---

[1] The union density rate in the USA and Canada tracked closely together for decades until they diverged in about 1980 when labor deregulation intensified in the USA. Currently the Canadian union density rate is almost triple that of the USA, despite the same technological and geopolitical forces suppressing organized labor.

agreement in some countries. Unions negotiate over a broad range of workplace issues. Collective bargaining can take place at the firm level, by industry or sector, nationally, or even globally in some unusual cases.[2] Union workers benefit from higher wages and better benefits (Freeman & Medoff 1984: 43). Typically in the USA, bargaining is done at the firm level. There is also a spillover positive effect that often enhances the compensation of the unorganized.

In addition to financial benefits, in some countries union members are protected from arbitrary termination through contract language that requires "just cause" for termination. Union contracts provide job security that is lacking throughout much of the private sector in the USA because of the employment-at-will doctrine, which provides employers the ability to terminate workers without cause. Unions also represent their members in workplace grievances that includes the legal requirement under the duty of fair representation to represent all bargaining unit members, regardless of whether they are union members or contribute financially to the union. In states that do not have "right to work" statutes,[3] private sector workers are still obliged to contribute a reduced sum to the union that represents them, but are not obliged to be a union member.

Unions build political power in local communities, as well as at the state, national, and global levels. At all levels unions and union federations advance policies that benefit working people and help to counterbalance the role of transnational capital. In the USA, the labor movement has been "the most prominent and effective voice for economic justice" (Rosenfeld 2014). A large body of research demonstrates that unions reduce inequality (Farber et al. 2018), which is important for bolstering democracy. Apart from wage and benefit enhancements for those workers covered by collective agreements, unions have been instrumental in the passage of labor protections and the social safety net, including social security, minimum wage and overtime, workplace health and safety, and medical leave, among others, confronting strenuous opposition from business interests. Labor was a "critical element" in the successful New Deal programs that so benefitted the working class (Kazin 2021). Labor additionally played a key role in the passage of civil rights legislation and prohibitions against housing discrimination.

By advancing democratic self-organization, labor unions play an important role in fostering civic and political participation by their members. *Schools of Democracy: A Political History of the American Labor Movement* provides a rich historical view of the labor movement's decades-long commitment to inculcating civic values in its working class members (Sinyai 2006). Unions routinely and systematically train their members in political action, through formal and informal training programs (Kerrissey & Schofer 2013). Union membership is associated with higher levels of political activism and participation (D'Art & Turner 2007). Empirical research confirms the broad positive impact of union membership on most types of political and civic involvement, including voting, protesting, signing petitions, association membership, etc. In research based on three nationally representative datasets that address the political behavior of Americans from 1973–1994, union membership positively affected electoral and collective action outcomes, particularly for low income voters (Kerrissey & Schofer 2013). In particular, union membership increases the likelihood of voting in a presidential election by 18 percent, volunteering for an election campaign by 43 percent, and participating in a protest by 73 percent to 93 percent.

---

[2] In the maritime industry there is a global collective bargaining agreement that covers workers all over the world. The United Steelworkers also have a global agreement with ArcelorMittal that covers workplace health and safety.

[3] Right to work statutes prohibit union security clauses that require a financial contribution from those workers represented by the union who benefit from the collective bargaining agreement.

Labor unions and mass parties have operated to invigorate those workers who are apathetic and instigate active participation. The impact is most significant among the working class and those with low levels of education. In discussing the ways in which unions' cultivation of political activity differ from that of other organizations or churches, Kerrissey and Schofer assert that "[u]nions arguably play a unique role, bringing the voices of working class individuals into American political life" (Kerrissey & Schofer 2013: 920). They go on to express concern about the consequences of shrinking union density, asserting that "[u]nions are powerful engines of political participation, and their decline betokens a less democratic future for American politics" (2013: 921).

Union organization advances meaningful decision-making roles at work, which makes a crucial difference in the advancement of political participation (D'Art & Turner 2007: 107). This experience helps to develop qualities that are necessary for active participation in a democratic system. In some situations, direct involvement in collective bargaining can also advance these qualities and other workplace negotiations that involve real power sharing (D'Art & Turner 2007).

Unions are civil society organizations, but they possess some features that are not characteristic of other organizations. For example, independent labor unions typically function democratically, which rarely is the case for other civil society organizations (Fick 2009). In some countries, internal union elections are regulated by law. For example, in the USA the Landrum-Griffin Act regulates internal union elections and provides union members with a range of statutory rights vis-a-vis their unions.[4] Under this statute, union members have the right to vote on contract ratification, union dues and other matters (Summers 2000). Members are provided access to the union's financial information and other documents. There are, additionally, a number of safeguards for internal union elections, including the secret ballot.

Independent unions face insurmountable obstacles in many countries under both authoritarian and democratic regimes. Authoritarian regimes target labor with particularly harsh treatment (Valenzuela 1989: 449). To take a notable historical example, Nazi Germany's persecution of trade unionists and dismantling of the independent trade union movement has been well documented.[5] The German Labor Front was created by the Nazis to replace the independent unions that had been banned shortly after coming to power while strikes and real collective bargaining were outlawed. The labor movement was instrumental in worker opposition to fascism, which garnered support from small and medium sized business owners and white collar workers (Mosimann et al. 2019). Similarly, fascists in Italy eliminated independent trade unions, as did Franco in Spain, who imprisoned labor leaders and imposed a new coopted labor organization (Fick 2009; Mosimann et al. 2019). Military regimes in Latin America in the 1970s and 80s targeted unions and trade unionists; thousands of trade unionists were detained, tortured, and murdered throughout the region. Latin America continues to be one of the most deadly regions in the world for trade unionists – even under democratic regimes. In 2018, thirty-four trade unionists were assassinated in Colombia with extreme violence also perpetrated against unionists in Guatemala, Honduras, Brazil, and Venezuela (International Trade Union Confederation 2019: 5).

Many authoritarian regimes would prefer to eliminate worker organizations, but choose to avoid the difficulty in squelching the trade union movement completely by eliminating independent trade unions and replacing them with a state-created worker organization

---

[4] Labor-Management Reporting and Disclosure Act (Landrum-Griffin Act), 29 USC §§ 401–531.
[5] Office of the US Chief Counsel for Axis Criminality, Nazi-Conspiracy and Aggression, Vol. II, 72 (1946).

(Valenzuela 1989). J. Samuel Valenzuela discusses two strategies employed by authoritarian regimes to contain and control unions: corporatist and the market mechanisms. The corporatist approach, as framed by Philippe Schmitter, involves the creation by the state of some form of worker organization, usually with state funding, compulsory membership, and the setting of strict boundaries to the sectors permitted to organize (Schmitter 1979: 20; Valenzuela 1989: 448). Leadership of these types of unions is typically designated by the state, or the slate of candidates is approved before an internal union election. Leadership in these coopted unions is thus "beholden to the authorities" (Valenzuela 1989: 448).

The market mechanism for union control, on the other hand, involves weakening unions as bargaining agents to the maximum extent, in order to lessen their capacity to push back against market pressures. Whereas, typically collective bargaining agreements can effectively insulate workers from the market insecurities. Valenzuela describes some of the characteristic ways unions can be constrained:

> ... collective bargaining can be decentralized completely; and strikes are rendered as ineffective as possible by such means as allowing them to be staged only when contracts have expired, preventing the use of union funds for strike support, permitting the hiring of strikebreakers, allowing lockouts, and designating many areas of the economy as "strategic," thereby prohibiting work stoppages in them ... (1989: 448).

Unions existing in these restrictive circumstances may appear to continue to exercise trade union rights, but their impact is severely curtailed. The market mechanism legal strategies effectively weaken any independent movement. Finally, corporatist and market mechanisms can also be used in combination for containment. Persecution of individual trade union leaders who are viewed as a threat can also be part of the containment strategy.

By no means is the heavy hand of restrictions and regulations used by the state to control the labor movement limited to authoritarian governments. Many democratic regimes around the globe have mirrored these labor containment policies and practices, with significant restrictions on the right to strike, collective bargaining, and other legal mechanisms that undermine democratic unions. Many countries that have previously had military regimes often continue to experience the lingering impact of these policies curtailing labor strength and undermining the development of independent labor unions, including much of Central and South America and Turkey. Several of these countries have labor laws that, in one aspect or another, significantly undermine freedom of association, impose impediments that make it impossible for workers to take advantage of statutory provisions that do exist, or lack effective enforcement.[6] They also tolerate practices that enable employers to either substantially limit trade union rights

---

[6] See, e.g. Complaint Against the Government of Guatemala Presented by the Guatemalan Trade Union, Indigenous and Campesino Movement, Case No. 3042 (ILO Committee on Freedom of Association 2013); Complaint Against the Government of Guatemala Presented by the Trade Union of Bank, Services, and State Employees of Guatemala and the Trade Union of Workers in the Municipal Development Institute, Case No. 3094 (ILO Committee on Freedom of Association 2014); Complaint Against the Government of Honduras Presented by the Latin American Federation of Education and Culture Workers, Education International, Federation of Teachers' Organizations of Honduras, General Confederation of Workers, Single Confederation of Workers of Honduras, and other national organizations supported by Education International for Latin America, Case No. 3032 (ILO Committee on Freedom of Association 2013); Complaint Against the Government of Honduras Presented by the Single Confederation of Workers of Honduras, Case No. 3268 (ILO Committee on Freedom of Association 2017); Complaint Against the Government of Turkey Presented by the Turkish Civil Aviation Union and International Transport Workers Federation, Case No. 3011 (ILO Committee on Freedom of Association 2013); Complaint Against the Government of Turkey Presented by the Union of Social Insurance, Education, Office, Commerce, Cooperative, and Fine Arts Workers of Turkey, Case No. 3021 (ILO Committee on Freedom of Association 2013).

or to create "yellow unions," which they control. Trade unions and union leaders endure persecution, and are subject to threats, detention, and even assassination in several of these countries with near or total impunity (International Trade Union Confederation 2019).

PERSPECTIVES FROM SOCIAL SCIENCE LITERATURE ON LABOR AND DEMOCRACY

Extensive research and empirical studies on unions and democracy have tended to show that organized labor plays a supportive and often crucial role in forging and defending democracies. In their seminal work *Capitalist Development and Democracy*, Rueschemeyer et al. provide a large scale historical cross-national analysis of democracy's origins (1992: 270). They assert that "[d]emocratization represents first and foremost an increase in political equality" (1992: 5). Their theoretical argument is that it is "power relations that most importantly determine whether democracy can emerge, stabilize, and then maintain itself in the face of adverse conditions" (1992: 5). Class and class coalitions have overwhelming importance in their research, and "the organized working class appeared as a key actor in the development of full democracy almost everywhere . . . " (1992: 270). The organized working class was the "primary carrier of democracy, playing a decisive role in the forging of democratic regimes" and the "most consistently prodemocratic force, which 'pushed forward' and 'fought for' democracy against the resistance of other class actors, often playing a 'decisively prodemocratic role'" (Collier 1999: 10–11).[7]

In the context of the struggle against authoritarianism, J. Samuel Valenzuela describes the "special place" labor occupies "among the forces of civil society," arguing that it "should not be discussed simply on the same plane with other segments of society" (Valenzuela 1989). According to Valenzuela, "at a certain point virtually all processes of redemocratization include a sharp increase in labor movement activism through strikes and demonstrations, usually in conjunction with a broader upsurge of mobilization by a wide variety of groups" (1989: 445). Ruth Collier's comparative research on twenty-one countries in Western Europe and South America documents the importance of the working class and the labor movement, more specifically the role of unions and labor-related political parties. In the context of democratic transitions from authoritarian regimes, she documents labor's "contribution to the delegitimization and destabilization of the authoritarian regime and hence its role in provoking the transition; and the oppositional role of labor during the process itself" (Collier 1999: 110–111). Valenzuela asserts that the labor movement is uniquely vital to redemocratization because it:

> has a greater capacity for extensive and effective mobilization at critical moments than other social groups. It has an organized network through its more or less permanently established unions which can provide an underlying grid for the choreography of demonstrations and protests. Its mass base normally has specific common interests and a politically tinged collective identity rooted in lived history. And, most important, unlike other segments such as students, church related groups, and neighborhood associations that in some national contexts may share with labor the previously mentioned attributes, the labor movement can disrupt the economy directly through work stoppages. Its wage demands are also an important element in the longer term macroeconomic context, and it can seek to redefine the conditions of employment and the character of labor-management relations. Labor's demands cannot be lightly ignored. (Valenzuela 1989: 447).

---

[7] Citing Rueschemeyer et al. (1992: 46, 59).

Along these lines Edward Shorter and Charles Tilly consider the strike to be "an instrument of working class political action" (Gentile & Tarrow 2009).[8]

Similar conclusions have been reached more recently in research on European unions and transnational democracy. In *European Unions: Labor's Quest for a Transnational Democracy*, Roland Erne concludes that "in addition to citizenship rights and constitutional bodies, a democratic polity needs tight networks of intermediate civil society organizations, like unions" (Erne 2008: 1). Independent trade union movements are "strategically and perhaps uniquely, placed to fulfill these functions which are so important to sustaining democratic government" (Fick 2009: 50). Among the specific advantages are the enhancement of citizen participation in the political system and the corresponding increase in its legitimacy (Erne 2008; Skocpol 2003). Additionally, "citizens' organizations, such as unions, also consolidate political democracy by holding corporations accountable when they subject citizens, as they frequently do, to autocratic rule in the production process or colonize the democratic process by pecuniary means" (Crouch 2004; Foot 2005; Sinyai 2006; Skocpol 2003). This is a version of what John Kenneth Galbraith referred to as "countervailing power," which emphasizes the importance of strong unions in an economy dominated by large corporations (Galbraith 1952).

Additionally, multi-country research on recent elections in Western Europe involving right-wing ethno-nationalist parties concluded that the unionized working and middle class are less likely to vote for the radical right than the non-unionized, even while the radical right expands its vote share among non-unionized workers (Mosimann et al. 2019). Radical right parties express concern over workers' interests, but undermine their interests. The study describes the agenda of the right and labor unions as being completely divergent with the radical right agenda undermining solidarity and unions advancing solidarity among workers. The research found that unions diffuse and reinforce values of solidarity among their members and this can effectively counter the exclusionary ideology of the radical right. It also referenced the ways in which workers of different origins and nationalities participate together in the union context. This research documents union members' resistance to the radical right parties.

Even in the context of recent presidential elections in the USA, union members were less likely to vote for Trump than the non-unionized white working class.[9] While a small number of unions, most specifically the police and border patrol, endorsed Trump, the vast majority of unions endorsed Biden and worked to support his election. UNITE-HERE alone knocked on 3 million doors in Nevada, Arizona, Pennsylvania, and Florida to get out the vote, including 575,000 in Philadelphia. Over 2/3 of those contacted were voters of color. The union also made 10 million phone calls. In the Georgia runoff election, the AFL-CIO made over 100,000 phone calls to Georgia union members, visited thousands of households, and sent 50,000 text messages to get out the vote.

Social science research helps to confirm the myriad ways independent trade unions strengthen democracy and resist authoritarian challenges to democratic institutions. Whether it's building solidarity among their own members who are less likely to support authoritarian-leaning candidates, or fighting to obtain or sustain democratic regimes, unions have unique strengths and are critically important to democratic governance.

---

[8] Citing Edward Shorter and Charles Tilly, *Strikes in France, 1830–1968*.
[9] Based on Exit Polling; See, CNN Politics 2020 Election Facts First Election 101.

LABOR IN THE INTERNATIONAL HUMAN RIGHTS FRAMEWORK

Labor rights have been identified as fundamental for a just society since the foundation of the International Labor Organization (ILO) in 1919; few international norms have enjoyed such widespread and historic recognition. The ILO founding documents in the Treaty of Versailles acknowledge the political significance of labor rights and the connection between social justice and securing peace. The Preamble of the ILO Constitution recognizes "the principle of freedom of association as an indispensable requirement for the attainment of universal and lasting peace."[10] The UN agency has played a critical role in establishing international labor standards and monitoring compliance through two separate complaint mechanisms. Conventions are the codifications of the labor standards passed by the tripartite body, which includes governments, unions, and employer representatives. Two of the most important conventions are the Freedom of Association and the Right to Organize (Convention 87) and the Right to Organize and Bargain Collectively (Convention 98). These two, along with the other core conventions, are recognized in the Declaration of Fundamental Principles and Rights at Work, which commits all member states (including the USA) to four categories of rights, including freedom of association and the effective recognition of collective bargaining, the elimination of forced or compulsory labor, the abolition of child labor, and the elimination of workplace discrimination. The Declaration is widely diffused throughout international instruments, bilateral and multilateral trade, and financial agreements as well as binding private contracts. The significant work of advancing human rights in the workplace and international labor standards earned the ILO the Nobel Peace Prize in 1969. The nexus between labor rights, social justice and political stability have long been acknowledged.

Recognized as both political and economic, labor rights hold the special status of being included in each of the core international instruments that comprise the International Bill of Human Rights: the Universal Declaration of Human Rights (UDHR),[11] the International Covenant on Civil and Political Rights (ICCPR)[12] and the International Covenant on Economic, Social, and Cultural Rights (ICESCR).[13] All three instruments recognize the significance of freedom of association and the right to form and join trade unions.[14] The ICESCR also requires that governments protect the right to strike and ensure that trade unions function freely.[15]

International law recognizes the dual character of labor rights, which are both individual and collective. Individuals have the right to join together with other workers to advance their collective interest, and trade unions play a critical role in the realization of these rights. Furthermore, labor unions have free-standing rights apart from their members and include the capacity to pursue relief and damages for human rights transgressions committed by a state.

Regional human rights instruments in Europe, Africa, and the Americas also recognize freedom of association and trade union rights (Ebert & Olez 2012). The European Convention for the Protection of Human Rights and Fundamental Freedoms acknowledges

---

[10] Constitution of the International Labor Organization preamble.

[11] Universal Declaration of Human Rights, GA Res. 217 (III) A, UN Doc. A/RES/217(III) (Dec. 10, 1948).

[12] International Covenant on Civil and Political Rights, Dec. 16, 1966, 999 UNTS 171, Article 22.

[13] International Covenant on Economic, Social, and Cultural Rights, Dec. 16, 1966, 993 UNTS 3, Article 8.

[14] James Gross provides a helpful framing of labor rights in the broader human rights framework in *Workers' Rights as Human Rights* (2003).

[15] International Covenant on Economic, Social, and Cultural Rights, Dec. 16, 1966, 993 UNTS 3, Article 8.

the right to freedom of association and "the right to form and to join trade unions for the protection" of interests.[16] The European Union's Community Charter of Fundamental Social Rights of Workers recognizes workers' freedom of association and the right to form trade unions, bargain collectively and to strike. The African Charter on Human and Peoples Rights also recognizes that "Every individual shall have a right to free association . . .".[17]

In the Inter-American Human Rights system, the Organization of American States Charter, Article 45(c) similarly recognizes freedom of association for workers and employers, the right to bargain collectively, and workers' right to strike as well as the right to recognition of the juridical personality for trade unions.[18] The important contributions of community organizations, including trade unions "in the life of the society and development process" is also acknowledged.[19] The American Convention and the Additional Protocol on Human Rights in the Area of Economic, Social, and Cultural Rights (Protocol of San Salvador) likewise reaffirm labor and trade union rights, with the latter also extending to trade unions the right to form federations and confederations, to function freely, and to strike. Although Economic, Social, and Cultural Rights are typically conceived to allow for gradual incorporation, labor rights referenced in Article 8(1)(a) – which include the right of workers to organize trade unions and the rights of unions to establish federations and confederations – are "immediately enforceable through the Inter-American System" (Ruiz-Chiriboga 2013: 167).[20] Only two articles hold this elevated status.

Although the ILO has been the primary international forum for addressing workplace violations of fundamental rights, other international human rights bodies have increasingly been addressing labor violations and their broader societal impact and implications. In 2010, the UN Human Rights Council created the mandate for a Special Rapporteur on Assembly and Association. In 2016, Special Rapporteur Maina Kiai published a report investigating freedom of assembly and association in the workplace, addressing the systemic violations of these rights around the world.[21] Globalization was the backdrop for the report, including the tremendous growth of multinational corporations and the erosion of states' capacity and political will to impose effective regulations on multinational corporations related to workers' rights. Kiai discusses the "worldwide crackdown [on peaceful assembly and workers' right to freedom of association] as contributing to a global crisis of governance."[22] The broader implications of this deregulation, according to the Special Rapporteur, have resulted in unconstrained public and private power and its very negative impact on vulnerable workers, including the approximately 60 percent worldwide in the informal sector who do not receive legal protection with migrant workers, domestics, and women suffering from more systemic discrimination. The failure of states to enforce laws and regulations, according to the report, has contributed to the inability of workers to exercise their assembly and associational rights, thus depriving them of "any realistic legal or democratic political recourse" and "a new poverty."[23] Citing the ILO on poverty, the

---

[16] European Convention for the Protection of Human Rights and Fundamental Freedoms, Nov. 4, 1950, ETS No. 5 (entered into force, Sept. 3, 1953), Article 11.

[17] African Charter on Human and Peoples' Rights, June 27, 1981, 1520 UNTS 217.

[18] Charter of the Organization of American States, April 30, 1948, OASTS No. A-41.

[19] Id. at Article 45 (g).

[20] The Standing of Legal Entities in the Inter-American Human Rights System, Advisory Opinion OC-22/16, ¶ 86 (Feb. 26, 2016); Additional Protocol to the American Convention on Human Rights in the Area of Economic, Social, and Cultural Rights, "Protocol of San Salvador," Article 19(6), OASTS No. 69.

[21] Maina Kiai (Special Rapporteur on the Rights to Freedom of Peaceful Assembly and of Association), *Fourth Rep. on the Freedom of Peaceful Assembly and of Association*, UN Doc. A/71/385 (Sept. 16, 2016).

[22] Id. at 4.

[23] Id. at 15.

report emphasizes that "[p]overty does not simply 'happen' to our world of work. Rather, our world of work and our labor markets are generating poverty, or at least proving inadequate to get rid of it."[24] The Special Rapporteur squarely places labor rights within the international human rights rubric and goes on to state that "[f]reedom of peaceful assembly and association are foundational rights precisely because they are essential to human dignity, economic empowerment, sustainable development and democracy. They are a gateway to all other rights; without them, all other human and civil rights are in jeopardy."[25] The work of the Special Rapporteur contextualizes and grounds labor rights as foundational, recognizing their broader significance for democracy.

With the increased precariousness of working people, and significant encroachments on freedom of association without recourse in domestic fora, regional human rights courts have played a more important role strengthening labor rights, solidifying unions, and acknowledging their significance for democracy. There is expanding labor-related jurisprudence from regional human rights bodies. The Inter-American Court of Human Rights has established an important foundation for labor rights and democracy. For instance, in *Ricardo Baena et al.* v. *Panama*, a 2001 case involving the dismissal of 270 public sector workers for engaging in a work stoppage, the Court rejected the Government of Panama's argument that the labor action was an attack against democracy and the constitutional order.[26] The walkout was framed by the government as a "savage stoppage" and characterized as militant, exceeding the bounds of law. The negotiations over labor issues between public sector unions and the government had failed, triggering the walkout. The government not only dismissed the workers, it also looted and took over union property, diverted union funds, and detained and expelled union members. Workers were targeted for dismissal because of their active membership in the union. The Court concluded that the government's actions violated freedom of association recognized in Article 16 of the American Convention, opining that "freedom of association is of the utmost importance for the defense of the legitimate interests of the workers, and falls under the *corpus juris* of human rights."[27] The Court emphasized that "in labor union matters, freedom of association consists basically of the ability to constitute labor union organizations, and to set in motion their internal structure, activities, and action program, without the intervention by the public authorities that could limit or impair the exercise of the respective right."[28]

In a more recent Inter-American decision that further elevates the status of labor unions, the Court in Advisory Opinion OC-22/16 (February 26, 2016) was asked by the government of Panama to interpret whether juridical entities, like unions and corporations, have standing in the Inter-American system (Cornell 2017). In a case of first impression, the Court distinguished the rights of labor unions from those of corporations, rejecting the claim that corporations have standing to direct access as presumptive victims of violations, while at the same time recognizing that labor unions do have standing to pursue such rights. Labor unions and indigenous communities were the only categories of juridical persons found to have standing to redress their own violations.[29]

---

[24] Id.

[25] Id. at 3.

[26] *Ricardo Baena* et al. v. *Panama*, Merits, Reparations, and Costs, Judgment, Inter-Am. Ct. HR (ser. C) No. 72 (Feb. 2, 2001).

[27] Id. at ¶ 158.

[28] Id. at ¶ 156.

[29] Article 44 of the American Convention enables juridical persons, including unions and corporations, to lodge a petition with the Inter-American Commission for violations of human rights on behalf of natural persons, but not to seek relief on their own behalf.

Protecting the rights of trade unions, the Court found, is "essential to safeguard the rights of workers to organize."[30] Unions are the "interlocutors of their members, facilitating, through this function, broader protection and the effective exercise of the workers' rights."[31] Unions are autonomous holders of rights in the Inter-American Human Rights system, which include the rights to form federations and confederations, function freely, implement their own plan of action, and to obtain a juridical personality.

The Court considered the broader societal benefits and cited the importance of reaffirming the protection of economic, social, and cultural rights to aid the consolidation of democracy in the Americas. The Court emphasized the importance of economic, social, and cultural rights as well as civil and political rights, asserting that "[d]ifferent categories of rights constitute an inseparable whole based on the recognition of the dignity of the human being, therefore require permanent protection and promotion in order to be fully realized." These rights "safeguard human dignity but also, and in equal measure, democracy."[32] The case reaffirms the far-reaching implications of workers' collective rights and their broader political significance.

The European Court of Human Rights (ECtHR) has also decided a number of important labor cases in the last twenty years, solidifying fundamental labor rights in the human rights jurisprudence. In 2008, the ECtHR issued a landmark decision, *Demir and Baykara* v. *Turkey*,[33] which recognized collective bargaining as "an essential" element of the right to freedom of association under Article 11 of the European Convention on Human Rights and Fundamental Freedoms (Ewing & Hendy 2010).[34] The case involved a public sector union that had negotiated a collective bargaining agreement with a municipality. The agreement was breached, and in the legal process to enforce it, the Turkish appellate court ruled that public sector workers do not have the right to bargain collectively or to take collective action. Reversing previous precedent, the ECtHR considered ILO and Council of Europe standards with regard to freedom of association and rejected the argument by the Turkish government that the restrictions on public sector unions were prescribed by law and had a legitimate aim. The court concluded that the government had failed to show that the "restriction was necessary in a democratic government" for any permissible purpose under Article 11(2).[35]

Demir and Baykara paved the way for subsequent decisions by the ECtHR on collective action. Perhaps most important was the recognition of the right to strike as a corollary to the essential right to bargain collectively and of freedom of association protected under Article 11. In *Enerji Yapi-Yol Sen* v. *Turkey*, public sector employees were barred from participating in a one-

---

[30] The Standing of Legal Entities in the Inter-American Human Rights System, Advisory Opinion OC-22/16, ¶ 96 (Feb. 26, 2016).

[31] Id. at ¶ 92.

[32] Id. at ¶ 98.

[33] *Demir and Baykara* v. *Turkey*, App. No. 34503/97, 48 Eur. HR Rep. 54 (2008); http://hudoc.echr.coe.int/fre?i=001-89558.

[34] The year prior, the Canadian Supreme Court in *Health Services and Support Facilities Subsector Bargaining Association* v. *British Columbia*, 2007 2 SCR 391, reached the same conclusion that collective bargaining is an essential element of freedom of association, reversing twenty years of precedent to find that Canadians have a constitutional right to bargain collectively based on international human rights law. In 2015, the Court in *Saskatchewan Federation of Labor* v. *Saskatchewan*, 2015 SCC 4, went on to recognize that there was a constitutionally protected right to strike in Canada, again as part of the fundamental right to freedom of association. The Canadian labor and industrial system was modeled after the USA and was similar in many respects and there was paralleled union density rates for decades, but decisions like these and the current stark differences in union density between the two countries with the USA holding on to only about a third of the density compared to Canada illustrate how far back the United States has fallen.

[35] Id.

day strike organized by the union federation in order to push for a collective bargaining agreement.[36] Citing ILO Convention 87, the ECtHR found the prohibition violated the European Convention since the right to strike is an inseparable part of freedom of association. Although the right to strike is not absolute and can be subject to restrictions with regard to certain categories of civil servants, the blanket ban imposed by Turkey was not permissible because it failed to demonstrate that the restriction was necessary for a democratic society. In subsequent cases where disciplinary actions against public sector workers for having participated in collective walkouts were challenged, the Court also found violations of Article 11 and 14.[37]

LEGACY OF REPRESSION OF WORKERS' COLLECTIVE RIGHTS IN THE USA

Despite the important recognition of labor rights as human rights in international law, the domestic labor law framework in the USA has never fully complied with these long-established norms, which now have far-reaching international recognition and acceptance. Millions of workers in the USA continue to be denied the ability to organize collectively, many state and municipal public sector workers have no legal mechanism to bargain collectively or are prohibited by law from doing so, and the vast majority of both private and public sector workers are deprived of any meaningful right to strike.[38]

The repression of workers' collective rights has a lengthy history in the USA. In the nineteenth century, common law legal doctrines that criminalized workers' collective activity were developed. When workers joined together to advance their collective interests, they were met with criminal prosecutions as conspiracies. After the capacity of the state to prosecute the criminal allegations began to face public disfavor, and convictions by juries waned, civil conspiracies gained ground (Lambert 2005). This legal mechanism enabled employers to sue workers and unions for financial damages and to obtain injunctions to block concerted activity. At the start of the twentieth century, judges interpreted the Sherman Anti-Trust Act to apply to unions.[39] Labor injunctions were not only used against strikes, but also to suppress strike announcements, strike rallies, picketing, private meetings, and boycotts. Employers could obtain

---

[36] *Enerji Yapi-Yol Sen v. Turkey*, App. No. 68959/01, http://hudoc.echr.coe.int/eng-press?i=003-2712212-2963054

[37] *Saime Ozcan v. Turkey*, App. No. 22943/04 http://hudoc.echr.coe.int/eng?i=001-93988 (government could not justify the prosecution of secondary school teacher who was tried for having abandoned her place of work during a walkout); *Danilenkov and Others v. Russia*, App. No. 67336/01, Eur. Ct. HR 1243 (2009) (longshoremen had hours and pay reduced, and were targeted for layoff after job action); *Kaya and Seyhan v. Turkey*, App. No. 30946/04 http://hudoc .echr.coe.int/eng?i=001-93994 (discipline of public sector worker for participating in strike day without permission and failing to perform work violated international law).

[38] See, e.g. Complaint Against the Government of the United States Presented by the Transport Workers Union of America AFL-CIO and Transport Workers Union of Greater New York AFL-CIO Local 100, Case No. 2741, Report No. 362 (ILO Committee on Freedom of Association 2011) ("The Committee ... considers that the restrictions of the right to strike in the transportation sector as set out in the Taylor Law are not in conformity with the principles of freedom of association."); Complaint Against the Government of the United States Presented by the United Electrical Radio and Machine Workers of America Supported by Public Services International, Case No. 2460, Report No. 344 (ILO Committee on Freedom of Association 2007) (denouncing the prohibition of collective bargaining for public sector workers "the Committee ... would like to emphasize that the voluntary negotiation of collective agreements, and therefore the autonomy of the bargaining partners, is a fundamental aspect of the principles of freedom of association."); Complaint Against the Government of the United States Presented by the American Federation of Labor and Congress of Industrial Organizations and the Confederation of Mexican Workers, Case No. 2227 (ILO Committee on Freedom of Association 2002) (denouncing the lack of meaningful remedies for undocumented workers under the NLRA); see also, Lance Compa, *Blood, Sweat, and Fear: Workers' Rights in the U.S. Meat and Poultry Plants* (Human Rights Watch 2004), *A Strange Case: Violations of Workers' Freedom of Association in the US by European Multinational Corporations* (Human Rights Watch 2010).

[39] *Loewe v. Lawlor*, 208 US 274 (1908).

treble damages with workers receiving criminal sanctions for strike-related activity. During this period, employers routinely required employees to sign agreements not to unionize, which are known as yellow-dog contracts. These agreements were legally enforceable, and violations could result in hefty financial damages against the workers. In addition to the severe legal action that could cause the financial ruin of workers engaging in union-related activity, private guards hired by employers and public law enforcement officers employed physical violence to intimidate or quash collective action. Workers who supported unions were often blacklisted and unable to find alternate employment.

The total assault on the interests of working people continued into the Lochner Era when for decades in the early twentieth century the Supreme Court struck down dozens of statutes that sought to curb the rampant exploitation and abuse. Statutes that dealt with issues of minimum wages, hours of work, health and safety protection, the ability of workers to engage in collective action and to organize, and even limitations on child labor were found unconstitutional in this pro-business distortion of liberty and substantive due process. Although this period is widely criticized, some of these same attributes are visible today in Supreme Court decisions that strike down statutes that seek to protect workers and consumers, exalt contractual rights, and elevate individual liberty at the expense of constitutionally protected collective rights.

Domestic labor laws in many countries obstruct workers' freedom of association, and in the USA the negative impact is particularly harsh. The union density rate in the USA is now lower than in 1935 – before we passed the National Labor Relations Act.[40] The statute no longer serves the policy goal of advancing collective bargaining. The current union density rate of 10.8 percent is completely out of sync with the level of union support among workers, which has only once dipped below 50 percent since 1936. The approval rate of unions in 2020 was 65 percent. Even as we saw union density slip in 2018, a Gallup poll shows support for unions increasing.[41] Earlier survey research by S. Martin Lipset and Noah M. Meltz showed that almost half of workers in the USA, who did not belong to a union, would vote for a union if they had the opportunity; when unionized workers were surveyed about whether they would keep their union if an election were held tomorrow, over 90 percent said they would vote to stay (Lipset & Meltz 2004: 94–96). There are a number of factors that have contributed to the decline in union density in the USA, but labor law and inadequate enforcement of the rights that do exist play no small role in constricting the labor movement. In the public sector, where union formation functions without the level of unfair labor practices found in the private sector, the union density rate is more than five times higher. The same types of labor containment practices documented in authoritarian regimes have been employed by the United States for decades and dramatically worsened under the Trump Administration and with the Trump appointed judiciary.

Labor law in the USA is also a prime example of a democratic regime that employs many of the labor containment policies that Valenzuela described in authoritarian regimes. The characteristics described that are present include constrained bargaining, significant strike impediments, extensive use of the lockout, and reducing obligations to support the designated union. Unlike in most industrial countries of the world, collective bargaining in the USA is highly decentralized, and sectoral bargaining is very rare, with bargaining typically taking place at the

[40] National Labor Relations Act, 29 USC §§ et seq. (1935), the federal statute that applies to most private sector workers.
[41] "At 65 percent, Approval for Labor Unions in the US Remains High," Gallup poll, Sept. 3, 2020, https://news.gallup .com/poll/318980/approval-labor-unions-remains-high.aspx; Gallup poll in 2018 showed 62 percent of Americans approve of labor unions (Syad 2018).

workplace level. This undermines the capacity and impact of organized labor. Furthermore, millions of workers fall outside statutory labor protections and therefore are deprived of the right to organize collectively.

Perhaps the most notorious impediment to freedom of association in the USA is the dramatic impairments of the right to strike. Most public sector workers do not have a right to strike. Federal workers can be fired and barred from federal employment for striking.[42] Many state and municipal workers are also barred from striking (Aaron 1986). Private sector workers have a statutory right to strike, under the National Labor Relations Act, but it is significantly impaired.[43] The right to strike is one of the triad of rights codified in the statute, along with the right to organize and bargain collectively. The right to strike was considered by Senator Wagner, the statute's architect, as essential in order to effectively pursue the other objectives of organizing and collective bargaining. The statute repeatedly emphasizes the critical importance of the right to strike: "[n]othing in this Act, except as specifically provided for herein, shall be construed so as either to interfere with or impede or diminish in any way the right to strike …".[44] Despite the explicit language of the statute, workers' right to strike is subject to numerous limitations and constraints, the most pernicious of which is the common law permanent replacement doctrine that permits employers to replace economic strikers (Weiler 1984).[45] Secondary boycotts, which can be particularly effective when used by organized labor, are explicitly barred and partial or intermittent strikes are impermissible as well.

So called "right to work" legislation in the USA may exemplify what Valenzuela denounces as voluntary union affiliation. Twenty-seven states currently have right to work statutes that make union affiliation voluntary in a workplace even where a majority of workers have already voted for union representation. At first glance this legislation looks innocuous, permitting individual employees to choose whether to contribute union dues. But these statutes are a deliberate effort to fatally weaken the ability of unions to function.

In right to work states, non-union members are exempted from all union dues. This creates what is known as a "free-rider" problem. Unions have a "duty of fair representation" that covers all workers in a bargaining unit.[46] Union representation of bargaining unit members is a time consuming and often costly endeavor and can involve hiring lawyers in the grievance/arbitration or litigation process. The "free-riding" employee who is not a union member thus receives the substantial benefits of the collective bargaining agreement – higher wages, job benefits, and the contractual requirement of just cause for termination – without paying a fair share of the expenses. "Right to work" legislation significantly undermines freedom of association and workers' choice to be represented collectively.

In 2018, in a decision that institutionalized free-riding and undermined freedom of association, the US Supreme Court in *Janus* v. *AFSCME* reversed the unanimous 40-year precedent *Abood* v. *Detroit Board of Education*, which upheld the constitutionality of mandatory union fees for public sector employees.[47] The Court had previously limited the use of mandatory fees exclusively to core union activities, like collective bargaining and grievance resolution, and

---

[42] 5 See USC § 7311 (1988); 5 USC § 333 (1988); Civil Service Reform Act of 1978, 5 USC §§ 7102(a)(2)(B)(v), 7116(b)(7) (1988). For example, in 1981, under the administration of President Ronald Reagan, over 11,000 air traffic controllers were fired for striking and barred from federal employment.

[43] National Labor Relations Act, 29 USC §§ 151–169 (1935).

[44] National Labor Relations Act § 2(3), 29 USC § 163 (1935).

[45] *NLRB* v. *MacKay Radio & Telegraph Co.*, 304 US 333, 345 (1938).

[46] *Smith* v. *Local No. 25, Sheet Metal Workers Int'l Ass'n*, 500 F.2d 741, 749 (5th Cir. 1974).

[47] *Janus* v. *AFSCME*, 138 S. Ct. 2448 (2018); *Abood* v. *Detroit Board of Education*, 431 US 209 (1977).

barred their use for political activities. But, rejecting the balanced approach that had existed for decades – in the 2018 split 5–4 decision – the Court in *Janus* v. *AFSCME* found requiring union fees that support core functions violated the First Amendment of public sector employees as a form of compelled speech.[48] Justice Elena Kagan's powerful dissent argued that the majority was "weaponizing the First Amendment, in a way that unleashes judges, now and in the future, to intervene in economic and regulatory policy."[49] In this decision and others, the Court is entrenching a toxic individualism that undermines critical collective rights. *Janus* challenges the financial viability of public sector unions, at the same time requiring these unions to service all workers covered by the collective bargaining agreements, even if they are contributing nothing. As has been recognized by the US Supreme Court previously, this is not a sustainable framework for advancing workers' collective rights and freedom of association.

CONCLUSION

At a time when democratic institutions have been weakened by populist and authoritarian-leaning regimes around the globe, it is imperative that we revisit the fundamentals of democracy building institutions, including the importance of strong, independent trade unions. Social science research has confirmed the critical role trade unions have played forging and sustaining democracies. The international human rights framework has long considered labor rights and labor unions as fundamental for social justice, securing peace, and bolstering democracy. Strengthening the meaningful exercise of labor rights is one important way to bolster democratic institutions. Union density in the USA reached its lowest point in over eight decades in 2019 and remains wildly out of sync with union approval. Labor law and judicial decisions that disfavor collective rights make it increasingly difficult for workers to realize their right to freedom of association.[50] Perhaps revisiting the broader significance of labor unions will increase the feasibility of legislative reform and lead to reconsideration on the part of the judiciary. The USA should join other advanced industrialized nations and comply with international norms by broadly protecting workers' right to organize, bargain collectively, and to strike in both the private and public sectors throughout the country. By doing so, the country can strengthen its ailing democracy.

REFERENCES

Aaron, Benjamin. 1986. "Unfair Labor Practices and the Right to Strike in the Public Sector." *Stanford Law Review* 38, 4: 1097–1122.

Collier, Ruth Berins. 1999. *Paths toward Democracy: The Working Class and Elites in Western Europe and South America.* Cambridge, UK: Cambridge University Press.

Cornell, Angela B. 2017. "Inter-American Court Recognizes Elevated Status of Trade Unions, Rejects Standing of Corporations." *International Labor Rights Case Law: Annotated Jurisprudence on Fundamental Rights at the Workplace* 3, 1: 39–44.

Crouch, Colin. 2004. *Post-Democracy.* Cambridge, UK: Cambridge University Press.

D'Art, Daryl, and Thomas Turner. 2007. "Trade Unions and Political Participation in the European Union: Still Providing a Democratic Dividend?" *British Journal of Industrial Relations*, 45, 1: 103–126.

Ebert, Franz Christian, and Martin Olez. 2012. "Bridging the Gap between Labour Rights and Human Rights: The Role of ILO Law in Regional Human Rights Courts." International Institute for Labor

---

[48] Id at 2482-86 (2018).
[49] Id. at 2501 (2018) (Kagan, J., dissenting).
[50] In 2019 the union membership rate dropped to 10.3%.

Studies Discussion Paper DP/212. International Labor Organization, Geneva, Switzerland. www.ilo .org/wcmsp5/groups/public/—dgreports/—inst/documents/publication/wcms_192786.pdf

Erne, Roland. 2008. *European Unions: Labor's Quest for a Transitional Democracy*. Ithaca, NY: Cornell University Press.

Ewing, K. D., and John Hendy. 2010. "The Dramatic Implications of *Demir* and *Baykara*." *Industrial Law Journal* 39, 1: 165–192.

Farber, Henry S., Daniel Herbst, Ilyana Kuziemko, and Suresh Naidu. 2018. "Unions and Inequality Over the Twentieth Century: New Evidence from Survey Data." Working Paper #620 Princeton University Industrial Relations Section, May 2018 Version. http://arks.princeton.edu/ark:/88435/dsp01gx41mm54w

Fick, Barbara. 2009. "Not Just Collective Bargaining: The Role of Trade Unions in Creating and Maintaining a Democratic Society." *Journal of Labor and Society* 12, 2: 249–264

Foot, Paul. 2005. *The Vote: How It Was Won and How It Was Undermined*. New York: Viking Press.

Freedom House. 2019. *Freedom in the World 2019*. Washington, DC: Freedom House. https:// freedomhouse.org/sites/default/files/Feb2019_FH_FITW_2019_Report_ForWeb-compressed.pdf

2020. *Freedom in the World 2019*. Washington, DC: Freedom House.

Freeman, Richard B., and James L. Medoff. 1984. *What Do Unions Do?* New York: Basic Books, Inc.

Galbraith, John Kenneth. 1952. *American Capitalism*. Boston: Houghton Mifflin.

Gentile, Antonina, and Sidney Tarrow. 2009. "Charles Tilly, Globalization, and Labor's Citizen Rights." *European Political Science Review* 1, 3: 465–493.

Ginsburg, Tom, Aziz Z. Hug, and Mila Versteeg. 2018. "The Coming Demise of Liberal Constitutionalism," *The University of Chicago Law Review*, 85 (March): 239–256.

Gross, James A., ed. 2003. *Workers' Rights as Human Rights*. Ithaca, NY: Cornell University Press.

International Trade Union Confederation. 2019. *Global Rights Index 2019*. Brussels: ITUC. www.ituc-csi .org/IMG/pdf/2019-06-ituc-global-rights-index-2019-report-en-2.pdf

Kazin, Michael, 2021. "The Cornerstone – What Is Living and What Is Dead in the New Deal." *The Nation (Book Review of Why the New Deal Matters by Erich Rauchway)*; www.thenation.com/article/society/ eric-rauchway-why-the-new-deal-matters/

Kerrissey, Jasmine, and Evan Schofer. 2013. "Union Membership and Political Participation in the United States." *Social Forces* 91, 3: 895–928.

Lambert, Josiah Bartlett. 2005. *If the Workers Took a Notion: The Right to Strike and American Political Development*. Ithaca, NY: Cornell University Press.

Lipset, Seymour Martin, and Noah M. Meltz. 2004. *The Paradox of American Unionism: Why Americans Like Unions More than Canadians Do but Join Much Less*. Ithaca, NY: Cornell University Press.

Mosimann, Nadja, Line Rennwald, and Adrian Zimmermann. 2019. "The Radical Right, the Labour Movement, and the Competition for the Workers' Vote," *Economic and Industrial Democracy* 40, 1: 65–90.

OECD. 2017. *Employment Outlook 2017*. Paris: OECD Publishing. https://dx.doi.org/10.1787/empl_out look-2017-en

Trade Unions, Employer Organizations, and Collective Bargaining in OECD Countries. Paris, France: OECD Publishing. www.oecd.org/els/emp/FlyerCollective%20bargaining.pdf

Rosenfeld, Jake. 2014. *What Unions No Longer Do*. Cambridge: Harvard University Press.

Rueschemeyer, Dietrich, Evelyne Huber Stevens, and John D. Stevens. 1992. *Capitalist Development and Democracy*. Chicago: Chicago University Press.

Ruiz-Chiriboga, Oswaldo R. 2013. "The American Convention and the Protocol of San Salvador: Two Intertwined Treaties." *Netherlands Quarterly of Human Rights* 31, 2: 159–186.

Schmitter, Philippe C. 1979. "Still the Century of Corporatism." In *Trends toward Corporatist Intermediation*, edited by Philippe Schmitter and Gerhard Lehmbruch. Beverly Hills, CA: Sage.

Schmitter, Philippe C., and Terry Lynn Karl. 1991. "What Democracy Is ... and Is Not." *Journal of Democracy* 2, 3: 3–16.

Sinyai, Clayton. 2006. *Schools of Democracy: A Political History of the American Labor Movement*. Ithaca, NY: Cornell University Press.

Skocpol, Theda. 2003. *Diminished Democracy: From Membership to Management in American Civic Life*. Norman: University of Oklahoma Press.

Summers, Clyde W. 2000. "From Industrial Democracy to Union Democracy." *Journal of Labor Research* 21, 1: 3–14.

Syad, Lydia. 2018. "Labor Unions Approval Steady at 15-Year High." *Gallup*, Washington DC. August 2018. https://news.gallup.com/poll/241679/labor-union-approval-steady-year-high.aspx?version=print

US Bureau of Labor Statistics. 2021. *Union Membership (Annual) News Release 2020*. Washington, DC: US Bureau of Labor Statistics. https://www.bls.gov/news.release/pdf/union2.pdf

Valenzuela, J. Samuel. 1989. "Labor Movements in Transitions to Democracy: A Framework for Analysis." *Comparative Politics* 21, 4: 445–472.

Weiler, Paul. 1984. "Striking a New Balance: Freedom of Contract and the Prospects for Union Representation." *Harvard Law Review* 98, 2: 351–420.

Weissbrodt, David, and Matthew Mason, Compliance of the United States with International Labor Law, 98 MINN. *L. REV.* 1842 (2014), available at https://scholarship.law.umn.edu/faculty_articles/368

World Justice Project, Rule of Law Index, https://worldjusticeproject.org/rule-of-law-index/

4

Right-Wing Populism, Illiberal Democracy, Trade Unions, and Workers' Rights

*Keith D. Ewing**

INTRODUCTION

In many countries in the immediate post-war era, trade unions were closely integrated into the processes of government and engaged in a regulatory capacity in collective bargaining. But that epoch appears to be passing, and with it the values and institutions it sustained. In the era of economic liberalism and austerity, the trade unions' role has diminished, and their industrial and political influence have declined. As if the changing economic paradigm were not difficult enough for workers' organizations world-wide, a new threat confronts them as their members are now, in large numbers, turning their backs on trade union achievements. This is the threat presented by populist movements offering populist solutions to popular problems. These are movements which are not only unsympathetic to what had been widely understood assumptions about the nature of liberal democracy, but also deeply suspicious of trade unionism.

At the time of writing it is impossible to say whether we are on the threshold of a new epoch, and whether populism reflects a transition to something altogether more sinister than even the inhospitable age of austerity. Recent experiences of the latter do not make it easy to advance the virtues of liberal democracy or the importance of trade unions – already marginalized – in making democracy work. Yet things could be even worse. My first aim in this chapter is to understand the nature and characteristics of new forms of government. In particular, I will consider the emergence of "illiberal democracy," the modern intellectual origins of which can be found in the writings of Carl Schmitt. My second aim is to examine the implications of illiberal democracy for trade unions. The issue here is not just that illiberal democracy continues to redefine and diminish the role of trade unions, but that it does so at a time when trade unions have been weakened by decades of economic liberalism.

POPULISM AND ILLIBERALISM

Populism is not a modern phenomenon, but it has spread quickly in recent years. The meaning of the term and the significance of its application vary from country to country. This section sets out:

- First, to contextualize populism as a species within the wider genus of democracy and to understand its ideological base;

* I wish to thank Professor Alan Bogg whose insights were invaluable in the preparation of this paper. I am solely responsible for the views expressed.

- Second, to explain how right wing populism is expressed as a form of illiberal democracy, populists repudiating the view that liberalism and democracy are synonymous; and
- Third, to consider some of the characteristics of populism/illiberal democracy as practiced in a number of jurisdictions.

But to emphasize that neither populism nor illiberal democracy are practiced in the same way everywhere, Trump's version of autarky (Polaski et al. 2020) is not to be found in Boris Johnson's commitment to free trade, one of the many contradictions of the latter explored below.

Populism and Democracy

I begin with the fundamental question: what is populism? This question provides no easy answer. True, many authors agree about several core characteristics of the phenomenon. But much of the writing avoids the critical issue of ideology, a point prompted by Alison Young's brilliant account of populism in the context of British constitutionalism. There she wrote about populism "as a thin-centered ideology which focuses on promoting the will of 'the people' against the will of the elites who currently occupy a position of governmental power" (Young 2018: 22). Yet having recently revisited Lenin's lecture on "The State" (Lenin 1919) and Miliband's *The State in Capitalist Society* (Miliband 1973), we see that the current wave of populism has an ideological purpose even more expansive than that identified by Young.

The starting point is thus that populism is a form of government in a capitalist society, albeit one that is less liberal than the forms of government that preceded it. As already pointed out, populism has emerged in the contemporary world as a form of government in different countries at different stages of economic and political development and in countries with different recent experiences. Here I am thinking of Hungary and Poland in contrast to the United Kingdom and the United States. So far as the United Kingdom is concerned, however, populism has emerged in an almost linear fashion from (1) the social democracy of the post-war era, to (2) the economically-liberal democracy of the Thatcher and post-Thatcher era, to (3) the populist democracy which finds expression in the current government, the origins of which predate the Brexit referendum of 2016 and the general election in 2019 (Bogg 2016; Bogg & Freedland 2018).

The emergence of populist forms of government has thus been gradual, with many of the features some identify as populist in the United Kingdom visible in earlier regimes. The seeds of populist forms are nevertheless to be found (ironically, perhaps) in the dismantling of "corporatist" structures of governance, the hollowing out of the state, and the privatization of public services. It was Blair's Labour government – not typically understood as a populist regime – that introduced the current fashion for referendums, and the Brown government that broke a promise to hold one on the Lisbon treaty in 2008. The Blair government also indulged in populist and draconian anti-terrorism legislation, and attacked the judges who held the legislation to violate human rights obligations (Blair 2010). And it was Cameron's Conservative government – which likewise would not self-define or be defined as populist as now understood – which not only authorized the Brexit referendum, but also introduced some of the populist labor laws in 2016.

Many features of the present populist forms in the United Kingdom echo the even more distant past of the right-wing populism of the 1930s. Central themes of Sir Oswald Mosley's *The Greater Britain*, published by the British Union of Fascists in 1934, prefigure the current populist ideology, including the claim that the British people (or "race") were no longer in control of their own destiny because of external influences; that political institutions (such as Parliament) and political elites (such as MPs) were frustrating the wishes of "the People;" and that traditional freedoms (by which he probably meant those secured by the Civil War in the seventeenth century) were now obstacles to freedom, insisting that "we must preserve the nation's right to decide how, and by whom, it shall be governed."

Right-wing populism is not only politically disruptive; it also has disruptive economic implications. Thus, the movement from one form of capitalist democracy to another has been accompanied by great upheavals within the organization of capitalism, marked by changes in the structure, dynamics, and geography of business. This is important to understand the significance of populist policies like Brexit being pursued against the wishes of many prominent corporations. This is neither to prove nor disprove a Leninist view of the capitalist state so much as to acknowledge that those whose interests it serves will be constantly changing. Writing about the current wave of populism in the United Kingdom, however, one distinguished journalist wrote in an essay with contested references to Schumpeter's kindred idea of creative destruction (1943):

> To them [the architects of the current wave], occasional bouts of chaos are necessary. As during wars, recessions and Thatcherism, Britain needs a therapeutic shock to jolt it into a new karma, a new inner greatness. To these no-dealers, sheep farmers and fishermen are the lackeys of Euro-protectionism. UK manufacturers have become slaves to Euro-conglomerates, forced to import bits of cars and planes because they can no longer fashion their own. They should get real. Likewise, it is humiliating that Britain should have Bulgarians picking its fruit, Poles building its houses, Portuguese staffing its clinics and care homes. Of course no deal will be painful in the short-term, but the short-term is for economic snowflakes. (Jenkins 2019)[1]

A key question, of course, is whether the movement from one species of capitalist democracy to another will lead to any significant changes in the distribution of resources and power. As Miliband points out, "it cannot be seriously disputed that a relatively small class of people do own a very large share of wealth in advanced capitalist societies" (Miliband 1973: 28). Under economic liberalism the concentration of wealth has increased, as revealed by multiple indicators. Here it is enough to note that in the United Kingdom, the share of GDP going to profits has increased year-on-year for nearly forty years, a mirror image of the diminishing proportion going to wages (65.1 percent to wages in 1976, falling to 49.5 percent in 2017 – and this includes the "wages" of CEOs, financiers, and professional footballers) (Ewing et al. 2018).

It will be a test of claims of populist governments whether the share of GDP to wage earners increases in the foreseeable future. Although the position may be different elsewhere, those who read the small print in the United Kingdom have reason to be skeptical:

> Our vision for the labour market, in other words, is not one where the state does everything for you. It is one where the state does everything it can to help you help yourself – by upgrading your skills, or by being able to balance work and family life. It is one in which a deep commitment to entrepreneurship and business is matched by a desire to ensure that the jobs that are created are highly skilled, well-paid, and fulfilling. (Conservative Party 2019: 39)

This and other clues suggest that populism is not only an ideology but, vitally, a political means to sustain an economic system. What distinguishes populism from the less primitive forms of government which preceded it (wherein its roots are to be found) is the intensity of the method deployed.

---

[1] On Schumpeter, compare Heaslip and MacGregor (2019).

Finally, in addressing its political origins and economic purpose, it is also important to note that populist government is not to be confused with *popular* government. A striking feature of recent British politics was the strong support for Jeremy Corbyn as Labour Party leader, especially in 2017. That support proved insufficient, as Labour lost the election in 2017 and decisively in 2019. Notwithstanding a trace of a "cult of the leader," Corbyn's short-lived popularity should not be confused with populism. Corbyn's reputation was won as a parliamentarian strongly committed to parliamentary democracy, and, when Labour leader, committed to restoring membership democracy within the Labour Party. The latter had been diminished by internal constitutional reforms driven by earlier leaders, notably Tony Blair – a once popular leader brought down by hubris and his own populist tendencies.

Populism and Illiberal Democracy

My claim so far is that populism is a form of capitalist democracy. Yet much of the criticism of populism is that it is an undemocratic phenomenon, for reasons outlined above. Its adherents maintain that, to the contrary, populism is a manifestation of what Victor Orban famously claimed was "illiberal" democracy (Plattner 2019). This is an idea that cannot lightly be dismissed, with an intellectual pedigree that can be traced back at least to the work of Carl Schmitt, an intellectual godfather of the far-right. Schmitt offered a searing critique of parliamentary democracy, "in which all public business has become an object of spoils and compromise for the parties and their followers, and politics, far from being the concern of an elite, has become the despised business of a rather dubious class of person" (Schmitt 1926: 4). But for our purposes the interest in Schmitt lies in his claim that democracy exists without liberalism, and the implications of that claim.

There are two aspects of Schmitt's work which are especially challenging, both of which are crystallized in the preface to the second edition of *The Crisis of Parliamentary Democracy* (Schmitt 1926). The first relates to his assertion that the belief in parliamentarism

> belongs to the intellectual world of liberalism. It does not belong to democracy. Both, liberalism and democracy, have to be distinguished from one another so that the patchwork picture that makes up modern mass democracy can be recognized. (1926: 9)

The point here seems to be that parliamentarism is based on the liberal values of "openness and discussion," reflecting the observations of the eighteenth century British parliamentarian Edmund Burke about the obligation of the Member of Parliament reflected in the Weimar constitutional government, which was the main focus of Schmitt's critique. Following Burke, the Weimar Constitution made clear that MPs were representatives, not delegates, with a deliberative duty to the nation as a whole, rather than to a party or faction. This was based on the liberal understanding that political discussion is "an exchange of opinion that is governed by the purpose of persuading one's opponent through argument of the truth or justice of something, or allowing oneself to be persuaded of something as true and just" (1926: 5).

But as Schmitt rightly points out, the "disinterestedness" required by "the liberal Burke" and others is "scarcely possible" in the modern world. Schmitt observed that, already in his day, "the development of modern mass democracy has made argumentative public discussion an empty formality," and continued as follows:

> Many norms of contemporary parliamentary law, above all provisions concerning the independence of representatives and the openness of sessions, function as a result like a superfluous

decoration, useless and even embarrassing, as though someone had painted the radiator of a modern central heating system with red flames in order to give the appearance of a blazing fire. (1926: 6)

This is a bleak assessment of parliamentarism, which also has a strong echo on the left (Lenin 1917, 1918, 1919; Miliband 1961, 1973, 1982): because the classical liberal function of Parliament is impossible as a matter of practice to achieve in a democratic state, the institution itself is irredeemably flawed, in the absence of any other compelling function of Parliament being identified. In Schmitt's view this is something his critics had been unable to provide.

Schmitt's populist critique of how Parliaments *do* behave has metamorphosed into a populist demand as to how Parliaments *must* behave, description transitioning to prescription. That is, while Schmitt intimated that Parliament was "finished" (Schmitt 1926: 8), the intolerance of liberal virtues of openness and discussion on which his view was based is now treated by modern populists as reason to marginalize and ignore the subsisting Parliament. Populists now insist that they represent the nation and the people, and that it is the role of Parliament to be the "practical-technical means" by which to govern and validate by sovereign *legal* authority the wishes of the executive in power. That Schmitt's critique has, in this way, been self-fulfilling was brought into sharp relief during the Brexit process in the United Kingdom, when Parliament was condemned for putting national interest above self-interest or factional interest as Edmund Burke instructed and in defiance of liberal constitutional law principles.[2]

Schmitt's critique of liberal values should not be mistaken for an attack on democracy. It is an attack on *liberal* democracy. For Schmitt, a precondition of democracy is homogeneity of the rights-bearing demos and, so, "a democracy can exclude one part of those governed without ceasing to be a democracy" (1926: 9). Indeed, "until now people who in some way were completely or partially without rights and who were restricted from the exercise of political power, let them be called barbarians, uncivilized, atheists, aristocrats, antirevolutionaries, or even slaves, have belonged to a democracy" (1926: 9–10). Here Schmitt was openly racist, asking rhetorically whether the British Empire rests on "universal and equal voting rights for all of its inhabitants." In answering his own question, Schmitt claimed that the Empire "could not survive for a week on this foundation: with their terrible majority, the coloreds would dominate the whites. In spite of that the British Empire is a democracy" (1926: 10).

Although readers will find this shocking, this was grist to the mill for Schmitt who argued that the "equality of all persons as persons is not democracy but a certain kind of liberalism" (1926: 13). For this, he drew inspiration from Rousseau's *Social Contract*, arguing that its central concept, the "general will," demonstrates that a true state "only exists where the people are so homogeneous that there is essentially unanimity." On this contestable reading of the great work "there can be no parties in the state, no special interests, no religious differences, nothing that can divide persons." This nevertheless raises questions about how the general will is to be determined. Even if it is the case that in democracy "there is only the equality of equals, and the will of those who belong to the equals" (1926: 16), how is the state to identify and act on the preferences of those who occupy such a position of relative political privilege?

Here we find a repudiation of elections and voting in parliamentary assemblies, a rejection of the liberal democratic conception that "a people could only express its will when each citizen voted in deepest secrecy and complete isolation" (1926: 16). According to Schmitt, such private acts even when expressing the "unanimous opinion of one hundred million private persons [are]

---

[2] *Amalgamated Society of Railway Servants* v. *Osborne* [1910] AC 87, per Lord Shaw of Dunfermline (fully discussed in Ewing 1983).

neither the will of the people nor public opinion" (1926: 16). For Schmitt, the will of the people is instead a spectral force detached from the individuals who create it and can be registered not through the aggregation of individual choice but "just as well and perhaps better through acclamation, through something taken for granted, an obvious and unchallenged presence, than through the statistical apparatus that has been constructed with such meticulousness in the last fifty years" (1926: 16).

This leads inevitably to a defense and justification of fascism and dictatorship, a close cousin if not the immediate sibling of illiberal democracy. For Schmitt, fascism like all dictatorships is "certainly anti-liberal but not necessarily anti-democratic;" on the contrary *fascism is a form of direct democracy*, political leaders representing the wishes of the people whose views paradoxically are never formally expressed and thus

> Parliament appears an artificial machinery, produced by liberal reasoning, while dictatorial and Caesaristic methods not only can produce the acclamation of the people but can also be a direct expression of democratic substance and power. (1926: 16–17)

Without suggesting that contemporary populist leaders go all the way with Schmitt, there is nevertheless enough here to alert us to the tendencies of illiberal democracy, and much here that has a contemporary resonance. This includes notably the faith in strong leadership, the contempt for Parliament, the willingness of leaders to divine the general will, the legitimation of inequality, and the demonization of "foreigners and aliens" (1926: 12).

Characteristics of Illiberal Democracy

If populism is a species of democratic government, Schmitt provides an indication of how it is distinguished from others in that genus. But although it need not be pursued with the same coarseness as he suggests, Schmitt nevertheless provides an important insight that uncouples liberalism from democracy, with far-reaching implications. Some of these implications are to be encountered in the practice of countries that have adopted "soft authoritarian" regimes, said to include the USA, Hungary, Poland, India, Brazil, the Philippines, and Turkey (Randeria 2019). Soft-authoritarianism seems to be synonymous with illiberal democracy, and both seem to involve a slide beyond if not a repudiation of liberal democracy as a form of government.

For our analytic purposes, we begin with a specification of core contemporary features of illiberal democracy that repudiate classical liberal values and democratic procedures:

- First, the seizure of power by lies, deceit, and manipulation, and often in breach of the rules and procedures designed to ensure fair electoral competition;
- Second, the democratic legitimacy which leaders claim to draw from their support by the People rather than from intermediary institutions such as Parliament;
- Third, the willingness of the proponents of illiberal democracy to govern in a way which is at best a-constitutional, and at worst unconstitutional; and
- Fourth, the tendency toward autocracy or oligarchy on the part of its proponents, and with it a tendency toward authoritarianism (Bogg 2016).

Although populist forms of illiberal democracy do not suddenly arrive, these are features of government that would be recognizable in the United Kingdom in 2020.

It is true that in uncoupling the "liberal" from the "democratic," there is not yet an infusion of the latter with the type of alternative procedures proposed by Schmitt, and that some form of popular mandate is still required. But it is clear that – as in the United States – this mandate may be provided by a minority of the people. Even Johnson with his landslide victory in the United Kingdom enjoyed the support of only 43.6 percent of those who voted (on an electoral turnout of 67.3 percent). In the same way, Johnson claims a mandate for a "hard Brexit" if necessary, despite having the support of only 51.8 percent in a national referendum in which the nations of Scotland and Northern Ireland voted to Remain and in which only 72.2 percent of eligible voters participated. The referendum was nevertheless regarded as a triumph of direct democracy over representative democracy, providing the government with a mandate to determine and to implement the will of the "People."

Putting aside the narrow majority and allegations not effectively dispelled of foreign interference in the campaign, the referendum at best determined the general preference of a significant minority, but did not settle the General Will as to the options by which that General Will might be implemented. In a system based on the principle of parliamentary sovereignty – itself the outcome of a popular revolution in the seventeenth century – the determination of the General Will was a job for Parliament, not for a minority of the electorate, as commentators made clear at the time (Robertson 2016). In the British constitution – as we have seen – Parliament exists as an elected, deliberative, and accountable body to represent the national interest rather than any geographical or sectional interest. This principle is propounded not only by Edmund Burke, but by the preeminent seventeenth and eighteenth century jurists Coke (1644) and Blackstone (1765–67), as well as by Locke who said, in a passage subsequently approved judicially at the highest level:[3]

> For the people having reserved to themselves the choice of their representatives, as the fence to their properties, could do it for no other end but that they might always be freely chosen, and so chosen freely act and advise, as the necessity of the commonwealth and the public good should upon examination and mature debate be judged to require. (Locke 1689)

In addition to the characteristics of illiberal democracy enumerated above, we might add others, some of which also have the virtue of being recognized as such by the European Union in its critique of Hungary and Poland (European Parliament 2017):

- Fifth, the attack on the rule of law, by undermining judicial independence, and initiatives to contain judicial scrutiny of government;
- Sixth, the lack of respect for human rights generally, and threats and steps to roll back legal protections of those rights;
- Seventh, marginalization or liquidation of other accountability mechanisms including the civil service, broadcasters, and civil society groups; and
- Eighth, the demonization of "migrants" and other vulnerable groups, and an associated strong sense of patriotism and national identity ("British Jobs for British Workers").

All of this alongside the simplification of complex problems, the use of simplistic slogans ("Take Back Control," "Get Brexit Done"), and the blaming of "elites" and "experts," provides simplifications which empower and legitimize the "People."

Some of the foregoing exposes the deep contradictions and hypocrisy of populism, notably in the attack on elites (Kuhner 2020). But for many the deepest concern is the attack on the courts as the defenders of the rule of law (Bingham 2011), a principle that populism strips of its liberal core and turns upside down to mean a source of government authority rather than government restraint. In the United States a populist-imbued President influences the judicial process by unabashedly political use of the power of appointment. For outsiders this is an extraordinary paradox: a

---

[3] *Amalgamated Society of Railway Servants v. Osborne*, supra.

constitution with the strongest separation of powers is also one that produces the most partisan judges of any hitherto liberal democracy. But although direct appointment in this way is not now possible in the United Kingdom, it has been proposed by right-wing think tanks nevertheless that greater political involvement in the appointments process should be restored (Falconer 2020).

Following misplaced claims about judicial activism in relation to Brexit, we have also seen an active campaign by politicians proposing to strip the judges of their powers. Just one of countless such pronouncements is Suella Braverman's posting on the *Conservative Home* website after the 2019 election but before her appointment as Attorney General. There she wrote:

> As we start this new chapter of our democratic story, our Parliament must retrieve power ceded to another place – the courts. For too long, the Diceyan notion of parliamentary supremacy has come under threat. The political has been captured by the legal. Decisions of an executive, legislative, and democratic nature have been assumed by our courts. (Braverman 2020)

Continuing in this vein, Braverman warned that "repatriated powers from the EU will mean precious little if our courts continue to act as political decision-maker, pronouncing on what the law *ought* to be and supplanting Parliament". "To empower our people," she wrote, "we need to stop this disenfranchisement of Parliament," comically unaware it seems of Parliament's already degraded role (Braverman 2020).

In joining the queue of senior politicians lining up to attack the courts, Braverman was simply expressing what had become received opinion on the Right, smarting from a number of judicial decisions restraining unconstitutional behavior by the government. Johnson's response has been not to respect the constitution but to change it:

> After Brexit we also need to look at the broader aspects of our constitution: the relationship between the Government, Parliament, and the courts; the functioning of the Royal Prerogative; the role of the House of Lords; and access to justice for ordinary people. The ability of our security services to defend us against terrorism and organized crime is critical. We will update the Human Rights Act and administrative law to ensure that there is a proper balance between the rights of individuals, our vital national security, and effective government. We will ensure that judicial review is available to protect the rights of the individuals against an overbearing state, while ensuring that it is not abused to conduct politics by another means or to create needless delays. In our first year we will set up a Constitution, Democracy, & Rights Commission that will examine these issues in depth, and come up with proposals to restore trust in our institutions and in how our democracy operates. (Conservative Party 2019: 48)

True, in the same manifesto the Conservative Party committed itself to "democracy and the rule of law," observing that "our independent courts and legal system are respected throughout the world" (2019: 47). But given the context in which parliamentary sovereignty is used paradoxically as a synonym for strong executive government, this was a mandate for a transition to a democracy where government speaks for and to the people unmediated by Parliament.

POPULISM, ILLIBERAL DEMOCRACY, AND TRADE UNIONS

It is perhaps obvious from the foregoing that illiberal democracy in the manner outlined above presents a threat to the very existence of trade unionism, for three different but overlapping reasons:

- Trade unions are generally committed to universal liberal values, including in particular social, economic, and political equality, which conflicts directly with Schmitt's homogeneity and his principle of equality of equals;

- Trade unions claim to have a voice in decision-making at the political level, and see themselves as the democratic element at the industrial level, which conflicts directly with Schmitt's requirement of no special interests; and
- Trade unions' claim to be the source of workplace regulation jointly with employers by means of collective bargaining conflicts with the view articulated by those in the Schmittian style of the responsibility of the State as protector.

The rest of this section seeks to explain and analyze each of these different threats to trade unionism in greater detail, focusing on the United Kingdom, while acknowledging that the experience may be different elsewhere.

Illiberalism and Inequality

The major driving force behind Brexit was a populist demand to take back control of national borders. Free movement of workers guaranteed by the EU treaty was a major issue, the United Kingdom being a net importer of labor. Many of the workers in question came from Eastern Europe following the expansion of the EU in 2004, countries like Poland being net exporters of labor, partly as a result of the severe economic liberalization pursued by Polish governments (Rogalewski 2020). According to the UK Office for National Statistics, in 2019 there were 28.94 million UK nationals, 2.38 million EU nationals, and 1.32 million non-EU nationals working in the UK (Office for National Statistics 2019). The numbers appeared to belie the toxic anti-immigration rhetoric from the far-right, but the concerns resonated loudly, however much inflated by such demagoguery. It was no consolation that some 800,000 British workers secured employment elsewhere in the EU.

The concerns were reinforced by a belief that freedom of movement and foreign workers were undercutting domestic standards, leading not only to unemployment amongst British workers, but forcing down wages and degrading workplace conditions. But just as the numbers of migrant workers was an exaggerated concern, it was equally misguided to blame EU nationals for the state of the British "labor market." Low wages and poor conditions were a consequence of government policy, with successive British governments of all three political parties pursuing variations of economic liberalism, which as explained below saw a steady decline in collective bargaining coverage and the statutory protection of employment standards. Actively promoted by the far-right, the myth was nevertheless allowed to circulate widely that low wages and poor working conditions were the responsibility of others, and that immigration must be stopped to protect British jobs.

This presented a dilemma for trade unions. Shortly before the Brexit referendum, Len McCluskey, the influential General Secretary of Britain's largest union – Unite the Union – wrote to encourage his members to vote to Remain, but not without some equivocation. He wrote that while his union was "fighting all the way for a Remain vote and for British workers to build their future in unity with workers in the rest of Europe," he refused "to lecture or to patronize those working people who take a different view," accepting that "in so many industrial areas, voting for the status quo is not a popular option." He continued:

> In the past ten years there has been a gigantic experiment at the expense of ordinary workers. Countries with vast historical differences in wage rates and living standards have been brought together in a common labour market. The result has been sustained pressure on living standards and a systematic attempt to hold down wages and cut the costs of social provision for working people. (McCluskey 2016)

So although "control of the labor supply in an industry or across society has always been the core of our mission, to ensure that workers get a fair share of the wealth they create . . . pulling up the drawbridge against the rest of Europe is the wrong answer." The right answer, McCluskey wrote, was "strong trade unions delivering the rate for the job, whoever you are and wherever you come from" (McCluskey 2016). And although to some extent he was driven by economic considerations and a fear of unemployment after Brexit, McCluskey was moved also by the logic of solidarity, along the lines identified by Marx in 1866:

> The only social power of the workmen is their number. The force of numbers, however, is broken by disunion. The disunion of the workmen is created and perpetuated by their unavoidable competition amongst themselves. (Marx 1866)

While not directly acknowledging Marx, for McCluskey the sentiment was the same: it was about equality, solidarity, and "working in unity across borders, rather than each isolated in our own country, turning our back on trade unions abroad" (McCluskey 2016).

Immigration was thus a big issue in the Brexit referendum, exploited ruthlessly by the populist right, with their demand for control of "our" borders. It was also an issue at the General Election in 2019, the Conservative Party standing on a populist "Get Brexit Done" platform, at the heart of which was a commitment on immigration:

> Only by establishing immigration controls and ending freedom of movement will we be able to attract the high-skilled workers we need to contribute to our economy, our communities and our public services. There will be fewer lower-skilled migrants and overall numbers will come down. And we will ensure that the British people are always in control. (Conservative Party 2019)

The promise is "a package of measures that is fair, firm and compassionate – that brings the immigration system, after so many years, into line with the British people's own sense of what is right". What is left unsaid is who will do the jobs that "lower-skilled migrants" will vacate.

As one often finds, the small print is telling. In this case the commitment to "invest in technical skills and work incentives so British workers take up as many jobs as possible" (Conservative Party 2019) should chill the enthusiasm of some Brexit supporters if "work incentives" means the same punitive and authoritarian zeal adopted for immigration control, which now deploys criminal sanctions (Bogg 2016). In any event – as McCluskey (2016) also pointed out – "leaving the EU will not stop the supply of cheap labour to Britain," the Conservative Party having already committed to increasing the number of seasonal workers who will be permitted to enter to work in agriculture (Conservative Party 2019). Nor is it clear on what terms these seasonal workers will be employed. Will freedom from EU law permit the United Kingdom to introduce "migrant rates"? Will this in turn also lead to a continuing depression of wages?

Immigration of course is not a uniquely British phenomenon, with Lynch pointing out that surveys of the 2019 European Parliament elections show that in some member states, up to a third of trade union voters favored right-wing parties (Lynch 2020). A major factor is free movement of workers and immigration, right-wing parties focusing their appeal on claims that "migrant workers are taking our jobs and a welfare chauvinism that views immigrants as undeserving and disproportionately drawing on welfare and public services and claims of welfare misuse by immigrants" (Lynch 2020). The dangers for trade unions as representative bodies which need to attract and retain members are obvious. Workers and their families are split on fundamental liberal questions of race, equality, and migration, and are prepared to reward political parties offering an unyielding xenophobic message.

The trade union strategy now is to address the problems that have created the conditions in which anti-migrant programs have flourished. These conditions include decades of deconstruction and deregulation of unions, Lynch (2020) arguing for the need to rebuild "real worker power by building up trade unions for the working class and advancing collective bargaining." But the 2019 British general election result shows how deeply ingrained these sentiments have become, and the easy allure of the simple message. Faced with a radical platform from the Labour Party that would reverse a generation of legal restrictions on trade unions and introduce an extensive suite of worker rights, British voters – including a majority of workers – rejected the offer, thereby "making Conservatives the party of the working classes," the Tories out-polling Labour "by double-digit figures among both manual workers and households with incomes below £20,000" (Woodcock 2019).

Illiberalism and "Special Interests"

So what are the implications for trade unions of illiberal democracy and the Conservative Party's apparent capture of the working classes? Other chapters in this volume confirm trade unions' past and present role, first in contributing to the development of liberal democracy, and second in defending democracy from attack. Yet as we witness the erosion of liberal democracy, we also witness trade unions as prominent victims of that process, in two separate but integrated ways: first, in terms of the role of trade unions as actors in the political process, and second, in terms of their role as the "democratic element in industry" (Bernstein 1898). So far as illiberal democracy is concerned trade unions are a hostile presence, challenging the claim that "there can be no parties in the state, no special interests, no religious differences, nothing that can divide persons" (Schmitt 1926). Trade unions, sometimes explicitly, promote a "hostile" political ideology, it being recognized judicially that

> [h]istorically, trade unions in the United Kingdom, and elsewhere in Europe, were, and though perhaps to a lesser extent today are, commonly affiliated to political parties or movements, particularly those on the left. They are not bodies solely devoted to politically-neutral aspects of the well-being of their members, but are often ideological, with strongly held views on social and political issues.[4]

It is important to say again that the emergence of illiberal forms of government has been gradual rather than sudden, and coincides with decades of economic liberalism in which trade unionism has been redefined by economics, politics, and law. The British Trade Union Act 2016 is, however, emblematic of both illiberal government and economic liberalism, introduced on the threshold of the populist era. Writing about labor law in an age of populism, Bogg and Freedland (2018) attribute to Muller (2016) the insight that "the suppression of a critical civil society is one of the core features of populist governance," and argue that this insight "provides a very powerful perspective on the political significance of the Trade Union Act 2016 in its broader context." Yet the motivation and the steps taken go beyond the containment of dissent or accountability, which we can see also in other recent initiatives, including the attacks on the civil service and the judiciary.

In a wide-ranging attack, provisions of the Trade Union Act 2016 are designed significantly to reduce the amount of money trade unions can raise and spend for political purposes. Without setting out the changes in detail here, it is enough to say that while the means chosen look

---

[4] *ASLEF* v. *United Kingdom* [2007] IRLR 361, para 50.

innocuous, the motivation is malign, and the effect likely to be profound (TULO 2016). While trade unions do raise and spend money on independent political activities, the great bulk of trade union political expenditure takes the form of affiliation fees and donations to the Labour Party, which historically has been heavily dependent on such money. The level of trade union support for the Party reflects its origins in the early twentieth century, having been formed by trade unions and socialist societies to promote working class representation in Parliament, the Party statutes retaining the Party's historic trade union based structures.

To attack trade union political activity is thus also to attack the Labour Party, currently Her Majesty's Opposition, to use British constitutional parlance. A nakedly partisan attack on the Labour Party is in turn an attack on parliamentary democracy, since the governing Conservative Party is using parliamentary power to change the rules with the purpose and effect of entrenching its control of the state. As the organization representing Labour Party affiliated trade unions made clear, at a "time when the Conservative Party already enjoys a significant financial advantage," the attack on Labour funding was "both politically unacceptable and democratically unsustainable" (TULO 2016). The changes would have been less objectionable if comparable restrictions had been imposed on the Conservative Party, or if the government had replaced union money with state funding, as is the practice in many countries throughout the world, though neither would compensate for the marginalization of trade union political voice.

Turning to the trade union role as the "democratic element in industry" (Bernstein 1898), here the reference is to trade unions not only raising wages and equalizing incomes to enable workers to participate more effectively in political society, but also extending liberal constitutional values from the political arena to the workplace (Flanders 1974). By means of collective bargaining in particular, these values include participation and accountability on the one hand and the restraint of power through legality and the rule of law on the other (Flanders 1974). Yet for those who adhere to illiberal democratic ideas, trade unions in performing this role are a hostile presence for reasons other than those already explained: they represent a conflict of interest in both society and the workplace; they put the private interests of their members above the "public interest" of public service users and others; and they are for equality, repudiating the idea that there are "equals and unequals."

This is not to suggest of course that trade unions would be crushed by modern-day populists in the way implied by authors like Schmitt. Authors and activists in the Schmittian tradition nevertheless make it clear that there will be "no place for the trade union leader who, from sectional or political motives, impeded the development of a vital service" (Mosley 1934: 36). But there would be "an honored place" for the trade unions that cooperate, "in the interest of members who are also members of the national community" (1934: 36). The worker as citizen was thus to take priority over the citizen as worker, and would be rewarded by the elimination of class war by "permanent machinery of government for reconciling the clash of class interests in an equitable distribution of the proceeds of industry" (1934: 36). Wages would not be "left to the dog fight of class war, but settled by the impartial arbitration of State machinery" (1934: 36).

With "existing organizations to be woven into the fabric of the Corporate State" (1934: 36), trade unions – along with employers' federations – were thus to be subordinated not only in the government of the state, but also in the government of industry, to represent an abstract national interest determined by a small but powerful executive government. Although this fantasy has yet to be realized, modern-day populists have nevertheless inherited a world bequeathed by economic liberalism in which the trade union role as the democratic element in industry has been largely vanquished (Ewing 2021). Not only has there been a steep decline in the levels of collective bargaining coverage, there has also been a sharp decline in strike activity, which is now at historically low levels (Office for National Statistics 2019a). That said, this decline has not prevented further restrictions being introduced, with the illiberal democratic view of homogeneity, no special interests, and a "General Will" to be seen at play in the emergence of the "public interest" as a new third party to labor law.

Although its traditional focus has been on the need to create countervailing sources of power between the employer and trade union in what was largely a private law relationship (Kahn-Freund 1983), it is true that the "public interest" is no stranger to labor law policy or analysis (Dukes 2009). There is a sense now, however, that the nature of that interest is different, with echoes of a concern to ensure that trade unions cooperate, "in the interest of members who are also members of the national community" (Mosley 1934: 36), as explained above. The Trade Union Act 2016 introduced further sweeping restrictions on the right to strike (despite the historically low levels of strike activity), reflecting an exaggerated concern with the "People" in the form of the "public interest" (ILO 2016, 2018). As Bogg (2016) suggests in a powerful and trenchant critique, the "public interest" is being invoked here to reflect the self-conscious role of the State as the protector, not only of citizens but also *workers*, from the trade union as an enemy of both.[5]

Illiberalism and the Role of the State

Apart from the "empowerment" of the "People" against trade unions as a hostile force, the other major dimension of right-wing populism for labor law is to empower the state on behalf of the People. There is nothing in the script that says that illiberal government is incompatible with social rights, and indeed it was part of Mosley's neo-Schmittian critique of parliamentary democracy that it failed to guarantee real freedom:

> A reasonable standard of life, a decent house, good wages, reasonable hours of leisure after hours of work short enough not to leave a man exhausted, unmolested private happiness with wife, children, and friends and, finally, the hope of material success to set the seal on private ambition: these are the realities of liberty to the ordinary man. (Mosley 1934)

Mosley anticipates a contemporary trend accelerating with the retreat of trade unionism and collective bargaining, namely the role of the state as the direct regulator of worker protection through legislation. This replaces the social democratic role of the state as facilitator of collective bargaining, as an autonomous process for worker engagement in decision-making and in regulation of worker protection.

The responsibility of the state in right-wing populist thought and practice is now well recognized in Europe (Lynch 2020) and can be seen most vividly in Poland where the success of the governing Law and Justice Party is due largely to the attack on social rights by its predecessor Civic Platform government, which "closely liaising with employers introduced anti-worker regulations such as those allowing employing workers on civil contracts (similar to zero-hours contracts)" (Rogalewski 2020: 8). At the same time, "the government did not conduct genuine negotiations with trade unions and left them without a choice [other] than to leave the tripartite committee and suspend their participation in the social dialogue" (2020: 8). Indeed, it has been said by a senior Polish trade unionist that since the replacement of the communist system in 1989, Polish workers have lived

---

[5] As Bogg points out, there has been a creation and exploitation of a "war" between the worker as producer and the worker as consumer (Bogg 2016: 324).

[i]n the neo liberal propaganda and policies which not only caused unemployment and dismantling [of the] collective bargaining system but most importantly they were told that they were responsible for their problems and if they were unable to find a job they should create their own company. (Rogalewski 2020: 9)

For many Polish workers, the only way to find employment and a decent life was to emigrate, with almost one million moving to the United Kingdom alone. In this context, explains Rogalewski (2020), the Law and Justice Party's program of pro-family and pro-social policies were attractive to many of those who had been left behind. These included measures to reduce the retirement age to sixty-five and to introduce a child allowance for poorer families. This was in addition to an increase in the minimum wage, which Rogalewski anticipated would eventually rise to 60 percent of the median wage. In these different ways, the working and living conditions of the poorest section of the Polish society were significantly improved (2020: 8). So while it is true that Law and Justice has also attacked the judges, and stands on a platform which is anti-women, anti-refugee, and anti-LGBT, in a telling phrase Rogalewski writes that "attachment to fundamental rights and [the] value of the rule of law become[s] somehow less important than social rights" (2020: 9).

The situation is different in the United Kingdom with neo-liberal policies having been pursued by a party now led by a populist leader, in what in effect has been a populist coup within the governing party. It is striking nevertheless that shortly before the election in 2019, the government announced plans to take the national minimum wage to two-thirds of median earnings by 2024, which "would on current forecasts equate to £10.50 ($12.93) an hour," reported to be "one of the highest levels, if not the highest, in the developed world" (Giugliano 2019), and reinforce the government's minimum wage initiative later in the same year, committing to "new protections for workers while preserving the dynamism and job creation that drive our shared prosperity" (Conservative Party 2019: 38). More specifically, the Conservative Party claims it is committed "to build on existing employment law with measures that protect those in low-paid work and in the gig economy." It asserts, for example:

- "We will create a single enforcement body and crack down on any employer abusing employment law, whether by taking workers' tips or refusing them sick pay."
- "We will ensure that workers have the right to request a more predictable contract and other reasonable protections."

All this is based on the understanding that "people cannot fulfil their potential if they do not have jobs that treat them with dignity and respect, and if they are not in control of their lives and their futures" (2019: 38). Other promises include steps to encourage flexible working as a default position, as well as to extend leave for neonatal care, and to improve entitlement to leave for unpaid carers. Such proposals represent a thoroughgoing reversal of the stern economic discipline hitherto promoted by Johnson and his ministerial team, five of whom had famously authored a book entitled *Britannia Unchained – Global Growth and Prosperity*, in which they claimed that "[t]he British are among the worst idlers in the world. We work among the lowest hours, we retire early and our productivity is poor. Whereas Indian children aspire to be doctors or businessmen, the British are more interested in football and pop music" (Kwarteng et al. 2012: 61).

One of this group of five Conservative ministers – now deputy Prime Minister – also argued for unfair dismissal reforms to make it easier for employers to fire workers without fear of legal liability, and to exempt small businesses from the minimum wage for workers under twenty-one. Johnson himself is on record as suggesting in relation to EU labor standards that, stuff such as the working time directive, ... the Data Protection Act, ... and the Insolvency II directive, many directives and regulations emanating from Brussels have, either through gold-plating in this country or simply because of poor drafting or whatever, been far too expensive.... They are not ideally tailored to the needs of this economy.[6]

It is not clear where Johnson has now landed on these latter issues, which are significant not least because the EU Working Time Directive to which he refers guarantees to British workers the right to four weeks' paid holidays, a requirement to which many employers appear to be opposed.

Adding to the uncertainty, Johnson has subsequently revealed an ideological promiscuity, famously attacking corporate critics with "fuck business,"[7] and allegedly freezing them out because of their pro-EU positions. Yet at the same time as promoting the interests of business, Johnson refused to accept alignment on social issues and workers' rights with the EU in the future trading relationship, despite the fact that for all its claims EU law provides only limited protection on an incomplete range of issues. The United Kingdom's preference was for a comprehensive free trade agreement in which there would be a standard labor chapter. This means a commitment to comply with the four core ILO principles, perhaps along with commitments to wages, working time, and health and safety. These have proved in other free trade agreements to be unenforceable soft law commitments, which will represent a poor deal if traded for the binding hard law of EU obligations.

That said, Johnson is apparently planning instead to "legislate to ensure high standards of workers' rights," these to be implemented in "parallel" with an EU free trade agreement (Conservative Party 2019) and similar such agreements with multiple other countries. But even if Johnson's and the Party's conversion to social rights is feigned, it was nevertheless pointed out pre Covid-19 that

> Boris Johnson has sensed the way the wind is blowing and tacked accordingly. Since becoming Prime Minister he has announced the biggest increase in public spending in more than fifteen years, abandoned a planned cut in corporation tax, raised the minimum wage, promised a budget that will boost spending on public infrastructure projects, and nationalized Northern Rail. Ministers are fully signed up to the idea that more needs to be done to tackle the climate crisis and are aware of how high the stakes are at the COP26 conference being held in Glasgow at the end of the year. If, as some of Johnson's critics say, this is the most right-wing government in history, it has a strange way of showing it. The above measures would be supported by those on the left if it was a Labour government responsible for them. (Elliott 2020)

Therein lies the dilemma of modern trade unionism identified also by Rogalewski (2020) above: the far right has made itself more appealing to trade union members, by "taking up some of the trade union demands, language, and narrative but none of our values nor the recognition of the legitimate role of trade unions to defend workers' rights and interests" (Lynch 2020).

CONCLUSION

Illiberal democracy thus presents three threats to trade unions: (1) it divides their membership; (2) it questions further their legitimacy; and (3) it reinforces the role of the state as provider. These threats are made all the more difficult by the context which has generated a populist response. Trade unions have been weakened by decades of economic liberalism and a decade of

[6] HC Treasury Committee, Oral Evidence, 23 March 2016, HC 499 (2015–16), Q 1148.
[7] See, e.g. *BBC News* (June 16, 2018).

austerity, weakened in other words by the conditions that have helped to fuel the populists' demands. Trade union decline is itself a symptom of the changes that have caused such discontent: commodification and insecurity at work, growing inequality of income and wealth, diminished public services, and a decaying public infrastructure. An opportunity radically to reverse these underlying causes by protecting workers and jobs, closing rather than widening the inequality gap, was presented in the United Kingdom to the British people at the election in 2019 but rejected.

The rejection at the general election in 2019 of a program that would reverse these trends indicates the extent of the difficulty facing trade unions as defenders of democracy against authoritarian challenges. That said, claims that populism and workers' interests are synonymous are nevertheless about to be sorely tested if the Johnson government realizes its ambition by negotiating free trade agreements with the EU and the USA respectively, which make no effective provision to protect workers' rights from the vagaries of the populists' whim. So far as we know, at least some (though by no means all) modern-day populists believe fundamentally in free trade and open markets on a global basis. That being the case, it seems doubtful that recreating the conditions that propelled them to power will satisfy the demands of the "People" on behalf of whom they claim implausibly to speak.

REFERENCES

Bernstein, Eduard. 1898. *The Preconditions of Socialism*. Cambridge, MA: Cambridge University Press.

Bingham, Tom. 2011. *The Rule of Law*. Harmondsworth: Penguin Books.

Blackstone, Sir William. 1765–67. *Commentaries on the Laws of England*. Oxford: Clarendon Press.

Blair, Tony. 2010. *A Journey*. London: Arrow Books.

Bogg, Alan L. 2016. "Beyond Neo-Liberalism: The Trade Union Act 2016 and the Authoritarian State," *Industrial Law Journal* 45, 3: 299–336.

Bogg, Alan L., and Mark R. Freedland 2018. "Labour Law in the Age of Populism: towards Sustainable Democratic Engagement," *Max Planck Institute for Comparative Public Law & International Law (MPIL). Research Paper No 2018-15*.

Braverman, Suella. 2020. "People We Elect Must Take Back Control from People We Don't, Who Include the Judges," *Conservative Home* (January 27, 2020).

Burke, Sir Edmund. 1774. "Speech to the Electors of Bristol, 3 November 1774," in *Edmund Burke on Government, Politics, and Society*. B.W. Hill, ed. Glasgow: Fontana.

Coke, Sir Edward. 1644. *Institutes of the Laws of England, Bk iv*. London: Lee and Pakeman.

Conservative Party. 2019. *Conservative Party Manifesto 2019*. London: Conservative Party.

Dicey, Albert V. 1959. *An Introduction to the Study of the Law of the Constitution*, 10th ed. E.C.S. Wade, ed. London: Macmillan.

Dukes, Ruth. 2009. "Otto Kahn Freund and Collective Laissez-Faire: An Edifice without a Keystone?," *Modern Law Review* 72, 2: 220–246.

Elliott, Larry 2020. "Boris Johnson Has Shifted the Tories Left on the Economy. Labour Should Watch Out," *The Guardian* (January 30, 2020).

European Parliament. 2017. "Resolution on the Rule of Law and Democracy in Poland" (November 15, 2017).

2018. "Rule of Law in Hungary: Parliament Calls on the EU to Act, Press Release" (September 12, 2018).

Ewing, K. D. 1983. *Trade Unions, the Labour Party, and the Law: A Study of the Trade Union Act 1913*. Edinburgh: Edinburgh University Press.

2021. "Contesting Austerity: The Role of Trade Unions," in Anuscheh Farahat and X. Arzoz, eds. *Contesting Austerity: A Socio-Legal Inquiry into Resistance to Austerity*. Oxford: Hart Publishing, forthcoming.

Ewing, K. D., John Hendy, and Carolyn Jones 2018. *Rolling Out the Manifesto for Labour Law*. Liverpool: Institute of Employment Rights.

Falconer, Lord. 2019. "The Government Has Plans That Would Destroy the Protection of the Law," *The Guardian* (February 12, 2020).

Flanders, Alan. 1974. "The Tradition of Voluntarism," *British Journal of Industrial Relations* 12, 3: 352–370.

Giugliano, Ferdinando. 2019. "Britain's Tories Become the Workers' Party," *Bloomberg Opinion* (October 1, 2019).

Heaslip, Michael, and Suzanne MacGregor, 2019. "Letter to the Editor," *The Guardian* (July 16, 2019).

ILO, Committee of Experts. 2016. *Observations, United Kingdom*. Geneva: ILO.
    2018. *Observations, United Kingdom*. Geneva: ILO.

Jacobs, Antoine. 1986, "Collective Self-Regulation," in B.A. Hepple, ed. *The Making of Labour Law in Europe: A Comparative Study of Nine Countries up to 1945*. London: Mansell.

Jenkins, Simon. 2019. "Trump Created a Storm over Kim Darroch. Boris Johnson Will Bring a Hurricane," *The Guardian* (July 11, 2019).

Kahn-Freund, Otto. 1983. *Labor and the Law*. 3rd ed. Paul L. Davies and Mark R. Freedland, eds. London: Stevens London.

Kuhner, Timothy K. 2020. *Tyranny of Greed – Trump, Corruption, and the Revolution to Come*. Palo Alto, CA: Stanford University Press.

Kwarteng, K. P., Patel, D. Raab, C. Skidmore, and L. Truss. 2012. *Britannia Unchained – Global Growth and Prosperity*. London

Labour Party. 2019. *It's Time for Real Change*. London: Labour Party.

Lenin, V.I. 1917. "The State and Revolution," in V.I. Lenin, *Selected Works, Volume 2*. 1971 ed. Moscow: Progress Printers.
    1918. "Letter to American Workers," in V.I. Lenin, *Selected Works, Volume 3*. 1971 ed. Moscow: Progress Printers.
    1919. "The State," in V.I. Lenin, *Selected Works, Volume 3*. 1971 ed. Moscow: Progress Printers.

Locke, John. 1689. *Two Treatises of Government*. Peter Laslett, Introduction, and Notes. New York: New American Library.

Lynch, Esther. 2020. "A New Social Contract to Resist the Rise of the Far-Right," *International Union Rights* 27, 1: 3–5.

Marx, Karl. 1866. "Instructions for Delegates to the Geneva Congress," in *The First International and After, Political Writings, Volume 3*, 1974 ed. David Fernbach, ed. Harmondsworth: Pelican Books.

McCluskey, Len. 2016. "A Brexit Won't Stop Cheap Labor Coming to Britain," *The Guardian* (June 20, 2016).

Miliband, Ralph. 1961. *Parliamentary Socialism*. London: Merlin Press.
    1973. *The State in Capitalist Society: The Analysis of the Western System of Power*. London: Quartet Books.
    1977. *Marxism and Politics*. Oxford: Oxford University Press.
    1982. *Capitalist Democracy in Britain*. Oxford: Oxford University Press.

Mosley, Sir Oswald. 1934. *The Greater Britain*. London: British Union of Fascists.

Muller, Jan-Werner 2016. *What is Populism?* Harmondsworth: Penguin Books.

Office for National Statistics, United Kingdom. 2019. "UK and Non-UK People in the Labour Market: May 2019" (May 14, 2019).
    2019a. "Labour Disputes in the UK: 2018" (May 17, 2019).

Plattner, Marc F. 2019. "Illiberal Democracy and the Struggle on the Right," *Journal of Democracy* 30, 1: 5–19.

Polaski, Sandra, Sarah Anderson, John Cavanagh, Kevin Gallacher, Manuel Perez-Rocha, and Rebecca Ray. 2020. "How Trade Policy Failed US Workers – And How to Fix It." *Institute for Policy Studies*, Boston University Global Policy Center, and Groundwork Collaborative.

Randeria, Shalini. 2019. "Is Each 'Illiberal' Democracy Illiberal in Its Own Way?" *LSE Brexit Blog* (November 28, 2019).

Robertson, Geoffrey. 2016. "How to Stop Brexit: Get Your MP to Vote It Down," *The Guardian* (June 27, 2016).

Rogalewski, Adam. 2020. "Right-Wing Populism in Poland: A Challenge for Trade Unions," *International Union Rights* 27, 1: 8–9.

Rousseau, Jean-Jacques. 1762. *The Social Contract*. 1976 reprint. Maurice Cranston, trans. Harmondsworth: Penguin Books.

Schmitt, Carl. 1988. *The Crisis of Parliamentary Democracy.* 1st ed., 1923; 2nd ed., 1926. Ellen Kennedy, trans. Boston: MIT Press.

Schumpeter, Joseph A. 1943. *Capitalism, Socialism, and Democracy.* London: Allen and Unwin.

TULO. 2016. *Written Evidence to House of Lords Select Committee on Trade Union Political Funds and Party Political Funding.* TUP0038.

Woodcock, Andrew. 2019. "Tories Won More Working Class Votes than Labour," *The Independent* (December 17, 2019).

Young, Alison L. 2018. "Populism and the UK Constitution," *Current Legal Problems* 71: 17–52.

PART II

History, Politics, and Law

5

Sectoral Bargaining in the United States

Historical Roots of a Twenty-First Century Renewal

Nelson Lichtenstein

The multiple, intertwined set of debilitations that have beset working-class Americans in recent years has had one salutatory impact: forcing us to think broadly and boldly about the political and organizational reforms necessary to empower workers, eliminate racial and gender discrimination, reduce inequality, and raise living standards. Yet even as we probe the historic New Deal for models of social reconstruction, it has become clear that the industrial relations system that emerged out of the Great Depression cannot be reconstructed to any useful twenty-first century purpose. The future for traditional, enterprise-based unionism in the USA looks bleak, not because workers don't want to be represented in a collective fashion or because new technologies have eviscerated the need for social solidarity and collective voice, but because opponents of such unionism – among employers, politicians, anti-union law firms, the conservative judiciary – have had decades to perfect the legal and organizational weapons they deploy against it.

Today, fully 62 percent of Americans support unions, according to a recent Gallup poll, a number that has increased 14 points over the last decade. But even the most robust and imaginative organizing drive can be defeated if corporate executives are willing to spend enough money, retaliate against those employees wishing to organize, or appeal any pro-union NLRB or court decision. Above all they seek to delay, delay, delay (Lichtenstein & Shermer 2012; Logan 2006: 651–675; Saad 2018). And of course, all this implies that workers know who is their real boss. The rise of fissured employment – sub-contracting, franchising, and the corporate transformation of millions of workers into "independent contractors" – has obscured where power, money, and responsibility lie in the employment relationship (Lichtenstein 2017: 329–358; Weil 2014).

Back in the first Gilded Age, workers knew who their boss was. Andrew Carnegie, John D. Rockefeller, and Henry Ford owned and controlled a set of giant enterprises, running them in a feudal, authoritarian fashion. President Franklin Roosevelt saw these "economic royalists" who had "created a new despotism" as a threat to the republic (Roosevelt 1936). The 1935 National Labor Relations Act (NLRA or Wagner Act) was therefore designed to empower workers by providing a set of legal rights and administrative mechanisms by which the employees of a Ford or Rockefeller could collectively organize and then bargain with the boss on behalf of all who worked in one or more factories, mills, and offices. Detroit unionists put out a leaflet right after FDR's sweeping victory in 1936: "You voted New Deal at the polls and defeated the Auto Barons: Now get a New Deal in the shop" (Fine 1969: 96).

Today, the translation of political power at the ballot box, even in reliably Democratic Party-aligned states and cities, into organizational power at the worksite is far more difficult. On the Western Front in the First World War a handful of German machine guns could mow down a regiment of stout-hearted British heroes. The same is true of union organizing in our twenty-first century era of industrial trench warfare. Under the system of firm-centered collective bargaining envisioned by the Wagner Act and refined by the National Labor Relations Board (NLRB) and the judiciary, virtually any employer can thwart the unionizing efforts of even the most enthusiastic and dedicated set of organizers. In consequence, says Larry Cohen, former president of the Communications Workers of America and later head of Our Revolution, "It is now clear that enterprise-based organizing and bargaining in the United States has a dim future." David Rolf, the Seattle labor leader who was a key activist in the "Fight for $15" movement, concurs. Of collective bargaining and private sector unionism he has said, "The twentieth century model is dead. It will not come back" (Cohen 2018; Matthews 2017; Rolf 2016).

Thus, if liberals and labor partisans continue to build power in a post-Trump America, they will not try to "revitalize" the existing labor movement. For more than half a century, from the mid-1960s effort to curb state "right to work" laws,[1] through the 1977–78 contest over legislation to strengthen the NLRB's enforcement powers, the attempt to ban "striker replacements" in the Clinton years, and the Obama Administration's proposal for an Employee Free Choice Act, labor and its allies have repeatedly sought to make the New Deal-era system of enterprise unionism function effectively. None of these legislative reforms passed, but even if they had, their impact on labor's capacity to organize and bargain for a better work life would have been marginal. The structures of capital have shifted too much, the managerial mindset has become too hostile, and neoliberalism has been embedded too securely within the nation's labor-law regime.

SECTORAL BARGAINING: A PATH FORWARD?

But is there a road forward, modeled on movements like "The Fight for $15" and recent campaigns against sweatshops, foreign and domestic? Many labor partisans think "sectoral bargaining" an answer for our times (Barenberg 2015; Block & Sacks 2020: 37–45). Sectoral bargaining encompasses an effort to win better wages and working conditions in an entire occupation or industry, usually in one state or city. In many countries – including in the USA, in the historical and contemporary instances discussed below – this has been achieved through a collective bargaining contract. But labor progressives throughout many advanced capitalist economies have also pressed for governmental standard-setting by the legislature or an agency – a "wage board" or other tribunal – that sets a floor on wages and working conditions once all the stakeholders have had their say. This is social bargaining with the state on behalf of all workers in a given occupational or industry category – at least when the putative labor representatives sitting on the wage board are genuinely representative of rank-and-file workers and are not merely technocratic appointees. Just as civil rights laws apply to all US workplaces regardless of the attitude of workers or employers, so too would a wage board promulgate a set of minimal work standards that are equally universal within the industries and regions over which the board has jurisdiction. As a consequence of either worksite collective bargaining or simple employer

---

[1] The federal Labor Management Relations Act of 1947 (Taft-Hartley Act) authorized state governments to enact "right to work laws," which prohibit collective bargaining agreements from requiring all workers covered by the agreement to pay union dues regardless whether the individual worker consents to do so.

preference, wages and labor standards might rise above these minimums in particular firms and workplaces. Thus, the employment law that arose out of the civil rights statutes enacted in the 1960s and Wagner-era labor law are conjoined and enhanced.

Although they had different historical origins, analogous systems that combine bargaining and administrative standard-setting are commonplace in Europe as well as Australia. In France the state ensures that collective bargaining contracts negotiated by key firms and unions in any given industry are "extended" to all workers and employees in that industrial sector, thus magnifying the impact of that nation's relatively small trade union movement. In Nordic Europe, Belgium, and Germany trade unions are much stronger, in some cases because they serve as mechanisms through which workers register for and then receive unemployment benefits, training, and other state-funded social provisions. The state-mandated extension of key wage bargains is not always necessary because peak associations of capitalists and union federations may hammer out an economy-wide "social pact," incorporating an incomes policy that sets a nationwide wage framework which is elaborated in sector-by-sector collective agreements and, in still greater detail, in local and occupational contracts within each sector. In Australia, about 36 percent of the workforce is covered by collective bargaining contracts, but another 23 percent have their labor standards set under a "Modern Awards" system of industry and occupation-specific minimums. These awards are set by a federal tribunal whose members, like many US judges, are appointed for life. There are 122 such Awards, and within each there are a host of wage rates based on skill requirements or experience. Whatever the formula or mechanism, wage-setting in Europe and Australia is far more likely than in the USA to take place at the sectoral level than that of the individual company or enterprise (Dube 2018; Wallerstein 1999: 649–680).

A variant of the wage board system took root in the USA during the Progressive Era when Massachusetts, Oregon, California, and some ten other states implemented a set of boards – sometimes called industrial commissions – designed to set wages and establish other labor standards for those workers, mainly women, without full citizenship rights or union representation. These boards would investigate both the "minimum subsistence budget" necessary for single women to survive and the "financial condition" of the business or industry in which they worked in order to arrive at a pay rate promulgated by a "wage decree." By 1919, in Massachusetts there were separate pay grades for candy, laundry, retail store, women's clothing, men's clothing, canning, and office cleaning industries. Although these wage boards were supervised by a state commissioner, most of the work was done by the direct representatives of employers and employees, who as board members themselves held hearings, took testimony, investigated conditions, and bargained with each other to reach a minimum wage for each occupation or industry (Douglas 1919: 701–738).

A board in the District of Columbia, which set minimum wages for women and children, was also tripartite in character – that is, composed of members representing employers, workers, and the public. The Board could inspect payrolls, subpoena information, and apply legal sanctions against defaulters. Appointed in 1918, the District board was abolished in 1923 by the infamous *Adkins* v. *Children's Hospital* decision of the US Supreme Court, which declared state-mandated minimum wage laws a violation of a worker's "freedom of contract" (261 US 525 [1923]). But while the board lasted it demonstrated how such an institution could empower and radicalize its constituents. Led by feminist reformers Clara Beyer and Elizabeth Brandeis – "conviction bureaucrats," in the term coined by historian Vivian Hart – the DC wage board sought to mobilize women workers to organize and participate in the agency's hearings and other activities. Beyer was constantly on the go, visiting department stores and other places of female employment to talk about the minimum wage and the role of the board. "Well it was amazing – I stood on boxes at quitting time . . . and I told them all about how, what the wage was going to be set and how we wanted to have their voice. And it was the first time that they had ever had any kind of group action." And, remembered Beyer, "it was a very good education for the employers" too (Hart 1992: 12).

The State of California also set up such a wage board in the Progressive Era, an Industrial Welfare Commission (IWC). It still exists, although it is "currently inoperative" according to its web page. But like an archeological dig, evidence for the existence of a once vital civilization is abundant, reflected in the seventeen industry and occupational wage orders still posted on the California IWC website. Among them are such traditional industrial sectors as manufacturing, logging, construction, and food processing (canning, freezing, and preserving), but the IWC also claimed responsibility for setting labor standards in regionally unique employment sectors, including "Amusements and Recreation," "Broadcasting," and "Motion Pictures" (State of California 2019).

The New Deal revived much of the Progressive-era spirit, subsuming it within the larger reforms that sought to reorganize US capitalism and provide a voice for labor. From the establishment in 1933 of the National Industrial Recovery Act's "codes of fair competition" through the powerful War Labor Board of the Second World War years, government entities used tripartite stakeholder mechanisms to establish, on a national level, uniform wage and union status guidelines in the auto, steel, rubber, trucking, electrical, and food processing industries, and also such highly competitive and low-wage sectors as textiles and garment manufacturing (Barenberg 1994: 1412–1432; Fraser 1991: 289–323; Gordon 1994: 166–203; Johnson 1979: 134–216; Lichtenstein 1993: 67–81).

Historians and legal scholars have argued that one of the prime functions of the early New Deal was to constrain the industrial chaos generated by a rising cohort of "competitively fragmented industries" in which individual enterprises were driven to slash wages and prices in an endlessly destructive battle to survive. To counter such industrial anarchy, trade unions and employer associations in the first third of the twentieth century episodically cooperated to standardize wages, working conditions, and market shares, especially in urban centers like Chicago, Detroit, and New York City. The giant steel mills and auto plants of the era captured the attention of the public – and a later generation of historians – but an equally consequential construction of a modern economy was underway among the jumble of far less imposing enterprises: at the building sites, trucking barns, breweries, eateries, and retail outlets where trade, governance, and unionism intersected (Cohen 2004: 273–276; Gordon 1994: 35–86).

Some unionists like Sidney Hillman of the Amalgamated Clothing Workers and Jett Lauck of the United Mine Workers had hoped that a species of what Colin Gordon calls "regulatory unionism" might bring economic order to those industries that failed to wield the pricing power or labor market controls deployed by the giant enterprises characteristic of the oligopolistic mass producers (Gordon 1994: 87–88). That project had clearly failed by the early Depression years. The unions and the local business associations with which they sometimes bargained were either too weak, too unpopular, or too constrained by Lochner-era legal edicts to make sectoral bargaining work on the municipal or regional level. For example, a pre-New Deal effort to set uniform wages and prices in the Chicago hand-laundry trade – there were more than 500 such establishments in Cook County – was challenged by an Illinois district attorney on the grounds that such an agreement constituted a form of "racketeering" not unlike Al Capone's equally expansive effort to corner the wholesale liquor business so as to bring a certain regulatory order to a set of economic endeavors that then stood outside the law (Cohen 2004: 59–97).

It would take the New Deal's National Industrial Recovery Act (NIRA) to legalize and popularize such sectoral bargaining agreements, abridge the antitrust laws, and eliminate what National Recovery Administration (NRA) chief Hugh Johnson called the "eye-gouging and knee-groining and ear-chewing in business" (Gordon 1994: 173). This effort to cartelize markets and establish uniform wages and prices on a sectoral basis incorporated patterns of investigation and industrial governance first employed by the Progressive Era wage board; thus also constituting the "racketeer's progress" so ironically identified by Andrew Wender Cohen in his study of municipal governance, local commerce, and the legally unprotected unionism of early twentieth century Chicago. Most of the NRA's 800 "codes of fair competition" were written by businessmen and their industry-specific associations and then certified by a set of overworked New Deal officials. "The Lumber Code is not an edict handed us by Congress or the President," reported a West Coast lumberman. "We went to Washington and asked for it" (Gordon 1994: 172). Here and in many other codes, labor's voice was absent from the sectoral bargaining legitimized by the state, notwithstanding the NIRA's nominal mandate of labor participation: much corporativist bargaining and standard-setting in the NRA years amounted to little more than the give and take between small producers and large, those with well-established markets versus the newcomers seeking to expand.[2]

NRA-era sectoral bargaining of the sort advocated in the twenty-first century took place only in those few industries, such as coal, textiles, apparel, and trucking, where markets were more than local and where actual unions existed. In many other economic sectors unionism was either entirely absent or all too anemic and embattled. New Dealers and unionists wanted uniform wage standards, but even more they wanted to ensure that workers did have a right, in law and practice, to the "unions of their own choosing" promised in the famous Section 7(a) of the NIRA. And here a contradiction arose. If enterprise-level collective bargaining was to become the essence of industrial freedom and a path toward higher standards of living in the New Deal era, then the very animation of such a bargaining regime threatened to subvert the sectoral standard-setting that was promised by and embodied in the NRA codes of fair competition and in later industry-specific regulatory regimes legislated for shipping, trucking, airlines, railroads, coal mining, and utilities.

As we will shortly see, "pattern bargaining" carried out between large, successful industrial unions – such as the United Auto Workers (UAW), United Steelworkers (USW), Teamsters, and Packinghouse Workers in the heyday of their power – and the giants of American industry resolved this contradiction for three or four mid-twentieth century decades, but the Wagner Act and Taft-Hartley Act, especially as interpreted by an increasingly hostile judiciary, propelled American industrial relations toward a far more centrifugal and decentralized terrain. Mark Barenberg has pointed out that the left-wing, pro-labor framers of the Wagner Act were hardly enthusiasts for enterprise unionism confined to a single worksite or company. On its face, the new labor law, especially Section 9(b), which gives the NLRB the authority to determine the appropriate bargaining unit, seemed to tilt against meso-corporatist arrangements, instead mandating workplace elections at the enterprise level to determine whether a majority of workers favored an independent union (Barenberg 1994: 770–793). But the drafters of the Act expected that, after workers poured into unions on an enterprise-by-enterprise basis, those units would merge into sectoral units in which one potent union would bargain with the multiple industrial combines extant in that sector.

---

[2] "NIRA" denotes the National Industrial Recovery Act. "NRA" denotes both the administrative agency that implemented the NIRA, and the industry codes hammered out through that agency-supervised process.

Barenberg shows that the 1935 NLRA's system for conducting majority-rule elections at the enterprise level was an "accidental" artifact of the labor relations experience in the NIRA years of 1933–34. At that time, Bethlehem Steel, Chrysler, Colorado Fuel and Iron, Thompson Products, and many other corporations created management-dominated "company unions" that claimed to enjoy the kind of employee support – at the single-enterprise level – that would fulfill the meaning of Section 7(a). To counter this corporate strategy, Senator Wagner and his advisers put a premium on the creation of a legal-administrative mechanism that could visibly demonstrate worker support for genuine trade unionism. The Wagner Act's ban on company unionism would therefore be combined with NLRB-supervised elections that would demonstrate workers' (presumptive) preference for independent unions over company unions. The resultant labor regime did for a time legitimate independent, even militant, trade unionism in key factories and companies. But those who crafted and enacted the Wagner Act did not anticipate that the NLRB and courts would permit employers to run ferocious and effective anti-union campaigns to obstruct unionization at the enterprise level and that the judiciary would prohibit those unions that did succeed in winning majority support in each of multiple enterprise units from insisting that employers merge the units into sectoral bargaining structures (Barenberg 2015: 12–13).

With the exception of the Second World War, the state was missing from the "pattern bargaining" that did come to characterize wage and benefit setting negotiations in some well-unionized industries. In an era when politics were moving to the right, unionists were wary of too much state regulation of the industrial relations system. A GOP-Dixiecrat coalition had passed the Taft-Hartley Act in 1947, immediately followed by a chorus of employer complaints that something should be done about the "monopoly unionism" that sought to organize all workers in a particular industry and set uniform wages and working conditions. As Walter Reuther, the visionary UAW leader put it at that time, "I'd rather bargain with General Motors than the US government. GM has no army." During the 1950s and 1960s, "pattern bargaining" in heavy industry did create a set of sectoral wage and benefit standards whereby key bargains, such as the 1950 UAW-GM "Treaty of Detroit," were not only replicated by Ford and Chrysler, but set a benchmark throughout mass production industry (Lichtenstein 1997: 261; Stebenne 1996: 120–153). Bargaining in steel, coal, commercial construction, and short-haul trucking was even more centralized, with a committee representing the entire industry sitting down with a big union like the United Mine Workers or the Steelworkers to structure a work regime for hundreds of thousands.[3]

Teamster president Jimmy Hoffa, for all his faults, used militant strike tactics and a strategic negotiating strategy to create a series of regional collective bargaining regimes that standardized wages and working conditions throughout an historically fragmented trucking industry. He even brought incomes for Southern over-the-road truckers up to Northern and Western standards (Russell 2001). In addition to the Teamsters, unions representing garment workers and bakers, printers and painters, the construction trades and longshore workers, encouraged and facilitated the organization of employer associations so that when they achieved a collective bargaining agreement it also constituted a de facto standard for an entire industry sector. This was sectoral bargaining without recourse to the state.

---

[3] As noted above, the NLRB and the judiciary do not permit unions to insist on, and strike to gain, merger of enterprise units into sectoral units, but the latter units are permitted where every employer voluntarily consents to multi-employer bargaining. Such consent might be explicit or, as proven by a history of sectoral bargaining, implicit. And in some key cases, multiple employers acceded to union power when they "consented" to multi-employer bargaining.

THE UNKNOWN FAIR LABOR STANDARDS ACT

At the very height of its post-war range and power, American trade unions never enrolled more than 35 percent of all non-farm workers; in 1938 when the federal minimum wage law – the Fair Labor Standards Act (FLSA) – became law, union density was barely half of that. Enterprise unionism, even as part of a system of pattern bargaining, could hardly encompass or set standards for the vast majority of employees, especially those oft-forgotten workers who labored in trades and occupations where a plethora of small enterprises made both organizing and standard-setting difficult. As the *New Republic* argued in support of the FLSA, there were "industries and regions where, for one reason or another, unions cannot make much headway, or severe competition prevents localized advances, and where as a consequence the conditions of labor lag behind the general standards." These were the "sweated industries" where state assistance was essential (Andrias 2019: 663).

As the legal scholar Kate Andrias reminds us, Roosevelt-era supporters of the FLSA hoped it would do more than what it does today, ensure subsistence-level wages. Rather, the bill's drafters saw it as a way to deliver on a set of "fundamental rights" and to ensure a "system of basic equality, extending into political, economic, and social realms" (Andrias 2019: 661). Indeed, the FLSA's backers in Congress expressly claimed that the law would expand the role of unions in politics and the economy, particularly in the non-union South, and would provide a kind of surrogate labor union representation for still-unorganized workers. In the words of Democratic Senator David Walsh, the FLSA promised that unorganized workers "will not be left helpless ... We will see to it that you, too, are given some of the benefits and some of the privileges of collective bargaining" (2019: 662).

Labor generally embraced the FLSA's approach, though not without important exceptions. In particular, the conservative, craft-dominated American Federal of Labor (AFL) sought to exempt unionized workplaces from FLSA coverage, on the ground that labor conditions were better left to private negotiation than to governmental supervision. But leaders of the unions affiliated with the insurgent Congress of Industrial Organizations (CIO) lauded the more universal and social democratic approach. They welcomed the idea of an intertwined labor and employment law; in their view, the FLSA would serve as a mechanism to help reduce downward, competitive wage pressure in shops already organized by the CIO. Unionist Sidney Hillman argued that in industries such as textiles, garments, and shoes, private collective bargaining could not cover the whole industry, and the only way to raise standards uniformly was to have it done by the government. Collective bargaining alone might well force high-wage employers out of business before the rest of the industry could be effectively organized (Fraser 1991: 378–395).

The FLSA's procedural mechanisms reflected these commitments. The law mandated the establishment of tripartite committees of labor, business, and the public in order to engage affected parties in the governance process. A sticking point soon arose: who would represent non-unionized workers? Business groups wanted employers to choose them, but labor convinced FLSA administrators – who were liberal laborites in any event – that unions, even if they represented but a small segment of workers in an industry, could nevertheless speak for the majority of all workers since they already bargained for a set of similarly situated workers (Andrias 2019: 271).

The industry committees' operation was a mix between collective bargaining and administrative decision-making, blending democratic deliberation with technocratic analysis, not unlike the wage boards of the Progressive Era or the code-making deliberations of the NRA. The committees conducted fact-finding investigations and grounded their conclusions within the framework of statutory law, while at the same time FLSA decision-making emerged from a negotiation between business and labor representatives with the public members acting as referees. For example, the first committee, representing much of the garment industry, met for over six months. Chaired by Donald Nelson, the Vice President of Sears, Roebuck, it counted among its members Sidney Hillman and several leaders from apparel-trade AFL and CIO locals, as well as industry executives from around the country. The committee issued a comprehensive report detailing many of the garment industry's chronic problems, including competition from abroad and the movement of capital from the organized and higher-wage North to the unorganized, low-wage South. Ultimately, the committee recommended a minimum wage for the whole industry of 32.5 cents an hour. Not unexpectedly, Southern members dissented in a separate report, objecting in particular to the committee's treatment of the "cotton growing" states and their insufficient representation (Andrias 2019: 672–673).

One virtue of the FLSA wage boards and of similar state-level wage-setting institutions is that they avoid the "preemption" trap whereby any effort on the part of a federal agency, or state or municipality, to encourage collective bargaining by either constraining employer power or enhancing the rights of workers is "preempted" by the NLRA which, as interpreted by the Supreme Court, reserves all such legislation to Congress. Eighty years ago, labor partisans saw such "preemption" as a great legal victory because it prevented reactionary politicians in places like Texas or Mississippi from enacting their own state-level obstacles to union organizing and bargaining. But as the decades passed this federal displacement of state activism soured when Republicans took periodic control of the NLRB and as the courts reinterpreted the meaning of the Wagner Act so as to turn labor's "magna carta" into an employer weapon. In contrast, the FLSA does not preempt state and local wage legislation, as long as the non-federal benefits exceed the floors set by federal statutes. States can pass, for example, higher minimum wages, more protective scheduling laws, and paid sick time provisions; so too can localities, as long as their state's home rule provisions permit them to do so. This is why there are so many different minimum wage and rest break standards across the USA.

While the Supreme Court has repeatedly emphasized the prohibition against state actors shifting the balance of power in privately negotiated agreements, it has never curtailed the ability of states and local governments to pass universally applicable standards of employment. Indeed, the Court has held that laws setting specific terms of employment contracts are not preempted even when they "alter the economic balance between labor and management." The Court has emphasized that "[w]hen a state law establishes a minimal employment standard not inconsistent with the general legislative goals of the NLRA, it conflicts with none of the purposes of the Act" (Andrias 2016: 91–92). Thus, the Court has upheld several state laws establishing workplace standards that could otherwise be negotiated in bargaining.

As it turned out, a conservative Congress eliminated the FLSA wage boards in the late 1940s, even as some states continued to maintain their own tripartite wage-setting agencies. The federal boards fell victim to intense hostility from the low-wage South, from Republicans and industrialists hostile to the Truman Administration's effort to boost the minimum wage to 75 cents an hour, and from the view held by some laborites who thought that unionism and collective bargaining were the only legitimate and effective roads forward for the unorganized and the poorly paid (Andrias 2019: 284–289).

An exception that offers us a quite different history, and therefore an alternative future, came in Puerto Rico. Congress had exempted the island from coverage by the FLSA in the late 1930s, and the apparel industry there, largely staffed by women workers, was overwhelmingly non-union in the early post-war years. Welcomed by Puerto Rican politicians seeking economic development at almost any cost, North American garment firms flocked to "the poor house of the Caribbean." It was a sweatshop colony.

This was the context in which a successful example of state-backed sectoral bargaining came to the fore. In lieu of an FLSA minimum wage, Puerto Rico set wages through a tripartite Minimum Wage Board administered by the island government. That board was inactive during its early years, but in the 1950s two developments animated the board and made it an effective locus of sectoral wage bargaining. First, the US labor movement began to lobby Congress for an extension of mainland FLSA wage standards to Puerto Rico. This proved unsuccessful during the 1950s, but Puerto Rican employers and politicians feared that AFL-CIO legislative success – the US union movement was then at the height of its organizational and political strength – might come with the next turn of the political tide. Second, the New York-based International Ladies' Garment Workers Union (ILGWU) sent organizers to the island to unionize runaway garment factories and agitate for higher wages, improvement of other labor standards, and enterprise-based collective bargaining along mainline US lines.

As Cesar F. Rosado Marzan argues in a recent essay, a sort of compact was put in place that made sector-wide wage setting by the Puerto Rican board highly advantageous to the ILGWU, as well as Puerto Rican employers and politicians. The union tacitly agreed not to press for an immediate extension of US minimum wage standards to Puerto Rico; instead the wage board would use its considerable investigative powers to summon witnesses, hold hearings, and issue a "mandatory decree" establishing minimum wages in the island's principal industry. With the most contentious wage issues already decided on a uniform, island-wide basis, Puerto Rican employers, often running branch plants of already unionized US firms, were normally willing to stand aside when the ILGWU sought to organize their workers. The union's appeal to Puerto Rican workers was based upon its capacity to negotiate wages that were somewhat above the wage board standard, and it also incorporated into its collective bargaining contracts the grievance procedures and arbitration mechanisms that were prevalent in unionized mainland shops. By the 1960s, reports Marzan, the ILGWU had organized almost 40 percent of all Puerto Rican garment workers (Marzan 2020: 144–148).

The Puerto Rican experience proved an ambiguous model for labor partisans, but one that nevertheless holds important lessons for contemporary reformers. The island wage board had the backing of the Puerto Rican government only because it proved an advantageous substitute for extension of the full FLSA to the Commonwealth. Once Congress extended US minimum wage coverage to the island in the late 1970s, the wage board lost employer and governmental support. Indeed, the ILGWU had come under much criticism from the late 1950s onward, because the union's bargaining strategy, on the mainland and in Puerto Rico, had been one of wage moderation, if not actual wage suppression. The union feared that an aggressive push for higher wages would lead to an epidemic of runaway shops, either to the non-union US South or to Central America and, still later, East Asia. Puerto Rican employers therefore had an incentive to welcome the ILGWU into their factories; and Marzan offers much evidence that they favored the North American union as a seemingly well-legitimized shield against the effort inaugurated by more radical, indigenous trade unionists to organize their shops (Marzan 2020: 149–154).

But the ILGWU was not merely a pawn of Puerto Rican employers. It won state backing for a tripartite, sectoral wage-setting mechanism because it had the political power, in conjunction with the rest of the US labor movement, to threaten the tax, regulatory, and labor-standard advantages enjoyed by island business interests. The board therefore proved to be a mechanism that won for the ILGWU an admittedly inferior wage standard, while at the same time advancing both the economic development program of the Puerto Rican government and the institutional strength of the union itself.

CONTEMPORARY EXAMPLES OF US SECTORAL BARGAINING

Apparel industry globalization in the 1970s and 1980s undermined the viability of the sectoral bargaining in Puerto Rico; likewise, the same rise of an international market, combined with the growth of employer anti-unionism and state hostility, subverted pattern bargaining where it had gained a foothold, thus putting wages and other work standards back in competition between one firm and another. By the early twenty-first century, the few remaining examples of sectoral bargaining were found in a set of occupational niches: major league sports, the Hollywood talent guilds at the major studios and broadcast networks, Ohio tomato harvesters, New York taxi drivers, and West Coast longshore workers. More recently, the teacher strikes that swept West Virginia, Oklahoma, and Arizona were also a species of sectoral bargaining, in which negotiations took place, not with the individual county boards of education, who were the formal employers of the school teachers, but at the state capitals where the real money and power were concentrated (Blanc 2019; Fisk 2016).

Sectoral bargaining in the private sector has always been far more difficult than among public employees. As in the Progressive Era and the New Deal, it requires the active engagement of the state to make sectoral bargaining once again work. The "Fight for $15" could only succeed when the struggle moved to the political realm, where states and municipalities passed local ordinances mandating higher wages (Rolf 2016: 97–121). Such initiatives might well be given more of a "bargaining" flavor in states like New York, California, New Jersey, Massachusetts, North Dakota, and Colorado, where wage boards still exist. They were put in place during the Progressive Era when they were designed to raise standards for workers – mainly women, in what were then called the sweated trades. And under the right circumstances they can still work. In New York in 2015 a wage board composed of representatives from labor, business, and the general public held an extensive series of hearings over a 45-day period in cities all across the state. Workers organized by the Service Employees International Union's (SEIU's) Fight for $15 were well represented at these meetings. As the *The New York Times* reported of one hearing, "[O]rganizers ... turned out a large and vocal crowd that included pizza makers, cashiers, unionized graduate students, economists, a venture capitalist from Seattle, and at least one rabbi" (McGeehan 2015b). On July 21, 2015, the New York State Board announced its decision: $15 per hour for fast food restaurants that are part of chains with at least thirty outlets, to be phased in over the course of six years, with a faster phase-in for New York City. The wage board order was a significant victory, followed by another victory: a bill to raise the state-wide minimum wage to $15 (McGeehan 2015a).

The SEIU official who served on the New York State wage board called the Fight for $15 experience "like collective bargaining on steroids. We were trying to bargain with society about what minimum wages and minimum living standards should be" (Greenhouse 2019: 246). That is undoubtedly an overstatement. The New York wage board was not the kind of tripartite entity resembling either the War Labor Board panels that regulated wages and working conditions during the Second World War or even the Puerto Rican board that modestly rationalized wage standards and advanced unionization during the 1950s and 1960s. For one thing the board did not itself formally set the new wage standard: it merely made a recommendation to the New York State Commissioner of Labor who made the final decision. Were the governorship in less labor friendly hands, the wage award might well have been less favorable. More importantly,

McDonald's and other fast food chains did nothing to recognize either a union of their workers or SEIU's right to speak for those employees. In contrast to the mid-twentieth century ILGWU, the twenty-first century SEIU had far less political or legislative leverage to deploy against firms whose business model was predicated upon the employment of millions of low-wage, high-turnover staff (Marzan 2020: 153–154).

Sectoral bargaining in the private sector has thus far worked far better among higher-waged workers whose skills are in demand. In the construction trades, "prevailing wage" standards – updated under the Bacon-Davis Act since the 1930s – ensure that on big government projects occupational wages of up to $80 an hour are paid to skilled craftsmen, unionized or not. To help imagine what a more full-fledged national version of this model could become, consider the National Football League (NFL) as well as TV-show writers. In each instance sectoral bargaining takes place between a union and an association of employers whose jurisdiction is coterminous with the national industry itself. And in both cases, we are talking about highly paid professionals whose compensation is often far more complex than a straight wage payment.

In the NFL, the players' union and the 32 team owners bargain collectively to divide up the total share of league revenue and provide minimum salaries for rookies and veterans. NFL players receive at least 47 percent of league revenue under their current agreement, and in 2017, rookies were paid a minimum season salary of $465,000 while veterans earned higher minimums based on their seniority. Of course, teams can – and many do – pay players more than league minimums (Madland 2018). The other major league sports – baseball, basketball, and ice hockey – have versions of the same model.

Similarly, the Writers Guild of America East and West negotiates a nationwide Minimum Basic Agreement with the Alliance of Motion Picture and Television Producers that provides for minimum wages, portable pension and health benefits, a process to receive proper credit for one's work, and residual payments to writers when produced content is exhibited outside of its initial window. Writers can – and frequently do – negotiate for higher standards, but employers cannot pay less than the agreed-upon minimums. In 2017, for example, a writer of a story and teleplay for a 30-minute primetime network TV show received a minimum fee of $26,303, and roughly 40 to 50 percent of that amount for each prime-time network rerun that airs, depending on the show's budget. Moreover, the company is required to pay an additional 19 percent contribution on top of the writer's salary and TV residual payments to the Writers Guild of America's pension and health fund to cover the writer's benefits. Minimum payments for non-network primetime shows are less, but follow a similar format. Even when writers change employers, their work is still covered by the Minimum Basic Agreement, and they therefore continue to receive the minimum pay and benefits that the collective bargaining agreement guarantees (Madland 2018).

SECTORAL BARGAINING FOR THE "GIG ECONOMY"

While both the football players and the TV writers collectively bargain with a set of private employers, this pattern could easily be transferred via the state-level wage board model to many of those gig economy workers whose actual employment status has been so ambiguous and contested: not just the Uber and Lyft drivers and the web-based temp workers, but those who develop video games, program social media connections, and build new apps for Apple. And of course, such sectoral bargaining is a natural for more traditional and normally lower-wage occupations, including those who labor in nursing homes, warehouses, and retail stores, and among the self-employed port truckers and grocery store delivery workers.

The door seems open to a new season of liberal-labor statecraft that puts high on its agenda the kind of wage boards discussed above. The Center for American Progress, a think tank with close ties to Obama and Clinton circles, is on board, likewise the Sanders and Warren wing of the Democratic Party; and of course advocacy of a $15 minimum wage is now standard fare for almost every Democrat. The enormous set of employment disruptions generated by the coronavirus pandemic has made both necessary and attractive the creation of new standard-setting mechanisms at the state and municipal levels. During the 2020 presidential election season Joe Biden's labor platform was the most progressive in recent history (Saenz & Mucha 2019). Wage boards and a higher minimum wage therefore are a natural fit for a leftward shifting Democratic Party: they are policies legitimized by history and current circumstance; large numbers of low-wage workers will benefit; and employer opposition will be muted because such governmental initiatives take wages out of competition throughout an entire labor market. If a union organizing drive were to force a handful of McDonald's restaurants in Manhattan to offer higher wages, while the rest pay two or three dollars less, then one can be sure that those McDonald's franchisees will loudly complain that they are burdened by unfair competition in the months before they close up shop. But if every fast food eatery in the borough pays the same wage, then burger prices might rise a bit, but wages are taken out of competition and the field of business contestation remains flat and equitable. This may be why McDonald's has announced that it will no longer lobby against a rise in the minimum wage (CBS News 2019).

Moreover, such sectoral bargaining is a tool that has the capacity to ameliorate the employment fissuring that has been the bane of so many organizing drives. If a wage board mandates that all janitors, home healthcare workers, or warehouse employees are paid the same, then unions can avoid the nearly impossible task of organizing the multitude of contractors and subcontractors in those sectors. Indeed, some of these subcontractors are likely to welcome a state-imposed wage standard, which would stop the chiseling and constant spin off of fly-by-night firms whose only competitive advantage is the exploitation or self-exploitation of those who work for them.

And finally, there is the dirty little secret that has long made even the most liberal Democrat wary of too close an identification with union organizing campaigns, contract fights, and the strike itself. The Wagner Act was premised upon the idea that social harmony might be achieved when and if capital and labor met on somewhat equal terms – both would be organized – and thereby they both would have the incentive and the power to construct a set of social bargains, with the strike weapon held largely in reserve. But if US employers ever thought this policy regime a good idea, they reject it today. In the private sector, certainly, and often in the public as well, managers seek domination and unilateral rule. Unions therefore are in the business of creating class conflict, when and if they have the chance, because it is only under such adversarial conditions that managers are incentivized to recognize and respond to the interests of their employees.

Liberal politicians may well offer support for contemporary strikes and organizing drives, but the turmoil created by union activism often plays havoc with a candidate's effort to build a constituency as broad and inclusive as possible even when, in the abstract, they stand with working people. Strikes are messy and often end in a partial victory, divisive defeat, or all sides losing. Many people, and not just those in the managerial strata, are repelled by such social conflict. So, while Democratic Party liberals may join the occasional picket line, they hesitate to identify their campaign with the fate of a union struggle. Though the Fight for $15 has, from the beginning, framed its demands as "$15 and a union," the wage plea has captured far more attention than the call for union rights. When it comes to the latter, even the most left-leaning liberals hesitate to put themselves squarely on the side of all those shrill and disruptive organizers. Instead they use a distancing rhetoric, with appeals to create a "level playing field" between management and labor, or they seek to avoid the conflictual narrative altogether by just condemning income inequality, tax breaks for the rich, and the role of the "billionaire class" in election campaigns.

But unionism, even when its chief objective is a higher wage for union workers, embodies far more than a mechanism for reducing income inequality. It raises consciousness among its members, creates an oppositional and continuously active locus of power in a society otherwise dominated by capital, and has the capacity to mobilize the community as well as its own members for social struggles, thereby demonstrating both social solidarity and a progressive vision of what would constitute a good society.

As presently constituted, wage boards do none of this, and while the Fight for $15 campaigns have often been genuine social movements, they have not won for the SEIU, the key funder and organizer of that movement, more than a handful of new members. And this is crucial, because without organization and the dues flow to sustain it, the labor movement will come to resemble a philanthropic foundation that makes incremental social changes, but is incapable of building a self-sustaining set of organizations that can intervene and win in the political arena or engage in the continuous effort needed to sustain a progressive consciousness among millions of working people.

Without unions to institutionalize them, waves of activism dissipate. The energy that went into the first Obama campaign evaporated after the thrilling election celebrations. The Occupy movement in 2011 fizzled when the tents cleared. And the anti-Trump "resistance" lacked an organizational structure independent of the people it has put into office or the political and legal campaigns it has waged. In contrast, effective trade unionism contributes not only to the mobilization of voters at the climax of a campaign season, but in the aftermath as well when the political and organizational trench warfare continues in a large array of legislative chambers, administrative agencies, and community political institutions. In recent years the political right – through megachurches, the National Rifle Association, and ad hoc donor formations – has proven far more potent than the political left in this kind of continuous partisan warfare.[4]

Now that the nation and the labor movement are shifting to the left, progressives need to push forward policies and politics that strengthen those working-class institutions so they can play a vigorous role in raising wages and begin to win the adherence of those elements of the working class who have defected. Here's how wage boards and sectoral bargaining can help. To institute wage boards at the national level, federal law would have to be changed. That will not happen soon, but in the meantime a number of liberal states, including Nevada, Maryland, Massachusetts, and Washington might well join the five jurisdictions (Arizona, Colorado, California, New Jersey, and New York) that already have wage board legislation on their books. These boards, old and new, need the funding and boldness that can once again make them a platform for the "conviction bureaucrats" who once helped give voice to Progressive Era workers.

In the USA, the preemption doctrine has long enabled an increasingly reactionary federal labor law to trump more progressive state legislation. But so long as the courts do not deem the activities of these state boards part of an NLRA-defined regulation of union organizing or the practice of collective bargaining, the anti-union preemption doctrine will not apply. The boards may therefore be sites for experimentation that encourages workers' self-organization in

---

[4] Some of these themes are discussed in Jake Rosenfeld (2014).

imaginative new ways, so that a collective employee voice will be well and democratically represented when the wage boards hold the periodic hearings so necessary to an informed decision. States that wish to test the legal boundaries of federal preemption might pass legislation that – when labor representatives are engaged in wage board activities – forbids employers from barring those representatives from their property, stiffens monetary fines against employers who demote or fire employees who seek to talk with those representatives, and bans employer-mandated "captive audience" meetings in which employers urge workers to oppose a wage board's raising of standards.

A funding stream for these organizations is also important so that workers seeking to make their voices heard before such a board can have their own staff and leaders to do the necessary research, member organizing, and political mobilization. Liberal states could therefore enact legislation, as in New York, that requires employers in a particular industry, such as fast food, to let their workers have a portion of their paycheck deducted in order to pay membership fees to a non-profit entity. Under that New York law, now being contested by a restaurant trade association, at least 500 workers would have to sign up before a group could receive contributions (Greenhouse 2018). To incentivize membership, liberal states could take a page from the northern European playbook and channel some social benefits, such as subsidized bus and subway cards, occupational training classes, and legal services for poor people, through these new working-class institutions.

The union movement, indeed democracy itself, has always advanced when will and circumstance conjoin to propel a great leap forward, as in the Civil War, the New Deal, and the 1960s. A new era of state-mandated sectoral bargaining may well be part of that reinvigoration, but its promise will fall short without the rebirth of a set of working-class organizations that give ordinary workers their own voice and the power to make it persuasive.

REFERENCES

Andrias, Kate. 2016. "The New Labor Law," *Yale Law Journal* 126, 1: 2–100.
    2019. "An American Approach to Social Democracy: The Forgotten Promise of the Fair Labor Standards Act," *Yale Law Journal* 128, 3: 616–709.
Barenberg, Mark. 1994. "Democracy and Domination in the Law of Workplace Cooperation: From Bureaucratic to Flexible Production," *Columbia Law Review* 94, 3: 753–983.
    1999. "The Political Economy of the Wagner Act: Power, Symbol, and Workplace Cooperation," *Harvard Law Review* 106, 7: 1379–1496.
    2015. *Widening the Scope of Worker Organizing: Legal Reforms to Facilitate Multi-Employer Organizing, Bargaining, and Striking.* New York: The Roosevelt Institute.
Blanc, Eric. 2019. *Red State Revolt: The Teachers' Strike Wave and Working-Class Politics.* New York: Verso.
Block, Sharon, and Benjamin Sachs. 2020. *A Clean Slate for Worker Power: Building a Just Economy and Democracy.* Cambridge, MA: Labor and Worklife Program, Harvard Law School.
CBS News. 2019. "McDonald's Now OK with Raising the Minimum Wage" (March 27, 2019).
Cohen, Andrew Wender. 2004. *The Racketeer's Progress: Chicago and the Struggle for the Modern American Economy, 1900–1940.* New York: Cambridge University Press.
Cohen, Larry. 2018. "The Time Has Come for Sectoral Bargaining," *New Labor Forum* 27, 3.
Douglas, Dorothy. 1919. "American Minimum Wage Laws at Work," *American Economic Review* 9, 4: 701–738.
Dube, Arindrajit. 2018. "Using Wage Boards to Raise Pay," Economists for Inclusive Prosperity Policy Brief 4. https://econfip.org/policy-brief/using-wage-boards-to-raise-pay
Fine, Sidney. 1969. *Sit-Down: The General Motors Strike of 1936–1937.* Ann Arbor: University of Michigan Press.

Fisk, Catherine. 2016. *Writing for Hire: Unions, Hollywood, and Madison Avenue*. Cambridge, MA: Harvard University Press.

Fraser, Steven. 1991. *Labor Will Rule: Sidney Hillman and the Rise of American Labor*. New York: Free Press.

Gordon, Colin. 1994. *New Deals: Business, Labor, and Politics in America, 1920-35*. New York: Cambridge University Press.

Greenhouse, Steven. 2018. "Fast Food Workers Claim Victory in a New York Labor Effort," *The New York Times* (January 9, 2018). www.nytimes.com/2018/01/09/business/economy/fast-food-labor.html

2019. *Beaten Down, Worked Up: The Past, Present, and Future of American Labor*. New York: Alfred A. Knopf.

Hart, Vivian. 1992. "Feminism and Bureaucracy: The Minimum Wage Experiment in the District of Columbia," *Journal of American Studies* 26, 1: 1–22.

Johnson, James P. 1979. *The Politics of Soft Coal: The Bituminous Industry from World War I through the New Deal*. Urbana: University of Illinois Press.

Lichtenstein, Nelson. 1983. *Labor's War at Home: The CIO in World War II*. New York: Cambridge University Press.

1997. *Walter Reuther: The Most Dangerous Man in Detroit*. Urbana: University of Illinois Press.

2017. "Two Cheers for Vertical Integration: Corporate Governance in a World of Global Supply Chains," in Naomi Lamoreaux, and William Novak, eds., *Corporations and American Democracy*. Cambridge, MA: Harvard University Press.

Lichtenstein, Nelson, and Elizabeth Shermer. 2012. *The Right and Labor in America: Politics, Ideology, and Imagination*. Philadelphia: University of Pennsylvania Press.

Logan, John. 2006. "The Union Avoidance Industry in the United States," *British Journal of Industrial Relations* 44, 4: 651–675.

Madland, David. 2018. "Wage Boards for American Workers." Washington, DC: Center for American Progress.

Marzan, Cesar F. Rosado. 2020. "Can Wage Boards Revive US Labor? Marshalling Evidence from Puerto Rico," *Chicago-Kent Law Review* 95, 1: 127–156.

Matthews, Dylan. 2017. "Europe Could Have the Secret to Saving America's Unions," *Vox* (April 17, 2017). www.vox.com/policy-and-politics/2017/4/17/15290674/union-labor-movement-europe-bargaining-fight-15-ghent

McGeehan, Patrick. 2015a. "New York Plans $15-an-Hour Minimum Wage for Fast Food Workers," *The New York Times* (July 22, 2015).

2015b. "Board Hears Support for Raising Food Workers' Minimum Wage," *The New York Times* (June 15, 2015).

Rolf, David. 2016. *The Fight for $15: The Right Wage for a Working America*. New York: New Press.

Roosevelt, Franklin D. 1936, "Acceptance Speech for the Renomination for the Presidency." Philadelphia (June 27, 1936).

Rosenfeld, Jake. 2014. *What Unions No Longer Do*. Cambridge, MA: Harvard University Press.

Russell, Thaddeus. 2001. *Out of the Jungle: Jimmy Hoffa and the Remaking of the American Working Class*. New York: Alfred A. Knopf.

Saad, Lydia. 2018. "Labor Union Approval Steady at 15-Year High," *Gallup News*. https://news.gallup.com/poll/241679/labor-union-approval-steady-year-high.aspx

Saenz, Arlette, and Sarah Mucha. 2019. "Joe Biden Releases Labor Plan in Middle-Class Pitch," *CNN Politics*. www.cnn.com/2019/10/25/politics/joe-biden-labor-plan/index.html

State of California, Department of Industrial Relations. 2019. "Industrial Welfare Commission Wage Orders." www.dir.ca.gov/IWC/WageOrderIndustries.htm

Stebenne, David. 1996. *Arthur Goldberg: New Deal Liberal*. New York: Oxford University Press.

Wallerstein, Michael. 1999. "Wage Setting Institutions and Pay Inequality in Advanced Industrial Societies," *American Journal of Political Science* 43, 3: 649–680.

Weil, David. 2014. *The Fissured Workplace: Why Work Became So Bad for So Many and What Can Be Done to Improve It*. Cambridge, MA: Harvard University Press.

6

The Lever and the Fulcrum

Organizing and Bargaining for Democracy and the Common Good

Sarita Gupta, Lauren Jacobs, Stephen Lerner, and Joseph A. McCartin

One way or another, the 2020s will very likely mark a decisive turning point in the political economy of the United States. Entering the decade, the USA was already teetering on a razor's edge. On one side, an authoritarian future loomed ever larger and more threatening, a dystopian one built on hyper-inequality, white supremacy, monopoly and financialized power, and surveillance capitalism, amidst the devastation of uncontrolled climate change. On the other, a future of economic and political justice is foreseeable, one foreshadowed by the antiracist Black Lives Matter protests, by the fight for a Green New Deal, and by new models of worker organization and struggle that brought labor and community together as never before, making it possible to imagine a country remade around the values of democracy, equality, racial and gender justice, and collective liberation.

As we teeter between these starkly different futures, the emergence of four crises has ensured that the 2020s will be a decade of momentous social and political outcomes. Covid-19 not only killed more Americans than any pandemic in a century, it revealed the failure of US healthcare, the insufficiency of the country's social welfare systems, and the extremity of its political dysfunction. Then, as the pandemic spread death and shuttered the US economy, the brutal police murder of George Floyd exposed again the gross inequity rooted in white supremacy and racism that continues to structure our economy and institutions, unleashing a wave of protest that exceeded in breadth and intensity any since 1968, a movement begetting calls to defund the police and a backlash by white supremacist defenders of "law and order." Meanwhile, the Covid-induced economic contraction depleted states and localities of revenue, threatening a renewal of the 2010 crisis of austerity politics. And, while each of these crises worsened, the climate-change clock ticked down toward the point of no return manifested by unprecedented wildfires in the West.

If social ruptures create opportunities proportional to their dangers, then this confluence of crises foretells that the 2020s will likely yield progressive transformation or reactionary descent. Which future prevails will be determined not so much by which party holds the White House as by the particular strategies for building and deploying power on each side of the political struggle. Of course, neither the set of alternative political paths in future years, nor the precise strategies that will successfully take us down one path or another, can be predicted with certainty. For future readers looking back at this moment with the benefit of hindsight, this chapter presents a strategic analysis made in the crucible of that contestation – a contemporaneous chronicle that may be useful not just for current strategists but for future actors who find themselves in the whirlwind of analogous moments of social fracture and political fluidity.

What strategies might best advance the forces for empowering labor, communities, and democratic governance? The ancient Greek polymath, Archimedes, provides a clue. Referring to that ancient device – the lever and fulcrum – with which humans first became able to build structures that would outlast their builders, he is reputed to have said: "Give me a lever long enough and a fulcrum on which to place it, and I shall move the world." The lever and fulcrum to move our nation, and thus our world, are worker organization and democracy. In the twentieth century, these two tools helped our forebears defeat fascism, overturn Jim Crow, and lift millions from poverty and exploitation. But, over the past half century, the lever of worker organization and the fulcrum of democracy have become detached from each other, neutralizing the effectiveness of each. Coupling them once again is necessary to move our world toward deep democratization of work, community, and national politics.

Events are foregrounding both the problem and its solution. Exploding wealth and income inequality, resurgent monopoly, hegemonic neoliberalism, judicial attacks on unions, and voter suppression and state violence targeted at communities of color put on sustained display the crises of politics and worker organization and clarified the relation between the two. Fortunately, a plethora of new initiatives point toward a reimagining of the dialectic of labor struggle and democracy. To understand the significance of these efforts, we must turn to the historical source and the stakes of the contemporary struggle.

HISTORICAL ROOTS OF THE CRISIS OF LABOR AND DEMOCRACY

For three-quarters of the twentieth century, the growth of worker organization and the expansion of democracy worked in tandem. As one progressed, so did the other. We often overlook the extent to which the United States was, at best, an aspirational democracy in 1900. The majority of citizens had no access to the ballot. The voting rights of African Americans were stripped by Klan terrorists who murdered black voters in the 1870s and 1880s and by racist state legislators who used poll taxes and literacy tests to drop them from voting rolls in the 1890s and early 1900s – with the approval of the US Supreme Court in *Williams* v. *Mississippi* (1898). And despite a half-century of women's suffrage agitation, they had won the right to vote only in Wyoming, Utah, Colorado, and Idaho. Granting women the franchise, anti-suffragists argued, would "corrupt" their "purer" natures (Goodier 2013: 7–11). Even white working men didn't fare much better. Many states maintained property requirements that barred those who lacked property or who had received public assistance from voting in local elections. Indeed, just when the Supreme Court upheld black disfranchisement, striking textile workers in New Bedford, Massachusetts, were told that receiving public relief would disqualify them from voting in the next election (Keyssar 2000: 117–171).

Even where the law entitled workers to vote in the early twentieth century, their exercise of that right was sharply limited. Many employers instructed them how to cast their ballots and punished them if they didn't comply. Pioneering sociologist John A. Fitch found this to be common in turn-of-the-twentieth-century steel towns, like Braddock, Pennsylvania. US Steel's New York headquarters sent voting instructions to mill superintendents in Braddock; foremen were then dispatched to escort workers to the polls to do their civic duty (Fitch 1910: 229–231). In other places, more drastic means were used. During a time of labor tension in 1914 in the coalfields of Huerfano County, Colorado, coal operators worked with local officials to draw the maps of seven electoral precincts so that they were entirely on company property. On election day, armed guards simply prevented anyone seen as potentially "disloyal" from entering those precincts to vote (Keyssar 2000: 160).

The abysmal quality of American democracy explains why workers and unions enjoyed few rights in the early 1900s. Thus, while workers had no legally protected right to organize, employers had a right to require as a condition of employment that workers sign a "yellow-dog contract," promising they would never join a union. Laws banning employer blacklists of union supporters or setting minimum wages or maximum hours were regularly struck down by courts during the Lochner era of Supreme Court jurisprudence (*Lochner* v. *New York*, 198 US 45 [1905]). Meanwhile, judicial injunctions forbidding picketing were so ubiquitous that, in the words of legal scholar William E. Forbath, they "enabled hostile employers and public officials to treat ordinary protest and mutual aid as the deeds of outlaws" (Forbath 1991: 126). Not surprisingly, in such an inhospitable environment, only skilled workers achieved much success in building durable unions capable of bargaining collectively. The vast majority of them were white men organized in craft unions that excluded women and people of color as a matter of course. Yet they represented a mere sliver of the early twentieth century working class.

Because workers' lack of union rights and their limited access to the ballot box were mutually reinforcing, the ensuing struggle to organize unions inevitably triggered a widening fight for increased political democracy. Similarly, workers' struggles to win voting rights energized efforts to unionize. Although the relationship between union organizing and the struggles of women, immigrants, and African Americans for their democratic rights was often complicated by tensions and conflicts, the dialectic that emerged between unionizing and deepening democracy transformed America between 1918 and 1968, as each step forward in one arena helped spur a step forward in the other.

The first such breakthrough occurred during the 1910s, when efforts by immigrant workers, African Americans, and women to win a greater measure of democracy became supercharged by US entry into World War I. While President Woodrow Wilson promised to make it a "war to make the world safe for democracy," workers insisted that the war must also result in an expanded democracy at home. In 1917, a wave of strikes nearly derailed the war effort, as workers began calling for the "de-Kaisering of industry" and insisting that "[s]elf government in the workshop" be "one part of the democracy for which our armies are fighting in France" (McCartin 1997: 119). Wilson found that he could not quash the militancy through the repression of radical members of the Industrial Workers of the World or the Socialist Party alone. Reforms were necessary. So, in 1918, he created a National War Labor Board (NWLB), giving union leaders an equal place with management in its membership. That board in turn promised to foster "industrial democracy" in return for workers' cooperation with the war effort.

The wartime fight for industrial democracy marked a turning point. The NWLB required that employers in war-related industries bargain with their employees, holding shop committee elections in settings where unions had never been established. Because shop committee elections were open to never before unionized semi-skilled workers in war industries – including immigrants, women, and African Americans who were unable to vote in political elections – the spread of these committees in turn had a profound impact on craft unions. If they hoped to win influence through shop committees, craft unionists realized they had to reach beyond skilled white men, to the broader base of war workers who claimed to be "sick and tired of Czar [Samuel] Gompers and his bunch of Grand Dukes," as one put it, and who demanded "DEMOCRACY in the labor movement as well as in politics and industry" (McCartin 1997: 200). This pushed unions like the International Brotherhood of Electrical Workers to embrace industrial union-like organizing drives in the steel and electrical manufacturing industries.

Those experiments in industrial democracy and mass unionization were cut short by the end of the war, the dissolution of the NWLB, and a furious post-war employer counteroffensive that rolled back union gains in 1919. But wartime struggles had left an indelible legacy. Women's participation in the war effort made it impossible to deny them suffrage any longer. By 1920, they had won the Nineteenth Amendment. African Americans who had moved north for jobs in war industries and sought a voice through shop committees increasingly chafed at discrimination and their continued exclusion from craft unions. Even employers knew they couldn't completely turn the clock back. After the dust from the battles of 1919 settled, companies such as General Electric realized they had to offer workers at least some form of workplace democracy if they hoped to avert a union resurgence, and they rushed to create company unions in the 1920s, putting them forward as "industrial democracy plans" (McCartin 1997: 209–220).

The unionization-democratization dialectic drove a second breakthrough during the New Deal and World War II. When Franklin Roosevelt came to office in 1933 promising to lift the country out of the Great Depression, he approved the inclusion of Section 7a in his National Industrial Recovery Act. Modeled on the NWLB's precedent, it extended bargaining rights to workers in vital industries, yet it failed to ban company unions. This initiated a furious struggle by workers who demanded real rather than sham industrial democracy, triggering a national strike wave in 1934. Those strikes paved the way for the passage of the National Labor Relations Act (NLRA or Wagner Act) of 1935 – which outlawed company unions. Senator Robert Wagner's law made it possible to resurrect the mass organizing experiments of 1918. Within months of the law's passage, a group of unions led by the Mine Workers' John L. Lewis broke with the craft-dominated American Federation of Labor (AFL) to create what would become the Congress of Industrial Organizations (CIO). CIO unions promptly launched mass organizing drives in steel, auto, and other industries. Addressing the nation in 1936, Lewis explained that the CIO sought an "industrial democracy" that would guarantee "the freedom, happiness, and security which should be the inheritance of all Americans" (Lewis 1937).

As happened during World War I, union organizing struggles energized those who sought to expand political democracy. To build effective unions in mass production industries, the CIO threw open its doors to the semi-skilled and the unskilled, to women and to African Americans. Although its unions generally avoided confronting racial and gender hierarchies head on, rarely challenging the prejudices of their racist and sexist members or the privileges of white men, they nonetheless served as incubators of a new wave of activism on behalf of equal rights for women and African Americans. The CIO created the space for the founding of the National Negro Congress (NNC), which elected union leader A. Philip Randolph as its president and launched a campaign for racial equality and the restoration of black voting rights, thus beginning what historians now call the "long civil rights movement" (Hall 2005).

The dynamics unleashed by World War II deepened this mutually reinforcing dynamic. Wartime policies solidified unionism in the nation's mass production industries. The rights won by workers during these years in turn propelled the post-war struggle for black freedom and women's rights (Cobble 2003; Jones 2013). In 1941, Randolph forced the federal government to ban racial discrimination in war industries, and during the war government agencies mandated that women get equal pay for equal work. Once more workplace organization helped expand democracy: by 1944 the US Supreme Court took its first momentous step in the effort to restore black voting rights in *Smith* v. *Allwright* (321 US 649 [1944]), declaring unconstitutional the whites-only political primaries that nominated Democratic candidates for office in the one-party Jim Crow South (Sullivan 1996).

Despite the post-war backlash against labor's gains, Republican takeover of Congress, and enactment of the union-hobbling Taft-Hartley Act over the veto of President Harry S. Truman in 1947, the expansion of unions and democracy over the previous decade had laid the foundation for a third momentous breakthrough for the union-democracy dynamic during the Cold War era. US aspirations to lead the "free world" against Stalinist communism created the context for two great and interconnected struggles, that of: (1) African Americans for civil rights and voting rights, and (2) public employees for union rights. Both arose simultaneously, beginning with the renewed African American civil rights struggle that started in earnest with the Montgomery Bus Boycott in 1955, in which veterans of the NNC and Randolph's Brotherhood of Sleeping Car Porters played an important role, and in which funding from unions like the United Auto Workers proved crucial. As African Americans began organizing and engaging in direct action protests against their second-class citizenship, the long-dormant aspirations of public sector workers for union rights were awakened.

The fights for civil and voting rights on the one hand and public sector unionism on the other were mutually reinforcing. Inspired by racial justice protestors, many government workers, who were disproportionately female and African American to begin with, chafed at being called "public servants," protested their exclusion from the Wagner Act, and insisted on winning the same rights as private sector workers. In 1962 they succeeded in getting President John F. Kennedy to issue an executive order granting limited union and bargaining rights to federal workers. That order in turn helped instigate a wave of state laws that granted bargaining rights to public employees. Growing government workers' unions, such as the American Federation of State County and Municipal Employees (AFSCME), meanwhile, became key allies of the civil rights struggle, pushing for passage of the Civil Rights Act of 1964 and the Voting Rights Act of 1965.

The Memphis sanitation strike of 1968, whose participants raised the cry "I Am a Man," in many ways marked the apogee of a half-century of intertwined struggle for democracy and union rights. The Memphis workers won their fight to unionize, but Rev. Martin Luther King Jr., who had by that point come to a deep realization of the intertwined nature of union rights, civil rights, and democracy, did not survive the battle (Honey 2007). Nor did the labor-liberal alliance that had emerged in the post-war era long survive the tumults of that momentous year, which witnessed a fracturing of the Democratic Party, the ascendance of Richard Nixon, and the Republican party's adoption of a Southern Strategy that would reconfigure politics by century's end.

Within years of Memphis, the relationship between democratization and unionization began to unravel, damaging both causes. By the late 1970s, deindustrialization was beginning to erode the membership of industrial unions, and stagflation and budget deficits began hardening opposition to public sector unions. At the same time, conservatives used busing, fair housing, and affirmative action as wedge issues to stoke the fears of white workers, undermining efforts to combat systemic racial inequality.

As repeated efforts to stem union decline either through reformed labor laws or new organizing initiatives failed and union strength ebbed, assaults on voting rights and democracy escalated. Major labor law reform efforts were consistently blocked by congressional filibusters, even as state-level campaigns achieved the enactment of "right-to-work" laws in a majority of states by 2015. Meanwhile, the well-funded State Policy Network, founded in 1992 (Hertel-Fernandez 2019) launched a long legal and legislative fight against public sector unions that culminated with Wisconsin Governor Scott Walker signing legislation stripping public employees of the right to bargain (2011 Wisconsin Act 10), and *Janus* v. *AFSCME*, the 2018 Supreme Court decision that outlawed union security provisions in the public sector (138 S. Ct. 2448). The very same forces that rolled back union gains also attacked voting rights and opposed efforts to curb the power of big money in politics. The Supreme Court again helped lead the charge, from

Buckley v. *Valeo* (424 US 1 [1976]), which ruled that limits on campaign spending amounted to an infringement on free speech, to *Citizens United* (558 US 310 [2010]), which opened the floodgates to oceans of "dark money" entering political campaigns, to *Shelby County* v. *Holder* (570 US 529 [2013]), which undermined the Voting Rights Act.

The interrelated decomposition of union strength and democratic rights since the 1970s created the political opening for neoliberalism's ascendancy. As neoliberalism's acolytes gained power and influence, they in turn furthered the projects of de-democratization and de-unionization, demonstrating in the process that, as Wendy Brown puts it, democracy can be "undone, hollowed out from within, not only overthrown or stymied by antidemocrats" (Brown 2015: 18).

CURRENT CORPORATE DOMINANCE AND ENCROACHING AUTHORITARIANISM

In this century, the United States has increasingly come to resemble the America of 1900 as both democracy and worker organization have atrophied – and, as a consequence, runaway economic inequality and corporate power have become markers of our Second Gilded Age. Voter suppression is becoming re-institutionalized in much of the nation, union membership threatens to dip below 10 percent of workers, and workplace rights are quickly eroding. These interrelated developments are turning our jobs into incubators of encroaching authoritarianism.

Anyone who has recently held a job in the United States where they were not an executive leader has had a taste of life under a dictatorship. Indeed, work for the vast majority entails an 8-, 10- or 12-hour-a-day sojourn in an authoritarian state. Work is a place where freedom of speech, assembly, or association, are relentlessly curbed; where people are subject to panopticon-like surveillance of their movements and communications by new technologies; where non-compete agreements, signed as a condition of employment, curtail the right of workers to leave their jobs to seek better ones, thereby weakening their bargaining power, as employer-mandated yellow-dog contracts once did; and where arbitration clauses strip them of their right to legal recourse when they have suffered discrimination, harassment, health or safety violations, and where, thanks to the Supreme Court's 2018 decision in *Epic Systems* v. *Lewis*, such clauses block their access to rights guaranteed by the NLRA (138 S. Ct. 1612).

As workers increasingly have become subjects who thrive or perish at the whims of corporate leaders, it is little wonder why one in four now say that their workplace is a "dictatorship," according to Elizabeth Anderson. More would say so, she argues, if they realized just how much power their employer has to arbitrarily regulate and punish their speech and conduct, not only on the job, but off it as well. In most workplaces today, "bosses govern in ways that are largely unaccountable to those who are governed," Anderson tells us. What's more, "employers don't merely govern workers; they *dominate* them" (Anderson 2017: xxii).

The impact on workers' lives of this daily domination is both demeaning of their dignity and corrosive of their democratic spirit. Workers in Amazon distribution centers are systematically tagged with personal sat-nav (satellite navigation) computers that not only tell them what route they must travel within the plant to fill orders, but also push them to meet target times for these journeys and rate them on whether their targets are met (Head 2014). Workers in poultry plants, meanwhile, consistently report being denied bathroom breaks. "I and many, many others had to wear Pampers," reported one worker, who added that she felt like she had "no worth, no right to ask questions or to speak up" (Oxfam America 2016: 6). Even as private prisons have proliferated to exploit the incarcerated for private profit, private employment of all kinds has come to seem increasingly prison-like for many workers. And just as incarceration disproportionately impacts black and brown communities, so too are black and brown workers more likely to face the most extreme forms of workplace authoritarianism.

It is a short step from domination in the workplace to domination in the political sphere. Alex Hertel-Fernandez finds that since 2010 corporations have succeeded in coercing workers to adopt their employers' political causes in ways not much different from those once employed by the steel workers John Fitch interviewed in the pre-World War I years. Whether they are forced to stand behind political candidates who visit their workplace for a "photo op," asked to write letters to legislators protesting bills their employers oppose, or urged to vote for the employers' favored candidates, workers are increasingly subjected to the influence of those who sign their paychecks (Hertel-Fernandez 2018).

Encroaching authoritarianism in work relations has begotten in turn illiberalism in the public square, relentlessly pushing us toward administering government "like a business," treating corporations and citizens alike as mere consumers of its services, and shifting from a "market economy" to a "market society," one in which, as Martha Minow observes, "market-style mechanisms are increasingly employed to provide what government had taken as duties" (Minow 2002: 1). This is an era of "market triumphalism," in which the consolidated rule of elites in politics, the economy, and culture has resulted in what Michael J. Sandel aptly calls "the skyboxification of American life" (2012: 6–11, 203).

The vast power imbalance in work relations acclimates Americans to an increasingly undemocratic political order as well. It is an order in which a political party whose presidential candidates have won the national popular vote for the presidency only once since 1988 has nonetheless named the majority of both Supreme Court justices and judges of the US Courts of Appeals; in which a man who lost the popular vote by a larger margin than any president in history elevated nearly one quarter of sitting circuit court judges (Economist blog 2020); in which Republicans have been able to control the US Senate with senators who were elected by 14 million fewer votes than those of the "minority" party (Brownstein 2020); in which forty-one senators, elected by perhaps a third of the nation's voters have held effective veto power over national legislation, including initiatives to protect unionizing and voting rights; in which "corporations are people too" and brandish the "free speech" rights of their corporate personhood to vitiate the voices of actual humans (Piety 2012). In such a context, it is not surprising that some conservative thinkers have gone so far as to suggest that we dispense with democracy altogether, overriding universal suffrage with an "epistocratic veto," exercised by those "knowledgeable" enough to pass "rigorous competency exams" – not surprising because self-described elites already exercise a semblance of such veto power (Brennan 2016: 215–216).

This undemocratic order gave rise to an economy characterized by privatization, financialization, and monopoly. Privatization and financialization both arose simultaneously from the economic crisis of the 1970s. As stagflation ballooned government deficits, privatizers launched what Donald Cohen calls a tireless "assault on public solutions and the common good" (Cohen 2018). Insisting that public workers were inefficient and overpaid, privatizers sought to contract out what government functions they could and administer the rest with market principles, in the process corroding "public things" such as schools, that, as Bonnie Honig puts it, "are necessary conditions of democratic life" (2017: 12).

As privatization advanced, so too did financialization as soaring inflation sent investors searching for those corporations most interested in "maximizing shareholder value" (Lazonick & O'Sullivan 2000). Thanks to the deregulation of the Reagan years, new pools of capital, organized in exotic new forms – hedge funds, private equity firms – began subordinating Main Street to Wall Street (Appelbaum & Batt 2014; Jacobs 2019). Resurgent monopoly was in turn a product of these economic shifts. We now live in an age of new goliaths, in which "bigness" has become a "curse" for workers and democracy (Stoller 2019; Wu 2018). Facebook, Apple, Google, Microsoft, Verizon, AT&T, Walmart, and Amazon dominate their respective economic niches, amidst an effective moratorium on antitrust regulation. Since its acquisition of Instagram, Facebook has successfully cleared 67 other mergers, while Amazon and Google cleared 91 and 214 respectively over the same period (Wu 2018: 123). These firms now bestride the economy much like the trusts that dominated America in 1900.

The combination of privatization, financialization, and growing monopoly places corporate interests in a position to control workers' lives far from work itself. Working families' access to housing, education, and healthcare is determined by an ever-smaller number of coactive financial actors than witnessed before in US history. Thus, as state and local governments market their bonds, as schools face threats of privatization and student debt mounts, as rent soars, evictions multiply, gentrification progresses, and medical bills accumulate, relatively few like-minded and powerful financial entities such as Blackstone, Wells Fargo, Goldman Sachs, and Citibank often drive these and similar processes across a wide spectrum of economic activity (Lerner & Bhatti 2016).

These developments have made the form of collective bargaining workers won in the twentieth century increasingly anachronistic. Whether they be in the public or the private sector, when unionized workers sit down at the bargaining table they are often negotiating with "employers" who either lack the power to deliver what the workers are seeking, or whose wealth and power defies workers' existing tools for exerting leverage. Under such conditions even unionized workers have found it difficult to win anything approximating self-governance or to practice what Yoni Appelbaum calls the "acquired habit" of democracy (Appelbaum 2018).

This is the world into which the Covid-19 pandemic came. Its disruptions created new opportunities for "disaster capitalism," and the mega-rich reaped rewards from the tragedy. Between mid-March and early August 2020, the fortunes of America's billionaires mushroomed by $685 billion (Helenowski 2020). As their wealth soared, the pandemic laid bare the results of decades of growing inequality and compounded the damage, taking a disproportionate toll on the poor, immigrants, and communities of color. Black and brown communities were disproportionately victimized not only by the virus (Oppel 2020), but by its economic fallout as well (Gould & Wilson 2020). Although frontline workers were often hailed as "essential workers" and heroes, they learned that while their work might be essential, they were expendable, and their families' health and finances were disregarded.

It was in this context that the uprisings in the streets in response to the murder of George Floyd and state sanctioned police violence against black bodies took place, reminding us of the important if ironic truth mentioned above: history shows that economic collapses, wars, pandemics, and other national and global crises, with all their horrors, can create conditions for transformational positive change. Such change is never inevitable, of course. But over the past decade new forms of organizing and struggle evolved in response to the financialized, racialized, privatizing, and monopolizing capitalism that we now face. These forms are beginning to find creative ways to bring the lever and fulcrum – worker organization and democracy – back into alignment with each other. As they do, they are making clear that the "old idea of industrial democracy," as Gareth Sitaraman puts it, is "making a comeback in different forms" (Sitaraman 2017: 291).

REVIVING DEMOCRACY THROUGH ORGANIZING AND BARGAINING
FOR THE COMMON GOOD

Given the current challenges that workers and unions face, the labor movement can no longer rely on the form of collective bargaining that emerged in the twentieth century. That form, which took shape before privatization, financialization, and resurgent monopoly transformed our economy, and before the democratic advances of the last century were stalled and forced into retreat, was largely confined to the narrowly economistic issues of wages, hours, and benefits within individual firms. It offered people a measure of empowerment on the job as workers, leaving largely unaddressed their needs as community members, renters and homeowners, students, and taxpayers, while also subordinating their distinctive needs as women, immigrants, and people of color to the common denominator of their status as employees. That form of collective bargaining presumed that a functioning representative democracy could work in tandem with economistic unionism to deal with the full range of issues on which working people needed a say. Yet that assumption no longer holds. If collective bargaining is to survive in the years ahead, it will have to be reconceptualized as more than a narrowly economic tool, but instead as the cutting edge of a powerful democracy movement, as an agent of liberation for those who have never before had the ability to bargain with the powerful over the things they need (Gupta et al. 2019).

Such a reconceptualization has already begun. For nearly a decade, experiments undertaken by unions and community organizations that have come together in a network called Bargaining for the Common Good (BCG) have helped lead this rethinking. BCG had its origins in resistance by progressive public sector union locals and their community allies to the austerity regime that was promoted after the Great Recession by antiunion governors such as Scott Walker of Wisconsin and Bruce Rauner of Illinois. Many unions began to realize that traditional bargaining no longer worked for them. They needed to be able to bring up issues such as school funding at the bargaining table and they needed to have community allies at their sides when they fought. Community and racial justice groups have long campaigned on a variety of issues, including getting police out of schools and foreclosure moratoriums. Community members, for their part, saw unions as the most effective partners in fighting for the restoration and preservation of the vital services upon which they depend. The embrace of these issues among unions in Bargaining for the Common Good opened up new opportunities for partnership and drew unions and their allies together in an effort to politicize the bargaining process in a broad sense, fighting for a democratic voice on issues that had long been determined by unaccountable financial and political elites. BCG unions built on and supported work that has been led by community and racial justice groups. Unions didn't invent these issues, but by partnering with community groups they learned to embrace and support them, initiating a positive feedback loop like that which emerged when organizations like the Brotherhood of Sleeping Car Porters and the National Negro Congress partnered to fuse civil rights and union rights struggles in an earlier era (Hall 2005).

BCG had its roots in the progressive ferment that flowed from convergent events in 2011. In a short span of time that year, the Service Employees International Union (SEIU) launched the Fight for a Fair Economy in January 2011, committing to organizing campaigns in dozens of cities, which within a few years would give birth to the Fight for $15; Jobs with Justice, the national network of unions and community allies, joined with the National Domestic Workers Alliance to create the Caring Across Generations campaign, a national initiative to transform the long-term care system and empower care workers; and the Occupy Wall Street movement erupted, crystallizing unexpected alliances and stirring public debate about inequality and the impact of financialization.

In the midst of this ferment, unions such as the St. Paul Federation of Teachers and the Chicago Teachers Union began consciously remaking collective bargaining. The St. Paul teachers started by fighting for the right of the parents of special needs children to participate in contract bargaining. Soon the union was demanding that negotiations be opened to parents at large, meeting with parents and other groups and drawing up an ambitious bargaining agenda which among other things insisted that schools break ties with banks that foreclosed on families during the school year. In Chicago, meanwhile, reformers led by Karen Lewis came to power with the Chicago Teachers Union (CTU) and immediately laid plans to challenge Chicago's neoliberal mayor Rahm Emanuel. The CTU's 2012 strike broke new ground. Before striking, the union built community relationships and involved allies in shaping their bargaining demands. They demanded things that weren't permissible in traditional bargaining: that the Chicago Public Schools claw back money it had squandered in predatory interest rate swaps; that Chicago use Tax Increment Financing (TIF) money for schools instead of lavishing it on the Chicago Board of Trade and developers; that schools provide wraparound services for their students; and others. In short they used the power of their strike and collective bargaining as leverage to try to win a democratic voice over decisions that had long been left to the city's elites (Ashby & Bruno 2016).

Other unions and their community allies followed with similar innovations, often targeting the domination of the public agenda by financial interests. In Los Angeles the Fix LA coalition of municipal unions and community groups demonstrated that the city paid more in fees to the Wall Street firms that marketed municipal bonds than it spent maintaining the city's streets and demanded a comprehensive overhaul of the city's relationship to Wall Street. In Oregon, SEIU Local 503 and its community allies fought austerity measures by insisting the state sue to recover money lost to predatory financial firms as a result of the LIBOR scandal.

By May 2014 the unions and community groups involved in these experiments convened and adopted Bargaining for the Common Good as the name of their strategy. Over the following three years other unions inspired by these efforts launched initiatives of their own. California university workers demanded that their employer prohibit the use of riot police or excessive police forces during non-violent student and worker actions; New Jersey teachers demanded their school district hire and support more black teachers, and mandate black history/ethnic studies; San Diego public employees demanded criminal justice reform to prioritize education, early intervention, and treatment over punitive measures; Maryland teachers demanded a Black Lives Matter Week of Action in Schools (Sneiderman & Fascione 2018).

When the #RedforEd movement erupted in 2018, its demands echoed the patterns that had begun to emerge in BCG campaigns. When West Virginia teachers refused to end their strike until all of the state's employees, not just teachers, received the same raise they had been promised, when Arizona teachers demanded a ballot initiative that would block tax cuts that had defunded their schools, and when North Carolina teachers called for Medicaid expansion, they pushed far beyond the boundaries of traditional bargaining by taking up issues that served a vision of the common good.

Leading BCG unions and their allies raised the ante in 2019 with major strikes led by the United Teachers of Los Angeles (UTLA) and the Chicago Teachers Union. When UTLA walked out in January 2019 it did so over issues not directly tied to teachers pay and benefits. The strike's priorities, developed in alliance with community members, focused on the hiring of nurses and librarians, the dedication of school property to green space, an end to the racially targeted searches of student backpacks, and legal support for immigrant families. Union members stayed out and, in the rain, held massive pickets, not aimed at increasing the school district's wage, but rather to secure these demands that were vital to community allies – and they won them. When the CTU struck nine months later, it also made community issues a priority. In alliance with community groups, it demanded an end to TIF-funded projects, like Lincoln Yards, that squandered subsidies on the ultrawealthy. Most important, it made housing justice a central demand of its strike, insisting that the school district provide resources for Chicago's thousands of homeless students. Mayor Lori Lightfoot and the Chicago press insisted that housing issues had "no place" at the bargaining table. But the union stuck to its position, ultimately winning housing assistance for the homeless (McCartin & Sneiderman 2020).

The thrust of BCG efforts was to break down the wall that separated the workplace from public space and workers from community members and taxpayers. Central to this effort was a shared analysis of the ways in which racialized capitalism was systematically undermining black and brown communities and the public services upon which they depended. Forging new alliances and forcing open the black box of collective bargaining, these efforts helped bring collective action to bear on festering public policy failures, giving community members a democratic voice on key issues that the political status quo denied them (Sneiderman & Fascione 2018).

The BCG network was not the only initiative that moved in this direction. Projects such as Caring Across Generations, the Better Banks Campaign, and the Athena Coalition shared a similar analysis and approach and often deep and overlapping ties with each other and BCG. In each of these efforts, a racial justice analysis guides the development of strategy and tactics. Eschewing the race neutral organizing language so common in the twentieth century heyday of old-model collective bargaining, this analysis leads to the building of large robust coalitions focused on bringing democratic force to bear against structural injustices. These coalitions, which are built around linking multiple goals, are not controlled by a single constituency. They seek to redefine workers' struggles as that of whole communities, in the process making issues like housing, caregiving, and environmental justice core labor issues.

Caring Across Generations, the most successful of these efforts to date, has built a national movement anchored by domestic workers and a coalition with more than one hundred other organizations and unions since its founding in 2011. It brings together families, care workers, people with disabilities, and aging Americans and works to transform the way care is provided so that all families and workers can live well and age with dignity. Through online and grassroots organizing and culture change work, the campaign is shifting how our nation values care and caregiving relationships and calling for policy solutions that create a much-needed care infrastructure that provides high-quality, affordable options for people who need care and support for family caregivers, and that strengthens the care workforce.

Caregiving has historically been done by unsupported women, immigrants, and women of color for free or for poverty wages – which perpetuates the idea that their work, in itself, is less valuable. Just prior to the Covid-19 pandemic, we still relied on $470 billion annually in free labor provided by family caregivers, over 75 percent of whom are women (Family Caregiver Alliance 2017), while care workers, who are overwhelmingly women of color and immigrants, powered a $78 billion industry (Crain 2017) on an average salary of $15,000 (PHI 2018). This essential work makes all other work possible by enabling those who work outside the home to go out to do their jobs; yet caregivers are treated as expendable. As domestic workers, most are excluded from the Fair Labor Standards Act and denied the right to collectively bargain under the NLRA.

The campaign has made significant gains. It paved the way for the Home Care Final Rule announced by the US Department of Labor in 2013 that took effect in 2015 after a successful court battle. In 2017 it won Hawaii's Kupuna Caregiver Program, that provides a financial benefit to working family caregivers. And, in 2019, it helped win the Washington Long-Term Care Trust Act, which established the first state-based public long term care program in the nation. By providing a vehicle through which worker organizations, unions, and those who need care support and services can come together, Caring Across Generation provides a vision of a care economy that replaces piecemeal components (paid leave, childcare, and elder care) with a comprehensive and public family care program that is portable and universally accessible, a program that will invest in our care infrastructure and support professionalizing, stabilizing, and growing the care workforce while increasing the stability of families and the productivity of all workers. This vision – the importance of which has been underlined by the coronavirus pandemic – would, if realized, ensure that care becomes a critical component of a twenty-first century social contract.

Another pioneering effort is the Committee for Better Banks (CBB), a project supported by the Communications Workers of America. It is organizing bank workers and bringing them together with consumers and community allies to demand both improved wages and benefits *and* an end to predatory banking practices with which workers have been forced to cooperate. Bank workers, who labor in the belly of the beast of our financialized economy, know better than anyone all the ways in which banks cheat and exploit consumers. They also see firsthand how badly government regulation has failed to stem these practices. Bank workers are therefore seeking to organize not only to improve their jobs but to "regulate from below." That effort led Wells Fargo employees connected to the CBB to become the whistleblowers who exposed the massive fake account scandal at their bank in 2016. The campaign has the synergistic goals of organizing bank workers into a union, exposing how banks cheat workers and consumers, and ultimately breaking up the big banks (Lerner et al. 2018).

An effort even more ambitious has emerged from Athena, the broad coalition that has come together to fight Amazon. Now the richest company in the world, Amazon's unparalleled power illustrates the need for a broad movement of workers and allies determined to organize on the job while also winning a democratic voice over the direction of our economy. Amazon's well-documented abusive labor practices affect not only the company's largely invisible black and brown logistics staff, but also its white collar operations. But labor abuses are only one of Amazon's destructive tendencies. The company targets communities of color through its Ring product, reporting "suspicious" people to the police, deploys its facial recognition technology to aid federal detention of immigrants, bankrupts small neighborhood businesses by forcing them to move their goods only through its platform, and contributes to climate change. It has also learned to dominate local politicians – as it did in its search for a location for its second headquarters. Simply unionizing a company of such destructive power while leaving the rest of its pathologies in place would be a partial victory, at best.

Realizing this, a coalition of close to one hundred groups, including labor, civil rights, racial justice, and immigrant organizations, and a host of others came together to form Athena in 2019. Athena aims to fight the surveillance capitalism which Amazon amplifies with the data collected from its vast retail and grocery delivery network. The coalition's pledge asks signers to agree that the campaign will not settle for small extractions of concessions in one arena. Athena welcomes incremental wins but refuses, for example, to trade the continued pollution of black and brown neighborhoods for new benefits like paid sick leave.

Ironically, because Amazon is so large and powerful it has helped coalesce a coalition of unparalleled size, breadth, and sophistication. Many Athena members have never worked together before. Athena has supported workers striking against Amazon in Minnesota by bringing engineering and other white collar staff to support Seattle warehouse workers organizing and striking around Amazon's environmental depredations. Its worker leaders meanwhile are learning about how monopolies damage local economies and undermine democracy. Through Athena, racial justice and technology reform organizations are making linkages among Immigration and Custom Enforcement's use of Amazon's facial recognition technology, police department use of thousands of Amazon's doorbell cameras across the country, and the company's surveillance of its logistics warehouse staff. Because Amazon is such a large foe, it ignites innovative ideas about its interconnected malignities.

Caring Across Generations, the Committee for Better Banks, and Athena share the central premises of Bargaining for the Common Good: old methods of organizing and bargaining are not up to the challenges presented by twenty-first century capitalism; and the fight to organize workers in this century cannot be separated from the effort to reverse the steady erosion of democracy in recent decades. As powerful forces are threatening to bring the US full circle from the "industrial autocracy" that workers battled a century ago to the "private dictatorships" they work under today, these initiatives help point the way forward. With the lever of worker organization, and the fulcrum of community-based demands for a democratic voice over the issues that impact working people, they intend to move our world forward toward a politics of hope, just as the struggles of the last century did – and we can feel it budging.

REFERENCES

Anderson, Elizabeth. 2017. *Private Government: How Employers Rule Our Lives (and Why We Don't Talk About It)*. Princeton, NJ: Princeton University Press.
Appelbaum, Eileen, and Rosemary Batt. 2014. *Private Equity at Work: When Wall Street Manages Main Street*. New York: Russel Sage Foundation.
Appelbaum, Yoni. 2018 "Losing the Democratic Habit," *The Atlantic* (September 13, 2018).
Ashby, Steven, and Robert Bruno. 2016. *A Fight for the Soul of Public Education: The Story of the Chicago Teachers Strike*. Ithaca, NY: ILR Press.
Brennan, Jason. 2016. *Against Democracy*. Princeton, NJ: Princeton University Press.
Brown, Wendy. 2015. *Undoing the Demos: Neoliberalism's Stealth Revolution*. Cambridge, MA: MIT Press.
Brownstein, Ron. 2020. "The End of the Filibuster, No Really," *The Atlantic* (July 20, 2020). www.theatlantic.com/politics/archive/2020/07/why-senate-filibuster-could-be-gone-2021/614278/
Cobble, Dorothy Sue. 2003. *The Other Women's Movement: Workplace Justice and Social Rights in Modern America*. Princeton, NJ: Princeton University Press.
Cohen, Donald. 2018. *Dismantling Democracy: The Forty-Year Attack on Government ... And the Long Game for the Common Good*.
Crain's. 2017. "Trends in Home Health Care: A Growing Industry Is Helping Seniors Age in Place," *Crain's Cleveland Business* (March 25, 2017). www.crainscleveland.com/article/20170325/CUSTOM2017/170329931/trends-in-home-health-care-a-growing-industry-is-helping-seniors-age
Derber, Milton S. 1970. *The American Idea of Industrial Democracy, 1865-1965*. Urbana: University of Illinois Press.
Economist Blog. 2020. "Donald Trump Is Appointing Federal Judges at a Blistering Pace," *The Economist* (February 12, 2020). www.economist.com/graphic-detail/2020/02/14/donald-trump-is-appointing-federal-judges-at-a-blistering-pace
Family Caregiver Alliance. 2019. "Caregiver Statistics: Demographics" (April 17, 2019). www.caregiver.org/caregiver-statistics-demographics
Fitch, John A. 1910. *The Steel Workers*. New York: Charities Publication Committee.
Forbath, William E. 1991. *Law and the Shaping of the American Labor Movement*. Cambridge, MA: Harvard University Press.

Goodier, Susan. 2013. *No Votes for Women: The New York State Anti-Suffrage Movement*. Urbana: University of Illinois Press.

Gould, Elise, and Valerie Wilson. 2020. "Black Workers Face Two of the Most Lethal Preexisting Conditions for Coronavirus – Racism and Economic Inequality," Economic Policy Institute (June 1, 2020). www.epi.org/publication/black-workers-covid/

Gramlich Gould, Elise, and Valerie Wilson. "How Trump Compares with Other Recent Presidents in Appointing Federal Judges," Pew Research Center FactTank (July 15, 2020). www.pewresearch.org/fact-tank/2020/07/15/how-trump-compares-with-other-recent-presidents-in-appointing-federal-judges/

Gupta, Sarita, Stephen Lerner, and Joseph A. McCartin. 2019. "Why the Labor Movement Has Failed and How to Fix It," *Boston Review* (June 10, 2019). http://bostonreview.net/forum/why-labor-movement-has-failed%E2%80%94and-how-fix-it/sarita-gupta-stephen-lerner-joseph-mccartin

Hall, Jacqueline Dowd. 2005. "The Long Civil Rights Movement and the Political Uses of the Past," *Journal of American History* 91, 4: 1233–1263.

Head, Simon. 2014. *Mindless: Why Smarter Machines are Making Dumber Humans*. New York: Basic Books.

Helenowski, Mark. 2020. "Billionaires Have Made an Absolute Killing during the Pandemic," *Mother Jones* (August 10, 2020). www.motherjones.com/politics/2020/08/billionaire-coronavirus-wealth-animation-covid-685-billion/

Hertel-Fernandez, Alexander. 2018. *Politics at Work: How Companies Turn Their Workers Into Lobbyists*. New York: Oxford University Press.

 2019. *State Capture: How Conservative Activists, Big Businesses, and Wealthy Donors Reshaped the American States – And the Nation*. New York: Oxford University Press.

Honey, Michael. 2007. *Going Down Jericho Road: The Memphis Strike, Martin Luther King's Last Campaign*. New York: W. W. Norton.

Honig, Bonnie. 2017. *Public Things: Democracy in Disrepair*. New York: Fordham University Press.

Jacobs, Lauren. 2019. "The American Corporation Is in Crisis – Let's Rethink It." *Boston Review* (October 2, 2019). http://bostonreview.net/forum/american-corporation-crisis%E2%80%94lets-rethink-it/lauren-jacobs-racist-lie-%E2%80%9Ctakers-and-makers%E2%80%9D

Jones, William P. 2013. *The March on Washington: Jobs, Freedom, and the Forgotten History of Civil Rights*. New York: W. W. Norton.

Keyssar, Alexander. 2000. *The Right to Vote: The Contested History of Democracy in the United States*. New York: Basic Books.

Lazonick, William, and Mary O'Sullivan. 2000. "'Maximizing Shareholder Value: A New Ideology for Corporate Governance," *Economy and Society* 29: 13–35.

Lerner, Stephen, Rita Berlofa, Molly McGrath, and Corey Klemmer. 2018. *Tipping the Balance: Collective Action from Finance Workers Creates Regulation from Below*. New York: Friedrich Ebert Stiftung (September 2018). http://library.fes.de/pdf-files/iez/14711.pdf

Lerner, Stephen, and Saqib Bhatti. 2016. "Organizing in a Brave New World," *New Labor Forum* 25, 3: 22–30.

Lewis, John L. 1937. *Industrial Democracy*. Washington, DC: Committee for Industrial Organization.

McCartin, Joseph A. 1997. *Labor's Great War: The Struggle for Industrial Democracy and the Origins of Modern American Labor Relations*. Chapel Hill: The University of North Carolina Press.

McCartin, Joseph A., and Marilyn Sneiderman 2020. "Combustible Convergence: Bargaining for the Common Good and the Teachers Uprisings of 2018," *Labor Studies Journal* 45, 1: 97–113.

Minow, Martha. 2002. *Partners, Not Rivals: Privatization and the Public Good*. Boston: Beacon.

Oxfam America. 2016. *No Relief: The Denial of Bathroom Breaks in the Poultry Industry*. Boston: Oxfam America.

Oppel Jr., Richard A., 2020. "The Fullest Look Yet at the Racial Inequity of Coronavirus," *The New York Times* (July 5, 2020). www.nytimes.com/interactive/2020/07/05/us/coronavirus-latinos-african-americans-cdc-data.html

PHI. 2018. "US Home Care Workers: Key Facts," *PHI* (August 31, 2018). https://phinational.org/resource/us-home-care-workers-key-facts-2018/

Piety, Tamara R. 2012. *Brandishing the First Amendment: Commercial Expression in America*. Ann Arbor: University of Michigan Press.

Sandel, Michael J. 2012. *What Money Can't Buy: The Moral Limits of Markets.* New York: Farrar, Straus, and Giroux.

Sitaraman, Ganesh. 2017. *The Crisis of the Middle-Class Constitution: Why Economic Inequality Threatens Our Republic.* New York: Alfred A. Knopf.

Sneiderman, Marilyn and Secky Fascione. 2018. "Going on Offense in Challenging Times," *New Labor Forum* 27, 1. https://newlaborforum.cuny.edu/2018/01/18/going-on-offense-during-challenging-times/

Stoller, Matt. 2019. *Goliath: The 100 Year War between Monopoly Power and Democracy.* New York: Simon & Schuster.

Sullivan, Patricia. 1996. *Days of Hope: Race and Democracy in the New Deal Era.* Chapel Hill: The University of North Carolina Press.

Wu, Tim. 2018. *The Curse of Bigness: Antitrust in the New Gilded Age.* New York: Columbia Press Reports.

7

"Industrial Democracy" in the United States, Past and Present

Wilma B. Liebman

In May 1919, in the aftermath of the Great War and during the Paris peace negotiations, US President Woodrow Wilson cabled Congress from Paris:

> The question which stands at the front of all others . . . amidst the present great awakening is the question of labor; . . . how are the men and women who do the daily labor of the world to obtain progressive improvement in the conditions of their labor, to be made happier, and to be served better by the communities and the industries which their labor sustains and advances? . . .
>
> The object of all reform in this essential matter must be the genuine democratization of industry. (Wilson 1919: 290–291)

Wilson's support for the democratization of post-war industry has been described as "largely rhetorical" (McCartin 1988: 189). Still, in 1919, there was widespread acknowledgment "that the 'labor question' was not merely the supreme economic question but the constitutive moral, political, and social dilemma of the new industrial order" (Fraser 1989: 55).

Historian Richard White describes the "core" of the labor question as "how to reconcile the democratic promise of the nation with the profoundly undemocratic organization of industry" (White 2017: 674). Throughout United States labor history, "industrial democracy" has been widely regarded as the answer to the labor question. But what that term means has been subject to radically diverse interpretations. This chapter traces key historical moments in the evolution of that concept and the glimmerings of its revival today.

INDUSTRIAL DEMOCRACY IN UNITED STATES LABOR HISTORY

> The term "industrial democracy" is an intricate one. . . . [It] covers a broad spectrum of meanings. (Muller-Jentsch 2008: 261–262)

After the Civil War, social reformers, labor and political activists, and employers debated the meaning of industrial democracy (Derber 1970: 22, 29–32). "With slavery in its grave, Americans had imagined a largely egalitarian society emerging from the war" (White 2017: 855). But the vision of free labor, which arose in an artisanal and agricultural economy and imagined the republican citizen as an independent producer, rested on the economic independence of working people. By the late nineteenth century, with the rise of mass production, wage labor had become the norm in industry, and dependence on wages prevailed as a new form of bondage.

In the late nineteenth century, in the era known as the Gilded Age, rapid industrialization and technological innovation in the United States economy were accompanied by periodic depressions, consolidation of industries into powerful monopolies, extreme inequality, political agitation, and massive labor strife, often bloody. These conditions propelled the growth of various social movements and national labor union organizations. "Labor Republicans" argued that the Constitution itself embodied the right of workers to "shape the conditions of their own work and to negotiate equitable returns on their labor" (2017: 810–811). Some unions championed worker ownership of factories, in which workers would own shares, have rights to elect management, and decide major enterprise policies. In the 1880s, for example, the Knights of Labor embraced the goal of establishing a system of cooperative production to overthrow the wage-labor system and private capitalism. It envisioned "eventually mak[ing] every man his own master, . . . his own employer" (Powderly 1890: 464) (quoted in Derber 1970: 48). Through the Social Gospel movement, Christian churches also played a major role in bringing worker ownership into the national dialogue, advocating for "making the laborer his own capitalist" (Gladden 1876) (quoted in Blasi et al. 2013: 132).

Eventually, many worker-owned companies failed and interest in worker ownership waned, leading many unions to focus on gains through collective bargaining (Blasi et al. 2013: 132) within the "existing private enterprise, wage-earner system" (Derber 1970: 40). The American Federation of Labor (AFL) – the alliance of craft unions that broke with the Knights of Labor – saw producers' cooperatives as unrealistic, at least in the foreseeable future (1970: 49–54). Instead, the AFL counted on the unions' own economic strength, insisted that workers have equal bargaining power with employers, defended the right to strike, and opposed reliance on government as a substitute for collective bargaining. Its objective was to secure "better wages, and shorter or normal workday . . . in a word, to make life the better worth living after all" (US Commission on Industrial Relations 1916: 719). Affirming a linkage between workplace democracy and political democracy, AFL president Samuel Gompers declared that "liberty can be neither exercised nor enjoyed by those who are in poverty" and that "[t]here never yet existed coincident with each other autocracy in the shop and democracy in political life" (AFL 1905: 14).

The abuses of industrial capitalism also gave rise to the Progressive Movement of the early twentieth century, allied with the labor movement. Progressive intellectuals and advocates sought to address the gap between the promise of democracy and the grim realities of industrial life. Among other prominent figures in that movement, Louis Brandeis (a future US Supreme Court Justice) argued for democracy in industry as a corollary to political democracy, for "while invention and discovery created the possibility of releasing men and women from the thralldom of drudgery, there actually came, with the introduction of the factory system and the development of the business corporation, new dangers to liberty" (Brandeis 1916: 463).

In 1912, in response to both labor strife and Progressive agitation, Congress established the US Commission on Industrial Relations to study the causes of "dissatisfaction in the industrial situation" (US Commission on Industrial Relations 1916: 29). Its final report highlighted four causes: unjust distribution of wealth and income; unemployment and denial of an opportunity to earn a living; denial of justice, with workers believing that the law was used to oppress them; and significant obstacles to the right to form voluntary organizations (1916: 29–68). The report concluded that the "only hope for the solution" of labor conflict lay in "the rapid extension of the principle of democracy to industry" (1916: 17). Importantly, it declared that "[p]olitical freedom can exist only where there is industrial freedom; political democracy only where there is industrial democracy" (1916: 18). Its key recommendation was the increase and improvement of organization and representation of workers, which should be protected by the Constitution.

In the first fifteen years of the twentieth century, many labor reformers focused on raising wages, limiting the workday, and restricting employers' control, while Socialist, anarcho-syndicalistic, and other radical groups sought more expansive transformation (Derber 1970: 54–59, 141–172). "Like labor, the employer group was not united in its views on industrial government" (1970: 128), but most employers sought to preempt the growth of radical challenges to capitalism that they saw erupting in Europe. Most were hostile to the notion of "industry as an arena for the democratic process" (1970: 128). They resorted to outright repressive tactics of firing and blacklisting union supporters and winning court-ordered injunctions against strikes and picketing, in order to beat back both moderate unions seeking collective bargaining rights and radical worker organizations. Still, in different ways some employers "attempted ... to accommodate to the rising democratic spirit of the times" (1970: 130). Some employers even supported collective bargaining with unions. Others advocated for welfare work or profit sharing, or experimented with forms of non-union employee representation, even using the title "Industrial Democracy" (Summers 1979: 33; see also Derber 1970: 130).

Economic mobilization for World War I disrupted patterns of labor relations and ignited explosive union activity. To avert impairment of the War effort, an array of new government agencies were quickly created to control labor conflict. Many employers, either on their own or pressured by government agencies, created shop committees, elected by workers and supervised by the government, to resolve disputes. "Billed as a non-union form of 'industrial democracy,' these representational structures ... provided for periodic joint meetings between elected worker representatives and selected management representatives, and ... emphasized conciliation, cooperation, and mutual gain" (Kaufman 1998: 735).

Intervention by the federal government during the War "transformed industrial relations, weakened 'authoritarian' management, and created opportunities for AFL leaders and labor militants alike to advance their own visions in the workplace" (McCartin 1988: 10, 64–93). "[E]ven the most militant unionists ... called ... for 'self-government in the workshop ... [as] part of the democracy for which our armies are fighting in France"' (1988: 7, 119). Government intervention into labor relations and quasi-representative shop committees altered workers' expectations about the possibilities for workplace and political democracy. Unions were hopeful that these shop committees would become union organizations when the War ended.

But trade unionists and progressives misjudged the reactionary forces unleashed by the War, and their fragile wartime coalition was shattered. The federal agencies were weak and retrenched after the war, destroying "any possibility that industrial democracy might be defined in the political arena" (McCartin 1988: 202). Unionists faced government and employer repression. By 1920, "despair reigned among those who had recently felt that the democratization of industry was imminent" (1988: 198).

During the 1920s, employers were eager to "forestall the emergence of powerful, independent union officials" (Summers 1979: 33). For the most part, "the trade unions fared badly in this period," in large measure because of employer resistance. While *industrial democracy* became [a] respectable term in the corporate lexicon, [t]he new lexicon did not, however, include *trade unionism*" (Derber 1970: 2013) (emphasis in original). Drawing from early twentieth century experimentation with a substitute model, "enlightened" employers sought to shape the landscape of labor relations through their own strategy of so-called welfare capitalism. In that decade, hundreds of non-union companies constructed recreational facilities, made safety and sanitation improvements, supplemented wages with profit-sharing, installed seniority systems, and launched shop committees, work councils, and employee representation plans (which labor unions attacked as phony "company unions"). While the aim of welfare capitalism was to avert both unionism and government-led reform, it did give legitimacy to demands for employee involvement and, in some cases, whetted workers' appetite for even greater voice and participation, including genuine unionism (Kaufman 1998: 734–735; see also Jacoby 1997: 11–18). Nonetheless, the United States' unique non-union conception of industrial democracy might well have persisted as the chief current of industrial relations if not for the economic crisis of the 1930s, which made it financially impossible for employers to sustain the cost of welfare capitalism (Jacoby 1997: 20–34).

THE COLLECTIVE BARGAINING MODEL: FROM PROMISE TO DISENCHANTMENT

> The Wagner Act was one of the most drastic legislative innovations of the decade.
> (Leuchtenburg 1963: 151)

Collective bargaining was the vision of industrial democracy advanced by the AFL and the newly emergent Congress of Industrial Organizations (CIO). That vision was, as a matter of federal policy if not yet in actual practice, fully realized in the summer of 1935, when Congress enacted the National Labor Relations Act (Wagner Act) (as amended, 29 USC §§151, et seq.) as a key component of President Franklin Roosevelt's New Deal. The law guaranteed employees the right to join unions and to strike free of employer retaliation, banned company unions, required employers to bargain with unions that had the support of a majority of workers at the enterprise or sub-enterprise level, and created an administrative agency to enforce those worker rights. The Wagner Act supplanted judge-made law restricting union activity with a system of state-supported collective bargaining.

The Act embodied the goals of both economic and political democracy – a giant step in crafting and legitimizing a certain concept of industrial democracy in US history. According to the framers of the Act, workers would "find freedom from the autocratic control of employers" (Summers 1979: 34). An equally important aim of the Act was to promote recovery from the Great Depression, and forestall future depressions, by equalizing bargaining power between labor and capital. By bargaining collectively with their employers through independent trade unions, workers would increase their incomes and thereby their purchasing power, with the Keynesian effect of reviving and sustaining mass consumption and production. In other words, industrial democracy was now presented not only as a moral exigency but as a foundation for the success of a complex industrial economy.

The Act also marked an intellectual revolution, in both economic and legal theory: "One of [its] most important yet oft-forgotten legacies ... was its challenge to the reigning theories of laissez-faire and liberty of contract ... upon which Gilded Age wealth and power resided" (Cobble 2011: 209–210). The Wagner Act advanced the idea that "actual liberty of contract" could occur only when parties had relative equality of bargaining power.

With the collective-bargaining model ascendant, earlier notions of industrial democracy receded. Interest in worker ownership faded yet further, and employer-sponsored non-union representation plans were outlawed as an obstacle to genuine collective bargaining (29 USC §158(2)) (subsequently renumbered as §158(a)(2)).

Unquestionably, the Wagner Act granted enormous protection for unionism, catalyzed workers' organizing efforts, and secured collective bargaining rights in the commanding heights of the US economy. For several decades, the New Deal labor policy delivered a measure of workplace democracy and economic advancement for workers and, indeed, for the general economy. Collective bargaining became an established part of American life. Millions of workers voted for union representation in elections conducted by the National Labor Relations Board (NLRB), the agency Congress created to enforce the Act. When the AFL and CIO merged in 1955, their combined membership was approximately 15 million (Filippelli 1990: xxix) and, even while the percentage of workers who were union members began its steep decline around that time, the absolute number continued climbing to its historical peak of about 21 million in 1979 (Hirsch 2007: App.). Millions achieved a middle-class way of life through collectively-bargained agreements that provided decent wages and benefits. Workers and management effectively shared the increased wealth generated by growth in productivity. Between 1945 and 1973, average wages grew at approximately the same rate as increases in labor productivity.

But the seeds of the New Deal labor policy's demise were planted as early as 1947. World War II had greatly increased the power of labor, amidst the tight labor market of wartime mobilization and the pressure for government resolution of labor disputes to avoid interruptions in armament production. Upon the War's end, the unions were unshackled from their wartime no-strike pledge, and the greatest strike wave in United States history ensued. Congress, newly controlled by the Republican Party, restricted union organizing and collective bargaining with the Labor Management Relations Act (Taft-Hartley Act) of 1947. Among other restrictions on union activity, the Taft-Hartley Act prohibited the unions' powerful weapon of secondary strikes and guaranteed employers' right to run intimidating anti-union campaigns. Since then, despite dramatic social and economic transformation, there have been no substantial revisions to the labor law governing labor-management relations. "[N]o other major American legal regime – no other body of federal law that governs a whole domain of social life – . . . has been so insulated from significant change for so long" (Estlund 2002: 1531).

For several institutional and historical reasons dating at least to the late nineteenth century, United States managerial culture has been and remains uniquely aggressive in its anti-unionism, compared to other advanced capitalist countries. Employers' campaigns against unionism intensified after Taft-Hartley and the recession of the post-Korean War years. While regulated actors typically come into compliance with new regulatory regimes, employers' labor policies followed the opposite path: employers' violations of the Wagner Act (as amended by Taft-Hartley) accelerated after the 1970s. The National Labor Relations Board's remedies for employers' violations were (and still are) so limited that employers' cost-benefit analysis comes out in favor of not just bending but often breaking the law, such as firing union supporters and refusing to bargain with duly elected unions. To avoid unionization, employers are willing to absorb the NLRB's weak penalties for violating the workers' rights nominally promised by the Wagner Act.

Further, the decisions of the NLRB are subject to judicial review, often by judges skeptical of or even hostile to the labor law's protection of collective activity. Jurisprudential battles between the NLRB and the courts are a constant, as are disagreements among the NLRB's members. By tradition, a majority of the NLRB's five members are of the President's party, with the other two of the opposing party. The rules and practices of the NLRB are unstable, with policy oscillating whenever the White House changes from one party's control to the other's. NLRB rulings predictably swing against labor unions under Republican Party administrations. As a general proposition from the 1940s to today, decisions by the courts and the NLRB deradicalized the Act, a law originally intended to accomplish perhaps the most dramatic economic transformation in United States history – namely, to redistribute income and power from capital to labor.

Since the 1980s, labor law scholars have described the United States labor law regime, which originated as the embodiment of one vision of industrial democracy, as "America's unfulfilled promise" (Summers 1979: 36), "an elegant tombstone for a dying institution" (Weiler 1983:

1769), and "an anachronism irrelevant for most workers and firms" (Freeman 2011: 330). While scholars and advocates agree that it is outdated, beyond that there is no consensus. Its defenders say the law, albeit in serious need of strengthening, is critical to a democracy and a fair economy. Its detractors, contesting any significant role of government in the free market, say the legal system should limit the power of trade unions as an impediment to the mobility of capital and efficient managerial decision-making. Since the Reagan-Thatcher revolution of the 1980s, free-market ideologies and deregulatory policies have largely been in the driver's seat.

With dramatic changes in the structure of production and distribution in the new era of globalization since the 1980s, additional limitations in the NLRA model became increasingly visible. The NLRA's protections turn on a narrow legal definition of "employee" status, excluding many workers and colliding with contemporary business models that seek "flexibility" by outsourcing, franchising, or using independent contractors. Enabled by technological advances, these arrangements hark back to early twentieth century market-mediated practices (Cappelli 1999; Weil 2014) and complicate union organization and effective collective bargaining. For workers, what was once secure employment has become increasingly precarious – and increasingly non-union.

One and a half centuries after the nation began to debate the labor question, the central story of American labor law is the progressively widening gap between its original promise of industrial democracy and its fading effectiveness in fulfilling that promise. Decades ago the "American standard of living" – a vision rooted in ever-increasing material consumption – became the "favored answer to the 'labor question', draining it of its moral preeminence, its political threat and its elemental social significance" (Fraser 1989: 56–57). As union density began to ebb after the 1950s, the United States labor movement faced a hard question: did labor law itself contribute to the relative weakness of the labor movement and thereby impede the achievement of democracy both in the workplace and in the wider polity?

THE LABOR QUESTION REEMERGES

> Now that America is back to a New Gilded Age of rabid inequality and arbitrary management, it seems fitting that industrial democracy is back on the table. (Reich 2019)

At this uncertain historical moment, the labor question has reemerged in America. The post-war social contract has unraveled, wages have stagnated, inequality has risen to levels not seen since the Gilded Age, union density in the private-sector workforce has plunged, workers' bargaining power has eroded, and corporate influence has gone largely unchecked. Democratic institutions are under stress, and a "specter of illiberalism" (Browning 2018) haunts America and threatens political democracy, exacerbated by authoritarian populism and pandemic-induced economic depression.

In the context of these crises, however, there are echoes today of the intellectual and activist ferment of a century ago. Older ideas about industrial democracy are being reimagined, new strategies explored. Workers are mobilizing in increasing numbers and in new ways. We are witnessing a potentially transformative dynamism of both thought and action not seen in decades.

Forms of industrial democracy that captured the imagination of the early labor and Progressive movements are reemerging and being adapted to today's radically different economic structures. Worker ownership (or shared capitalism) is again being pursued in various shapes (e.g. worker cooperatives, employee stock ownership, and profit- and gain-sharing plans), each with a distinct legal structure. Some of these schemes give employee shareholders not just an ownership, but also a governance role. Experimentation with worker-developed and worker-owned gig-economy platform cooperatives has also begun. These initiatives are still limited, but they are expanding. While unions generally have not broadly advanced ownership opportunities, some unionists see good reason to promote these developments, in order to increase workers' capital stake in their firms, to allow them more control over their own work, and to enhance firm performance. A widening circle of scholars – reaching even the traditionally conservative fields of corporate law and financial regulation – are convinced that a more inclusive capitalism, with worker ownership of capital, is a critical step to solving the challenge of glaring inequality in America, saving the middle class, and – for champions of market economies – salvaging capitalism itself (Blasi et al. 2013).

Pre-Wagner Act interest in works councils has also returned, now propelled by the contemporary lesson of European-wide adoption of that organizational form (Weiler 1990). Volkswagen's exploration of a works council at its Tennessee plant with the United Auto Workers (UAW) (Greenhouse 2014: sec. B, p. 4), so far unfulfilled, garnered public attention for the German model of co-determination – with its establishment-level works councils and worker representation on corporate boards. While there is no consensus on the continuing wisdom of the Wagner Act's restriction on non-union dealing with employers, many argue that it needlessly limits the choice of democratic forms of workplace representation and decision-making. Recently, two bills calling for reforms to corporate governance – the Reward Work Act (S. 2605, 115th Congress, 2d Session 2017–2018)), and the Accountable Capitalism Act (S. 3348, 115th Congress, 2d Session (2017–2018)) – were introduced into Congress, both requiring that a percentage (2/5 or 1/3) of a public corporation's board of directors be selected by workers.

Collective action has also shown renewed vitality, some driven by social media and by movements such as #MeToo and Black Lives Matter. Almost 500,000 workers participated in work stoppages in 2018, more than in any year since 1986. A large proportion of them were teachers who struck, often illegally, in several states. Conventional unions have undeniably faltered, yet they have not been abandoned in practice or in popular opinion (Pew Research Center 2018). Surveys reveal that workers value the possibility of collective bargaining and would also support labor organizations if they offered certain benefits and services (e.g. portable health and retirement benefits, job training, and legal representation) and expanded roles in organizational governance (e.g. informal participation, worker-management committees, and representation on company boards) (Hertel-Fernandez et al. 2019).

One worker movement, the Fight for $15, began in 2012 when 200 fast-food workers walked off their jobs in New York City, seeking a union and a $15-an-hour wage. It has grown to a series of one-day strikes and rallies in cities across the country and globally, involving thousands of low-wage workers. While it has not yet won union representation, the campaign has introduced workers to the power of collective action and triggered a wave of minimum-wage hikes in cities and states around the USA. Many worker advocates are looking to new models of unionism, including structural changes in worker representation and membership, and imaginative law reform that might encourage those new models.

Workers excluded from the basic labor law's coverage, including public-sector employees, domestic workers, and platform workers treated as independent contractors, are also mobilizing. Some are joining traditional labor unions. Others are creating their own organizations or allying with alternative worker advocacy groups, such as workers centers and non-union employee associations, making their voices heard outside of established collective-bargaining structures and testing novel strategies to organize for improved conditions and empower themselves.

Activists are shaking up even the so-called knowledge economy – including the core firms in Silicon Valley's tech industry – often protesting about community or national issues that extend beyond traditional workplace topics, reflecting a rising commitment to "bargaining for the public good." For example, when Google announced that it had partnered with the Pentagon to analyze drone videos using artificial intelligence (AI), several thousand employees signed a petition decrying the project, and dozens resigned in protest. The backlash led Google to announce that it would not renew the contract and would unveil new ethical guidelines regarding its use of AI. In 2018, 20,000 Google workers walked off the job worldwide after the *The New York Times* reported that the company had awarded a $90 million severance package to an executive while concealing details of his alleged sexual misconduct (Wakabayashi & Benner 2018: sec. A, p. 1). Among the strikers' demands were employee representation on the company's board and the elimination of a forced arbitration policy requiring that employees waive their right to enforce legal protections in court. Facing pressure on social media, Google agreed to end forced arbitration.

The threat to industrial and political democracy posed by the relentlessly diminishing power of workers in the last forty years has become stark and a matter of public debate. Scholars, policy analysts, and workers cannot ignore the labor question, much as that question was unavoidable in the early decades of industrial mass production. And the relationship between disempowerment in the workplace and the corrosion of political democracy is again indisputable. Apart from corporate dominance in the political system via campaign contributions and lobbying, managers mobilize their employees to lobby on political issues (Hertel-Fernandez 2018), lecture workers in captive-audience speeches against union representation and in support of certain political and religious beliefs, and subject them to surveillance not only in their workplace conduct but also in their political and personal lives outside of work. Elizabeth Anderson shines a light on the "private government" at work, warning of workplace autocracy with diminished limits on employer discretion (Anderson 2017). In light of corporate power in workplace and public life, many scholars seek to renew the nineteenth century Labor Republicans' thinking about the contradiction between economic dependency and the rights of equal citizenship (Gourevitch 2013).

In a highly polarized political climate, conflicting proposals for a way forward are of course inevitable, and business and right-wing opposition to labor law protections is a constant. Still, even before the Covid pandemic, some state and local governments had begun to address social and economic tensions by, for example, enacting family leave and fair-scheduling laws and exploring rights and benefits for domestic and platform workers. Once the pandemic brought massive job losses, business closings, and a staggering workplace health and safety crisis in spring of 2020, a wave of worker protests followed, along with congressional enactment of an array of worker safety nets that were unthinkable in the US context just a few months before. Current agitation in a wholly unprecedented context of intersecting social, economic, and political crises, then, may provide a laboratory for testing a new social compact and foretell yet another great reimagining of "industrial democracy." It must embrace a multifaceted, visionary approach to the labor question, befitting a large, complex political economy in a moment of stunning upheaval the likes of which have not been seen since the 1930s.

A century ago, the post-World War I negotiations in Paris launched the International Labor Organization (ILO), the body that, to this day, sets international labor standards and promotes global labor rights. The labor question, as framed by President Wilson in the Paris negotiations that gave birth to the ILO, is a good starting place for understanding the present and reimagining democracy for the twenty-first century workplace. At its heart a "clash of interests" (Adams 1880: 17), democracy in both the workplace and the polity has been an experiment in America from its birth, in a repeated cycle of promise, disappointment, and renewal – renewal that often comes in times of crisis, when the fault lines in society are laid bare.

REFERENCES

Adams, Henry. 1880. *Democracy: An American Novel*. New York: Holt & Co.

American Federation of Labor. 1905. *Report of the Proceedings of the Fourteenth Annual Convention of the A.F. of L. Held at Denver, Col., Dec., 1894*. Bloomington, IN: AFL.

Anderson, Elizabeth. 2017. *Private Government: How Employers Rule Our Lives (And Why We Don't Talk About It)*. Princeton, NJ: Princeton University Press.

Blasi, Joseph R., Richard B. Freeman, and Douglas L. Kruse. 2013. *The Citizen's Share: Reducing Inequality in the Twenty-First Century*. New Haven, CT: Yale University Press.

Brandeis, Louis D. 1916. "The Living Law," *Ill. L. Rev.* 10: 461.

Browning, Christopher R. 2019. "The Suffocation of Democracy," *New York Review of Books* (Oct. 25, 2019).

Cappelli, Peter. 1999. *The New Deal At Work: Managing the Market-Driven Workforce*. Boston: Harvard Business School Press.

Cobble, Dorothy Sue. 2011. "The Intellectual Origins of an Institutional Revolution," ABA *Journal of Labor & Employment Law* 26: 209.

Derber, Milton. 1970. *The American Idea of Industrial Democracy 1865–1965*. Urbana: University of Illinois Press.

Estlund, Cynthia L. 2002. "The Ossification of American Labor Law," *Colum. L. Rev.* 102: 1531.

Filippelli, Ronald F., ed. 1990. *Labor Conflict in the United States: An Encyclopedia*. New York: Garland Publishing, Inc.

Fraser, Steve. 1989 "The 'Labor Question," in Steve Fraser, and Gary Gerstle, eds. *The Rise and Fall of the New Deal Order 1930–1980*. Princeton, NJ: Princeton University Press.

Freeman, Richard B. 2011. "What Can We Learn from the NLRA to Create Labor Law for the Twenty-First Century?" *ABA J. Lab. & Emp. L.* 26: 327.

Gladden, William. 1876. *Working People and Their Employers*. Boston: Lockwood, Brooks, and Co.

Gourevitch, Alex. 2013. "Labor Republicanism and the Transformation of Work," *Political Theory* 41, 4: 591–617.

Greenhouse, Steven. 2014. "VW Workers in Tennessee to Vote on Union," *The New York Times* (Feb. 3, 2014), sec. B, p. 4.

Hertel-Fernandez, Alexander. 2018. *Politics at Work: How Companies Turn Their Workers Into Lobbyists*. Oxford: Oxford University Press.

Hertel-Fernandez, Alexander, William Kimball, and Thomas Kochan. 2019. "How US Workers Think About Workplace Democracy," *Working Paper*, MIT Sloan School of Management.

Hirsch, Barry. 2007. "Sluggish Institutions in a Dynamic World: Can Unions and Industrial Competition Coexist?," *Journal of Economic Perspectives*, Fall 2007.

Jacoby, Sanford M. 1997. *Modern Manors: Welfare Capitalism Since the New Deal*. Princeton, NJ: Princeton University Press.

Kaufman, Bruce. 1998. "Does the NLRA Constrain Employee Involvement and Participation Programs in Non-Union Companies? A Reassessment," *Yale L. & Pol'y Rev.* 17: 729.

Leuchtenburg, William E. 1963. *Franklin D. Roosevelt and the New Deal*. New York: Harper & Row.

McCartin, Joseph A. 1988. *Labor's Great War: The Struggle for Industrial Democracy and the Origins of Modern American Labor Relations, 1912–1921*. Chapel Hill: University of North Carolina Press.

Muller-Jentsch, Walther. 2008. "Industrial Democracy: Historical Development and Current Challenges," *Management Revue* 19, 4: 261–262.

Pew Research Center, 2018. "More Americans View Long-Term Decline in Union Membership Negatively than Positively" (June 5, 2018).

Powderly, Terence. 1890. *Thirty Years of Labor: 1859 to 1889*. Columbus, OH: Excelsior Publishing.

Reich, Robert. 2019. "US Must Return to Industrial Democracy to Restore Workers' Rights," *San Francisco Chronicle* (Feb. 1, 2019).

Summers, Clyde. 1979. "Industrial Democracy: America's Unfulfilled Promise," *Clev. St. L. Rev.* 28: 29.

US Commission on Industrial Relations. 1916. *Final Report and Testimony*. v. 1. Washington, DC: Government Printing Office.

Wakabayashi, Daisuke, and Katie Benner. 2018. "How Google Protected Andy Rubin, the 'Father of Android'," *The New York Times* (Oct. 26, 2018), sec. A, p. 1.

Weil, David. 2014. *The Fissured Workplace: Why Work Became So Bad For So Many and What Can Be Done to Improve It*. Cambridge, MA: Harvard University Press.

Weiler, Paul. 1983. "Promises to Keep: Securing Workers' Rights to Self-Organization Under the NLRA," *Harv. L. Rev.* 96: 1769.

1990. *Governing the Workplace*. Cambridge, MA.: Harvard University Press.

White, Richard. 2017. *The Republic for Which It Stands: The United States during Reconstruction and The Gilded Age, 1865–1896*. New York: Oxford University Press.

Wilson, Woodrow. 1919. Cable to the Congress (May 20, 1919), in Arthur S. Link, ed. *The Papers of Woodrow Wilson*, v. 1. Princeton, NJ: Princeton University Press (1988).

8

Holding On

The Decline of Organized Labor in the USA in Historical Perspective and the Implications for Democracy

Timothy J. Minchin

In June 1983, when production began at Nissan's new assembly plant in Smyrna, Tennessee, the United Automobile Workers (UAW) declared that they would organize the factory, as they had almost every auto plant in America (Bob King, interview with author; Zieger 1994: 178). In a sign of the changing times, however, Nissan America CEO Marvin Runyon called the union a "third party" that the company's workers did not need (Holusha 1983). Selected from non-union backgrounds, early employees imbibed the message, and when the union finally contested an election at the plant in July 1989, it lost heavily. In nationally-televised pictures that graphically illustrated labor's decline, rank and file workers celebrated the result by dancing and singing, with many sporting company shirts and waving banners that proclaimed "Union Free and Proud" (Levin 1989; Papathanasis 1989; Zieger 1994: 197). Explaining the outcome, former city clerk and lifelong Smyrna resident Mike Woods returned to Runyon's mantra. Workers' reasoning, he recalled, was that "we don't need a third party to speak for us, as long as they're treating us fairly" (Mike Woods, interview with author).

Events in Smyrna highlighted how many Americans portrayed unions not as guarantors of democracy, but the opposite. Rather than speaking for workers, unions were outsiders who took away their voice, along with their hard-earned money. "There's really two companies when the UAW's there," claimed Tennessee senator Bob Corker, leading the charge (DePillis 2014). Powerful opponents like Corker advanced many other arguments to stymie unions, portraying them as harmful, corrupt, and undemocratic. Because union membership was concentrated in struggling manufacturing industries, opponents also blamed them for job losses. Labor unions, summarized a southern business recruiter, had "failed miserably" in protecting workers' jobs (Phillip Dunlap, interview with author). Pointing to the auto industry's decline in Michigan, Corker dismissed the UAW's efforts to organize foreign-owned plants as little more than a cynical ploy. "This is all about money for them," he summarized (DePillis 2014).

These arguments took their toll, both on the UAW and other unions. The UAW's failure to organize the foreign-owned sector – which in 2018 made nearly half of all cars produced in North America – was an important part of the longer-term decline of organized labor in the USA. Once one of the most powerful and influential unions in the country, the UAW saw its membership fall from over 1.5 million to less than 700,000 in the 1980s and 1990s. By 2010, it had dipped below 500,000 (Bunkley 2018; Hakim 2001; UAW 2010: 43, 58). Over the same period, union density in the USA tumbled dramatically, particularly in manufacturing. As measured by the Bureau of Labor Statistics, density peaked at 35 percent in the mid-1950s but fell to 20 percent in 1983 – the year Smyrna started making vehicles – and 12 percent in 2006. By 2019, it had dropped to 10.3 percent, with just 6.2 percent of private sector workers holding union cards (Bureau of Labor Statistics 2020; Greenhouse 2007).

As scholars have demonstrated, labor's decline reflected many factors, including deindustrialization, weak labor laws, workplace deregulation, and unions' own conservatism and lethargy (Geoghegan 1991; Getman 2010; Goldfield 1987; Moody 1988; Rosenfeld 2014; Stein 2010). Over the course of the post-war period, moreover, policy makers and intellectuals pushed a neoliberal agenda that was able to, as Quinn Slobodian has put it, "inoculate capitalism against the threat of democracy," with independent trade unions forced to defer to the power of the "world economy" (Slobodian 2018: 2, 283). As Michael Goldfield and others have demonstrated, growing opposition to union influence – particularly from corporate leaders, think tanks, and conservative politicians – was integral to labor's decline. One study, for example, found that unions won 95 percent of elections where there was no employer resistance but only 43 percent where union activists were fired or demoted (Goldfield 1987; Moberg 1988). Management's growing power was especially important as more industry – like Nissan – moved to the South, a region with the lowest levels of union density in the USA. In the 1990s, for example, the South attracted more than half the foreign businesses drawn to the USA, with union avoidance being a key drawcard (Cobb 1980, 2005). In this regard, Runyon's tale was typical; he had previously dealt with the union when managing Ford's plant in Dearborn, Michigan, but now decided that he did not have to do so. Like Runyon, many Americans felt that their country was better off without unions (Lindsay Chappell, interview with author; Holusha 1983).

In reality, however, unions were not a third party, but an important force for democracy. Throughout the post-World War II era, organized labor provided a voice for all working people, not just its members. While labor had its flaws, its decline had troubling implications for American democracy that were elided by the increasingly dominant voices of Corker, Runyon, and others. Unions were a much-needed watchdog, consistently fighting for safer workplaces, higher pay, and workplace democracy. They also gave a stronger voice to working people in politics. Despite their imperfections, no other organization performed this role in quite the same way. As union leader John Sweeney commented in 2001, "If unions aren't there for working people, who will be?" (Hetter 2001). Although opponents continued to refer to "labor bosses," by the early 2000s unions were very much on the defensive in the world's most powerful democracy (Patterson & Kovacs 2012).

The country's largest union federation, the AFL-CIO, illustrated this broader role very well. Almost all of America's labor unions belonged to the AFL-CIO, which had over 15 million members when it was formed in 1955 (Minchin 2017: 6–7; *The New York Times* 1955).[1] Like its affiliates, the AFL-CIO did not always endear itself to progressive groups. There were good reasons for this. The Federation was slow to respond to the concerns of women workers and racial minorities, while long-term presidents George Meany and Lane Kirkland also supported US foreign policy throughout the Cold War. These shortcomings have attracted criticism from scholars, who have generally overlooked the Federation's positive contributions (Buhle 1999; Goldfield 1997; Hill 1977; Moody 2007; Radosh 1969; Scipes 2010; Wehrle 2005).

When it came to domestic politics, the AFL-CIO acted as an important voice for all working people, carrying out a lot of little-known lobbying work that was easy to miss. The Federation, summarized long-term staffer Susan Dunlop, fought "a constant battle, to not go so far back that we were going back to the workers' stone age" (interview with author). When the AFL-CIO was

---

[1] Some of the arguments laid out here are developed in Minchin 2017, and this chapter also draws on some material from that book.

strongest, in its first decade or so, it was able to not just defend progressive legislation but also pass it, benefiting millions of Americans in the process. In the 1950s and 1960s, the Federation acted as what President John F. Kennedy called "the people's lobby" (Driscoll 1983). It advocated for most of the important progressive legislation of the 1960s, including the Voting Rights Act, the Social Security Amendments of 1965, and the Elementary and Secondary Education Act (Johnson 1964, 1965). The "labor-endorsed" Education Act, for example, was very significant, as it was the biggest aid to education legislation ever to be considered by Congress. In its first year alone, the Act granted over $1.3 billion to assist poor children from both rural and urban areas (Perlman 1965). When he left office in January 1969, President Johnson presented the AFL-CIO with one hundred signed pens that symbolized the group's "contribution to legislation beneficial to all Americans."[2] Each pen carried the name of a piece of legislation passed during the Johnson presidency. The AFL-CIO, proclaimed Meany in 1967, spoke for the "forgotten many," a claim it was less able to make decades later (Townsend 1967).

In the 1970s, the AFL-CIO – despite increasing corporate resistance to organizing, especially in the South – was still able to fulfil its "People's Lobby" function. Even during the Nixon-Ford presidencies, organized labor and a Democratic Congress secured the passage of important progressive legislation. In 1970 and 1971, for example, the AFL-CIO helped to steer through a pioneering Occupational Health and Safety law, as well as a five-year extension of the Voting Rights Act, which had become a liberal landmark. It also advocated effectively for a public service employment bill, with Nixon reluctantly signing the law at a time of high unemployment (AFL-CIO 1971: 220–221). Both Nixon and Ford also took organized labor seriously, keeping what one Nixon aide called "open and friendly communications, notwithstanding any political differences" (Colson 1970).

Organized labor was particularly important in putting a floor under wages for American workers. By 1972, for example, the federal minimum wage – created during the New Deal partly because of labor pressure – stood at $1.60 an hour, and it covered some 45 million workers. The Federation pushed for further improvements, especially for a $2.20 minimum to be implemented by 1974 (Stulberg 1972). In that year, Congress – following lobbying from the Federation's legislative department – amended the Fair Labor Standards Act, increasing the minimum wage to $2.00 an hour immediately, with a further increase to $2.30 by January 1, 1976. The law was also changed to cover federal, state, and local government employees, as well as domestic workers – expansions that helped millions of vulnerable Americans (AFL-CIO 1975: 155). The improvements in coverage represented a major breakthrough and were secured despite some objections from the Nixon White House (Nixon 1974). At the state level, collective bargaining laws for public workers were also becoming common, often because of union pressure. In 1978, following a campaign by government unions, organized labor also secured collective bargaining rights for federal workers in the Panama Canal Zone (AFL-CIO 1989a: B1).

Organized labor was also an important part of the Democratic coalition. With its numbers, any Democratic president had to take note. In the 1960s, both Kennedy and Johnson had a close relationship with the union movement, particularly when it came to legislative matters (Minchin 2017: 25–27). Although he lacked a labor background, Carter still understood the need to consult closely with unions, ensuring that important protective legislation remained in place. In September 1978, Carter wrote Meany that the AFL-CIO had provided "a voice for millions of workers who might otherwise not be heard," uplifting the working standards of all

---

[2] The quotation from Johnson, and the description of the pen display, is based on the author's visit to view this item in November 2015, which is on display in the AFL-CIO's headquarters in Washington, DC.

American workers. According to Carter, "most of the major social advances of the last fifty years," in areas that included welfare, health, and education, "would have been impossible without the able assistance of the organized labor movement" (Carter 1978).

As union density began to fall precipitously, especially in the early 1980s, the AFL-CIO's role became more defensive. As former staffer Gerry Shea put it, the Federation now had to "build power" rather than "wield" it (Gerry Shea, interview with author). During the Reagan presidency, a period of sharp decline, organized labor still defended vital gains and fought off conservative efforts to gut social programs. In early 1982, the AFL-CIO helped to defeat sweeping cuts in social security, citing opinion polls that illustrated the program's popularity with working Americans (AFL-CIO 1982: 73–74). Throughout the recession of the early 1980s, the Federation consistently protected the vital program. "Thank goodness for the AFL-CIO," recalled Dunlop. "We were big supporters of social security" (interview with author). In 1983, the AFL-CIO also successfully resisted Republican proposals to raise the retirement age and repelled efforts to establish a separate "sub-minimum" wage for young workers (AFL-CIO 1983: 78–79).

Many other examples from the 1980s showed unions benefiting all American workers. In the summer of 1982, organized labor mobilized to defeat the administration's Balanced Budget Amendment, which passed the Republican-controlled Senate and would have led to massive cuts in vital social programs. A massive labor lobbying campaign contributed to the House vote of 236–187 for the amendment, forty-six votes short of the two-thirds majority needed to send it to the states for ratification. After the vote Speaker Tip O'Neill, Majority Whip Tom Foley, and other congressional leaders credited organized labor with defeating the Amendment (AFL-CIO 1983: 96–99; Perlman 1982). Between 1981 and 1983, the AFL-CIO also successfully fought off damaging Department of Labor regulations that would have allowed for more industrial homework and child labor, and defended the Davis-Bacon and Service Contracts Act, upholding labor standards on public works projects and federal service contracts. It also helped to secure congressional inquiry into proposed guidelines for federal contractors, ensuring that important affirmative action provisions were maintained (AFL-CIO 1983a: 23; Minchin 2017: 106–107). There were also important initiatives in maintaining workplace safety. In the 1970s, it was unions that had pushed OSHA to issue its first regulatory guidelines on asbestos exposure, helping millions and saving untold lives. In the Reagan era, as further details emerged of how damaging asbestos was, labor pressed for stronger enforcement, preventing harsh cuts at OSHA from occurring. "The standards governing occupational exposure to asbestos in this country have never been adequate," testified AFL-CIO staffer Margaret Seminario in 1983 (Kirkland 1981; Seminario 1983).

When it came to upholding wage standards, labor continued to play a particularly important role. In the summer of 1989, the AFL-CIO successfully pressured the Bush administration to increase the minimum wage from \$3.35 to \$4.25 an hour, a long overdue increase. Without unions, the minimum wage – while hardly satisfactory – would have been even less. Indeed, the Bush White House, like its predecessor, wanted a "sub-minimum" wage for new employees (AFL-CIO 1989: 6; AFL-CIO 1991: 12, B5; Kilborn 1990). In 1996, organized labor was also crucial in pushing the Republican Congress to endorse a 90-cent rise in the minimum wage, with Republicans conceding after some of the costs to small businesses were compensated by tax breaks (Stevenson 1996). The increase, which unions had consistently pushed for, helped more than 10 million low-paid workers. As the Clinton administration noted proudly, the hike – along with the expansion of tax credits to low-income earners – brought "financial independence to many of America's poorest working families" (AFL-CIO 1995: A9; Clinton 2000: 8).

At the state level, unions also succeeded in raising the minimum wage well above the federal level. In 2012 it was organized labor – and especially the large Service Employees International Union – that launched "Fight for $15," a high-profile push for a substantial increase in the federal minimum wage, with active campaigns in a number of states, including California, Illinois, Massachusetts, Michigan, New York, Oregon, and Washington. As part of this campaign, there were fresh initiatives and civil disobedience, including flash strikes by fast-food workers in major cities. Across the country, the fight had an extraordinary impact, lifting many workers out of poverty. It was particularly effective in California, which in 2016 agreed to a $15 state-wide minimum wage, to be introduced incrementally (Porter 2012; Andy Stern, corr). Because 40 percent of California's work force earned less than $15 an hour, this move helped over 10 million workers (Drier 2016).

Unions' work, however, continued to stretch well beyond wages. In 1998, the AFL-CIO defeated congressional attacks on not just wage and hour laws, but also vital safety and health protections that many Americans took for granted. The Federation successfully protected OSHA's ergonomics standard – a central initiative of Clinton's Department of Labor – from congressional interference, helping millions of union and non-union workers as a result. It also continued to fight hard for an effective OSHA, resisting conservative efforts to let industry police itself. By the end of the twentieth century, fatalities in the American workplace had been halved since OSHA was created forty years earlier, and occupational injury and illness rates had declined by 40 percent (AFL-CIO 2010; Clinton 2000: 83–90). While there were many reasons for these improvements – especially improved enforcement by OSHA and the decline of the heavy industrial sector, where accidents were rife – labor's vigilance had also played its part. "Much of it is defensive," long-serving AFL-CIO health and safety director Peg Seminario summarized in 2013, discussing her work. "Keeping funding for agencies, and keeping our law, (plus) keeping an enforcement approach . . . it makes a difference" (Peg Seminario, interview with author).

In politics, unions also performed a vital democratic function, again doing much more than simply representing their members. In particular, they fostered civic participation and voter turnout, especially among lower-income Americans. In a 2006 study, for example, political scientists Jan Leighley and Jonathan Nagler found that the decline in union membership since 1964 had reduced turnout from low and middle-income individuals more than among high-income citizens. Throughout the post-war period, union members were more likely to vote for progressive candidates, and they were also more likely to vote. Other observers reached similar conclusions. As organizer Helen Marot put it, "The labor unions are group efforts in the direction of democracy" (McElwee 2015).

Results from several recent elections highlight these broader themes well. The AFL-CIO always gave a high priority to political mobilization; as staffer Craig Becker put it, it was in this area "where the value is added by a federation" (interview with author). This was because affiliates had considerable independence in other areas, especially organizing and bargaining. In 1955, the merger of the AFL and CIO was partly designed to increase labor's political power, and early leaders placed a heavy emphasis on political mobilization ("Meany Lays Down AFL-CIO Policy," *The New York Times*, Nov. 5, 1955). As declining density led to more attacks on unions, politics became even more important. Elected in 1995, reformist president John Sweeney revitalized the political program, securing some impressive results (John Sweeney, interview with author; Steve Rosenthal, interview with author). In the 1998 mid-term elections, union households – those that contained a union member – accounted for 17 percent of the population but comprised 23 percent of those who went to the polls. Some 71 percent of union voters, moreover, backed union-endorsed candidates (AFL-CIO 1999: 5). Partly as a result of labor's mobilization, the anticipated Republican gains did not materialize, and the GOP actually lost five seats in the House of Representatives. This was only the second time since the Civil War that the President's party had gained seats in a midterm election. No wonder that labor's opponents were so keen to gut its political power (Gigot 1997; Kopecki 1997).

In the crucial 2000 election, unions launched a huge campaign in favor of Democratic candidate Al Gore, who they endorsed as early as October 1999. The political program had been centralized under Sweeney, and it secured results. Overall, the Democrats received an unprecedented 26.3 million votes from union households, up substantially from 1996. This comprised 26 percent of all voters, almost double the percentage of union members in the USA. Organized labor, observed *Industry Week*, had "brought Democrats to within a whisker of sweeping Congress and the White House" (Miller, "Sweeney Sees Organization Gains," *Industry Week*, March 5, 2001). Through the AFL-CIO's 2000 in 2000 program – formulated to elect union members to public office – more than 2,600 rank and filers won office, exceeding the target. "Labor 2000" volunteers mobilized tens of thousands of working people to knock on doors, work the phones, disseminate literature, and talk with co-workers. The AFL-CIO's "Working Families Toolkit," which allowed unions at the state and local level to customize candidate fliers for their members, was also a great success. In all, workers ordered over 3.5 million worksite fliers through the website (AFL-CIO 2010; Minchin 2017: 256; Steve Rosenthal, interview with author). During the election, the *US News and World Report* described unions as "the most powerful force in the Democratic Party" (Barone, "Will Unions Rule?", March 6, 2000). Although Gore's narrow – and controversial – defeat was a blow for American unions, their importance to the democratic process was clear. "Whatever labor's problems," summarized Steven Greenhouse in the *New York Times* in 2004, "few deny that unions remain one of the most formidable forces in politics, especially because of their ability to turn out the vote" ("Labor is Feeling Embattled as Union Leaders Convene," *The New York Times*, March 9, 2004).

Following continued investment in the political program, unions also played a key role in electing America's first African-American president. In the months before the 2008 election, organized labor persuaded many white workers – particularly men – to vote for Barack Obama, overcoming their misgivings about race and focusing instead on the Democrat's support for economic justice (Minchin 2017, 287–289; Richard Trumka, interview with author). This was important work. As *The Washington Post* summarized, Obama's "biggest challenge" was trying to win over white working-class voters in crucial Rust Belt States where unions were still strong (MacGillis 2008). For forty years white voters had preferred Republican presidential candidates. In the 2004 election, for example, exit polls by CNN showed that 58 percent of white voters had backed President Bush. In the summer of 2008, about 15.4 million workers still belonged to unions, and 73 percent of them were white (Berzon & Mishak 2008; "Selling" 2008). If Obama was to win, the AFL-CIO – along with the newly-formed Change to Win federation – needed to reach their white members (Greenhouse 2005; Andy Stern, interview with author). Early results graphically illustrated the problem. In March and April, Obama lost the Ohio and Pennsylvania primaries. He was "struggling to connect with working-class White voters," concluded *The Washington Post* staff writer Shailagh Murray. Soon afterwards, Obama also lost the Indiana primary to Hillary Clinton, his appeals for the AFL-CIO's help coming too late ("Two Candidates, Two States, and One Big Day: Indiana and North Carolina Shape Up as Big Pieces of the Democratic Puzzle," *The Washington Post*, May 6, 2008).

The labor movement helped to turn things around. The AFL-CIO launched an educational campaign that was designed to, as political director Karen Ackerman put it, combat "fear and hesitancy" among white members (MacGillis 2008). Particularly important efforts were carried out by Working America, which was set up in 2003 and allowed Americans who were not union members to join the Federation and support its work, particularly during elections. Sweeney established Working America because he was convinced that "the AFL-CIO must represent the interests of all working people" (AFL-CIO 2007). Within two years, the nonprofit association had become the fastest-growing organization for working people in the country, and it secured some important gains in the 2004 and 2006 elections ("Country's Fastest-Growing Labor Organization," *Management Report*, February 2008; Nussbaum 2006). As director Karen Nussbaum recalled, over 80 percent of Working America's membership – which topped 2.5 million in 2008 – were white, making the group a "trusted messenger" for the Obama campaign within white neighborhoods, which they targeted (AFL-CIO 2008; Karen Nussbaum, interview with author). An important role was also played by AFL-CIO secretary-treasurer Richard Trumka, who in July used his speech at the United Steelworkers convention to tackle racism in the labor movement head on (Karen Ackerman, interview with author). "There's no evil that's inflicted more pain and suffering than racism," he told a heavily white audience, "and it's something we in the labor movement have a special responsibility to challenge" (Trumka 2008). The speech had a broader impact, attracting more than half a million views online. As *The Washington Post* observed, this was "surely the first YouTube moment" in the AFL-CIO's history (MacGillis 2009a; YouTube 2008).

These efforts reaped results. According to date from leading pollster firm Peter D. Hart, Obama won among white men who belonged to unions by some eighteen points. In the population as a whole, however, Obama lost this group by sixteen points. A similar pattern prevailed among white union members who were gun owners, regular church attendees, veterans, and those without a college education, all difficult groups to crack. Obama thus lost each of these groups in the overall population, yet won among white union members. An important role was also played by Change to Win, which endorsed the Illinois senator early. Working together, the two labor federations helped Obama to win key states, particularly Florida and North Carolina in the South and Ohio and Pennsylvania in the North. In the Keystone State, labor's push in the closing two months meant that backing for Obama among union card holders jumped 16 percent, resulting in a 68 to 24 percent advantage. Union members, summarized Michael A. Fletcher in *The Washington Post*, had played a "pivotal role" in Obama's victory (Fletcher 2008; Minchin 2016: 300).

Labor's opponents admitted its political effectiveness, both in 2008 and earlier. In December 1997, for example, *Fortune* ranked the AFL-CIO as the third most influential lobby group in the country. Based on an extensive survey among elected representatives, their congressional offices, and White House staff, the survey ranked the AFL-CIO highly partly because of its ability to mobilize grassroots Americans (Gigot 1997; Kopecki 1997). After the 2008 election, meanwhile, labor's role was widely noted by both liberals and conservatives, with the latter determined to reverse the trend. Editorialist Gary Andres wrote in the *Washington Times* that, "No special interest group deserves more credit for electing and expanding a Democratic majority in Congress than organized labor. Unions infused Democrats with money, manpower, and message support across America. Their resources are both concentrated and large, and they continue to provide electoral and legislative lifeblood" (Rosenfeld 2014: 178; Zieger 2008).

Unions were also an important part of democracy because of their ability to mobilize and put people in the streets. Even in an era of decline – and at the most unlikely of times – labor performed this function, putting conservative elites on notice and protecting important social programs. In September 1981, for example, America's beleaguered unions – under attack from

the new Reagan administration, which had just dismissed 11,000 striking air traffic controllers –
hit back (Morton Bahr, interview with author; Tom Donahue, interview with author; McCartin
2011: 338–351). Joining with over one hundred civil rights, religious, and civic groups, the AFL-
CIO initiated "Solidarity Day," a mass march in Washington DC that was designed to protest
against President Reagan's cuts and his claim to speak for working Americans directly, without
needing the third party of unions. According to the National Park Service, over 260,000 people
attended the rally, more participants than either the iconic March on Washington in 1963 or the
anti-Vietnam War Moratorium in 1969 attracted. Despite this, Solidarity Day – and labor's
important contribution to Democratic protest – has been largely overlooked (Bonitati 1981; Dray
2011; Minchin 2015; Pianin & Brown 1981).

Crucially, many of the participants did not belong to unions, but were mobilized by labor's
call. "I'm not a radical," explained Mildred Donahue, a middle-aged Connecticut librarian.
"But Ronald Reagan made me come here. I wanted to make the point that this Administration
doesn't have a mandate for what they're doing." Others commented on the diversity of the
marchers, especially the fact that many were mature-age Americans who were taking to the
streets for the first time: "These people are older. They're all working people. I've been to twenty
different demonstrations. There hasn't been one like this before" (Shribman 1981: 1). The crowd
was massive, snaking for over a mile from Constitution Avenue toward the Capitol. Attendance
may even have exceeded the official count, especially as Park Service calculations were cautious.
A count from the Washington DC mayor's office recorded that 400,000 people had showed up,
and several big newspapers also used this higher figure (AFL-CIO 1981; Willhelm 1983;
Woodard 1983).[3] As labor historians Melvyn Dubofsky and Foster Rhea Dulles have noted,
Solidarity Day was "perhaps the largest mass march in US history to that time" (Dubofsky &
Dulles 2004: 389).

Although they publicly denied it, the Reagan White House certainly took notice of Solidarity
Day. Its archives show that the president's top aides kept a full list of all the groups – labor or
otherwise – that supported the protest. While many unions were listed, there were also
numerous other organizations, such as the Sierra Club, the Consumer Federation of
America, and Americans for Democratic Action, an independent political organization that
promoted a wide range of progressive policies. A week before the march, Elizabeth Dole –
Reagan's public liaison chief – reported that "as much as 50 percent" of participants were drawn
from outside the labor movement. Solidarity Day, she concluded, was "clearly no longer just a
labor rally" (Blackwell 1981; Bonitati 1981; Dole 1981).

There was also a congressional response. Following Solidarity Day, the House extended the
crucial Voting Rights Act, which had greatly improved black access to the ballot, and blocked
cuts to the departments of Labor, Education, and Health and Human Services, approving
funding for those important agencies. More aware of progressive sentiment, Congress also
stymied the White House's push efforts to undermine the Occupational Safety and Health
Act, which protected millions of union and non-union workers (AFL-CIO 1981a: 18; "Inside
Report: Did Organized Labor's Solidarity Day Sway Congress?" *Christian Science Monitor*,
October 16, 1981). The protest also helped the labor movement's successful fight against tuition
tax credits in Washington, DC, helping to uphold funding for public education in the racially-
divided District. Rather than ignoring the labor movement, President Reagan also met with
union leaders after the march and directed his labor liaison, Robert Bonitati, to establish regular

---

[3] While covering the 1983 Solidarity Day march, a follow-up protest that is discussed further below, the Willhelm and
Woodard stories give attendance figures for the original 1981 march.

dialogue with them. This was part of Reagan's new "labor strategy," with the president also promising an "open door policy" with unions and improved "dialogue" (Bonitati 1981a, 1981b; McCartin 2011: 320–321). Solidarity Day also played a part in the gains the Democrats secured in the 1982 mid-term elections, when they kept control of the House of Representatives, winning twenty-seven seats. No longer could Reagan claim that unions were "out of step" with rank and file workers, as he had after the 1980 election (AFL-CIO 1982: 6; Strout 1981; "Kirkland Leading the AFL-CIO on a New Course," *Miami Herald*, August 1, 1982).

On numerous other occasions, unions brought Americans into the streets, acting to protect the interests of all working people. In 1982, 1983, and 1984, there were large follow-up Solidarity Day marches, ensuring that the Reagan administration continued to consult with unions and did not repeat the "third party" trope. Again, the impact of budget cuts was blunted, and important social programs maintained. In August 1991 another national labor march – timed to celebrate Solidarity Day's tenth anniversary – drew some 250,000 people to the capital, demanding strong rights for strikers, healthcare reform, and a greater focus on domestic issues. The AFL-CIO's executive council called it "massive" (AFL-CIO 1995a: 6). Raising his fist in the air as a symbol of solidarity, former presidential contender Jesse Jackson stole the show, giving an impassioned speech in which he demanded that President Bush "come home now … [and] rebuild America." As *The Washington Post* put it, labor had sent politicians "a message" that was "hundreds of thousands strong" (Swoboda & Torry 1991).

Drawing on Jackson's performance, labor used the march to mobilize support behind Bill Clinton's presidential campaign, which succeeded in evicting President Bush from office in an unlikely turnabout. During Clinton's presidency, there were gains that reflected labor pressure, particularly passage of the 1993 Family and Medical Leave Act, a long-held goal. It granted up to twelve weeks unpaid (but job-protected) leave to workers for family medical needs. Opposed by the Bush administration, the measure was popular with American workers, with a Gallup poll finding that 83 percent of adults backed the measure (Clymer 1992). Legislators who pushed the law through the Democratically-controlled House and Senate understood the grassroots sentiment. "For the parents whose employers do not provide this benefit voluntarily, the choice between keeping one's job or caring for a new child or sick family member is a choice no American should have to make," summarized House leader Richard A. Gephardt. Once the law was passed, it helped millions of American workers – it covered about two-thirds of workplaces – and was seen by the Clinton administration as one of its main accomplishments. During Clinton's two terms, the White House also issued an executive order allowing the dismissed air traffic controllers to re-apply for federal employment, appointed more sympathetic officials to the NLRB, and consulted closely with labor officials (Chira 1993; Clinton 2000: L0017–L0022; Clymer 1992; Minchin 2017: 187).

Helped by the election of reformist John Sweeney in 1995 – who came into power drawing on his use of civil disobedience and mass protest during the SEIU's "Justice-for-Janitors" campaign – the pace of union decline also slowed (Melillo 1995). Sweeney placed a much greater emphasis on organizing and brought more women and minorities onto staff. On the ground, the efforts began to pay off. Between 1994 and 1996, union density increased from 14 percent to 14.5 percent, while in 1999 the number of union members jumped by the biggest margin in two decades (AFL-CIO 2010; Rosenthal 2013; Lane Windham, interview with author). "The two-decade hemorrhaging of union membership has been staunched," declared *The Nation* in 1999. Labor, added the *New York Times*, had ended its "long slide" ("Labor's Labors," *The Nation*, November 1, 1999; "Labor Ends Its Long Slide," *The New York Times*, January 22, 2000).

These headlines proved to be overly optimistic. Many of the forces causing labor's decline, especially deindustrialization, remained in place. Between 2000 and 2010, the USA lost 5.5 million manufacturing jobs, wiping out around one third of the sector. Many unions were devastated (Greenhouse 2009). Moreover, the contested election of George W. Bush in 2000 – with labor being among the groups that wanted Gore to fight the result and put protesters in the street – dramatically changed the political climate. During the eight years of the Bush presidency, labor was very much on the defensive (Stewart Acuff, interview with author; John Sweeney, interview with author). The NLRB became more hostile, the courts ruled against workers, and the president barely consulted with unions. Summing up the mood, laborers' union leader Terry O'Sullivan termed the Bush presidency "eight years of torture and hell" (MacGillis 2009).

Still, unions continued to speak for all workers, performing valuable defensive work. Labor in these years mounted what organizer Stewart Acuff termed a "huge campaign" to pass the Employee Free Choice Act, which made organizing easier and increased the penalties for violating the National Labor Relations Act (interview with author). Both congressional representatives and the public were lobbied heavily, and several polls indicated that most Americans supported labor law reform. Reflecting this, on March 1, 2007 Congress passed the Employee Free Choice Act by a margin of 241 to 185, raising supporters' hopes. Although the measure was subsequently blocked in the Republican-controlled Senate, it focused attention on organizing and exposed the weaknesses of American labor law in international forums. Unions also continued to push for healthcare reform, which became increasingly urgent as many Americans lost coverage with their jobs. These efforts bore fruit in 2010, when labor played a vital role in helping President Obama to squeeze his comprehensive healthcare reforms through Congress, overcoming virulent opposition from their powerful conservative opponents. It was also unions that spoke for what new AFL-CIO leader Richard Trumka called the millions of Americans who were "trapped in the twilight of the contingent economy," usually without health insurance and pensions. Without unions, underpayment and exploitation would have been even worse (Mishak 2009).

Unions' ability to bring citizens into the streets – a feature its opponents detested – is also vital for American democracy. In 2011, when Wisconsin governor Scott Walker proposed a legislative package eviscerating the rights of almost all public employees to engage in meaningful collective bargaining, unions led a broad public mobilization. During the protests, some rallies drew 100,000 demonstrators. The campaign, claimed AFSCME president Gerald McEntee, "showed our ability to put boots on the ground" (Whoriskey & Balz 2012; Zieger et al. 2014: 295–297). Labor played a key part in collecting nearly 1 million signatures to force a recall election in Wisconsin, as well as organizing rallies in several other state capitols. Although Walker – amply funded by conservative lobbyists – narrowly survived the recall vote, a *New York Times*/CBS poll indicated that the public opposed efforts to weaken the collective bargaining rights of public employee unions by nearly a two to one margin. The following year in Ohio, unions mobilized widespread public support after Republican governor John Kasich included police, firefighters, and other public safety workers in similar anti-union legislation. In April, Ohio voters, following a labor-led campaign, repealed Kasich's legislation. Partly because of lingering anger over his attack on workers, Walker was also later voted out of office (Brady 2011; Gowen 2018; Hananel 2011).

Unions are also vital in raising wages – for all workers. History again provides plenty of examples, even in unlikely settings. In the southern textile states of North and South Carolina, Alabama, and Georgia – which consistently had the lowest levels of union density in the country – unions never organized more than 10 percent of the work force, but for decades unorganized companies matched union pay scales, especially in the immediate post-war period, in order to keep the union out. As organizer John Neal reported from a losing campaign in 1948 at Standard Knitting Mills in Knoxville, Tennessee, workers told him "that they did not need a union at the Standard Knitting Mill, that the union couldn't give them anything that the company hasn't, they get wage increases every time the union gets one" (Daniel 2001; Neal 1948). Even as unions weakened nationally, the practice persisted, an implicit compliment to union's effectiveness. There were numerous other examples. When the first foreign-owned car plants were established in the 1970s and 1980s – again largely in the South to avoid unions – companies such as Honda, Toyota, and Nissan kept wages and benefits close to levels at the Big Three plants in Michigan. Workers enjoyed higher wages as a result, making their jobs highly sought after. As UAW attorney Lynn Agee put it, workers at unorganized plants "get the benefits without paying any dues" (Minchin 2005a: 154). In the airline industry, meanwhile, Delta Airlines – which was also southern-based – consistently avoided unionization of its 20,000 or more flight attendants through the same tactic. "Over the years," commented Association of Flight Attendants' leader Patricia Friend in 2001, "Delta Airlines has maintained its union-free status by keeping wages up near the top of the industry and basically treating its employees well." The phenomenon illustrated the important role that unions have played in reducing income inequality and ensuring better treatment for all workers (AFL-CIO 2001: 68).

For union members, particularly in the affluent decades after World War II, the benefits of high wages were especially palpable. It was unions that provided stable jobs with good pay, enabling workers with high school educations to buy homes and send their children to college. As such, organized labor was at the heart of the "American Dream" of upward mobility. It was a role that some well-placed observers acknowledged. As President Obama told a group of UAW members in 2012, "it's unions like yours that forged the American middle class." The auto industry, added *The New York Times* in 2015, "served as the twentieth-century trailblazer in spreading prosperity to millions of workers and their families and fostering middle-class security through higher wages and company-sponsored benefits." Workers in many other unionized industries certainly experienced the same uplift (Obama 2012; "UAW and the Auto Industry," *The New York Times*, October 8, 2015).

Given labor's role in building the middle-class, union decline threatened wage levels for all workers. As unions disappeared and the workplace casualized, more and more Americans became trapped in low-paying jobs with little prospect of mobility. As several scholars have shown, it is no coincidence that income inequality in the USA has increased as union density has fallen. The level playing field that unions fought for has disappeared in recent decades, with profits kept at the top rather than distributed. In 1978, for example, the top 1 percent of Americans earned 8.9 percent of US income, but by 2007 their share had jumped to 23.5 percent (Wright 2016: 969). In 1965, CEOs earned about twenty times more than their line workers, but by 2000 the ratio had increased to 376 to 1 (Clarke 2017). Over the same period, the wages of workers stagnated. Between 1978 and 1996, for example, workers' real wages tumbled by 12 percent, at a time when productivity rose by 24 percent (Sweeney 1996: 33). The problem continued in the twenty-first century. "Labor's decline," concluded one data-rich analysis by senior reporter Kevin Clarke, "just about matches up to the swan dive of middle-class income in the United States since the 1970s" (Clarke 2017).

As unions have declined, income inequality has worsened, bringing with it a host of other problems, including increased homelessness, poverty, and social polarization. Pointing to research that union members feel more empowered and have better mental health, some concerned observers have even asserted that union decline is a public health crisis. This was partly because union members were more likely to vote and to engage in community activities, including voluntary work (Economic Policy Institute 2012; Mosher 2007: 225–227; Patterson 2005: 351–353; Wright 2016: 969). As research by senior scholars Raymond L. Hogler, Herbert Hunt, and Stephan Weiler has concluded, unions not only underpinned a "thriving American middle class" in the post-war era; they were also associated with other critical dimensions of material well-being. Weaker unions were associated with regressive and unfair tax regimes, whereas when unions were stronger citizens had more opportunity for development and there was more income equality. "The higher amount of generalized trust linked with greater union density promotes beneficial social and economic outcomes for all citizens," they concluded (Holger et al. 2015: 76–77).

Union decline had other negative consequences for democracy. As scholars Julius Getman and F. Ray Marshall have written, throughout the post-war period unions acted as "a barometer of liberty," in the USA and beyond. Whenever democratic societies arose – from South Africa to Eastern Europe – unions were integrally involved. Organized labor offered an independent source of power and could unite groups that totalitarian regimes want to keep separate (Getman & Marshall 2003). The precedents went back to World War II itself. Thus, the Allies stimulated the revitalization of an independent labor movement in Germany, which had been brutally suppressed by the Nazi regime. In April 1946, for example, Assistant Secretary of State Maj. Gen. John Hilldring commented that, "promotion of labor unions will be a basic part of United States occupation policy in both Germany and Japan as the best means for teaching democracy." In the "first instance," labor unions were encouraged in the American zone to achieve cooperation ("Labor Unions in US Zones Backed as Aid to Democracy," *Christian Science Monitor*, April 29, 1946).

Despite this history, many commentators – particularly in the conservative press – continued to see unions as a special interest, pursuing narrow policies to please their members at the expense of the social good (Barro 2011; Levitz 2018; Mix 2008). "Labor unions," summarized economist Bryan Caplan in 2007, "thwart the will of the majority" ("Special Interest Secret," *Wall Street Journal*, May 12, 2007). Of course, unions fight for their members, and occasionally abuse their power (Martinez 2019). In general, however, they defend a broad range of interests for the majority, lifting wages, reducing inequality, expanding civic participation, and ultimately strengthening American democracy. Often occurring behind the scenes, this work is easy to overlook, and under-appreciated. History illustrates that when unions disappear, the consequences are profound – for all of us (Levitz 2018; Richard Trumka, interview with author).

When unions decline, workers lose their collective voice. With no vehicle to challenge the powers that be, they are more likely to look for scapegoats (Goldfield 2019). In his unlikely 2016 presidential campaign, Donald Trump mobilized working-class voters who felt they needed a stronger voice after decades of union decline, along with bipartisan support of trade deals that had cost America millions of manufacturing jobs. By promising to bring back industrial jobs and by demonizing "others," particularly undocumented immigrants, Trump did well among blue-collar groups, notably in crucial Rustbelt states such as Michigan, Pennsylvania, and Wisconsin, all of which he won. "I just think he's good for the economy," summarized Pennsylvania roofer Ted Lunger, who claimed that more than half the members of his local union supported Trump (Leary & Maher 2019). Exit polling and data from the Cooperative Congressional Election Study found that as many as 37 percent of union members voted for Trump in 2016. Overall, Hillary Clinton's labor numbers were down about 18 percent compared to Barack Obama in 2012 (Lynch 2019). In the election, the effects of union decline were clear. In Wisconsin, for example, where labor had mobilized against Walker just a few years earlier, union membership had dropped by 176,000 between 2008 and 2016; Trump ended up winning the state by less than 23,000 votes (Leary & Maher 2019). As president, Trump undermined labor's political programs, peeling off white voters, especially men, in a way that unions – hurt by a series of hostile Supreme Court decisions, particularly in the public sector – were unable to recover from. At the same time, he maintained grassroots support by continuing to profess his preference for American jobs (Johnson 2018).

Union evisceration had troubling consequences for all American workers. While opponents continued to talk of "Big Labor" – partly to justify further attacks on working conditions – in reality unions had shrunk beyond recognition (Maher 2009). Under Trump, moreover, the situation reached a new low. As President Trump saw little need for unions, or even the National Labor Relations Act, posing worrying questions for American democracy that labor leaders articulated best. "I believe our democracy itself is in grave danger of being corrupted," claimed NEA leader Lily Eskelsen Garcia in 2019. "Donald Trump is pushing our beautiful, imperfect nation toward something that would break the hearts of our Founding Fathers and Mothers. Towards authoritarianism and despotism." Attacking unions – and taking away their "People's Lobby" function – was at the heart of the plan. As Garcia explained: "You suppress wages. You kill unions. You want people underpaid and fearful of the future. You intentionally create insecurity so you can scapegoat some group as the cause and offer yourself as the savior" (Strauss 2019). Business leaders and conservative politicians, however, continued to argue that unions were outsiders, a corrupt and greedy "third party" that America was better off without. History showed otherwise. While they had their flaws, for decades unions had represented popular interests, and their decline hurt democracy, in the USA and beyond. "When unions are under attack," summarized Australian Council of Trade Unions president Michele O'Neill in 2019, "all working people suffer" (Michele O'Neill, email to author).

REFERENCES

AFL-CIO. 1971. Executive Council Report, November 18–22, AFL-CIO Papers. Hornbake Library, University of Maryland (hereafter "AFL-CIO Papers").

1975. Executive Council Minutes, February 17–24. AFL-CIO Papers.

1981. "Solidarity Day Sends Powerful Message From Workers," Press Release, September 24, 1981. AFL-CIO Papers.

1981a. Executive Council Minutes, November 14–18. AFL-CIO Papers.

1982. Executive Council Minutes, February 15–22. AFL-CIO Papers.

1983. Executive Council Minutes, February 21–28. AFL-CIO Papers.

1983a. Executive Council Minutes, May 24–25. AFL-CIO Papers.

1989. Executive Council Minutes, August 8–9, 1989. AFL-CIO Papers.

1989a. Executive Council Minutes, November 16. AFL-CIO Papers.

1991. Executive Council Minutes, February 18–22. AFL-CIO Papers.

1995. Executive Council Minutes, February 20–23. AFL-CIO Papers.

1995a. Executive Council Report, October 23–26. AFL-CIO Papers.

1999. "Report to the AFL-CIO Convention," August 2, 1999. AFL-CIO Papers.

2001. Proceedings of the 24th Biennial Convention, December 3–6, 2001. AFL-CIO Papers.

AFL-CIO. 2007. "Talking Points/WA Core Staff Meeting – January 18, 2007 – Working America Leadership Training, Washington, DC." AFL-CIO Papers.

2007a. "Talking Points for JJS: Transportation Trades Department Executive Board Meeting, Las Vegas, NV – March 4, 2007 – TTD Executive Committee Mtg. Las Vegas." AFL-CIO Papers.

2008. "TPs for Pres. Sweeney for Greenhouse, Chicago Tribune, Major Interviews – 6/18 and 6/19 2008 Meetings w/Barack Obama Washington, DC." AFL-CIO Papers.

2010. "Chronology of AFL-CIO and Sweeney Initiatives, 1995–2009." AFL-CIO document provided to the author by the AFL-CIO (copy in author's possession).

Barone, Michael. 2000. "Will Unions Rule?" *US News and World Report.* 128: 9, March 6, 2000.

Barro, Robert. 2011. "Unions vs. The Right to Work." *Wall Street Journal.* February 28, 2011. www.wsj.com/articles/SB10001424052748704150604576166011983939364

Berzon, Alexandra, and Michael Mishak. 2008. "Tackling Race to Negate It," *Las Vegas Sun.* September 10, 2008.

Blackwell, Morton. 1981. "National Non-AFL-CIO Organizations That Have Endorsed Solidarity Day," August 1981. Morton Blackwell Files, Ronald Reagan Presidential Library, Simi Valley, CA.

Bonitati, Bob, to Elizabeth H. Dole. 1981. "Solidarity Day 09/19/1981." Joseph W. Canzeri Files, Ronald Reagan Presidential Library, Simi Valley, CA.

1981a. "A Suggested Labor Strategy." Robert Bonitati files, Ronald Reagan Presidential Library, Simi Valley, CA.

1981b. "Notes – AFL-CIO Executive Board Meeting with President," December 2, 1981. Robert Bonitati files, Ronald Reagan Presidential Library, Simi Valley, CA.

Brady, Dennis. 2011. "Supporters Rally for Wis. Governor's Bill." *The Washington Post.* February 20, 2011.

Buhle, Paul. 1999. *Taking Care of Business: Samuel Gompers, George Meany, Lane Kirkland, and the Tragedy of American Labor.* New York: Monthly Review Press.

Bunkley, Nick. 2018. "Transplants Set to Dominate North American Production; Global Automakers Pull Even with Detroit 3." *Automotive News.* January 15, 2018. www.autonews.com/article/20180115/OEM01/180119937/transplants-set-to-dominate-north-american-production

Bureau of Labor Statistics. 2020. "Union Members – 2019," US Department of Labor. January 22, 2020. www.bls.gov/news.release/pdf/union2.pdf

Carter, Jimmy, to George Meany. 1978. "AFL-CIO 6/3/78–12/18/78." Chief of Staff files (Landon Butler files), Jimmy Carter Presidential Library, Atlanta, GA.

Chira, Susan. 1993. "Family Leave Is Law; Will Things Change?" *The New York Times.* August 15, 1993. www.nytimes.com/1993/08/15/weekinreview/the-nation-family-leave-is-law-will-things-change.html?searchResultPosition=1

Christian Science Monitor. 1981. "Did Organized Labor's 'Solidarity Day' Sway Congress?" *Christian Science Monitor.* October 16, 1981.

Clarke, Kevin. 2017. "The Decline of Unions Is Part of a Bad 50 Years for American Workers." *America Magazine.* September 4, 2017. www.americamagazine.org/politics-society/2017/08/23/decline-unions-part-bad-50-years-american-workers

Clinton, William J., administration. 2000. "A History of the US Department of Labor during the Clinton Administration, 1993–2001." White House Oral History Project. William Jefferson Clinton Presidential Library, Little Rock, AR.

Clymer, Adam. 1992. "Family-Leave Bill Sent to President." *The New York Times.* September 11, 1992. www.nytimes.com/1992/09/11/us/family-leave-bill-sent-to-president.html?searchResultPosition=1

Cobb, James C. 1980. *The Selling of the South: The Southern Crusade for Industrial Development, 1936–1980.* Baton Rouge: Louisiana State University Press.

2005. "Beyond the 'Y'All Wall': The American South Goes Global." in James C. Cobb and William Stueck, eds. *Globalization and the American South.* Athens: University of Georgia Press.

Colson, Charles W. 1970. Memorandum for the President, November 30, 1970. Charles W. Colson files (White House Special Files-Staff Member and Office Files). Richard Nixon Presidential Library, Yorba Linda, CA.

Daniel, Cletus E. 2001. *Culture of Misfortune: An Interpretive History of Textile Unionism in the United States.* Ithaca, NY: ILR Press.

DePillis, Lydia. 2014. "Sen. Bob Corker Can't Stand the United Auto Workers: An Annotated Interview." *The Washington Post,* February 12, 2014. www.washingtonpost.com/news/wonk/wp/2014/02/12/sen-bob-corker-cant-stand-the-united-auto-workers-an-annotated-interview/

Dole, Elizabeth H. to Edwin Meese III et al. 1981. September 11, 1981. "Solidarity Day (2)." Elizabeth Dole files, Ronald Reagan Presidential Library, Simi Valley, CA.

Dray, Philip. 2011. *There Is Power in a Union: The Epic Story of Labor in America.* New York: Anchor Books.

Drier, Peter. 2016. "How the Fight for 15 Won." *American Prospect*. April 4, 2016. https://prospect.org/economy/fight-15-won

Driscoll, John J. 1983. "How US Labor Is Tackling the 'Fix' It Is In," *The New York Times*. December 19, 1983. www.nytimes.com/1983/12/19/opinion/l-how-us-labor-is-tackling-the-fix-it-is-int-o-the-editor-117646.html?searchResultPosition=2

Dubofsky, Melvyn, and Foster Rhea Dulles. 2004. *Labor in America: A History*. 7th ed. Wheeling, IL: Harlan Davidson.

Economic Policy Institute. 2012. "As Unions Decline, Inequality Rises." June 6, 2012. www.epi.org/press/unions-decline-inequality-rises/

Fletcher, Michael A. 2008. "Labor Seeks Election Rewards; Union Organizing Rights Could Be Early Obama Test." *The Washington Post*. November 6, 2008.

Geoghegan, Thomas. 1991. *Which Side Are You On? How to Be for Labor When It's Flat on Its Back*. New York: Farrar, Straus, and Giroux.

Getman, Julius G. 2010. *Restoring the Power of Unions: It Takes a Movement*. New Haven, CT: Yale University Press.

Getman, Julius, and F. Ray Marshall. 2003. "Democracy and Unions Go Together." *Los Angeles Times*. July 6, 2003. www.latimes.com/archives/la-xpm-2003-jul-06-oe-getman6-story.html

Gigot, Paul A. 1997. "Terminator II: Why Big Labor Keeps on Coming." *Wall Street Journal*. April 11, 1997. www.wsj.com/articles/SB860708545278550000

Goldfield, Michael. 1987. *The Decline of Organized Labor in the United States*. Chicago: University of Chicago Press.

  1997. *The Color of Politics: Race and the Mainsprings of American Politics*. New York: New Press.

  2019. "Working-Class Roots of Trumpism." Lecture delivered at the History Program Research Seminar, La Trobe University. September 12, 2019. (notes in author's possession).

Gowen, Annie. 2018. "How the Democrats Finally Defeated Wisconsin Gov. Scott Walker." *The Washington Post*. November 7, 2018. www.washingtonpost.com/politics/how-the-democrats-finally-defeated-wisconsin-gov-scott-walker/2018/11/07/3377ed17-9cbe-4537-8b2a-acd0c37a8d35_story.html

Greenhouse, Steven. 2004. "Labor Is Feeling Embattled as Union Leaders Convene." *The New York Times*. March 9, 2004. www.nytimes.com/2004/03/09/us/labor-is-feeling-embattled-as-union-leaders-convene.html

  2005. "Breakaway Unions Start New Federation." *The New York Times*. September 28, 2005. www.nytimes.com/2005/09/28/us/breakaway-unions-start-new-federation.html

  2007. "Sharp Decline in Union Members in '06." *The New York Times*. January 26, 2007. www.nytimes.com/2007/01/26/us/26labor.html

  2009. "Labor Leader Is Stepping Down Both Proud and Frustrated." *The New York Times*. September 13, 2009. www.nytimes.com/2009/09/13/us/13labor.html

Hakim, Danny. 2001. "Nissan Workers Reject Bid to Join Union in Tennessee." *The New York Times*. October 4, 2001. www.nytimes.com/2001/10/04/business/nissan-workers-reject-bid-to-join-union-in-tennessee.html

Hananel, Sam. 2011. "AFL-CIO Leader: Wisconsin Fight Energizing Unions." *Associated Press Archive*. March 2, 2011. www.deseret.com/2011/3/2/20176677/afl-cio-leader-wisconsin-fight-energizing-unions

Hetter, Katia. 2001. "Labor Convention Addresses 9/11." *Newsday*. December 4, 2001. www.newsday.com/business/technology/labor-convention-addresses-9-11-1.754882

Hill, Herbert. 1977. *Black Labor and the American Legal System: Race, Work, and the Law*. Madison: University of Wisconsin Press.

Hogler, Raymond L., Herbert G. Hunt III, and Stephan Weiler. 2015. "Killing Unions with Culture: Institutions, Inequality, and the Effects of Labor's Decline in the United States." *Employee Responsibilities and Rights Journal* 27, 1: 63–79.

Holusha, John. 1983. "In Tennessee, the US and Japan Mesh." *The New York Times*. June 16, 1983. www.nytimes.com/1983/06/16/us/in-tennessee-the-us-and-japan-mesh.html?searchResultPosition=1

Johnson, Katie. 2018. "Under Trump, Labor Protections Stripped Away." *Boston Globe*. September 3, 2018. www.bostonglobe.com/business/2018/09/02/under-trump-labor-protections-stripped-away/jbr9aClCWyca8SbQCdtKJP/story.html

Johnson, Lyndon B. 1964. Signing invitation, August 18, 1964. White House Central Files-Name File (George Meany), Lyndon Baines Johnson Presidential Library, Austin, TX.

cense

1965. Signing invitation, April 10, 1965. White House Central Files-Name File (George Meany), Lyndon Baines Johnson Presidential Library, Austin, TX.

Kilborn, Peter T. 1990. "Dole Winning Applause for Labor Dept. Actions." *The New York Times*. January 4, 1990. www.nytimes.com/1990/01/04/us/dole-winning-applause-for-labor-dept-actions.html

Kirkland, Lane. 1981. "Statement Before the Labor Subcommittee of the Senate Committee on Labor and Human Resources, on Legislation to Establish a Sub-Minimum Wage." March 25, 1981. AFL-CIO Legislation Department files, AFL-CIO Papers.

Kopecki, Dawn. 1997. "Grassroots Lobbies Bygone Era's Cigar Chompers." *Washington Times*. November 24, 1997.

"Labor Ends Its Long Slide." 2000. *The New York Times*. January 22, 2000. www.nytimes.com/2000/01/22/opinion/labor-ends-its-long-slide.html

"Labor's Labors." 1999. *The Nation*. November 1, 1999.

"Labor Unions in US Zones Backed as Aid to Democracy." 1946. *Christian Science Monitor*. April 29, 1946.

Leary, Alex, and Kris Maher. "Democrats Labor to Stem Flow of Union Voters to Trump." *Wall Street Journal*. September 2, 2019. www.wsj.com/articles/democrats-labor-to-stem-flow-of-union-voters-to-trump-11567422002

Levin, Doron P. 1989. "Showdown for Nissan: Union Vote by Workers," *The New York Times*. July 26, 1989. www.nytimes.com/1989/07/26/business/showdown-for-nissan-union-vote-by-workers.html

Levitz, Eric. 2018. "Unions Are Not a Special Interest Group." *New York Magazine*. May 25, 2018. https://nymag.com/intelligencer/2018/05/unions-are-not-a-special-interest-group.html

Lynch, James Q. 2019. "Union Members Say 2020 Labor Support for Trump Won't Match 2016." Cedar Rapids (IA) *Gazette*. September 9, 2019. www.thegazette.com/subject/news/iowa-labor-unions-2020-presidential-election-donald-trump-20190909

McCartin, Joseph A. 2011. *Collision Course: Ronald Reagan, The Air Traffic Controllers, and the Strike That Changed America*. New York: Oxford University Press.

McElwee, Sean. 2015. "How Unions Boost Democratic Participation." *The American Prospect*. September 16, 2015. https://prospect.org/labor/unions-boost-democratic-participation/

MacGillis, Alec. 2008. "Labor Leaders Stress Unions' Importance for Obama." *The Washington Post*. August 29, 2008.

2009. "For Unions, a Time of Opportunity and Worry; Obama to Address AFL-CIO as Labor Faces Its Divisions." *The Washington Post*. September 15, 2009.

2009. "No Getting Around This Guy." *The Washington Post*. September 7, 2009.

Maher, Kris. 2009. "Big Labor Leader Is Old School Writ Large." *Wall Street Journal*. September 1, 2009.

Management Report. 2008. "Country's Fastest-Growing Labor Organization." *Management Report*. February 2008.

Martinez, Michael. "New UAW Boss Aims to Contain the Crisis." *Automotive News*. November 11, 2019. www.autonews.com/manufacturing/new-uaw-boss-aims-contain-crisis#:~:text=UAW%20President%20Rory%20Gamble%20had,comment%2C%20a%20union%20spokesman%20said

Melillo, Wendy. 1995. "150 Arrested in Downtown DC Protest: 650 Union Activists, Supporters Block Commuter Traffic for 2nd Day." *The Washington Post*. March 22, 1995.

Miami Herald. 1982. "Kirkland Leading the AFL-CIO on a New Course." *Miami Herald*. August 1, 1982.

Miller, William H. 2001. "Sweeney Sees Organization Gains." *Industry Week*. March 5, 2001.

Minchin, Timothy J. 2005. *'Don't Sleep With Stevens!': The J.P. Stevens Campaign and the Struggle to Organize the South, 1963–1980*. Gainesville: University Press of Florida.

2005a. *Fighting Against the Odds: A History of Southern Labor since World War II*. Gainesville: University Press of Florida.

2015. "Together We Shall Be Heard: Exploring the 1981 'Solidarity Day' Mass March." *Labor: Studies in Working-Class History of the Americas* 12:3: 75–96.

2016. "A Pivotal Role? The AFL-CIO and the 2008 Presidential Election." *Labor History* 57:3: 299–322.

2017. *Labor Under Fire: A History of the AFL-CIO since 1979*. Chapel Hill: University of North Carolina Press.

Mishak, Michael. 2009. "AFL-CIO Sees Young as Challenge, Opportunity." *Las Vegas Sun*. September 20, 2009.

Mix, Mark. 2008. "Labor Unions Prolonged the Depression." *Wall Street Journal*. October 28, 2008. www.wsj.com/articles/SB122515112102674263

Moberg, David. 1988. "US Management and Unions Contribute to Labor's Decline." *In These Times.* August 17–30, 1988.

Moody, Kim. 1988. *An Injury to All: The Decline of American Unionism.* New York: Verso.

2007. *US Labor in Trouble and Transition: The Failure of Reform from Above, the Promise of Revival from Below.* New York: Verso.

Mosher, James S. 2007. "US Wage Inequality, Technological Change, and Decline in Union Power." *Politics and Society* 35, 2: 225–264.

Murray, Shailagh. 2008. "Two Candidates, Two States, and One Big Day: Indiana and North Carolina Shape Up as Big Pieces of the Democratic Puzzle." *The Washington Post*, May 6, 2008.

Neal, John. 1948. *Organizing Report, May 22, 1948.* Operation Dixie Archives, Perkins Library, Duke University.

The New York Times. 1955. "Meany Lays Down AFL-CIO Policy." *The New York Times*, Nov. 5, 1955.

1955. "AFL-CIO, with 15,000,000, Largest Free World Labor Unit." December 1, 1955.

Nixon, Richard. 1974. "Statement on Signing the Fair Labor Standards Amendments of 1974." April 8, 1974. The American Presidency Project. www.presidency.ucsb.edu/ws/?pid=4169 (accessed February 5, 2015).

Nussbaum, Karen. 2006. "A 'Shadow PAC'? Not Us – We're Growing by the Day." *Wall Street Journal.* April 19, 2006. www.wsj.com/articles/SB114541306066529589

Obama, Barack. 2012. "Remarks to UAW Conference." February 28, 2012. available from the Obama White House (archived) at: www.whitehouse.gov/the-press-office/2012/02/28/remarks-president-uaw-confer ence(accessed March 2, 2020).

Papathanasis, Tas. 1989. "Smyrna: The Crucible of American Labor." *The Christian Science Monitor.* August 11, 1989. www.csmonitor.com/1989/0811/epapa.html

Patterson, James T. 2005. *Restless Giant: The United States From Watergate to Bush v. Gore.* New York: Oxford University Press.

Patterson, Matt, and Trey Kovacs. 2012. "Labor Bosses Demand Their Dues." *Washington Times.* May 10, 2012. www.washingtontimes.com/news/2012/may/10/labor-bosses-demand-their-dues/

Perlman, David L. 1965. "House Votes School Aid 'Breakthrough.'" *AFL-CIO News.* April 3, 1965.

1982. "Labor Hails Defeat of Balanced Budget Amendment Move." *AFL-CIO News.* October 9, 1982.

Pianin, Eric, and Warren Brown. 1981. "Crowd Proclaims Labor's Solidarity." *The Washington Post.* September 20, 1981.

Porter, Eduardo. 2012. "Unionizing at the Low End of the Pay Scale." *The New York Times.* December 5, 2012. www.nytimes.com/2012/12/05/business/unionizing-at-the-low-end-of-the-pay-scale.html

Radosh, Ronald. 1969. *American Labor and United States Foreign Policy.* New York: Random House.

Rosenfeld, Jake. 2014. *What Unions No Longer Do.* Cambridge, MA: Harvard University Press.

Rosenthal, Steve. 2013. "Union Household Share of Vote and Workforce Percentage, 1992–2012," copy in author's possession.

Scipes, Kim. 2010. *AFL-CIO's Secret War Against Developing Country Workers.* Lanham, MD: Lexington Books.

"Selling the Man to the Membership: Calling Union Members Who Don't Vote Democratic 'Racist' Is Risky." 2008. Charleston (WV) *Daily Mail.* September 1, 2008.

Seminario, Margaret. 1983. "Testimony before the House Committee on Government Operations on Regulation of Occupational Exposure to Asbestos." June 28, 1983. AFL-CIO Legislation Department files, AFL-CIO Papers.

Shribman, David. 1981. "A Potpourri of Protesters." *The New York Times.* September 20, 1981. www.nytimes .com/1981/09/20/us/a-potpourri-of-protesters.html

Slobodian, Quinn. 2018. *Globalists: The End of Empire and the Birth of Neoliberalism.* Cambridge, MA: Harvard University Press.

"Special Interest Secret." 2007. *Wall Street Journal.* May 12, 2007. www.wsj.com/articles/ SB117893365787300771

Stein, Judith. 2010. *Pivotal Decade: How the United States Traded Factories for Finance in the Seventies.* New Haven, CT: Yale University Press.

Stern, Andy. 2019. Correspondence with author. June 14, 2019 (copy in author's possession).

Stevenson, Richard W. 1996. "Clinton Signs a Bill Raising Minimum Wage by 90 Cents." *The New York Times*. August 21, 1996. www.nytimes.com/1996/08/21/us/clinton-signs-a-bill-raising-minimum-wage-by-90-cents.html

Strauss, Valerie. 2019. "Leaders of Teachers Unions: America's Democracy Is at Risk." *The Washington Post*. July 12, 2019. www.washingtonpost.com/education/2019/07/12/leaders-teachers-unions-americas-democracy-is-risk/

Strout, Richard L. 1981. "Worried Unions Aim for Biggest Mass Rally Ever in Capitol." *Christian Science Monitor*. September 15, 1981.

Stulberg, Louis. 1972. "Address, AFL-CIO Fraternal Delegate to the Trades Union Congress." Brighton, England, September 4–8, 1972. Charles W. Colson files, White House Special Files-Staff Member Office Files. Richard M. Nixon Presidential Library, Yorba Linda, CA.

Sweeney, John J. 1996. *America Needs a Raise: Fighting for Economic Security and Social Justice*. Boston: Houghton Mifflin.

Swoboda, Frank, and Saundra Torry. 1991. "Labor Sends Politicians a Message Hundreds of Thousands Strong." *The Washington Post*. September 1, 1991.

Townsend, Ed. 1967. "Unions Top 19 Million Members; Ratio Dip Continues." *Christian Science Monitor*. September 9, 1967.

Trumka, Richard. 2008. "Remarks by Richard L. Trumka, USW Convention." July 1, 2008. Transcript supplied by the AFL-CIO (in author's possession).

"UAW and the Auto Industry." 2015. *The New York Times*, October 8, 2015. www.nytimes.com/interactive/2015/10/08/business/uaw-auto-union-timeline.html

United Automobile Workers. 2010. "Submitted Resolutions, 35th UAW Constitutional Convention." June 14–17, 2010. UAW Papers, Walter P. Reuther Library, Wayne State University, Detroit.

Wehrle, Edmund F. 2005. *Between a River and a Mountain: The AFL-CIO and the Vietnam War*. Ann Arbor: University of Michigan Press, 2005.

Whoriskey, Peter, and Dan Balz. 2012. "Governor's Triumph Deals Major Blow to Unions." *The Washington Post*. June 7, 2012.

Willhelm, Noreen. 1983. "Labor Makes it Day of Protest." Dayton, OH *Journal Herald*. September 6, 1983.

Woodard, Catherine. 1983. "Unions Working Today – to Beat Reagan." *Fort Worth Star-Telegram*. September 5, 1983.

Wright, Michael. 2016. "The Decline of Unions Is a Threat to Public Health." *American Journal of Public Health* 106, 6: 968–969.

YouTube. 2008. "AFL-CIO's Richard Trumka on Racism and Obama." July 20, 2008. www.youtube.com/watch?v=7QIGJTHdH50

Zieger, Robert H. 1994. *American Workers, American Unions*. 2nd ed. Baltimore: Johns Hopkins University Press.
    2008. "'Labor Did It' Again." Gainesville (FL) *Sun*. November 9, 2008.

Zieger, Robert H., Timothy J. Minchin, and Gilbert J. Gall. 2014. *American Workers, American Unions*. 4th ed. Baltimore: Johns Hopkins University Press.

9

Unions and the Democratic First Amendment

Charlotte Garden

After it became clear that former Vice President Joe Biden had won a majority of votes in the 2020 presidential election and was also likely to win the electoral college, AFL-CIO President Richard Trumka declared at a press conference that "Joe Biden's firewall was union made!" (Trumka 2020). Trumka cited a post-election survey showing that union members voted for Biden and Senator Kamala Harris at a greater rate than did the general public, and also touted union "get out the vote" efforts (Trumka 2020). He also noted a more unusual effort: as pro-Trump protestors gathered outside the Detroit convention center to urge an end to vote-counting, the "Michigan AFL-CIO put out an email Wednesday at 3 am asking members to show up and protect our democracy ... Union members showed up, peacefully defused the tension and the count proceeded" (Trumka 2020).

That unions interceded on behalf of democracy itself by supporting the process of vote-counting was unusual,[1] but the other election-related activities Trumka noted were more routine. Going back just four years, the Culinary Union – that is, the UNITE HERE local union that represents 60,000 casino and hotel employees in Las Vegas – was credited with triggering "a mini blue wave" in Nevada (Murphy 2018). One remarkable thing about this wave was who accomplished it – hospitality workers, many of whom were people of color and/or immigrants. Without the Culinary Union, these workers might have been ignored or taken for granted by elected officials; with it, they became a political powerhouse.

This volume is about unions and democracy, rather than unions and politics. But one result of unions' activities – including their political activity – is to strengthen American democracy by amplifying workers' voices.[2] In part because unions are themselves run in a relatively democratic fashion, they can be "schools for democracy," helping refine members' civic skills; they also

---

[1] In a related development, the "AFL-CIO's executive council approved a resolution on 19 October saying: 'Democracies are not, in the last analysis, protected by judges or lawyers, reporters or publishers. The survival of democracy depends on the determination of working people to defend it. And America's labor movement is indeed determined to defend our democratic republic" (Greenhouse 2020). Around the same time, at least a handful of unions and labor federations began discussing a call for a general strike in the event that President Trump refused to accept the results of the election (Greenhouse 2020).

[2] There are many conceptions of "democracy." I have in mind Charles Tilly's definition, in which "a regime is democratic to the degree that political relations between the state and its citizens feature broad, equal, protected, and mutually binding consultation" (Tilly 2007: 13–14). In other words, democratic government must be inclusive and responsive – it should not systemically exclude the poor and working class from public policy decision-making, and it should not impede members of those groups from associating. In this account, an institution that helps equalize workers' participation in electoral politics is an institution that strengthens democracy.

encourage voting and other forms of civic participation among represented and non-represented workers and their families; and union representation increases workers' access to material conditions that allow full participation in democracy (Radcliff & Davis 2000; Zullo 2004, 2008).

This chapter contrasts unions' beneficial effects on workers' participation in democracy – and therefore for democracy itself – with the limited regard in which the Court has held unions' political advocacy in cases involving union agency fees. However, it also closes on a note of optimism, looking ahead to a time when scholars and advocates can realistically begin the work of rebuilding a First Amendment that treats labor unions as democracy-enhancing institutions.

UNIONS AND AMERICAN DEMOCRACY

This section discusses briefly the significant body of literature showing that unions strengthen American democracy in at least two ways. First, union representation helps reduce economic inequality, which is important because economic inequality undermines democracy. Second, unions increase workers' abilities to have their voices heard and preferred policies enacted. More concretely, unions organize voter outreach aimed at workers and voters of color, lobby elected officials, encourage members to run for office, and similar activities. Of course, there is significant overlap between these two mechanisms, and they can be pro-cyclical. For one example, just as unions may decrease inequality by raising wages in bargaining, they may also decrease inequality by working to raise the minimum wage with lobbying, get-out-the-vote efforts, and other forms of support. For another, unions might win secure and predictable work schedules during bargaining, which in turn make it easier for workers to plan to vote.

"Scholars have shown that democracy fares best when the working class enjoys economic prosperity" (Klarman 2019: 148–149). It is "well established that economic inequality is associated with increasing acceptance of authoritarian rule" (Huq & Ginsburg 2018: 81).[3] Readers will probably not be surprised to learn that these sentences appeared in articles focused on the health (or lack thereof) of American democracy. But income inequality was growing long before the Trump Administration – perhaps one was a necessary condition for the other – with consequences for democracy. As early as 2004, a group of political scientists formed a task force that linked the health of American democracy to income inequality. They warned: "The privileged participate more than others and are increasingly well organized to press their demands on government. Public officials, in turn, are much more responsive to the privileged than to average citizens and the least affluent" (APSA 2004: 1). Relatedly, a body of research argues that in the USA, government is relatively unresponsive to the concerns of the poor and working class, though there is disagreement about the extent of the problem (Branham et al. 2017; Gilens 2015; Gilens & Page 2014).[4]

There is little doubt that one cause of increasing income inequality in the USA is union decline (Farber et al 2018). Bruce Western and Jake Rosenfeld estimate that this decline is

---

[3] The concern with the effect of income inequality on US democracy can be traced back at least as far as 1787, when James Madison wrote in Federalist Number 10 that "the most common and durable source of factions has been the various and unequal distribution of property."

[4] For example, whereas Gilens and Page conclude that "when a majority of citizens disagrees with economic elites ... they generally lose" (Gilens & Page 2014: 576), Branham et al. (2017) argue that there is a lot of policy agreement between the rich and middle class, and that when the two diverge, the rich win just over half the time. However, Branham et al. also agree that policies supported by only the poor are relatively unlikely to be adopted, because "the middle and rich may be effective at blocking policies that the poor want" (Branham et al. 55).

responsible for "a fifth to a third of the growth in inequality" (2011: 1).[5] They argue that unions reduce income inequality through a mix of mechanisms: collective bargaining in unionized workplaces; "union threat" in non-union workplaces; successful union advocacy for pro-equality policies; and unions' roles in creating moral and economic workplace norms.

The link between unions, inequality, and democracy is reflected in work showing that where unions increase workers' participation in the electoral process – and therefore can make politicians pay a price for ignoring them – elected representatives may become more responsive to workers' concerns (Ahlquist 2017; Kerrissey & Schofer 2013). One remarkable recent study found that "in districts with relatively strong unions legislators are about equally responsive to rich and poor Americans" (Becher & Stegmueller 2020). This result is consistent with earlier research also finding that the strength of organized labor in a state affects substantive policy outcomes. As two researchers put it in an earlier paper, the "greater the organizational strength of labor, the more states spend on welfare, education, and other activities" that reduce social inequality – but where "organized labor has receded as an institution capable of representing class interests, those interests have become increasingly less represented" (Radcliff & Saiz 1998:121–122; *see also* Freeman and Medoff 1984).

One explanation for all this rests in the fact that the working class and the poor are relatively unlikely to vote, contribute to elected officials, or otherwise try to exert political influence. But areas with greater levels of unionization also have greater voter turnout (Radcliff & Davis 2000). More granular work suggests that union voter-outreach efforts have a disproportionate effect on low-income workers and workers of color, helping narrow the voter participation gap (Radcliff 2001; Zullo 2006). Zullo (2006) found that working class voters and voters of color were more likely to vote in the 2000 election if they lived in a district containing a "Union City" – that is, where an AFL-CIO labor council had made a coordinated effort to "participate in community coalitions, perform political outreach in working-class neighborhoods, diversify and train labor-friendly political leaders, and expand labor's voice through the media" (Zullo 2006: 196). Another study focused on state and local elections found that Latino voters who were contacted through the Los Angeles County Federation's outreach program were more likely to turn out. Observing that other research had shown that out-of-state telemarketing calls to voters made relatively little difference to turnout, the author of the LA County Federation study suggested that the Federation's outreach was more effective because the "Los Angeles individuals who contacted voters were local community and union members with close ties to the candidates . . . and they often shared key similarities" with contacted voters (Lamare 2010: 466).

Conversely, where unions have been weakened through right-to-work laws or laws limiting or eliminating bargaining for public-sector employees, voter turnout is lower. Zullo (2008) found that when states both had a right-to-work law and limited collective bargaining for public employees, voter turnout was nearly 5 percent lower than in states with neither. More recently, another group of researchers found that right-to-work laws decreased voter turnout, decreased vote share for Democratic party candidates for President, Governor, and the US Senate and House of Representatives, and pushed policy in a more conservative direction (Feigenbaum et al. 2019).

Voting is not the only way to participate in the political arena – citizens also work or volunteer for campaigns, make contributions, do outreach to other voters, and run for office themselves.

---

[5] IMF researchers agree that union decline is linked to income inequality in advanced economies, including in the USA; they argue this is mainly because unions check the ability of top earners to capture a greater share of income and that they do this through bargaining and by influencing public policy (Jaumotte & Buitron 2015, see also Freeman 1980).

But rates of participation in these activities reflect even greater disparities between the poor and working class as compared to Americans who are better off than do voting rates (APSA 2004; Carnes 2013). Again, unions can help decrease these inequalities (Carnes 2013; Feigenbaum et al. 2019). Unions make contributions, funded by member dues, to candidates running for office, and some hold "lobby days," during which workers who have received union training visit legislators and urge particular courses of action. In addition, unions run a variety of programs aimed at recruiting, training, and supporting union members to run for office, which increase working-class representation in government (Sojourner 2013). For example, the recent "Red for Ed" protests by teachers reportedly inspired some of the participants to run for office, often with union support.

Finally, unions can increase workers' participation in civic life writ large. From Alexis de Tocqueville to Robert Putnam and beyond, authors have linked strong civil society organizations to strong democracies. These organizations increase social cohesion, trust, and interdependence, and they also help channel and amplify citizens' voices (Edwards & Foley 2000). And, as Barbara Fick suggests, unions are "archetypal" civil society organizations because of the degree to which they reflect "democratic representation, demographic representation, financial independence, breadth of concerns, and placement within society for access to both elites and grass roots" (Fick 2009: 254).[6] The link between active participation in a union and worker empowerment outside of work is reflected in Veronica Terriquez's study of Latino workers who had been active in a "social movement" union – SEIU Local 1877, which represents janitors and other service workers in Los Angeles (Terriquez 2011). Terriquez found that workers who were active in union campaigns often went on to become activists in their children's schools; as one immigrant parent and union member observed, "Here at the union they teach you how to speak up … that helps you share your point of view when you go to meetings at your children's school" (2011: 581). Other parents whom Terriquez interviewed had similar trajectories – their union activism taught them how to agitate for change or to assume leadership roles at their children's schools.

This section has given an overview of literature on the relationship between American unions and American democracy. The next section shifts gears, turning to the Supreme Court's treatment of unions' political advocacy.

UNIONS' POLITICS IN COURT

Both campaign finance law and labor law recognize political advocacy as an important component of unions' overall advocacy for workers. But in another line of cases – those considering the legality of certain union security clauses – the Court has implied that unions' political activities are peripheral to their core work at the bargaining table. These cases culminated in *Janus* v. *AFSCME*,[7] which held that public sector workers could not be required to contribute anything to the union that represents them. One effect of this line of cases has been to weaken unions' ability to play a role in American democracy; as discussed above, "right to work" rules lower voter turnout and diminish the funds that unions have available for get-out-the-vote efforts, canvassing support, and more. This section discusses these cases, emphasizing how both the

[6] Regarding unions' breadth of concerns, Gilens and Page argued that while interest groups generally advance views that are not closely related to "the preferences of average citizens," labor unions are among the best "interest groups" at "represent[ing] average citizens' views" (Gilens & Page 2014: 576).
[7] 138 S. Ct. 2448 (2018).

Court and advocates have framed arguments about unions' political activities. This discussion lays the groundwork for the final section in this chapter, which discusses an alternative way to approach cases involving the relationship between unions and represented members.

In some contexts, courts regard unions' and workers' political activity as expected, or even important. Perhaps the most to-the-point example involves campaign finance cases, in which unions and labor federations are frequent plaintiffs and amici. To give one early illustrative example, in *United States* v. *CIO*, the CIO challenged on First Amendment grounds a criminal fine imposed because the federation had endorsed a political candidate in its weekly periodical, *The CIO News*.[8] The Court construed the relevant statute narrowly and decided it did not cover the CIO's conduct, observing that the circulation of newspapers and journals by unions (and corporations) to their members (or shareholders) was a "normal organizational activit[y]" that was part of "advocacy ... of governmental policies affecting their interests, and the support thereby of candidates thought to be favorable."[9]

CIO is considered a campaign finance case, but the Court has also held that labor law protects union-to-member political education and advocacy. In a foundational case about the scope of the NLRA's protection for concerted activity, *Eastex, Inc.* v. *NLRB*, the Court again acknowledged that unions routinely advocate for workers in the political process as well as in the workplace.[10] The majority opinion by Justice Powell – who was no champion of labor unions – observed that when Congress passed the NLRA, it "knew well enough that labor's cause often is advanced on fronts other than collective bargaining and grievance settlement within the immediate employment context."[11]

However, when it comes to another set of cases – those involving the rights of union-represented workers who object to paying union dues or fees – the Court has implied that unions' core function is to engage in bread-and-butter unionism via collective bargaining, and that their engagement in the democratic process is a sort of add-on. This came about in cases holding that the "agency shop" was the most that could be required in either the private or public sector, thereby making contributing to union politics an à la carte option for represented workers.

The two foundational cases for my purposes are *International Association of Machinists* v. *Street*, and *Abood* v. *Detroit Board of Education*. In *Street*, a group of railway employees challenged on constitutional grounds a contractual requirement that they pay union dues and fees.[12] The Court avoided the constitutional question by construing a provision of the Railway Labor Act[13] to authorize unions and employers to require represented employees to pay agency fees, but not full union dues. This rule implemented a distinction between union bargaining

---

[8] *United States* v. *CIO*, 335 US 106 (1948).

[9] P. 123.

[10] *Eastex, Inc.* v. *NLRB*, 437 US 556 (1978).

[11] P. 565. In recent years, disputes have arisen as to the outer boundaries of this protection – for example, whether advocacy on immigration reform relates closely enough to workplace issues to qualify as protected concerted activity under the NLRA – but the basic tenet of labor law established in *Eastex* remains settled.

[12] 367 US 740 (1961).

[13] The statutory provision permits covered employers and unions "to make agreements, requiring, as a condition of continued employment, that within sixty days following the beginning of such employment, or the effective date of such agreements, whichever is the later, all employees shall become members of the labor organization representing their craft or class: Provided, that no such agreement shall require such condition of employment with respect to employees to whom membership is not available upon the same terms and conditions as are generally applicable to any other member or with respect to employees to whom membership was denied or terminated for any reason other than the failure of the employee to tender the periodic dues, initiation fees, and assessments (not including fines and penalties) uniformly required as a condition of acquiring or retaining membership." 45 USC § 152, Eleventh.

and union politics that exists in the private sector to this day.[14] *Street* adopted this distinction after reviewing the legislative history of the relevant provision, which revealed that Congress sought to prevent represented workers from free-riding on dues paid by their colleagues. The Court then reasoned that "the conclusion to which this history clearly points is that [the RLA's union-shop provision] contemplated compulsory unionism to force employees to share the costs of negotiating and administering collective agreements ... [o]ne looks in vain for any suggestion that Congress also meant ... to provide the unions with a means for forcing employees ... to support political causes."[15]

Of course, one can free-ride on political efforts designed to improve working conditions at least as easily as one can free-ride on union representation in collective bargaining; union-supported legislation requiring improvements to worker safety or increasing the minimum wage will usually apply to wide swaths of workers. Further, bargaining and legislative strategies can be closely intertwined. Making this point in dissent, Justice Frankfurter argued that the majority ignored the link between unions' political activity and their workplace goals, with the former "indissolubly relating to the immediate economic and social concerns that are the raison d'être of unions."[16] Although Frankfurter did not tie his analysis to unions' role in strengthening American democracy itself, he did repeatedly reference the idea of majority rule within unions, noting unions' similarities not just to other types of associations, but also to representative government – a point that would be at home in an article arguing that unions are "schools for democracy." Frankfurter also articulated a full-throated defense of unions' role in the political process, at one point declaring that "[t]he notion that economic and political concerns are separable is pre-Victorian."[17]

Street lay the groundwork for *Abood*, which ultimately imported into the public sector *Street's* approach to mandatory agency fees. However, the *Abood* plaintiffs had argued for a broader rule that would have barred public sector unions and employers from requiring represented workers to pay any amount to the union that represented them. In support of that argument, the plaintiffs argued that public-sector unions' collective-bargaining activities were more political than equivalent work by their private-sector counterparts: "[I]f politics determine all governmental programs and all public administration, and if public-sector collective bargaining plays an

---

[14] The *Street* Court apparently did not consider itself to be writing on an entirely blank slate, as it repeatedly referenced *Railway Employees' Department* v. *Hanson*, 351 US 225 (1956), which rejected a facial challenge to the constitutionality of the Railway Labor Act's union-shop provision. In relevant part, the *Hanson* Court had observed that the RLA provision allowed only those mandatory payments that related "to the work of the union in the realm of collective bargaining," and noted that the employee-objector had argued that "the union shop agreement forces men into ideological and political associations which violate their right to freedom of conscience, freedom of association, and freedom of thought protected by the Bill of Rights" (pp. 235–236). However, neither of those statements was aimed squarely at the distinction between union bargaining and union political advocacy. The *Hanson* Court's observation about the "realm of collective bargaining" distinguished financial support for union representation of members from "fines and penalties" imposed through a system of union discipline. And the Court responded to the second argument by observing that there was no evidence before the Court that "compulsory membership will be used to impair freedom of expression," and that "Congress endeavored to safeguard against that possibility by making explicit that no conditions to membership may be imposed" beyond financial obligations. That suggests the Court was thinking of situations in which unions require members to take certain political positions, rather than the union taking its own political positions.

[15] 367 US at 763–764. In addition, the Court argued that Congress had "incorporated safeguards" to protect dissenters – but then cited legislative history concerning the possibility that employees would face union discipline or loss of employment because of the employees' own political activity or criticism of unions, rather than the possibility that the union would spend dues money on politics.

[16] P. 800.

[17] P. 814.

integral part in this process, then it too acquires an inherently and ineradicably political character."[18]

That argument used as a baseline the (flawed) assumption that private-sector employers share one goal: economic efficiency. In contrast, the *Abood* plaintiffs argued, elected officials might have two goals: efficient provision of public services, and reelection. Further, those goals might conflict because unions can campaign against intransigent bargaining partners. To support this contention, the plaintiffs included in their brief a list of situations in which unions, frustrated at the bargaining table, pursued their goals through political channels. Some of these examples involved union commitments to campaign against or try to recall public officials who antagonized unions during bargaining. In another example, when a "fire fighters union in Syracuse, New York failed to negotiate a 40-hour week with city officials," it "succeeded in getting the state legislature to enact legislation establishing a 40-hour work-week."[19]

These examples might have been aimed at distinguishing public- from private-sector bargaining in either (or both) of two ways. First, the plaintiffs might have been arguing that public-sector unions have different options than private-sector unions for exerting pressure on employers. In the private sector, a union might strike, or protest at shareholders' meetings, or urge the public to boycott. In the public sector, the union might use similar tactics (though certain activities, such as strikes, might be illegal), but they also might try lobbying or electoral politics. In other words, accepting the premise that "economic activities" and "political activities" are distinguishable from each other, a public-sector union might engage in economic activities during bargaining, and then later pursue politics as another method of winning gains for its members. And – to make the *Abood* plaintiffs' further leap – the public-sector employer might make concessions during bargaining in order to avoid the later, political stage.

Second, the *Abood* plaintiffs might have been arguing that public employers have different mindsets than private employers when they interact with unions. As the *Abood* plaintiffs set up the argument, unions are pursuing essentially the same goals in both the public and the private sectors – higher wages and better working conditions for represented workers. But, they continued, bargaining is economic in the private sector because managers are assumed to be focused on keeping costs down.

In response, the government and union parties argued that the bargaining process was "essentially economic, not 'political.'"[20] First, there was an essentially economic rationale for the agency fee itself – avoiding free riding that could otherwise occur because of the union's duty of fair representation. Further, the parties responded to the second iteration of the argument above, arguing that "it is the public employer, rather than the public employee union, whose bargaining posture is significantly affected by budget and tax considerations. On the union side the process is essentially the same economic exercise as in the private sector."[21] In other words, a public employer might consider political issues, such as "the taxpayers' tolerance limits," but the union's advocacy would be focused on the bread-and-butter concerns of its members.

The Supreme Court majority ultimately adopted a view of the nature of public-sector bargaining that was closer to that of the employee-objectors than that of the government and the unions:

[18] Brief for Appellants at 63, *Abood* v. *Detroit Board of Education*, 431 US 209 (1977).
[19] P. 71.
[20] Brief for Appellees at 31, *Abood* v. *Detroit Board of Education*, 431 US 209 (1977).
[21] Pp. 28–31.

An employee may very well have ideological objections to a wide variety of activities undertaken by the union in its role as exclusive representative. ... To be required to help finance the union as a collective-bargaining agent might well be thought, therefore, to interfere in some way with an employee's freedom to associate for the advancement of ideas, or to refrain from doing so, as he sees fit.[22]

In other words, the Court baked into its analysis its view of public-sector bargaining as belonging to the realm of the political: "decision[-]making by a public employer is above all a political process."[23] Further, in part because employees could "exercise ... their political influence as part of the electorate," it was "surely arguable ... that permitting public employees to unionize and a union to bargain ... gives the employees more influence in the decision[-]making process than is possessed by employees similarly organized in the private sector."[24]

But the Court also held that "interference" with objectors' "freedom to associate" was permissible because of "the legislative assessment of the important contribution of the union shop to the system of labor relations" in preventing free-riding and maintaining stable labor relations. The difference between a union charging for its representation activities and its other activities was not that one was economic and one was political, but instead that one was justified by a sufficient government interest, and the other was not. That interest – first articulated in *Street* and then carried forward into *Abood* – was "the legislative assessment of the important contribution of the union shop to the system of labor relations established by Congress."[25] *Street* and *Abood* further linked this interest to the duty of fair representation, implying what Cynthia Estlund has framed as a "quid pro quo," in which unions are constrained by the duty of fair representation (DFR) but empowered to negotiate agency fee provisions that cover those representation costs (Estlund 2015). One distinction between the costs of collective bargaining and the costs of political activity is that unions are not constrained by the DFR when choosing to lobby for legislation or support candidates for office – though they may be constrained by other factors, such as the threat of decertification, or the likelihood that unpopular union decisions could lead to leadership challenges.

The absence of one justification does not imply the absence of any justification – yet the *Abood* Court did not discuss any others.[26] There could be any number of reasons for this, but one is that, despite having the benefit of Frankfurter's dissent in *Street*, the Court simply did not think political activity was a necessary part of representing workers, which in turn meant that it was not important to prevent free riding on the cost of political advocacy. Whatever the reason, though, *Street* and *Abood* (as well as a later decision extending *Street* to the NLRA context)[27] gave the impression that what a union does in the political realm is peripheral: a distraction or even a work-around from the core activity that takes place at the bargaining table.

Still, as a political and legal compromise, *Street* and *Abood* reached an outcome that unions and represented workers could and did live with. It is even one that unions defended in later cases, which saw unions try to shore up *Abood*'s reasoning, including by arguing that public-sector collective bargaining should be viewed through the lens of employee management, which would trigger lower First Amendment scrutiny. Nonetheless, the Court overruled *Abood* in *Janus*.

[22] *Abood*, 431 US at 222.
[23] P. 228.
[24] Pp. at 228–229.
[25] P. 222 (identifying this interest as "the judgment clearly made in Hanson and Street").
[26] Nor did the *Street* Court – though this is explained by the fact that *Street* was a statutory decision.
[27] *Communications Workers of America v. Beck*, 487 US 735 (1988).

The road to *Janus* began with a little-noticed case called *Knox v. SEIU Local 1000*.[28] The events that gave rise to *Knox* involved a mid-year dues increase or "special assessment" levied by a California public-sector union. The union told workers that the assessment would go to a "Political Fight-Back Fund," which would aid the union in its fight against two 2005 ballot initiatives – one to require unions to obtain annual written consent from represented workers before spending dues or fees on "political activity," and another to give the governor new powers to reduce state spending, including on public employee compensation.[29] These initiatives were advanced by Republican governor Arnold Schwarzenegger, and they were packaged with two others: one to extend the timeline for teachers to be awarded tenure; and one to change the state redistricting process.

In keeping with the Court's holding in *Abood*, the workers represented by the SEIU Local 1000 fell into one of three categories: members who paid full dues; non-members who, at the start of the year, had not opted out of the increment of dues to be spent on politics that year; and agency-fee payers, who paid 56 percent of full dues (a reduction based on the percentage of total union spending that went to political purposes in the previous year – the method of calculation endorsed by the Court's precedents). When the union imposed the assessment, it simply continued each represented worker's original choice for the year, charging member and non-member full-freight payers the full increment, and charging agency-fee payers 56 percent of the increase.

The plaintiffs in *Knox* maintained that the union should have given all non-members an opportunity to opt out of the entire special assessment given that it was slated to be spent on politics, whether or not the non-member had previously agreed to pay full dues for the year. Notably, however, the union's defenses included not just legal arguments, but also a factual one: as it turned out, by the end of the year in which the assessment was imposed, the union had actually spent a smaller percentage of dues and fees on politics than it had done the previous year, even when the special assessment was included in the total of the year's political spending by the union. Therefore, as Justice Breyer noted in dissent, "the objecting non[-]members ended up being charged too little, not too much, even with the special assessment thrown into the mix."

The Court rejected all of these arguments. But it did not decide only that the union should have given non-members the opportunity to opt out of the special assessment, as the plaintiffs had asked. Instead, the Court held that the First Amendment required that the union obtain affirmative consent from non-members before collecting any of the special assessment. The result was that the plaintiffs obtained by Court decision part of what they did not win at the ballot box – by the time *Knox* was decided, California voters had already rejected the ballot initiative that would have required written consent to a union's use of dues or fees for politics. In addition, *Knox*'s solicitude for the First Amendment rights of objecting workers signaled that several Justices were open to reconsidering *Abood*'s holding. Groups including the National Right to Work Legal Defense Foundation, the Center for Individual Rights, and organizations linked to the right-wing State Policy Network answered the call.

The Court's next significant decision was *Harris v. Quinn*,[30] which struck down agency fees in the context of homecare workers who were paid directly by the state to care for individuals with disabilities. The workers bargained collectively under an Illinois statute that designated the state

---

[28] *Knox v. Service Employees International Union, Local 1000*, 567 US 298 (2012).

[29] P. 304.

[30] 573 US 616 (2014).

as the workers' employer for purposes of collective bargaining over those working conditions that the state controlled. A wave of these laws were passed – mainly by states with Democratic leadership – in the 1990s and 2000s, and unionization of tens of thousands of home healthcare aides followed (Smith 2008).

The *Harris* plaintiffs stressed that, in their view, a union that engaged in collective bargaining on behalf of homecare workers was indistinguishable from a union engaged in lobbying. And, in a 5–4 decision, the Court agreed, writing that "*Abood* failed to appreciate the conceptual difficulty of distinguishing in public-sector cases between union expenditures that are made for collective bargaining purposes and those that are made to achieve political ends."[31]

However, *Harris* did not overrule *Abood* – instead, it distinguished it on the basis of the nature of the workers involved. For the majority, it was significant that the homecare workers were jointly employed by individual customers and the state – in the Court's idiosyncratic parlance, they were "partial" or "quasi" public workers. This status, the Court continued, meant that homecare unions did not fulfill all the same contract-related representation functions as a union that represented traditional workers, thereby diminishing the importance of agency fees in ensuring that unions could meaningfully represent workers to whom they owed a duty of fair representation.

After *Harris* came *Friedrichs* v. *California Teachers Association*, in which the plaintiffs asked the Court to go beyond *Harris* and overrule *Abood* by holding that it was unconstitutional to require public employees to pay anything to the union that represents them.[32] Like *Abood*, *Friedrichs* involved public school teachers. Also like *Abood*, the plaintiffs wove throughout their argument the idea that teachers who have divergent views on state and local education policy should not have to pay union fees, given that their union might take disagreeable positions in bargaining. In response, the state and union defendants and several of their amici argued in part that collective bargaining was a fair and effective way of managing a large and professionally diverse workforce.[33]

That theme – collective bargaining as a management technique – would have had at least two advantages from the state's and the union's perspective at the time of briefing and oral argument. First, there is evidence that it is historically accurate for at least some public-sector workplaces. Joseph Slater has recounted that some states and localities decided to formalize bargaining with their public sector workforces – and to require or allow agency fees – either because the practice had sprung up informally between workers and managers, or as a way to quell public workers' discontent that threatened the provision of public services (Slater 2004). Second, the cases rejecting public employees' First Amendment claims in other contexts often emphasized the need for managerial flexibility in the public sector. For example, in one case, Justice Kennedy wrote for a 5–4 majority that public employees' First Amendment rights had to give way to employers' need to make decisions free of "invasive judicial superintendence."[34] Despite all this, oral argument strongly implied that five Justices would have voted to overrule *Abood*, although *Friedrichs* ultimately resulted in a tie at the Supreme Court following Justice Scalia's death.

Finally, in *Janus* v. *AFSCME*, the Court did what it had been threatening since *Knox*, and overturned *Abood*. *Janus* involved many of the same themes as *Harris* and *Friedrichs*, including

---

[31] This sentence misrepresents *Abood*, which held that required dues payments for a union's political expenditures were justified by the government's interests if the political spending was related to collective bargaining.
[32] *Friedrichs* v. *Cal. Teachers Ass'n*, 136 S. Ct. 1083 (2016).
[33] This theme was also echoed in amicus briefs filed in support of the union and state defendants in *Harris*, *Friedrichs*, and *Janus*, including in briefs that I co-authored.
[34] *Borough of Duryea* v. *Guarnieri*, 564 US 379 (2011).

that public sector collective bargaining is inherently political, and that agency fees therefore demand "exacting" First Amendment scrutiny.[35] One exchange during oral argument was especially telling. Counsel for the state of Illinois asserted that the state had "an interest . . . in being able to work with a stable, responsible, independent counterparty that's well-resourced enough that it can be a partner with us in the process of not only contract negotiation . . ." Justice Kennedy's response was incredulous: "It can be a partner with you in advocating for a greater size workforce, against privatization, against merit promotion . . . for teacher tenure, for high wages, for massive government, for increasing bonded indebtedness, for increasing taxes? That's . . . the interest the state has?" Then, moments later, Kennedy added, "Doesn't it . . . blink reality to deny that that is what's happening here?" These questions were notable for their implication that, at least for Justice Kennedy, collective bargaining was a subterfuge through which states dodged the democratic process to adopt policies – and specifically, policies that were typically associated with the Democratic party.

Justice Alito's opinion for the majority echoed Justice Kennedy's view of public-sector bargaining. For example, to distinguish other public-employee free speech cases, the *Janus* majority wrote that individual employees' concerns and demands usually are not matters of public concern, unlike collective demands, which (if granted) could implicate state budgets. Illustrating this point, the majority offered a dire view of Illinois's budget, including that the state "had nearly $160 billion in unfunded pension and retiree healthcare liabilities" and had a credit rating that was "one step above junk." And, Justice Alito wrote, the "Governor, on one side, and public-sector unions, on the other, disagree sharply about what to do about these problems," with the state offering unspecified "cost-saving proposals," and the union counter-proposing "wage and tax increases, cutting spending 'to Wall Street financial institutions,'" and progressive tax reforms.[36] Based on this description, it is not hard to imagine which set of solutions Justice Alito thought was more realistic.

The result is a First Amendment that protects workers who object to paying for union representation, to the detriment of workers' collective power to influence both working conditions and government. The next section works towards a new approach, albeit one that rests on the optimistic assumption of a change in the composition of the Supreme Court: we should apply the First Amendment to questions about the powers and duties of labor unions in a way that promotes participation by workers in American democracy.

LABOR AND THE DEMOCRACY-PROMOTING FIRST AMENDMENT

There is broad agreement that one purpose of the First Amendment is to protect and promote speech that is necessary for a functioning democracy, including democratic participation and deliberation. That agreement does little to resolve most hotly disputed First Amendment

---

[35] *Janus*, 138 S. Ct. 2448 (2018).

[36] The majority did not discuss what leverage the union funded by agency fees had to influence whether or not the state would accept its proposals. This is a significant gap in the majority's reasoning, because its distinction between matters of public and private concern rested on the likelihood that demands by a public-sector union funded by agency fees would result in a greater change in public finances than would demands by public-sector union not funded by agency fees. However, the majority did not require any proof that either the AFSCME union involved in *Janus* or any other public-sector union was likely to affect government decision-making. To be clear, I am not suggesting that public-sector bargaining by an agency-fee funded union commonly concludes without significant changes in wages or working conditions. However, we should expect the Court to at least address whether its rationale is grounded in fact – especially in jurisdictions where the scope of public-sector bargaining is very limited.

questions,[37] but it provides a foundation to link the findings discussed in the first part of this chapter to the legal questions discussed in the second – if the First Amendment is about facilitating functional democracy, then it would be logical for Courts resolving First Amendment cases involving unions to consider that they improve American democracy by making it more responsive to workers.

First Amendment scholars with a range of priors and commitments have urged that First Amendment doctrine should account in various ways for the role of civil society organizations in facilitating democracy-promoting speech.[38] For example, focusing on the media, Cass Sunstein has urged that some pro-democratic legislative interventions aimed at facilitating deliberation should not be considered abridgements of free speech at all. Sunstein also argues that an important function of the First Amendment is to facilitate changes in the political status quo, which is likely to happen only through collective action (Sunstein 1993). Frederick Schauer urges that the Court's unwillingness to account for the unique functions or character of institutions in First Amendment doctrine has led to "sub-optimal" and sometimes incoherent results (Schauer 1998: 120). Taking that point further, Paul Horwitz argues for an "institutional First Amendment," that allows certain civil society institutions considerable autonomy (Horwitz 2013). Robert Post argues for an approach that links the First Amendment to governmental decision-making that is "rendered accountable to public opinion," which is in turn embedded within social networks and relationships (Post 2011: 482). These authors have little to say about labor unions, instead focusing on institutions such as the media, libraries, or churches. But, for the reasons discussed in the first part of this chapter, it is a mistake to overlook unions in the conversation about democracy-promoting institutions.

Looking through lens of effective democratic deliberation, the examples offered by the plaintiffs in *Abood* – such as the Syracuse firefighters who won a 40-hour work-week through legislation after they could not win it at the bargaining table – take on a different cast. Perhaps workers' diffuse desires for a more humane work-week would have gone unheeded but for the union's organizing and advocacy; perhaps success on that issue led union members to engage politically on other issues or to run for office. Of course, this does not obviate the fact that some represented workers might have objected to the unions' actions. But, assuming – as the Court has since *Abood* – that the First Amendment is implicated when government requires someone to pay money to a private entity that later engages in speech, the Court could still consider a fuller picture of the relevant interests, including that unions have a net positive effect on workers' abilities to make themselves heard in the political arena. Without retreading the discussion from the first part of this chapter, one risk of decisions like *Abood* and *Janus* is that financially weakening duly-elected and internally democratic unions could mean that workers of any political persuasion will ultimately have less ability to turn their political preferences into reality.

Along those lines, Professor Kate Andrias has suggested that courts could adopt an approach to the First Amendment in which courts:

> would recognize that labor organizations serve a role that is not limited to advancing managerial efficiency, nor to the commercial sphere. Rather, unions enable workers' effective participation in the political process, they facilitate worker voice, and they serve as a critical countervailing

---

[37] For example, in *Citizens United v. Federal Election Commission*, 558 US 310 (2010), both the majority opinion of Justice Kennedy and the partial dissent of Justice Stevens invoked the relationship between the First Amendment and democracy to reach opposing results.

[38] The Court, however, has mostly been quite reluctant to adopt an approach to First Amendment cases that is sensitive to institutional context (Schauer 1998). Further, in recent years, the Court's approach has grown more rather than less formalist and context-blind (Krotoszynski 2019; Lakier 2018).

force to organized business interests in the public square. They also help achieve social equality. This version of the First Amendment would allow democratic processes to pursue these interests at least when incursions on other speech rights are minimal. Indeed, it would recognize these interests as essential to an overall system of free speech, expression, and association. (Andrias 2018: 56)

Similarly, Professor Jedediah Purdy argues that "a democratic polity has an interest in structuring economic power and its translation into political power in ways that counteract the structural advantages of wealth and coordination that otherwise strengthen owners and employers" (Purdy 2018: 2185). Accordingly, elected unions' membership rules "should be assumed to be compatible with First Amendment interests unless there is a very strong showing to the contrary" (Purdy 2018: 2185).

An approach that was structured in this way would have salience beyond the subject of union dues and fees. In recent years, union opponents have also challenged other aspects of unions' relationships with represented workers and with public and private employers. For example, objectors have challenged the use of the exclusive representation system in the public sector, unions' use of membership incentives, and public employer rules granting unions opportunities to communicate with newly hired workers. Conversely, private-sector organizations have argued that their own constitutional rights should defeat rules designed to empower unions or workers (Garden 2016). Many of these cases can and should be resolved in unions' favor based on existing doctrine – but to the extent difficult questions arise, courts should weigh heavily the fact that union interests and First Amendment values are often aligned.

CONCLUSION

This chapter has contrasted how the Supreme Court has sometimes viewed union political advocacy – with indifference or disdain – with research showing that unions play a key role in strengthening American democracy. Of course, the latter is unlikely to make any difference to the current Supreme Court. However, if the Court's composition changes in a way that is likely to improve its receptivity to labor unions, those unions may find that they no longer need narrow arguments – designed to appeal to Justice Scalia or Justice Gorsuch – that focus on collective bargaining as a system of employee management. Instead, they may be able to stand on their record of raising up workers and workers' concerns in political discourse.

REFERENCES

Ahlquist, John S. 2017. "Labor Unions, Political Representation, and Economic Inequality," *Annual Review of Political Science* 20: 409–432.

American Political Science Association Task Force on Inequality and American Democracy. 2004. "American Democracy in an Age of Rising Inequality," accessed at www.apsanet.org/portals/54/Files/Task%20Force%20Reports/taskforcereport.pdf

Andrias, Kate. 2018. "Janus's Two Faces," *Supreme Court Review*: 21–58.

Becher, Michael, and Daniel Stegmueller. 2020. "Reducing Unequal Representation: The Impact of Labor Unions on Legislative Responsiveness in the US Congress," *Perspectives on Politics* (forthcoming). https://people.duke.edu/~ds381/SB_representation_April2020_web.pdf

Branham, J. Alexander, Stuart N. Soroka, and Christopher Wlezien. 2017. "When Do the Rich Win?," *Political Science Quarterly* 132, 1: 43–62.

Carnes, Nicholas. 2013. *White-Collar Government*. Chicago: University of Chicago Press.

Edwards, Bob, and Michael W. Foley. 2000. "Civil Society and Social Capital: A Primer," in Bob Edwards, Michael W. Foley, and Mario Diani eds., *Beyond Tocqueville: Civil Society and the Social Capital Debate in Comparative Perspective*. Middlesex, MA: Tufts University Press: 1–14.

Estlund, Cynthia. 2015. "Are Unions a Constitutional Anomaly?," *Michigan Law Review* 114, 2: 169–234.

Farber, Henry S., Daniel Herbst, Ilyana Kuziemko, and Suresh Naidu. 2018. "Unions and Inequality Over the Twentieth Century: New Evidence from Survey Data," NBER, accessed at www.nber.org/system/files/working_papers/w24587/w24587.pdf

Feigenbaum, James, Alexander Hertel-Fernandez, and Vanessa Williamson. 2019. "From the Bargaining Table to the Ballot Box: Political Effects of Right to Work Laws," NBER, accessed at www.nber.org/system/files/working_papers/w24259/w24259.pdf

Fick, Barbara J. 2009. "Not Just Collective Bargaining: The Role of Trade Unions in Creating and Maintaining a Democratic Society," *WorkingUSA: The Journal of Labor and Society* 12: 249–264.

Freeman, Richard B. 1980. "Unionism and the Dispersion of Wages," *Industrial and Labor Relations Review* 34, 1: 3–23.

Freeman, Richard B., and James L. Medoff. 1984. *What Do Unions Do?* Basic Books.

Garden, Charlotte. 2016. "The Deregulatory First Amendment at Work," *Harvard Civil Rights-Civil Liberties Law Review* 50: 323–362.

Gilens, Martin. 2015. "Descriptive Representation, Money, and Political Inequality in the United States," *Swiss Political Science Review* 21, 2: 222–228.

Gilens, Martin, and Benjamin I. Page. 2014. "Testing Theories of American Politics: Elites, Interest Groups, and Average Citizens," Perspectives on *Politics* 12, 3 (September): 564–581.

Greenhouse, Steven. 2020. "Unions Discussing General Strike If Trump Refuses to Accept Biden Victory," *The Guardian,* accessed at www.theguardian.com/us-news/2020/oct/30/us-unions-general-strike-election-trump-biden-victory

Horwitz, Paul. 2013. *First Amendment Institutions.* Cambridge, MA: Harvard University Press.

Huq, Aziz, and Tom Ginsburg. 2018. "How to Lose a Constitutional Democracy," *UCLA Law Review* 65 (February): 78–169.

Jaumotte, Florence, and Carolina Osorio Buitron. 2015. "Inequality and Labor Market Institutions," *IMF Staff Discussion Note,* accessed at www.imf.org/en/Publications/Staff-Discussion-Notes/Issues/2016/12/31/Inequality-and-Labor-Market-Institutions-42987

Kerrissey, Jasmine, and Evan Schofer. 2013. "Union Membership and Political Participation in the United States," *Social Forces* 91, 3: 895–928.

Krotoszynski, Jr., and Ronald J. 2019. *The Disappearing First Amendment.* New York: Cambridge University Press.

Lakier, Genevieve. 2018. "Imagining an Antisubordinating First Amendment," *Columbia Law Review* 118: 2117–2159.

Lamare, J. Ryan. 2010. "Union Influence on Voter Turnout: Results from Three Los Angeles County Elections," *ILR Review* 63, 3 (April): 454–468.

Klarman, Michael. 2019. "Foreword: The Degradation of American Democracy – and the Court," *Harvard Law Review* 134, 1: 1–264.

Madison, James. 1787. "The Federalist Number Ten," accessed at https://founders.archives.gov/documents/Madison/01-10-02-0178

Murphy, Tim. 2018. "What the Democratic Party Can Learn from Nevada Casino Workers, Cooks, and Housekeepers," Mother Jones, accessed at www.motherjones.com/politics/2018/10/what-the-democratic-party-can-learn-from-nevada-casino-workers-cooks-and-housekeepers/

Post, Robert. 2011. "Participatory Democracy and Free Speech," *Virginia Law Review* 97: 477–489.

Purdy, Jedediah. 2018. "Beyond the Bosses' Constitution: The First Amendment and Class Entrenchment," *Columbia Law Review* 118: 2161–2186.

Radcliff, Benjamin. 2001. "Organized Labor and Electoral Participation in American National Elections," *Journal of Labor Research* 22, 2: 405–414.

Radcliff, Benjamin, and Patricia Davis. 2000. "Labor Organization and Electoral Participation in Industrial Democracies," *American Journal of Political Science* 44, 1 (January): 132–141.

Radcliff, Benjamin, and Martin Saiz. 1998. "Labor Organization and Public Policy in the American States," *The Journal of Politics* 60, 1 (February): 113–125.

Slater, Joseph. 2004. *Public Workers: Government Employee Unions, the Law, and the State, 1900–1962.* Ithaca, NY: Cornell University Press.

Smith, Peggie R. 2008. "The Publicization of Home-Based Care Work in State Labor Law," *Minnesota Law Review* 92 (May): 1390–1423.

Sojourner, Aaron J. 2013. "Do Unions Promote Members' Electoral Office Holding? Evidence from Correlates of State Legislatures' Occupational Shares," *ILR Review* 66, 2: 467–486.

Schauer, Frederick. 1998. "Principles, Institutions, and the First Amendment," *Harvard Law Review* 112: 84–120.

Sunstein, Cass R. 1993. *Democracy and the Problem of Free Speech*. New York: The Free Press.

Terriquez, Veronica. 2011. "Schools for Democracy: Labor Union Participation and Latino Immigrant Parents' School-Based Civic Engagement," *American Sociological Review* 74, 4: 581–601.

Trumka, Richard. 2020. "Trumka: Joe Biden's Firewall Was Union Made," accessed at https://aflcio.org/speeches/trumka-joe-bidens-firewall-was-union-made

Tilly, Charles. 2007. *Democracy*. New York: Cambridge University Press.

Western, Bruce, and Jake Rosenfeld. 2011. "Unions, Norms, and the Rise in US Wage Inequality," *American Sociological Review* 76, 4 (August): 513–537.

Zullo, Roland. 2004. "Labor Council Outreach and Union Member Voter Turnout: A Micro-Analysis from the 2000 Election." *Industrial Relations* 43, 2 (April): 324–338.

2006. "Union Cities and Voter Turnout," in *Proceedings of the Annual Meeting – Industrial Relations Research Association*. Labor and Employment Relations Association: 193–205.

2008. "Union Membership and Political Inclusion." *Industrial and Labor Relations Review* 62, 1: 22–38.

PART III

Labor, Diversity, and Democracy

10

Coming Apart

How Union Decline and Workplace Disintegration Imperil Democracy

*Cynthia Estlund**

In the immortal words of Joni Mitchell, "Don't it always seem to go, that you don't know what you've got 'til it's gone."[1]

For decades, much of the mainstream American left regarded organized labor as one interest group among many; its shrinkage was regrettable but seemingly not a burning issue. Now that unions have nearly passed from the scene – with private sector union density down to 6 percent – that might be changing. Union decline is now widely recognized as a major factor in growing economic polarization and in labor's declining share of income vis-à-vis capital (Farber et al. 2018; Rosenfeld 2014; Scholzman et al. 2012; Stiglitz 2015: 70–75). A high level of economic inequality itself threatens the sustainability of democratic self-governance (Fishkin & Forbath 2014: 669; Purdy 2017: 235; Sitraman 2017; Stiglitz 2012: 118–186). Union decline is also exacerbating other inequalities in the political sphere. Unions are among the few organized groups that advocate politically for non-professional workers (Scholzman et al. 2012: 87, 598–599). And they help to disseminate political information, boost voter participation, and cultivate "civic skills" among ordinary workers (Iverson & Soskice 2015: 1792; Kerrissey & Schofer 2013; Rosenfeld 2014: 159–181; Scholzman et al. 2012: 599; Sinyai 2019; Wang 2020).

Here I want to focus on a less-noticed political function of unions: their ability to sway working-class voters away from authoritarian or ethno-nationalist politics (Cohen 2019: 20–23; Gest 2016; Lipset 1959: 484; McUsic & Selmi 1997; Nussbaum 2019). This chapter briefly surveys the rise of ethno-nationalist politics and the attendant threat to democratic governance (in the first section) before exploring why unions may be uniquely situated to counter that threat. In the second section, I will argue[2] that the daily experience of working together in comparatively integrated workplaces is a favorable medium for intergroup sociability, cooperation, and solidarity, and a predicate for appeals that harken to solidarity versus intergroup hostility and conflict. The third section will argue that trade unions, with their roots in common work and shared economic interests, are well-equipped not only to strengthen social solidarity but also to elevate it from the workplace up to the highest tiers of national political discourse. Provided that their constituents are demographically diverse, unions are (or were) uniquely well-situated to promote cross-racial cooperation and comity. The fourth section will return to the present political moment, in which the capacity of both workplaces and unions to perform those crucial political

* I wish to thank Molly Jacobs-Meyer for extraordinary research assistance.
[1] Joni Mitchell, 'Big Yellow Taxi' (1970).
[2] As I have before at length (Estlund 2003).

functions has been degraded by the decline of union density and the rise of fissuring, fragmentation, precarity, and virtuality at work. Those trends should spur reform efforts for the sake of both economic justice and political democracy.

DIVERSITY, DIVISIVENESS, AND THE RISE OF RIGHT-WING POPULISM

In the past few decades, the developed world has experienced growing demographic diversity as ambitious or desperate residents of poor and war-torn regions make their way to richer and more stable ones (Collier 2019; Smith 2019). In Europe, immigration has transformed linguistically and ethnically homogeneous populations into multiethnic, multiracial, multilingual ones. In North America, demographic diversity has long been a fact of life; but in recent decades immigration has altered the demographic and cultural make-up not only of large cities but also of rural and suburban communities that were overwhelmingly white (Cramer 2016: 103-104; Frey 2015; Hochschild et al. 2012: 21–55; Parker et al. 2018). The proportion of US residents born abroad is now higher than it has been since the 1920s (Issacharoff 2018: 507–508). All in all, demographic diversity and change are now facts of collective life shared by the industrial democracies of the world (Alesina et al. 2013).

Growing diversity and cross-border migration have been flashpoints in regional and national politics across the Global North in recent decades, and pose a major challenge for the solidaristic social models that put a human face on capitalism in the twentieth century. History suggests that it is much easier within relatively homogeneous societies to cultivate the social solidarity that underpins those social models (Alesina et al. 2001; Alesina & Glaeser 2004; Collier 2018; Costa & Kahn 2003; Jäntti et al. 2014). The European strongholds of social democracy all constructed their labor-friendly industrial relations structures and generous social welfare programs in a context of ethnic, racial, and linguistic homogeneity; and those programs are coming under pressure in the face of growing demographic diversity.[3] In the USA, racial cleavages growing out of slavery and apartheid have contributed to the comparative weakness of organized labor and left-leaning political parties (Alesina & Glaeser 2004). And in recent decades, historically high immigration levels have helped fuel popular skepticism toward progressive and redistributive policies based on the belief that they might benefit and attract undocumented immigrants.[4]

Demographic change has both eroded support for traditional social democratic and center-left parties and fertilized the political ground for their rivals to the right, especially those who would sow discord along racial and ethnic lines. Of course, growing diversity alone does not explain the rise of right-wing populist politics. Growing economic insecurity across a broad swath of the income distribution since the 1970s, and especially since the 2008 financial crisis, has contributed to the recent populist turn in political discourse (Autor et al. 2017; Cohen 2019: 20; Stiglitz 2018: xxxix–xli, 3–4, 9).[5] And both ethno-nationalist ideologues and partisan opportunists have worked mightily to bend that populist turn in a rightward direction.[6] But actual

---

[3] On one empirical account, demographic heterogeneity dampens social welfare generosity through two separate mechanisms: attenuated empathy across group lines and greater political conflict (Jäntti et al. 2014).

[4] The so-called magnet hypothesis claims that migrants are drawn to countries with more generous benefits (Borjas 1999). There is, however, empirical evidence countering the hypothesis (Kaushal 2005; Zavodny 1999).

[5] Others dispute the centrality of economics to the rightward shift of the white working class (Cox et al. 2017; Ingraham 2016).

[6] The Republican Party in the USA has a long history of using subtle or overt racist appeals to peel blocks of white voters away from the Democratic Party and the policies that would benefit those voters economically (Haney-López 2013).

demographic change in recent decades has softened the ground, especially among white rural and working-class voters, for the propagation of divisive narratives of us-versus-them, of invasion and predation, and of an embattled heartland of authentic citizens versus outsiders (Cohen 2019; Cramer 2016: 74, 103–104; Gest 2016).[7]

Growing demographic diversity in a context of economic insecurity can set in motion a political contest for hearts and minds between those who would widen the tent and those who would batten down the hatches (Cohen 2019: 20–21; Rodrik 2018). There is little doubt that white working-class and rural voters have experienced economic setbacks, including the loss of secure and dignified jobs. The political contest is largely over where to locate responsibility for those grievances: the left points upward toward economic elites and the policies that have enabled them to capture the lion's share of economic gains (Reich 2020; Stiglitz 2018). The right – as richly illustrated by Donald Trump's Twitter feed and campaign speeches – points toward the "others" who are competing over what is left, and toward cosmopolitan cultural elites who are seen as siding with those others (Lamont et al. 2017; Pain & Chen 2019).[8]

In that political contest, those who would appeal, overtly or more subtly, to ethno-nationalism, racism, and xenophobia are unfortunately able to tap into a reservoir of biases – both negative attitudes toward racial and ethnic out-groups and own-group affinities and preferences, such as a greater sense of identification, comfort, and empathy with those of one's own race or ethnicity.[9] Those biases are widespread and deeply rooted in human psychology and history – though not equally pronounced, entrenched, or conscious across individuals and over time – and they may be all too easy to activate and manipulate, especially in a climate of economic insecurity and demographic change (Klein 2020a: 120–123). Those biases pose a challenge for the proponents of inclusive, cross-racial working-class politics, and create an opportunity for the proponents of ethno-nationalist populism, as well as for those who use such appeals to divide working people and distract them from the promotion of policies that favor the rich.

Intergroup divisions jeopardize not only the pursuit of an economically egalitarian political agenda but also the health of democratic institutions (Issacharoff 2018: 505–513). At the extreme, some early democratic theorists held that ethnic and linguistic homogeneity was a precondition for republican self-government (Issacharoff 2018: 505–506; Mill 2009: 344–345). Today scores of multiethnic democracies exist in defiance of that proposition. Yet the jury is still out on how and how well those democracies will fare going forward.

Scholars of democratic resilience and decay generally agree that democracy requires at least a thin sense of shared identity and shared membership – some reservoir of common values and constitutional commitments (Collier 2019; Issacharoff 2018: 506). There are bound to be social cleavages, including along ethnic or religious lines. But right-wing populist narratives cast some as the "real" people, and others as outsiders, aliens, or interlopers, poison and polarize political discourse, as we are seeing across the world today (Cohen 2019; Moffit 2016; Müller 2016). Those narratives from the right tend to delegitimize political adversaries on the left, and to provoke charges of racism and fascism from the latter. Democracy is in danger when political contests

---

[7] Some commentators have criticized the media's focus on "white working class" voters in the 2016 election of Donald Trump, pointing out that the average Trump voter, like the average Republican voter for much of the past century, was above the median income level (Carnes & Lupu 2017). Still, the rightward shift of some white working class voters from 2008 and 2012 to 2016, especially in the industrial Midwest, was pivotal in Trump's electoral college victory (Monnat & Brown 2017: 236; Cohn 2017).

[8] For more on how right-wing and left-wing populists diverge in their assignment of blame for economic distress, see Judis (2016).

[9] For an excellent recent overview of the social science literature on these biases, see Klein, *Why We're Polarized* (2020a: 49–79).

become apocalyptic battles for the nation's soul, and when an electoral loss is seen as delivering the nation to demonic forces.

Powerful counternarratives of solidarity and common interests and values across ethnic and racial lines can contest and defuse the divisive rhetoric and politics of ethno-nationalism and right-wing populism. That brings us to a crucial question: what does it take to successfully propagate that essential counternarrative of intergroup solidarity, especially given the pervasive presence of conscious and unconscious in-group affinities and out-group biases? Surely it takes powerful institutional proponents of intergroup solidarity. But that message will be more credible if it is grounded in the actual interests of both the messenger and the audience, and if it resonates in some way with the lived experience of the audience. Let us begin with that last element.

SHARED WORK AS A MEDIUM FOR THE MESSAGE OF INTERGROUP SOLIDARITY

Recall the consensus among democratic theorists that a sustainably democratic society requires at least a thin sense of shared identity and shared membership in the polity. That sense of shared identity and membership must be nourished by a rich substrate of social ties – not just intimate ties among close family and friends, but thinner ties among strangers, or once-strangers, from outside those small circles who can serve as emissaries for, and a social bridge to, the larger society. Tocqueville and his successors, like Robert Putnam, teach that those ties come from associating and cooperating toward shared ends (Putnam 2000). Overlapping networks of purposeful cooperative activity generate diffuse feelings of trust and reciprocal obligation that are part of the glue that holds a society and a polity together (Fung 2003). It is among the crucial functions of civil society to cultivate "social capital," or the bonds and norms of reciprocity that enable people to cooperate in pursuit of shared objectives, including collective self-governance (Putnam 2000).

On most accounts of civil society and social-capital formation, like Putnam's, voluntary associations formed around charitable, religious, political, cultural, or even recreational aims are at the center (Cohen & Arato 1992: ix; Ehrenberg 1999: 235; Habermas 1996: 366–367; Post 1991: 289; see also Arendt 1998). That generally includes trade unions – albeit with little regard for the distinctive nature of those associations.[10] But most accounts of civil society exclude ties and associations formed at the workplace itself, in part because of their infusion with economic necessity and hierarchical authority structures (Cohen & Arato 1992: ix; Ehrenberg 1999: 235; Habermas 1996: 366–367; Post 1991: 289; see also Arendt 1998).[11] Yet it turns out that those very aspects of work-based ties contribute to their distinctive value in a diverse democratic society (Estlund 2003).

To begin with, given the need to make a living, most working adults spend much of their waking lives at work and interacting with co-workers, often face-to-face.[12] Co-workers interact in the course of doing the job, before and after work, during breaks, around the proverbial (and

[10] Trade union decline thus counts for Putnam as just one more sign of declining group membership (2000: 80–82). The distinctive features of trade union associations draw little scrutiny.
[11] Putnam, more than most, does consider workplace ties as a potential source of social capital (2000: 83–92). But he finds them to be tainted (2000: 91), and in any case thin and wearing thinner (2000: 86–91). After concluding that "[t]he workplace is not the salvation for our fraying civil society," he proceeds to largely ignore those ties (2000: 92).
[12] American adults spend, on average, 4.35 hours per day engaged in "work and work-related activities," and just over 15 minutes per day in "organizational, civic, and religious activities" (Bureau of Labor Stat., *American Time Use Survey – 2018 Results*).

increasingly metaphorical) water cooler, and in the digital sphere. They talk about the work itself, about shared working conditions – a speed-up of production, a rumor of layoffs, a "handsy" supervisor – and about kids, parents, politics, popular culture, sports, and other stuff of daily life. Over weeks, months, or even years of working together, co-workers often develop ties of affection, empathy, loyalty, solidarity, and friendship. Obviously, workplace ties can also be fraught and tainted by conflict, resentment, abuse, or humiliation. But given all that is at stake in a job, people often find ways to work through or around conflicts and to get along, or at least get the job done, despite friction. That tends to give bonds among co-workers a resilience that is rarely replicated in voluntary associations unrelated to work.

Some evidence of the strong bonds that form among co-workers can be found in the history of the labor movement and in contemporary bursts of worker activism. I will return to the role of unions and labor organizing in these dynamics in the third section. For now, let us just note that shared workplace grievances have long provided a rich medium for the growth of solidarity – a willingness to take risks and make sacrifices for the group – and a platform for organizing and collective action. The point here is not that shared grievances are essential to the growth of bonds among co-workers. Both "good" and "bad" work environments create a base of common experience and material interests and can generate valuable social ties whether grounded in shared pride and purpose, shared frustration, or both.

The relative resilience and density of workplace ties is especially important because co-workers are *comparatively* likely to come from different cultural, religious, racial, and ethnic backgrounds – compared, that is, to the people one meets within families, neighborhoods, religious congregations, or clubs, and voluntary associations other than unions (Estlund 2003: 7–10, 61–69; see also Briggs 2007; Darling-Hammond et al. 2019; Tomaskovic-Deney et al. 2006). As compared with those groups, workplaces tend to reflect a wider swath of the larger community. That is partly because employment discrimination law has countered (though far from eliminated) forms of exclusion and segregation that are far less regulated, harder to regulate, or even constitutionally shielded from regulation in other social settings (Estlund 2003: 120–130).

The combination of relative diversity and density of interactions among co-workers makes the workplace a relatively prolific site of sustained interaction, and the most frequent source of friendships, among adults of different racial and ethnic identities (Estlund 2003: 9–12; see also 33–35). Interracial friendships are important not because they offer a magical solution to racial exclusion and subordination but because those strong ties of friendship attest to the reservoir of weaker positive ties that can flourish among co-workers. Daily cooperation, informal sociability, and shared experiences and interests among comparatively diverse co-workers generate interpersonal connections that can render the unfamiliar more familiar and can counter stereotypes and biases.[13] Social scientists widely agree that sustained cooperative interaction across group lines tends to produce more positive and egalitarian intergroup relations and attitudes (Estlund 2003: 74–76; see also Darling-Hammond et al. 2019; Paluck et al. 2019; Tropp & Pettigrew 2006). A recent empirical study finds, for example, that white individuals with at least one black co-worker manifest significantly less racial bias than those who do not, and finds clues that the link is causal (Darling-Hammond et al. 2019; Tropp & Pettigrew 2006).

Obviously out-group biases and in-group affinities persist, and inflict harm on groups that are still underrepresented in good jobs, and especially in management where workplace power is concentrated (Estlund 2003: 77–83). Legal institutions have a limited capacity, and perhaps a limited willingness, to prohibit, punish, or even detect the unconscious or well-hidden biases

---

[13] For discussion of qualitative and quantitative studies making this point, see Estlund (2003: 9–12, 60–69, 77–83).

and stereotypes that infect relations among individuals and groups. But the law can help, and has helped, to create integrated social environments in which these destructive attitudes might gradually wane (Llewellyn 1957: 32).

More is at stake here than the reduction of intergroup biases, crucial as that is in a diverse society. Personal connections across group lines provide a medium for the exchange of experiences and opinions, for the discovery of commonalities and differences, and for the cultivation of diffuse qualities of empathy and broad-mindedness that shape political preferences, enable compromise, and enrich public discourse. The daily experience of working together, multiplied across legions of adult citizens, strengthens the social foundations for democratic governance in a heterogeneous society.

Let me be clear: the claim here is *not* that demographic diversity – at work or elsewhere – enhances the formation of solidaristic and friendly ties; sadly that appears not to be the case. The claim is rather that societies that are in fact diverse must find ways to foster individuals' ability to transcend the differences that may come with diversity, or to get along in spite of those differences; and that the experience of working together is a comparatively promising medium for doing so.

Paradoxically, the crucial convergence of diversity and intense cooperation among co-workers is possible partly *because of* the economic hold that the workplace has on individuals and the power that managers exercise there. The economic compulsion that forces workers to sell their labor to make a living, and the managerial compulsion to cooperate in production once they have done so, are at the heart of enduring critiques of capitalism.[14] But those elements of compulsion also give workers a powerful motivation to find ways to deal with conflict and friction, and to carry on cooperating with co-workers with whom they might not choose to associate, rather than simply walking away. Moreover, managers have powerful means and motives to induce or compel workers to overcome differences and cooperate in production. Those managerial imperatives have generated a cottage industry of corporate diversity consultants and initiatives. To be sure, some of those initiatives are window-dressing or even counterproductive.[15] But the point is that employers, at least once they have some degree of diversity in their workforces, have good bottom-line reasons for figuring out what actually works in promoting integration at work.

Another kind of compulsion – state regulatory compulsion – is also crucial to these workplace dynamics: managers manage and workers work under the shadow of antidiscrimination laws, which help both to make workplaces more diverse and, through the law of discriminatory harassment, to counter the interpersonal conflict that diversity might entail. Liability pressures reinforce managers' operational reasons for promoting or even compelling a measure of civility among co-workers, and for fostering constructive intergroup relations at work.[16] Those relatively civil and constrained relations among diverse co-workers help to enrich public discourse at its roots in daily life.

Again, I do not mean to overstate either the demographic diversity of existing workplaces or the law's efficacy in combatting discrimination, stratification, and intergroup conflict at work. Workplaces are not as diverse or integrated as they could or should be after all these years. But compared to what? Compared to the non-work-based voluntary associations at the core of

[14] Elizabeth Anderson has a recent excavation and elaboration of these critiques (2017), which I later reviewed (2018).
[15] Some research takes a relatively positive view of those programs (Hawkins 2017). Others, however, are more skeptical (Leong 2013: 216); (Kim et al. 2012).
[16] Up to a point, that is. Managers operating under the shadow of liability can go too far in suffocating sociability among co-workers (Estlund 2003: 157–159, 163–164).

conventional conceptions of civil society? Unfortunately, we see all around us ample evidence that many people choose – when their choices are unconstrained – to live and associate with others from similar backgrounds and racial and ethnic identities. That is both a lesson and a consequence of human history. Now more than ever, diverse societies must find ways and places to cultivate empathy and reciprocity across group lines. That is not easy to do, and may in fact require the kinds of legal, economic, and organizational compulsion that operate at work.

This "working together" thesis – besides underscoring the imperative of combatting discrimination and promoting integration in parts of the labor market that are still predominantly white – raises concerns about the changing organization of work to which I will return below. But first let us turn to the role that unions can sometimes play in forging diffuse workplace ties into solidaristic bonds that are strong enough to withstand divisive appeals to ethnic identity and competition.

UNIONS AS AGENTS OF INTERGROUP SOLIDARITY

We should begin with the bad news: although racially-inclusive labor organizing in the United States dates back at least to the mid-nineteenth century,[17] much of the US labor movement for much of its history was dominated by native-born white workers, and fought to preserve patterns of racial exclusion, segregation, and discrimination against racial and ethnic outsiders (Marshall 1965: 113, 128–129; 1968: 128–154). That history generated what Charlotte Garden and Nancy Leong call the "conventional wisdom" about the antagonism between organized labor and civil rights goals (Garden & Leong 2013: 1141–1159). They argue that more recent history, by contrast, supports an "occasionally complicated but ultimately hopeful relationship between labor and race" (2013: 1139).

My main point here is that the hopeful side of that history rests on firm institutional foundations. Trade unions' distinctive capacity to cultivate interracial solidarity, both at work and in the political sphere, stems from three ways in which unions' and workers' material interests reinforce the moral case for intergroup solidarity. First, trade unions connect with workers at and through work, where they are comparatively likely to cooperate and socialize, and to share material interests, with diverse others. Second, trade unions that represent or aspire to represent diverse workforces have a strong institutional self-interest in promoting solidarity and combatting divisions, for that is how they can win gains for workers and thrive as organizations. Third, trade unions can often make a credible case to workers that their own economic interests are best served by intergroup solidarity. That pitch is more likely to resonate with workers – especially if it leads to gains on the ground – than abstract appeals to equality and the value of diversity. These three interconnected dynamics can be glimpsed in several historical accounts that both reinforce the basic "working together" thesis and illustrate the potential for unions to promote intergroup solidarity.

First, consider the early history of the Congress of Industrial Organizations (CIO), as recounted by historian Lizbeth Cohen in her book *Making the New Deal* (1990).[18] The rise of mass manufacturing had opened factories to less skilled workers who could be hired off the street, and doomed craft union strategies that depended on monopolizing scarce skills. The industrial unions sought instead to organize whole factories with highly heterogeneous

[17] Interracial organizing efforts in the South after the Civil War met violent repression (Pope 2016: 1584–1585). In the late nineteenth century, the Knights of Labor were famously committed to interracial solidarity (Forbath 1991: 12–13, 23).
[18] Discussed in Estlund (2003: 71–72).

workforces. They also sought to overturn the prevailing anti-union, anti-regulatory regime in favor of a political New Deal. Both their industrial and political goals required them to bring diverse workers together in a common struggle.

Conditions seemed inhospitable in the 1930s. Ethnic loyalties were strong and reinforced by language differences, and racial subordination was widely institutionalized and unregulated by law. Employers sought to thwart collective action in part by deliberately mixing ethnic groups at the workplace. Yet the convergence of diversity within workplaces, the increasingly integrated nature of work along the assembly line, and broader opportunities for sociability among co-workers helped lay the groundwork for industry – and plant-wide organizing (Cohen 1990: 292, 333). The cause was inadvertently aided by some paternalistic employers that sought to build loyalty to the firm in place of ethnic loyalties by sponsoring sports teams, social clubs, English classes, and other occasions for interaction across ethnic divisions.

The hero of Cohen's account, however, is CIO leadership, which sought to blunt potential racial and ethnic divisions by fostering a "culture of unity" among diverse workers (1990: 333–336). CIO unions organized their own racially- and ethnically-integrated recreational activities, and some undertook to integrate the taverns and restaurants near their factories – using the familiar union tool of the boycott – so they could be used for union meetings (1990: 340–341). As Cohen recounts:

> Racial unity became a watchword of the CIO's campaign in the 1930s, and to an astonishing degree in those early years … it became a reality in locals everywhere. A black butcher in Armour's sheep kill, filled with optimism, boasted to a WPA interviewer in 1939 that whereas once "the white butchers hated the Negroes because they figured they would scab on them when trouble came, … with the CIO in, all that's like a bad dream gone. Oh, we still have a hard row, but this time the white men are with us and we're with them." (1990: 337)

Cohen concludes: "The CIO hardly created a racially integrated society, but it went further in promoting racial harmony than any other institution in existence at the time" (1990: 337). It did so for instrumental reasons – reasons that converged with ideological and moral commitments within the union (1990: 261–267; Goldfield 1993: 5) but that resonated with workers mainly because they appealed to workers' shared self-interest and drew on their shared experiences at work.

While Cohen focused on blue collar workers in Chicago in the 1930s, William Kornblum studied their successors, South Chicago steelworkers in the early 1970s (1974: 36–67). By that time, the Civil Rights Act of 1964 had prohibited discrimination by both employers and unions, and desegregation efforts were underway. The since-merged AFL-CIO was officially committed at the top to equal opportunity and desegregation; but its component unions had a decidedly mixed record on race – still worse in the craft unions, but also uneven among industrial union locals (Frymer 2008: 69–71; Lee 2014: 12–20, 35–55, 81–96). Race relations in Chicago, as elsewhere, were tense at best, and working-class neighborhoods were sharply segregated.

Against this inauspicious backdrop, Kornblum found that workers formed attachments "over a lifetime in the mills [that] often cut across the racial, ethnic, and territorial groupings which may [and did] divide men in the outside community" (1974: 36). Forced to depend on each other at work, sometimes for their physical safety, workers formed interracial ties that were simply unimaginable outside the mill. And those ties carried into the otherwise-segregated outside world, as "men from interracial work-groups routinely share[d] wakes, funerals, retirement parties, weddings, and a host of family activities over the course of their lives in the mill" (1974: 66). Racial tensions were not dissolved but were leavened by feelings of solidarity, respect, and friendship.

While work relations and long job tenures helped to bridge "potential cleavages based on race and ethnicity," those positive dynamics were reinforced by shared involvement in union politics and the need to build coalitions across group lines (1974: 57). For example, the "leadership of the union's grievance system in No. 3 Mill was an extremely heterogeneous" bunch (1974: 57). Those well-respected workers "over years of common experience in the heterogeneous aggregation of mill activists" came to "define [their] solidarity upon grounds of common fate and mutual respect rather than any prior criteria such as ethnicity, race, or neighborhood affiliation" (1974: 58).

Kornblum found that, in South Chicago, "the unionists [were] agents of ethnic adaptation, for the union is not a closed society of workers but one which bridges the barriers of local segmentation and in various ways channels the participation of racial and ethnic groups in other community institutions" (1974: 130). These processes spilled into the community, providing "precedents in managing of ethnicity for participation in other community political processes" (1974: 132). Union leadership sometimes led to community and political leadership. And "in the process of winning power in the union, the cleavages which divide a group are overcome, attachments among group leaders are reconstructed, and alliances are formed with outsiders" (1974: 130).

Sociologist Rick Fantasia found some of those dynamics operating in a New Jersey steel plant in the mid-1970s, when it became the site of several spontaneous strikes (1988). Fantasia describes a highly diverse workforce, with roughly equal numbers of black, Hispanic, and non-Hispanic white workers, and various ethnic subgroups.[19] Race relations were no better in New Jersey than in Chicago. Yet "the actual activities and requirements of work, combined with certain patterns of social interaction, served to minimize ... divisions" among these diverse workers (1988: 77). Fantasia found that "[k]idding and joking about racial, ethnic, and cultural matters provided a safe outlet for the expression of prejudices and differences," and often led to "a real sharing of culture" (1988: 79). Racial dynamics were complex, and individual attitudes contradictory. Even white "workers who had worked closely with, been on friendly terms with, and ... staunchly defended black workers in the plant" sometimes reverted to racist comments and epithets when speaking with white co-workers (1988: 92). Despite the divisions that remained, however, diverse groups of workers joined in two spontaneous "wildcat" strikes, putting their jobs at risk, in support of fellow workers.

Fantasia argues that "the conditions of work and the day-to-day social interaction they shaped created at least a surface level of mutuality, a foundation of trust among the workers" (1988: 92). Working together created weak ties, and acting together galvanized and strengthened those ties. Fantasia's account of the union's role in promoting solidarity is more mixed. The workers viewed their union as far too compliant with management (1988: 81, 89–90). But *unionism* played an unambiguously positive role, as suggested by the words of a young black worker to his co-workers during the strike: "The union's more worried about the company's profits than our working conditions. But remember... *we're* the union; black and white united, right here.... *This* is the union, and we can't let them forget that!" (1988: 89).

These stories may evoke a bygone era. On the one hand, they are especially impressive because they unfolded against the backdrop of the unreconstructed racial and ethnic divisions of the 1930s, and the still-volatile race relations of the 1970s. On the other hand, one might well

[19] "'Whites' included Poles, Italians, Irish, Portuguese, and white Southerners; 'Hispanics' consisted of Argentinian, Puerto Rican, and Dominican workers; '[B]lacks' included Haitians and Jamaicans as well as native-born Americans from both the South and the North" (Fantasia 1988: 77).

question their relevance for today. For one thing, all three accounts involved industrial work-places in which workers' physical interdependency and relatively long job tenures helped to forge stronger bonds; nearly everything about that world of work has changed to the detriment of workplace ties. For another, all three accounts involved overwhelmingly male workforces; shared masculine identity might have facilitated the crossing of racial lines.[20] That is one small caveat to the salutary (if limited) changes wrought by the legal prohibition of sex discrimination, along with changing gender norms and aspirations. Still, these historical accounts underscore both how workplace cooperation can serve as a medium for intergroup solidarity, and how unions can cultivate that solidarity.

In virtually any union organizing campaign or strike that occurs within a racially-mixed workforce, the union must strive to forge trust and solidarity across racial and ethnic divisions even if management seeks to exploit those divisions. Race is not necessarily submerged in those campaigns; successful unions have instead learned to appeal to racial and ethnic loyalties in ways that unite workers rather than divide them (Guinier & Torres 2002).[21] Lani Guinier and Gerald Torres develop that theme in their book, *The Miner's Canary*, which features several union campaigns from the 1990s (2002: 43–44). For example, during an organizing drive at the largest textile plant in the United States:

> [i]t was only when union organizers found they could draw on the strengths of Chicano and [B]lack communities that the organizing effort made progress.... [T]he organizers helped [W]hite workers see that the racial pride of minority communities strengthened the coalition.... Racial pride became a vehicle for building worker, and ultimately community, solidarity. (2002: 101)

In short, the organizing effort initially sought to ignore racial issues, but only succeeded when it embraced them.

Guinier and Torres report similar dynamics in a union's effort to organize a K-Mart distribu-tion center in Greensboro, North Carolina. The organizers had found that "the Greensboro plant – the only K-Mart distribution center with a majority nonwhite workforce – received the worst wages and benefits of any center in the country" (2002: 132). Organizers had to figure out how to use the issue of racial discrimination to unite rather than divide workers and the community. They found allies in a group of black ministers that had come together in the civil rights struggles of the 1960s. The ministers argued to their parishioners that "K-Mart's refusal to pay a living wage was a threat to all those in Greensboro who wanted to build a sustainable community" (2002: 133). With the problem thus framed, the union led white workers and community members to join in the ministers' weekly protests on K-Mart's property and in the resulting arrests for trespass. A turning point came when K-Mart sued to enjoin the protests, but named only black workers and black ministers. Against that bid to divide-and-conquer, the black community reached out to white workers and their ministers, who promptly held a news conference to ask why they, too, were not sued for their participation in the protests.

Guinier and Torres argue that the black community's experience of racial injustice was a resource in mobilizing the wider community, and that racializing the struggle in that way was a key to broadening and energizing it. They argue that racial injustice can serve as a kind of "miner's canary," a powerful indicator of broader economic injustice and a potential catalyst for cross-racial action. In the context of union organizing, shared workplace experiences and

---

[20] Fantasia makes this point (1988: 79–80).
[21] These efforts also face legal constraints (Crain 2002).

concerns supply a foundation for the challenging project of building solidarity that both draws on and transcends racial identity, and that puts the weight of economic interests behind moral appeals. Given the prevalence of racial injustice in labor markets, it is heartening that it can sometimes be a resource in cross-racial struggles for economic justice.

Undoubtedly, uplifting stories of solidarity across lines of social division could be countered with innumerable stories of hostility or exclusion, sometimes with active union support. The potential for building cross-racial ties is no guarantee of its realization. Still, that potential rests on firm ground. Trade unions that seek to organize or represent racially mixed workforces have compelling reasons to cultivate the potential for unity and to overcome divisions that are all too easy for employers to exploit. In organizing campaigns and disputes with management, both the unions' institutional interests and the workers' shared material interests often depend on holding together against divide-and-conquer tactics and damaging divisions and defections.

Collective bargaining – both the process and the results – could also help to unify workers and dampen divisions. Job security and seniority rights played that role, while also yielding long job tenures and enduring co-worker relationships. To be sure, in the early years of desegregation, collectively bargained seniority rights privileged incumbent white workers over newer black and Hispanic entrants; and unions fought hard in courts and legislatures to preserve those seniority rights. But over the longer haul, both seniority and job-security rights served as a hedge against discrimination by sharply constraining the role of subjective employer judgments in discipline, discharges, and promotions. They tended to align worker interests, minimize interpersonal competition, and limit managers' ability to target union activists, favor compliant workers, and sow divisions (Freeman & Medoff 1984: 21, 104–107; Kochan et al. 1986: 37–39; Wachter & Cohen 1988: 1362). That was crucial in maintaining the solidarity that was required to carry off or threaten a strike; and those periodic episodes of collective mobilization in turn generated experiences and memories of shared sacrifice that further bonded workers to each other.

Where union membership is itself diverse, internal union politics afford additional occasions for intergroup cooperation and compromise. Beyond their role within the workplace, unions are among the intermediate associations that are glorified and, in their decline, mourned by those who emphasize their critical role in the stability and vitality of democratic governance (Kohler 1993, 1995; Putnam 2000). Most of those associations are unregulated by, or even constitutionally shielded from, laws promoting equal treatment and democratic governance. For historical reasons, however, US labor law regulates both union membership practices and internal union politics to a degree that is unique among Western democracies (Estlund 2015: 202–203, 211). The statutory "bill of rights" for union members,[22] along with unions' duty of fair representation[23] and the legal prohibition of union discrimination,[24] all aim to protect minority groups and dissident voices and to fortify internal union democracy.

Unions at their best can promote intergroup connectedness at the workplace and within unions, and can make mutually reinforcing moral and material arguments for intergroup solidarity. That can make them especially credible proponents of racial inclusion and progressive class-based policies and politics beyond the workplace. Union appeals for cross-racial solidarity in political organizing and at the ballot box – especially when those appeals resonate with workers' experiences of cooperation and shared grievances, gains, and losses in their

[22] Labor-Management Reporting and Disclosure [Landrum-Griffin] Act, [LMRDA], 29 USC §411.
[23] Originally read into the Railway Labor Act by the Supreme Court in *Steele* v. *Louisville & Nashville RR Co.*, 323 US 192 (1944).
[24] See Title VII of the Civil Rights Act of 1964, 42 USC §2000e-2(c).

working lives – are far more likely to resonate with workers than are the more abstract moral appeals of liberal elites.

REFLECTIONS ON SOLIDARITY AND DEMOCRACY IN AN ERA OF SHRINKING UNIONS AND FRACTURED WORKPLACES

The question is whether all this amounts to a mournful eulogy for a dying order – an order that was in fact just coalescing when it began to collapse. In principle, the combination of public regulation and industrial relations practices could have worked out well for workers of color as well as for cross-racial politics. Litigation, along with federal government pressure on contractors to desegregate, opened good jobs to black workers in heavily unionized manufacturing and transportation sectors (Blumrosen 1984: 317–320; Donohue & Heckman 1991a, 1991b; Heckman & Verkerke 1990). Increasingly diverse workforces came within the ambit of organized labor and the protections of the traditional collective bargaining model, which tended to reinforce solidarity, fairness, and equality, as well as long-term ties among co-workers. But the felicitous convergence of civil rights and trade union aims had barely begun to take hold when deindustrialization started to ravage its economic foundations, taking a devastating toll on black male employment as well as union strength (Rosenfeld 2014: 100–130; see also Wilson 1996, 1999: 46–50).

The problems go well beyond the blue-collar fields of manufacturing and transportation. Even as workplaces and unions became more diverse and integrated beginning after the 1960s, work in other ways became less conducive to the formation of strong workplace bonds than it was in the factories and the large integrated organizations that dominated twentieth century labor markets. Major workplace trends since the 1970s – deindustrialization, the decline of job tenures and the rise of contingency and precarity, the "fissuring" of vertically integrated firms and the rise of extended supply chains,[25] the disintegration of internal labor markets, and the rise of "gig" work and independent contracting – all tend to undercut the density and durability of co-worker ties (Katz & Krueger 2016).[26]

Those same labor market trends also contributed along several vectors to the decline of unions. Thinner and shorter-term ties between co-workers provide a poorer social medium for building and sustaining unions. The decline of manufacturing struck at the historic heartland of the labor movement, and unions never managed to make up for the membership losses by organizing the lower-skilled, higher-turnover service sectors. Deregulation of heavily-unionized sectors like transportation and communications, fissurization, and the liberalization of trans-national trade and capital flows, have all conspired to both motivate and enable firms to avoid the costs and constraints of unionization. Faced with more competitive product markets and more demanding capital markets, managers fought back against the traditional union model – with its intentional rigidities and constraints on managerial discretion, not to mention generous wage and benefit packages – with escalated campaigns of union avoidance and union suppression (Katz & Darbishire 2000). Weak and ossified labor laws, which unions and their allies fought in vain to reform, did too little to constrain them. A rising tide of anti-union laws (such as

[25] "Fissuring," as used by David Weil, encompasses a variety of mechanisms by which firms increasingly outsource labor-intensive phases of production and distribution to contractors (Weil 2017).
[26] Other data suggest less dramatic changes in job tenure and "self-employment," (Bureau of Labor Statistics 2018; Pew Research Center 2016; Applebaum et al. 2019).

right-to-work laws) and legal rulings (like the Supreme Court's *Janus* decision)[27] compounded unions' troubles.

All in all, it is hard to avoid a depressing dual conclusion: common work has become a less fertile source of the sturdy co-worker bonds that can bridge racial and ethnic divisions, while unions have grown smaller, weaker, and less capable of nurturing those workplace bonds into forms of cross-racial solidarity that can carry beyond the workplace into the political domain. Both the fragmentation of work and the decline of unions have been devastating for workers' economic security and well-being. The impact of those trends on democratic discourse is more diffuse, but it is profound. Trade unions' waning ability to propound a credible, racially-inclusive, cross-class political message makes it more likely that divisive ethno-nationalist appeals will continue to poison our politics, and more challenging to build political support for progressive pro-worker policies.

One might find reasons for hope on several fronts: a recent uptick in worker activism and strikes,[28] including in sectors that have not historically been unionized;[29] the turn toward organizing and bargaining "for the common good" and in alliance with constituencies beyond the workplace (Gupta et al. 2019); the rise of organizing outside the traditional "exclusive representation" model (Andrias 2016; Oswalt 2019); among those, the Fight for Fifteen and its alliance with Black Lives Matter activists (Elk 2018); and renewed debate over structural changes in the law and institutions governing work and the links between economic and racial inequality (Bazelon 2020; Greenhouse 2020a; Labor and Worklife Program 2019). And that is apart from growing awareness of the environmental and economic unsustainability of markets run amok (Chomsky 2019; Taylor 2019). Hopeful signs emerged as well amidst the converging crises of public health and police violence that marked 2020. That summer's explosion of cross-racial protests over police killings might be the harbinger of a more profound reckoning with the roots of racial subordination, and an anti-racist backlash against the racism that Trump has nurtured (Klein 2020b; Worland 2020).

These recent developments point in a more optimistic direction than much of this chapter, and are deserving of much more attention than I can give them here. My main point is that organizations grounded in the experience of shared work have a distinctive and perhaps irreplaceable role to play in shifting the political and cultural climate in the direction of cross-racial comity and cooperation. Many workers and their allies are committed to the necessary though difficult project of building and rebuilding workers' organizations that can credibly propound and amplify a political message of inclusive and sustainable economic justice both to the broader polity and to their own constituents. To turn Margaret Thatcher's famed phrase on its head, "there is no alternative"[30] for those aiming to right the listing, embattled ship of American democracy.

REFERENCES

Alesina, Alberto, and Edward Glaeser. 2004. *Fighting Poverty in the US and Europe*. Oxford: Oxford University Press.

Alesina, Alberto, Edward Glaeser, and Bruce Sacerdote. 2001. "Why Doesn't the United States Have a European-Style Welfare State?" NBER Working Paper No. 8524. National Bureau of Economics Research, Cambridge, MA, October 2001. www.nber.org/papers/w8524

---

[27] *Janus* v. AFSCME, Council 31, 138 S. Ct. 2448 (2018).
[28] After years of declining strike levels, the number of strikes and strikers surged in 2018 and 2019 to levels last seen in the 1980s (Scheiber 2019; Shierholz & Poydock 2020).
[29] Many of those efforts have been led by young workers (Greenhouse, 2020b).
[30] The phrase "there is no alternative," or "TINA," was used by Margaret Thatcher "to mean that certain debates were over, especially debates over capitalism" (Laura Flanders 2013).

Alesina, Alberto, Johann Harnoss, and Hillel Rapoport. 2013. *Immigration, Diversity, and Economic Prosperity*. London: Vox CEPR Policy Portal. https://voxeu.org/article/immigration-diversity-and-eco nomic-prosperity

Anderson, Elizabeth. 2017. *Private Government: How Employers Rule Our Lives*. Princeton, NJ: Princeton University Press.

Andrias, Kate. 2016. "The New Labor Law," *Yale Law Journal* 126, 1: 2–100.

Applebaum, Eileen, Arne Kalleberg, and Hye Jin Rho. 2019. *Nonstandard Work Arrangements and Older Americans, 2005–2017*. Washington, DC: Economic Policy Institute. www.epi.org/publication/non standard-work-arrangements-and-older-americans-2005-2017/

Arendt, Hannah. 1998. *The Human Condition*. 2nd ed. Chicago: University of Chicago Press.

Autor, David, David Dorn, Gordon Hanson, and Kavesh Majlesi. 2017. "Importing Political Polarization: The Electoral Consequences of Rising Trade Exposure." Working Paper No. 22637. National Bureau of Economics Research, Cambridge, MA, September 2016, revised December 2017. www.nber.org/papers/w22637

Bazelon, Emily, 2020. "Why Are Workers Struggling? Because Labor Law Is Broken," *The New York Times* (February 19, 2020), www.nytimes.com/interactive/2020/02/19/magazine/labor-law-unions.html

Blumrosen, Alfred W. 1984. "The Law Transmission System and the Southern Jurisprudence of Employment Discrimination," *Industrial Relations Law Journal* 6, 3: 313–352.

Borjas, George J. 1999. "Immigration and Welfare Magnets," *Journal of Labor Economics* 17, 4: 607–637.

Briggs, Xavier de Souza. 2007. "'Some of My Best Friends Are...': Interracial Friendships, Class, and Segregation in America," *City and Community* 6, 4: 263–290.

Bureau of Labor Statistics. 2018. *Contingent and Alternative Work Arrangements-May 2017*. www.bls.gov/news.release/pdf/conemp.pdf

    2019. *American Time Use Survey – 2018 Results*. Table 8a. www.bls.gov/news.release/archives/atus_06192019.pdf

Carnes, Nicholas, and Noam Lupu, 2017. "It's Time to Bust the Myth: Most Trump Voters Were Not Working Class," *Washington Post* (June 5, 2017), www.washingtonpost.com/news/monkey-cage/wp/2017/06/05/its-time-to-bust-the-myth-most-trump-voters-were-not-working-class/

Chomsky, Aviva. 2019. "Sorry Conservatives – Unions Do Support the Green New Deal," *The Nation* (August 7, 2019), www.thenation.com/article/archive/unions-support-green-new-deal/

Cohen, Jean L. 2019. "Populism and the Politics of Resentment," *Jus Cogens* 1, 1: 5–39.

Cohen, Jean L., and Andrew Arato. 1992. *Civil Society and Political Theory*. Cambridge, MA: MIT Press.

Cohen, Lizbeth. 1990. *Making a New Deal: Industrial Workers in Chicago 1919–1939*. Cambridge: Cambridge University Press.

Cohn, Nate. 2017. "The Obama-Trump Voters Are Real. Here's What They Think," *The New York Times* (August 15, 2017), www.nytimes.com/2017/08/15/upshot/the-obama-trump-voters-are-real-heres-what-they-think.html

Collier, Paul. 2018. *The Future of Capitalism*. New York: HarperCollins.

    2019. *Exodus: How Migration Is Changing Our World*. Oxford: Oxford University Press.

Costa, Dora L., and Matthew E. Kahn. 2003. "Civic Engagement and Community Heterogeneity: An Economist's Perspective," *Perspectives on Politics* 1, 1: 103–111.

Cox, Daniel, Rachel Lienesch, and Robert P. Jones. 2017. *Beyond Economics: Fears of Cultural Displacement Pushed the White Working Class to Trump*. Washington, DC: Public Religion Research Institute. www.prri.org/research/white-working-class-attitudes-economy-trade-immigration-election-donald-trump/

Crain, Marion. 2002. "Whitewashed Labor Law, Skinwalking Unions," *Berkeley Journal of Employment and Labor Law* 23, 2: 211–258.

Cramer, Katherine J. 2016. *The Politics of Resentment*. Chicago: University of Chicago Press.

Darling-Hammond, Sean, Rodolfo Mendoza-Denton, and Randy Lee. "Interracial Contact at Work: Can Workplace Diversity Reduce Bias?" *SSRN* (April 2019) https://papers.ssrn.com/sol3/papers.cfm?abstract_id=3379069

Donohue, John J., and James J. Heckman. 1991a. "Continuous Versus Episodic Change: The Impact of Civil Rights Policy on the Economic Status of Blacks," *Journal of Economic Literature* 29, 4: 1603–1643.

    1991b. "The Law and Economics of Racial Discrimination in Employment: Re-Evaluating Federal Civil Rights Policy," *Georgetown Law Journal* 79: 1619–1657.

Ehrenberg, John. 1999. *Civil Society: The Critical History of an Idea*. New York: New York University Press.

Elk, Mike. 2018. "Justice in the Factory: How Black Lives Matter Breathed New Life Into Unions," *The Guardian* (February 10, 2018), www.theguardian.com/us-news/2018/feb/10/black-lives-matter-labor-unions-factory-workers-unite

Estlund, Cynthia. 2003. *Working Together: How Workplace Bonds Strengthen a Diverse Democracy*. Oxford: Oxford University Press.

  2015. "Are Unions a Constitutional Anomaly?" *Michigan Law Review* 114, 2: 169–234.

  2018. "Rethinking Autocracy at Work," *Harvard Law Review* 131, 3: 795–826.

Fantasia, Rick. 1988. *Cultures of Solidarity*. Berkeley: University of California Press.

Farber, Henry S., Daniel Herbst, Ilyana Kuziemko, and Suresh Naidu. 2018. "Unions and Inequality Over the Twentieth Century: New Evidence from Survey Data," NBER Working Paper No. 24587. National Bureau of Economics Research, Cambridge, MA, May 2018. www.nber.org/papers/w24587

Flanders, Laura. 2013. "At Thatcher's Funeral, Bury TINA, Too," *The Nation*. (April 12, 2013). www.thenation.com/article/archive/thatchers-funeral-bury-tina-too/

Fishkin, Joseph, and William Forbath. 2014. "The Anti-Oligarchy Constitution," *Boston University Law Review* 94, 3: 669–696.

Forbath, William E. 1991. *Law and the Shaping of the American Labor Movement*. Cambridge, MA: Harvard University Press.

Freeman, Richard, and James Medoff. 1984. *What Do Unions Do?* New York: Basic Books.

Frey, William H. 2015. *Diversity Explosion: How New Racial Demographics Are Remaking America*. Washington, DC: Brookings Institution.

Frymer, Paul. 2008. *Black and Blue: African Americans, the Labor Movement, and the Decline of the Democratic Party*. Princeton, NJ: Princeton University Press.

Fung, Archon. 2003. "Associations and Democracy: Between Theories, Hopes, and Realities," *Annual Review of Sociology* 29: 515–539.

Garden, Charlotte, and Nancy Leong. 2013. "'So Closely Intertwined': Labor and Racial Solidarity," *George Washington University Law Review* 81, 4: 1135–1210.

Gest, Justin. 2016. *The New Minority*. Oxford: Oxford University Press.

Goldfield, Michael. 1993. "Race and the CIO: The Possibilities for Racial Egalitarianism during the 1930s and 1940s," *International Labor and Working-Class History* 44 (Fall): 1–32.

Guinier, Lani, and Gerald Torres. 2002. *The Miner's Canary: Enlisting Race, Resisting Power, Transforming Democracy*. Cambridge, MA: Harvard University Press.

Gupta, Sarita, Stephen Lerner, and Joseph A. McCartin. 2019. "Why the Labor Movement Has Failed – And How to Fix It," *Boston Review* (June 06, 2019), http://bostonreview.net/forum/sarita-gupta-stephen-lerner-joseph-mccartin-why-labor-movement-has-failed%E2%80%94and-how-fix-it

Greenhouse, Steven. 2020a. "Overhaul US Labor Laws to Boost Workers' Power, New Report Urges," *The Guardian* (January 23, 2020), www.theguardian.com/us-news/2020/jan/23/overhaul-us-labor-laws-unions-workers-power-report

  2020b. "The Faces of a New Union Movement," *The New Yorker* (February 28, 2020).

Habermas, Jürgen. 1996. *Between Facts and Norms*. Cambridge, MA: MIT Press.

Haney-López, Ian. 2013. *Dog Whistle Politics: How Coded Racial Appeals Have Reinvented Racism and Wrecked the Middle Class*. Oxford: Oxford University Press.

Hawkins, Stacy L. 2017. "The Long Arc of Diversity Bends towards Equality: Deconstructing the Progressive Critique of Workplace Diversity Efforts," *University of Maryland Law Journal of Race, Religion, Gender, and Class* 17, 1: 61–116.

Heckman, James J., and J. Hoult Verkerke. 1990. "Racial Disparity and Employment Discrimination Law: An Economic Perspective," *Yale Law and Policy Review* 8, 2: 276–298.

Hochschild, Jennifer L., Velsa M. Weaver, and Traci R. Burch. 2012. *Creating a New Racial Order*. Princeton, NJ: Princeton University Press.

Ingraham, Christopher. 2016. "Two New Studies Find Racial Anxiety Is the Biggest Driver of Support for Trump," *Washington Post* (June 6, 2016), www.washingtonpost.com/news/wonk/wp/2016/06/06/racial-anxiety-is-a-huge-driver-of-support-for-donald-trump-two-new-studies-find/

Issacharoff, Samuel. 2018. "Democracy's Deficits," *University of Chicago Law Review* 85, 2: 485–519.

Iverson, Torben, and David Soskice. 2015. "Information, Inequality, and Mass Polarization: Ideology in Advanced Democracies," *Comparative Political Studies* 48, 13: 1781–1813.

Jäntti, Markus, Gerald Jaynes, and John E. Roemer. 2014. "The Double Role of Ethnic Heterogeneity in Explaining Welfare-State Generosity," Cowles Foundation Discussion Paper No. 1972. Cowles Foundation for Economic Research, New Haven, CT, December 2014. https://cowles.yale.edu/sites/default/files/files/pub/d19/d1972.pdf

Judis, John B. 2016. *The Populist Explosion: How the Great Recession Transformed American and European Politics*. New York: Columbia Global Reports.

Katz, Harry C., and Owen Darbishire. 2000. *Converging Divergences: Worldwide Changes in Employment Systems*. Ithaca, NY: ILR Press.

Katz, Lawrence F., and Alan B. Krueger. 2016. "The Rise and Nature of Alternative Work Arrangements in the United States," NBER Working Paper No. 22667. National Bureau of Economics Research, Cambridge, MA, September 2016. www.nber.org/papers/w22667.pdf

Kaushal, Neeraj. 2005. "New Immigrants' Location Choices: Magnets without Welfare," *Journal of Labor Economics* 23, 1: 59–80.

Kerrissey, Jasmine, and Evan Schofer. 2013. "Union Membership and Political Participation in the United States," *Social Forces* 91, 3: 895–928.

Kim, Soohan, Alexandra Kalev, and Frank Dobbin. 2012. "Progressive Corporations at Work: The Case of Diversity Programs," *NYU Review of Law and Social Change* 36, 2: 171–213.

Klein, Ezra. 2020a. *Why We're Polarized*. New York: Simon & Schuster.

    2020b. "The Ezra Klein Show: Why Ta-Nehisi Coates Is Hopeful," Vox (June 5, 2020), www.vox.com/2020/6/5/21279530/ta-nehisi-coates-ezra-klein-show-george-floyd-police-brutality-trump-biden

Kochan, Tomas A., Harry C. Katz, and Robert B. McKersie. 1986. *The Transformation of American Industrial Relations*. New York: Basic Books.

Kohler, Thomas C. 1993. "Individualism and Communitarianism at Work," *BYU Law Review* 1993, 2: 727–741.

    1995. "Civic Virtue at Work: Unions as Seedbeds of the Civic Virtues," *Boston College Law Review* 36, 2: 279–304.

Kornblum, William. 1974. *Blue Collar Community*. Chicago: University of Chicago Press.

Labor and Worklife Program, Harvard Law School. 2019. *Clean Slate for Worker Power: Building a Just Economy and Democracy*. Cambridge, MA: Harvard Law School.

Lamont, Michèle, Bo Yun Park, and Elena Ayala-Hurtado. 2017. "Trump's Electoral Speeches and His Appeal to the American White Working Class," *British Journal of Sociology* 68, supplement S1: S153–S180.

Lee, Sophia Z. 2014. *The Workplace Constitution from the New Deal to the New Right*. Cambridge: Cambridge University Press.

Leong, Nancy. 2013. "Racial Capitalism," *Harvard Law Review* 126, 8: 2151–2226.

Lipset, Seymour Martin. 1959. "Democracy and Working-Class Authoritarianism," *American Sociological Review* 24, 4: 482–501.

Llewellyn, Karl. 1957. "What Law Cannot Do for Inter-Racial Peace," *Villanova Law Review* 30, 1: 30–36.

Marshall, F. Ray. 1965. *The Negro and Organized Labor*. New York: Wiley.

    1968. "The Negro in Southern Unions," in Julius Jacobson, ed. *The Negro and the American Labor Movement*. Garden City, NY: Anchor Books, 1968, pp. 128–154.

McUsic, Molly S., and Michael Selmi. 1997. "Postmodern Unions: Identity Politics in the Workplace (An Essay)," *Iowa Law Review* 82, 5: 1339–1374.

Mill, John Stuart. 2009. *Considerations on Representative Government*. Auckland: The Floating Press. First Published 1861 by Parker, Son, and Bourn (London).

Moffit, Benjamin. 2016. *The Global Rise of Populism*. Redwood City, CA: Stanford University Press.

Monnat, Shannon M., and David L. Brown. 2017. "More than a Rural Revolt: Landscapes of Despair and the 2016 Presidential Election," *Journal of Rural Studies* 55: 227–236.

Müller, Jan-Werner. 2016. *What Is Populism?* Philadelphia: University of Pennsylvania Press.

Nussbaum, Karen. 2019. "Unions and Democracy," *Labor Studies Journal* 44, 4: 365–372.

Oswalt, Michael M. 2019. "Alt-Bargaining," *Law and Contemporary Problems* 82, 3: 89–139.

Parker, Kim, Juliana Horowitz, Anna Brown, Richard Fry, D'Vera Cohn, and Ruth Igielnik. 2018. "What Unites and Divides Urban, Suburban, and Rural Communities," Pew Research Center, Washington, DC, May 2018. www.pewsocialtrends.org/2018/05/22/what-unites-and-divides-urban-suburban-and-rural-communities/

Pain, Paromita, and Gina Masullo Chen. 2019. "The President Is In: Public Opinion and the Presidential Use of Twitter," *Social Media + Society* 5, 2: 87–96.

Paluck, Elizabeth Levy, Seth A. Green, and Donald P. Green. 2019. "The Contact Hypothesis Reevaluated," *Behavioural Public Policy* 3, 2: 129–158.

Pew Research Center. 2016. *The State of American Jobs*. www.pewsocialtrends.org/2016/10/06/1-changes-in-the-american-workplace/

Pope, James Gray. 2016. "Why Is There No Socialism in the United States? Law and the Racial Divide in the American Working Class, 1676–1964," *Texas Law Review* 94, 7: 1555–1590.

Post, Robert C. 1991. "Racist Speech, Democracy, and the First Amendment," *William and Mary Law Review* 32, 2: 267–327.

Purdy, Jedediah. 2017. "Wealth and Democracy," in Jack Knight and Melissa Schwartzberg, eds. *Wealth – Nomos LVIII*. New York: New York University Press, pp. 235–260.

Putnam, Robert. 2000. *Bowling Alone: The Collapse and Revival of American Community*. New York: Simon & Schuster.

Reich, Robert B. 2020. *The System: Who Rigged It, How We Fix It*. New York: Penguin Random House.

Rodrik, Dani. 2018. "Populism and the Economics of Globalization," *Journal of International Business and Policy* 1, 1-2: 12–33.

Rosenfeld, Jake. 2014. *What Unions No Longer Do*. Cambridge, MA: Harvard University Press.

Scheiber, Noam. 2019. "In a Strong Economy, Why Are So Many Workers on Strike?" *The New York Times* (Oct. 19, 2019), www.nytimes.com/2019/10/19/business/economy/workers-strike-economy.html

Scholzman, Kay Lehman, Sidney Verba, and Henry E. Brady. 2012. *The Unheavenly Chorus*. Princeton, NJ: Princeton University Press.

Shierholz, Heidi, and Margaret Poydock. 2020. *Continued Surge in Strike Activity Signals Worker Dissatisfaction and Wage Growth*. Washington, DC: Economic Policy Institute. www.epi.org/publication/continued-surge-in-strike-activity/

Sinyai, Clayton. 2019. "Schools of Democracy," *Labor Studies Journal* 44, 4: 373–381.

Sitraman, Ganesh. 2017. *The Crisis of the Middle-Class Constitution: Why Economic Inequality Threatens Our Republic*. New York: Penguin Random House.

Smith, Stephen. 2019. *The Scramble for Europe*. Medford, MA: Polity Press.

Stiglitz, Joseph E. 2012. *The Price of Inequality: How Today's Divided Society Endangers Our Future*. New York: W. W. Norton & Company.

2015. *Rewriting the Rules of the American Economy*. New York: W. W. Norton & Company.

2018. *Globalization and Its Discontents Revisited*. New York: W. W. Norton & Company.

Taylor, Matthew. 2019. "Trade Unions Around the World Support Global Climate Strike," *The Guardian* (September 19, 2019), www.theguardian.com/environment/2019/sep/19/trade-unions-around-the-world-support-global-climate-strike

Tomaskovic-Deney, Donald, Kevin Stainbeck, Tiffany Taylor, Catherine Zimmer, Corre Robinson, and Tricia McTague. 2006. "Documenting Desegregation: Segregation in American Workplaces by Race, Ethnicity, and Sex, 1966–2003," *American Sociological Review* 71, 4: 565–588.

Tropp, Thomas, and Lind Pettigrew. 2006. "A Meta-Analytic Test of Intergroup Contact Theory," *Journal of Personality and Social Psychology* 90, 5: 751–783.

Wachter, Michael L., and George M. Cohen. 1988. "The Law and Economics of Collective Bargaining: An Introduction and Application to the Problems of Subcontracting, Partial Closure, and Relocation," *University of Pennsylvania Law Review* 136, 5: 1349–1417.

Wang, Tova. 2020. "Union Impact on Voter Participation – And How to Expand It," Harvard Kennedy School Ash Center for Democratic Governance and Innovation, Cambridge, MA, June 2020. https://ash.harvard.edu/files/ash/files/300871_hvd_ash_union_impact_v2.pdf

Weil, David. 2017. *The Fissured Workplace*. Cambridge, MA: Harvard University Press.

Wilson, William Julius. 1996. *When Work Disappears: The World of the New Urban Poor*. New York: Alfred A. Knopf.

1999. *The Bridge Over the Racial Divide*. Berkeley: University of California Press.

Worland, Justin. 2020. "America's Long Overdue Awakening to Systemic Racism," *Time* (June 11, 2020), https://time.com/5851855/systemic-racism-america/

Zavodny, Madeline. 1999. "Determinants of Recent Immigrants Locational Choices," *International Migration Review* 33, 4: 1014–1030.

11

Unions Can Help White Workers Become More Racially Tolerant

Paul Frymer, Jacob M. Grumbach, and Thomas Ogorzalek

> Probably the greatest and most effective effort toward interracial understanding among the working masses has come about through the trade unions. The organization of the CIO in 1935 was an attempt to bring the mass of workers into the union movement as contrasted with the AFL effort to unionize only the skilled workers of industry. As a result, numbers of men like those in the steel and automotive industries have been thrown together, black and white, as fellow workers striving for the same objects. There has been on this account an astonishing spread of interracial tolerance and understanding. Probably no movement in the last 30 years has been so successful in softening race prejudice among the masses.
>
> (W. E. B. Du Bois 1948: 236)

To many progressives, the labor movement has long embodied the vehicle with which to establish and harness not just class consciousness and working-class solidarity, but an organizational bridge that can cross the nation's longstanding and deeply entrenched racial divisions. In a nation with a political system marked by its halting and incomplete development of a social welfare state and the longstanding dominance of corporate power, the prospect of a racially and ethnically diverse working-class coalition could serve as the backbone of a stalwart electoral coalition promoting greater equality in economy and society (e.g. Hacker & Pierson 2011; Haider 2018; Marable 2009; Reed 2013).

The history of the labor movement in the United States is replete with powerful examples of when such coalitions of workers have united to champion democracy and economic justice (e.g. Arnesen 1991; Biondi 2006; Jones 1998; Kelley 1990; McLean 2008). The above epigraph by the famous civil rights activist, writer, and social scientist, W. E. B. Du Bois, well reflects this aspiration and possibility. Writing during the 1940s, Du Bois saw in the relatively new, politically aggressive, and racially progressive union, the Congress of Industrial Organizations (CIO), a way to mobilize a multi-racial workforce around its strategic interests to fight employer exploitation and pass state and federal laws that would expand workplace rights. CIO organizing drives at the time such as Operation Dixie targeted the overwhelmingly non-unionized workforces in southern states, including large numbers of African American workers (e.g. Goldfield 1993; Griffith 1988; Honey 1992; Korstad & Lichtenstein 1988). The CIO's efforts were part of a larger movement of workers, students, religious organizations, and progressive activists in the early to mid-twentieth century fighting against racial discrimination and prejudice. Combined, these efforts spearheaded a fundamental transformation of public opinion in the nation around civil rights and racial toleration, and a partisan realignment (Schickler 2016). Representing the majority of unions, the merged AFL-CIO served as a legislative liaison in the 1950s and '60s for many aspects of civil rights policy, providing a critical funding arm for the NAACP and a leading interest group in the fight for the passage of the 1964 Civil Rights Act.

Since the Civil Rights Era, the labor movement's presence and authority in the workplace and American politics has declined significantly. Labor unions currently represent merely 10 percent of workers, in sharp contrast with the 1950s when more than a third of workers were unionized (Goldfield & Bromsen 2013). The early CIO's aspirations to mobilize southern workers produced only mixed results and, to this day, the southern United States remains the region with the lowest rate of union members, at just 5 percent, with further organizing stymied by anti-union "right to work" laws in those states (Garcia 2019). Labor's influence within the Democratic Party has also notably declined, as the party leadership has not only allowed labor law to ossify over the last half century, it has notably shifted toward more neo-liberal policies to enhance and expand global trade and corporate power in non-unionized work sectors such as the expanding gig economy (Estlund 2002; Prasad 2006; Stein 1998).

Despite its history of civil rights activism, the labor movement also has a problem with racism within its ranks of workers. This problem is not new, as we will discuss in greater length below, but it has received renewed attention since the 2016 election of Donald Trump, a candidate who promoted a populist, often pro-white and anti-immigrant agenda that attracted a majority of the white working class vote and a significant minority of white union members. In the exceedingly close 2016 election, many of these voters coming from the declining steel, coal, and auto industries of the Midwest proved to be decisive in turning those states toward Trump and enabling him to win the Electoral College. The protests in 2020 promoting Black Lives Matter (BLM) have further put unions in a controversial place between civil rights and labor activists, with BLM supporters demanding the expulsion of police unions from the AFL-CIO and other national unions, and most union leaders promoting slower reform efforts through the collective bargaining process.

In this paper, we discuss both the promise and the difficulties of unions in the promotion of greater racial justice, and greater racial toleration among workers. Unions are critical in many ways to the promotion of civil rights in the workplace and society. They are a chief mobilizer of voters for civil rights causes as well as leading advocates within the legislative branches for political reform. Union contracts provide protections for workers against unjust termination that serve to strongly aid in the fight against discriminatory behavior by employers in the hiring, promotion, and termination process. Unions provide their members greater access to benefits (Hertel-Fernandez & Gould-Werth 2020), as well as an important wage boost, particularly for minority workers compared to their nonunionized counterparts. In 2019, African American union members made nearly $200 more per week than non-union workers; unionized Latino workers made $270 more per week than nonunionized Latino workers (Bureau of Labor Statistics 2020).

Our primary focus here is more specifically on the question of whether unions impact the attitudes that its members have toward questions of civil rights and racial tolerance. Recent work has offered evidence that unions can positively influence the racial attitudes of its membership, and specifically its white members to be more racially tolerant and supportive of civil rights (Frymer & Grumbach 2021). Unions offer unique advantages that can promote greater toleration for civil rights among its members. The workplace is a site that brings people in lengthy and concentrated contact with those of different socioeconomic and demographic backgrounds than just about every other aspect of their daily lives. Unions have always been ideologically allied with challenging societal hierarchies, and have long attracted people who view the labor movement as a leading way of promoting greater tolerance and equality in society. But more practically, union vitality is predicated on attaining and maintaining majorities in the workplace, something that – in today's increasingly diverse work environment – incentivizes unions to actively engage with the socioeconomic divisions within the work community and promote greater toleration and unity. The labor movement's longstanding alliance with the Democratic Party only furthers the degree to which its messaging and engagement incorporates messages of racial toleration and greater coalition building among diverse communities. In this chapter, we will provide longitudinal data that is suggestive of the historical variation that unions play toward promoting further racial tolerance, and the ongoing role that union leadership can offer. Most notably, the activism we are currently seeing from many sectors of the labor movement suggests a meaningful opportunity to work beyond our existing political moment of division, polarization, and seemingly active support for white supremacy among large minorities of the US population.

At the same time, there is nothing inherent in this union activity and effect: all of the positive features just listed can change with different workplace environments, historical contexts, and political alliances. The promise that unions provide further necessitates active participation by labor leaders and activists. And, the challenges these leaders and activists face in promoting racial toleration amongst their members is evident both historically and within many union contexts today – an intersection of roles and actions by employers, union leadership, and union members that can potentially exacerbate existing racial divides as much as they can potentially promote greater toleration.

We begin with an overview of the recent evidence. We then put it in historical context, moving through to the current era. We end with broader organizational reasons why, with the right context, unions are not just significant but unique in their ability to promote diversity in this moment of racial backlash and white populism.

THE PROMISE OF UNIONS IN OUR CURRENT ERA: UNIONS PROMOTE GREATER RACIAL TOLERANCE AND SUPPORT FOR CIVIL RIGHTS POLICIES AMONG WHITE WORKERS

Can the labor movement aid the cause of racial justice and civil rights in America by influencing the attitudes of its rank and file toward civil rights goals and greater tolerance? Recent research shows the profound potential of the labor movement to promote greater racial tolerance among white unionized workers: union membership and the social, organizational, and institutional ties and engagements that come with it, can reduce racial resentment among white workers toward African Americans (Frymer & Grumbach 2021). Drawing on a variety of large national survey datasets, including the novel use of panel data, the research explored the responses among whites who were unionized as opposed to those who were not members of a labor union, examining their responses to different statements about racial equality. For example, one of the four survey questions used to identify people's views towards African Americans asked people to respond to the statement: "It's really a matter of some people not trying hard enough; if blacks would only try harder they could be just as well off as whites." The authors also examined questions that asked respondents about their support for different policies, such as racial preferences in hiring and government action in support of fair treatment in employment, and a broader question about the role that the government should play in improving the social and economic position of African Americans.

In the article, Frymer and Grumbach found compelling and statistically significant evidence that white union members are less likely to have racist attitudes than white workers in similar

TABLE 11.1. *CCES panel results of union membership and racial resentment among whites*

	Outcome: Racial Resentment			
	Model 1	Model 2	Model 3	Model 4
Gained Union Membership	-0.055** (0.018)	-0.055** (0.018)	-0.051** (0.019)	-0.049** (0.018)
Lost Union Membership	0.0002 (0.032)	-0.00001 (0.032)	-0.003 (0.033)	0.009 (0.033)
R. Resentment (t - 1)	0.899*** (0.005)	0.899*** (0.005)	0.884*** (0.005)	0.797*** (0.007)
Party ID (Dem)				-0.124*** (0.005)
Income			0.0004 (0.001)	-0.0005 (0.001)
Female			-0.007 (0.003)	0.002 (0.003)
Age			0.0003* (0.0001)	0.0002 (0.0001)
Education			-0.010*** (0.001)	-0.010*** (0.001)
Constant	0.056*** (0.004)	0.054*** (0.004)	0.084*** (0.012)	0.215*** (0.014)
Year FEs	No	Yes	Yes	Yes
N	10,908	10,908	9,726	9,617
R-squared	0.749	0.749	0.749	0.764
Adj. R-squared	0.749	0.749	0.749	0.764
Residual Std. Error	0.165	0.165	0.165	0.161

***$p < .001$; **$p < .01$; *$p < .05$

industries who are not in a union. Perhaps most notably, with the aid of longitudinal panel data from the 2010s, they compared those who joined unions with those who did not, finding that those who joined a union increased their support for racial tolerance and civil rights by between 4–4.8 percent. Even within a very short time period, unionized respondents showed markedly greater toleration in their preferences on civil rights policies and tolerance towards African Americans (see Table 11.1, reproduced from Frymer & Grumbach 2021: 10).

What explains this dynamic? There are a number of different mechanisms by which unions might promote greater support for civil rights and racial tolerance amongst its members, ranging from structural incentives for union leadership to promote racial equality to the labor movement's institutional ties to the comparatively diverse Democratic Party. In particular, unions provide opportunities for people of different racial backgrounds and identities to not merely work side by side – which may itself relax prejudice through sheer exposure – but to work toward a common goal together, promoting cooperation, and enhancing respect and mutuality across racial lines. In many workplaces, the goal of building a strong union cannot be achieved without diverse workers joining together.

Organizations of all kinds shape their members' political views and broader social attitudes. But unions are unique among non-governmental organizations due to the fact that federal labor law under the National Labor Relations Act requires unions to adopt democratic forms of governance and that, in carrying out the union's collective-bargaining functions, the union has a legal duty to fairly represent all workers in the relevant bargaining unit.[1] Furthermore, unions establish contracts with their employers via collectively bargained agreements that provide just cause protections against termination, enabling further protections against racial and other forms of discrimination in the workplace.

Unions influence their members' political and social preferences through a number of different means, such as exposing them to relevant political knowledge (Kim & Margalit 2017) and increasing interactions with other unionized workers (Ahlquist et al. 2014). Research has shown that direct interactions between a diverse group of workers can promote greater tolerance toward politically distant individuals, leading to interpersonal links that ultimately motivate more encompassing political views (Mutz 2002). Unions' organizational structures can be important for their ability to facilitate political socialization through the dissemination and sharing of political information among workers as well as the mobilization of those workers in union election drives and contract negotiations (Ahlquist & Levi 2013; MacDonald 2020; Rosenfeld 2014; Sobieraj & White 2004).

Most people work to sustain themselves. In an increasingly diverse society, the workplace is often the site with which people interact with others, at least sometimes engaging with people demographically different from themselves. At the very least, such exposure is greater than many voluntary sites of congregating and networking, such as churches, neighborhoods, and many social activities. By extension, the membership of unions, as workforce representatives, is likely to feature a degree of diversity that's higher than in other types of community formations. Unlike other organizational vehicles, unions have incentives to mobilize large numbers within a workforce to maintain their presence; as such, unions frequently pull from disparate backgrounds and encourage those workers to see commonalities. Union leaders need to recruit workers of color in order to achieve majority memberships in racially diversifying labor sectors, and as such have ideological and strategic incentives to mitigate racial resentment among the rank and file in pursuit of organizational maintenance and growth (Rosenfeld & Kleykamp 2012).

As already noted, unions are, by law, democratic institutions (not without warts and complexities, of course) that are required to represent fairly all the workers covered by their contracts. They also provide an organizational space for workers to make collective decisions about how they want their union to be run, and to work together to secure common victories. The more cooperative union members are, the greater unity they will have heading into a workplace struggle, and the greater the eventual reward for all. In that sense, diverse democratic unions can be unique sites of cross-racial cooperation. It is in the active effort at cooperation that people are more likely to confront and challenge their inherited prejudices, find unrecognized common ground, and potentially have their worldview transformed or at least meaningfully shaped.

There is an additional mechanism working to promote greater tolerance and support for civil rights causes among union members. Because of historic institutional and ideological ties to the Democratic Party, union leaders have incentives to encourage support for the party, an organization with its own strategic and ideological incentives. Since the New Deal era, the Democratic Party has been strongly identified with the promotion of civil rights, particularly since its championing of the Civil Rights Act of 1964 and Voting Rights Act of 1965. Since 1964, African Americans have been the most supportive and loyal demographic group within the Democratic Party, typically with rates upwards of 80 and 90 percent for the Democratic

---

[1] The "duty of fair representation" comes from the Supreme Court decision, *Steele* v. *Louisville and Nashville Railroad* (323 US 192, 1944), where African American workers successfully sued their union for racial discrimination, demanding that the union represent all of its workers the same regardless of race.

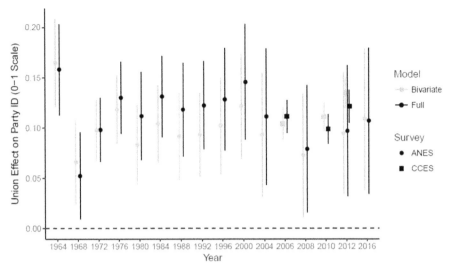

FIGURE 11.1 Union membership and Democratic Party ID over time

candidates (Frymer 1999). Given the close relationship between unions and the Democratic Party, it is not surprising that union membership increases identification in national surveys among respondents with the Democratic Party (see Figure 11.1, reprinted from Frymer & Grumbach 2021, supplemental materials, 3). Indeed, recent research has shown a direct relationship between union members being more likely to identify with the Democratic Party (see Figure 11.2, reprinted from Frymer & Grumbach 2021, supplemental materials, 3; see too, MacDonald 2020, who finds specifically that whites affiliated with labor unions are more likely to identify with the Democratic Party).

The relationship between union membership and party identification is of further consequence. Frymer and Grumbach (2021, supplemental materials, 19, reprinted as Table 11.2) find evidence that in addition to union membership directly promoting greater tolerance on its own, the fact that being a union member promotes greater support for the Democratic Party has additional benefits, notably a further increase in support for racial tolerance and civil rights policy. By this, we mean that because union membership makes identification with the Democratic Party more likely, being a supporter of the Democratic Party leads union members to associate and engage more directly with the rhetoric of the Party, and correspondingly, less so with the Republican Party and its messaging. For instance, in national campaigns, like 2016 and 2020, unions distributed millions of fliers and made millions of phone calls to its membership on behalf of the Democratic Party and its candidates; they further provided direct information about legislation, highlighting the benefits of Democratic Party goals (MacDonald 2020: 3–5). All of this targeting by unions of its members with the messaging of Democratic Party priorities simply compounds and reinforces the benefits already coming from being a union member.

These are promising findings. With an increasingly diversifying workforce, we ought to expect more and more unions to rally around their membership and promote greater toleration and unity. But, again, while there are organizational and statutory benefits of being in a union that serve to promote greater civil rights engagement and racial intolerance, there is nothing inherent in the union ultimately playing this role. Our research findings are from a specific moment in time and are contextually and temporally bounded. We would not expect, for instance, that segregationist unions allied with a pre-civil-rights-era Democratic Party would have the same

TABLE 11.2. *Mediation models of union membership and racial resentment among whites (CCES cross-sectional)*

	Bivariate Model			Full Model	
Est.	95% CI	Relationship	Est.	95% CI	Relationship
-0.053	(-0.058, -0.048)	Union mediated by party ID	-0.048	(-0.052, -0.043)	Union mediated by party ID
-0.003	(-0.011, 0.006)	Union direct relationship	0.006	(-0.002, 0.014)	Union direct relationship
-0.055	(-0.065, -0.046)	Union direct relationship + Union mediated by Party ID	-0.042	(-0.05, -0.032)	Union direct relationship + Union mediated by Party ID

Note: **The relationship between union membership and racial resentment appears mediated by party ID.** Results from mediation analysis using the Baron and Kenny (1986) estimator, implemented with the Mediate package in R (Tingley et al 2014). 95 percent confidence intervals (two-tailed) are estimated with nonparametric bootstrapping.

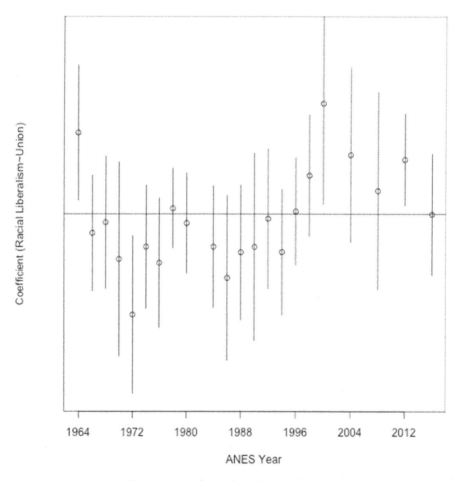

FIGURE 11.2 Bivariate and covariate analysis of racial attitudes among white union members

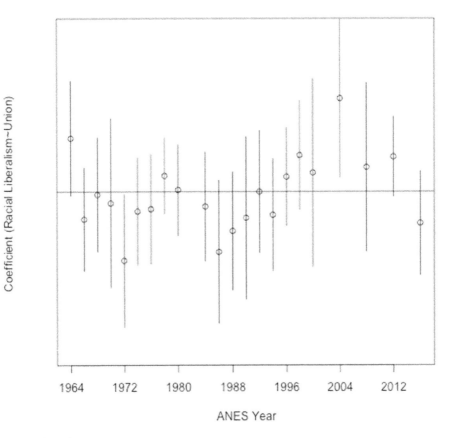

FIGURE 11.2 *(cont.)*

incentives, behavior, and impact as more racially diverse unions allied with the modern-day Democratic Party. Nor would we expect in the modern era that all unions would act and impact equally: Our theory is predicated on the perceived coalitional needs of the union, driven both internally and externally through its alliances with political parties.

Using the American National Election Study (ANES) cumulative data file, we identified those variables that assessed attitudes about race and civil rights for African Americans, including attitudes about racial stereotypes, perceptions of values held by African Americans, government treatment of racial groups, and civil rights policy issues, such as employment and housing non-discrimination. It is important to note that these survey questions vary by year, meaning the question wording is not identical and can lead to meaningful differences in interpretation among respondents, but in each year at least two questions addressed these issues.[2] Moreover, it is also important to note that this data is cross-sectional with less than ideal sample sizes, since we could not benefit from the unique panel data in the manner that Frymer and Grumbach were able to utilize in the 2010s. We estimated each respondent's racial liberalism using

[2] The questions included from the ANES cumulative datafile include: VCF0811, VCF0813–19, VCF0830, VCF9037–42, VCF9270–73, and VCF9275. We recoded each variable with the liberal/anti-racist position at the high end and performed a principal components analysis on each year's pool of respondents to estimate racial liberalism for each of the respondents. The figures plot the relationship between this measure and union membership among white respondents in an OLS regression, in bivariate and multivariate relationships. The overall trends and relationships are largely the same when estimated for members of union household instead of union members.

principal components analysis using all of the variables engaging with racial attitudes from that year's survey. In each year, a clear first factor emerged, which we interpret as "racial liberalism." We then estimated the relationship between union membership and this measure of civil rights liberalism using OLS regression year-by-year in both bivariate and multivariate equations. The multivariate equations include similar covariates to those in Frymer and Grumbach: occupational status, education, family/household income, region, urbanicity, and sex (see Figure 11.2, which displays the bivariate analysis first, followed by the covariate analysis). The results show two distinct phenomena: one, a great deal of variation over time; two, a noted trend since the 1990s towards greater racial liberalism among white union members.

Over time, there is, in general, no consistent or precisely estimated relationship between union membership and civil rights liberalism. But since 1996, the relationship clearly appears to have trended notably more positive over time. Even in 2016, where significant numbers of white workers turned to Trump, the results remain quite muted given the historical context. In 2012, the relationship was at its strongest positive peak, no doubt in part representing the less suggestive intersection of a more diverse and progressive union movement championing and mobilizing directly around civil rights causes with a Democratic Party campaign headed by the nation's first and only African American president, Barack Obama. In the decades before, there's evidence that white union members were more racially liberal than the rest of the public at large.

Unions' taking on the task of promoting greater racial tolerance generally necessitates leadership action, something that historically has been motivated by the active demands of a demographically diverse union membership. Unions in which racially progressive leadership and membership demands are absent will not necessarily become promoters of racial justice. But, as we will see, unions have indeed moved in the direction of racial activism when confronted with memberships' greater diversity and pressure.

PUTTING THE LABOR MOVEMENT'S PROMOTION OF RACIAL JUSTICE IN HISTORICAL PERSPECTIVE

The labor movement has been a pivotal and prominent place for understanding the possibilities and pitfalls of greater racial equality in America. From its very beginnings, the idea that class can overcome racial divisions has attracted many an activist, political leader, and scholar to the potential role of the labor movement. It is centered on a belief that workers of all races will join in the common goal of furthering their class power. Important leaders of both labor and civil rights recognized the need for an alliance: as Martin Luther King famously wrote, "the coalition that can have the greatest impact in the struggle for human dignity here in America is that of the Negro and the forces of labor, because their fortunes are so closely intertwined." Indeed, we can find such aspirational language from many labor and civil rights leaders from A. Philip Randolph of the Brotherhood of Sleeping Car Porters to Walter Reuther of the United Autoworkers and Cesar Chavez of the United Farm Workers, from the president of SEIU Mary Kay Henry to longstanding activist Bill Fletcher Jr.

Labor historians have documented a multitude of examples of both national and local unions forging cross-racial alliances, not just in northern industrial states, but in the heart of the Jim Crow South: the multi-racial Triple Alliance consortium of three New Orleans port worker unions championing its diversity in the course of achieving a huge victory for workers in the 1890s (Arnesen 1991); the Great Riverfront Strike in Memphis combining all black AFL unions with interracial CIO unions (Trotter 2019); the R. J. Reynolds strike in 1940s Salem, North Carolina, where a majority black union with substantial numbers of white members, successfully used a series of work stoppages to achieve significant gains in worker protections (Korstad 2003); and many others.

A large body of literature focuses on the particular role of communist organizing in predominantly black southern workplaces that helped reconfigure both class and race relations within the factories (Biondi 2006; Kelley 1990; Korstad 2003; Nelson 2009). Other scholars emphasize the role of all-black unions in the South, some segregated affiliates with white unions, and others like the porters union, led by A. Philip Randolph – all of which were, in different ways, critical in promoting economic and political change for African Americans (Arnesen 2002; Trotter 2019). These union movements had implications that extended far beyond their worksites. Randolph, for instance, would go on to lead the fight for the first workplace protections in the 1940s with the establishment of the Fair Employment Practices Committee (FEPC). Some of the more progressive union organizations, notably within the CIO, merged their activism into party politics, both within the south and nationally, importantly re-configuring the alliances of the Democratic Party (Korstad 2003; Schickler 2016).

But by no means is this the sole or even primary experience of the labor movement. In *Black Reconstruction in America*, W. E. B. Du Bois (1935: 700) famously wrote that, due to "a carefully planned and slowly evolved method" by demagogues, planters, and capitalists, racism came to so perniciously separate black and white workers in the South that "there probably are not today in the world two groups of workers with practically identical interests who hate and fear each other so deeply and so persistently and who are kept so far apart that neither sees anything of common interest." These workers, faced with an historic opportunity to combine with black workers across the southern region of the country in an act of unified class defiance of employer oppression and coercion, chose to follow their racial status instead of their class status. White workers joined employers in helping cement and entrench a generation of Jim Crow and white supremacy. To Du Bois, white workers' psychological wage of racial privilege was ultimately more powerful than the potential economic wages gained from working-class formation. Du Bois does not simply ascribe this to psychology: capitalism forces workers into competition, and employers further seize on this to promote divisions on grounds that they perceive as advantageous.

But, for much of the labor movement's early history, numerous unions actively advocated for racial discrimination against African Americans and immigrants from Asia and Latin America, notably leading the fight for Chinese Exclusion at the end of the nineteenth century (Mink 1986; Ngai 2004). As Bill Fletcher (2020) has recently written, the labor movement and trade unions were formed during a time of, and actively sustained, national redefinition premised formally and informally on white supremacy: "[T]he acceptance of the racial settler state was part of [the early labor movement's] DNA. It was not just a matter of racial prejudice but the identification of populations who were not acceptable for the union movement." Many union locals and some national unions expressly prohibited non-white workers from membership, and others isolated non-white members into segregated and inferior auxiliary locals (Frymer 2008). It took many decades, for instance, for A. Philip Randolph's influential Brotherhood of Black Porters to be admitted into the AFL (Arnesen 2002; Bates 2001).

In order to gain the congressional majority to enact the National Labor Relations Act (NLRA) in 1935, the Democratic Party needed votes from its southern wing of legislators representing Jim Crow districts (Katznelson 2005). For the most part, the inequalities and discrimination facing black workers did not come up at all in the legislative conversation, and when they were raised in congressional debates in years surrounding the legislation, it was largely in reference to their role as strike breakers and as threats to the rights and wages of white workers. The New Deal legislation ultimately served to protect racial apartheid by limiting labor's reach in the South.

Large numbers of African American and Latino workers were excluded from the protections of the Act, since agricultural and domestic workers were carved out of the Act's definition of employees. Nor did the NLRA contain provisions prohibiting race discrimination by unions, despite protests from civil rights organizations at the time. As mentioned, only with *Steele* v. *Louisville*[3] in 1944, did the Supreme Court mandate that unions had a duty to represent all workers fairly and equally regardless of race. A few years later, the FEPC held hearings around the country that delved into both employer and union hiring practices, particularly within the craft industries. These hearings received national media attention for their findings of deep-seated racism in the sector, angering unions who felt unfairly targeted and scrutinized (Bates 2001; Chen 2009; Sullivan 1996). A number of building trade leaders advocated white supremacy and resistance to civil rights well into the 1970s, with some, like the New York City Sheet Metal Workers, fighting anti-discrimination laws in federal courts into the twenty-first century.

CIO unions were not immune to discrimination within their ranks. Numerous locals engaged in often widespread practices of racial and gender discrimination, and its leaders, while including notable civil rights progressives such as Walter Reuther, also included many of lesser influence and weaker resolve in fighting racial inequality within their unions. Even Reuther's UAW faced concerted protests from African American workers, such as those by the Dodge Revolutionary Workers of the late 1960s and '70s. Few unions avoided Title VII racial discrimination lawsuits in the 1970s, and many felt coerced into signing consent decrees (Frymer 2008; Schiller 2015). Perhaps most notably, the US Steelworkers Union joined as a full partner with employers in, for instance, signing a major consent decree in 1974 admitting fault for a wide range of discriminatory practices against black workers and agreeing to changes in hiring practices, seniority, and future affirmative action policies.

The civil rights movement and partisan realignments of the 1960s in certain ways represented important turning points for American labor. On the one hand, the AFL-CIO was both a leading funder of the NAACP and other civil rights organizations as well an important lobbyist for the 1964 Civil Rights Act, the fundamental statutory achievement of the era, which prohibited discrimination in the workplace on the basis of race and sex, among other categories. The statute's passage, and specifically its Title VII provisions, leveraged the power of the federal government in unprecedented ways against workplace discrimination, leading to signature victories over large corporations and in many cases the unions that represented their workers.

On the other hand, this was also a moment in which the AFL-CIO leadership and rank and file seemingly trended in a conservative direction, especially on the social and racial cleavages that increasingly divided the Democratic Party (Lichtenstein 2001; Minchin 2001). Led by the politically and racially moderate George Meany who both formally endorsed the civil rights movement and publicly distanced himself from many of its substantive implications, the AFL-CIO became identified – fairly or unfairly – in the national public sphere with its more conservative and often racially reactionary construction and craft trades, the supposed "hard hat" protestors who turned to Richard Nixon and the Republican Party, driven by a mix of opposition both to rising economic inequality and to different "rights" movements in the Democratic Party.

Throughout much of the labor movement's history, these fractures were derided by many labor activists as being entirely the fault of employers. Employers, union supporters argued, cynically used African American, Chinese, and Mexican labor (among other groups) to break strikes, divide workforces, and weaken union resolve. This is not wrong: employers did this,

[3] *Steele* v. *Louisville & NRR Co.*, 323 US 192 (1944).

strategically wielding different features of labor law, societal racism, and the fundamental inequities that exist between employer and employee to weaken union movements in both workplace campaigns and national politics (Frymer 2005). Since the prohibition of the closed shop, through which unions had substantially controlled hiring decisions, and the proliferation of right-to-work states, unions have lost much of what modicum of influence they had over the hiring process. Employers, of course, have structural interests in sustaining divisions among workers. Indeed, the historical development of capitalism and the construction and establishment of racial identities and divisions are deeply intertwined, albeit contingent. Capitalism's competitive nature incentivizes not simply economic inequality and hierarchical labor structures but transposes a variety of constructed human differences into explicitly racial categories as a means to enable and maintain those economic hierarchies (Bonacich 1972; Cox 1948; Gilroy 1987; Marable 1999; Reed 2013; Robinson 1983).

But notable numbers of workers and union leaders within the labor movement have contributed and participated in both the establishment and maintenance of these racial divisions. Their views and actions were not just constitutive of capitalism, they were constitutive of white supremacy and the ongoing establishment of a settler state, finding their interests deeply invested in racial inequality (Du Bois 1935; Frymer 2017; Gilroy 1987; Roediger 1991). Any argument, then, that promotes the importance of unions for promoting greater racial equality needs to assess these contradictory features within the historical record. It also must take account of the varying demographics across occupations and sectors, and of the different union leadership and organizational structures that place varying emphases on mobilization and outreach (Milkman & Luce 2019).

All unions, like any organizations, develop historically out of specific political and social circumstances and demographic configurations, and this evolution continues even when union leadership and bureaucracy are entrenched. Moreover, the nature of capitalism – its incessant competition and consequent expansion of product and labor markets – continually reconstructs demographics and inequalities. The modern gig economy, for instance, thrives on an immigrant working class population in a way strikingly different than the building trades of the 1960s. Industry unions evolve too, responding to new demographics and changes in leadership and vision. Construction trades, for instance, once bastions of racially conservative white male workers, have now become more diverse with a governing structure that is frequently progressive and politically active. On the other hand, unions of law enforcement employees, from local police to federal border agents, are, at this moment, in a struggle with civil rights activists over their violence towards minority populations and are using their collective bargaining agreements to resist reform efforts.

But as a, if not the, chief source of resistance to capitalist inequality, unions are constantly searching for new alternatives to confront worker inequality. Recognizing inherent differentials in power between employers and workers and responding to exploitation in the workplace are at the heart of labor's mission. It is not surprising then, especially with the changing demographic workforce in the post-civil rights era, that unions come to engage minority communities and oppose discrimination.

DECLINE AND DIVERSIFICATION OF THE LABOR MOVEMENT IN THE POST-CIVIL RIGHTS ERA

African Americans and Latinos entered the union workforce at much higher rates starting in the 1960s with simultaneous changes to employment discrimination and immigration laws that eased non-white migration to the United States. As mentioned above, civil rights activists within the labor movement pushed unions to make changes, often getting help from the US Department of Justice and federal court litigation to push resistant unions and employers to make structural changes to hiring and promotion (Frymer 2008; Gould 1977; McCann & Lovell 2020; Minchin 2001). Moreover, public employee unions surged at this time; starting in the 1960s, rapidly increasing categories of state and federal government employees, a large proportion of whom were African American, received bargaining rights.

The first EEO data compiled by the Equal Employment Opportunity Commission found many sectors of the labor force, particularly in the building trades, to be overwhelmingly white and male, and the 1970s were filled with lawsuits and resulting consent decrees (Frymer 2008). But by 1983, the first year in which the Bureau of Labor Statistics reported national statistics on the question, the numbers of African Americans and Latinos within the labor movement were quite high, with close to a third of African Americans represented by the labor movement at the time. Over the next few decades, the raw numbers of workers from these racial categories have declined significantly, as have the overall number of union members. The relative percentages of black and Latino workers, however, have continued to climb: more than a third of union members are now non-white, with African Americans the most likely minority group to be represented by unions at 13.8 percent, and African American men represented at 14.7 percent (BLS 2020). The increased presence of minority workers in the labor movement alters the incentives of union leaders looking to find strategies that unify and mobilize for collective action and bargaining and alters the types and substance of issues they promote and the language they communicate. Indeed, this changing coalition has not only made the union movement undoubtedly more diverse than ever, but as an emergent civil rights organization, unions have become the largest mass membership organization of people of color (Bronfenbrenner & Warren 2007).

The movement's increasing diversity brought internal debates about organized labor's stance on civil rights and particularly immigration policy. In the 1980s, the AFL-CIO supported the passage of the Immigration Reform and Control Act (IRCA) of 1986, including the employer sanctions provision, which was designed to curb employer hiring of undocumented workers. The statutory reform didn't work, as employers took advantage of the law's failure to impose fines, enabling them to hire more and more undocumented workers with impunity. With increasing numbers of immigrants entering the workforce, the national labor movement divided over policy direction; a number of unions, notably HERE and SEIU – unions that would lead a split from the AFL-CIO a decade later – promoted a repeal of the employer sanctions provision (Fine & Tichenor 2009; Haus 1995).

In 1997, the new president of the AFL-CIO, John Sweeney, pushed a strong new agenda to focus on organizing. The former SEIU president allocated 30 percent of the union's budget to organizing (in the contrast both to the prior years' much smaller fraction and to recent years' regression to less than 10 percent). The AFL-CIO also made immediate efforts to diversify the unions' leadership, significantly increasing both racial and gender diversity among its 54-member Executive Council, and appointing Linda Chavez-Thompson to Executive Vice President (Minchin 2013). In Sweeney's earliest speeches endorsing this new emphasis, he made at most vague comments to questions of race. But shortly after, the AFL-CIO shifted its organizing strategy to put greater emphasis on immigrant labor, particularly workers coming from Mexico and Central America. Unions in sectors with large immigrant populations quickly saw the damaging effect of the employer sanctions provisions, and particularly the ways in which the provision impeded the organization of these new workers. In 2000, Sweeney issued a formal statement demanding unconditional amnesty for undocumented workers. Labor leaders increasingly pushed the federal government to deny the INS access to union worksites, filing lawsuits to block the federal government from enforcing employer efforts to threaten and fire undocumented workers. By 2005, the tension within the union movement was acute, and seven AFL-CIO unions split away to create Change to Win, a separate federation of unions, which was committed to the organizing of sectors dominated by immigrant labor.

With this increasing diversity comes the potential for conflict, as we have seen in recent years reflected in national politics. But because of labor's long history as an instrument in the mobilization of white working-class voters, it also provides a unique opportunity for the movement to communicate and engage with these workers more directly. Unions, as we have argued earlier, have opportunities and access to engage workers in a way that most institutional actors do not. In 2008, the president of the AFL-CIO, Richard Trumka, embarked on a national tour targeted at labor's white working-class members, with special emphasis on those in midwestern states thought to be resistant to voting for Barack Obama, who at the time was vying to be the nation's first African American president. Trumka made frequent and frank speeches to workers around the country about his own white working-class upbringing and support (Minchin 2016: 310–311). He responded similarly to the racial conflicts produced by the 2014 police shooting of Michael Brown in Ferguson, Missouri, noting in a speech widely disseminated to union workers by the AFL-CIO and through its locals that both the police officer and Brown's mother were union members. "Our brother killed our sister's son and we do not have to wait for the judgment of prosecutors or courts to tell us how terrible this is." Noting the difficult history of union racial division and the fight for equality, Trumka declared that ongoing racism within the labor movement is "our problem. That is what solidarity means" (AFL-CIO 2017).

Unions have further amplified this messaging to their members in the past decade, making a much more concerted, often multilingual, effort to communicate support for civil rights and interracial solidarity. A report from the AFL-CIO Commission on Racial and Economic Justice in 2017 challenged its leaders and members to address matters of diversity directly: "Talking about racial bias and the impact of racial politics can be challenging, but it lies at the core of strengthening solidarity, growing labor's membership and allies, and creating a movement that lifts all working people. Without an understanding of the intersection between class and race, we are vulnerable to the divisive tactics of corporations and unscrupulous politicians" (AFL-CIO 2017: 32). The report recommended race training courses in all affiliates and requires it of all state federations and central labor councils in large metropolitan areas. "[H]aving tough and facilitated conversations about race within our respective union families will help build empathy, and bridge gaps in lived experiences across race and ethnicity that will make our unions stronger and more unified" (AFL-CIO 2017: 33). The report was only the most high-profile of union efforts, as different unions, both at the national and local levels engaged in these discussions throughout the decade. A report of the American Federation of Teachers (2015), for instance, predated the AFL-CIO's, recognizing the "blunt, tough, uncomfortable, but important conversation to determine how our union could address the lingering effects of racism and inequality and, in particular, the impact on black males." The AFT launched these conversations at its policy meetings around the country, questioning its own history and ongoing role in promoting greater equity, and looking for ways to move forward in promoting greater progress within the union, within the schools that they teach, and in society at large.

The BLM protests in 2020 inspired another round of efforts by locals around the country both to critically engage with labor's past history of racial discrimination and to champion further tolerance and diversity within their membership. Hundreds of unions, national and local, protested with BLM activists and started discussions among their members about racial legacies, the present problems with racism that unions face within their ranks, and proposals for the future. Numerous unions went on day long strikes, including the Longshore Workers union, which went on strike on Juneteenth. To help connect with their members, these union leaders emphasized that the people being killed by police were workers, and frequently union members or part of union families. The president of the 29,000 member Northwest Carpenters Union (2020), Evelyn Shapiro, stressed that "there are generations of people of color who do not trust unions because of our actions" and urged her members to see the importance of labor for helping to engage with societal and structural racism: "Unionism means uniting over the important stuff. It means we care. Care does not mean we like each other. But it does mean we value and respect each other. If we believe that Unionism is simmered down to pay and benefits, we are missing the point" (Northwest Carpenters Union 2020).

At this point, we can only conjecture what direct impact this communication will have on labor members in the wake of the recent BLM uprisings, and particularly on white trade unionists and their electoral choices. Initial election data so far has indicated that there was a slight uptick of two to three percentage points in white union workers supporting the Democratic candidate, Joe Biden, over Donald Trump. Labor's role in turning out these voters for Biden in percentages that far contrast with the overall white vote in the 2020 election is something to highlight and champion. It remains critical that we explore further the politics and messaging of unions so as to further understand the ways in which specific environments impact what is communicated by union leaders and organizers and what is heard by rank and file workers.

CONCLUSION

In the midst of the demonstrations demanding recognition that Black Lives Matter in the summer of 2020, protestors in the nation's capital damaged the headquarters of the AFL-CIO. Perhaps the reason for this was incidental, given the building's geographic proximity to Lafayette Park and the White House where protests were centered. But at least some of the protestors recognized that a significant number of police officers are protected by unions, many of which are affiliated with the AFL-CIO. Amongst the graffiti on the building were the words, "Disband Cop Unions" and "AFL must disaffiliate with Cop Unions!"

The AFL-CIO quickly responded to the protestors by posting large "Black Lives Matter" banners to different sides of the building. Some local union supporters posted fliers to the building walls linking the fight for unionism with the fight against racism. Leaders of the AFL-CIO and other national unions such as SEIU and UNITE-HERE, and dozens of their local affiliates, have since made notable public statements on behalf of the Black Lives Matter movement. Some of these unions have advocated for the firing of certain police officers and the removal of certain police union leaders (Rainey & Otterbein 2020). Some, such as SEIU, have shown support for abolition movements and have debated expelling police officers affiliated with the union, whereas the AFL-CIO has largely remained more cautious, with prominent voices arguing that police officers should remain unionized and that efforts at reform should be consistent with the right of all employees, including those in law enforcement, to workplace representation. Equally noteworthy is that the AFL-CIO headquarters was not spared from attack because of their role advocating civil rights and racial justice. This lack of recognition is understandable given their mixed history on such matters.

But unions offer a too often overlooked vehicle for civil rights advancement. Changes to their memberships over the past few decades have turned many unions from bastions of white male dominance to movements of extremely diverse workforces, and in many cases establishing them as some of the largest and most vocal civil rights organizations in America. Labor leadership has, in the last two decades, been much more responsive to these changes. In conjunction with similar demographic changes in Democratic Party constituencies, labor has not only actively promoted civil rights legislation and other policies that benefit workers of all races, but has also engaged with a debate about their history and future around diversity and racial equality. Because of their organizational power, they have the already built-in structures to mobilize their workers, inform and engage their politics and preferences and, as our previous research shows, successfully promote greater tolerance amongst their white members. Again, there is much more work that needs to be done, to concretize initiatives that can be construed as more symbolic, and to continue often difficult conversations among members with very different worldviews. Indeed, the last four years should be a clarion call for labor activists: in supporting President Trump, a significant number of its white members are seemingly expressing their opposition to the future of a diverse America. The labor movement can make and has made important inroads against this, but it takes continued concerted action. Because of labor's increasingly diverse workforce and leadership, we believe that it can and will play this role.

REFERENCES

AFL-CIO. 2017. *AFL-CIO Labor Commission on Racial and Economic Justice Report.* Racial-justice.aflcio. org.

AFT. 2015. *Reclaiming the Promise of Racial Equity.* www.aft.org/sites/default/files/racial_equity_taskforce_ 10-8-15.pdf

Ahlquist, John S., Amanda B. Clayton, and Margaret Levi 2014. "Provoking Preferences: Unionization, Trade Policy, and the ILWU Puzzle," *International Organization* 68, 1: 33–75.

Ahlquist, John S., and Margaret Levi 2013. *In the Interest of Others: Organizations and Social Activism.* Princeton, NJ: Princeton University Press.

Arnesen, Eric. 2002. *Brotherhoods of Color: Black Railroad Workers and the Struggle for Equality.* Cambridge, MA: Harvard University Press.

1991. *Waterfront Workers of New Orleans: Race, Class, and Politics, 1863–1923.* New York: Oxford University Press.

Baron, Reuben M., and David A. Kenny, 1986. "The Moderator-Mediator Variable Distinction in Social Psychological Research – Conceptual, Strategic, and Statistical Considerations," *Journal of Personality and Social Psychology* 51, 6, 1173–1182.

Bates, Beth Tompkins. 2001. *Pullman Porters and the Rise of Protest Politics in Black America, 1925–1945.* Chapel Hill: University of North Carolina Press.

Biondi, Martha. 2006. *To Stand and Fight: The Struggle for Civil Rights in Post-War New York City.* Cambridge, MA: Harvard University Press.

Bonacich, Edna. 1972. "A Theory of Ethnic Antagonism: The Split Labor Market," *American Sociological Review* 37, 5: 547–559.

Bronfenbrenner, Kate, and Dorian T. Warren. 2007. "Race, Gender, and the Rebirth of Trade Unionism," *New Labor Forum* 16, 142–148.

Bucknor, Cherrie. 2016. "Black Workers, Unions, and Inequality," *Center for Economic and Policy Research.* https://cepr.net/images/stories/reports/black-workers-unions-2016-08.pdf?v=2

Bureau of Labor Statistics. 2020. "Union Members, 2019." www.bls.gov/news.release/pdf/union2.pdf

Chen, Anthony S. 2009. *The Fifth Freedom: Jobs, Politics, and Civil Rights in the United States, 1941–1972.* Princeton, NJ: Princeton University Press.

Cox, Oliver C. 1948. *Caste, Class, and Race.* New York: Doubleday.

Du Bois, W. E. B. 1935. *Black Reconstruction: An Essay toward a History on the Part Which Black Folk Played in the Attempt to Reconstruct Democracy*. New York: Harcourt Brace.

    1948. "Race Relations in the United States, 1917-1947," *Phylon* 9, 3: 234-247.

Estlund, Cynthia. 2002. "The Ossification of American Labor Law," *Columbia Law Review* 102, 6, 1527–1612.

Eveland, William P. 2004. "The Effect of Political Discussion in Producing Informed Citizens: The Roles of Information, Motivation, and Elaboration," *Political Communication* 21, 2: 177–193.

Fine, Janice, and Daniel J. Tichenor. 2009. "A Movement Wrestling: American Labor's Enduring Struggle with Immigration, 1866–2007," *Studies in American Political Development* 23: 84–113.

Fletcher, Bill Jr. 2020. "Race Is About More than Discrimination," *Monthly Review*. https://monthlyreview.org/2020/07/01/race-is-about-more-than-discrimination/

Frymer, Paul. 1999. *Uneasy Alliances: Race and Party Competition in America*. Princeton, NJ: Princeton University Press.

    2005. "Racism Revised: Courts, Labor Law, and the Construction of Racial Animus," *American Political Science Review* 99, 3: 373–387.

    2008. *Black and Blue: African Americans, the Labor Movement, and the Decline of the Democratic Party*. Princeton, NJ: Princeton University Press.

    2017. *Building an American Empire: The Era of Territorial and Political Expansion*. Princeton, NJ: Princeton University Press.

Frymer, Paul, and Jacob M. Grumbach. 2021. "Labor Unions and White Racial Politics," *American Journal of Political Science* 65, 1: 225–240.

Garcia, Ruben J. 2019. "Right-to-Work Laws: Ideology and Impact," *Annual Review of Law and Social Science* 15, 509–519.

Gilroy, Paul. 1987. *"There Ain't No Black in the Union Jack": The Cultural Politics of Race and Nation*. New York: Verso.

Goldfield, Michael. 1993. "Race and the CIO: The Possibilities for Racial Egalitarianism during the 1930s and 1940s," *International Labor and Working-Class History* 44: 1–32.

    2020. *The Southern Key: Class, Race, and Radicalism in the 1930s and 1940s*. New York: Oxford University Press.

Goldfield, Michael, and Amy Bromsen. 2013. "The Changing Landscape of US Unions in Historical and Theoretical Perspective," *Annual Review of Political Science* 16, 231–257.

Gould, William B. 1977. *Black Workers in White Unions: Job Discrimination in the United States*. Ithaca, NY: Cornell University Press.

Griffith, Barbara S. 1988. *The Crisis of American Labor: Operation Dixie and the Defeat of the CIO*. Philadelphia: Temple University Press.

Hacker, Jacob S., and Paul Pierson 2011. *Winner-Take-All Politics: How Washington Made the Rich Richer – And Turned its Back on the Middle Class*. New York: Simon and Schuster.

Haider, Asad. 2018. *Mistaken Identity: Race and Class in the Age of Trump*. New York: Verso.

Hamlin, Rebecca. 2008. "Immigrants at Work: Labor Unions and Noncitizen Members," in S. Karthick Ramakrishnan and Irene Bloemraad, eds. *Civic Hopes and Political Realities: Immigrants, Community Organizations, and Civic Engagement*. New York: Russell Sage Foundation.

Haus, Leah. 1995. "Openings in the Wall: Transnational Migrants, Labor Unions, and US Immigration Policy," *International Organization* 49, 2: 285–313.

Hertel-Fernandez, Alex, and Alix Gould-Werth. 2020. "Labor Organizations and Unemployment Insurance: A Virtuous Circle Supporting US Workers' Voices and Reducing Disparities in Benefits," *Washington Center for Equitable Growth*. https://equitablegrowth.org/wp-content/uploads/2020/10/100920-ui-workerpower-ib.pdf

Honey, Michael. 1992. "Operation Dixie: Labor and Civil Rights in the Post-War South," *Mississippi Quarterly* 45, 4: 439-452.

Jeffery, Steven. 2007. "Why Do Unions Find Fighting Workplace Racism Difficult?" *European Review of Labour and Research* 13, 3: 377–395.

Jones, Jacqueline. 1998. *American Work: Four Centuries of Black and White Labor*. New York: W. W. Norton.

Katznelson, Ira. 2005. *When Affirmative Action Was White: An Untold History of Racial Inequality in Twentieth-Century America*. New York: Norton.

Kelley, Robin D. G. 1990. *Hammer and Hoe: Alabama Communists during the Great Depression*. Chapel Hill: University of North Carolina Press.

Kim Sung Eun, and Yotam Margalit. 2017. "Informed Preferences? The Impact of Unions on Workers' Policy Views," *American Journal of Political Science* 61, 3: 728–743.

Korstad, Robert. 2003. *Civil Rights Unionism: Tobacco Workers and the Struggle for Democracy in the Mid-Twentieth Century South*. Chapel Hill: University of North Carolina Press.

Korstad, Robert, and Nelson Lichtenstein. 1988. "Opportunities Found and Lost: Labor, Radicals, and the Early Civil Rights Movement," *Journal of American History* 75, 3: 786–811.

Lichtenstein, Nelson. 2001. *State of the Unions*. Princeton, NJ: Princeton University Press.

MacDonald, David. 2020. "Labor Unions and White Democratic Partisanship," *Political Behavior*, https://link.springer.com/article/10.1007/s11109–020-09624-3

MacLean, Nancy. 2008. *Freedom Is Not Enough: The Opening of the American Workplace*. Cambridge, MA: Harvard University Press.

Marable, Manning. 1999. *How Capitalism Underdeveloped Black America: Problems in Race, Political Economy, and Society*. New York: Haymarket Press.

Marable, Manning. 2009. *Beyond Black and White*. New York: Verso Press.

McCall, Leslie. 2001. "Sources of Racial Wage Inequality in Metropolitan Labor Markets: Racial, Ethnic, and Gender Differences," *American Sociological Review* 66, 4: 520–541.

McCann, Michael W., with George I. Lovell. 2020. *Union by Law: Filipino American Labor Activists, Rights Radicalism, and Racial Capitalism*. Chicago: University of Chicago Press.

Milkman, Ruth. 2006. *LA Story: Immigrant Workers and the Future of the US Labor Movement*. New York: Russell Sage Foundation.

Milkman, Ruth, and Stephanie Luce. 2019. "The State of the Unions 2019: A Profile of Organized Labor in New York City, New York State, and the United States." https://slu.cuny.edu/wp-content/uploads/2019/08/Union_Density-2019.pdf

Minchin, Timothy J. 2001. *The Color of Work: The Struggle for Civil Rights in the Southern Paper Industry, 1945–1980*. Chapel Hill: University of North Carolina Press.

2013. "'Labor Is Back?': The AFL-CIO during the Presidency of John J. Sweeney, 1995-2009," *Labor History* 54, 4: 393-420.

2016. "A Pivotal Role? The AFL-CIO and the 2008 Presidential Election," *Labor History* 57, 3, 299–322.

Mink, Gwendolyn. 1986. *Old Labor and New Immigrants in American Political Development: Union, Party, and State, 1875–1920*. Ithaca, NY: Cornell University Press.

Mishel, Lawrence. 2017. "Diversity in the New York City Union and Nonunion Construction Sectors," *Economic Policy Institute*. 1–27.

Mutz, Diana C. 2002. "Cross-Cutting Social Networks: Testing Democratic Theory in Practice," *The American Political Science Review* 96, 1: 111–126.

Nelson, Bruce. 2009. *Divided We Stand: American Workers and the Struggle for Black Equality*. Princeton, NJ: Princeton University Press.

Ngai, Mae M. 2004. *Impossible Subjects: Illegal Aliens and the Making of Modern America*. Princeton, NJ: Princeton University Press.

Northwest Carpenters Union. 2020. "EST Shapiro's Statement on BLM and Racism in the Industry." www.nwcarpenters.org/est-shapiros-statement-on-blm-racism-in-the-industry/

Office of Speechwriting, and Lowell Weiss. 2020. "AFL-CIO [2]," *Clinton Digital Library*, accessed September 22, 2020. https://clinton.presidentiallibraries.us/items/show/47367

Parker, Christopher S., and Matt A. Baretto 2014. *Change They Can't Believe In: The Tea Party and Reactionary Politics in America*. Princeton, NJ: Princeton University Press.

Prasad, Monica. 2006. *The Politics of Free Markets: The Rise of Neoliberal Economic Policies in Britain, France, Germany, and the United States*. Chicago: University of Chicago Press.

Rainey, Rebecca, and Holly Otterbein. 2020. "Local Unions Defy AFL-CIO in Push to Oust Police Unions," *Politico* (June 30, 2020). https://politi.co/38i4ieJ

Reed, Adolph. 2013. "Marx, Race, and Neoliberalism," *New Labor Forum* 22, 1: 49–57.

Robinson, Cedric. 1983. *Black Marxism: The Making of the Black Radical Tradition*. Chapel Hill: University of North Carolina Press.

Roediger, David. 1991. *The Wages of Whiteness: Race and the Making of the White Working Class*. New York: Verso.

Rosenfeld, Jake. 2014. *What Unions No Longer Do*. Cambridge, MA: Harvard University Press.

Rosenfeld, Jake, and Meredith Kleykamp 2012. "Organized Labor and Racial Wage Inequality in the United States," *American Journal of Sociology* 117, 5: 1460–1502.

Schickler, Eric. 2016. *Racial Realignment: The Transformation of American Liberalism, 1932–1965*. Princeton, NJ: Princeton University Press.

Schiller, Reuel. 2015. *Forging Rivals: Race, Class, and the Fate of Postwar Liberalism*. New York: Cambridge University Press.

Sobieraj, Sarah, and Deborah White. 2004. "Taxing Political Life: Reevaluating the Relationship between Voluntary Association Membership, Political Engagement, and the State," *Sociological Quarterly* 45, 4: 739–764.

Stein, Judith. 1998. *Running Steel, Running America: Race, Economic Policy, and the Decline of Liberalism*. Chapel Hill: University of North Carolina Press.

Sullivan, Patricia. 1996. *Days of Hope: Race and Democracy in the New Deal Era*. Chapel Hill: University of North Carolina Press.

Tingley, Dustin, Teppei Yamamoto, Kentaro Hirose, Luke Keele, and Kosuke Imai. 2014. "Mediation: R Package for Causal Mediation Analysis," *Journal of Statistical Software* 59, 5, 1–38.

Trotter, Joe William, Jr. 2019. *Workers on Arrival: Black Labor in the Making of America*. Berkeley: University of California.

Watts, Julie. 2002. *Immigration Policy and the Challenge of Globalization: Unions and Employers in Unlikely Alliance*. Ithaca, NY: Cornell University Press.

Western, Bruce, and Jake Rosenfeld. 2011. "Unions, Norms, and the Rise of US Wage Inequality," *American Sociological Review* 76, 4: 513–537.

12

Attacking Democracy through Immigration Workplace Raids

Bill Ong Hing

INTRODUCTION

On a cold, raw December morning in Marshalltown, Iowa, Teresa Blanco woke up to go to work at the local Swift meat packing plant. Hundreds of others across the town were doing the same thing, in spite of the miserable mixture of sleet, mist, and slush that awaited them outside their front doors. As they made their way to the plant, the workers, who were from Mexico, did not mind the weather.

Unfortunately, the workers' day turned into a nightmare soon after they reported for work. Not long after the plant opened, heavily armed agents from the US Immigration and Customs Enforcement agency (ICE) stormed onto the scene. Pandemonium broke out. The workers panicked; many began to run; others tried to hide, some in dangerous and hazardous areas. As the ICE agents began rounding up all the workers, they ordered those who were US citizens to go to the cafeteria. Noncitizens were directed to a different section of the plant. Agents shouted out instructions: "documenteds" in one line, "undocumenteds" in another. If an agent suspected that the person in the documenteds' line was undocumented, the agent would instruct the person to get into the undocumented line. More than one individual was told, "You have Mexican teeth. You need to go to that line [for undocumented persons] and get checked" (National Commission on ICE Misconduct & Violations of Fourth Amendment, Commission Hearing, Des Moines, Iowa 2008).

The nightmare was only beginning. Although supervisory ICE agents carried a civil warrant for a few individuals, the squad demanded that all plant employees be held, separated by nationality. That included US citizen workers who were interrogated and detained. No one was free to leave – not even those who carried evidence of lawful status or proof they were in the process of seeking proper permission to be in the country. Each was interrogated individually. The process took the entire day, and phone calls were not permitted until later in the day. By the end of the day, ninety were arrested, but hundreds, including citizens, had been detained for hours. The entire community was shaken to its core.

The Marshalltown raid was one of the more egregious operations under the George W. Bush administration, conducted not long after his push for immigration reform in 2004. Although Barack Obama's administration focused more on "silent raids" of I-9 paper audits instead of armed operations, the Donald Trump administration picked up right where the Bush administration left off (Bacon & Hing 2010). Armed workplace raids by ICE agents were instituted again soon after Donald Trump took office. The Trump ICE raid that received the most notoriety took place on August 7, 2019, when almost 700 workers were arrested at food processing plants in central Mississippi. Those arrested included two single mothers – each with three minor children – whose children had to be cared for by friends or other family members. A breastfeeding mother was separated from her four-month old baby. Video and photos posted after the initial stages of the raid showed men and women walking in boots with their hands zip-tied behind their backs. Other detained employees sat on the grass or near large, white silos on the company property. Neighbors worried about a twelve-year-old girl whose mother was being questioned by officers inside the plant. Another girl could be heard wailing in the background. A girl no more than three feet tall slowly waddled toward the metal gate to look, with other workers, at those who were being detained.

I had the opportunity to learn more about the effects of several Bush ICE raids first hand as part of a commission that was established by the United Food and Commercial Workers International Union (UFCW) in 2008. The Commission spent more than a year holding regional hearings, interviewing witnesses, and soliciting input from a wide range of workers, elected officials, policy experts, psychologists, and religious and community leaders. Commissioners learned about the abuse that ICE officials visited upon workers, their families, and the communities.

Analysis of workplace ICE raids expose racial profiling and the attendant trauma to children and families as well as social and economic damage to communities. However, the manner and timing of these raids also represent an attack on democracy that we should not ignore. These raids have come at a time when immigrants are playing a vital role in the labor movement.

ICE raids challenge us to think seriously about their underlying implications. The tragic effects on families and communities, as well as the serious constitutional violations committed by ICE agents during the raids, provide ample moral and legal justification to end the raids. However, the inherent racism at the center of the ICE raids and other ICE and Border Patrol operations raises further concern that receives little public attention. With few exceptions, the ICE operations target Latinx – usually Mexicans. Suppression of the labor movement, racism, violation of constitutional rights, and toleration of a subaltern class of exploited workers who have no right to participate in government are, separately, and even more so together, inconsistent with democratic governance.

The structure of immigration laws has institutionalized a set of values that dehumanize, demonize, and criminalize immigrants of color. The result is that these victims stop being Mexicans, Latinx, or Chinese and become "illegal immigrants." We are aware of their race or ethnicity, but we believe we are acting against them because of their status, not because of their race. This institutionalized racism makes the Bush and Trump ICE raids natural and acceptable in the minds of the general public. Institutionalized racism allows the public to think ICE raids are freeing up jobs for native workers without recognizing the racial ramifications. Objections to ICE raids are debated in non-racial terms. Failing to recognize these operations from the perspective of institutional racism is problematic, of course. But ignoring how raids inhibit labor organizing and constitute an attack on democracy is also a problem.

While workplace raids are emblematic of blatant and structural racism, workplace raids are blatantly anti-democratic: ignoring the Fourth Amendment during raids, violating civil rights, engaging racial profiling, and disrupting labor organizing. In short, democratic principles are jeopardized. Given the American labor movement's shift toward including noncitizen workers, the attack on such workers is properly viewed as an attack on the labor movement.

ENTERING THE ICE AGE OF ENFORCEMENT

The ICE age of immigration enforcement began when the Department of Homeland Security (DHS) was established in 2003. The new DHS took over the old Immigration and Naturalization Service (INS) from the Department of Justice. Repackaged, interior enforcement functions were channeled into ICE.

Immigration raids, including worksite operations, have been part of immigration enforcement for decades. However, the courts had placed constraints on INS and Border Patrol agent activities during raids. For example, in *INS* v. *Delgado*, although the US Supreme Court did not find the particular worksite operation in question unconstitutional, the Court held that without a warrant, INS agents cannot seize an entire worksite, workers have the right to remain silent, and workers can leave if agents have no reasonable suspicion that the workers are unauthorized to be in the United States.[1]

But in January 2004, after Republicans showed little interest in a guest worker proposal, Bush implemented the current ICE raid strategy to garner support for his plan. His detractors on the right argued the proposal was too lenient and amounted to amnesty. Bush responded with a strong enforcement program. In the process, ICE agents ignored the legal constraints that had been imposed on the old INS raids. The actions suggested that the well-established rules were no longer applicable to the new DHS. Homeland Security Secretary Michael Chertoff and ICE Assistant Secretary Julie Myers ushered in the new ICE age seemingly free of the old constraints.

The Swift Raids

Early on the morning of December 12, 2006, the feast day of Our Lady of Guadalupe and a holy day of special significance to Catholics of Mexican descent, ICE conducted a massive military style raid on six Swift & Company meatpacking plants across the nation's heartland. Hundreds of federal agents in riot gear, armed with assault weapons, descended upon plants in Cactus, Texas; Greeley, Colorado; Grand Island, Nebraska; Worthington, Minnesota; Marshalltown, Iowa; and Hyrum, Utah.

ICE was there to execute arrest warrants for a handful of named workers – less than 1 percent of the workforce. The sheer number of ICE agents on the scene and the manner in which the operation was conducted made clear that the execution of those warrants was not the government's real purpose. Rather, the raids seemed designed to ramp up the number of arrests and capture the headlines on the evening news. ICE rounded up nearly 13,000 workers – the vast majority of them US citizens – holding them against their will for hours.

According to witness testimony, there were about one hundred people standing at the fence in front of the Marshalltown plant by the end of the day. Many were people who had family members working the first shift.

While Sister Christine (a Catholic nun) and family members held vigil outside, the workers inside were caught in a frightening, military-style assault. Instead of searching out the 133 individuals named on the arrest warrants, heavily armed ICE agents fanned out through each of the affected plants, sealed the exits, and ordered workers into lines, where they were patted down and searched for weapons. After the weapons search, ICE agents herded workers en masse into the plant cafeterias or other holding areas and divided them by race and national origin. Many were denied food, water, or the use of bathroom facilities; some were handcuffed. No one was

---

[1] *Immigration & Naturalization Service v. Delgado*, 466 US 210 (1984).

advised of their rights or provided access to legal representation at the raid site. The overwhelming majority of those held that day were US citizens. In Marshalltown, Michael Graves, a US citizen, got to work that morning and was instructed to go to the cafeteria.

> [Heavily-armed] ICE agents ... questioned me about my status as a US citizen and I said my mother and father were born and raised in Mississippi. He questioned me about that and asked me, did I know my route to Mississippi? And I said no, but I can find my way there because I had been there a lot of times with my parents. He looked at my ID again, told me to sit down with my hands behind my back, still handcuffed. (United Food and Commercial Workers Union 2009)

Graves was forced to sit in that position for over an hour. ICE continued to hold him and co-workers – still deprived of food, water, and external communication – until he was finally released after eight hours of captivity and told to "go home."

Another US citizen, Melissa Broekemeier, had worked at the Swift plant in Marshalltown for more than eight years. But the "longest day [she] ever worked was on December 12, 2007." Broekemeier described her experience on the day of the Swift raid this way:

> I, like all my co-workers that went to work that day.... we were instructed by our supervisors to finish up ... and report to the cafeteria, where we were inspected, and our private lives were scrutinized by ICE agents as if we were illegal convicts.... The power that runs our machines should have been shut off first, but it was not.... The Federal government jeopardized our safety and health without care. We were overlooked. We were ignored. We were treated like criminals. We were not free to leave.... We had people who really lost control, we had people rolling on the floor... upset and distressed. They really lost their dignity.... (National Commission on ICE Misconduct & Violations of Fourth Amendment, Commission Hearing, Des Moines, Iowa 2008)

During their interviews with ICE agents at the plant, the alleged undocumented workers were asked if they had children, but were not told that one of the parents would be allowed to remain to care for them. Many parents were afraid to say "yes" because they feared their children would be taken away from them and placed in foster care. In one case, a six-year-old and two-and-a-half-year-old stayed with a babysitter for three weeks until the mother was deported. In another family, an elderly woman had been living with her daughter. The daughter was detained, and the mother spoke no English, did not drive, and was not familiar with Marshalltown.

Immigrant rights attorney Sonia Konrad concluded that the ICE agents "conducted themselves as if they were dealing with terrorists[,] entering the premises in uniform, black jackets, strapped down guns, shouting and leaving no doubt to all workers that ... they were not free to go" (2018). ICE made sure that people were uprooted and moved out of Iowa quickly, some of them within twenty-four hours of their arrests and detention. Once arrested, people were coerced into signing stipulated orders of deportations without an opportunity to consult with an attorney. Konrad and her colleagues were relegated to quickly writing powers of attorneys and guardianships for those detainees.

Other Raids

Stillmore, Georgia

One ICE raid in Stillmore, Georgia, the Friday before Labor Day weekend in 2006, evoked outcry from local residents who labeled the ICE action as nothing short of "Gestapo tactics." Descending shortly before midnight, ICE agents swarmed the area, eventually arresting and deporting 125 undocumented workers. Most of those rounded up were men, while their wives fled to the woods to hide children in tow. In the weeks after the raid, at least 200 more immigrants left town. Many of the women purchased bus tickets to Mexico with their husband's final paycheck. The impact underscored how vital undocumented immigrants were to the local economy. Trailer parks lay abandoned. The poultry plant scrambled to replace more than half its workforce. Business dried up at stores. The community of about a thousand people became little more than a ghost town. The operator of a trailer park that was raided, David Robinson, commented, "These people might not have American rights, but they've damn sure got human rights. There ain't no reason to treat them like animals" (Bynum 2006).

Local residents witnessed the events, as ICE officials raided local homes and trailer parks, forcing many members of the community out of Stillmore. Officials were seen stopping motorists, breaking into homes, and even threatening people with tear gas according to reports. Witnesses reported seeing ICE officials breaking windows and entering homes through floorboards. Mayor Marilyn Slater commented, "This reminds me of what I read about Nazi Germany, the Gestapo coming in and yanking people up" (Bynum 2006).

San Rafael, California

On March 6, 2007, ICE officials raided the small communities of San Rafael and Novato in Marin County, arresting roughly thirty undocumented immigrants. This raid was also part of ICE's "Operation Return to Sender," the federal effort to crack down on immigrants who have stayed past their deportation orders. ICE officials armed with warrants bearing dated and/or incorrect information stormed homes and began arresting violators regardless of whether they were named in the original warrant. The San Rafael raid became a national symbol of the traumatic effects raids have on children. Juan Rodriguez, principal of Bahia Vista Elementary School, noted that on a typical day the school might have eight to ten children absent, but seventy-seven children were absent the day of the raid. San Rafael's Mayor Alberto Boro criticized federal officials, noting that the raid resulted in a drop in calls to local law enforcement agencies, signaling a heightened level of mistrust of police within the community.

New Bedford, Massachusetts

In March 2007, nearly 500 ICE officials descended upon the small southern New England community of New Bedford, Massachusetts. ICE officials targeted the local Michael Bianco, Inc. plant, a leather goods manufacturer that had manufactured goods for brands such as Coach, Rockport, and Timberland. As with other larger raids, the event split families and underscored the negative effects the raids have on communities. Because many of Bianco's employees were women, this created a crisis with caring for their children. Roughly one hundred children were stranded with babysitters and other caregivers as their mothers were seized during the raid. The majority of those arrested were moved to detention centers halfway across the country in Texas.

Postville, Iowa

One of the largest immigration raids in US history occurred in April 2008 in the small Midwestern town of Postville, Iowa. The raid occurred at the kosher meat plant, Agriprocessors, Inc., the largest employer in town and one of the largest in northeastern Iowa. ICE seized over 400 undocumented workers, including eighteen juveniles.

Agriprocessors employed approximately 970 workers, 80 percent of whom were believed to have fraudulent identification. After the raid, the entire Postville community was in recovery mode. Mayor Robert Penrod speculated on the effect of a possible Agriprocessors closure, estimating that "two-thirds of the homes here will sit empty [and] 95 percent of downtown business ... will dry up." One witness labeled the government strategy "criminal" as hundreds of women and children were faced with the threat of being left "homeless and starving" (Newman 2008).

As in other communities, the school system also felt the immediate impact of the raids. The local school district estimated that 150 of the 220 students from immigrant families were absent the day after the raid.

Northern California Chinese Restaurants

On September 17, 2008, ICE special agents executed federal criminal search warrants at four sites in the northern California towns of Vacaville, Vallejo, and Hercules, in the North Bay area northeast of San Francisco, as part of an investigation into the hiring and possible harboring of unauthorized workers at local Chinese restaurants. ICE agents made no criminal arrests but arrested twenty-one workers on administrative immigration violations. The arrested workers were from six countries: nine from China, five from Mexico, three from Guatemala, two from Indonesia, one from Singapore, and one from Honduras.

Racial Profiling

The United Food and Commercial Workers Commission I was a part of heard repeated testimony about racial profiling. Witnesses testified that workers who appeared to be of Latinx national origin or minorities were singled out by ICE and subjected to the greatest scrutiny. John Bowen, General Counsel for UFCW Local 7, said "race was, almost without question, the sole criteria for harsher interrogations" to which the workers were subjected at the Greeley, Colorado, plant. Fidencio Sandoval, a US citizen and Swift worker at the Grand Island, Nebraska, plant, recounted how he was released only after his sister was able to go to his home, "break the window from my kitchen and go straight to my closet and get my citizen certificate" (National Commission on ICE Misconduct & Violations of Fourth Amendment, Commission Hearing, Des Moines, Iowa 2008).

Other US citizen co-workers were not as fortunate. Those who did not have a way to prove their citizenship were arrested and taken to Camp Dodge, located nearly 300 miles from Grand Island. Manuel Verdinez was finally released after twelve hours: "They called a cab for me and I had to pay $90 for the cab ride back" (National Commission on ICE Misconduct & Violations of Fourth Amendment, Commission Hearing, Boston (2008).

The increased racial profiling and selective enforcement are also evident in the manner in which local police enforce immigration law pursuant to section 287(g) of the Immigration and Nationality Act.[2] In Nashville, Tennessee, a police officer pulled over Juana Villegas, who was nine months pregnant at the time, for a routine traffic violation. The arrest was made pursuant to a section 287(g) agreement and resulted in Villegas' detention in county jail. According to *The New York Times*, Villegas went into labor and delivered her baby with a "sheriff's officer standing guard in her hospital room, where one of her feet was cuffed to the bed most of the time" (Preston 2008). Although the Obama administration severely reduced and more carefully controlled 287(g) agreements with state and local law enforcement agencies, the Trump administration reinstated the 287(g) program with full force (Pham 2018). More than 145 jurisdictions across 25 states currently have 287(g) agreements (Agarwal 2021).

---

[2] Title 8, United States Code, Section 1357(g).

Effect on the Labor Movement

At the height of the American labor movement in the 1950s, more than a third of American workers were union members (Figueroa 2019). However, today only 10.3 percent of workers are union members – the lowest unionization rate among wealthy nations.

Federal actions contributed to the decline. For example, the Taft-Hartley Act of 1947 restricted unions and hampered organizing efforts by facilitating state right-to-work laws, allowing non-union members to enjoy union benefits without paying dues. President Reagan sharpened the assault with new regulations. In 1981, he fired 11,000 striking air traffic controllers who refused his back-to-work order after they walked out to protest poor working conditions and low pay. A 2018 Supreme Court case created a major hurdle, ruling that state governments cannot force public employees who do not join unions to pay fees that support collective bargaining.[3] More than twenty states had required these fair-share fees (Figueroa 2019).

Besides those real challenges, some labor leaders understand that the tough work of organizing, convincing members to expand ranks, and putting more resources toward those efforts have been neglected. One union that understands, the Service Employees International Union (SEIU), now spends 20 percent of its budget to bring in workers who are not already union members (Figueroa 2019). Its strategy has paid off, as its membership increased by adding immigrant workers (Figueroa 2019).

The key to SEIU's growth – and that of other expanding unions – is a focus on immigrant workers, including those workers without employment authorization. Historically, many rank-and-file union members have had problems with undocumented workers, perhaps with good reason. Developers and construction companies have often turned to an undocumented workforce to undercut union costs. A stark example is Donald Trump's real-estate company that, in 1980, recruited 200 undocumented Polish workers to demolish the Bonwit Teller building to clear ground for the 58-story Trump Tower. The workers – some of whom were only paid $4 an hour – worked 12-hour shifts, without basic safety on very dangerous work (Hennelly 2019). Management also exploited racial division and anti-immigrant sentiment in this arena. The tactic pitted one group against another, often establishing a "certain color hierarchy and class pecking order" (Hennelly 2019).

Many labor activists recognize that the future of their movement depends on incorporating immigrants. For them, this is about survival – not just about social justice on behalf of workers. They are relying on the basic tenet of the labor movement – a collective effort to empower workers irrespective of background. Often, union members are placed on job sites to work alongside undocumented workers. The unions realize that aside from safety concerns, the immigrant workers face other challenges, such as immigration, housing, and health. Those are matters that the union can help address.

Labor leaders increasingly see alignment with immigrant workers as an opportunity. When Trump unveiled a plan to penalize noncitizens for using government assistance, New York Attorney General Letitia James filed a lawsuit opposing the move. A big part of the crowd cheering her on were members of 1199 SEIU, the nation's largest healthcare union (Hennelly 2019).

Low-wage workers from Mexico and Central America are at the center of the efforts to rebuild the US labor movement. Not only have they been the focus of this dynamic effort, but the immigrant workers themselves are on the front lines of worker center organizing and advocacy

---

[3] *Janus* v. *AFSCME*, 138 S. Ct. 2448 (2018).

efforts. This has occurred in parallel with a vibrant immigrant rights movement, which combines civil rights and labor rights elements. The work has infused the US labor movement with new energy, new tactics, and new ideas (Milkman 2009).

The mutual attraction between labor and migrant workers is obvious. Low-wage and working-class immigrants come to the United States with dreams of economic advancement, but they arrive with few resources. They are often confined to the bottom of the labor market, where wages are low, working conditions are poor, benefits are limited, and chances for promotion are extremely restricted. Many immigrants are concentrated in job segments where wage theft and other labor law violations are prevalent. This abuse and lack of resources make the labor movement appealing to low-wage immigrants. And, even though many such workers lack legal status, much of the wider public is sympathetic when their abuse is highlighted (Milkman 2009).

Foreign-born workers make up 175 percent (29 million) of the nation's 165 million workers (Budiman 2020). Many are high-wage earners, including professionals and entrepreneurs. More than a quarter (7.6 million) are not authorized to work, most of them Latinx (Budiman 2020). They typically hold low-wage jobs in agriculture, construction, food and garment manufacturing, hotels and restaurants, and low-wage service industries. Many noncitizens with lawful permanent or refugee status are also employed at or near the bottom of the labor market. Others hold jobs with better pay and conditions. That possibility motivates many at the low end to join the new immigrant labor movement (Milkman 2009).

Traditional trade unionism is important to the immigrant labor movement today. In spite of the fact that many unions supported restrictive immigration policies historically, beginning in the 1980s, several leading unions began to organize Latinx immigrants employed in low-wage sectors, including janitorial, retail, hospitality, residential construction, and manufacturing. In 2000, the AFL-CIO supported legislation that would have granted legalization to undocumented workers. Although immigrant union organizing is uneven across industries and occupations, today virtually all US labor unions offer at least some support for immigrant workers (Milkman 2009).

When labor organizers first began recruiting more immigrant workers in the 1980s, many movement officials were skeptical that the workers would be receptive. Why would workers who intended to return home after earning a certain amount invest time and effort into organizing? Furthermore, the low wages here were still probably better than what the workers made back home. Would they really be concerned about raising US labor standards? Organizers assumed that immigrants unauthorized to work would worry about apprehension and deportation if they became active in unionization (Milkman 2009).

However, countervailing factors actually made organizing Latinx immigrant workers easier than expected. Immigrant social networks that help newcomers adjust and find jobs can be strong. Those social networks become a resource for union organizing. Latinx immigrants also have a sophisticated worldview of how their individual fate is tied to that of their community as a whole. Collective action is viewed as an opportunity for community advancement. And some of the workers also have backgrounds in political and/or union activism in their home countries (Milkman 2009). The communal experience that many Latinx workers endure in being subordinated for lacking immigration documents creates an open-mindedness toward organizing efforts. The shared stigmatization creates a natural comradery. Also, any fear related to participating in unionization efforts pales in comparison with crossing borders or living under threat of immigration enforcement. Still, like most American workers, the vast majority of immigrant workers are not part of organized labor (Milkman 2009).[4]

---

[4] Recent surveys indicate that 64 percent of Americans approve of unions, much higher than during the Great Recession more than a decade ago (Jones 2019).

The matter of organizing immigrant workers invariably raises the effect of the 2002 US Supreme Court ruling in *Hoffman Plastic Compounds, Inc. v. National Labor Relations Board*.[5] In an earlier case, *Sure-Tan, Inc. v. National Labor Relations Board*, the Supreme Court held that immigrant workers without work authorization are still protected by the National Labor Relations Act.[6] It is an unfair labor practice for an employer to report such workers to immigration authorities in retaliation for engaging in union activities. But in *Hoffman*, the Court held that if unauthorized immigrant workers are fired unlawfully for organizing activities, they are not entitled to back pay or reinstatement (the legal remedies available to workers under the NLRA). However, the impact of *Hoffman* may be less significant than originally feared.

In spite of the *Hoffman* decision and the fact that workers without immigrant documents are denied many basic civil rights, in principle they still are protected by nearly all laws covering wages, hours, and union representation. The basic principles of the earlier *Sure-Tan* decision still stand. Since all workers, regardless of immigration status, are protected under the NLRA, the broader purpose of the labor movement to have all workers represented remains legitimate (Milkman 2009).

Of course, serious challenges persist for immigrant workers. All workers have witnessed an erosion of employment and labor laws over the past few decades. At the same time, punitive immigration laws have increased along with enforcement strategies like the workplace raids. Low-wage immigrant workers are more vulnerable, as deportation enforcement renders employment and labor law meaningless for those who are removed (Milkman 2009).

After 9/11, the prospects for immigration reform that would include legalization for undocumented immigrants faded. President Bush tried to get immigration reform talks started again by putting forward a large guest worker plan. But the plan got pushback from both the right and the left (Hing 2006). So the Bush administration turned its enforcement attention to a new strategy.

The tragic events of 9/11 led to the profiling of Arabs, Muslims, and Sikhs in America. But anti-immigrant forces took advantage of the events to focus on other noncitizens as well. In response to those pressures and perhaps also in response to the huge immigrant rights marches in the spring of 2006, the Bush ICE began to orchestrate the series of high-profile workplace raids discussed previously (Milkman 2009). Immigration raids and deportations were by no means a new phenomenon, but the scale was unprecedented.

The raids created a climate of fear. As a result, immigrants without documents who experienced labor and employment law violations were even less likely to pursue whatever legal remedies that might be available, chilling participation in the labor movement (Milkman 2009).

RAMPING UP UNDER TRUMP

The Trump administration's well-documented anti-immigrant agenda included the Bush era workplace raids playbook. The Mississippi raid that resulted in the arrest of almost 700 workers was one example. Although ICE took a pause when the Covid-19 pandemic first hit, ICE soon resumed its enforcement tactics. In a two-month period beginning in mid-July 2020, immigration agents arrested more than 2,000 people in their homes, workplaces, and other sites (Jordan 2020).

---

[5] *Hoffman Plastics Compounds, Inc. v. NLRB*, 535 US 137 (2002).
[6] *Sure-Tan Inc. v. NLRB*, 467 US 883 (1984).

As enforcement resumed at the workplace, some US unions saw an opportunity and responsibility; Trump's focus became a new battlefront between the Republican party and organized labor. Unions understand that ICE agents, the National Labor Relations Board, and the courts are firmly on the side of the rich and powerful. The labor movement understands that its challenge is not simply to organize workers shop by shop. This is about the need for widespread efforts to mobilize large numbers of workers. This "big tent approach" calls for a deep understanding of the economics and competitive dynamics within industries, and unions can help address inequality, division, and attacks on democracy that Trump and his supporters have sowed (Figueroa 2019).

This broader vision incorporates defending their membership facing immigration enforcement as well. Take the case of Hugo Mejía Murguía, an undocumented worker from northern California who got a call to report to work in May 2017. When he arrived at Travis air force base in California, military police called ICE, suspicious of his immigration status. ICE also detained a second worker, Rodrigo Núñez (Elk 2018). Hugo's union, the Painters Union Local 82, hired a lawyer to represent him, and eventually he won political asylum. Rodrigo was less fortunate and was deported back to Mexico. Their different fates highlight the continuing split personality in the union movement and its attitude toward undocumented workers. Rodrigo's union, the United Brotherhood of Carpenters, did not defend him (Elk 2018). The leadership of North America's Building Trades Unions has traditionally been one of the whitest sectors of the labor movement. However, over the last two decades as some construction unions sought to organize larger numbers of undocumented workers, the attitude of labor has slowly changed (Elk 2018).

Neidi Dominguez, a thirty-year-old Mexican immigrant who lived in the United States without legal status until she was twenty-five, is the Painters Union's national strategic campaign coordinator. As the first Latina woman to head a major department at the Painters Union, Dominguez has led efforts not only to make her union more vocal and active on immigration, but also to push other unions to be more proactive. Dominguez understands that since the majority of new members in the construction workforce are Latinx, building trades unions must do more to embrace immigrant workers to survive. In response to the Trump administration's enforcement focus on undocumented workers, the Painters Union is one of many that has become a "sanctuary union" and developed programs to defend their membership against the threat of deportation (Elk 2018).

A New York coalition of organized labor and immigrant rights advocates in New York also has emerged. In January 2019, both camps celebrated the passage of the state DREAM Act, which made undocumented immigrants eligible for in-state college tuition assistance. Months later, the state legislature authorized drivers' licenses for undocumented immigrants, a critical measure for migrant workers. Then the legislature passed the landmark Farmworkers Fair Labor Practices Act, which focused on working conditions, overtime pay, a day off, unemployment benefits, and the right to organize (Hennelly 2019).

Make no mistake. Labor unions are playing defense following a string of adverse decisions from the US Supreme Court and the National Labor Relations Board – both bolstered by Trump appointees – while right-to-work laws have decimated union membership in a number of states. However, an alliance between unions and immigrants offers a path forward. The relationship between immigrants and labor is important in the battle over how the United States chooses to define itself. The immigrants' rights movement has been lauded for its successful organizing models, often drawing upon the vitality and ingenuity of immigrant-based worker centers, which themselves have emerged as alternatives to traditional labor unions (Rathod 2014). This collaboration is revitalizing the US labor movement.

ATTACK ON DEMOCRACY DURING THE TRUMP ICE AGE

Viewed as an assault on workers who represent the future of the American labor movement, workplace raids by ICE are aptly regarded as an attack on democratic attempts to advocate for workers' rights in the United States. Certainly, going through three versions of the Muslim ban before it passed constitutional muster, diverting billions from the Pentagon's budget to fund border wall construction, and using faulty legal arguments to terminate DACA are emblematic of the Trump administration's disregard for the rule of law and democratic principles. However, specifically targeting workers without papers who are otherwise protected by the NLRA strikes at the heart of organizing efforts.

While difficult to quantify precisely, the election of Donald Trump "unleashed" ICE officers bent on greater enforcement who felt constrained under the Obama administration. Many ICE agents did not like the lenient prosecutorial discretion memos issued by the Obama administration; the ICE union unsuccessfully tried to sue the Obama administration over the DACA program, arguing that the deferred action program undermined their duty to enforce the law. The border patrol union threw its support behind candidate Trump during the 2016 primaries, stating that he would "embrace the ideas of rank-and-file Border Patrol agents" (Davidson 2016).

Critics of President Trump may focus on one or more substantive issues, such as the insurrection at the Capitol on January 6, 2021, racial justice, the environment, handling of the pandemic, the growing deficit, Russian interference in the election, the Emoluments Clause, and, of course, immigration policy. Like so many authoritarian rulers around the world, Trump engaged in an attack on the rule of law and essential democratic institutions. Like anti-democratic leaders around the world, Trump sought to undermine the free press and erode the independence of law enforcement and the judiciary (McMullin 2018). He called the press the "enemy of the American people," repeatedly labeled reputable media outlets as "fake news," and undermined media watchdogs (Feffer 2018).

We saw these strategies used repeatedly in the immigration realm. This began with Trump's claim that Barack Obama was not a US citizen (repeated with a similar suggestion about Kamala Harris) and included his false assertions that "Mexico is sending us rapists and criminals," that asylum seekers approaching the US southern border are terrorists, that people from "shithole" countries like Haiti and Africa did not deserve temporary protected status, and that sanctuary cities harbor dangerous felons. Trump was also quick to criticize federal judges who ruled against some of his immigration orders. For example, in the space of one week in 2017, President Trump belittled all four judges who ruled against him in separate lawsuits challenging his first Muslim travel ban. He referred to Judge James Robart, a George W. Bush appointee who temporarily suspended the travel ban, as a so-called judge whose decision was "ridiculous." When the case was heard by an appeals court panel, Trump told a group of police chiefs that even a "bad high school student" could understand the ban was authorized by law (Totenberg 2017). In fact, former Acting Attorney General Sally Yates was fired for refusing to defend Trump's first version of the "shameful and unlawful Muslim travel ban." She called Trump's decision to restrict travel to the United States from several majority-Muslim nations "the start of his relentless attacks on our democratic institutions and countless dedicated public servants" (Moreno 2020).

Perhaps the most blatant attack on the judiciary came on the heels of the Supreme Court's decision that the Trump administration's attempt to terminate the Deferred Action for Childhood Arrivals (DACA) program violated the Administrative Procedures Act.[7] While the Court did not doubt that the administration had the authority to terminate DACA if done

---

[7] *Dep't. of Homeland Security v. Regents of the Univ. of California*, 140 S. Ct. 1891 (2020).

properly, its justification at that juncture constituted an "arbitrary and capricious" action. So the DACA program was reinstated by the Court. In spite of the Court's decision – and in a challenge to the fundamental principles of *Marbury* v. *Madison* – the Trump administration refused to adhere to the Supreme Court's authority, refusing to accept new DACA applications after the decision. A federal court subsequently had to order the administration to accept new applications (Rose 2020).

As underscored above, the Trump administration returned to using high-profiled, armed, physical raids. And early in his administration, it became clear that workplace raids were a big priority. ICE oversaw a massive surge in the number of workplace immigration raids in 2018, with more than four times the number of raids aimed at finding and arresting undocumented immigrants compared to the year before. Agents opened 6,848 worksite investigations in the fiscal year of 2018, compared to 1,691 investigations opened in 2017 (Mindock 2018).

The Trump assault also illustrates the vulnerability of undocumented workers. They become targets of ICE at times based on information that ICE has obtained from informants, employer records, or instincts of agents; or they may be targeted by the employers themselves, who may be threatened by organizing activity. A pattern between workers' labor activism and immigration enforcement has been documented, where employers actually call agents to act against workers who seem inclined to organize (Wishnie 2004).

These efforts are appropriately viewed as part of the Trump assault on democracy. The surge in workplace raids comes at a time when unions are making outreach to undocumented workers a priority. Removing the workers strikes at the heart of the today's union movement.

CONTEXTUALIZING THE RACIALIZED EVOLUTION OF IMMIGRATION LAWS AND WORKPLACE RAIDS

The evolution of immigration policy, beginning with the forced migration of African workers through the infamous Asian exclusionary period and then to the southwest border regime, is critical in understanding today's policies and enforcement approaches. The history informs our understanding of today's enforcement regime. Associated institutions exacerbate the effects of the racialized immigration system.

From Dehumanization and Demonization to Criminalization

The institutionalized racism of US immigration laws and enforcement policies reflects the evolution of immigration laws that grappled with constant tension over who is and who is not acceptable as a true American. Early in US history, preferential treatment for Western Europeans was constantly asserted in battles over immigration laws. That perspective was apparent in the forced migration of African workers and in Asian exclusion laws, as well as in the anti-Southern and Eastern European quota system of the 1920s, and is maintained to this very day in the controversy over our southwest border. The Euro-centrism of the nation's identity has enabled the institutionalization of an immigration regime that commodifies those immigrants who are left out – namely, newcomers of color – into a faceless group that can more easily be demonized and even criminalized.

The process of criminalizing the immigrant and their dreams requires multiple steps. First the immigrant is dehumanized, then demonized and labeled a problem, then further degraded until at last their actions or conditions are criminalized. This parallels what Charles Lawrence terms "stigmatization, . . . the process by which the dominant group in society differentiates itself from others by setting them apart, treating them as less than fully human, denying them acceptance by the organized community, and excluding them from participating in that community as equals" (1987).

As Professor Rhonda Magee has pointed out, the immigration system began the dehumanizing dynamics of racism with the forced migration of black laborers called slaves (2009). Although early Chinese immigrants were welcomed with mixed greetings, eventually the anti-Chinese lobby that could not tolerate this "yellow peril" prevailed. Recruited then rejected through efforts like Operation Wetback, Mexican migrants also felt the sting of racial animus. Each of these groups were dehumanized through racism (Hing 2004).

The next step – identifying immigrants as a problem through demonization – involves familiar allegations: they take jobs (thus the need for raids); they cost a lot; they commit crimes; they do not speak English; they damage the environment; they do not share our values; and they simply are different. This problematization-demonization process is implemented by the likes of Donald Trump, Stephen Miller, Lou Dobbs, Steve King, the Center for Immigration Studies, and the Federation of American Immigration Reform. And their tactics are successful in many quarters despite questionable empirical support for their positions. They attack with hysterical statements. While Trump and Steve King do use racial attacks, many in the anti-immigrant ranks do not mention race in their attacks and find a ready audience in members of the public (some gullible, others who themselves are racist) who look around, see immigrants with accents working, and facilely conclude that they must be taking jobs that Americans would otherwise be holding. This brand of xenophobia is recycled from the worst nativist periods of the nation's history.

After hysteria is heightened, the demonization process continues by asking the public if immigration is a problem. Modern day polls and surveys claim to reveal that if asked specifically about immigration, 80 percent of respondents think that current immigration is bad for the country. But when general polls ask respondents to name serious societal problems, immigration is either ranked low or not mentioned. Or when the public is asked whether legalization should be granted to undocumented workers and families who pay a fine, the resounding answer is yes.

Even in the midst of a robust economy, the modern problematization-demonization process has proven wildly successful. Restrictionist strategies have worked, as their proponents define the issues largely in their own terms of alleged economic and fiscal impact. Pro-immigrant sentiment and immigrant rights groups essentially are silenced in the media. The media offers unproven economic claims that blame immigrants for job loss and wage depression in place of the more complex reality. Politicians point fingers at the disenfranchised, voiceless alien to grab the attention of voters. The media and these politicians serve as convenient and effective conduits for demonizing aliens. Their effectiveness is striking, as little attention is paid to the economic benefits of immigration.

As the level of demonization through anti-immigrant rhetoric reaches new heights, popular talk radio hosts, Fox news anchors, conservative columnists, and politicians (Democrats and Republicans alike) chime in. The notion of America as the land of immigrants is brushed aside. The neo-nativists claim that things are different today. Much of the rhetoric strikes a chord with well-meaning, but misguided, members of the public who sense a lack of control over a variety of things that affect their lives and who are looking for simple answers. Scapegoating is in, and the blame can be dispensed in non-racial terms, using phrases like "porous" borders, "broken" immigration system, "illegal" aliens, or "criminal" aliens. The framework of the visa and enforcement systems do the dirty work of exclusion and deportation of those noncitizens.

Once demonized, immigrants can be further dehumanized. Dehumanization at this stage commodifies immigrants, stripping them of race and ethnicity. The dominant group further advances the immigrant-as-commodity notion to ignore race and view the immigrant as a labor-providing commodity. This facilitates the dehumanization that follows. Like the black-migrant commodities (enslaved African workers), the modern immigrant commodity is not treated as human. Rather, even the Supreme Court likens immigrant commodities to "hazardous waste dumps."[8] The Court has ruled that dangerous and hazardous materials are "commerce" subject to Commerce Clause scrutiny; and the immigrant-toxic-waste-dump commodity has little constitutional protection in this dehumanized state. Dehumanization thus silences the immigrants. Dehumanization allows the public to ignore their faces and their humanity. Once dehumanized, deportation is easily facilitated without asking why particular migrants come here in the first place.

Employer sanctions – the statutory provision that justifies the arrest of undocumented workers – is a major step in the dehumanization-demonization-commodification-criminalization process. Previously rejected, the employer sanctions effort was accomplished as part of IRCA in 1986. Throughout the debate, Mexican workers were largely the focal point, but they became dehumanized and commodified simply as "unauthorized" workers once sanctions were enacted (Hing 2009). The groundwork was laid for workplace raids.

Structural Relationships

Based on the manner in which immigration laws and enforcement policies have evolved, racism has been institutionalized in those laws and policies. However, writers such as john a. powell urge us to do more and to examine how different institutions interrelate with one another to produce an even more sinister dynamic. Thus, powell would encourage us to look beyond the institutionalized racism within US immigration laws and enforcement policies that have become part of the "structure" of those laws and policies, and to look at the interaction between institutions for what he terms "structural racism." powell invites us to take the institution of immigration laws and policies and see how that institution relates to other institutions that can produce racial outcomes (Grant-Thomas & powell 2006).

It does not take long to realize that while immigration laws and enforcement policies have evolved in a manner that continues to prey on Asians, Mexicans, and other Latinx migrants, the relationship of those laws and policies with other racialized institutions underscores the structural challenges that immigrants of color face. Consider the North American Free Trade Agreement (NAFTA) and the World Trade Organization (WTO). NAFTA placed Mexico at such a competitive disadvantage with the United States in the production of corn that Mexico now imports most of its corn from the United States, and Mexican corn farmworkers have lost their earnings. The US-embraced WTO implements global free trade and favors lowest-bid manufacturing nations like China and India, so that manufacturers in a country like Mexico cannot compete and must lay off workers. It is of little wonder that so many Mexican workers look to the United States for jobs (Hing 2010). Think also of refugee resettlement programs as an institution. When Southeast Asian

---

[8] In *INS* v. *Lopez-Mendoza*, 468 US 1032 (1984), the Supreme Court refused to extend the exclusionary rule derived from the Fourth Amendment to deportation proceedings. In the process, Justice Sandra Day O'Connor reasoned: Presumably no one would argue that the exclusionary rule should be invoked to prevent an agency from ordering corrective action at a leaking hazardous waste dump if the evidence underlying the order had been improperly obtained, or to compel police to return contraband explosives or drugs to their owner if the contraband had been unlawfully seized.

refugees are resettled in public housing or poor neighborhoods, their children find themselves in an environment that can lead to bad behavior or crime. Consider US involvement in wars and civil conflict in Central America. Think also of US involvement in places like Vietnam, Afghanistan, or Iraq – places that have produced involuntary migrants of color to our shores. Other racialized institutions that interact with immigration laws and enforcement also come to mind: the criminal justice system, inner-city schools, and poor neighborhoods. These institutions can lead to situations that spell trouble within the immigration enforcement framework, providing further foundation for workplace immigration raids.

LABOR ORGANIZING AS AN INGREDIENT OF DEMOCRACY

The interference to labor organizing exemplified by raids at noncitizen worksites is an assault on democracy. The right to organize is closely related to the constitutional right to free association and assembly. In a democracy, the right of individuals to band together and pursue their interests with like-minded people is considered an essential element of freedom. Although the Constitution does not specifically mention "freedom of association," the Supreme Court long ago recognized that First Amendment free speech and freedom of assembly provisions necessarily imply a corollary right to freedom of association.[9] Moreover, the Supreme Court has specifically applied the right of association to labor unions, striking down government efforts to quash union-based associational rights.[10]

Unions play a critical role in democracy. Unions decrease employers' discretion to make arbitrary and abusive decisions to fire workers or to pay some workers more than others – which can reduce opportunities for discrimination. Many Americans do not realize that most employees work "at will," meaning they can be fired for any reason or no reason at all. Unions, by contrast, usually bargain for the right to be fired only for "just cause." This higher standard for termination helps minority or female employees who are discriminated against because it is much easier to prove that a termination was unjust or arbitrary rather than having to go further and prove that it was also motivated by race or sex discrimination (Kahlenberg & Marvit 2019: 105).

The protections that unions provide against discrimination are especially important in low-wage jobs, where employers are more likely to act arbitrarily, women and employees of color are more likely to be concentrated, and the low value of lost wages makes it difficult to attract an attorney for litigation on a contingency-fee basis. Plaintiffs in unionized firms are more likely to be successful with their employment discrimination suits, and they are less likely to be dismissed or to settle early. Thus, for a variety of reasons – including more uniform pay scales and the availability of grievance procedures – there appears to be "less discrimination among union workers" (Kahlenberg & Marvit 2019: 106). Guarding against unjust discrimination is an important democratic principle.

More broadly, at a time when American democracy is under tremendous stress – with attacks on the free press, an independent judiciary, and religious and racial minorities – we need a strong labor movement more than ever. Democracies need a strong middle class, and unions help create shared prosperity (Kahlenberg & Marvit 2019: 110). Civic organizations that are run democratically can also be an important mechanism for acculturating citizens to the inner workings of democracy. Unions are among the most important of these organizations, bringing

---

[9] *NAACP v. Alabama*, 357 US 449 (1958).
[10] *Thomas v. Collins*, 323 US 516 (1945); *see also Smith v. Arkansas State Highway Employees Local*, 441 US 463 (1979).

together rank-and-file workers from a variety of ethnic, racial, and religious backgrounds, and serving as "schools for democracy" (Putnam 2000: 80–81). Labor unions can also help create a culture of participation among workers. Being involved in workplace decisions and the give-and-take of collective bargaining, voting on union contracts, and voting for union leadership all have been called important drivers of "democratic acculturation" (Kahlenberg & Marvit 2019: 110).

Historically, unions have participated in the democratic political process, collaborating with political parties and influencing policy. They can facilitate the social compromise necessary to enact vital legislation. Politically active unions are also more likely to work within legal frameworks to resolve disputes, strengthening the government's institutional legitimacy and the rule of law (Becker 2011).

Freedom of association and collective bargaining are crucial components of a well-functioning democracy. While it may seem tempting to limit the ability of organized labor's political participation – either as a means to political expediency or economic growth – such actions can easily backfire, undermining the institutions for dispute resolution that are important in any well-functioning democratic society (Becker 2011).

The democratic goal of protecting civil rights also is bolstered by the labor movement. Both are concerned about the same principles: "the dignity of individuals, who have the right to be respected and valued whatever their job or race; the importance of equality, both racial and economic; the centrality of the right to vote – both for elected representatives in government and for union leadership – to bring about greater political and workplace democracy; and the salience of human solidarity, that is, the need to rise above our atomized existence to join together to improve the larger society" (Kahlenberg & Marvit 2019: 101).

CONCLUSION

Democracy is under attack through immigration workplace raids. Labor unions have finally come to realize that noncitizen workers – documented and undocumented – are their future. ICE raids have been timed – particularly by the Bush and Trump administrations – to thwart organizing efforts. Through a process of demonizing and commodification of immigrant workers, the public has been conditioned to ignore the racial implications of ICE raids. But even a cursory examination reveals the racist effects of these enforcement efforts. However, closer analysis reveals how these attacks are an attack on democracy as well. ICE raids are an attack on labor organizing, which in turn represents an assault on freedom of association, freedom from discrimination, a strong middle class, and democratic acculturation.

REFERENCES

Agarwal, Neel. 2021. "Biden's Unfulfilled Promise to End 287(g) Agreements with Local Law Enforcement," *Immigration Impact* (June 24, 2021). https://immigrationimpact.com/2021/06/24/biden-287g-agreements-police/#.YPSLTuhKjcs

Bacon, David, and Bill Ong Hing. 2010. "The Rise and Fall of Employer Sanctions," 38 *Fordham Urban Law Journal* 38, 1: 77–105.

Becker, Jeff. 2011. "Organized Labor's Role in Democratic Transitions," Center for American Progress, June 20, 2011. www.americanprogress.org/issues/security/news/2011/06/20/9744/organized-labors-role-in-democratic-transitions/

Budiman, Abby. 2020. "Key Findings About US Immigrants," *Pew Research Center* (August 20, 2020). www.pewresearch.org/fact-tank/2020/08/20/key-findings-about-u-s-immigrants/

Bynum, Russ. 2006. "Immigration Raids Leave Georgia Town Bereft, Stunned," *Seattle Times* (Sept. 16, 2006).

Davidson, Joe. 2016. "Border Patrol Agents Union Endorses Trump." *The Washington Post* (March 30, 2016). www.washingtonpost.com/news/powerpost/wp/2016/03/30/border-patrol-agents-union-endorses-trump/

Elk, Mike. 2018. "Undocumented Workers Find New Ally as Unions Act to Halt Deportations," *The Guardian* (March 22, 2018). www.theguardian.com/us-news/2018/mar/22/unions-undocumented-workers-immigration-deportation-painters

Feffer, John. 2018. "Donald Trump's War on Democracy," *The Nation* (Sept. 24, 2018). www.thenation.com/article/archive/donald-trumps-war-on-democracy/

Figueroa, Hector. 2019. "The Labor Movement Can Rise Again," *The New York Times* (July 12, 2019) www.nytimes.com/2019/07/12/opinion/hector-figueroa.html

Garcia, Ruben J. 2012. Ten Years After *Hoffman Plastic Compounds, Inc.* v. *NLRB*: The Power of a Labor Law Symbol, *Cornell Journal of Law & Public Policy* 21: 659 (2011–2012).

Grant-Thomas, Andrew, and John A. Powell. 2006. "Toward a Structural Racism Framework," *Poverty & Race* 15, 6: 3–6.

Hennelly, Bob. 2019. "There's a Future for Organized Labor – If It Welcomes Immigrants and Supports Them," *Salon* (Sept. 1, 2019). www.salon.com/2019/09/01/theres-a-future-for-organized-labor-if-it-welcomes-immigrants-and-supports-them/

Hing, Bill Ong. 2004. *Defining America through Immigration Policy*. Philadelphia: Temple University Press.

    2006. *Deporting Our Souls: Values, Morality, and Immigration Policy*. Cambridge, MA: Cambridge University Press.

    2009. "Institutional Racism, ICE Raids, and Immigration Reform," *USF Law Review* 44, 2: 307–352.

    2010. *Ethical Borders: NAFTA, Globalization, and Mexican Migration*. Philadelphia: Temple University Press.

Jones, Jeffrey M. 2019. "As Labor Day Turns 125, Union Approval Near 50-Year High," *Gallup*, August 28, 2019. https://news.gallup.com/poll/265916/labor-day-turns-125-union-approval-near-year-high.aspx

Jordan, Miriam. 2020. "After a Pandemic Pause, ICE Resumes Deportation Arrests," *The New York Times* (Sept. 14, 2020). www.nytimes.com/2020/09/12/us/ice-immigration-sweeps-deportation.html#:~:text=The%20Trump%20administration%20says%20it,caught%20up%20in%20immigration%20sweeps

Kahlenberg, Richard D, and Moshe Z. Marvit. 2019. "Making Labor Organizing a Civil Right," in Bales, Richard, and Charlotte Garden, (Eds.) 2019. *The Cambridge Handbook of US Labor Law for the Twenty-First Century*. Cambridge: Cambridge University Press.

Lawrence, Charles R. 1987. "The Id, the Ego, and Equal Protection: Reckoning with Unconscious Racism," *Stanford Law Review* 39, 2: 317–388.

Magee, Rhonda V. 2009. "Slavery as Immigration." *University of San Francisco Law Review* 44, 2: 273–306.

Milkman, Ruth. 2009. "Immigrant Workers and the Future of American Labor," *ABA Journal of Labor & Employment Law* 26, 2: 295–310.

Mindock, Clark. 2018. "US Workplace Immigration Raids Surge 400% in 2018," *The Independent* (Dec. 12, 2018). www.independent.co.uk/news/world/americas/us-politics/ice-immigration-workplace-migrants-undocumented-immigrants-raids-trump-obama-2018-a8678746.html

McMullin, Evan. 2018. "An Attack on the Rule of Law," *The Atlantic* (Apr. 13, 2018). www.theatlantic.com/politics/archive/2018/04/assault-on-democracy/557912/

Moreno, Edward. 2020. "Sally Yates Appears at Democratic Convention to Rip Trump Travel Ban," *The Hill* (Aug. 18, 2020). https://thehill.com/homenews/campaign/512634-sally-yates-appears-at-democratic-convention-to-rip-trump-travel-ban

National Commission on ICE Misconduct & Violations of Fourth Amendment, Commission Hearing, Boston (2008) (unpublished transcript on file with author).

Newman, Jonah. 2008. Letter to the Editor, *The New York Times* (June 3, 2008).

Putnam, Robert. 2000. *Bowling Alone: The Collapse and Revival of American Community*. New York: Simon & Schuster.

Pham, Huyen. 2018. "287(g) Agreements in the Trump Era," *Washington & Lee Law Review* 75, 3: 1253–1286.

Preston, Julia, "Immigrant, Pregnant, Is Jailed Under Pact," *The New York Times*, July 20, 2008.

Rathod, Jayesh M. 2014. "Riding the Wave: Uplifting Labor Organization through Immigration Reform," *UC Irvine Law Review* 4, 2: 625–654.

Rose, Joel. 2020. "Federal Court Orders Trump Administration to Accept New DACA Applications," *NPR* (July 17, 2020). www.npr.org/2020/07/17/892413311/federal-court-orders-trump-administration-to-accept-new-daca-applications

Totenberg, Nina. 2017. "Trump's Criticism Of Judges Out of Line With Past Presidents." *NPR* (Feb. 11, 2017). www.npr.org/2017/02/11/514587731/trumps-criticism-of-judges-out-of-line-with-past-presidents

United Food and Commercial Workers Union. 2009. "Raids on Workers: Destroying Our Rights."

Wishnie, Michael. 2004. "Introduction: The Border Crossed Us: Current Issues in Immigrant Labor," *NYU Review of Law & Social Change* 28, 3: 389–395.

13

The Care Crisis

Covid-19, Labor Feminism, and Democracy

Deborah Dinner

What is the role of caregiving labor in our democracy? Scholars often consider the relationship between labor and democracy with reference to the role that male-dominated unions and formal labor laws have played in struggles for civil and political rights. Yet that frame obscures the place of care work in social citizenship, which T.H. Marshall defined to include rights that range from basic economic security to the enjoyment of a nation's cultural heritage and prevailing living standards (Marshall 1950: 11, 43–44). Marshall's explanation of the progression from civil, to political, to social rights was based on the experience of white working-class men. He portrayed the subordination of women and racial minorities as an anachronism in liberal societies, ignoring that the historical development of full citizenship for white men in England and the United States rested on coverture and slavery (Fraser & Gordon 1992: 48–60). Feminists have criticized theories of social citizenship for failing to take account of injustices within the family, the social and legal construction of divides between private and public spheres, the existence of cultural pluralism, and the limitations of the nation state (Nakano Glenn 1992; Kymlikca & Norman 1994: 358–359, 369–371). Notwithstanding their trenchant critiques, feminists have also used the idea of social rights as a theoretical foundation in arguing that the state should recognize and support caregiving labor (Fineman 2005: 208–213; McClain 2001: 1691–1698; McCluskey 2003: 818). To understand the historical development of social citizenship in the United States, including political mobilization for its expansion and contraction, researchers must analyze the intersecting legal regulation of caregiving labor in the home and in the workplace.

Expansive literatures in history, law, and the social sciences analyze the gendered and racialized organization of care work. This form of work, whether paid or unpaid, involves the affective and physical labor extended to meet the needs of dependents, including children, the elderly, and people who are disabled and sick (England & Folbre 1999; Folbre 2006: 186–187).[1] Women have historically cooked, cleaned, and performed child and elder care without remuneration in the home, in their roles as mothers, wives, and daughters and, during the antebellum era, as slaves (Boydston 1990, Giddings 1984: 33–55; Jones 2009). Women of color have disproportionately occupied low-wage, contingent jobs as domestic workers, childcare providers, and home healthcare aides (Hunter 1997). Historically, this labor was often invisible in economic analyses and undervalued within law and policy.

---

[1] Care work also includes labor to meet the needs of able-bodied adults and the self, but feminist scholars and this chapter generally focus on care for dependents.

Covid-19 moved caregiving labor from the margins to the center of national debate, high-lighting a scholarly imperative to do the same. Neoliberal policies implemented over the last half century rendered the nation ill prepared to address the coronavirus. As the pandemic gripped the United States, it exacerbated an existing care crisis. Nurses and home care workers provided essential services to elderly and sick persons in need of care, while risking their own lives (just a few of the headlines illuminating this: "Hundreds of Healthcare Workers Lost Their Lives Battling the Coronavirus," *The Washington Post*, June 17, 2020; "How Coronavirus Could Forever Change Home Healthcare, Leaving Vulnerable Older Adults without Care and Overburdening Caregivers," *The Conversation*, May 18, 2020). Middle-class professionals juggled Zoom meetings from the kitchen table with childcare and home-schooling (another headline: "Work From Home Is Here to Stay," *The Atlantic*, May 4, 2020). Approximately half of the nation's childcare slots were placed at risk of elimination (Jessen-Howard & Workman 2020; Sohn 2020). A political showdown pitted teachers' safety against an economic interest in getting students' parents back to work ("'Not Knowing, It's Just Killing Us' – Parents, Teachers Wrestle with Reopening Schools," *Los Angeles Times*, July 15, 2020). The devastating social conse-quences of Covid-19 highlighted the critical importance of caregiving labor, paid and unpaid, to public health and to a market economy.

Beyond its material consequences, the Covid care crisis has threatened our democracy. To begin, it jeopardizes "social reproduction:" the resources, relationships, and labor necessary to replicate the next generation and to sustain individuals across the life course (Nakano Glenn 1992: 1). Social reproductive labor is essential to the survival of society and, consequently, the state, market, and social institutions are indebted to those who perform it (Fineman 2001: 1409–1413). The care crisis undermines the functioning of key social reproductive institutions including hospitals, schools, nursing facilities, and families. In addition, the care crisis has deepened gender and racial hierarchies in the labor market and in families. African-American and Latinx workers, particularly women of color, suffered the economic devastation of the pandemic disproportionately. They were more likely both to serve as low-wage, essential workers and to be laid off (Powell 2020). These inequities render our social and political fabric even more fragile. Furthermore, the Covid care crisis has exacerbated the class inequality that contributes to populist enthusiasm for authoritarian government.

This chapter draws on the history of labor and socialist feminist activism to explore the roots of the Covid care crisis and its potential solutions. Since the New Deal, labor and socialist feminists have fought for justice in the organization of care work. They have pursued social insurance support for families, workplace policies that accommodate workers' family lives, better job conditions for paid care workers, and a more equitable division of caregiving labor within families. Yet market and social conservatives defeated their most ambitious proposals and thereby weakened the social and economic citizenship rights at the core of a healthy democracy. This chapter suggests the need for a broader understanding of the relationship between labor and democracy – one which links caregivers' struggles for justice in the workplace and in the home.

THE CARE CRISIS AND ITS GENDERED AND RACIALIZED CONSEQUENCES

The coronavirus pandemic intensified a care crisis within families, in welfare state policies, and in labor law. First, the pandemic has deepened gender inequality in the allocation of responsi-bility for unpaid caregiving labor. Parents navigated the care crisis by squeezing paid work time into the wee hours, juggling newborn infants in their arms while homeschooling older children, and making excruciating decisions to leave their own jobs ("In the Covid-19 Economy, You Can Have a Kid or a Job. You Can't have Both," *The New York Times*, July 8, 2020; "The Coronavirus Is a Disaster for Feminism," *The Atlantic Magazine*, Mar. 19, 2020). As daycare centers, schools, and camps shut their doors, families needed to take on the childcare functions that these institutions ordinarily perform. Many parents were also cut off from informal sources of care provided by kin and by neighbors. All parents bore the burdens of the care crisis. It is important to note that single parents and primary caregivers in two-parent households (most often mothers) experienced the crisis most intensely.

Single parents and queer families are under-represented within the media coverage and the nascent social science literature discussing Covid-19's consequences for care work. That is not surprising given the normative image of the family in US political culture remains that of two, married parents caring for children (Fineman 1995: 143–144; Polikoff 2008: 1–3). Same-sex marriage has broadened that image but not fundamentally disrupted it. In reality, single mothers care for nearly a quarter of the nation's children. In the context of the pandemic, they faced a nearly impossible task navigating the conflicting demands of family and work, especially if they became sick.[2] Queer families faced particular challenges in the pandemic arising from social stigma, discrimination in family law, and the logistical challenges of raising children across multiple households. But past experience co-parenting, forging caregiving networks across multiple households, and chosen kin also may have invested queer families with greater resilience to weather the crisis (Kessler 2008: 176–183; "How Co-Parenting Equipped Queer Families to Handle the Coronavirus Pandemic," *HuffPost Canada*, April 24, 2020).

Survey data and media reports suggest that the pandemic had mixed effects on gender roles within heterosexual couples. Some couples split housework and childcare in a more egalitarian manner. In other families (according to some researchers, in most families) the pandemic intensified women's primary responsibility for caregiving labor (Carlson et al. 2020; "Women Already Do Most Domestic Work. The Coronavirus Makes the Gap Worse," *The Philadelphia Inquirer*, May 11, 2020). Mothers took on the work of supervising home-schooling, in particular ("Nearly Half of Men Say They Do Most of the Home-Schooling. 3 Percent of Women Agree," *The New York Times*, May 8, 2020). Outraged commentators sounded the alarm that the pandemic pushed back the feminist cause by decades ("COVID-19 Should Be a Wake-Up Call for Feminists," *Jacobin Magazine*, April 15, 2020). More accurately, the pandemic exposed the fact that late-twentieth century feminism changed the composition of the workforce more than it transformed the social organization of care. Mothers of children under age eighteen increased their labor force participation rates, from 47 percent in 1970 to 72 percent in 2019 (US Bureau of Labor Statistics 2008: Table 7; US Bureau of Labor Statistics 2020). Yet their caregiving responsibilities within the family did not decrease in corresponding degrees. Rather, middle- and working-class mothers have long performed a "second shift" in the home at the end of the paid workday, sacrificing time available for leisure and for self-care (Hochschild & Machung 1989). The pandemic rendered that shift more arduous and more visible.

---

[2] In 2016, 23 percent of the nation's children lived with single mothers (The Majority of Children Live with Two Parents, Census Bureau Reports [Nov. 17, 2016], available at www.census.gov/newsroom/press-releases/2016/cb16-192.html. For personal accounts, see Tracy Clark-Flory, "Imbalancing Act: A Single Mom with Covid-19 Symptoms Self-Isolates Away from Her Daughters," *Jezebel*, April 8, 2020, available at https://jezebel.com/imbalancing-act-a-single-mom-with-covid-19-symptoms-se-1842727661; Eli Saslow, "Jessica Santos-Rojo on Working, Teaching, and Parenting at Home in the Coronavirus Crisis," *The Washington Post*, Sept. 5, 2020, available at www.washingtonpost.com/nation/2020/09/05/working-while-parenting-coronavirus-pandemic/?arc404=true.

In her influential essay "The Politics of Housework," radical feminist Pat Mainardi called upon men to take on their fair share (1970). Activists of the period imagined that gender equality, and a more humane lifestyle for both sexes, might be achieved by parents sharing the rewards and the burdens of employment and caregiving labor (Swinth 2018: 70–133). That is not what happened, however. Even as women's socioeconomic roles transformed, hegemonic masculinity and its role in the organization of work proved resistant to change (Dinner 2017b: 292–294; Dowd 2008: 231–232; McGinley 2011: 1–5). Employers discriminated against male caregivers (Bornstein 2012; Cunningham-Parmeter 2013; Garcia 2012). They also resisted implementing workplace accommodations, such as prohibitions on mandatory overtime, reduced hours, and job-sharing, that would have made jobs more amenable to family life (Williams 2008: 68–108). In lieu of both mothers and fathers working less in the market, women increased their total hours of paid and unpaid labor (Folbre et al. 2005: 388; Sayer et al. 2004: 17–20). Higher-income families solved their care problems by purchasing the services of nannies, home healthcare workers, and maids, often immigrant women of color (Guarnizo & Rodriguez 2017: 8; Sassen 1991: 254–255; Zimmerman 2006).

The pandemic laid bare the fragility of such privatized workarounds around the absence of workplace accommodations for caregiving. The combination of intensified family responsibilities and employer inflexibility regarding work arrangements pushed many mothers out of their jobs ("Real Life Horror Stories from the World of Pandemic Motherhood," *The New York Times*, Aug. 26, 2020). According to advocates at the Center for WorkLife Law, employers also discriminated against mothers by blocking their unemployment assistance claims. Although Congress modified unemployment insurance during the pandemic to allow claims when an employee leaves a job due to lack of childcare, many employers nonetheless characterized such departures as personal. Meanwhile, paid caregivers, often women of color who themselves contracted the virus at higher rates, suffered additional economic hardships. Due to public health officials' fear that daycare centers would be vectors of community spread and parents' fear of their households' exposure, many home-based caregivers were laid off.

The second, related dimension of the care crisis is the inadequacy of welfare state supports for working parents. Since the 1970s, federal policies have facilitated market-based rather than public childcare (Michel 1999: 247–280). Yet the market has proven incapable of consistently delivering affordable, high-quality care (Blau 2001: 10–11; Harbach 2015: 669–672; Zigler et al. 2009: 9–12). In 2018, more than half of American families lived in a "childcare desert" – a census tract with three times more young children than available childcare slots. Middle-income communities were more likely than either high- or low-income communities to lack sufficient childcare, and such deserts were rampant in rural areas (Malik et al. 2020: 2, 4–5). The pandemic threatened to devastate the nation's already fragile childcare infrastructure. By late April 2020, 60 percent of licensed childcare providers had closed; others reduced their spaces and hours. Because providers operate on such tight margins, they were unlikely to survive extended closure (Malik et al. 2020: 4–5). Congress' coronavirus relief bill allocated $3.5 billion to the Child Care Development Block Grant,[3] but this fell far short of the $50 billion experts say is required to preserve an adequate childcare supply (Jessen-Howard & Workman 2020). In stark contrast,

---

[3] Since the Coronavirus Aid, Relief, and Economic Security Act (CARES) Act, HR 748, which allocated $3.5 billion for childcare, Congress has evaluated two bills which would provide financial resources for childcare services. The Moving Forward Act, HR 2, passed the House on July 20, 2020. The Child Care is Essential Act, S.3874, was introduced in the Senate on June 3, 2020.

other countries responded to the coronavirus by expanding government-funded public childcare ("Australia Is Providing Free Childcare to Help Flatten the Curve," *Jezebel*, April 3, 2020).

The childcare emergency reflected the broader paucity of welfare state supports for working families. The dearth of social insurance systems supporting workers' family care responsibilities has resulted from dual aspects of US political culture. To begin, throughout the twentieth century, policymakers subscribed to a public/private divide. According to sociologist Gøsta Esping-Andersen's famous typology, the United States developed a liberal welfare regime (1990: 9–34). The defining value of such regimes is that the family and not government should be primarily responsible for social reproduction. The political scientist Jacob Hacker argues that the hallmark of American exceptionalism is not the paucity of the welfare regime, but rather its privatized character. The United States provides for social welfare via employment benefits and tax subsidies. This policy design, Hacker explains, deepens class inequalities in the provision of benefits (2002: 4–24). Professional women workers, for example, are significantly more likely to have access to maternity leave or family leave than low-income women workers (O'Leary 2007: 6–8). The dearth of universal entitlements means that many fall through the cracks of welfare provisioning altogether. By contrast, social democratic countries have comprehensive systems of social insurance – government entitlements funded by mandatory contributions that spread the costs of risk across society. A significant percentage of Americans shoulder routine care obligations without public support. They consequently experience periods of heightened need triggered by childbearing, unemployment, sickness, disability, and old age.

In addition, gender stereotypes have shaped the few social insurance programs that do exist. During the Progressive Era and New Deal, policymakers designed social insurance programs on the model of the family-wage ideal: the notion that a male breadwinner should preside at the helm of the family and earn a wage sufficient to support a dependent wife who cared for children within the home (Kessler-Harris 2001: 7, 42–44; Woloch 2015: 22–23). While this ideal provided a foundation for white workingmen's demands for a living wage, it also reinforced a gendered division of labor within the family. Accordingly, policymakers modeled workers' compensation, unemployment insurance, Social Security, and temporary disability insurance (in a handful of states) on white male industrial workers (Mettler 1998; Witt 2009). At their origins, many of these programs explicitly discriminated on the basis of sex. For example, injured male but not female workers received benefits to support their families; female widows but not male widowers caring for young children were eligible for "mothers' benefits." Even when rendered sex neutral from the 1940s through the 1970s, social insurance programs modeled on male workers fell short of extending to women workers protection for specifically gendered needs. For example, states denied unemployment benefits to women workers separated from the workforce because of pregnancy, even when their employers fired them solely because of their pregnant status. Social Security channeled economic support for dependent homemakers via their marital status, rendering women economically vulnerable upon divorce (Dinner 2022).

The public/private divide in social provision and the gendered design of social insurance has contributed to the socioeconomic insecurity of working mothers. The United States is notorious as the only industrialized nation that does not offer paid maternity leave ("The World's Richest Countries Guarantee Mothers More than a Year of Paid Maternity Leave. The US Guarantees Them Nothing," *The Washington Post*, Feb. 5, 2018). The Pregnancy Discrimination Act of 1978 prohibits discrimination on the basis of pregnancy. But it creates a comparative right to equal treatment rather than an affirmative entitlement to pregnancy-based accommodations in the workplace or to maternity leave (Dinner 2017a: 1110–1113, Grossman & Thomas 2009: 41–49).

Only eight states and the District of Columbia have enacted paid family leave laws.[4] The Family and Medical Leave Act of 1993 (FMLA) provides twelve weeks of unpaid leave to eligible employees who cannot work because of their own serious health conditions or because they need to care for a newborn infant, for a child placed with the employee for adoption or foster care, or for an immediate family member with a serious health condition.[5] The FMLA's eligibility criteria, however, exclude 40 percent of the nation's private-sector workers. Furthermore, many of those who are covered cannot afford to take unpaid leave (Barzilay 2012).

The Families First Coronavirus Response Act, for the first time in the nation's history, enacted a federal mandate for paid leave. The Act amended the FMLA to provide leave and to replace lost income when an employee needed to care for a son or daughter due to Covid-related school or childcare closures. In addition, the Act created two weeks of paid sick leave available to covered employees who could not work because they were quarantined or experiencing Covid symptoms, were caring for an immediate family member who was quarantined, or were caring for children due to school or childcare closures.[6] The Coronavirus Response Act had the potential to act as a wedge that cracked open political opportunity for broader paid leave. Even the reference to "Emergency" in the title of the Act, however, suggested its political framing as exceptional legislation, restricted to the apex of the pandemic.

The lack of state support helping to reconcile work and family life forces many women to make agonizing choices between them. A "motherhood penalty," ongoing sex segregation in the labor market, and the undervaluation of "women's jobs" have yielded a persistent earnings gap between women and men (Blau & Kahn 2017; Budig & England 2001; Waldfogel 1997). This has made it more likely that mothers rather than fathers will cut back on their work hours or quit their jobs entirely when family caretaking needs increase. Economic incentives influence the allocation of domestic work between partners, though they are also determined by culture (Andrew et al. 2020; Pew Research 2013: 12, 22–24, 56–58). The coronavirus pandemic heightened the economic and cultural forces pushing women out of the labor market. In part

---

[4] "State Paid Family and Medical Leave Insurance Laws," *National Partnership for Women & Families*, available at www.nationalpartnership.org/our-work/resources/economic-justice/paid-leave/state-paid-family-leave-laws.pdf

[5] 29 USC § 2612(a)(1) (2006).

[6] Both the Emergency Family and Medical Leave Expansion Act (EFMLEA) and the Emergency Paid Sick Leave Act (EPSLA) applied to government agencies and to those private employers with fewer than 500 employees operating in interstate commerce. The EFMLA provided for two weeks unpaid leave and another ten weeks paid leave at two-thirds the employee's average rate. The Department of Labor's temporary regulations exempted business with fewer than fifty employees. Eligibility was extended to those employees on payroll in the thirty calendar days prior to the leave. EPSLA provided for two weeks of paid sick leave at the employee's regular rate of pay if the employee was subject to quarantine or experiencing Covid-19 symptoms and for two weeks of paid leave at two-thirds the regular rate of pay if the employee was caring for an individual subject to quarantine or for a child whose school or childcare provider was unavailable for Covid-related reasons. EPSLA did not have an eligibility requirement for employees related to days or hours of work. The Department of Labor's temporary regulations allowed for exemption of small businesses under EPSLA, only with respect to leave for school or childcare closures. The FFCRA allowed employers to excluded "healthcare providers" and "emergency responders" from leave under both EFMLEA and EPSLA. See Emergency Family and Medical Leave Expansion Act, Pub. L. No. 116–127, Div. C, 134 Stat. 189 (to be codified as amended at 29 USC § 2611 et seq.) Emergency Paid Sick Leave Act, Pub. L. No. 116–127, Div. E, 134 Stat. 195 (to be codified at 29 USC § 2601 note); Paid Leave Under the Families First Coronavirus Response Act, 85 Fed. Reg. 19,326 (April 6, 2020) (temporary rule). At the time of the writing of this chapter, a US District Court in the Southern District of New York struck down the FFCRA's definition of "healthcare provider" along with other provisions of the statute, holding that the Department of Labor exceeded its administrative authority. *New York v. US Dep't of Labor et al.*, 20-cv-03020-JPO (SDNY August 3, 2020). The decision sowed confusion, in part because of a lack of a clarity about whether it applied to employers in states other than New York (Ben Penn, "Judge Creates Regulatory Vacuum, Mass Confusion on Paid Leave," *Bloomberg Law News* [Aug. 5, 2020], available at https://news.bloomberglaw.com/daily-labor-report/ny-judge-creates-regulatory-vacuum-mass-confusion-on-paid-leave).

because work conflicts with family responsibilities and in part because of the differing impacts of the pandemic on specific economic sectors, women experienced Covid-related unemployment at higher rates than men (Sohn 2020).

At the same time, women – in particular women of color – were disproportionately represented within the low-wage "essential" workforce. Nurses and nursing assistants, grocery checkout workers, pharmacists, and home health aides compose the care infrastructure that, in the words of sociologist Mignon Duffy, "holds everything together" (Robertson & Gebeloff 2020). In the context of the pandemic, one in three jobs held by women were deemed essential. Of the nearly 6 million healthcare workers who earn less than $30,000 annually, 83 percent are women. In a cruel irony, many lack health insurance themselves. In some but not all regions, essential workers were provided public childcare. Even as they cared for others on the job, essential workers struggled – alone and in cooperation with each other – to perform caregiving within their own families (Alon et al. 2020: 66–69; Robertson & Gebeloff 2020; "Being a Childcare Worker Has Always Meant Living on the Frontlines," *Jezebel*, March 17, 2020).

The third dimension of the care crisis is the insufficiency of social insurance and labor protections for care workers. Because the federal Fair Labor Standards Act of 1938 regulated only interstate commerce and excluded agricultural and domestic workers, it failed to extend wage and hour protections to the vast majority of women and minority workers (Katznelson 2013: 267–272; Mettler 1998: 198–204). Although a 1974 amendment to the FLSA brought domestic workers within its coverage (Palmer 1995), home care workers only recently came under the coverage of the FLSA.[7] State labor standards regulating wages and hours exclude many low-income care workers. These exemptions from coverage eliminate a critical floor of protection for care workers, disproportionately women and minorities. They also reduce care workers' power to bargain for better job terms. The dearth of protective legislation thus contributes to the economic insecurity of caregivers and lowers the quality of care for clients.

The United States' failure to value care work rendered it unprepared to address the social, health, and economic consequences of the coronavirus. The pandemic, in turn, heightened the care crisis by expanding women's unpaid labor in the home, pushing women out of the workforce, and imperiling the health of essential workers and their families. The care crisis is not an inevitable result of the pandemic. Rather, it is the historical product of politics and policy designs – ones that labor and socialist feminists contested.

VALUING CARE: THE LABOR AND SOCIALIST FEMINIST TRADITIONS

In the popular imagination, late-twentieth century feminists aimed to gain employment opportunity by fighting for equal treatment with men. Certainly, tearing down glass ceilings was an important component of feminists' goals (Schultz 2015). Working-class women fought to escape pink-collar and service-sector ghettos to gain access to higher-paying, blue-collar jobs (MacLean 2008, 117–154). Yet this was only half the story. Historians of gender and labor are now showing that significant strains of the feminist movement in the late 1960s, 1970s, and beyond fought for a more just organization of care work in law, policy, and society. Feminists advocated along three axes: government support for care in the home, workplace policies toward families, and the organization of paid care workers (Cobble 2004; Dinner 2022; Swinth 2018; Turk 2016). This history illuminates alternative paths that law and social policy might have taken, which would

[7] "Home Care Final Rule," 78 Fed. Reg. 60454–60557.

have rendered the nation better prepared to perform the care work necessary to navigate the pandemic.

Women's rights advocates have long argued that society should remunerate women for the care work they perform in their homes. The first argument for "home as work" dated to the antebellum period, when feminists argued that wives held property rights in their household labor. In the postbellum period, feminist argumentation shifted toward challenging the gendered division of labor and arguing for women's rights to work outside the home (Siegel 1994). This strand of modern feminism is the one that predominated over the next century. In the early 1970s, however, socialist feminists revitalized an alternative conception of equity. Socialist feminists fought for policies that would value women's caregiving within the home, rather than for policies that would redistribute this labor to facilitate women's engagement in the formal labor market. The Wages for Housework movement emerged among Marxist feminists in Italy, who fought for state support for social reproduction in the form of improved housing, women-centered healthcare, and better schools. Activists argued that women's household labor merited a wage because childrearing was necessary to replenish the workforce – the fundamental commodity in capitalism.[8]

Though never dominant within US feminism, Wages for Housework nevertheless exerted a powerful influence. From the late 1960s to the mid-1970s, various elements of the women's movement fought for recognition for the social and economic value of housework within US law and policy (Swinth 2018: 100–102). African-American household workers organized to professionalize household employment and successfully advocated legislation amending the FLSA to cover domestic work (Nadasen 2015: 127–130; Palmer 1995). In 1975, the largest feminist advocacy group, the National Organization for Women (NOW), held a Strike for Women's Equality that emphasized women's labor in the home (Dinner 2022). Modernizing the arguments of antebellum women's rights activists for joint property, NOW's Task Force on Marriage and Divorce advanced legal doctrines that would vest homemakers with property rights stemming from their economic contributions to the marriage and, thereby, protect these women if they divorced (Lefkovits 2018: 53–71). Welfare rights activists used the wages for housework theory to support their claim that single mothers and their children deserved public support. Racist hostility to welfare rights, however, undermined political support for the idea of universal remuneration of mothers' caregiving. Ultimately, Wages for Housework proved too threatening

---

[8] Western European nations provide far more economic support for childbearing and childrearing than does the United States. In some countries, maternalist supports helped women maintain labor-force attachment across childbirth but did not disrupt the gendered division of labor. France, for example, introduced job protection for women for the twelve weeks following childbirth in 1966. By 1970, France had enacted fourteen weeks paid maternity leave at 90 percent of earnings. In 1977, the country enacted an additional two years' unpaid parental leave, which the child's father could utilize only if the mother declined her right to the parental leave. Italy's maternity leave policy was coercive rather than voluntary. Since 1950, Italy has required mandatory, job-protected leave in industry of three months prior to childbirth (and of lesser duration in other sectors) and of eight weeks following childbirth. By contrast, other countries developed explicitly egalitarian leave policies. For example, in 1963, Sweden instituted six months paid maternity leave at 80 percent of earnings. In 1974, Sweden replaced this leave with sex-neutral parental leave. Over the next two decades, Sweden both increased the duration of parental leave and modified eligibility criteria to put in place an incentive for fathers to take at least some leave. See OECD Family Database, available at: www.oecd.org/els/family/PF2_5_Trends_in_leave_entitlements_around_childbirth_annex.pdf. The socialist feminist vision came closer to fruition in Italy in recent years. In 2019, Italy's law was amended to allow healthy women to work until childbirth and take five months' leave afterward. In June 2020, Italy passed a Family Act including a universal monthly allowance, paid for each child from the seventh month of pregnancy until the child reaches eighteen years of age. It also implemented mandatory paid paternity leave for ten days. But Italy still lags behind Sweden in terms of both the generosity and the gender egalitarianism of family leave policy. See "How Italy's New 'Family Act' Aims to Increase the Plunging Birth Rate," *The Local*, June 12, 2020, available at: www.thelocal.it/20200612/what-you-need-to-know-about-italys-new-family-act

to the New Right ascendant in the 1970s and to its intertwined ideologies: male authority within home and fiscal conservatism (Dinner 2022).

Feminists' most feasible policy proposal to support unpaid caregiving centered on Social Security reform. The Social Security Act of 1935, and subsequent amendments, entrenched the family-wage ideal within the design of the nation's premier social insurance system. Social Security, meant to protect against economic insecurity at old age, provided benefits directly to wage-earners and indirectly to married women, as dependents of their husbands. Although divorced and widowed women were entitled to some benefits, these were inadequate to protect non-wage earning women upon changes in their marital status. By the mid-1970s, as no-fault divorce swept across the country, both feminists and conservative activists such as Phyllis Schlafly were calling for "homemakers' rights." While conservatives wanted to restore patriarchal family structures and male breadwinners' support for wives, feminists fought for Social Security credits for homemakers (Dinner 2022; Swinth 2018: 100, 107–108, 115–116). Homemakers would be entitled to these benefits even if they divorced or became widowed, in the same way that wage-earners kept their credits when they changed jobs. By directly supporting individuals (mostly mothers) who performed caregiving labors without pay in the home, homemaker credits would enhance caregivers' economic security and reduce women's dependence on men for financial support. In a period of political enthusiasm for Social Security reform during the late 1960s,[9] it seemed that homemakers' credits might have political legs. But, escalating conservatism limited reforms to enhancing divorced spouses and widows' dependency benefits and blocked advocacy for homemaker credits (Dinner 2022).

In addition to economic support for caregiving in the home, feminists pursued workplace policies and welfare entitlements to assist mothers in the workplace. The historian Dorothy Sue Cobble has excavated the activism of "labor feminists," who from the New Deal through the post-World War II period fought for both employment opportunity and social supports for life outside of the workplace. Labor feminists advocated shorter workdays, more flexible hours, and increased sick leave that would help women reconcile employment with daily caregiving responsibilities in the family. In the late 1940s, they advocated that Congress pass the Murray-Dingell bills, which would have created a system of national health insurance including paid maternity leave (Cobble 2004: 127–129). Several labor feminist leaders served as powerful voices on John F. Kennedy's Presidential Commission on the Status of Women, setting forth policy positions that catalyzed subsequent feminist advocacy. These included job security for pregnant workers, childcare services for all women, more family-friendly tax policy, and Social Security reform (Cobble 2004: 142–178; Harrison 1988: 138–167).

After the passage of Title VII of the Civil Rights Act of 1964, which prohibited employment discrimination because of sex, race, color, religion, and national origin, labor feminists fought for expansive conceptions of workplace fairness. They were concerned not only with disparate treatment of men and women, but also with the conditions in sex-segregated jobs that made it harder for working-class women to care for their families (Boris 2014: 45; Turk 2016: 12–42). They did not want simply to vitiate the sex-based state labor standards enacted in the Progressive Era, which regulated the hours and conditions of women's work. Rather, they fought to extend state protective labor standards to men and women alike (Dinner 2017b). In 1974, labor feminists founded the Coalition of Labor Union Women (CLUW), dedicated to organizing for women's rights within both unions and the workplace (Cobble 2004: 200–205). CLUW was instrumental in Congress' passage of the Pregnancy Discrimination Act and the FMLA. Yet labor feminists'

---

[9] Richard Nixon, "Social Security," Compilation of Presidential Documents vol. 5 (September 29, 1969): 1319–1320.

most capacious objectives – voluntary overtime laws, the expansion of state temporary disability insurance, heightened safeguards for reproductive health, and paid parental leave – met with defeat in the face of conservative opposition (Dinner 2022).

Feminists also fought hard for public childcare. In the late 1960s, the women's liberation movement built on the childcare activism of black freedom activists. They argued that free, government-funded, community-controlled childcare should be a right of social citizenship. Activists believed the *right* to childcare, as opposed to market-based daycare, would do more than enable women to engage in paid employment. It would transform gender relations in the family, empower minority communities, and foster the liberation of both children and women from oppressive societal values (Dinner 2010). The confluence of feminist activism and advocacy by child development scholars, anti-poverty reformers, and black freedom activists resulted in Congress' passage of the Comprehensive Child Development Act of 1971 (CCDA). The CCDA would have allocated $2.1 billion to a federal childcare program, providing free services below a lower-middle-class income cutoff and services on a sliding-fee scale above that threshold. The CCDA, however, got caught up in the crossfires of conservative mobilization against the welfare state and for patriarchal gender norms. President Richard Nixon's veto of the CCDA marked the last time that the United States came close to enacting universal childcare. It entrenched a bifurcation between public childcare for the poor and market-based childcare for the middle-class (Dinner 2010; Michel 1999; Morgan 2001).

Even as feminist proposals for a more expansive welfare state succumbed to political opposition, paid care workers organized for better jobs. In 1968, the Service Employees International Union (SEIU) formed to defend the labor rights of home healthcare workers, nurses, cleaners, and other service professionals.[10] Workers and care recipients joined together to demand state funding for states' investment in care services. Over the next several decades, the SEIU challenged sexism in the labor movement, extended organizing campaigns to workers outside traditional union strongholds, and developed into one of the movement's most dynamic sectors (Boris & Klein 2012). Despite the SEIU's achievements, paid household workers continued to face significant obstacles to labor organizing: isolated labor, affective ties to clients that could also deepen exploitation, ongoing exclusion from the National Labor Relations Act (NLRA) and other federal and state labor and employment statutes, doctrinal limitations on union activities, and many workers' immigration status (Lin 2016: 77–78; Rivchin 2004: 410–415; Smith 2000: 57–71; Smith 2007: 1839–1841).

The last two decades have witnessed new and creative forms of labor activism among household workers. One major question for labor organizers was how to identify the entity that employed home care workers, who labored in complex institutional and administrative schemes that involved state funding, county administration, and individual clients. In a protracted legal and political struggle that began in the late 1980s, the SEIU won legislation in California that provided for the establishment of public agencies that serve as the legal employer for home care workers. In 1999, two years after Los Angeles County established such an authority, the SEIU won a campaign to organize the county's 74,000 home care workers (Smith 2000: 71–80). Since the victories in California, labor advocates have established similar legal provisions in at least an additional eight states, establishing an employer of record to facilitate collective bargaining by home care workers. Beginning in Illinois in 2005, at least ten states have taken legal action to enable union organization by family-based childcare providers (Smith 2008: 1404–1420).

[10] The SEIU was originally founded in 1921 as primarily a janitors' union and was called the Building Services Employees Union. It was renamed in 1968 to reflect its diversified membership.

In addition to such legal advocacy and formal unionization campaigns, household workers and their advocates have pursued strategies outside of the NLRA. One of the more powerful ones are worker centers: community-based nonprofits that provide support for low-income workers excluded from unions. These centers emphasize grassroots leadership, communal empowerment, building connections to broader social justice movements, and democratic governance norms. The National Domestic Workers Alliance has successfully organized for better work conditions, respect, and states' passage of domestic workers' bills of rights. The Alliance partnered with SEIU to form Caring Across Generations, an advocacy campaign which argues that better work conditions lead to improved care for clients (Ashar & Fisk 2019: 143–144, 158; Kennedy & Runnels 2013: 910–917; Rivchin 2004: 399–401; Smith 2007: 1839–1841).

Had socialist and labor feminists' visions come to fruition, the United States would not be enmeshed in a care crisis of the severity we now face. Mothers and other caregivers would have received support, such as Social Security credits, for their social reproductive labors. Workplaces would have policies in place, including paid sick and family leave, enabling workers to attend to their families at moments of heightened need. Paid care workers would be entitled to safe job conditions, health protections, and a living wage. Although history can never serve as a blueprint for the future, scholars and advocates may find inspiration to navigate and remediate the current crisis in this past feminist activism. Indeed, the pandemic revitalized labor and socialist feminism precisely because of the threats it posed to social reproduction in the absence of a more robust welfare state. These feminist traditions are evident in worker activism ranging from teacher resistance to a recent landslide election in which 40,000 childcare providers in California voted for union representation.[11]

CARE WORK AND DEMOCRATIC VITALITY

The pandemic highlighted the democratic imperative to build a comprehensive vision for just care work – both unpaid caregiving in the home and paid caregiving services in the market. The Covid care crisis cost health and lives, further weakened the US economy, and destabilized democratic institutions. The inability to meet the care needs of young children and elderly parents both cut lives short and undermined the flourishing of the next generation. It also contributed to unemployment and thereby exacerbated economic fragility. The care crisis has been experienced universally and unevenly at the same time – all families feel its pain but, on average, women do more than men and people of color more than whites. Such inequalities undercut the social citizenship of women and minorities both by restricting their standard of living and constraining their choices respecting the activities they pursue (Korpi 2010). The care crisis also reduced the time and resources women and people of color could invest in movements for gender and racial justice. These movements are both ends in themselves and also essential to activate an engaged citizenry and a robust democracy (Young 1990: 156–191). Last, the care crisis contributed to downward mobility and a sense of precarity in middle-class families, creating conditions that are ripe for authoritarian populist leaders and movements (Rohac et al. 2018).

A just care work system is a feminist issue, not only because women perform a disproportionate share of caregiving labor. A healthy society must account for what the legal theorist Martha Albertson Fineman terms inevitable dependency – the youth, sickness, and aging that all

---

[11] "California's Child Care Providers Win Historic Union Election in a Landslide," *Portside*, July 29, 2020, available at https://portside.org/2020-07-29/californias-child-care-providers-win-historic-union-election-landslide.

experience across the life cycle – and derivative dependency – caregivers' need for societal resources (Fineman 2004). Historically, the family has been the repository of such dependency, subsidizing both markets and the state through the performance of unpaid labor (Fineman 1995: 161–166). The Covid care crisis pierced the veil of this labor's invisibility and rendered painfully obvious the ongoing critical role that families play in social reproduction. The last half century has seen the shift of caregiving functions – ranging from food preparation to childcare – from the family to the market. Yet such commodification has limits – ones more fundamental than mere market failures that may be fixed with minor government interventions. Rather, families – including extended kin, nonmarital romantic partnerships, and chosen families of all kinds – are an inextricable building block of the care infrastructure (Polikoff 2008). Families require and deserve support from the whole of society to perform their caregiving functions.

Care work complicates easy dichotomies between employers and employees, as well as between the economy and public health. The dilemma of how to handle the opening of schools in 2020 illustrated the impossibility of severing economic from caregiving interests. The pandemic highlighted the fact that schools perform dual educational and childcare functions. Aside from the developmental needs of children, parents rely on schools as institutions that perform daycare for their children so that they can participate in the workforce. Teachers, conversely, thus perform dual jobs as educators and care providers. The Trump administration placed pressure on schools to open as a necessary jumpstart to the flailing economy. This framing of the issue pit the interests of students and parents in in-person education against those of teachers and other school staff in their own health and safety ("Reopening Schools Is Way Harder than It Should Be," *The New York Times*, July 23, 2020). Concerned about the health and safety of teachers, staff, and students, the demands of online teaching, and the quality of education, the American Federation of Teachers authorized its state and local chapters to strike. Planned teacher absences and sick-outs, as well as threatened strikes, forced some school districts to reverse plans to reopen or implement more stringent safety measures.[12] Only a comprehensive societal solution that protected both students and school workers had the potential to safeguard the economy and to advance educational purposes in the context of a pandemic. The false dichotomy between market imperatives and public health ended up undermining both the economy and community well-being.

Activists, scholars, and policymakers have advanced policies that hold the potential to transform care work in the United States. All Our Kin, a Connecticut-based nonprofit, recommended that states include support for the health and financial stability of family-based childcare providers as critical components of their economic recovery plans (2020). In the *Boston Review*, Gregg Gonsalves and Amy Kapczynski called for a Community Health Corps that would offer employment to people who need paid work while promoting health and social solidarity

---

[12] For a small sampling of accounts, see: Tommy Beer, "Sick Days, Resignations, and Potential Strikes over Schools Reopening," *Forbes*, Aug. 16, 20202, available at www.forbes.com/sites/tommybeer/2020/08/16/teachers-organize-mass-sick-days-resignations-and-potential-strikes-over-schools-reopening/#12c79d403fe1; Kalyn Belsha, "Influential National Teachers Union Backs Reopening Fight," *Chalkbeat* (Jul. 28, 2020), available at www.chalkbeat.org/2020/7/28/21345279/influential-national-teachers-union-backs-strikes-as-tool-in-school-reopening-fight; James David Dickson and Jennifer Chambers, "20-Student Cap among Terms of DPSCD, Union Agreement to Resume School in Detroit," *The Detroit News*, Aug. 28, 2020, available at www.detroitnews.com/story/news/local/detroit-city/2020/08/28/detroit-public-schools-community-district-union-agreement/5653904002/; Dana Goldstein and Eliza Shapiro, "Teachers Are Wary of Returning to Class, and Online Instruction Too," *The New York Times*, Aug. 13, 2020, available at www.nytimes.com/2020/07/29/us/teacher-union-school-reopening-coronavirus.htmlhttps://www.nytimes.com/2020/07/29/us/teacher-union-school-reopening-coronavirus.html.

("The New Politics of Care," April 27, 2020). The Hawai'i State Commission on the Status of Women proposed the nation's only "feminist economic recovery plan for COVID-19." The plan resisted the notion that widespread unemployment – among the highest rates in the country – represented an economic shutdown. Rather, the plan recognized that the care economy, much of it unpaid, is busier than ever. It called for a reimagining of the state's economy in ways that target social services to women, native communities, and other marginal populations while building sustainable and equitable industries.[13]

President Joe Biden campaigned on a platform of support for both familial and paid caregivers. He endorsed twelve weeks' paid family and medical leave. He also proposed a $775 billion investment in three dimensions of the caregiving infrastructure. First, the proposal involved creating free, universal preschool for three- and four-year olds, and expanding access to quality childcare for children up to five years old via tax credits and sliding-scale subsidies. The plan referenced tax and Social Security credits for informal, unpaid caregivers in the family. Second, Biden's plan expanded community- and home-based care for the elderly and disabled, through Medicaid reform and state innovation funds. Third, the plan proposed improving wages and job conditions for care workers. This would include access to paid family and sick leave and protections for union organizing among care workers, as well as professional training opportunities.[14] Biden's plan echoed labor and socialist feminist activism, revitalizing its commitment to support both working families and paid care workers. In his first months in office, Biden continued to advance this vision. He pressed for the extension of Covid-related paid leave in the American Rescue Plan and expressed a commitment to a national family leave and childcare policy beyond the pandemic ("President Biden Announces American Rescue Plan,"[15] "Biden Is Open to Mandating Paid Family Leave in Future Legislation, Yellen Says," *The Washington Post*, Feb. 7, 2021).

An ambitious proposal for reform at the state level is Universal Family Care, advocated by Ai-jen Poo, director of the National Domestic Workers Alliance and Caring Across Generations ("Coronavirus Will Change the World Permanently. Here's How," *Politico Magazine*, March 19, 2020). Universal Family Care would involve the creation of state social insurance programs, funded either solely by worker contributions or via additional funding sources. Individuals could then use the insurance credits to pay for family or medical leave from work, childcare, or long-term health services. Universal Family Care would thus address families' changing care needs across the life course, recognizing that such needs are interrelated. For example, a worker might need time off to care for both children and an aging parent, or a family caregiver might themselves become sick (National Academy of Social Insurance 2019: 227–297). An advantage of both Biden's proposal and Universal Family Care is that they present integrated approaches to caregiving for children, the elderly, and sick or disabled persons. Too often, these caregiving issues are isolated from one another, fragmenting both the political constituencies organizing for reform and the policy remedies advanced ("Biden's Quietly Radical Care Plan," *The New York*

---

[13] Hawai'i State Commission on the Status of Women, Department of Human Services, State of Hawai'i, "Building Bridges, Not Walking on Backs: A Feminist Economic Recovery Plan for COVID-19," April 14, 2020.

[14] Joe Biden, "The Biden Plan for Mobilizing American Talent and Heart to Create a Twenty-First Century Caregiving and Education Workforce," *Medium* (July 21, 2020), available at https://medium.com/@JoeBiden/the-biden-plan-for-mobilizing-american-talent-and-heart-to-create-a-21st-century-caregiving-and-af5ba2a2dfeb; Christina Wilkie, "Biden Announces $775 Billion Plan to Fund Universal Child Care and In-Home Elder Care." *CNBC* Aug. 3, 2020). Available at www.cnbc.com/2020/07/21/biden-to-unveil-775-billion-plan-to-fund-child-care-and-elder-care.html.

[15] www.whitehouse.gov/briefing-room/legislation/2021/01/20/president-biden-announces-american-rescue-plan/.

Times, Aug. 2, 2020). Both proposals represent holistic visions for just care – an urgent priority for the nation.

Covid-19 did not create, but rather exacerbated a care crisis, which was the product of policy design rather than nature. In the late twentieth century, labor and socialist feminists spoke to the heart of capitalism. They showed that waged labor and its contributions to capital accumulation rest on unpaid labor in the home and low-wage caregiving in the market. Activists fought for the workplace policies, social insurance systems, and welfare entitlements that would support care. Conservatives, however, countered their claims with the argument that law should insulate families from government interference. When conservatives won in political battles, they implemented neoliberal policies that place responsibility for social reproduction on families with minimal public support (Cooper 2017: 21–22; Eichner 2020: 176–192). The care crisis, intensified in the context of a pandemic, has undermined democracy by eroding the already thin social citizenship rights of caregivers – paid and unpaid. It has pushed women out of their jobs and widened gender inequalities in the labor market; jeopardized the health of low-wage workers and communities of color; and threatened the most fundamental institutions of social reproduction, from families to hospitals to schools.

Although neoliberal ideology renders caregiving labor invisible, the disruption in our capitalist system precipitated by the pandemic highlighted this essential form of labor as a political headline. In the face of widespread suffering and fear about the future, democratic movements have argued that the country needs to move from media headlines into action for just care. As devastating as the pandemic has been, it has also presented an opportunity to reimagine social reproduction. It threw into relief the need to allocate the burdens and rewards of caregiving in an egalitarian manner. To build a democracy that promotes the full social belonging of all its members, law and policy must recognize the universality of care needs and the value of caregiving labor.

REFERENCES

All Our Kin. 2020. *A Strong Economy Needs Strong Family Child Care: Principles and State Policy Recommendations.* New Haven, CT: All Our Kin. http://allourkin.org/sites/default/files/A%20Strong%20Economy%20Needs%20Strong%20Family%20Child%20Care%20-%20All%20Our%20Kin.pdf

Alon, Tittan, Matthias Doepke, Jane Olmstead-Rumsey, and Michele Tertile. 2020. "The Impact of Covid-19 on Gender Equality," in Center for Economic Policy Research, *Covid Economics: Vetted and Real-Time Papers* 4: 62–85.

Andrew, Alison, Sarah Cattan, Monica Costa Dias, Christine Farquharson, Lucy Kraftman, Sonya Krutikova, Angus Phimister, and Almudena Sevilla. 2020. "The Gendered Division of Paid and Domestic Work under Lockdown," in Center for Economic Policy Research, *Covid Economics: Vetted and Real-Time Papers* 39: 109–138.

Ashar, Sameer M., and Catherine L. Fisk. 2019. "Democratic Norms and Governance Experimentalism in Worker Centers." *Law and Contemporary Problems* 81, 3: 141–190.

Barzilay, Arianne Renan. 2012. "Back to the Future: Introducing Constructive Feminism for the Twenty-First Century: A New Paradigm for the Family and Medical Leave Act." *Harvard Law & Policy Review* 6, 2: 407–436.

Blau, David M. 2001. *The Child Care Problem: An Economic Analysis.* New York: The Russell Sage Foundation.

Blau, Francine D., and Lawrence M. Kahn. 2017. "The Gender Wage Gap: Extent, Trends, and Explanations." *Journal of Economic Literature* 55, 3: 789–865.

Boris, Eileen. 2014. "Where's the Care?" Labor: Studies in Working-Class History of the *Americas* 11, 3: 43–47.

Boris, Eileen, and Jennifer Klein. 2012. *Caring for America: Home Care Workers in the Shadow of the Welfare State*. New York: Oxford University Press.

Bornstein, Stephanie. 2012. "The Law of Gender Stereotyping and the Work-Family Conflicts of Men." *Hastings Law Journal* 63, 5: 1297–1344.

Boydston, Jeanne. 1990. *Home and Work: Housework, Wages, and the Ideology of Labor in the Early Republic*. New York: Oxford University Press.

Budig, Michelle J., and Paula England. 2001. "The Wage Penalty for Motherhood." *American Sociological Review* 66, 2: 204–225.

Carlson, Daniel, Richard Petts, and Joanna Pepin. 2020. "US Couples' Divisions of Housework and Childcare during COVID-19 Pandemic." *SocArXiv Papers*. https://osf.io/preprints/socarxiv/jy8fn

Cobble, Dorothy Sue. 2004. *The Other Women's Movement: Workplace Justice and Social Rights in Modern America*. Princeton, NJ: Princeton University Press.

Cooper, Melinda. 2017. *Family Values: Between Neoliberalism and the New Social Conservatism*. Cambridge, MA: MIT Press, Zone Books.

Cunningham-Parmeter, Keith. 2013. "Men at Work, Fathers at Home: Uncovering the Masculine Face of Caregiver Discrimination." *Columbia Journal of Gender & Law* 24, 3: 253–301.

Dauber, Michele Landis. 2012. *Sympathetic State: Disaster Relief and the Origins of the American Welfare State*. Chicago: University of Chicago Press.

Dinner, Deborah. 2010. "The Universal Childcare Debate: Rights Mobilization, Social Policy, and the Dynamics of Feminist Activism, 1966–1974." *Law & History Review* 28, 3: 577–628.

    2017a. "Beyond 'Best Practices': Employment Discrimination Law in the Neoliberal Era." *Indiana Law Journal* 92, 3: 1059–1118.

    2017b. "Equal by What Measure? The Lost Struggle for Universal State Protective Labor Standards," in Martha Albertson Fineman and Jonathan W. Fineman, eds., *Vulnerability and the Legal Organization of Work*. New York: Routledge: 283–304.

    2022 (forthcoming). *The Sex Equality Dilemma: Work, Family, and Legal Change in Neoliberal America*. New York: Cambridge University Press.

Dowd, Nancy E. 2008. "Masculinities and Feminist Legal Theory." *Wisconsin Journal of Law, Gender & Society* 23, 1: 201–248.

Eichner, Maxine. 2020. *The Free-Market Family: How the Market Crushed the American Dream (and How It Can Be Restored)*. New York: Oxford University Press.

Esping-Andersen, Gøsta. 1990. *The Three Worlds of Welfare Capitalism*. Princeton, NJ: Princeton University Press.

England, Paula, and Folbre, Nancy. 1999. "The Cost of Caring." *Annals of the American Academy of Political and Social Science* 561, 1: 39–51.

Fineman, Martha Albertson. 1995. *The Neutered Mother, the Sexual Family, and Other Twentieth Century Tragedies*. New York: Routledge.

    2001. "Contract and Care." *Chicago-Kent Law Review* 76, 3: 1403–1440.

    2004. *The Autonomy Myth: A Theory of Dependency*. New York: The New Press.

    2005. "The Social Foundations of Law." *Emory Law Journal* 54, 5: 201–237.

Folbre, Nancy, Jayoung Yoon, Kade Finnoff, and Allison Side Fuligni. 2005. "By What Measure? Family Time Devoted to Children in the United States." *Demography* 42, 2: 373–390.

Folbre, Nancy. 2006. "Measuring Care: Gender, Empowerment, and the Care Economy." *Journal of Human Development* 7, 2: 183–199.

Fraser, Nancy, and Linda Gordon. 1992. "Contract Versus Charity: Why Is There No Social Citizenship in the United States?" *Socialist Review* 22, 3: 45–67.

Garcia, Kelli K. 2012. "The Gender Bind: Men as Inauthentic Caregivers." *Duke Journal of Gender Law & Policy* 20, 1: 1–43.

Giddings, Paula. 1984. *When and Where I Enter: The Impact of Black Women on Race and Sex*. New York: HarperCollins.

Grossman, Joanna L., and Gillian L. Thomas. 2009. "Making Pregnancy Work: Overcoming the Pregnancy Discrimination Act's Capacity-Based Model." *Yale Journal of Law & Feminism* 2, 1: 15–50.

Guarnizo, Luis Eduardo, and Guadalupe Rodriguez. 2017. "Paid Domestic Work, Globalization, and Informality." *Population, Space and Place*: 1–16.

Hacker, Jacob S. 2002. *The Divided Welfare State: The Battle over Public and Private Social Benefits in the United States*. New York: Cambridge University Press.

Harbach, Meredith J. 2015. "Childcare Market Failure." *Utah Law Review* 2015, 3: 659–719.

Harrison, Cynthia. 1988. *On Account of Sex: The Politics of Women's Issues, 1945–68*. Berkeley: University of California Press.

Hochschild, Arlie, and Machung, Anne. 1989. *The Second Shift: Working Parents and the Revolution at Home*. New York: Viking Press.

Hunter, Tera W. 1997. *To 'Joy My Freedom: Southern Black Women's Lives and Labors After the Civil War*. Cambridge, MA: Harvard University Press.

Jessen-Howard, Steven, and Simon Workman. 2020. "Coronavirus Pandemic Could Lead to Permanent Loss of Nearly 4.5 Million Childcare Slots," *Center for American Progress*, April 23, 2020. www.americanprogress.org/issues/early-childhood/news/2020/04/24/483817/coronavirus-pandemic-lead-permanent-loss-nearly-4-5-million-child-care-slots/

Jones, Jacqueline. 2009. *Labors of Love, Labors of Sorrow: Black Women, Work, and the Family, from Slavery to the Present*. New York: Basic Books.

Katznelson, Ira. 2013. *Fear Itself: The New Deal and the Origins of Our Time*. New York: W. W. Norton & Company.

Kennedy, Elizabeth J., and Michael B. Runnels. 2013 "Bringing New Governance Home: The Need for Regulation in the Domestic Workplace." *University of Missouri-Kansas City Law Review* 81, 4: 899–941.

Kessler, Laura T. 2008. "The Politics of Care." *Wisconsin Journal of Law, Gender, & Society* 23, 2: 169–199.

Kessler-Harris, Alice. 2001. *In Pursuit of Equity: Women, Men, and the Quest for Economic Citizenship in Twentieth-Century America*. New York: Oxford University Press.

Korpi, Walter. 2010. "Class and Gender Inequalities in Different Types of Welfare States: The Social Citizenship Indicator Program." *International Journal of Social Welfare* 19: S14–S24.

Kymlikca, Will, and Wayne Norman. 1994. "Return of the Citizen: A Survey of Recent Work on Citizenship Theory." *Ethics* 104, 2: 352–381.

Lefkovits, Alison. 2018. *Strange Bedfellows: Marriage in the Age of Women's Liberation*. Philadelphia: University of Pennsylvania Press.

Lin, Shirley. 2016. "'And Ain't I a Woman?': Feminism, Immigrant Caregivers, and New Frontiers for Equality." *Harvard Journal of Law and Gender* 39, 1: 67–114.

Maclean, Nancy. 2008. *Freedom Is Not Enough: The Opening of the American Workplace*. Cambridge, MA: Harvard University Press.

Malik, Rasheed, Katie Hamm, Won F. Lee, Elizabeth E. Davis, and Aaron Sojourner. 2020. "The Coronavirus Will Make Childcare Deserts Worse and Exacerbate Inequality." *Center for American Progress*.

Mainardi, Pat. 1970. *The Politics of Housework*. Boston: New England Free Press.

Marshall, T.H. 1950. *Citizenship and Social Class and Other Essays*. Cambridge: Cambridge University Press.

McClain, Linda C. 2001. "Care as a Public Value: Linking Responsibility, Resources, and Civic Republicanism." Chicago-Kent Law Review 76, 3: 1673–1731.

McCluskey, Martha T. 2003. "Efficiency and Social Citizenship: Challenging the Neoliberal Attack on the Welfare State." *Indiana Law Journal* 78, 2: 783–876.

McGinley, Ann C. 2011. "Work, Caregiving, and Masculinities." *Seattle University Law Review* 34, 3 (2011): 703–723.

Mettler, Suzanne. 1998. *Dividing Citizens: Gender and Federalism in New Deal Public Policy*. Ithaca, NY: Cornell University Press.

Michel, Sonya. 1999. *Children's Interest/Mothers' Rights: The Shaping of America's Child Care Policy*. New Haven, CT: Yale University Press.

Morgan, Kimberly J. 2001. "A Child of the Sixties: The Great Society, the New Right, and the Politics of Federal Child Care." *Journal of Policy History* 13, 2: 215–250.

Nadasen, Premilla. 2015. *Household Workers Unite: The Untold Story of African American Women Who Built a Movement*. Boston, MA: Beacon Press.

Nakano Glenn, Evelyn. 1992. "From Servitude to Service Work: Historical Continuities in the Racial Division of Paid Reproductive Labor." *Signs: Journal of Women in Culture and Society* 18, 1: 1–43.

2000. "Citizenship and Inequality: Historical and Global Perspectives." *Social Problems* 47, 1: 1–20.

National Academy of Social Insurance. 2019. *Designing Universal Family Care: State-Based Social Insurance Programs for Early Childcare and Education, Paid Family and Medical Leave, and Long-Term Services and Supports.*

O'Leary, Ann. 2007. "How Family Leave Laws Left Out Low-Income Workers." *Berkeley Journal of Employment and Labor Law* 28, 1: 6–8.

Palmer, Phyllis. 1995. "Outside the Law: Agricultural and Domestic Workers under the Fair Labor Standards Act." *Journal of Policy History* 7, 4: 416–440.

Pew Research Center. 2013. *On Pay Gap, Millennial Women Near Parity – For Now.* Washington, DC: Pew Research Center.

Polikoff, Nancy D. 2008. *Beyond (Straight and Gay) Marriage: Valuing All Families Under the Law.* New York: Beacon Press.

Powell, Catherine. 2020. "Color of Covid: The Racial Justice Paradox of Our New Stay-at-Home Economy," *CNN Opinion.* www.cnn.com/2020/04/10/opinions/covid-19-people-of-color-labor-market-disparities-powell/index.html

Rivchin, Julie Yates. 2004. "Building Power among Low-Wage Immigrant Workers: Some Legal Considerations for Organizing Structures and Strategies." *New York University Review of Law and Social Change* 28, 3–4: 397.

Robertson, Campbell, and Robert Gebeloff. 2020. "How Millions of Women Became the Most Essential Workers in America." *The New York Times*, April 18, 2020.

Rohac, Dalibor, Liz Kennedy, and Vikram Singh. 2018. "Drivers of Authoritarian Populism in the United States." *Center for American Progress.*

Sassen, Saskia. 1991. *The Global City: New York, London, Tokyo.* Princeton, NJ: Princeton University Press.

Sayer, Liana C., Suzanne M. Bianchi, and John P. Robinson. 2004. "Are Parents Investing Less in Children? Trends in Mothers' and Fathers' Time with Children." *American Journal of Sociology* 110, 1: 1–43.

Schultz, Vicki. 2015. "Taking Sex Discrimination Seriously." *Denver University Law Review* 91, 5: 995–1119.

Smith, Peggie R. 2000. "Organizing the Unorganizable: Private Paid Household Workers and Approaches to Employee Representation." *North Carolina Law Review* 79, 1: 45–110.

2007. "Aging and Caring in the Home: Regulating Paid Domesticity in the Twenty-First Century." *Iowa Law Review* 92, 5: 1835–1900.

2008. "The Publicization of Home-Based Care Work in State Labor Law." *Minnesota Law Review* 92, 5: 1390–1423.

Sohn, Emily. 2020. "When Child Care Centers Close, Parents Scramble to Adapt." *The New York Times*, June 10. www.nytimes.com/2020/06/10/parenting/virus-day-care-bright-horizons.html

Siegel, Reva B. 1994. "Home as Work: The First Woman's Rights Clams Concerning Wives' Household Labor, 1850-1880." *Yale Law Journal* 103, 5: 1073–1217.

Swinth, Kirsten. 2018. *Feminism's Forgotten Fight: The Unfinished Struggle for Work and Family.* Cambridge, MA: Harvard University Press.

Turk, Katherine. 2016. *Equality on Trial: Gender and Rights in the Modern American Workplace.* Philadelphia: University of Pennsylvania Press.

US Bureau of Labor Statistics. 2008. *Women in Labor Force: A Databook.* Washington, DC: US Bureau of Labor Statistics. www.bls.gov/cps/wlf-table7-2008.pdf

2020. *Employment Characteristics of Families Survey.* Washington, DC: US Bureau of Labor Statistics. www.bls.gov/news.release/famee.nro.htm

Waldfogel, Jane. 1997. "The Effects of Children on Women's Wages." *American Sociological Review* 62, 2: 209–217.

Woloch, Nancy. 2015. *A Class by Herself: Protective Laws for Women Workers, 1890s–1990s.* Princeton, NJ: Princeton University Press.

Williams, Joan C. 2008. *Reshaping the Work-Family Debate: Why Men and Class Matter.* Cambridge, MA: Harvard University Press.

Witt, John Fabian. 2009. *The Accidental Republic*. Cambridge, MA: Harvard University Press.

Young, Iris Marion. 1990. *Justice and the Politics of Difference*. Princeton, NJ: Princeton University Press.

Zigler, Edward, Katherine Marsland, and Heather Lord. 2009. *The Tragedy of Childcare in America*. New Haven, CT: Yale University Press.

Zimmerman, M. K., J. S. Litt, and C. E. Bose. 2006. "Globalization and Multiple Crises of Care," in M. K. Zimmerman, J. S. Litt, and C. E. Bose, eds. *Global Dimensions of Gender and Carework*. Palo Alto, CA: Stanford University Press: 9–27.

PART IV

Country and Regional Perspectives

14

Labor, Workers' Rights, and Democracy in Latin America

Mark Anner

Latin America's labor movements are marked by their long, tumultuous struggles for workers' rights, equity, and democracy. Most Latin American countries have experienced prolonged periods of authoritarian rule in which workers' rights were violently suppressed. For periods of time, labor union organizations ceased to operate, as movement leaders were arrested, killed, or forced into exile. At times, segments of organized labor were coopted by the state and economic elites. Yet, many other labor movement leaders risked their lives as they demanded not only better wages for the workers they represented, but also an end to authoritarian rule and democratization.

This chapter traces these complex dynamics. It begins by examining theoretical debates on labor and democracy. It then examines crucial periods in regime formation and transitions in Latin America, and the corresponding interaction between labor and the state. Next, the chapter explores processes of democratization and the economic and labor reforms that accompanied these processes. Finally, it traces recent reversals in democracy and the impact on workers' rights before concluding.

THE RELATIONSHIP BETWEEN LABOR AND DEMOCRACY

Questions on the relationship between labor and democracy have long been debated in the literature. This debate was revived in the 1990s with the publication of *Capitalist Development & Democracy* by Rueschemeyer et al. (1992), who argued that the working class is a pro-democratic force because workers have the most to gain from democracy. As a consequence, strong labor movements make democratic outcomes more likely. In response, Levitsky and Mainwaring argued that, in the case of Latin America, labor has not been a consistent champion of democracy after 1945. Rather, its support for democracy has been contingent on its partisan alliances and regime context (Levitsky & Mainwaring 2006).

This chapter argues that, while segments of Latin America's labor movements have, at times, collaborated with autocratic elites, a significant share of labor leaders and members have fought for democracy not out of perceived partisan advantage, but rather out of commitment to the principles of liberal democracy – and labor has often realized that commitment by strengthening democracy. Democracy is understood here as a political system that goes beyond electoral democracy to include civilian control over the military, horizontal accountability of office-holders, and extensive provisions for individual and collective freedoms of opinion, assembly, and demonstration (Diamond 1999).

This positive view of democracy and labor is reflected in the findings of Adler and Webster in what they refer to as "the centrality of the labor movement in the South African transition to democracy" (1995: 99). Adler and Webster take issue with Przeworski's (1991) narrow economic-interest based conceptualization of labor. Rather, they argue that the objectives of labor include democracy and equity (1995). Survey research spanning a ten-year period provides support for this argument: South African labor unionists have maintained a strong preference for liberal democracy (Buhlungu 2006). Labor's contribution to democracy has been noted in other developing regions, including Poland (Ost 1990) and South Korea (Kwon & O'Donnell 1999). Most recently, in Hong Kong we have seen trade unionists take to the streets at great personal risk to demand the withdrawal of the bill authorizing extradition to mainland China and the direct elections of the chief executive and all legislature members (Wan Chan & Pun 2020). In established democracies, Baccaro argues that the weakening of trade unions is correlated to a perceived crisis of democracy "as it has corroded a pillar of capitalism's democratic legitimation and hampered the potential of 'associational democracy'" (Baccaro et al. 2019: 6).

What this literature indicates is that labor has a direct and an indirect influence on democracy. It directly influences democracy through its commitment to liberal, democratic principles. Indeed, the existence of trade unions helps to define a robust democracy since freedom of association is a defining component of democratic regimes. Labor has an indirect influence on democracy by doing what labor unions do every day: negotiating for better wages. This is because better wages reduce the gap between the highest and lowest income brackets in society, and equity in society both increases the legitimacy of democratic systems of governance and helps equalize opportunities for participation in elections and governance, hallmarks of robust democratic processes.

LABOR AND DEMOCRACY IN LATIN AMERICA: A LONG, TUMULTUOUS HISTORY

As Latin American states achieved independence from Spain and Portugal in the early 1800s, all the constitutions of emerging states recognized the right to associate, congregate, and make collective petitions (Alba 1968: 28). Organizations of craft unions emerged during the colonial era that functioned largely as mutual aid societies. In the nineteenth and early twentieth centuries, southern European migrants brought with them militant labor ideologies, notably anarchism in the late 1800s and early 1900s, anarcho-syndicalism following World War One, and Marxism in the 1930s (Alba 1968). Motivated by such ideas, labor became very involved in the political process. If many of these immigrants were swayed by radical ideologies and not supportive of electoral participation at the time, it was in part because immigrant workers did not enjoy the right to vote during this period.

Latin American unions increasingly not only engaged the electoral process, but also targeted the state in their campaigns more than labor movements in more developed market economies because the former's labor market power was often significantly weaker. High unemployment and underemployment meant that there were a large number of workers competing for a limited number of formal sector jobs. Since workers could easily be replaced, their bargaining power at the workplace level was very limited. In this context, labor unions found that one of the best strategies for improving the lives of large numbers of workers was to target the state and demand higher minimum wages and other state-mandated benefits (Payne 1968).

In one of the more substantial studies on labor and the political process in Latin America, David and Ruth Collier argue that, by the 1930s and 1940s, not only was labor politically engaged, but it had also become formally "incorporated" into the political process, by which they mean the "institutionalization of a labor movement sanctioned and regulated by the state" (Collier & Collier 1991: 3). For Collier and Collier, a key factor in understanding labor today is to understand this process of incorporation and control. While some labor movements were incorporated directly into the political process through the state (e.g. Brazil, Chile), in other cases labor's incorporation was done through a dominant political party (e.g. Peronism in Argentina and the Institutional Revolutionary Party, or PRI, in Mexico).

How labor was incorporated into the political process had important implications for labor's ability to leverage its economic, social, and political demands. Incorporation meant that institutionalized political access gave labor influence over everything from labor laws to minimum wage levels and state-mandated benefits. However, it also meant a loss of autonomy. Direct state incorporation meant trade unionists did not gain access through a political party. This meant, of course, that these labor movements were often even less autonomous from, and more controlled by, the state than were movements with party-mediated relations with states. In Brazil, for example, unionization was encouraged and facilitated by the state, but the state also ensured that labor unions would remain fragmented by promoting unions at the municipal level. The state also made striking very difficult. Access through a political party potentially gave labor unions more strength, but this varied by types of parties. Some parties gave their union members more autonomy and influence (notably in Uruguay and Argentina), whereas other parties expected unions to play a more subordinate role to the party.

While in the early twentieth century political incorporation and economic insertion shaped labor's legacy, in the latter years, authoritarian rule would leave permanent scars on the movement. With very few exceptions (e.g. Costa Rica and Mexico), Latin American countries went through periods of highly repressive authoritarian rule that profoundly weakened labor movements in the region (Drake 1996). The killings of unionists in the region were motivated by two elite objectives. First, it was assumed that organized labor would stand in the way of market-oriented economic reforms. As Drake explains, authoritarian rulers "wanted to foster economic growth, encourage investment, increase competitiveness, curb inflation, and reduce wages. To do so, they curtailed union interference with market mechanisms" (Drake 1996: 2).

The second goal – shared by local elites and the US government during the Cold War – was to weaken the power of the political left and its union allies, often in the name of anti-communism. The US government, notably through the CIA, played a particularly prominent role in this effort, at times signaling to regimes which trade unionists should be eliminated (Agee 1975). The government-funded American Institute for Free Labor Development (AIFLD) provided very generous funding to conservative, anti-communist unions. In the process, it often orchestrated divisions in the movement (Norton 1985).

The attacks against unionists were particularly severe in countries in the midst of civil war. In El Salvador, over 5,000 labor activists were killed during the period of authoritarian rule and civil war, in part because the mere act of organizing and demanding wage increases were perceived as threatening to the economic interests of the ruling elite, and in part because many had joined massive protests for regime change, which was perceived as threatening to the political interests of the ruling elite (Anner 2011). In Colombia, for decades more unionists were killed each year than in the rest of the world combined (ITUC 2009). Guatemala has had the highest per capita killings of trade unionists in the world (Levenson-Estrada 1994). Today, Guatemala has the lowest unionization rate in the region; only 2.6 percent of workers belong to labor unions. In El Salvador, in the aftermath of the civil war and US intervention in unions, the movement had divided into thirteen national trade union centers that, combined, represented under 4 percent of workers (Anner 1996).

DEMOCRACY, REFORM, AND UNION DECLINE

The contemporary period begins with the process of democratization that swept the region in the 1980s and 1990s. Neoliberal, market-oriented reforms complicated this otherwise positive political transition. Often, these reforms were forced on the region following the debt crisis of the 1980s and the corresponding International Monetary Fund conditionality that accompanied the loans needed to bail out economies in the region. This led to a debate among labor scholars and practitioners as to which force had a greater impact on organized labor: the positive effect of democratization or the adverse impact of market-oriented reforms.

For many observers, neoliberalism entailed an unambiguous attack on labor rights in Latin America. Maria Lorena Cook, however, challenges this assumption and argues that in some cases the forces of democratization had a more powerful and positive impact on labor (Cook 1998, 2007). Cook documents which countries made their labor laws more flexible (that is, weakened workers' rights) and which countries enacted more worker-protective labor legislation. What she finds is that only five countries had unambiguously flexible labor reforms, while the remaining ten countries she studied had either protective or a mix of protective and flexible labor reforms.

An examination of unionization rates by Anner (2008) before and after reforms in countries with protective, flexible, and mixed reforms reveals an unexpected finding: unionization rates declined in *all* cases. Indeed, some of the countries with protective reforms (such as the Dominican Republic and Paraguay) had the most dramatic declines in unionization rates (Anner 2008). This apparent paradox can be explained in two ways. First, while many countries enacted pro-labor reforms, they failed to improve their labor inspectorates. Inspectorates remained under-funded, and inspectors had limited power to fine violators. Second, and perhaps more important, the reforms made relatively minor adjustments to very old labor laws. In some countries, including Paraguay, the vestiges of decades of authoritarian rule, in law and practice, has undermined independent labor unions' capacity to advance. As such, they failed to meet the challenges presented by neoliberal reforms and structural changes to the region's economies, which included informality and the growth of global supply chains.

The fate of labor took a positive turn in the late 1990s and early 2000s as the political direction of Latin America moved to the left. In 2000, the left was elected in Chile. This was followed by left/labor party victories in Brazil (2002), Argentina (2003), Uruguay (2004), Bolivia (2005), Nicaragua and Ecuador (2006), Paraguay (2008), and El Salvador (2009). The electoral success of these left parties was seen as a response to the adverse impacts of neoliberalism. The left promised not only to reduce inequality but also to improve the quality of democracy in the region. However, as Levitsky and Roberts (2011) observe, the left came to power in very different ways in the region with very different impacts on work and labor. This includes the old populist "machines" in Nicaragua and Argentina, new populist movements in Venezuela and Bolivia, and institutionalized partisan left parties in Chile, Brazil, and Uruguay (Levitsky & Roberts 2011).

Handlin and Collier find that, during this period, left parties placed more of an emphasis on ties to popular associations, such as community groups and informal vendors' unions. The mobilization of informal sector workers for electoral gain is not new; moderate right and conservative political forces had done this for decades in the region, particularly at the municipal level (Hawkins 2011). What was new was the focus of left parties on this sector

(Handlin & Collier 2011). Handlin and Collier note, however, that new ties with associations were "often weaker and [took] on a more instrumental quality than traditional party-union ties" (Handlin & Collier 2011: 147).

For Handlin and Collier, with the exception of Uruguay, there has been a perceived general decline in organized labor's influence on the political process in the early twenty-first century (Handlin & Collier 2011). They suggest that left party mobilization had previously relied on a degree of delinking between parties and organized labor. In their stead, these parties placed more of an emphasis on mass media and ties to popular associations, such as community groups and informal vendor unions. Handlin and Collier link this trend to a general decline in unions and a proliferation of associations. They also find that it is partly because the party system has become more fractionalized in some countries, such as Brazil and Chile. This creates an incentive for old labor-based parties to enter into pacts with a range of parties and social organizations in order to win elections and enact legislation (Handlin & Collier 2011).

Roberts (2019) builds on these insights, arguing that there is a crisis of representation that is affecting party system dynamics rooted in neoliberal reforms, which has contributed to social fragmentation. This creates, he argues, "openings for populist contenders to politicize economic insecurities and cultural resentments, in opposition to traditional political establishments" (Roberts 2019: 188). Left populists in countries such as Argentina, Bolivia, Ecuador, and Venezuela, in response to growing labor market insecurities, promise voters redistributive policies and social protections (Roberts 2014). In contrast, right populists "construct 'the people' in terms of ethno-national and/or religious particularisms, more than socioeconomic stratification … Although right-populist parties often began with anti-tax, pro-market economic platforms …, many have shifted leftward over time on the economic axis, enhancing their appeal to working class constituencies" (Roberts 2014: 197).

Levitsky & Ziblatt (2019) observe that during the Cold War, the end of democratic regimes was the result of a violent coup d'état in 75 percent of cases. Currently, they argue, democracies are dying due to an undermining from within. Representatives of political opposition parties are not seen as opponents, but rather as enemies. These leaders feel entirely unencumbered by historic democratic norms and use all the power at their disposal to achieve their narrow political goals. In the process, they "subvert the very process that brought them to power" (Levitsky & Ziblatt 2019: 3).

Since 2018, the left has won some important elections. For example, Mexico's 2018 election was won by progressive Andrés Manuel López Obrador in Mexico. In December 2019, Argentina saw a return of the Peronists to power. Yet, elsewhere the tide turned against the left and toward both the right and extreme right. The most recent examples of this trend are the elections of Jair Bolsanaro in Brazil and Iván Duque Márquez in Colombia in 2018, and the displacement of leftist Evo Morales by Jeanine Áñez Chávev of the center-right Democrat Social Movement as Bolivia's interim president in 2019.

These changes are more than the swinging of a political pendulum from left to right. Rather, they also reflect a weakening of democratic institutions. The election of Bolsanaro followed a process by which a left ex-president of Brazil, Luiz Inácio Lula da Silva, was imprisoned (2018–2019) and his successor, Dilma Rousseff (the first woman president in Brazil's history), was removed from office (2016) in a highly political impeachment on questionable legal grounds. Democratic institutions have also been undermined under once progressive governments in Venezuela and Nicaragua. In El Salvador, a young president with autocratic tendencies, Nayib Bukele, turned to the Armed Forces on February 9, 2020 to briefly take over the National Assembly to pressure the legislative body to approve his request for extra security funding (McDonnell & Renderos 2020: A3).

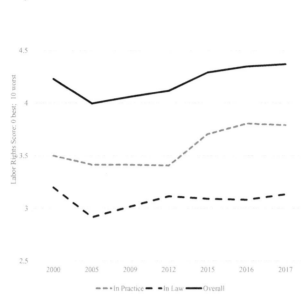

FIGURE 14.1 Workers' rights violations in law and practice in Latin America
Source: Author's calculations based on the Labour Rights Indicators (LRI) data.

This turn to the right and undermining of democratic institutions has weakened workers' rights in the region. Brazil is notable in this regard. The Brazilian Labor Reform Act of 2017 weakened collective rights substantially by eliminating representation fees (e.g. the union "tax") and by allowing for the primacy of negotiated agreements over national legislation (Anner & Veiga 2020). Yet, the trend is not limited to Brazil. Using data from the Center for Global Workers' Rights Labor Rights Indicators, it is possible to track how widely labor laws and labor practices in the region violate international standards on the rights to form unions, bargain, and strike (Kucera & Sari 2019).[1]

What the data indicate is that there is a significant number of laws in the region that violate standards, for example, by placing too many restrictions on union formation or the right to strike. On average, ten laws per country violate international freedom of association standards. Patterns of violations in the implementation of formal laws are even more numerous, on average fourteen per country. This includes states' arbitrary arrest of unionists, repression of strikes, or inadequate protection of unionists from unfair dismissal and blacklisting, notwithstanding workers' legal entitlements to organize and strike. Violations in practice are particularly high in countries with a history of violent repression of trade unionists, such as Colombia, Guatemala, and Peru. There has been a general rise in workers' rights violations throughout the region as a whole (see Figure 14.1).

As workers' rights violations increase, unionization rates have declined in the region. Since unions increase the share of national income in society that goes to labor relative to capital, it follows that low unionization rates correlate with high degree of inequality in society. The two countries with the highest unionization rates in the region, Argentina and Uruguay, have the lowest relative levels of inequality, measured in terms of the share of national income received

[1] Center for Global Workers' Rights (2020). Labour Rights Indicators. Retrieved from http://labour-rights-indicators.la.psu.edu/ (Date accessed: June 28, 2020.).

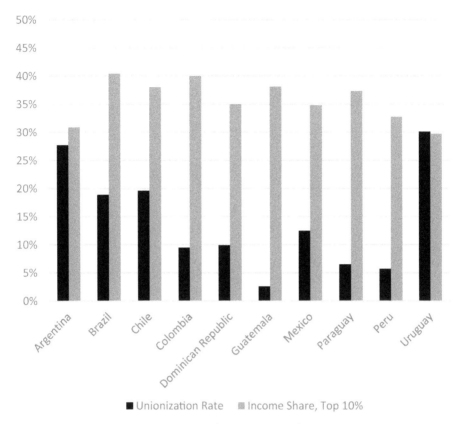

FIGURE 14.2 Unionization rates and income inequality in Latin America (2016)
Sources: ILOSTAT (*data for 2014; **data for 2013), and World Bank.

by the top 10 percent of the population. In contrast, countries with lower unionization rates tend to have higher levels of inequality (see Figure 14.2).

Reviewing detailed studies of democracy in Latin America, Diamond et al. identify "substantial, persistent, and even increasing inequalities of wealth and income as a serious challenge to democracy" (Diamond et al. 1999: 53). This is because progress toward reducing poverty is needed to ensure the legitimacy required for democratic consolidation. Otherwise, they noted ominously and prophetically when writing in 1999, these democracies are likely "to be susceptible to the appeals of future populist demagogues who might (like Fujimori in Peru) seriously diminish the institutional foundations of democracy" (1999: 53). What this suggests is a potentially vicious circle in which a declining quality of democracy contributes to an erosion of workers' rights and unionization, which in turn contributes to greater inequality, which then further erodes the quality of democracy (see Figure 14.3).

The arrows in Figure 14.3 go in both directions because the vicious circle could be transformed into a virtuous circle. Changes in governments could improve the quality of democracy, which would strengthen workers' rights, increase unionization rates, and lessen inequality, and thus contribute to a reinforcement of democratic institutions. A reduction in the rate of inequality, as Diamond et al. (1999) suggest, is also important to ensure the legitimacy required for democratic consolidation. But change does not need to begin at the top. It could instead begin with a strengthening of labor movements in the region through new strategies for organizing.

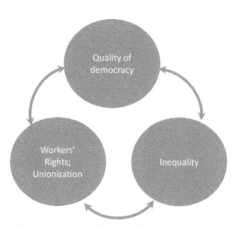

FIGURE 14.3 Democracy, workers' rights/unionization, and inequality

TRANSFORMATIVE AND ALTERNATIVE WORKER MOVEMENTS
IN LATIN AMERICA

As outlined above, conditions in Latin America suggest a very challenging environment for workers and organized labor. However, there are a range of emerging strategies and organizing dynamics that suggest labor and workers are refocusing, organizing different sectors of the economy, leveraging new domestic and transnational targets, and turning to alternative forms of power such as "symbolic power," understood as the ability to shame opponents into respecting workers' rights. Worker organizations are also realizing the importance of strategic research and campaigns as they take on increasingly sophisticated corporations and their local, regional, and global supply chains.

Trade unions in Latin America have long been organized into national centers[2] that have unified trade union strategies and engaged in the political arena. These national centers have been subject to a range of political influences and international trade union orientations. For much of the Cold War period, national centers chose whether to affiliate with the communist-line World Federation of Trade Unions (WFTU), the Social Christian World Confederation of Labour (WCL), or the International Confederation of Free Trade Unions (ICFTU). The latter considered itself as "social democratic" in orientation, but in the Americas, it was largely influenced by the anti-communist orientation of the United States at the time (Anner 2011; Jakobsen 2001; Norton 1985). In the second half of the twentieth century, in almost every country there was at least one national trade union center affiliated with each of the three international trade union organizations. The notable exception was Bolivia, where the Bolivian Workers' Center (*Central Obrera Boliviana*, COB) was and remains independent (Alexander 2005). In many countries, there were also a significant number of "independent left" unions. These were progressive groups that often split with local communist-oriented unions, and refused to join the more conservative ICFTU or WCL (Anner 2011).

In the aftermath of the Cold War, there was a considerable degree of adjustments in alliances and affiliations. The ICFTU, no longer driven by an anti-communist agenda, began to affiliate independent left trade union centers in Latin America, such as the CUT in Brazil. In 2006, the

---

[2] We are using the term "national center" to cover national-level trade union organizations that represent multiple sectors of the economy, such as the AFL-CIO in the United States, which is a federation. In Latin America, national centers are legally recognized as federations, confederations, "centrals," or similar entities.

ICFTU and the WCL merged to form the International Trade Union Confederation (ITUC), which has come to dominate trade union politics in the region and internationally. Rather than using this international consolidation to force the merger of national centers in Latin America, the ITUC opted to allow for multiple affiliations from each country. And old tensions between "official" corporatist unions and independent left unions never fully dissipated.

Along these lines, in 2015, the Americas' section of the ITUC (TUCA) suffered a split when thirteen of its fifty-six organizations walked out of a TUCA congress in a dispute with the leadership and the political direction of the organization. Several of these groups, which represent the old-line corporatist tendency in the region, formalized their disaffiliation (CGT-Colombia, CROC-Mexico, and Força Sindical, Brazil). The groups that remain have continued to develop a "social democratic" orientation, demanding reforms such as greater accountability of MNCs in global supply chains, free trade agreements with strong social clauses, gender-inclusion, and action to protect the environment. Currently, the TUCA represents 50 million workers in the Americas.[3]

One of the biggest struggles for labor has been to become independent of the old, official corporatist structures that often made some unions a conservative force in society (La Botz 1999). In Brazil, in the 1970s and 1980s, workers famously formed new organizations and took on the authoritarian state through waves of protests and strikes in what became known as "new unionism" (Keck 1989). In El Salvador and Guatemala, progressive labor movements emerged during authoritarian rule and allied with other progressive forces to oppose their respective political regimes and demand democratization and respect for human rights (Anner 2011; Levenson-Estrada 1994). Some of these organizations later became more institutionalized and lost some of their initial progressive tendencies. But in many cases, such as in Mexico, workers continue to fight for independent unionism that is capable of adequately defending workers' interests (Marinaro 2018). For example, in November 2018, seven independent unions in the auto sector joined together to form the Federation of Independent Unions in Automobiles, Auto Parts, Aerospace, and Tires.[4]

A developing challenge for labor has been how to respond to workplace fissuring caused by global supply chains and outsourcing (Weil 2014). In earlier efforts, unions attempted to organize workers through traditional, local campaigns. However, without fully appreciating the cost and time pressures faced by supplier factories in these global supply chains, the end result was that thousands of workers, rather than being organized, lost their jobs and were blacklisted (Anner 2011). It took a lot of reflection for labor to realize how it might align with labor and non-labor advocates in developed market economies to put pressure on buyers in global supply chains. In the 1990s, Salvadoran garment workers targeted the Gap and Honduran garment workers targeted Liz Claiborne, in alliances not only with labor unions, but also with labor rights groups in the USA and Canada, such as the National Labor Committee and the Maquila Solidarity Network. When this was done well, these new labor-civil society trans-national alliances proved remarkably effective at naming and shaming companies to defend workers' rights in individual factories (Anner 2011).

Today in El Salvador local labor organizations such as the *Federation of Associations and Independent Unions of El Salvador* (FEASIES) and women's organizations – such as *La Asociación Movimiento de Mujeres Melida Anaya Montes* (Las Melidas), Organization of Salvadoran Women for Peace (ORMUSA), and Women Transforming (MT) – have been

---

[3] See: http://library.fes.de/pdf-files/iez/13861.pdf
[4] www.industriall-union.org/es/sindicatos-independientes-de-mexico-conforman-la-federacion-fesiiaaan

involved in struggles for decent work in global supply chains.[5] They have allied themselves with international advocacy organizations, including the Canadian Maquila Solidarity Network.[6] In Argentina, organizations that emerged out of the economic crises of the early 2000s – notably the Alameda Foundation – today organize against sexual exploitation and forced child labor, including in clandestine textile workshops tied to global supply chains.[7]

Attempts have been made to transform limited factory campaigns into sustained, global organizations such as the International Union League for Brand Responsibility (García Dueñas & Montalvo 2017). The League comes out of the successful campaign to organize Fruit of the Loom factories in Honduras. A crucial component of the campaign was research and advocacy carried out by the US-based Worker Rights Consortium (WRC). This led to regional meetings among unions to discuss how to better coordinate campaigns that targeted the same multinational firms. The strategy has been to pressure MNCs to commit to broad agreements that would cover all their facilities. The pressure to achieve this goal would come from local unions and international allies, including the WRC, the Solidarity Center of the AFL-CIO, and United Students Against Sweatshops (USAS) (García Dueñas & Montalvo 2017). Those allies continue to provide vital campaign support for transnational labor organizing efforts throughout the region.

As noted above, more than half of laborers work in the informal sector in Latin America. Hence, organizing this sector is of strategic importance for labor. Rosaldo documents how, in one noteworthy case, waste pickers in Colombia organized and improved their working conditions and income (2016). They did so, Rosaldo argues, through innovative organizing models, NGO alliances, and leveraging key human rights protections in the Colombian Constitution of 1991. Notably, Colombian waste pickers won seven cases in Colombia's Constitutional Court that affirmed their right to be paid by the state for their work. Similar to workers in the retail sector, Rosaldo finds that informal workers used symbolic power by framing their issues in ways that mobilized support in society (2016).

Another important sector dominated by informality is the domestic sphere. As Maich shows, for domestic workers – despite their isolation in homes, racialization, migration status, and gender discrimination – there have been significant organizational gains in countries such as Peru (2014). Their demands and targets reflect their particular status and economic sector. Notably, they are often organizing for "defined benefits as state-recognized workers" (Maich 2014: 73). That is, the struggle of these domestic workers is for legal inclusion. Blofield, like Maich, finds that the main focus of women domestic workers' struggles is the state, not the employer. Through alliances, mobilizations, and political openings with left parties, Blofield finds that domestic workers have achieved limited, but nonetheless important, improvements in their rights (2012).

Organizing migrant workers is of strategic importance given the number of workers who have migrated to other countries in Latin America, the United States, or Canada. In Guatemala, organizing is a bit less dynamic due to the more limited local capacity. Yet, groups such as *Asociación de Guatemaltecos Unidos por Nuestros Derechos*, AGUND (Association of United Guatemalans for our Rights) have been organizing and denouncing the substandard living and working conditions of Guatemalan migrant workers in Canada. AGUND has developed a

---

[5] Valeria Scorza, correspondence with author, December 18, 2018.
[6] See: www.maquilasolidarity.org/
[7] See: www.fundacionalameda.org/2011/06/historia.html

collaboration with the United Food and Commercial Workers Union of Canada (UFCW Canada n.d.). A similar cross-border effort exists among Canadian and Mexican groups.

ProDESC, a human rights organization based in Mexico, has worked with the *Centro de los Derechos del Migrants* (Center of Migrant Rights) to establish the Binational Labor Justice Initiative. The Initiative brings together labor lawyers, workers' rights and human rights advocates, and organizers from Mexico and the USA to coordinate campaigns to strengthen migrant workers' rights and to improve organizing and enforcement in the USA and Mexico (Gordon 2009). Through its work, ProDESC has helped to organize migrant guest workers and agricultural workers tied to global supply chains by effectively using legal strategies, policy promotion, strategic research, and organizing and leadership development.

Brazil has provided an example in organizing agricultural workers. As shown by Tarlau, the Landless Movement (MST) became Latin America's largest social movement not only by pursuing aggressive strategies of land takeovers, but also by developing popular education programs within the movement (2019). Tarlau argues that social movements can provide "pedagogical spaces" that facilitate the emergence, growth, and sustainability of movements. This strategy of developing educational programs within movements is an approach worth studying and perhaps replicating.

CONCLUSION

This chapter has argued that Latin America's labor movements have had a positive impact on democracy in the region. This is because most labor unions in the region have directly supported democratic institutions. At the same time, strong labor unions have an indirect impact on democracy by reducing inequality and thus increasing the legitimacy and strengthening the institutions of democratic regimes. Recent trends toward the erosion of workers' rights have contributed to rising inequality, which has correlated with an erosion of democracy. Labor movements in the region are looking to new and creative ways to organize workers. The degree to which they are successful will impact not only the quality of the lives of the workers they represent, but also the quality of democracy in the region.

REFERENCES

Adler, Glenn, and Edward Webster. 1995. "Challenging Transition Theory: The Labor Movement, Radical Reform, and Transition to Democracy in South Africa." *Politics & Society* 23, 1: 75–106.

Agee, Philip. 1975. *Inside the Company: CIA Diary*. New York: Stonehill.

Alba, Victor. 1968. *Politics and the Labor Movement in Latin America*. Stanford, CA: Stanford University Press.

Alexander, Robert J. 2005. *A History of Organized Labor in Bolivia*. Westport, CT: Praeger.

Anner, Mark. 1996. "¿Hacia la Sindicalización de los Sindicatos?" *Estudios Centroamericanos* 573–574: 599–614.

2008. "Meeting the Challenges of Industrial Restructuring: Labor Reform and Enforcement in Latin America." *Latin American Politics and Society* 50, 2: 33–65.

2011. *Solidarity Transformed: Labor's Responses to Globalization and Crisis in Latin America*. Ithaca, NY: ILR Press, an imprint of Cornell University Press.

Anner, Mark S., and João Paulo Veiga. 2020. "Brazil." In Carola M. Frege, and John Kelly, eds. *Comparative Employment Relations in the Global Economy*, 2nd Ed. New York: Routledge, pp. 404–426.

Baccaro, Lucio, Chiari Benassi, and Guglielmo Meardi. 2019. "Theoretical and Empirical Links between Trade Unions and Democracy." *Economic and Industrial Democracy* 40, 1: 3–19.

Blofield, Merike. 2012. *Care Work and Class: Domestic Workers' Struggles for Equal Rights in Latin America*. University Park: The Pennsylvania State University.

Buhlungu, Sakhela, ed. 2006. *Trade Unions and Democracy: Cosatu Workers' Political Attitudes in South Africa*. Cape Town: HSRC Press.

Collier, Ruth Berins, and David Collier. 1991. *Shaping the Political Arena: Critical Junctures, the Labor Movement, and Regime Dynamics in Latin America*. Princeton, NJ: Princeton University Press.

Cook, Maria Lorena. 1998. "Toward Flexible Industrial Relations? Neo-Liberalism, Democracy, and Labor Reform in Latin America." *Industrial Relations* 37,3: 311.

2007. *The Politics of Labor Reform in Latin America: Between Flexibility and Rights*. University Park: The Pennsylvania State University Press.

Diamond, Larry. 1999. *Developing Democracy: Toward Consolidation*. Baltimore: Johns Hopkins University Press.

Diamond, Larry, Jonathan Hartlyn, and Juan J. Linz. 1999. "Introduction: Politics, Society, and Democracy in Latin America." In Larry Diamond, Jonathan Hartlyn, Juan J. Linz, and Seymour Martin Lipset, eds. *Democracy in Developing Countries: Latin America, Second Edition*. Boulder, CA: Lynne Rienner Publishers.

Drake, Paul W. 1996. *Labor Movements and Dictatorships: The Southern Cone in Comparative Perspective*. Baltimore: Johns Hopkins University Press.

García Dueñas, Gilberto, and Karla Molina Montalvo. 2017. *Trade Unions in Transformation: Building Power in Global Networks: The International Union League in Central America*. Berlin: Friedrich-Ebert-Stiftung.

Gordon, Jennifer. 2009. *Towards Transnational Labor Citizenship: Restructuring Labor Migration to Reinforce Workers' Rights: A Preliminary Report on Emerging Experiments*. New York: Fordham Law School.

Handlin, Samuel, and Ruth Berins Collier. 2011. "The Diversity of Left Party Linkages and Competitive Advantages." In Steven Levitsky and Kenneth Roberts, eds. *The Resurgence of the Latin American Left*. Baltimore: The Johns Hopkins University Press, pp. 139–161.

Hawkins, Daniel. 2011. *The Struggles over City Space: Informal Street Vending & Public Space Governance in Medellín, Colombia*. Baden: NOMOS Verlagsgesellschaft.

ITUC. 2009. "*Annual Survey of Violations of Trade Union Rights 2009*." Brussels: International Trade Union Confederations. http://survey09.ituc-csi.org

Jakobsen, Kjeld. 2001. "Rethinking the International Confederation of Free Trade Unions and Its Inter-American Regional Organization." *Antipode* 33, 3: 363–383.

Keck, Margaret E. 1989. "The New Unionism in the Brazilian Transition." In Alfred Stepan, ed. *Democratizing Brazil: Problems of Transition and Consolidation*. New York: Oxford University Press, pp. 252–296.

Kucera, David, and Dora Sari. 2019. "New Labour Rights Indicators: Method and Trends for 2000–2015." *International Labour Review* 158, 3: 419–446.

Kwon, Seung-Ho, and Michael O'Donnell. 1999. "Repression and Struggle: The State, the Chaebol, and Independent Trade Unions in South Korea." *Journal of Industrial Democracy* 41, 2: 272–294.

La Botz, Dan. 1999. *Mask of Democracy: Labor Suppression in Mexico Today*. Boston: South End Press.

Levenson-Estrada, Deborah. 1994. *Trade Unionists Against Terror: Guatemala City 1954–1985*. Chapel Hill: The University of North Carolina Press.

Levitsky, Steven, and Scott Mainwaring. 2006. "Organized Labor and Democracy in Latin America." *Comparative Politics* 39, 1: 21–42.

Levitsky, Steven, and Kenneth Roberts. 2011. "Latin America's 'Left Turn,' A Framework for Analysis." In *The Resurgence of the Latin American Left*. Baltimore: The Johns Hopkins University Press, pp. 1–28.

Levitsky, Steven, and Daniel Ziblatt. 2019. *How Democracies Die*. New York: Broadway Books.

Maich, Katherine. 2014. "Marginalized Struggles for Legal Reform: Cross-Country Consequences of Domestic Worker Organizing." *Social Development Issues* 36, 3: 73–91.

Marinaro, Paolo. 2018. "'We Fight Against the Union!': An Ethnography of Labor Relations in the Automotive Industry in Mexico." In Maurizio Atzeni and Immanuel Ness, eds. *Global Perspectives on Workers' and Labour Organizations*. Singapore: Springer.

McDonnell, Patrick J, and Alexander Renderos. 2020. "Is El Salvador's Millennial President a Reformer or an Autocrat?" *Los Angeles Times*, February 28.

Norton, Chris. 1985. "Build and Destroy." *NACLA Report on the Americas* XIX (6): 26–36.

Ost, David. 1990. *Solidarity and the Politics of Anti-Politics: Opposition and Reform in Poland since 1968.* Philadelphia: Temple University Press.

Payne, James L. 1968. "The Oligarchy Muddle." *World Politics* 20, 3: 439–453.

Przeworski, Adam. 1991. *Democracy and the Market: Political and Economic Reforms in Eastern Europe and Latin America.* Cambridge: Cambridge University Press.

Roberts, Kenneth M. 2014. *Changing Course in Latin America: Party Systems in the Neoliberal Era.* New York: Cambridge University Press.

2019. "Crises of Representation and Populist Challenges to Liberal Democracy." *Chinese Political Science Review* 4: 188–199.

Rosaldo, Manuel. 2016. "Revolution in the Garbage Dump: The Political and Economic Foundations of the Colombian Recycler Movement, 1986–2011." *Social Problems* 63: 351–372.

Rueschemeyer, Dietrich, Evelyne Huber Stephens, and John D. Stephens. 1992. *Capitalist Development & Democracy.* Chicago: University of Chicago Press.

Tarlau, Rebecca. 2019. *Occupying Schools, Occupying Land: How the Landless Workers Movement Transformed Brazilian Education.* New York: Oxford University Press.

UFCW Canada. n.d. "UFCW Canada Supports Migrant Workers in Guatemala." www.ufcw.ca/index .php?option=com_content&view=article&id=2971:ufcw-canada-supports-migrant-workers-in-guate mala&catid=259:directions-1259&Itemid=6&lang=en (accessed July 14, 2020)

Wan Chan, Debby Sze, and Ngai Pun. 2020. "Economic Power of the Politically Powerless in the 2019 Hong Kong Pro-Democracy Movement." *Critical Asian Studies* 52, 1: 33–43.

Weil, David. 2014. *The Fissured Workplace: Why Work Became So Bad for So Many and What Can Be Done to Improve It.* Cambridge, MA: Harvard University Press.

15

African Perspectives on Labor Rights as Enhancers of Democratic Governance

*Evance Kalula and Chanda Chungu**

INTRODUCTION

The ravaging and still unfolding Covid-19 pandemic, with its disproportionate impact on the poor and working people, has heightened the urgency of addressing the democratic deficit globally – a deficit that has grown worse in recent years (Fasih et al. 2020). An effective response to what political scientists call widespread "democratic backsliding" makes all the more vital a renewed focus on the crucial role played by labor in promoting democracy (Bermeo 2016).

Labor and employment are at the center of the struggle to overcome the challenges to democracy everywhere, not least in Africa (Wood & Dibben 2008: 677). Indeed, labor has been at the center of the struggle for democracy in Africa for many years, since the acceleration of the movements for decolonization and political emancipation (Rossi 2014: 1, 23). In many African countries, labor formations, in particular trade unions and other related organizations, were instrumental in giving support to nationalist campaigns. Owing to their power as organized entities, labor formations could operate more effectively than dispersed dissenters in many colonial jurisdictions.

The importance of labor rights in the quest for decolonization and democracy in Africa was further amplified during the heady 1960s. In other words, the struggle for labor rights, in particular freedom of association, enhanced and reinforced decolonization efforts; and trade union formations continued to have relatively stronger capacity and wider collective space to support agitation for political emancipation. Post-colonial developments present an interesting mixed experience for labor unions and challenges to democracy, particularly in the relationship between labor movements and the state. This chapter explores selected perspectives on the role of labor rights as enhancers of democratic governance in Africa, using a number of countries as proxies for the rest of the continent.[1]

Our exploration is informed, to a large extent, by the ILO's recent Centenary reflections, in particular the inevitable link between labor rights and social justice, issues initially canvassed by the ILO Global Commission on the Future of Work. The Commission's report has provided a basis for continuing intense and vibrant debate among scholars and policy makers alike, which

---

* We gratefully acknowledge Theodore Kamwimbi for his advice and kind assistance.
[1] Labor rights encompass both procedural rights, such as freedom of association and collective bargaining rights, and substantive ones, such as freedom from forced labor and the right to equal treatment, which are greatly affected by the procedural rights.

culminated in a rejuvenation and renewal of its mandate at the Centenary International Labor Conference in June 2019 (ILO 2019: 55).

LABOR RIGHTS AS ENHANCERS OF DEMOCRATIC GOVERNANCE

Undeniably, the body of persons who make up the working population in each country across the African continent are political agents in African democracy. Researchers too often limit their analysis of democratic political actors to elected leaders, candidates who are running for election, and relatively high-level policy makers who directly formulate and execute government policies (Wolfsfeld 2015: 1). Wolfsfeld's examination of democratic governance, for example, highlights those elected or appointed to critical positions in government institutions (2015: 1).

This notwithstanding, in the African context, workers and trade unions were often among the earliest and most energetic demonstrators in the African countries witnessing democratic protests (Kraus 1995). Coalitions of working-class decolonization protestors crystallized into labor movements that were largely the core internal constituents of, or external allies with, various political organizations in fighting for decolonization (Huntington 1991).

Whereas it is apparent that in most African countries labor movements and trade unions were suppressed rather than recognized, they formed a key cog in organizing society against the colonial power's persistent domination. To overcome these challenges, labor movements galvanized as many workers as possible to fight outside the legal order for the rights of people and the overthrow of the authoritarian colonial regimes (Seidman 1994: 30).

Against this backdrop, labor movements had a strategic organizational interest in promoting the creation and consolidation of democratic regimes. Of course, the essential objective of trade unions and labor movements was the safeguarding of workers' interests – but it was recognized very early on that a necessary condition for pursuing this objective was independence and political freedom. In turn, this necessary condition could be fully guaranteed only through democratic institutions. The existence of free and independent unions is a reliably strong indicator of democracy (Calenzo 2009: 2).

This is consistent with the freedom to associate and unionize regarded by Dahl as an essential element of polyarchy (1971: 24). It is precisely for this strategic interest that unions had a prominent role in being often willing to defy regimes with an historical reputation of corruption and repression. In several cases, organized labor made an essential contribution to the creation of a political space favorable to the development of democratic institutions (Jose 2002: 9).

Pre-independence and authoritarian regimes found their strength in particular economic and social conditions, which were a product of history and conquest. As such, the labor movement's role as a mouthpiece of the working population was, in each colony, adapted to those particular conditions. The movements recognized that each regime would continue to make strategic use of its distinctive conditions, just as the movement would strategically cooperate with other relevant political and democratic actors to change both the regime and the underlying conditions that sustained it. Cardoso, for example, argues that authoritarian regimes are weakened by the social mobilization that they themselves produce and fail to strategically avert (1985: 32). Assuming his conclusion is correct, the observation of particularly high levels of mobilization among workers can be an indication that the given society is undergoing deep changes that undermine the status quo.

As early as 1859, Marx noted that society may radically change when the material forces of production in society come in conflict with the existing relations of production or, what is but a legal expression for the same thing, with the property relations that generated those forces (1904:

12). Without falling into sociologism or determinism, it is reasonable to expect that, in such contexts, those groups interested in change – organized labor in our case – would adapt their strategies and efforts to create the optimal conditions for the realization of such change (Hyman 1971: 44).

Consistent with Marx's principles, trade unions in Africa played an important role in the struggle for the independence of their respective countries and collaborated closely with nationalist parties (Kester & Sidibé 2019: 11). By doing so, they imagined that independence would guarantee greater freedom for union action and would promote development and – consequently – better life and work conditions for their members (Kester & Sidibé 2019: 11–12). However, once independence had been achieved, political leaders began to distrust unions, whose claims were excessive from their point of view.

It, therefore, follows that the forms and practices of social movement unionism, which have proved their potential political efficacy, especially in South Africa, emerged under certain favorable conditions (Calenzo 2009: 18). These relate essentially to the social and political basis of the authoritarian regime in question. High levels of social conflict and attendant social fragmentation – along ethnic, religious, or even ideological lines – may obstruct multiple groups' perception of a common interest around which the struggle for democracy can be organized (Calenzo 2009:18). Calenzo concludes that an ideal background for the emergence of a solidarity network among social movements may be one in which the greatest sections of the population see their life conditions threatened by the regime's policies: this would allow the various movements to overcome mutual differences and work together for a common project of democracy.

Thus, authoritarian African governments – no matter whether civil or military – strove to provide unions with minimal space for participation in the making of development plans. Even when participation was accepted, this occurred within a framework that confined unions to a passive role of transmission of instruction to workers. Unions often accepted this role in order to avoid repression and thus survive, with the hope of finding some room for maneuver.

Kester and Sidibé (2019: 12) argue that this strategy did, in fact, enable African trade unions to maintain some degree of autonomy, although varying from one country to another. Even though union leaders generally fell under substantial (but again varying) degrees of government control, intermediate structures and – most importantly – the base, often had greater autonomy. This difference frequently rested on greater direct contact between union officials and political leaders and on the opportunities for corruption occasioned by such contact.

In light of the leaderships' exposure to pressures and influences from the state, union democracy was stronger at the base than at the top. This led to protest from below that intensified after the 1970s. Nigeria, Benin, and Togo are good examples: the strongest stances against governments have often been assumed by local or sector labor leaders. Governments have weakened those currents in the labor movements perceived as hostile, by promoting those that enhance the state's strategic capacity to control and manipulate union leadership.

LABOR MOVEMENTS AND DEEPENING DEMOCRACY IN AFRICA

The manner in which labor movements were able to deepen democracy during decolonization and afterwards depended, of course, on the relative strength of the labor movement. The greater the unionization rate, the less able were the main actors in the transition process able to ignore the position and the demands of trade unions without generating discontent and regime destabilization (Calenzo 2009: 11). Conversely, a low unionization rate made it easier for the government and the employers to take labor claims into little account and to construct a system of industrial relations relatively unfavorable for the workers. Further, when the labor movement failed to achieve significant economic and social gains, workers were less likely to exhibit loyalty to the overall political and industrial-relations regime, thus creating the conditions for widespread anti-system tendencies within the labor movement (Calenzo 2009: 11). As will be seen below, the increased informality of labor in the 1990s to date is one change in the labor-market regime that has yielded strong challenges to labor movements across the continent.

Two other key factors accounting for whether labor movements in African countries thrived or weakened are the relative centralization or decentralization of the relevant labor movement and its respective political unity or division. A mobilization sequence was more likely to succeed if union organizations and collective bargaining were highly centralized, and if the leadership was politically united rather than factionalized (Calenzo 2009: 4).

The regime's response and counter-response to labor and its political allies – while a highly complex and variable phenomenon – is for obvious reasons essential to the way the labor movement shapes democracy. The greater the regime's hostility toward unions and the closure of space for unions' political and economic action, the more likely is an alliance between unions and opposition parties (Calenzo 2009: 4).

The problem of the regime's treatment of labor is complex, because it encompasses not only the qualitative containment strategy adopted toward unions, but also the relative harshness of state repression of labor. Harsh regimes are more inclined to exclude unions and limit their channels of voice, while "mild" regimes tend to the opposite. Closely linked to this factor is the degree of openness or closure of the political space, such as the regime's greater or lesser tendency to tolerate the political activities of opposition groups, including those connected to the labor movement (Calenzo 2009: 12)

Valenzuela finds a particularly strong relationship between the labor movement's achievement of political democratization and both the modalities of the post-colonial transition and the connection between the labor movement's political leadership and the other primary transition elites (1989: 465) – the ruling coalition and opposition parties, to mention but two such elites (Calenzo 2009: 4).

If the labor movement and the parties connected to it were included in, or fully constituted, the coalition that led the transition but did not formally occupy positions in the government (leaving these to other trusted groups), then there was greater likelihood of stabilization of the democratic regime – and greater chance of long-term benefits for the movement, since leaders could avoid being identified with potentially unpopular economic measures (Calenzo 2009: 13).

The analysis of transitions to democracy relies in a decisive way on the concept of civil society. Its role – in a context of multilateral acceptance of the formal procedures that allow electoral competition and alternation in government – can be illuminated through the concept of the reinforcement and control of institutional responsibility. Parties play a particularly important role in this analysis, since they often assume the task of aggregating different social interests and absorbing the anti-systemic potential of certain social forces, which in some cases include the labor movement (Calenzo 2009: 14). For that reason, many African states and dominant parties prioritized the institutionalization of the labor movement to secure its commitment to the state's and ruling party's preferred path of transition. Valenzuela highlights, in particular, the labor movement's constitutive role and political integration in institutionalized systems of tripartite bargaining (1989: 464).

It is the perpetual ambiguity between labor as an organization and labor as a movement that permitted and encouraged the state strategy of reducing labor's non-institutionalized features and the political consequences of such features: African states, like those of other continents, sought to achieve a normative model of "responsible unionism" – when, of course, the state did not adopt a model of all-out repression (Calenzo 2009: 14). In light of this analysis and the often decisive role of civil society in democratization processes, it is essential to examine the particular non-institutional dynamics of labor as a movement. That is, civil society – including, most prominently, the labor movement – is critical to the distribution of power in a non-institutional public sphere and associational life (Cohen & Arato 1995: 7).

In this regard, it is critical to recognize that civil society in Africa is characterized by deep inequalities of influence and access to power, and by the existence of informal models of subordination that have to do with elements such as personalization of politics, ethnicity, religion, gender, and language. Therefore, the power of the working class in the distribution mentioned above – conceptualized as the allocation of power for realizing interests that are multiple and often conflicting – is, without question, influenced by elements of identification and aggregation other than class (Cohen & Arato 1995: 14).

The policy ambitions of labor movements were also weighty factors in the transition to democracy. It was crucial that labor movements in Africa became the most fervent advocates for social welfare programs. As a consequence, socialist and social democratic political parties that were either labor-based or in coalition with labor movements were elected and at the forefront of those post-colonial national governments that implemented radical redistribution and took on the features that are characteristic of social democracies. Even when the labor movement did not succeed in constructing a social democratic state, the role of labor organizations as social movements with particular political programs is central to understanding the strength of post-colonial civil society's capacity to articulate alliances and define political agendas with a broader basis of support, even in open conflict with the state.

Broadly speaking, the modalities of involvement of labor in the mobilization for democracy depended greatly on whether it took the form of social movement unionism or, instead, top-heavy labor organizations entering into alliances with other powerful elites (Cohen & Arato 1995: 14). Labor movements were much likelier to succeed in deepening democracy if they did not limit themselves to merely occasional collaboration with communitarian groups and other social movements, and instead created a durable common front against the pre-democratic regime. In such cases, the labor movement became a vanguard social movement, one that may not alone have secured full democratization but around which relevant allies gravitated in effecting democratic transition (Cohen & Arato 1995: 14).[2]

TRADE UNIONS AND THE CHANGING NATURE OF WORK

The ongoing decline of trade unions comes at a time when they are most needed in their role as champions of democracy. In some African countries, the period immediately following the end of colonization was characterized by the nationalization of several state entities, which meant that large segments of workers served in state-owned institutions (Prasnikar 1991: 3). As highlighted above, the new governments sought to give new shape and direction to labor relations as they controlled much of the workforce, and this allowed for trade unions and other labor movements to influence democracy across the continents (Unni & Rani 2003: 1–5).

---

[2] It is worth pointing out that in some countries, the development of a similar model of collaboration among the different sectors of the society in a common mobilization for democracy was more difficult (Cohen & Arato 1995: 15).

Yet difficulties for African unions began to increase considerably in the 1980s when, with the introduction of structural adjustment programs in every country on the continent, governments completely removed participation from their political agenda, promoting economic liberalism and constricting the role of the state. This has put unions at the forefront of the struggle for a new direction, even as the unions are politically embattled and, indeed, *because* they are under attack. Democracy, it is often argued, is incompatible with the existence of extreme inequalities (Lipset 1959: 52). Since participation promotes social cohesion and a socially sustainable development, the labor movement may contribute to forward movement in this direction.

The trade unions' decline comes at a time when they are most needed in their role as foundations of democracy. The consequences of trade union decline were increasingly evident in the 1990s as the world of work was transformed radically. In that decade, democratization – not just a critical consequence, but also a key cause of work relations – was stopped in its tracks by the consolidation of many non-party or one-party governments, and therewith also the symbiotic relationship between government and trade unions (Tangri 1995: 4).

Compounding the profound implications for the labor movement of democratic backsliding was structural adjustment, which was characterized by privatization and liberalization (Kayizzi-Mugerwa 2002: 1–2). This change of control and ownership in various sectors of the economy weakened the influence of trade unions (Mengistu & Vogel 2009: 688), owing to the withdrawal of the government as the principal employer, and trade unions' reorganization to deal with the more adversarial relationship with profit-driven private employers (Lindell 2009: 122–136).

Despite the lauded pre-pandemic economic growth of many African economies, other economic trends create yet further obstacles and challenges to trade union renewal, even as the labor movement continues to keep the struggle for democracy alive. One of the key trends is the decline in formal employment, which continues at a rapid rate. The informal economy is now dominant in most African countries, particularly in Sub-Sahara. In many African countries, formal employment stands at less than 10 percent (Smit & Fourie 2010: 49–51). This is largely due to the inability of the formal sector to produce and generate jobs, with the consequence that a larger percentage of the population falls into the informal economy. Even in some of the older industrialized countries where the informal sector does not occupy a majority of the labor force, it is becoming increasingly significant, particularly for women (Pitcher 2002: 1).

This continuing decline in the formal sector seems irreversible, at least in the medium term, and has adverse implications for the role of labor in the struggle for democracy in Africa. The heterogeneous nature of employment relations, the difficulties of locating and contacting workers in informal employment and – in some instances – obstacles created by legislation make organizing difficult (Lindell 2009: 131–132). With the decline in formal employment, trade unions continue to lose membership and resources, not only to organize workplace-centered campaigns, but also to sustain meaningful solidarity for democratic change in the wider polity (ILO 2002). Simultaneously, unions and other labor formations, particularly those in the service sector, face significant problems in trying to organize in the formal part of the economy, and therefore have even less incentive to use scarce resources for the seemingly greater challenge of organizing in the informal sector (Gallin 2001: 227).

With such loss of ground, is it then feasible to sustain efforts to attain working people's demands for decent work and broader social justice? What strategies could be conceived to reverse the democratic deficit in Africa? Answers to these questions need not be pessimistic (ILO 2010). Recall that labor movements managed to have a profound impact on nationalist movements in the 1950s and 1960s through creative strategic programs and action, in the face of the many glaring challenges of colonization. Indeed, labor movements have throughout their history in Africa – in the post-colonial period, not just in the period of decolonization – demonstrated the ability to overcome severe tests (Freund 1984: 1). Likewise, trade unions in the current modern era need to find innovative ways to address the challenges of the changing world of work and politics, and again make a decisive impact on the growth of democracy across the continent (Sundar 2006: 1).

Even now in some African states, the importance of organizing informal sector workers is not fully recognized by all sections of the trade union movement (Lindell 2009: 127). Part of the reason for this position is the confused and contradictory perception of the informal sector by some trade unions. It is still an accepted assumption by some that the informal sector is a transitory phenomenon, and that it will be absorbed by the formal sector in time without the need for action by trade unions or the state (Bonner & Spooner 2011: 13).

Based on what has been outlined above, it is patently clear that trade unions need to rise to the challenge of the growing informal economy. As such, trade unions need to find creative ways to ensure that they are able to make an impact, notwithstanding the growth of the informal economy. The most obvious route would be for trade unions to extend their field and sphere of activity to include these workers, given the seeming irreversibility of the growth of this sector (ILO 2010). This would require, in some countries, national-level action in order to remove impediments to the long-term development of the formal sector and, concurrently, facilitate trade-union organizing in the informal sector (Birchall 2001: 34).

Trade unions, thus, need to begin by engaging in basic research into the informal economy (Anner & Caraway 2010: 151). Once unions feel they understand what is needed and implement what is necessary, their power to use labor to entrench democracy can only be limited by the incapacity of innovative strategy and action to overcome the concededly high hurdles canvassed above. A starting point for such an understanding is this: it is no longer accurate today to describe the informal economy in Africa as "atypical" (Mazumdar 1976: 660). In most so-called developing countries, it is the formal sector – regular, direct employment with a formal-sector company – that is "atypical" in the literal sense (Smit & Fourie 2010: 43).

The experience of the last two decades shows that the assumption of gradual formalization is unrealistic and only fosters dangerous complacency (Gallin 2001: 227). On the contrary, organizing in the informal economy should not be viewed as intractable and resource-draining, but must be driven by the ability to reach out to groups of workers who are survival experts and therefore, in many cases, extraordinarily dynamic and resourceful (Pontusson 2013: 79).

Further, given their role in sustaining democracy, it is imperative for trade unions to create links with other organizations that work in the informal sector, such as various informal economy representative bodies or relevant non-governmental organizations (Wood & Dibben 2008: 671). Together, the trade unions, and other bodies tasked with providing assistance and representation for the informal economy, could help them define a wider role and identify joint projects at the local level (Jütting & de Laiglesia 2009: 11). This would strengthen democracy across the board as a more unified labor movement would be able to engage more effectively in joint lobbying not only of local, but also of national governments for progressive extension of social security schemes, the provision of infrastructure, land rights, and application of labor protections that will, in turn, strengthen their bargaining power in economic and political democracy (Birchall 2001: 34).

Indeed, there is much evidence that workers in the informal economy are already organizing, partly within existing union structures originating in the formal sector, partly into new unions created by themselves, and partly into associations (Vosko 2007: 287). What is required is for this form of organization to strengthen and build on the successes of the labor movements witnessed during decolonization and the immediate post-colonial period (Berg 2011: 54).

We have briefly surveyed earlier in this chapter the conventional wisdom about the strategies and actions that optimize organized labor's contribution to democratic transition and consolidation (Calenzo 2009: 16). The lessening of repression, especially decreases in violations of personal and legal rights, civil liberties, and freedom of association (Donnelly 2017: 506), that accompanies liberalization of a regime – often flowing from crises of the kind that have become endemic to, and perhaps more frequent in, contemporary capitalism – will very likely encourage the mass of workers to present a long list of unexpressed claims (Calenzo 2009: 16). This will stimulate the mobilization and participation of workers in union activities, while their leaders will attempt to reaffirm the role of negotiators with other political actors, inside and outside the state apparatus. Unions will reorganize and establish new links with parties. The claims of workers, however, can go beyond the capacity or will of employers and economic policy makers to respond in a satisfactory way – for example, leaders' demands for the modification of labor laws can face strong opposition from employers (Calenzo 2009: 16) – and a wave of strikes can prolong crises and create conditions for deepening democratic transition.

On the other hand, conservative and even moderate politicians, the military, and other pivotal actors may become alarmed by the popular support for labor and political leaders they regard as too radical and may push for renewed political closure (Calenzo 2009: 16). It is possible, therefore, that a strategy of militant mobilization in certain critical moments, followed by a decrease of such a mobilization combined with the will and capacity of union leaders to show moderation when the political agenda turns in favor of democratization, would be the sequence to optimize labor's contribution to a successful transition (Valenzuela 1989: 449–450). However, it is imprudent for researchers to propose a single template for labor movement strategy in unpredictably complex and fluid critical moments in political and economic circumstances. Consider the current period of multiple crises in global economics, finance, public health, and democratic backlash. In such circumstances, there is no substitute for shrewd, experienced strategic capability among union leaders, activists, and their allies.

INTERNATIONAL DIMENSIONS: ILO AND THE QUEST FOR DEMOCRACY

No review of labor and the challenge to democracy in Africa would be complete without considering the role the ILO has played through the propagation of international labor standards, in particular freedom of association (Kilpatrick 2019: 665). Since it was established a hundred years ago, the ILO has played a special role in heightening and reinforcing freedom of association, which has been a cornerstone of trade unions' ability to support the development of democracy in Africa (Milman-Sivan 2009: 110).

Karen Curtis, the current chief of the ILO's Freedom of Association branch, gives an insightful analysis and outline of the impact of freedom of association worldwide, including significant developments in Africa (Curtis 2004: 82–89). As she recounts, with the adoption of several instruments after World War II, namely the *Freedom of Association and Protection of the Right to Organize Convention No. 8, 1948*, and the *Right to Organize and Collective Bargaining Convention No. 98, 1949*, reinforcing the 1944 *Declaration of Philadelphia*, the international quest for democracy in the workplace, with ramifications for broader democracy in the body politic, was truly underway (2004: 90). In due course, these instruments were enhanced by the creation of special procedures and structures, such as the Fact-Finding and Conciliation Commission on Freedom of Association and the ILO Governing Body Committee on

Freedom of Association (CFA). These further reinforced Article 26 of the *ILO Constitution*, which provided for the establishment of Commissions of Inquiry (2004: 89).

The link between freedom of association (at its core, a freedom to ensure the independence of trade unions from both state and employer control) and democracy is unassailable. Curtis aptly quotes the ILO's Director General's observations in the 2004 Global Report: "Over the past four years, it has become increasingly apparent that, to promote freedom of association as a human right at work, we need to understand its intimate connection with the enlargement of democracy, the efficiency of market-oriented development and social justice" (2004: 89) (quoting ILO [2004: 90]). Under the ILO's core instruments, freedom of association requires that workers and employers elect their representatives in full freedom and that they are able to organize their administration and activities without interference by the public authorities (ILO 2006: Par. 454). Governments are urged to observe the rights of unions to administer their own affairs and activities without obstacle or hindrance and in line with the principles of freedom of association and democracy to ensure that the elected leaders of the union are free to exercise the mandate given to them by their members and to enjoy the recognition of the government as a social partner (ILO 2018: Par. 668).

Freedom of association and democracy share the same roots: liberty, independence, pluralism, and a voice in decision-making. These fundamental freedoms cannot be suppressed in one sphere and flourish in another (Dahl 1971: 12). If there is no democracy at the political level, there will likely be no right for workers and employers to join freely the organization of their own choosing and exercise their legitimate activities. If freedom of association, including the associational rights of workers, is not recognized as a human right, the foundations of a democratic political system will likely be shaken (Curtis 2004: 91). The ILO has already pronounced itself on the view that a system of democracy is fundamental for the free exercise of trade union rights, and vice-versa (ILO 2006: Par. 32; 2012). And, the ILO's recognition of these fundamental relationships, in its formal legal instruments and its public pronouncements, has had the material effect of strengthening the power of labor movements to deepen democracy across its membership.

The ILO has strengthened the quest for democracy by placing a duty on governments to maintain a social climate in which the rule of law secures respect for and protection of the rights of workers and, by extension, all individuals (ILO 2018: Par. 72). The ILO mandates that appropriate measures be taken to ensure that, irrespective of trade union affiliation, organizational rights can be exercised with respect for basic human rights and in a climate free of violence, pressure, fear, and threats of any kind (ILO 2018: Par. 73).

As outlined above, labor movements in Africa have had and continue to contend with many restrictions imposed by non-democratic regimes. In order to find space to operate, they have to find more creative strategies, such as forming alliances with other social movements. As more and more nations ratified ILO instruments, the environment within which labor movements operated was made more favorable, assisting them in carrying out their functions in a climate of greater freedom and security. Even apart from any tangible sanctions imposed to enforce ILO instruments, the international legitimacy those instruments provided for basic labor rights strengthened the credibility and political capacities of trade unions, including those in Africa.

What is needed, as discussed above, is for African labor movements to overcome the challenges brought on by those changes in their particular polities, economies, and labor markets that run counter to the positive effects of ILO instruments. If these impediments are not mitigated, the progress made in deepening democracy through the entrenchment of ILO instruments will be hampered.

The ILO itself is taking action to respond to those countervailing challenges. To better understand and respond effectively to changes in the world of work, the ILO has launched the "Future of Work Initiative." This initiative was launched in a context of great uncertainty and insecurity, and of fear that the direction of change in the world of work was moving away from, not towards, the achievement of social justice (ILO 2015: 2) – uncertainty and fear that characterize African societies as much as others.

The establishment of the Global Commission on the Future of Work in August 2017 marked the start of the second phase of the ILO's Future of Work Centenary Initiative (ILO 2019: 5). The six thematic clusters of the Future of Work Initiative focus on the main points of what must be addressed to frame effective policies and laws to ensure that work provides security, equality and prosperity (ILO 2019). A series of twelve Issue Briefs were prepared under each of the clusters.

The rationale underpinning the Future of Work Initiative stems from the fact that it is difficult for the ILO (or any comparable international organization) to address all the implications of transformational change in its regular day-to-day activities. While all such activities are relevant, even taken together they are not enough. This is because, by their nature, they tend to be short-term and specific – necessary responses to immediate policy challenges (ILO 2015: 1). The Future of Work initiative will, therefore, need to operate at a high level of ambition to succeed. It needs to involve its tripartite constituency (labor, business, and governments) fully and universally, but must also reach beyond them to the academic world, and indeed to all other relevant and interested actors, including in the African countries. This should not be understood as a threat to tripartism; a greater threat would lie in failure to connect with that wider public (ILO 2015: 2).

Success will also depend on providing the right mechanisms and framework for engagement, and above all on clear recognition that this initiative must have consequences and not just pronouncements. The Centenary is certainly an occasion to look back at past history and achievements (and to learn from them). But the value of the Future of Work initiative will be measured by how it provides concrete guidance for the future activities of the ILO (2015: 2). African labor movements must provide continuous input into that ambitious project.

The ILO Centenary initiative seeks to reinvigorate the ILO's efforts in driving the renewal of democracy that is the focus of this chapter. To achieve this objective, the ILO's stated priorities are specific drivers to keep the Future of Work human-centered in the face of rapid technological change, aimed at affirming the role of labor in enhancing and deepening democracy across the African continent and elsewhere.

CONCLUSION

In this brief discussion, we have sought to show that while the challenges of attaining, let alone entrenching, democracy in Africa remain formidable, it is far from impossible for labor to make meaningful contributions to keep the flame of democracy burning, despite the difficult circumstances in which labor movements find themselves across the continent.

Thanks to alliances with social movements and other strategies, workers were able to play an important part in the formation of democratic institutions in Africa by igniting mass mobilizations that served social needs and claims not only in the workplace, but across society and the polity. However, concerted efforts to renew such mobilization through innovative workplace and political campaigns need to be pursued, in the face of epochal changes in the world of work and in broader economic and political circumstances.

Such efforts should entail both domestic goals and support for the fundamentals of the ILO's program of Decent Work and other imperatives of social justice enunciated in the ILO's agenda for the Future of Work. While it is very much a moving target, deepened democracy in Africa through strengthened labor movements is an attainable goal that calls for creative strategy and for solidarity among labor and other progressive social formations.

REFERENCES

Anner, Mark, and Teri Caraway. 2010. "International Institutions and Workers' Rights: Between Labor Standards and Market Flexibility," *Studies in Comparative International Development* 42, 2: 151–169.

Berg, Janine. 2011. *Labour Markets, Institutions, and Inequality: Building Just Societies in the Twenty-First Century*. Geneva: International Labor Office.

Bermeo, Nancy. 2016. "On Democratic Backsliding," *Journal of Democracy* 21, 5–19.

Birchall, Johnston. 2001. "Organizing Workers in the Informal Sector: A Strategy for Trade Union-Cooperative Action." COOP Working Paper 01-1, International Labor Organization, Geneva, Switzerland.

Bonner, Christine, and Dave Spooner. 2011. "Organizing in the Informal Economy: A Challenge for Trade Unions," *International Politics and Society* 2: 87–105.

Calenzo, Gaetano. 2009. "Labour Movements in Democratisation: Comparing South Africa and Nigeria." Paper presented at the 5th CEU Graduate Conference in Social Sciences, *Old Challenges in a New Era: Development and Participation*. Budapest (June 19–21 2009).

Cardoso, Fernando. 1985. "Transizione politica in America Latina?" In Riccardo Scartezzini, Luis Germani, Roberto Gritti, and Massimo Paci, eds. *I limiti della democrazia. Autoritarismo e democrazia nella società moderna*. Napoli: Liguori.

Cohen, Jean L., and Andrew Arato. 1995. *Civil Society and Political Theory*. Cambridge, MA: MIT Press.

Collier, Ruth Berins, and David Collier. 1991. *Shaping the Political Arena: Critical Junctures, the Labor Movement, and Regime Dynamics in Latin America*. Princeton, NJ: Princeton University Press.

Curtis, Karen. 2004. "Democracy, Freedom of Association, and the ILO," in Jean-Claude Javillier and Bernard Gernigon, eds. *Les Normes Internationales du Travail: Un Patrimoine pour L'avenir*. Geneva: International Labour Organisation.

Dahl, Robert. 1971. *Polyarchy: Participation and Opposition*. New Haven, CT: Yale University Press.

Donnelly, Jack. 2017. "Human Rights," in John Baylis, Steve Smith, and Patricia Owens, eds. *The Globalization of World Politics: An Introduction to International Relations, 7th ed.* Oxford: Oxford University Press, pp. 497–513.

Fasih, Tazeen, Harry Patrinos, and Najeeb Shafiq. 2020. "The Impact of COVID-19 on Labor Market Outcomes: Lessons from Past Economic Crises," *Education for Global Development*, World Bank (May 20, 2020) https://blogs.worldbank.org/education/impact-covid-19-labor-market-outcomes-lessons-past-economic-crises

Freund, Bill. 1984. "Labor and Labor History in Africa: A Review of the Literature." *African Studies Review* 27, 2: 1–58.

Gallin, Dan. 2001. "Propositions on Trade Unions and Informal Employment in Times of Globalisation," in Jane Willis and Peter Waterman, eds. *Place, Space, and the New Labor Internationalisms*. Oxford: Blackwell Publishers.

Huntington, Samuel. 1991. *The Third Wave: Democratization in the Late Twentieth Century*. Norman: University of Oklahoma Press.

Hyman, Richard. 1971. *Marxism and the Sociology of Trade Unionism*. London: Pluto Press.

ILO. 2002. *Women and Men in the Informal Economy: A Statistical Picture*. Geneva: International Labor Organization.

2004. *International Labor Conference, 92nd Session, 2004, Record of Proceedings*. Geneva: International Labor Organization.

2006. *Digest of Decisions and Principles of the Freedom of Association Committee of the Governing Body of the ILO, 5th ed.* Geneva: International Labor Organization.

2010. *Manual on Surveys of Informal Employment and Informal Sector.* Geneva: International Labor Organization.

2012. *ILO Committee on Freedom of Association. Complaint against the Government of Swaziland Presented by the Trade Union Conference of Swaziland and the International Trade Union Confederation,* Case No. 2949, Report No. 367, Interim Report. Geneva: International Labor Organization.

2013. *367th Report of the Committee on Freedom of Association.* Presented at the 317th Session of the Governing Body. Geneva: International Labor Organization.

2015. *Report of the ILO's Director General: The Future of Work Centenary Initiative.* Presented at the 104th Session of the International Labor Conference. Geneva: International Labor Organization.

2018. *Compilation of Decisions of the Committee on Freedom of Association,* 6th ed. Geneva: International Labor Organization.

2019. *Work for a Brighter Future—Global Commission on the Future of Work.* Geneva: International Labor Organization.

Jose, A. V. 2002. "Organised Labour in the twenty-first Century – Some Lessons for Developing Countries," in A. V. Jose, ed. *Organised Labour in the Twenty-First Century.* Geneva: International Institute for Labour Studies, pp. 1–20.

Jütting, Johannes, and Juan Ramón de Laiglesia. 2009. *Is Informal Normal? Towards More and Better Jobs in Developing Countries.* Paris: OECD.

Kayizzi-Mugerwa, Steve. 2002. "Privatisation in Sub-Saharan Africa: On Factors Affecting Implementation." UNU-WIDER Working Paper Series DP20002–12. Helsinki: United Nations University World Institute for Development Economics Research.

Kester, Gerard, and Ousmane Oumarou Sidibé. 2019. "Trade Unions, It's Your Turn!" in Gerard Kester, and Ousmane Oumarou Sidibé, eds. *Trade Unions and Sustainable Democracy in Africa.* London: Routledge, pp. 1–18.

Kilpatrick, Claire. 2019. "Taking the Measure of Changing Labour Mobilisation at the International Labour Organisation," *International and Comparative Law Quarterly* 68, 3: 665–697.

Kraus, Jon. 1995. "Trade Unions in Africa, Democratic Renewal and Transitions: An Introduction," in Jon Kraus, ed. *Trade Unions and the Coming of Democracy in Africa.* New York: Palgrave Macmillan, pp. 1–33.

Lindell, Ilda. 2009. "Global Movements: Place, Struggle, and Transnational Organising by Informal Workers," *Geografiska Annaler: Series B, Human Geography* 91, 2: 123–136.

Lipset, Seymour. 1959. "Some Social Requisites of Democracy: Economic Development and Political Legitimacy," *The American Political Science Review* 53, 1: 69–105.

Marx, Karl. 1904. *A Contribution to the Critique of Political Economy.* N.I. Stone, trans. Chicago: Charles H. Kerr Publishing.

Mazumdar, Dipak. 1976. "The Urban Informal Sector," *World Development* 4, 8: 655–679.

Mengistu, Berhanu, and Elizabeth Vogel. 2009. "Public Perceptions of Privatization in Ethiopia: A Case for Public Good or Private Gain?" *International Journal of Public Administration* 32, 8: 681–703.

Milman-Sivan, Faina. 2009. "Freedom of Association as a Core Labor Right and the ILO: Toward a Normative Framework," *Law & Ethics of Human Rights* 3, 2: 109–153.

Pitcher, M. Anne. 2002. *Transforming Mozambique: The Politics of Privatisation, 1975–2000.* Cambridge: Cambridge University Press.

Pontusson, Jonas. 2013. "Unionisation, Inequality, and Redistribution," *British Journal of Industrial Relations* 51, 4: 797–825.

Prasnikar, Janez. 1991. *Workers' Participation and Self-Management in Developing Countries.* San Francisco: West View Press.

Rossi, Benedetta. 2014. "Migration and Emancipation in West Africa's Labor History: The Missing Links," *Slavery & Abolition* 35, 1: 23–46.

Seidman, Gay. 1994. *Manufacturing Militance: Workers' Movements in Brazil and South Africa, 1970–1985.* Berkeley: University of California Press.

Smit, Nicola, and Elmarie Fourie. 2010. "Extending Protection to Atypical Workers, Including Workers in the Informal Economy in Developing Countries," *The International Journal of Comparative Labor Law and Industrial Relations* 26, 1: 43–60.

Sundar, K. R. Shyam. 2006. "Trade Unions and the New Challenges: One Step Forward and Two Steps Backwards," *Indian Journal of Labour Economics* 49, 4: 895–910.

Tangri, Roger. 1995. "The Politics of Africa's Public and Private Enterprise," *The Journal of Commonwealth & Comparative Politics* 33, 2: 169–184.

Unni, Jeemol, and Uma Rani. 2003. "Employment and Income in the Informal Economy: A Micro-Perspective," in Renana Jhabvala, Ratna Sudarshan, and Jeemol Unni, eds. *Informal Economy Center Stage: New Structures of Employment*, 39–61. New Delhi: Sage.

Valenzuela, J. Samuel. 1989. "Labor Movements in Transitions to Democracy: A Framework for Analysis." *Comparative Politics* 21, 4: 445.

Vosko, Leah. 2007. "Representing Informal Economy Workers: Emerging Global Strategies and Their Lessons for North American Unions," in Dorothy Cobble, ed. *The Sex of Class: Women Transforming American Labor*. Ithaca, NY: ILR Press, pp. 272–292.

Wolfsfeld, G. 2015. INFOCORE Definitions: "Political Actors." Herzliya, Interdisciplinary Center. www.infocore.eu/results/definitions

Wood, Geoffrey, and Pauline Dibben. 2008. "The Challenges Facing the South African Labour Movement: Mobilisation of Diverse Constituencies in a Changing Context." *Relations Industrielles/Industrial Relations* 63, 4: 671–693.

16

Why (Which) Workers Often Oppose (Which) Democracy?

David Ost

Do workers support democracy? As democracy comes under attack, this has become one of the most important questions of our era. Reading the changing opinion on this subject is a dizzying experience. In the 1980s, union movements were leading democratization struggles in a variety of countries, symbolized by Lula and the Workers Party in Brazil, Lech Wałęsa and Solidarity in Poland, and Cyril Ramaphosa and COSATU in South Africa. This came soon after the critical role labor played in ending dictatorships in Spain and Portugal. Scholarship at the time focused not just on workers in this so-called third wave of democratization (Fishman 1990; Ost 1990), but on the crucial role of workers in the origins of democracy (Rueschemeyer et al. 1992). Earlier scholarship had focused on the importance of the bourgeoisie to democratization, epitomized by Barrington Moore's summation of his famous work on the social origins of political regimes with the pithy line, "no bourgeoisie, no democracy" (Moore 1966: 418). But the new scholarship stressed that while the bourgeoisie in Europe fought against the aristocracy in the name of liberal ideas and thus made democratic evolution possible, they had regularly made peace with the old elites once they secured *their* political inclusion, leaving workers, not to mention the rural poor and non-whites, still without political rights (Aminzade 1981; Berman 2019). Instead of the bourgeoisie, this literature demonstrated, it was workers, with their trade unions and socialist parties, that fought consistently for the end to class restrictions on political citizenship, thereby ushering in democracy.

Today, however, a different narrative is popular. Nowadays it is common to see workers presented as dangers to democracy, as they flock to new far right parties. We hear about the "White working class" in the United States, enthralled by Donald Trump, or about labor support for the anti-immigrant "populists" in Europe building up the radical right. The basic facts are hard to dispute. Donald Trump did decisively win the white working class vote. In France, manufacturing workers who used to line up behind the Communist Party have become the base of Le Pen's National Front. Large numbers of workers in Germany and Sweden have deserted their social democratic parties for the far-right Alternative for Germany and Swedish Democrats. In Poland, manufacturing workers constitute a strong part of the illiberal Law and Justice Party's base, with the Solidarity trade union a loyal ally. In Turkey and India, urban workers have become a crucial part of the electoral support for Erdogan and Modi. To read these accounts is to think of workers today as enemies of democracy.

Of course, such accusations are often met by the riposte that even if workers are voting for radical right parties, they are, after all, *voting*, thus taking part in democracy, and are voting for parties that respect the democratic rules in that they don't "seize" power but take hold of it only upon winning free elections. Critics then counter that democracy has often been toppled by electoral means, and that democratic institutions can be undone by their supposed protectors.

Obviously, we need to slow down. Before we can answer the question of whether workers support democracy, we need to say what we mean by democracy. We also need to say who we mean by workers. In this chapter, I show a complex relationship between different types of workers to different understandings of democracy. I argue that while there is a strong positive link between workers and support for basic political inclusion, the association frays when we look at understandings of democracy more prominent today, such as the full inclusion of all citizens and the relative autonomy of state institutions from direct political control.

Throughout I develop three different understandings of democracy, which I label political, egalitarian, and formal-institutional, or Democracy I, II, and III. I argue that while workers in capitalist society have had a strong association with Democracy I, their relationship to the other aspects of democracy has always been ambivalent. They have no special reason to be particularly supportive of inclusive democracy, and are likely to value concrete, substantive outcomes more than the autonomy of state institutions.

As for workers, I mean those who depend for their survival chiefly on selling their labor power for a wage. This includes both those workers with what Beverly Silver (2003: 13) calls "market-place bargaining power," and those without, or what are commonly referred to as skilled and unskilled workers, respectively. I discuss the question of workers and democracy historically, talking first about differences among manual workers, which appeared with the rise of factory work, and then about differences between blue- and white-collar workers (or physical and intellectual laborers), which distinguishes the working class today. I should stress that while much academic discussion of workers and democracy focuses on the role of organized labor, or workers' unions and parties, I am equally interested in whether workers as individuals support democracy. Workers became important in the fight for democracy because of their organizations. But those organizations are much weaker today, and access to information much greater. With all parties appealing to them, workers do not strongly follow the recommendation of their organizations. Also, with union density today often higher for jobs requiring higher education, focusing on union attitudes to democracy doesn't tell us much about workers in general.

One important qualification: my focus here is on those I call "dominant-essence" workers. This refers to those workers with the ascriptive, identity-based cultural characteristics that make them appear to be a natural and inexorable part of the given national community. In the United States, where the enslavement of black people from the earliest times created a divide that still profoundly shapes politics and social relations, the phrase "White working class" evokes this group. In Europe, where colonial legacies and immigration have reshaped the working class, I am speaking about those known as the "native" French, or the "real" Germans, Poles, or any other national group whose "dominant essence" is understood to be white and Christian. I use the term "dominant-essence" rather than dominant race or nationality because the relevant categorical division can be based along any number of cultural factors, including also religion, ethnicity, language, or political creed. Maleness, of course, is a typical part of the dominant essence almost everywhere. Workers lacking the dominant features – "marginalized-essence" workers, we might say – have often been simply excluded from the political community. Such workers, to use the terms developed below, are sometimes still fighting to be included within Democracy I, are fully committed to Democracy II, and are not likely to care much about Democracy III. They are not invited to join today's new right, and are thus not able at all to be a threat to democracy today. If we are interested in workers who might oppose democracy, the focus must be on dominant-essence workers.

I conclude the chapter with a discussion of Poland's trade union movement Solidarity, which arose in opposition to the state socialist system in 1980. Solidarity has been seen, very correctly, as a powerful movement for democracy (Beem 1999; Cohen & Arato 1992; Ost 1990). Ironically, however, whereas workers and union movements in capitalist societies are consistently associated with political democracy, that is the one aspect of democracy that Solidarity did *not* formally pursue. And whereas workers and unions in capitalist societies are generally ambivalent today toward egalitarianism or institutional autonomy, Solidarity was an energetic proponent of Democracy II and III. Yet when state socialism fell and Solidarity became a union in a capitalist society, its positions began to change. Today it is one of the strongest bastions of support for the Law and Justice government that, since winning elections in 2015, has been pushing hard to dismantle Democracy II and III. Understanding the transformation of Solidarity can therefore illuminate how the overall nature of the system affects workers' attitudes toward different aspects of democracy.

A final point: if I spend more time here showing the reasons why workers often ally with the political right and oppose contemporary understandings of democracy, it is not to blame workers for these developments. Much of the history I discuss here is not new. Labor *has* often been a key player in an anti-democratic political alliance. Workers haven't just passively supported non-democracies. They've also contributed actively to making places less democratic. Labor advocates know this well, but often find it desirable to ignore, for fear of aiding cynical liberal elites all too ready to blame *only* workers for the crisis of democracy. That is a legitimate fear. All too often we do see accounts blaming workers, blaming those without higher education, as the problem today. So let me be clear: I believe that neoliberalism and the exclusion of workers from decision-making and wealth-sharing lie at the root of the crisis of democracy today by generalizing a fear of insecurity. But the political right has always gained at times of crisis by recruiting dominant-essence workers around a program centering on attacks on others and the delegitimation of state institutions. Fascism crushed trade unions, but won over plenty of workers (Aly 2006; Mason 2007). It is the historical susceptibility of workers to right-wing, anti-democratic appeals that is my concern here.

VARIETIES OF DEMOCRACY

Current debates about the decline of democracy and whether workers support democracy do not usually specify terms, but typically they seem to be speaking about three different meanings of democracy, which I label political, egalitarian, and formal-institutional, or Democracy I, II, and III.

Political democracy, or Democracy I, is the most basic, referring to the right to vote, inclusion in the political game, and gaining some voice in the formulation of the universally binding decisions of the state. Democracy II, or egalitarian democracy, refers to the inclusion of minorities and other non-dominant-essence groups within the political community. Egalitarian democracy means that those who lack the dominant ascriptive and cultural traits are treated as fully legitimate members of the polity, with interests whose satisfaction the state is equally compelled to realize. Formal-institutional democracy, or Democracy III, concerns the rules guaranteeing fair political competition, including a free press, ensured access of opposition parties, and the general rule of law, meaning state institutions run by professionals committed to administering the law in an impartial fashion.

So, what is the connection of workers to democracy? Scholars working on this have mostly focused on the onset of democracy, or what I have called political democracy or Democracy I.

Understanding democracy chiefly as the "extent to which the right to vote transcends class boundaries," Rueschemeyer et al., in perhaps the most comprehensive book on the topic, demonstrate that historically, "[t]he working class was the most consistently pro-democratic force" (1992: 8, 43). The landed upper-classes were the chief enemy of democracy, since their economic model was dependent on cheap, plentiful, and vulnerable labor. Middle class liberals, meanwhile, played an "ambiguous" role (1992: 8). In Europe they typically initiated the struggle for democracy, against the old nobility's efforts to maintain all power in their hands. Sometimes they allied with workers in the struggle. But from the French Revolution and for a century afterwards, they almost invariably abandoned workers when winning gains for themselves, as happened in much of Europe in 1848. In the later part of the century, as capitalism grew, workers became more prominent, more important to the economy, and thus more powerful. They certainly wanted more than political democracy. Already in 1848, many workers were pushing not only for the right to vote, which they lacked, but for a "social republic" as well (Berman 2019: 88). But every workers' movement pushed for the end of property qualifications for voting, thereby setting the grounds for a universal franchise. Without a strong workers' movement, there would have been no political democracy.

Who were these nineteenth century workers, and why did they play such a crucial role in the coming of political democracy? Workers are those who survive by selling their labor power for a wage. But in the nineteenth century, wage work was just *becoming* a phenomenon of central importance. According to Eric Hobsbawm, wage workers emerged "mainly by transfer from the two great reservoirs of preindustrial labor, the handicrafts and the agricultural countryside" (Hobsbawm 1989: 113). Each of these groups – the craftsmen trying to resist a descent into wage work and recent agricultural laborers now surviving only by wage work – developed a vital interest in Democracy I, but for different reasons. Artisans sought a voice in public decision-making via the franchise to help maintain themselves as autonomous producers and arrest their descent into dependents. They saw the right to vote as a chance to offset in the political world the changes driving them down in the economic world. For wage workers emerging from the countryside, the political world was now the arena that could provide them some of the security they lost when they left the land. Accustomed to a role as subordinates, they did not initiate the fight for democracy, but they eagerly supported it as a chance to use the political arena to provide what they needed to survive.

Pre-capitalist times were halcyon days for artisans. With guilds protecting them and elites needing them, artisans constituted the middle class, between rural or day laborers and established elites. This changed in the early nineteenth century with the emergence of sub-contracting. In this arrangement, "the merchant bought the products of the handicraftsman ... for sale in a wider market," turning the craftsman "into little more than a worker paid on piece-rates" (Hobsbawm 1996: 19, 20). Realizing there was no return to the past, yet wary of further class and status descent as capitalism expanded, craftsmen saw political democracy as a chance to "re-right" the economic order. The Chartist movement in Britain emerged in 1836, just as it became clear that there was no stopping the new wage-labor system. The skilled workers behind Chartism demanded voting rights for all men, secret ballots, and remuneration and no property qualifications for serving in Parliament. Political democracy, they reasoned, could ensure that society rewards labor, not just landowners or merchants. They figured they could win, too, since, as "the most active, educated, and self-confident element in the developing proletariat" (Hobsbawm 1989: 115), craftsmen were among the most important non-aristocratic intellectuals of the time, with significant powers of persuasion. Skilled workers went on to become, throughout Europe, the backbone of the socialist parties, whose first major battles were simply for political democracy, which they saw as the vehicle to making socialism possible.[1]

For the working class emerging from the countryside, the desire for political democracy stemmed from the need to regain some semblance of security. Squeezed off their land by poverty and enclosures (privatization), only wage work allowed them to survive. The demise of feudalism and other forms of enforced rural peonage meant they were free, yet also meant that no elites any longer had an interest in their survival. For while capitalism needs laborers, unlike feudalism it doesn't depend on any specific laborers. Anyone will do, so no one had protection. For workers emerging from the countryside, without any marketplace bargaining power, Democracy I meant that political actors seeking votes might be compelled to address their concerns, which no powerful groups now cared about. Unlike in the feudal past, they now *needed* a say in public affairs and decision-making because, no longer a legal subordinate, they no longer had a benefactor who needed to keep them alive, even for the purpose of exploitation. Political democracy could solve this new problem by making the state responsive also to their needs.

THE RATIONALITY OF WORKING CLASS INEGALITARIANISM

Is there any reason for workers to be as committed to Democracy II, egalitarian democracy, as they are to Democracy I? For socialists, workers *ought* to be, out of a moral sense of class solidarity and the practical gains that come from the struggles of a united working class. And workers, particularly unionized ones, have frequently led the struggle for egalitarianism. History keeps showing, however, that dominant-essence workers often feel they have more to gain by rejecting egalitarianism than embracing it. In the end, the relationship of workers to Democracy II is an ambivalent one.

Let's look first at the perspective of skilled workers. We can imagine that artisans in the early capitalist world would be supporters of ascriptive egalitarianism, since they themselves traveled across imprecise borders, often working or training with craftsmen in other countries. Early artisan fighters for democracy, from Franklin or Paine in America to the printers of France's Third Estate and the die makers of Britain's Chartist movement, welcomed craftsmen from other countries as part of their struggle. To be sure, race was for almost all of them an impassable stumbling block. Nevertheless, their (limited) internationalism bespeaks a deep acceptance of other identities and peoples.

A key factor underpinning such egalitarianism is that artisans possess the scarce skills giving them what Silver (2003) calls high "marketplace bargaining power" (MBP). They cannot easily be replaced. Nineteenth century artisans naturally regretted the erosion of guilds, which ensured them a legal monopoly. Still, they could be highly active in socialist and pro-democracy movements because they knew their own livelihood would be protected even if the landless or unskilled ethnic others got the vote, since those groups could not perform the skilled trades. Comforted by their own resources, they could be magnanimous to those lacking them.

Yet it is this same logic that can make skilled workers *hostile* to Democracy II. For when production becomes mass production, and non-dominant-essence workers become available to

---

[1] August Bebel, a founder of the German Social Democratic Party, was a wood-turner; Pablo Iglesias of the Spanish Socialist Party a printer. Shoemakers also played an important role in the radical democratic movements of the nineteenth century, due to their independence, itinerancy, close contact with the poor (and everyone else), and familiarity with the news, due to sometimes employing "readers" to read newspapers and books to them while they worked, a practice also common among cigar-makers, who also played an outsized role in democratic movements (Hobsbawm & Scott 1980).

employers, the skilled have an incentive to oppose egalitarianism since now they face real competition. Their interests, in other words, give them an ambivalent relationship to egalitarianism.

For skilled workers who rely on formal education, the situation is different. Today, the correlation of higher education to egalitarian politics is one of the most common findings in political science (Kitschelt & Rehm 2019). Higher education correlates strongly with opposition to Brexit, support for Black Lives Matter, and general opposition to the populist right. Yet it was not always this way. In interwar Hungary, Poland, or Romania, college students and the university-educated were strong supporters, even leaders, of nationalist, anti-Semitic, and fascist movements, leading the campaign to oust Jews from positions of influence (Sachar 2003). In the United States, through much of the twentieth century, university-educated professionals tended to be racist, country-club Republicans.

It is only when higher education changed from being exclusively an elite matter to a more mass phenomenon that the correlation began to change. When expanding states after World War II needed the teachers, healthcare workers, and intellectuals to power their modernizing drive, university education became open to non-elites. Graduates got jobs in new kinds of institutions and industries supported by state funding devoted to an expanded welfare state and a post-industrial economy. With the peak of the post-war boom promoting "post-materialist" thinking among ever more numbers of college-educated youth, and with women and ethnic minorities advancing into white-collar positions for the first time, higher education started being associated with egalitarianism. Left parties which had, before World War II, often muted their identity-egalitarianism in order to organize traditionalist dominant-essence workers, now grew explicitly anti-sexist and anti-racist in response to these new voting blocs and constituencies. In short, changes in the nature, purpose, and social profile of higher education, along with the growth of the knowledge economy, help explain why education today correlates highly with support for Democracy II.

What about those lacking MBP, or the so-called unskilled? First of all, we should note that the very label "unskilled" is often an unjust invective deployed by already-existing workers (the "skilled") to protect their own privileges. That is, the term "unskilled" can itself be part of the anti-egalitarian arsenal used by some workers to protect themselves, both by keeping *people* designated as "unskilled" away from their own jobs, and by maintaining preferential wages for themselves by designating other *jobs* as "unskilled."[2]

On the one hand, dominant-essence workers with limited MBP often have a natural affinity for Democracy II, since they have always been more likely to live and work with racial and ethnic minorities, due to shared poverty and, until nationalism began changing this, shared cultural subservience. (Most languages have derogatory terms – "hicks," for example – for new workers from the agricultural countryside, making clear that even these workers, despite their race, language, and religion, lack the traits granting them entry into the dominant-essence.) Exclusionary nationalists have often had a tough time winning lower-class support in diverse areas, since the dominant-essence unskilled usually have close personal relations with the "enemy-other" such nationalists are proposing. Studies of ethnic cleansing consistently show the great efforts to which nationalists must go to carry out their goals. Serbian nationalists, for example, finding that low-MBP Bosnian Serbs did not want to turn against their Muslim

---

[2] Lizzie O'Shea has recently examined this point (2020).

neighbors, had to murder individual recalcitrant Bosnian Serbs in public in order to force other local Serbs to join their cause (Rieff 1996).[3]

On the other hand, if presented with a credible opportunity to improve their economic lot by joining an effort to collectively subordinate a different group, many will take it. In other words, if offered a chance to take dominant-essence status, and enjoy the privileges thereof, plenty of lower-skilled workers are likely to do so. For example, newly arriving Irish immigrants to America typically lived among and had good relations with black people, since they too were cruelly marginalized, as both Catholics and Irish. But when offered a chance to advance via "whiteness," many eagerly took it, sometimes through a racism enacted with particular fierceness so as to "prove" their whiteness to skeptical Anglo natives (Roediger 2007).[4]

Of course, the unskilled are not destined to latch on to racism. When there is a realistic opportunity for *class-wide* advance, the unskilled can be particularly receptive to egalitarian democracy, as seen, for example, in the 1930s in the multi-ethnic and multi-racial engagement in the CIO. Socialist parties and left-wing trade unions have long played an important role in thwarting working class racism.[5]

Let's consider two theoretical accounts of the problem. In a well-known article, Edna Bonacich (1972) argues that dominant-essence workers, when faced with a challenge from lower-payable (because of their identity) marginalized-essence workers, have historically tried to maintain or improve their own class position via two different ways of ethnically "splitting" the labor market, which she calls "exclusion" and "caste." Exclusion obtains when workers organize to keep out or remove class comrades of a different identity who, by virtue of their lower status and often shorter time horizons, are desirable for capitalists seeking to lower wage costs. The USA's Chinese Exclusion Act of 1882 and the "White Australia Policy" of the early twentieth century are prime examples of dominant-essence (white) workers defending *their* class position by preventing employers from exploiting (i.e. employing) others. Caste, meanwhile, refers to the arrangement sought by dominant-essence workers when ascriptive others cannot be kept out, either because they're already present or because elites defy laws and keep bringing them in. In this situation, the dominant-essence seek to restrict the others' possibilities to marginalized and "dirty" jobs, and to reinforce inequality by supporting limitations on others' educational and political opportunities. Here, as Bonacich puts it, "the solution to the devastating potential of weak, cheap labor is, paradoxically, to weaken them further, until it is no longer in business's immediate interest to use them as replacements" (Bonacich 1972: 556). South African apartheid and the Jim Crow South are classic examples of this.

Both these approaches point to the fact that while capitalists are equal-opportunity exploiters, a group of workers can obtain an advantage by being the *only* workers that capitalists exploit, as this gives them a bargaining power they otherwise lack. Of course, this is available only to dominant-essence workers, who alone can use their cultural identity for class advantage. Unlike

---

[3] Other literature on ethnic cleansing shows similar difficulties nationalists have had in inciting violence against minorities in MBP-poor regions (Mann 2005; Snyder 2004).

[4] In his account of how whiteness in America became so crucial for working class advance, Roediger (2007) focuses on artisans, who sought to limit any further descent into exploited wage work by embracing an anti-black racism that privileged themselves as "producers," in contrast to black people who were "slaves," even if formally free. In Frank Parkin's (1979) terms, discussed below, artisans unable to usurp the exclusionary strategies of those above them thus sought economic exclusion against those culturally below them.

[5] The Communist Party USA consistently fought against racial divides within the labor movement (Kelley 2015). Sometimes, though, even left parties have caved to racism and defended only the dominant-essence working class, the most notorious being the South African Communist Party in 1922, supporting the miners' strike with the remarkable slogan, "Workers of the World, Fight and Unite for a White South Africa" (Marks 2019).

the above examples, however, it is not limited only to whites. Note, for example, South African workers' strenuous efforts to keep out Zimbabweans: an attempt to gain an advantage by exclusion, not caste, on behalf of workers long subject themselves to caste exploitation (Polakow-Suransky 2017).

Whereas Bonacich, rooted in a Marxist approach, shows us why working class racism, and thus opposition to Democracy II, can unfortunately make sense for dominant-essence workers, for Frank Parkin (1979) racism is a natural strategy pursued by whatever social groups in the subordinate class are able to do so. Parkin's Weberian approach to class is based not on a group's place in economic production but on how any group seeks to gain and maintain an advantage. In premodern society, position in a social hierarchy was preordained and permanent. Non-elites were excluded from power and wealth by law. With capitalism and modernity, elites seek to keep privileges for themselves by precluding entry to others. Property and credentials (education) have been the main way elites manage the trick, in a process Parkin calls "social closure." The capitalist rules over the worker and not vice versa because only the former owns the means of production. Professionals gain advantages for supplying services by inventing the credentials required for entry. Elites get the law to institutionalize property rights and credentialization. By thus limiting but, unlike in the past, not formally excluding others, elites maintain class hierarchy in democratic times.

Workers, however, fight back. Having been excluded due to their lack of property, their chief method of defense is what Parkin calls "usurpation," or pushing back against the privileges of those above them. If ownership allows employers to pay wages of mere subsistence, workers can refuse to work unless they are paid more. This is of course what the best unions do: they limit exploitation by enforcing wages higher than capital is willing to provide. But – and here is the link to workers' opposition to egalitarian democracy – challenging exclusion by elites is not the only way, and *often not the easiest way*, for workers to advance their interests. Parkin introduces the concept of "dual closure," whereby some sectors of the subordinate class, besides pursuing a usurpation strategy against the bourgeoisie, pursue their own exclusionary social closure against *other* subordinate class groups, mainly those that have already been stigmatized by state and society on the basis of their identity (Parkin 1979: 89). Those pursuing such a strategy, says Parkin, might not necessarily wish to do so. They might well prefer uniting with others to fight together against the dominant class. But dominant class power is *hard to challenge*. Those at the top of the ranks of social exclusion also control the state, the military, and usually the dominant cultural norms as well. (In Michael Mann's terms, they possess economic, political, military, and ideological power.) Thus, for those workers who are able to, initiating downward exclusion against more marginalized groups is "a rational response to their own exploited condition" (Parkin 1979: 91).

In other words, the white Afrikaner miners discussed by Bonacich could have joined together with black workers on class grounds, and adhering to the principles of Democracy II would require that they did. Yet it was clearly *easier* for exploited Afrikaners to accept an offer of advance via whiteness than to create a cross-race alliance against British capitalist mine owners, particularly since British *co-workers*, already benefiting because of their national identity, would have been very unlikely to join.

It is often said that trade unions and workers' parties prevent the turn to racism by promoting class unity instead. For Silver, workers' "associational power" is what unites workers against capital, winning gains for the class as a whole. And of course workers' associations have very often done just that. The problem, though, is that anti-egalitarian working class associational power is also possible. Unions have fought racism, but they have also supported exclusion.

Socialists have organized workers, but so have fascists. Workers' associational power does not necessarily tackle racism.

The discussion above of why workers don't support Democracy II boils down in essence to what rational choice theorists call a collective action problem. Workers are best off if they join together, but because success is so difficult, those of the dominant-essence reject egalitarianism and seek advance by persecuting those below, by becoming racists. The collective action required for downward exclusion, moreover, is easier to organize because the persecuted are already culturally marginalized (low status), and because capitalists, while preferring equal exploitation of all, take the super exploitation of some and the limited inclusion of others as an acceptable way to thwart unified class pressure from below. Capitalists gain also by having dominant-essence workers expend their energy excluding below rather than "usurping" above.

Theoretically, the problem can be solved by inculcating egalitarian norms among workers, and providing emotional and material incentives not to defect (into racism). This is what many unions do. This is what socialist parties have done. But today we are faced with the phenomenon not of massive working class unity against capital. Rather, with neoliberalism so seemingly unbeatable (Hassel 2003; Ost 2011), we see workers turning *against* leftist workers' movements and being lured by a nationalist, neo-fascist right. We should not assume that just because associations represent workers, they will defend egalitarian democracy.[6]

THE PUZZLE OF DEMOCRACY III

Democracy III, or formal-institutional democracy, concerning the fairness and neutrality of state institutions, has been the focus of most of the recent discussion today about the decline of democracy. Hungary and Poland, under Viktor Orbán and Jarosław Kaczyński respectively, have been undermining democracy because they attack its institutions. Their party wins power, and they proceed to take over the judiciary, limit the parliamentary rights of the opposition, reduce the reach of opposition media, direct state resources to party allies alone, and replace professionals in state institutions with party hacks. Gerrymandering and voting restrictions limit Democracy I, and abusive attacks on marginalized-essence others (mostly refugees and gays, with Jews often as a subtext) damage Democracy II, but with voting for the opposition still possible, and with too few minorities to make identity persecution a winning strategy, the undermining of institutions is the main way today's radical right clamps down on democracy. Donald Trump's refusal to accept limitations on executive power, firing of independent-minded state professionals, and efforts to restrict voting shows the spread of such practices.[7]

Formal-institutional democracy has always been frail. Indeed, one of the puzzles is why any political contenders should support it, since insistence on the state following the law as interpreted by professionals can hurt both those in power and in opposition. Embracing Democracy III requires taking a longer time horizon and accepting short-term defeats. For those with urgent needs, it can seem like a privilege they cannot afford. Democracy III first

---

[6] One recent effort arguing otherwise, that unions consistently support democracy, runs into a lot of problems. Mosimann et al. (2019) (discussed in this volume by Roberts) begin with the dubious assertion that "solidarity among workers irrespective of nationality, origin, race, or gender" is an eternally core principle of labor movements, which flies in the face of apartheid, the Chinese Exclusion Act, and White Australia. Empirically, they argue that unionized workers are less likely than the non-unionized ones to switch to the radical right, yet acknowledge that they're more likely to move right than previously. Moreover, by failing to distinguish between higher-educated and lower-educated unionists, they risk misidentifying as a unionization linkage what in fact is an educational one.

[7] For a recent account of the global diffusion of right-wing ideas originating in eastern Europe, see Ost 2019.

became a focus of liberal democratic governance in the early twentieth century, and was quickly deemed not to have passed the test, as country after country entered into crisis (Mazower 2000). Fascism promised to take care of people's needs without any formal democracy to worry about, and when it did, it won over many workers, even former socialists, to the cause.

Democracy III returned as a central feature of democracy only after World War II, driven by the expanded role of the state and of state bureaucracies, now responsible for administering and regulating large swaths of society. Maintaining public support for such state expansion was understood to require the professionalization of administrators. Courts also took on an increasing role, even in Europe which lacked the tradition of a strong judiciary. Constitutional courts empowered to overturn legislation were imposed on eastern European countries as a condition of joining the European Union. Stripping such courts of their independence and autonomy was the first order of business for both Orbán and Kaczyński.

How workers relate to Democracy III probably depends on where they stand in terms of access to the state. The huge expansion of the state in the 1960s and 1970s meant a concomitant expansion in the number of higher-educated state workers: teachers, researchers, and (outside of the USA) healthcare workers, many of them the professionally educated children of blue collar workers. We would expect these workers to defend the professional autonomy of institutions since, with their qualifications, they would be among the ones participating in and leading them. We would expect them to support formal procedures since, lacking an old elite pedigree, they owe their own advance to the following of formal rules. We need not believe in pure meritocracy to see how these workers would be committed to Democracy III. Indeed, Moshe Lewin (1988) explains the massive democratic mobilization of the Gorbachev period in the Soviet Union precisely on these grounds: newly confident educated workers and professionals feeling they no longer need the oppressive guidance of the ruling party, come to believe that citizens can and should govern on their own.

For workers without such educational resources, however, who might not expect to see the inside of a courtroom except perhaps as a defendant, the formal independence of state institutions can seem like an irrelevant abstraction, especially in tough economic times.

Support for Democracy III thus hinges largely on a feeling of competence and proximity to state institutions. Those workers and organizations that believe they can shape the law are likely to support institutional independence, and those who see themselves as outsiders will be focused on outcomes, not procedures. There is no clear allegiance of workers to Democracy III.

THE RIDDLE OF *SOLIDARNOŚĆ*

How then are we to understand the Polish Solidarity movement, which pushed for egalitarianism and institutional autonomy when it emerged in 1980, yet, soon after the collapse of state socialism and the introduction of Democracy I in 1989, turned dramatically to the right, becoming today one of the key bastions of the Law and Justice party's (PiS, in Polish initials) campaign against Democracy II and III?

Solidarity arose in the summer of 1980, as a result of strikes that began with the skilled workers in the Gdansk shipyard. As the country was part of the Soviet bloc, governed by a communist party claiming to be the only true representative of the working class, neither strikes nor independent trade unions were allowed. But the strikes occurred in a context of deep economic crisis and a long-lasting legitimacy crisis, and within days they had spread to factories and institutions throughout the country, winning the support even of intellectuals and technicians. On August 31, the government signed an accord allowing the formation of Solidarity as an "independent self-governing trade union." Within a year it had close to ten million members, in a country with about 38 million inhabitants. Because the Soviet-type system was neither politically nor economically structured to incorporate independent voices, the state never reconciled itself to Solidarity, and in December 1981 it arrested most leading unionists and imposed martial law. Solidarity survived as an underground organization and rose again as a legal trade union after communist party rule collapsed in 1989.

Democracy I, or free elections for state power, was the one aspect of democracy that Solidarity did not demand. For most, this was simply a recognition of reality: anything that could jeopardize communist party rule was the one thing the government, and its Soviet sponsors, would not allow. This does not mean Solidarity did not care about political democracy. For if, as Philippe Schmitter (1983: 891) has argued, political democracy "in its most generic sense" means citizenship opportunities for an increasingly "wider range of eligible participants," able to influence decisions "binding upon all," Solidarity's commitment to political democracy was present in the Gdansk strikers' first, and only non-negotiable, of their twenty-one demands: the right to form independent trade unions. In a state socialist system, where there are no independent parties, but where the working class is recognized as the source of political power, independent unions open up precisely the *political* sphere to more participants, since the ruling party would now have to take into account other voices in making decisions.

The fact that Solidarity in 1980 did not highlight free elections as part of its fight for democracy does, however, tell us something important about the systemic basis of labor support for Democracy I: when states are formally committed to governing in the interests of the working class, policy can be more important to workers than voting rights. Workers fought for basic political democracy in capitalist societies because both the political and economic structures of those states excluded them. Voting was the only way to gain a guaranteed voice. State socialism, however, claimed to be *privileging* workers' voice. Workers didn't necessarily feel they needed a vote to be heard; they just needed to *be* heard. Contemporary Chinese workers, for example, engage in all kinds of protests to get themselves heard, without campaigning for formal democracy (Lee 2007), which would not be likely to benefit them, at least in the short term, since they would lose their special resonance. Polish strikers wanted changed policies, not free parliamentary elections, and built an independent union to compel the government to make those changes. Today's Solidarity supports the authoritarian Law and Justice government because the latter has made some key reforms that Solidarity sought. In other words, where authoritarianism promises to defend workers, the latter might reasonably seek inclusion within the system rather than risk their symbolic centrality to fight for political democracy.

Again, no one in Solidarity *opposed* Democracy I, but, knowing it was unattainable, they sought to get their interests accommodated via a democratic union instead. Workers acted differently in the Latin American and southern European dictatorships of the 1970s. Because these regimes explicitly opposed workers, the latter pushed for formal democracy and free elections as the way to get heard.

What about Democracy II and III? In its initial period of 1980–81, Solidarity went to great pains to stress its openness to all. Five factors seem to explain this union's unusually unambivalent commitment to Democracy II. First, there was the state socialist context with its official ban on ascriptive inequality, which made any who advocated identity-based exclusion subject to state sanction.[8] Second, state socialism's social structure prevented the kind of downward exclusion

---

[8] The state-socialist state could conduct its own identity-based exclusion campaigns, as Poland's did in 1968, launching an anti-Semitic purge, but any opposition seeking political recognition had to adopt universality.

strategies discussed by Parkin. There was no group with a systemically enforced subordinate status easily subject to (or "worthy of") exclusion, and no economic conflicts among different social groups since all grievances were directed to the state. A third factor was Poland's homogeneity. Once one of Europe's most ethnically and racially divided countries (Jews were typically labelled a "race"), Poland became, as a result of the war, the holocaust, and post-war deportations, one of the most homogeneous. This meant there was little temptation for ascriptively dominant workers to gang up on others, and little reward for doing so. Fourth, Solidarity's leadership and top advisers included many former socialists and emerging liberals, for whom solidarity across national borders was a natural principle. Finally, Solidarity in the factories was led by skilled workers. Many had worked and trained in neighboring socialist countries, and developed the kind of artisanal respect for the craftsmanship of others typical of the highly skilled.

At its National Congress in 1981, Solidarity issued a call to the people of Eastern Europe, asking them to join in the struggle for democratic change. The union established contacts with South Africa's COSATU union of black workers and with Brazil's Workers Party, both still fledgling movements also fighting against dictatorships. In the generalized free public sphere that Solidarity's existence created, anti-Semitic propaganda directed at the ruling party did appear, and individual union leaders sometimes uttered ethnocentric and anti-Semitic remarks. The union as a whole, however, took pains to resist such divisiveness, and to embrace the egalitarianism of Democracy II as a key part of its program.

Because it possessed no actual political power yet aimed to transform the political system, Solidarity comported itself in a way that can be called "anticipatory democracy," or acting in a way that sets a model for the desired future. This is why it adhered so closely to Democracy III. It aimed to show, in contrast to the ruling party, that it could conduct affairs in a democratic manner, and that its institutions would be accorded the kind of independence that the existing state institutions lacked. Support for formal-institutional democracy came easily. Solidarity called itself an "independent, self-governing trade union." Support for independent associations of any kind were central to the program its key intellectual advisers had promoted in the 1970s (Ost 1990). Solidarity stayed loyal to institutional autonomy even when doing so seemed counterproductive. For example, its press agency, *Agencja Solidarności*, sat in on top union leadership meetings and was allowed to publish detailed accounts of internal conflicts, despite the obviously damaging use Party authorities would make of such material.[9] Solidarity treated institutional autonomy as a hallowed achievement, and applied the principle also to the state. It did not criticize state institutions as such but only their "dependence" on the ruling party, symbolized by the "nomenklatura" principle of empowering loyalists rather than experts. With their practice of endorsing independent experts for top positions in factories and ministries, Solidarity unionists showed that they were all for letting professionals do their jobs.

Solidarity also put outsized emphasis on formal democracy within the union. At its First National Congress in 1981, before collecting presidential election ballots, the organizers performatively held up the ballot boxes to show they were empty. Democracy prevailed over efficiency. Union meetings often dragged on for hours, according to the principle that everyone who raised their hand had a right to be heard. Critical voices were not shouted down. Opposing views were contested, never excluded. Fair competition, a free press, rights for critics, institutional autonomy: Solidarity in 1980–81 was a staunch and uncompromising supporter of the principles of Democracy III.

---

[9] Personal conversation with Joanna Stasińska of Agencja Solidarności, New York, 1983.

Our main indicator of Solidarity's turn to the anti-democratic right is its wholehearted support for the Law and Justice (PiS) party, which came to power in 2015 promising to bring "a change for the better," and quickly set about dismantling key constitutional provisions and inciting constant cultural war against critics at home and abroad. Like Viktor Orbán's Fidesz party in Hungary, PiS does not reject formal democracy, though it reduces the fairness of elections by making it harder for the opposition to participate. PiS tried to push an election during the 2020 pandemic, when no opposition candidates could campaign; forced to abandon it, its state media devoted its news programs to lies about the opposition. PiS is more openly hostile to both Democracy II and III. Islamophobia has become state policy. It denounces anti-racist movements as leftist "political correctness." With its so-called *polityka historyczna* (historical politics), PiS has rebranded nationalist anti-Semitic warriors from the 1940s as great Polish patriots. It belittles feminism as "gender ideology," equating it to both Nazism and communism. It focused its 2020 presidential campaign around the struggle against "LGBT ideology," which priests have called "worse than communism." PiS doesn't call for violence, but it neither acknowledges the increases of identity-based assaults nor denounces them. It stokes hatred, and denies responsibility for the consequences. PiS insists also on an everyday division among Poles based on political views or creed. When in opposition from 2007 to 2015, PiS leader Jarosław Kaczyński denied the "Polishness" of the elected leaders. Upon coming to power, Kaczyński started referring to opponents as the "worst sort of Poles." In 2020, Kaczyński claimed the liberal candidate for president lacked "even a tiny bit of Polish soul." PiS asserts not just that only it represents the nation, but also that only its supporters constitute the nation. It is a consistent opponent of egalitarian Democracy II.

As for Democracy III, the attack on institutional autonomy has been pervasive. Within weeks of coming to power, PiS opened a war on the Constitutional Court. It openly violated court rulings, justifying this on the authoritarian grounds that since it had won national elections, its views were endorsed by "the nation," and thus final. "Any law which does not serve the nation is lawlessness," one parliamentarian proclaimed, to a PiS standing ovation (Ost 2016). Soon it set to work on the media, turning public radio and TV stations into government mouthpieces openly lying about the opposition. In 2020, the PiS-installed director of the state pop radio station even annulled the results of a "best song of the month" contest when listeners selected one with critical words about Kaczyński. It reversed civil service rules mandating professionalism, essentially returning state administration to the nomenklatura system of the past.

And all of this, Solidarity has supported. Why?

First of all, obviously, different people are in charge. The left-liberal activists who were so prominent in the early Solidarity departed after 1989 for positions in government, media, civil society, and business, opening the way for previously marginalized conservatives to become the dominant group in the union. By the early 1990s national Solidarity was explicitly defining itself as a "right-wing" union movement fighting for "traditional Catholic" values.

The erosion of the left was a huge second factor. That a right-wing ideological group *could* take charge of Solidarity was the result of the fall of state socialism, which ended the need to appear egalitarian in order to take part in public debate. A bigger problem was the abandonment of class discourse. In a colossal intellectual misunderstanding and political blunder, left-leaning activists after 1989 treated class as a concept relevant only to state socialism (Ost 2015a). Nothing could be more mistaken. State socialism *talked* about class, but by turning everyone into state employees, it wasn't class but political access that shaped antagonisms. The post-socialist transformation, meanwhile, set as its *goal* the creation of a class society, and by refusing to talk about it, the left had nothing to counteract the right-wing perspective holding that culture and identity shaped social stratification. Opposition to Democracy II follows easily from there.[10]

Third, PiS's economic policies keep Solidarity loyal. Upon coming to power in 2015, PiS introduced several policies the union had called for: mandating secure labor contracts, lowering the retirement age, limiting Sunday work, and providing cash benefits for parents. The policies do not empower trade unions or improve public services; they can be seen as state paternalism that keeps neoliberalism intact (Pawłowski 2020). They are, nevertheless, more pro-worker than the policies of any other post-1989 government, and they help Solidarity members more than other workers.

The union's changing make-up is thus a fourth factor facilitating Solidarity's devotion to PiS. The worker-intellectual unity of Solidarity in 1980, when all had the same employer and opponent, broke down after the fall of state socialism, with blue-collar workers in mines and privatized manufacturing plants becoming dominant in Solidarity, and white-collar higher educated employees either abandoning unions altogether or concentrating in their own inde-pendent unions. The lower status of today's Solidarity members makes them open to a PiS right-wing nationalism that promises both status and class elevation. PiS rhetoric about "real Poles" offers those with weak bargaining power a dominant-essence status they have so far lacked – a lack made evident in the many hundreds of thousands who have decamped to the west for higher-paid work where they are still paid less and treated worse than western natives. PiS's language disparaging diversity, belittling immigrants, denouncing the educated, and lauding traditional values discursively elevates Polish workers to dominant-essence status, and its modest pro-worker policies can be treated as concrete steps towards realizing this goal. PiS's anti-Islamism, meanwhile, is an assertion that Poles are whites and should be treated as such. If western European white workers secured their dominant-essence status in part through their states' former colonialism, a legacy that western right-wing populists still cherish, it is not so surprising that Polish or Hungarian workers believe campaigns against others might benefit them too. Identity-based exclusion often facilitates some class advance (Ost 2015b).

Poland's higher-educated workers in health and education, now mostly in unions other than Solidarity, have largely opposed PiS's attacks on democracy (Ost 2018). Their greater market-place bargaining power and scarce skills, obtained through extensive interaction with others, give them the security that the lesser-skilled lack, allowing them more liberal views on Democracy II. (Skill seems to affect outlook in other sectors too: one of the most anti-PiS workers I have met is an oil rig operative frequently stationed in Angola, who sees himself as a craftsman among others and considers PiS racism an endorsement of mediocrity.) As discussed above, there also seems to be a correlation with Democracy III: Polish skilled workers with high MBP, mostly outside of Solidarity, appear more sympathetic to the ideas of autonomous insti-tutions run by professionals and to full opposition rights, since they can imagine being among the decision-makers.

In the end, then, Solidarity was one of the most consistent pro-democratic union movements in history when it emerged in opposition to state socialism. But when the union began to represent workers in a capitalist context, at a time of peak neoliberalism, it ended up quite susceptible to the anti-democratic right, as other workers' movements have been.

---

[10] I have previously probed how class conflicts lead to democratic outcomes while identity-based conflicts facilitate authoritarianism (Ost 2005, Chapter 1).

CONCLUSION

This chapter has argued that workers and unions are not necessarily a pro-democratic force. Historically, they secured Democracy I. But today it is Democracy II and III that are under attack, and labor is not a natural ally. Dominant-essence workers have "rational" reasons to fight only for themselves, even at the cost of others. Unions are a more natural ally for democracy, being often internally diverse and committed to maintaining their autonomy. But even unions can go with authoritarians that claim to look out for them. A union presence democratizes the firm, but unions and their members cannot be relied on to support democratic government, if by that we mean a system open to citizens of all identities, with institutions run by civil servants enforcing laws binding equally upon all. Whether labor supports democracy or helps undermine it depends on their view of democracy, on which party or ideology they accept as their own. Being a worker or a union doesn't determine much in itself.

REFERENCES

Aly, Götz. 2006. *Hitler's Beneficiaries: Plunder, Racial War, and the Nazi Welfare State.* New York: Metropolitan Books.

Aminzade, Ronald. 1981. *Class, Politics, and Early Industrial Capitalism.* Albany: SUNY Press.

Beem, Christopher. 1999. *The Necessity of Politics.* Chicago: University of Chicago Press.

Berman, Sheri. 2019. *Democracy and Dictatorship in Europe.* New York: Oxford University Press.

Bonacich, Edna. 1972. "A Theory of Ethnic Antagonism: The Split Labor Market." *American Sociological Review* 37, 5: 547–559.

Cohen, Jean, and Andrew Arato. 1992. *Civil Society and Political Theory.* Cambridge, MA: MIT Press.

Fishman, Robert F. 1990. *Working-Class Organization and the Return to Democracy in Spain.* Ithaca, NY: Cornell University Press.

Hassel, Anke. 2003. "The Politics of Social Pacts." *British Journal of Industrial Relations* 41, 4: 707–726.

Hobsbawm, Eric. 1989. *The Age of Empire: 1875–1914.* New York: Vintage.

Hobsbawm, Eric. 1996 (orig. 1962). *The Age of Revolution, 1789–1848.* New York: Vintage.

Hobsbawm, Eric, and Joan Wallach Scott. 1980. "Political Shoemakers." *Past and Present* 89: 86–114.

Kelley, Robin D. G. 2015 (orig. 1990). *Hammer and Hoe: Alabama Communists during the Great Depression.* Chapel Hill: University of North Carolina Press.

Kitschelt, Herbert, and Philipp Rehm. 2019. "Secular Partisan Realignment in the United States: The Socio-Economic Reconfiguration of White Partisan Support Since the New Deal." *Politics and Society* 47, 3: 425–479.

Lee, Ching Kwan. 2007. *Against the Law: Labor Protests in China's Rustbelt and Sunbelt.* Berkeley: University of California Press.

Lewin, Moshe. 1988. *The Gorbachev Phenomenon.* Berkeley: University of California Press.

Mann, Michael. 2005. *The Dark Side of Democracy.* Cambridge: Cambridge University Press.

Marks, Steven G. 2019. "'Workers of the World Fight and Unite for a White South Africa': The Rand Revolt, the Red Scare, and the Roots of Apartheid." In Choi Chatterjee, Steven G. Marks, Mary Neuburger, and Steven Sabol, eds. *The Global Impacts of Russia's Great War and Revolution, Book 2.* Bloomington, IN: Slavica Publishers, pp. 195–226.

Mason, Timothy. 2007. *Nazism, Fascism, and the Working Class.* Cambridge: Cambridge University Press.

Mazower, Mark. 2000. *Dark Continent: Europe's Twentieth Century.* New York: Vintage.

Moore, Barrington. 1966. *Social Origins of Dictatorship and Democracy.* Boston: Beacon.

Mosimann, Nadja, Line Rennwald, and Adrian Zimmermann. 2019. "The Radical Right, the Labour Movement, and the Competition for the Workers' Vote." *Economic and Industrial Democracy* 40, 1: 65–90.

O'Shea, Lizzie. 2020. "We Keep You Alive: Unskilled Labor Does Not Exist." *The Baffler,* (March). https://thebaffler.com/salvos/we-keep-you-alive-oshea

Ost, David. 1990. *Solidarity and the Politics of Anti-Politics.* Philadelphia: Temple University Press.

2005. *The Defeat of Solidarity: Anger and Politics in Postcommunist Europe*. Ithaca, NY: Cornell University Press.

2011. "'Illusory Corporatism' Ten Years Later: Has an East European Anomaly Become the Norm?" *Warsaw Forum of Economic Sociology* 2, 1: 19–49.

2015a. "Stuck in the Past and the Future: Class Analysis in Postcommunist Poland." *East European Politics and Societies* 29, 3: 610–624.

2015b. "Class and Social Order: Political Consequences of the Move from Class to Culture." In Victoria Goddard and Susana Narotzky, eds. *Industry and Work in Contemporary Capitalism: Global Models, Local Lives*. New York: Routledge, pp. 64–77.

2016. "Regime Change in Poland, Carried Out from Within." *The Nation*, January 8. www.thenation .com/article/regime-change-in-poland-carried-out-from-within

2018. "Workers and the Radical Right in Poland." *International Labor and Working-Class History* 93, Spring: 113–124.

2019. "The Endless Innovations of the Semi-Periphery and the Peculiar Power of Eastern Europe." In John Frederick Bailyn, Dijana Jelača, and Danijela Lugarić, eds. *The Future of (Post) Socialism*. Albany: State University of New York Press, pp. 19–50

Parkin, Frank. 1979. *Marxism and Class Theory*. New York: Columbia University Press.

Pawłowski, Łukasz. 2020. *Druga fala prywatyzacji: Niezamierzone skutki rządów PiS* ("The Second Wave of Privatization: Unintended Effects of PiS Governance"). Warsaw: Kultura Liberalna.

Polakow-Suransky, Sasha. 2017. *Go Back to Where You Came From: The Backlash Against Immigration and the Fate of Western Democracy*. New York: Nation Books.

Rieff, David. 1996. *Slaughterhouse: Bosnia and the Failure of the West*. New York: Touchstone.

Roediger, David. 2007 (orig. 1991). *The Wages of Whiteness*. New York: Verso.

Rueschemeyer, Dietrich, Evelyne Stephens, and John Stephens. 1992. *Capitalist Development and Democracy*. Chicago: University of Chicago Press.

Sachar, Howard M. 2003. *Dreamland: Europeans and Jews in the Aftermath of the Great War*. New York: Vintage.

Schmitter, Philippe. 1983. "Democratic Theory and Neocorporatist Practice." *Social Research* 50, 4: 885–928.

Silver, Beverly J. 2003. *Forces of Labor*. Baltimore: Johns Hopkins University Press.

Snyder, Timothy. 2004. *The Reconstruction of Nations: Poland, Ukraine, Lithuania, Belarus, 1569–1999*. New Haven, CT: Yale University Press.

17

Reclaiming Democracy

The Challenge Facing Labor in India

Anibel Ferus-Comelo

INTRODUCTION

Although attacks on unions take place around the world and in all eras, in India the threat to democracy with the reelection of Narendra Modi as Prime Minister in 2019 is unprecedented since the country's independence. India's global ranking in the Economist Intelligence Unit's Democracy Index dropped precipitously to 51st place in 2019, the proverbial *annus horribilis* for democracy in the country (PTI 2020b). The index measures five factors – electoral process and pluralism; the functioning of government; political participation; political culture; and civil liberties – in which India's overall score fell from 7.23 in 2018 to 6.90. This is the lowest score that India has earned since the inception of the index in 2006, putting it in the same "flawed democracy" category that the United States has occupied since 2016. Both countries had held the torch of democracy aflame in their claim to adult franchise in "free and fair" elections. Yet, the corrosion of India's democratic structures corresponded to the general elections in May 2019 that resulted in a landslide victory for the right-wing Bharatiya Janata Party (BJP) led by Modi, who the award-winning writer Arundhati Roy called "our nakedly fascist Prime Minister" (Roy 2020).

Modi's elections first with "false hopes" in 2014 and again in 2019 with "false pride" consolidated a brazen Hindu nationalism that was the cornerstone of a calamitous legislative and policy agenda centered on authoritarian rule (Bardhan 2019). Ideologically rooted in the hard-line "Brahminical patriarchal" Hindu supremacy, also known as Hindutva,[1] propagated by the Rashtriya Swayamsevak Sangh (RSS), Modi exploited the intersection of class, caste, gender, and religion in a rapid succession of alarming pronouncements (Chakravarti 2004). In July 2019, the BJP government introduced aggressively anti-labor measures in the new national Wage Code, as part of a broader set of labor law reforms detailed below. Next came the Citizenship (Amendment) Act (CAA) that parliament passed in December 2019 to create a pathway to citizenship for non-Muslim migrants already in India from Afghanistan, Bangladesh, and Pakistan, treating them as refugees fleeing religious persecution. The blatantly anti-Muslim law was the first time since India's independence that religion was made a criterion for determining citizenship. It was intended to pave the path to a National Register of Citizens (NRC) proposed to identify and expel "illegal migrants" but that, in effect, harasses and

---

[1] Hindutva is a political ideology that selectively coopts Hindu traditions into dogma and is separate from the heterogeneous religious faith of India's majority population.

intimidates Muslims, and worse, as was amply demonstrated by the implementation of the NRC in the border state of Assam, strips millions of impoverished families of Indian citizenship. In fact, the 2020 annual report of the United States Commission on International Religious Freedom (USCIRF) designated India as a "country of particular concern" (CPC), placing it in the same category as North Korea, China, and Pakistan, for "engaging in and tolerating systematic, ongoing, and egregious religious freedom violations, as defined by the International Religious Freedom Act (IRFA)" (USCIRF 2020).

With the BJP at the helm, foundational pledges to pluralism and federalism that shaped India's path for most of its post-colonial history were callously revoked. Democracy in contemporary India is indeed in dire danger with assaults on some universities by thugs and politicians, the repression of dissent, and the harassment and arrest of prominent journalists, lawyers, intellectuals, and human rights activists. Besides "turning nearly 200 million people in our country into intimidated, second-class citizens," Modi's regime has engendered a crisis of Constitutional democracy:

> Concentration of power in one person, intimidation of critics and dissenters, weakening of institutions of checks and balances and misuse of police, bureaucracy, tax and investigative agencies against political opponents, are all gross violations of the Constitution which can put the world's largest democracy to shame. (Bardhan 2019)

At a time when Constitutional ideals of a fair and just economy and a democratic polity have been gravely undermined, the Indian labor movement faces the key question of how to respond to the decline in democracy. One of the twelve national unions has expressed in the following words a widespread recognition that the intersection of class-, caste-, and religion-based oppression calls for concerted action: "The working class movement bears a special responsibility in advancing the defense of our democracy as cardinal to its fight for working people's rights and to ensure that it is sustained until we can bring gains to working people and all of society."[2]

This chapter discusses the tremendous challenges that the labor movement faces – and will doubtless continue to face for many years – in the fight to reclaim democracy in India. It begins with a political economic context that explains why the targets of Prime Minister Modi's exclusionary policies are precisely the same segments of the working-class population that require the protective power of the labor movement in a highly stratified labor market. The next section focuses on the politically fragmented state of unions, while drawing attention to the tremendous potential that organizing the unorganized could have to expand workers' economic and political power in the Modi era. The third part of the chapter delves into the recent and ongoing overhaul of the legal framework that governs industrial relations and workers' rights by the BJP to curtail worker power through representative organizations. The concluding section proposes ways in which the labor movement might reclaim democracy in twenty-first century India by renewing its raison d'être as the collective voice of the most economically *and* politically marginalized citizens under BJP rule.

POLITICAL ECONOMY OF INDIA

Modi's audaciously systematic assault on civil and human rights through the CAA, the NRC, and the labor law "deform" need to be considered in the political economic context of an India marred by jobless growth, stagnant wages, grinding poverty, and gross inequalities. The three

---

[2] NTUI press statement on the General Strike 2020.

new laws were preceded by beef bans and state laws against cow slaughter to carry out Modi's 2014 election promise of protecting cows, considered sacred in the Hindu religion, while controversially disrupting India's multimillion dollar meat industry – the largest exporter in the world – which provided over 2.5 million direct and indirect jobs, mostly to poor Muslims and *Dalits* (Alam 2017; Anonymous 2017; Bhardwaj & Mohanty 2017; Gowan 2018).[3] With the institutionalization of "cow protection" policies, a long history of caste- and religion-based oppression gained legitimacy in lynchings of meat traders, transporters, and leather workers by "beef vigilantes," atrocities against Dalits, hate speech, and anti-Muslim rhetoric from legislators (Lakshmi 2015).

Muslims, who constitute 14 percent (172 million) of India's population, in addition to millions of Dalits and migrants, are the most exploited and marginalized segments of the Indian population. Protecting their rights as workers and citizens needs to be at the forefront of any transformative political project toward democracy. Yet, in February 2020, the world witnessed an unleashing of state-sanctioned violence against Muslims in the northeastern part of the capital, Delhi (Wilson 2020). This premeditated, systematically executed attack was a frontal assault on the lives, livelihood, and homes of a religious minority community, in an expression of Hindi-Hindu-Hindustan supremacy.

Since the election of Modi, the Indian labor movement has renewed its active resistance against the state. Although, as discussed later, the Indian labor movement has historically been fragmented; unions were spurred into collective action in opposition of the New Economic Policy of liberalization, privatization, and deregulation introduced in 1991. Thus, recognizing the need for unity in the Modi-era of *Hindutvadi* neoliberalism, an alliance of India's national trade union federations issued a strike call in September 2019 to protest the BJP government's anti-labor measures, including the dismantling of workplace and environmental protections, cuts in social spending, and the de facto endorsement of child labor and precarious contracted jobs. Unions also issued a joint call for the BJP government to rescind its anti-Muslim Citizenship Amendment Act.

On January 8, 2020, one day after the official report of an annual growth rate of 5 percent – the lowest in eleven years – a coalition of national unions mobilized around 250 million students, workers, and rural and urban poor across the country in a General Strike against the BJP's 'anti-people' policies.[4] Hailed as possibly "the largest in world history," the strike drew attention to the unions' 12-point common demands that included: (1) a minimum wage of at least INR 15,000 (USD 210) per month; (2) equal pay for equal work; (3) stricter enforcement of all basic labor laws; (4) an end to pro-employer, anti-labor laws; (5) a job generation scheme to combat India's unemployment problem; (6) universal social security with a guaranteed pension for the entire working age population; (7) urgent measures to restrict price rises through a universalized public distribution system and banning of speculative trading on the commodities market; and (8) a halt to privatization by stealth through the sale of India's natural resources and national assets and foreign direct investment in key industries like rail, defense, and finance (Macleod 2020). The 24-hour national shutdown disrupted financial transactions as well as train and road transportation, erupting in violent clashes and arrests as protesters took over streets and railroad tracks to shut down the central arteries of the country (Dhillon & Harding 2020). Significantly, the

---

[3] "Dalit," denoting the oppressed, is the term adopted by the lowest castes (or caste-less) to describe themselves in defiance of derogatory labels such as the "untouchables" or romanticized references such as Gandhi's "Harijan" (God's people).

[4] The BJP affiliated labor federation, Bharatiya Mazdoor Sangh, did not participate in the call for a strike.

General Strike demonstrated unity among different sections of the population against the Modi government. Popular opposition to the CAA and NRC was fueled by general anxiety and anger about two fundamental features of the Indian economy, discussed later, which have had profound effects on the extent and nature of employment, particularly in their intersection with deep social inequalities rooted in gender, religion, and caste hierarchies.

JOBLESS GROWTH

Although the country has seen a growth rate of 7 percent per year recently, there has been a decline in labor force participation (Dhar & Kumar 2020). Employment was considered to be the single most important issue for voters in the 2019 elections. The *Business Standard*, a premier financial newspaper, leaked a report produced in 2019 by the National Sample Survey Office (NSSO), a government agency that revealed that India's unemployment rate in 2017–18 was 6.1 percent (Jha 2019). This was not only an all-time 45-year high, but was also approximately triple the rate five years earlier when the last national survey was conducted. More importantly, the report undercut a basic premise of Modi's 2014 election campaign – to create jobs for India's workers under the age of thirty-five, who represent roughly two-thirds of the 1.35 billion population. The government tried to cover up the report to avoid allegations of not fulfilling its pre-electoral promises (Gettleman & Kumar 2019). With a working population of about 500 million, roughly 30 million people, including 10 to 12 million young people who enter the labor market each year, could not find jobs.

In 2015, Modi launched the Skill India Mission in order to decrease unemployment by providing job skills to the unemployed in over thirty-five sectors and across 1,800 occupations. Data from the Ministry of Skill Development and Entrepreneurship show that, as of mid-2020, only 23 percent of those who were trained since the program's inception found jobs (Vikram 2020). The failure of remedial programs to stimulate employment was compounded by two disruptive economic changes that Modi imposed during his administration. First, the "grand hoax" of demonetization in November 2016, that was ostensibly intended to shut down illicit cash transactions, instead imposed enormous hardships on marginalized people who depend on cash currency, and wreaked havoc on India's economy (Bardhan 2019). Second, in July 2017, Modi implemented a new single tax code, the Goods and Services Tax (GST), that economists claim "crippled small businesses."

There were other signs of "employment distress" in India, including data from the All India Manufacturers' Organization in December 2018 that revealed 3.5 million jobs had been lost since 2016 (Gettleman & Kumar 2019). Another study that corroborated the NSSO report was published in January 2019 by the Center for Monitoring Indian Economy, a Mumbai-based business data company, revealing that 11 million jobs were lost in 2018 alone, as an indirect consequence of demonetization and the GST (Gettleman & Kumar 2019). Job losses and retrenchment of workers dramatically increased during the global pandemic (Crump 2020; Kumari & Krishna 2020; Lankesh 2020; PTI 2020a). Reduced investment in the rural economy, droughts, and losses in Indian manufacturing exacerbated India's rising unemployment trend under BJP rule.

SEGMENTED LABOR MARKET

The second feature of the Indian labor market that has posed a tremendous challenge to unionization and, interrelatedly, has caused a deterioration of labor standards is its segmentation into the formal and informal sectors. Consistent with a global trend toward the informalization and casualization of employment, workers in India have been caught in a regime of "flexibility" that has deeply transformed the nature of employment and resulted in mass unemployment, under-employment, contract jobs, and endemic poverty.

Formal employment in India is predominately in the public sector which has gradually been squeezed through cuts in social spending, privatization, and public-private partnerships. Labor force surveys show that the proportion of regular wage and salaried employees in the non-agricultural sector who have no written job contract, and therefore no job security, increased from 59 percent in 2004–05 to 65 percent in 2011–12 and 71 percent in 2017–18 (Dhar & Kumar 2020). This increase was the result of contingent and contractual forms of labor that gradually "fissured" the formal sector by employing workers on a part-time, seasonal, and temporary basis, or through third-party intermediaries. These workers are kept as a reserve pool of labor to provide employers the maximum level of flexibility with the minimal amount of financial and legal liability. Consequently, such workers cannot aspire to job security and associated economic stability.

Besides the informalization of formal employment, nearly 90 percent of the workforce (more than 435 million people in India) work outside the ostensibly formal economy altogether. Workers in the informal economy are largely without any legal protection or income security. They are deprived of their Constitutional rights to adequate means of livelihood (Article 39), just and humane conditions of work (Article 42), and a living wage and conditions of work ensuring a decent standard of life (Article 43). Although the female percentage of the labor force fell from 31.2 percent in 2011–12 to 23.3 percent in 2017–18, women are disproportionately represented in the informal economy, and face poorer conditions of work than men (Anonymous 2020). Most of the informal workers are neglected by Indian labor law and therefore have no legal recourse to address low wages, job insecurity, inadequate employment opportunities, a lack of social security, or retirement benefits. Approximately 18.4 million people work as bonded laborers, trapped in deplorable working conditions. India's indigenous communities from rural regions in economic distress migrate in search of livelihoods and end up working in some of the most dangerous occupations in brick kilns, mines, plantations, and construction. The existence of a parallel economy with workers in indentured servitude and conditions of quasi-slavery at the intersection of caste, class, gender, and religion is antithetical to democracy.

Adverse labor market conditions have contributed to the suppression of wages in every segment of the labor market. In the organized sector, which is the best protected, wages slumped from approximately 30 percent of value-added in the early 1980s to around 11 to 12 percent in recent years. India does not have a universal wage floor for all workers, as minimum wages are set by state governments for employees in select industries. This has led to more than 1,500 different rates across the country which only apply to about 66 percent of wage workers (ILO 2018). The legally non-binding national minimum wage is INR 176 (USD 3) for an eight-hour workday, but state governments can set a lower rate, and six states do. According to a 2018 International Labor Organization (ILO) report, approximately 41 percent of Indian workers said they were poorly paid and 31 percent were working in unhealthy conditions, relegating India to 19th place among 22 countries in the Asia-Pacific region.

STATE OF LABOR

Indian unions do not have a significant base among the working-class because they represent a tiny fraction of the organized sector and are predominately engaged in defensive fights due to changes in employment structure, discussed previously, as well as proposed reforms of labor law described later. Union density in India was a low 10.7 percent in 2011–12, just slightly higher than it was in 1993–94, and among non-agricultural workers was 17.7 percent in 2011–12 (ILO 2018). However, estimates of union density are highly unreliable and virtually impossible to calculate (Bhattacherjee 1999; Frenkel & Kuruvilla 2002).

Furthermore, some argue that in India's case, owing to fragmentation and alignment with the state, union density does not accurately reflect worker power or weakness (Kuruvilla et al. 2002). Unions in India are affiliated to one of the twelve national union federations, which are in turn extensions of major political parties, thus reducing their autonomy from the state. The five biggest labor federations are: the Indian National Trade Union Congress (INTUC) which belongs to the Indian National Congress; the All India Trade Union Congress (AITUC) affiliated with the Communist Party of India; the Centre of Indian Trade Unions (CITU) affiliated with the Communist Party of India–Marxist; the Hind Mazdoor Sabha (HMS) linked to the Janata Dal; and the Bharatiya Mazdoor Sangh (BMS) affiliated with the ruling Bharatiya Janata Party (BJP). Parallel to the political party labor federations, there is a high number of "independent" unions, including the New Trade Union Initiative (NTUI), founded in 2006 "on the basis of independence from government, employers, and political parties" and committed to the principles of democracy, organizing the unorganized, and building solidarity across organizational, industrial, and geographical boundaries.[5]

This ideological heterogeneity among unions and within labor structures has often translated into self-defeating divisions on critical issues facing Indian working-class. Since the mid-1990s, however, the need for unity against neoliberal policies has brought together coalitions of unions at the state and regional levels including those affiliated with the ruling parties. There are signs that Indian unions are also connecting to international union structures more than ever before in order to raise awareness of domestic working conditions, mobilize resources, connect with union counterparts across national boundaries, and push for higher labor standards for Indian workers.

Despite fragmentation and being trapped in defensive fights, unions and workers' organizations have been waging protracted campaigns toward significant victories. For instance, the Right to Food campaign demand for livelihood security was partially realized in the National Rural Employment Guarantee Act (NREGA), enacted by the Congress-led United Progressive Alliance (UPA) government in 2005. The Act strengthened the bargaining power of rural workers. Two workers' campaigns deserve special mention – the sanitation workers in Mumbai who won significant gains after a ten-year struggle despite great challenges of contract labor and caste oppression as Dalits; and domestic workers who waged their campaign at local, state, national, and international levels to gain ratification of the 189th ILO Convention on Domestic Workers, health insurance, and legal protection from sexual harassment at work. Given that over 90 percent of India's workers are employed in the informal sector and are sorely unrepresented, it is important to examine these positive cases of worker organization.

Garbage collection and street cleaning in urban areas of India are predominately done by workers in the lowest social strata marked by class, caste, gender, and migration. They are relegated to the most dirty, dangerous, and demeaning work, including manual scavenging.[6] The socioeconomic vulnerability of these workers is further entrenched by the contractual

---

[5] Report on the Founding Conference of New Trade Union Initiative.
[6] The practice of clearing, carrying, and disposing of human excreta is almost exclusively done by Dalits without any tools or personal protective equipment.

nature of their employment, thus limiting their power in local labor markets. Despite Constitutional protections of the right to organize, such workers, who do not have political party backing, lack protections against discharge for exercising their rights. However, in recent decades, workers' organizations have actively organized sanitation and sewer workers and manual scavengers, notably in Mumbai and Bangalore. Formed in 1997, the Garbage Transport Workers Union in Mumbai faced an uphill battle against the broad anti-Dalit, anti-migrant social environment that the BJP inflamed to challenge an insidiously entrenched subcontracting system in the courts (Fernandes 2019). The organized sanitation workers had to stand up to the combined power of the Bombay Municipal Corporation, private contractors, and political representatives who were hostile to their cause in order to gain job security. When 2,000 sanitation workers in Bangalore went on a one-day strike in July 2017 to protest wage theft and the lack of toilets and safety gear, they won a promise from the municipal corporation to be moved from contractual to permanent or regular employment. In Delhi, the sanitation workers' union has pressed demands for quarantine facilities for these "essential workers" exposed to the coronavirus and for compensation to the dependents of workers who died from it (Correspondent 2020).

Similarly, domestic workers are ubiquitous in local labor markets but lack power due to the structural nature of their employment in private, spatially scattered workplaces. Paid domestic work is overwhelmingly done by migrant women from lower castes, who suffer the brunt of intersectional forms of oppression that translate into low education levels, social isolation, and grinding poverty. Although they lack formal union protection, domestic workers have benefited from the services and advocacy efforts of numerous local women's organizations and community-based legal clinics. Moreover, the National Domestic Workers' Movement (NDWM) has organized local domestic workers' organizations in eleven states into unions and brought them together into one federation. As a result of organizing and direct action of the National Platform for Domestic Workers, led by the Self-Employed Women's Association (SEWA), the government extended the Rashtriya Swasthya Bima Yojana (RSBY), a health insurance plan covering hospitalization expenses, to domestic workers in 2012, and included domestic workers in a 2013 law prohibiting sexual harassment in the workplace (HRW 2013).[7]

Both of these examples come from the informal and casualized workforce. The collective forms of organization that these workers developed are outside the mainstream union structures and present compelling lessons. Together these and many other workers' struggles across the country demonstrate the potential of a determined labor movement to organize for greater worker power in the face of great obstacles. Such ambitions require investment of resources, a long-term organizing strategy at different levels from the local to the international, and cultivation of political alliances.

LABOR LAW "DEFORM"

Contemporary industrial relations in India are governed by both national and state laws embodying the overriding principles of industrial peace and economic growth. Hard-won labor protection has been dismantled at an alarming speed in recent years, effectively facilitating the exploitation of workers. The legal framework for working conditions is undergoing an overhaul,

---

[7] For the sexual harassment in the workplace act, see Sexual Harassment of Women at Workplace (Prevention, Prohibition, and Redressal) Act 2013 (No. 14 of 2013), http://wcd.nic.in/wcdact/womenactsex.pdf (accessed September 19, 2013).

ostensibly to streamline complex labor laws and to boost India's competitiveness on the global business stage. The Indian government is in the process of subsuming over forty national labor laws into four new labor codes to cover: wages, industrial relations, social security, and industrial safety and welfare. Based on the recent changes at the national and state levels, the current legal reforms tilt the already grossly unfair industrial relations equation still further in favor of employers by permitting short-term, temporary, contractual work, legalizing child labor and bonded labor through ambiguous clauses, placing new restrictions on the rights to organize and to strike, decriminalizing the non-payment of wages, reducing current penalties in case of non-compliance, and institutionalizing corporate self-certification of legal compliance, thereby stripping any semblance of regulatory control in India's woefully lenient and ineffective system of labor law enforcement.

Proponents of the law reforms point to a reduction in labor costs and greater flexibility for employers, for purposes of attracting foreign direct investment (FDI). Employers' Covid-19 lockdowns cast doubt on the widespread narrative that the "rigidity" of Indian labor laws deprives employers of the flexibility to shut down their companies and downsize their workforce when needed. In fact, companies have done so with impunity for a long time (Dhar & Kumar 2020). During the same period that India's Ease of Doing Business Index (designed by the World Bank) ranking climbed from 130 in 2016 to 63 in 2019, the country sank to the bottom quintile of the International Trade Union Confederation's (ITUC's) Global Rights Index based on 97 indicators, falling into the category of countries where there is "no guarantee of rights" (ITUC 2019a). Between 2019 and 2020, India jumped fourteen notches on the same Ease of Doing Business Index to be named among ten countries that improved the most on business regulatory reforms, along with Saudi Arabia, China, Nigeria, Pakistan, Jordan, Kuwait, Tajikistan, Togo, and Bahrain, several of which are indisputably authoritarian states (Sharma 2019).

One of the most egregious forms in which international labor rights are curtailed in India is the freedom of association and right to strike. The 2020 ITUC Global Rights Index identified India as a new entry among the ten "worst in the world for working people" among 144 countries for its brutal repression of strikes, mass dismissals, and regressive laws (ITUC 2020; Liew 2020). Besides two ILO core conventions that protect workers' freedom of association (no. 87) and the right to organize collectively (no. 98), Indian workers' freedom of association is guaranteed under Article 19 of the Constitution and recognized under the amended Trade Unions Act of 2001. However, the government complicit with employers use many egregious means, sometimes violence, to disrupt and discourage union activities, particularly in high-stake global industries such as automobiles (ICLR 2013) and electronics manufacturing (Ferus-Comelo & Pöyhönen 2011). A United Nations (2016: 17) report on freedom of association globally highlights the increasing "legislative precariousness" or flexibility of labor laws in India that makes it easier for employers to fire workers and for the state to restrict workers' right to assemble in protest. For example, in April 2016, the state government of Karnataka used section 144 of the Criminal Procedure Code, which prohibits assemblies of more than ten people, to prevent garment workers in Bengaluru from taking collective action (UN 2016). The law in India also allows the government to ban strikes in the public sector and government-owned enterprises. For example, before the General Strike of 2020, discussed earlier, the central government issued an order to employees in all its departments warning that: "Any employee going on strike in any form would face the consequences which, besides deduction of wages, may also include appropriate disciplinary action" (PTI 2020d). In a notable shift away from standard judicial activism, the Supreme Court reinforced the threat against public employees' right to strike as a "grave misconduct."

Although attacks on workers' rights and anti-labor policies have been the mainstay of the Indian government for decades, they have taken a virulent turn under the Modi regime. In mid-2019, the Indian Parliament passed the Code on Wages, the first of the four labor bills designed to replace forty-four labor laws, in order to set a standard rule for minimum wages and bonus payments for millions of workers across the country (Srivastava 2019). The Code applies only to commercial establishments employing ten or more employees, effectively neglecting 85 percent of the Indian labor market, or about 97.39 million who work in own-account and home-based enterprises (Deka 2019). While this law will cover formerly excluded casual, daily wage workers across all sectors for the first time, the wage standard is far below a "fair" or "living" wage, and leaves workers in contractual arrangements, such as those in brick kilns and tea plantations, vulnerable to exploitation. Moreover, a provision in the law allows employers to make deductions for staff benefits such as food, travel, and housing payments.

Unions and labor law experts have been unanimously and stridently critical of the dilution of protections and vulnerability of millions of workers who remain invisible and abandoned under the newly framed laws. On August 2, 2019, ten union confederations announced a Day of Action against the government's new Occupational Health and Safety Code that replaced thirteen sector-specific laws while covering only 10 percent of Indian workers. Representing the global labor movement, the ITUC General Secretary, Sharan Burrow said:

> The global trade union movement supports the Indian unions in demanding that democracy works for working people. We stand for dignity not exploitation, and we are side-by-side with our affiliates in India who are standing up for workers' rights in every workplace, a national minimum wage that people can actually live on, and a new social contract for every worker. The world is watching whether Modi's government can override basic principles of social justice and decent work, so the struggle of our Indian sisters and brothers is our struggle too. (ITUC 2019b)

Labor activists anticipate that the Wage Code and the OHS Code will deepen the informalization of the formal sector, deteriorate employment conditions, compromise health and safety on the job, and lower incomes. This recent deformation of labor law required that the government overcome a "somewhat coordinated working class movement" (Sapkal 2020). However, resistance in the form of organized protest is especially challenging during the lockdown, leaving the working-class extraordinarily vulnerable to the whims of the business and political elite. Six global union federations joined the ITUC in June 2020 to condemn the Indian government for "using the coronavirus crisis as an excuse to suspend labor laws and attack workers' rights as the central government of Narendra Modi continues its assault on the trade union movement."[8]

The labor law reforms have been on the anvil for a long time. In 2014, the BJP government in the northwestern state of Rajasthan began dismantling labor protections by reducing the scope of legal coverage, for example, by amending the Contract Labor Act to apply to businesses that employ over fifty workers rather than twenty, and increasing the number of employees who could be laid off without government permission under the Industrial Disputes Act from 100 to 300. Following this model, the states of Uttar Pradesh (UP), Madhya Pradesh (MP), and Gujarat suspended essential labor laws, under cover of the Covid-19 crisis (Bhattacharjee 2020; Sapkal 2020). The suspensions included allowing non-hazardous factories in MP employing less than fifty workers to use third-party certification instead of routine state inspections for the next 1,000 days

---

[8] Labourstart: www.labourstartcampaigns.net/show_campaign.cgi?c=4378 (accessed June 27, 2020).

and extending the hours for business from 6 am to midnight. The UP government exempted all factories from the timely and bank payment of wages, payment of minimum wages, occupational safety and security, compensation for death and disability, all laws relating to women's and children's employment, and various other labor laws. Similarly, Gujarat exempted new industrial units from all labor laws except minimum wages, industrial safety, and employees' compensation for at least 1,200 days. The magnitude of the effect of these exemptions is staggering because, according to the Sixth Economic Census, 118 million (55 percent) work in establishments with at least one hired worker and fall under the purview of the Factories Act.

As the country went under stringent lockdown against Covid-19, thousands of migrant workers were left to fend for themselves (Chaudhry & Prasad 2020). They were the easiest to retrench as they were the least protected under labor laws that cover formal employment. They were stranded without any means of livelihood or roofs over their heads (Frayer & Pathak 2020). They trekked on foot for days with meager belongings, trying to reach their home villages, as state governments suspended all forms of transportation. Not only are they the most exploited workers, they are also denied access to education, a living income, and decent housing. During their journeys back home, they were stopped and harassed at state borders, sprayed with disinfectant, and held in cages (Heijmans et al. 2020). To entice them back to their worksites, state governments offered various incentives, but not living wages, employment security, housing and health services, or quality education for their children.

Unions protested the gross violations of the government's own directives and advisories in relation to payment of full wages to workers during the lockdown and job protection. They noted the systemic failure that deprived targeted beneficiaries of food grains distribution and meager cash transfers to women and senior citizens, despite governmental rhetoric. For instance, a day before the Covid-19 lockdown began, the Union Labor Minister issued an advisory to states to distribute cash relief funds to an estimated 50 million building and construction workers who were registered with the state welfare boards for the Building and Construction Workers Welfare Fund. While the cash amount varied across states, and over 200,000 unregistered workers were excluded, three states and union territories did not release any funds at all to nearly 4.5 million registered workers (Das Gupta 2020).

In May, 2020, the national union federations issued a joint press statement to mobilize workers against the undemocratic and hostile changes in India's labor laws, accusing the national and state governments of using the Covid-19 pandemic to further curtail the rights of workers who were already in "deep distress" due to the health and economic crises caused by the virus, and "aggressively moving to push the working people into virtual slavery."[9] Taking note of the disproportionate effects of the quarantine on migrant workers, national leaders of ten unions organized a day-long hunger strike on May 22 demanding immediate safe transport to stranded workers, universal food grains distribution, and cash transfer to all informal workers (PTI 2020c).[10]

---

[9] "Central Trade Unions to Fight Back Attempts of Draconian Changes in Labor Laws: Nationwide Protest on 22nd May 2020," a Joint Press Statement by Central Trade Unions released on May 15, 2020.

[10] The ten unions were INTUC, AITUC, HMS, CITU, AIUTUC, TUCC, SEWA, AICCTU, LPF, and UTUC. The RSS-affiliated Bharatiya Mazdoor Sangh, also the labor wing of the BJP, issued a belated protest against labor law suspension on May 20th.

CONCLUSION: A CLASS-BASED POLITICAL AGENDA

As India undergoes remarkable political upheaval, the primary challenge is to harness the recent retrograde mobilization around identity and religious minority chauvinism into class politics for greater democracy. One of the most important goals of the collective Indian labor movement is to establish institutional independence from party politics in order to organize and educate workers as a class, and represent their interests and aspirations through action and in public policy beyond elections.

The labor movement has a unique role in three arenas of struggle that have emerged in sharp relief for the post-pandemic world. First, established unions could support the organization of rural workers such as farmers, sharecroppers, peasants, and agricultural workers around the fundamental issues of food security, debt relief, access to water, electricity, and sources of livelihood; and social security coverage could be instrumental in drawing national and international attention to the rural-urban disparities that define India. Recent farmer protests proved quite effective to shake the political establishment out of a stupor to enact relief schemes.

Second, unions might assume the forefront of a youth movement against unemployment. Despite the government's suppression of quantitative data and its dissemination of misinformation, unemployment and underemployment are deeply and viscerally experienced by young people around the country. Protests by urban, educated unemployed youth are harder for media to ignore than pleas by the economically and politically marginalized in rural parts of the country. The labor movement's mid- to long-term mission could be to organize four different groups of the unemployed: (1) the aspirants to, or those currently unemployed and enrolled in, training institutes or coaching classes in order to upgrade their skills for greater employability; (2) the underemployed, or those who are eking out a living through two or more jobs in the informal and platform-based gig economies; (3) contract laborers, or those employed in perennial long-term, "perma-temp" employment arrangements that deprive them of job security and the full benefits of employment; and (4) those who are being retrenched in large numbers as companies claim bankruptcy or geographically move operations.

A post-pandemic economic recovery plan could comprise the creation of decent jobs, defined by the ILO as centered around opportunities to be productive and earn living wages with core human rights at work. In the midst of the coronavirus crisis, the ITUC re-articulated the aspiration of the global labor movement for an economy with "a new commitment to workers' rights and renewed investment in compliance and the rule of law," starting with workplace democracy (ITUC 2020). The Indian labor movement could position itself to raise extraordinary public pressure toward this goal. The words of a leader in the Muslim meat trading community, Gulzar Qureshi, uttered in the context of the beef bans, begs the question of what poor Indian workers can expect of their government if they do not have access to decent employment: "We are not asking for fancy roads and schools. Just let us earn whatever little amount we make for our children. I think that's the least a citizen can expect from his [sic] government" (Pandey 2017).

Finally, the labor movement could engage actively in the anti-corruption movement to address a chronic bane of Indian democracy that led to the decline in power of the Congress Party. This would entail prioritizing transparency and people's participation in decision-making at all levels. It would mean leading by example – by developing rank and file leaders in local workplaces, enabling local activists to rise to office-bearing positions while maintaining their accountability to members, and creating pathways to public office for union members and community allies.

India is reeling from unprecedented authoritarianism that has changed the contours of people's participation in the country's future. The antidote in this context is independent unions, operating at a national level across industries, sectors, and companies. They must unite the formal and informal workforces with contractual labor, and place organizing the unorganized workforce at the forefront of their mission. This will take years to accomplish. The core goals of the labor movement must be to educate the working class on issues beyond the workplace in order to fight bigotry and discrimination; to build organizations among the unemployed and soon-to-be unemployed; and to transform union culture from patriarchal and lawyer-driven to social movement unionism. In sum, a deep transformation of the institutional framework and modes of operation of labor are essential to reclaim democracy in twenty-first century India.

REFERENCES

Alam, Afroz. 2017. "'Cow Economics' Is Killing India's Working Class." *Quartz India*, June 23.

Anonymous. 2017. "India Tightens Meat Industry Laws Amid Fierce Protests." *The Guardian*, May 30. www.theguardian.com/world/2017/may/30/india-rocked-by-protests-meat-industry-tighter-laws

———. 2020. "India's Social Justice Agenda Is Unfulfilled as the Labor Market Remains Gendered, Classist, and Casteist." *Economic and Political Weekly* *(EPW) Engage*, 20 February. www.epw.in/engage/article/indias-social-justice-agenda-unfulfilled-labour

Bardhan, P. 2019. "India Has Gone from False Hopes in 2014 to False Pride in 2019." *The Indian Express*, June 15. https://indianexpress.com/arti

Bhardwaj, Mayank, and Suchitra Mohanty. 2017. "India's Top Court Suspends Ban on Trade in Cattle for Slaughter." *Reuters*, July 11. www.reuters.com/article/us-india-politics-meat/indias-top-court-suspends-ban-on-trade-in-cattle-for-slaughter-idUSKBN19W0IH

Bhattacharjee, Saurabh. 2020. "Demystifying the Changes to Labor Laws in States: Madhya Pradesh." May 15. https://clllnujs.wordpress.com/2020/05/15/demystifying-the-changes-to-labour-laws-in-states-madhya-pradesh/?fbclid=IwAR31sQ8hrEADgWFWeEVrXpYg2E_mM1utXRQFH6sryjwIv_0lHUq5YXKU8U8

Bhattacherjee, Debashish. 1999. "Organised Labour and Economic Liberalisation in India: Past, Present, and Future." International Institute for Labor Studies Labor and Society Program Discussion Paper Series DP/105/1999. Geneva, Switzerland.

Chakravarti, Uma. 2004. "Conceptualizing Brahminical Patriarchy in Early India: Gender, Caste, Class, and State." In *Class, Caste, Gender*, edited by Manoranjan Mohanty, 271–295. New Delhi: Sage.

Chaudhry, Suparna, and Shubha Kamala Prasad. 2020. "How India Plans to Put 1.3 Billion People on a Coronavirus Lockdown." *The Washington Post*, March 20. www.washingtonpost.com/politics/2020/03/30/how-india-plans-put-13-billion-people-coronavirus-lockdown/

Correspondent. 2020. "Sanitation Workers' Union Demands Dedicated Quarantine Centers for Staff Members." *Hindustan Times*, June 23. www.hindustantimes.com/cities/sanitation-workers-union-demands-dedicated-quarantine-centres-for-staff-members/story-WP9zRIxLf128dR8wB9COHP.html

Crump, James. 2020. "Indian Factory workers Protest after 'H&M Cancels Orders' Leaving 1,000 Jobless." *The Independent*, June 24. www.independent.co.uk/news/world/asia/hm-garment-workers-factory-india-jobs-a9579856.html

Das Gupta, Moushumi. 2020. "Bihar, Jharkhand, Chhattisgarh Did Not Release a Rupee for Construction Workers during Lockdown." *The Print*, June 23.

Deka, Kaushik. 2019. "Rationalisation at the Cost of Rights?" *India Today*, August 9. www.indiatoday.in/magazine/up-front/story/20190819-rationalisation-at-the-cost-of-rights-1578658-2019-08-09

Dhar, Biswajit, and Ramaa Arun Kumar. 2020. "Can't Justify Attack on Workers' Rights." *The Hindu Businessline*, May 21. www.thehindubusinessline.com/opinion/cant-justify-attack-on-workers-rights/article31634217.ece#

Dhillon, Amrit, and Luke Harding. 2020. "Indian Towns and Cities Grind to Halt as Workers Stage 240 Hour Strike." *The Guardian*, January 8. www.theguardian.com/world/2020/jan/08/india-towns-and-cities-grind-to-halt-as-workers-stage-24-hour-strike

Fernandes, Sujatha. 2019. "How Mumbai's Sanitation Workers Won Their Rights." *The Nation*, March 5. www.thenation.com/article/archive/hmumbai-india-sanitation-workers-union-organizing/

Ferus-Comelo, Anibel, and Päivi Pöyhönen. 2011. *Phony Equality: Labor Standards of Mobile Phone Manufacturers in India*. Finnwatch, Cividep, and SOMO.

Frayer, Lauren, and Suchmita Pathak. 2020. "Coronavirus Lockdown Sends Migrant Workers on a Long and Risky Trip Home." *NPR*. March 31. www.npr.org/sections/goatsandsoda/2020/03/31/822642382/coronavirus-lockdown-sends-migrant-workers-on-a-long-and-risky-trip-home

Frenkel, Stephen, and Sarosh Kuruvilla. 2002. "Logics of Action: Globalization, and Employment Relations Change in China, India, Malaysia, and the Philippines." *Industrial and Labor Relations Review* 55, 3: 387–412.

Gettleman, Jeffrey, and Hari Kumar. 2019. "India's Leader Is Accused of Hiding Unemployment Data before Vote." *The New York Times*, January 31. www.nytimes.com/2019/01/31/world/asia/india-unemployment-rate.html

Gowen, Annie. 2018. "Cows Are Sacred to India's Hindu Majority. For Muslims Who Trade Cattle, That Means Growing Trouble." *The Washington Post*, July 16. www.washingtonpost.com/world/asia_pacific/cows-are-sacred-to-indias-hindu-majority-for-muslims-who-trade-cattle-that-means-growing-trouble/2018/07/15/9e4d7a50-591a-11e8-9889-07bcc1327f4b_story.html

Heijmans, Philip, Bibhudatta Pradhan, and Pauline Bax. 2020. "Locked in Cages, Beaten and Shamed: Virus Laws Lead to Abuses." *Bloomberg*, April 1, www.bloomberg.com/news/articles/2020-04-02/locked-in-cages-beaten-and-shamed-virus-laws-lead-to-abuses

HRW. 2013. *Claiming Rights: Domestic Workers' Movements and Global Advances for Labor Reform*New YorkHuman Rights Watch

ICLR. 2013. *Merchants of Menace: Repressing Workers in India's New Industrial Belt*New YorkInternational Commission for Labor Rights

ILO. 2018. *India Wage Report: Wage Policies for Decent Work and Inclusive Growth*International Labor Organizationwww.ilo.org/newdelhi/whatwedo/publications/WCMS_638305/lang–en/index.htm

ITUC. 2019a. *2019 Global Rights Index: The World's Worst Countries for Workers*. Brussels: The International Trade Union Confederation (ITUC). www.ituc-csi.org/IMG/pdf/2019-06-ituc-global-rights-index-2019-report-en-2.pdf

2019b. "Don't Bulldoze Workers' Rights in India, Says Global Trade Union Movement." www.ituc-csi .org/workers-rights-in-India-2019

2020. *2020 ITUC Global Rights Index: The World's Worst Countries for Workers*. Brussels: International Trade Union Confederation. www.ituc-csi.org/IMG/pdf/ituc_globalrightsindex_2020_en.pdf

Jha, Somesh. 2019. "Unemployment Rate at Four-Decade High of 6.1 percent in 2017–2018: NSSO Survey." *The Business Standard*, February 6. www.business-standard.com/article/economy-policy/unemployment-rate-at-five-decade-high-of-6-1-in-2017-18-nsso-survey-119013100053_1.html

Kumari, Neha, and Swati Krishna. 2020. "The Lions of 'Make in India' Companies Fire 15,000 Employees." June 22. https://gaurilankeshnews.com/make-in-india-startup-companies-fires-15000-employees-lockdown-worsening-the-economy

Kuruvilla, Sarosh, Subesh Das, Hyunji Kwon, and Soonwon Kwon. 2002. "Trade Union Growth and Decline in Asia." *British Journal of Industrial Relations* 40, 3: 431–461.

Lakshmi, Rama. 2015. "Hindu 'Cattle Patrols' in India Seek to Protect Cows from Beef Eaters." *The Washington Post*, October 28. www.washingtonpost.com/world/asia_pacific/hindu-cattle-patrols-in-india-seek-to-protect-cows-from-beef-eaters/2015/10/28/89da1cc8-7c08-11e5-bfb6-65300a5ff562_story .html?itid=lk_inline_manual_9

Lankesh, Gauri. 2020. "Ashok Leyland Fires 5800 Workers without Notice." June 23. https://gaurilankeshnews.com/ashok-leyland-suddenly-fires-5800-workers-without-notice

Liew, Shawn. 2020. "Violation of Workers' Rights at Seven-Year High." *HRM Asia*, June 23. https://hrmasia .com/violation-of-workers-rights-at-seven-year-high

Macleod, Alan. 2020. "In What May Be the Largest Strike in World History, Millions in India Protest PM Modi's Policies." *The Portside*, January 13. https://portside.org/2020-01-13/what-may-be-largest-strike-world-history-millions-india-protest-pm-modis-policies

Pandey, Vikas. 2017. "'You May As Well Kill Us': Human Cost of India's Meat Ban." *BBC News Daily*, 30 March. www.bbc.com/news/world-asia-india-39427552

PTI. 2020a. "Apparel Giant Raymond Fires More than 1000 Workers to Tide Over COVID-19 Woes." *The Indian Express*, June 22. www.newindianexpress.com/business/2020/jun/22/apparel-giant-raymond-fires-more-than-1000-workers-to-tide-over-covid-19-woes-2159923.html

PTI. 2020b. "India Falls to 51st position in EIU's Democracy Index." *The Economic Times*, January 23. https://economictimes.indiatimes.com/news/politics-and-nation/india-falls-to-51st-position-in-eius-democracy-index/articleshow/73519661.cms

2020c. "Trade Unions to Go on Strike on May 22 to Protest Against Labour Law Suspension." *Hindustan Times*, May 15. www.hindustantimes.com/india-news/trade-unions-to-go-on-strike-on-may-22-to-protest-against-labour-laws-suspension/story-nwTLgMYycBlBBUSZYJ1vKP.html 2020d. "Face Consequences If You Go on Strike: Government to Employees." *The Times of India*, January 7. https://timesofindia.indiatimes.com/business/india-business/face-consequences-if-you-go-on-strike-government-to-employees/articleshow/73137102.cms

Roy, Arundhati. 2020. Statement at Hum Dekhenge All India Convention of Writers and Artists Against CAA-NPR-NRC in Delhi, March 2. www.newsclick.in/There-is-Fire-in-the-Ducts-The-System-is-Failing-Delhi-Riots

Sapkal, Rahul Suresh. 2020. "The Road to Modern Serfdom." *India Legal Live*, May 23. www.indialegallive.com/top-news-of-the-day/the-road-to-modern-serfdom-100286

Sharma, Yogima Seth. 2019. "India Jumps to 63rd Position in World Bank's Ease of Doing Business 2020 Report." *Economic Times*, October 24. https://economictimes.indiatimes.com/news/economy/indicators/india-jumps-to-63rd-position-in-world-banks-doing-business-2020-report/articleshow/71731589.cms?from=mdr

Srivastava, Roli. 2019. "India Passes 'Historic' Minimum Wage Law Amid Activist Worries." *Thomson Reuters Foundation Asia section*, https://in.reuters.com/article/india-labour-lawmaking/india-passes-historic-minimum-wage-law-amid-activist-worries-idINKCN1UV1Y2

UN. 2016. *Report of the Special Rapporteur on the Rights to Freedom of Peaceful Assembly and of Association*, A/71/385. Geneva: United Nations.

USCIRF. 2020. Annual report of the US Commission on International Religious Freedom (USCIRF). www.uscirf.gov/sites/default/files/USCIRF%202020%20Annual%20Report_Final_42920.pdf

Vikram, Kumar. 2020. "Just 23 percent of Trainees Got Jobs under Skill India Mission Since 2015." *New Indian Express*, June 8. www.newindianexpress.com/nation/2020/jun/08/just-23-per-cent-of-trainees-got-jobs-under-skill-india-mission-since-2015-2153636.html

Wilson, Audrey. 2020. "Uneasy Calm in Delhi after Days of Riots." *Foreign Policy*, February 27. https://foreignpolicy.com/2020/02/27/uneasy-calm-delhi-days-riots-religious-violence-citizenship-law-modi-bjp

18

A Critical Assessment of Democratic Labor Unionism in South Korea from a Feminist Standpoint

Jaok Kwon

INTRODUCTION

Kwanghwamun Plaza in Seoul is a place of great historical significance, since it is one of the iconic places where demonstrations were held in the time before the transition to democracy in contemporary South Korea (hereafter, Korea) (Hong 2018). Under the successive oppressive authoritarian regimes from the 1960s to the 1980s in Korea, kwanghwamun Plaza became the central place where the strong aspiration for democracy among the people expressed itself. During this period, when student movements and labor movements spearheaded the combat to achieve democracy, kwanghwamun Plaza was repeatedly and defiantly occupied by well-organized and militant male demonstrators.

The Great Workers' Struggle, which climaxed in 1987, was led by the middle-class workers of large enterprises – so-called neck-tied military troops (*nekt'aibudae*). It was a milestone in the achievement of class consciousness and solidarity among Korean workers (Koo 2001). At the same time, the well-organized strategies of aggressive combat became a symbol for the political struggles against militant authoritarianism, as well as the ongoing guardian of democracy in Korea (Y. Lee 2011). In this sense, unions in Korea have been positioned as "forces for national democratization" (Chun 2005: 500). In particular, the nationwide umbrella union, the Korean Confederation of Trade Unions (*chŏn'guk minju nodong johap ch'ongyŏnmaeng*) (KCTU), which was established in 1995, has functioned as the "moral force" for new social movement organizations which blossomed after democratization in 1987. This umbrella union is literally translated as the "nationwide federation of the democratic trade union." The establishment of the KCTU itself, therefore, expresses a strong will to represent working class solidarity and guard democracy, maintaining a clear distance from the pro-government labor unions, including the Federation of Korean Trade Unions (*han'guk nodong chohap ch'ongyŏnmaeng*) (FKTU), which was built in 1961 by the repressive authoritarian regime. FKTU functioned as a single national center until 2000, by which point "the outgoing authoritarian regime feared that independent and democratic unions would challenge the existing labor relations that had been dominated by the government-sponsored national center, FKTU" (Y. Lee 2009: 55), even though it was detached from a dictatorial state after democratization and in part allied with the KCTU.

Thirty years later in 2016 and 2017, kwanghwamun Plaza was again occupied by demonstrators who were standing up for democratization by seeking to topple the corrupt President Park Geun-hye (2013–2017). However, the configuration of demonstrators at that time, as well as the nature of the protests, had dramatically changed. In the new so-called Candlelight movement, people held candles in their hands and handed out flowers to the policemen as an expression of a peaceful, but steadfast, commitment to democracy, instead of resisting with tear gas, wooden sticks, and steel pipes, as had been the symbol of the earlier labor strikes and protests. Indeed, members of the KCTU who have stood at the center of previous democratic movements in Korea were blocked by the mass of other protestors, when the union attempted to confront the police in a violent and aggressive way.

Unorganized groups of individuals marched together peacefully in the Candlelight movement, in contrast with the conventional labor protests, which were led by well-organized male workers with militaristic red flags, red bands on their heads and arms, and red vest jackets, while chanting slogans emblematic of their clubs and asserting their resolve to fight for workers' rights. In contrast, the participants in the new protests comprised different genders, regions, ages, and class backgrounds, had diverse agendas, and expressed their opinions on a range of topics through speeches on self-arranged stages.

What do these changes signify? What message does the Candlelight movement send to the democratic labor unions, which have symbolized support for democratization in Korea? There has been little discussion about the role of democratic labor unionism in the further development of democratization after the transition to democracy in 1987. This is likely based on the belief that the Great Workers' Struggle in 1987 and the following establishment of the KCTU in 1995 represented a single decisive landmark in the transition to democracy in Korea. This chapter seeks to address this lacuna by exploring critically, from a feminist perspective, the trajectories of democratic labor unionism after the transition to democracy.

Among the limited research conducted on the question, one prominent political scientist in Korea, Choi Jang Chip (2013), argues that the leadership as well as the primary beneficiaries in the democratization movements were the middle classes, such as university students, intellectuals, and regular workers, but not the lower-class workers that were most in need of empowerment. In particular, since the Asian financial crisis, the aim of democratic unionism has changed from class-wide solidarity to securing the economic interests of the middle class centered around union members. Choi further maintains that decreasing union density in Korea is not only a natural outcome of the neoliberalized labor market after the financial crisis in the late 1990s, but also the result of the politicization and institutionalization of democratic labor unionism after 1987. As a result, even though democratic labor unionism has remained a symbol of political democratization at the level of public discourse since 1987, nevertheless it has gradually lost its commitment to broad working-class solidarity extending beyond the already-unionized sector. Choi denotes this process, somewhat hyperbolically, as a "democracy without labor." Similarly, Roh Jung Gi (2010) maintains that labor unionism was the greatest beneficiary of democratization as well as the strongest driving force for democratization in the transition to democracy in 1987, but concludes that democratic labor unions have rested on their laurels and on the memory of their past political triumph.

Feminist studies have also raised critical questions about the relation between the conception of democratic labor unionism and the reality of gender inequality in both the labor market and the union movement. Park (2001) argues that the democratization process driven by Korean labor unions constitutes "democratic unionism without democratization," since it marginalized the value of gender equality among unionists. Likewise, the author of this chapter (Kwon 2018) has recently described the Great Workers' Struggle as a "great victory of masculinities" (2018: 641). I have also critically questioned, from a gender perspective, the type of democratization achieved by democratic labor unionism. I demonstrated that the victory of masculinities in Korean democratic labor unionism specifically entails "the standardization of male workers in the labor unionism," the "representation of the male regular workers' issues from large enterprises," and the "normalization of masculine organizational culture of the trade union." I therefore concluded that the historical legacy of the victory of the Great Workers' Struggle, such as a militaristic culture, male- and regular-worker-centeredness, and nationalistic sentiment, all hindered the advancement of feminist principles within democratic labor unionism.

Political science and feminist perspectives have provided insights into the limitations of democratic labor unionism, notwithstanding its role in the democratization of Korea. But the precise ways that civic actors critically view the "democracy" achieved by the democratic labor unions, as well as the ways that conventional labor unionism has influenced the struggles of marginalized, non-union workers, have yet to be deeply analyzed.

To date, labor unionism in Korea has been categorized as "social movement unionism" that is comparable to the labor movements in Brazil and South Africa (Moody 1997; Seidman 1994; Waterman 1993) in building a broad coalition of social movements for social reforms and democratization. The following discussion critically interrogates whether this conception of "social movement unionism" has been historically sustained in Korea. By focusing on the Candlelight movement, which "marks the first nation-wide political struggle since the June Uprising of 1987" (Kim 2018: 1), this chapter maintains that the "democratic norm" in Korean labor unionism should be assessed critically, by parsing the concepts of the "militant culture" of labor unionism, the meaning and possibility of "collectiveness," and the scope of "democratic values" internalized by the unions. It further argues that these current critical questions on the (dis)continuity and sustainability of democratic labor unionism are illuminated by feminist ideology, and correspond with the growing diversity in the Korean labor market.

A CRITICAL EXAMINATION OF THE MILITANT CULTURE OF KOREAN UNIONISM

The Candlelight movement, which emerged in the early 2000s, marked a new form of civic protest in Korea. The first eruption of the Candlelight movement (in 2002) was a mass rally that memorialized the death of two school girls who were struck to death by a US military vehicle. The Candlelight movement's second large-scale campaign, which was organized by female teenagers in order to protest the import of US beef in 2008, attracted attention on account of the novel demographics of its participants. Middle- and upper-school girls, who had widely been considered apolitical and social minorities (Kim & H. Lee 2010), held candles on the kwanghwamun Plaza, raising questions about food security and the danger of importing mad cow. Young mothers with baby strollers joined the school girls in the peaceful demonstrations. In the face of trade unionists' injection of some acts of violence into the demonstrations, the girls and women attempted to protect the peaceful protests from the involvement of conventional demonstrators such as university students, labor union leaders, and farmers, groups often comprised of well-organized militaristic male protestors (S. Lee et al. 2010). In particular, they intentionally attempted to establish a clear distance from militant trade unionists, out of fear that violence would trigger a coercive reaction by the government.

During the Candlelight movement's actions in 2016 and 2017, there were no barricades, and no violent conflicts between police and the demonstrators, as in the earlier union protests. The peaceful protests included displays of visual art, and presentation of literary works, street concerts, musical performances, theater, and speeches. When darkness came, the participants lit up their candles and marched through the streets in order to express their collective demand for the impeachment of President Park Geun-hye. After the peaceful march, participants voluntarily cleaned the streets. Between October 2016 and March 2017 there were twenty-three demonstrations, conducted every Saturday – but there was not a single arrest or fatality, in marked contrast with the Great Workers' Struggle. The behavior of the civic actors in the Candlelight movement seemed to display an "obsession towards nonviolence" (G. Lee 2018: 528).

"Proletarian masculinity and militancy" (Wajcam 2000: 187) was a key social norm of the labor unions, rooted in the power, and latent or manifest violence, of the male workers in the manufacturing sector. Dubin (1973: 54) viewed labor militancy as the "willingness to use economic and physical force in gaining collective bargaining ends." While labor unionism is, of course, not inevitably violent, militant unionism in Korea is entangled with several historical elements that inflect labor unionism, or at least the perception of labor unions, as violent in nature. The outbreak of the Korean War (1950–1953) and the subsequent national division between North and South Korea strongly influenced industrial relations, as well as the form of the protests by labor unions. Under the US military government (1945–1948), all political protests and labor organizations were suppressed in the name of anti-communism. The successive authoritarian regimes from the 1960s into the 1980s continued to repress labor unions' collective action (Park 2007).

Even after the transition to democracy, the Korean government and employers persisted in labor-repressive strategies. The political activities of unions were prohibited by law. Participation of labor unions in the policymaking process was not permitted in the ten years following democratization (Yoo 2012). Consequently, the Korean labor unions' strategies were to build an aggressive form of unionism to exert combative power against both the state and the employers.

In fact, militant unionism in Korea did contribute to the strengthening of workers' bargaining power and solidarity. Furthermore, in a broader vein, militant labor unionism stood as a reminder of the vanquishing of authoritarianism and achievement of democratization. It was therefore welcomed by social movement activists and scholars alike as a continuing force in the process of democratic transition (Koo 2001; Y. Lee 2011).

However, the well-organized militant power of the labor unions is no longer the central force for social reform or class-wide solidarity across the increasingly diverse Korean labor market. In the late 1990s, after the Asian financial crisis and subsequent economic restructuring, trade union ideology evolved from its political and solidaristic focus into a "militant economism" (Cho 2005). As a result, this well-structured militancy began to function as a tool to maximize the unions' "organizational resources and bargaining power to realize a short-term" economic gain limited to the regular workers of large companies (Yoo 2012: 183). Therefore, the labor union bloc used its militant power to secure a "league of its own" (Yoo 2012: 184), thereby defending the interests of its privileged members. The historical legacy of the militant Great Workers' Struggle became not just the democratization of the state, but also the normalization of masculine organizational culture both in trade unions and in social movements more generally (Kwon 2018).

In this respect, the emergence of the nonviolent Candlelight movement itself demonstrates that civic actors began to question the legitimacy of the militancy of democratic labor unions long revered as emblems of the triumph of Korean democracy. In short, union militancy has come to be seen not as the central force for social reform, but as the strategy of an interest group seeking narrowly defined interests. Indeed, both the nationwide spread of the peaceful Candlelight movement and the participation of social groups previously marginalized from social movements – notably girls and women, including stay-at-home mothers – deliver a strong message that the normalization of militant demonstration culture, which had become the central "democratic norm" of labor unionism, had limited civic involvement in social movements in the post-1987 period.

Militant unionism is also problematized by the recent struggles of contingent workers. As labels such as "elite labor unionism" and "labor aristocracy" have become attached to democratic labor unionism, "non-regular" workers' struggles are the new symbols of militant resistance to the neoliberal capitalist regime (B. Lee 2016: 3).

It is true that some of the militaristic characteristics of democratic labor unionism have been adopted, at least in part, by non-regular workers. Irregular workers express their desperation and hostility arising from their precarious condition and the discriminatory employment practices not only by the state and their own employers, but also by mainstream labor unions devoted mostly to the interests of their own members. Ironically, the resentment of non-regular workers has often been expressed in the militant sorts of protests pioneered by the democratic labor unions that exclude them (Chun 2009, 2012).

At the same time, as Y. Lee (2015) argues, the precarious workers' struggles cannot be monolithically categorized as "militant" protests. The militancy of the massively organized workers' struggles of the conglomerate unions cannot be fully replicated by the unorganized precarious workers of the small- and medium-sized enterprises, on account of the dispersion and instability of their employment (Yoo 2012). The emergence of a new form of protest by the non-regular workers in Korea "resembles an extreme form of workers' resistance," but is inflected by the more recent aversion, described earlier, to excessively confrontational tactics by contemporary movement actors (Y. Lee 2016: 457).

THE "COLLECTIVENESS" OF THE WORKING CLASS: ITS MEANING
AND POSSIBILITY

Democratic unionism has been positioned as a "moral force" despite its fundamental transformation from an avatar of workers' solidarity and democratization to an interest group for union members (Chun 2005: 500). During the campaign by the Candlelight movement in 2008, a younger generation became inspired by the "vernacular memories of the 1987 pro-democracy movement" (K. Lee 2014), even as they distanced themselves from university students, labor unions, and peasant movement activists. The memory of the 1987 protest inspired the younger generation, who had not experienced political struggles of such breadth, to "mobilize actions for the present, legitimize the current events, and to reimagine the future community" (K. Lee 2014: 72). Furthermore, in the Candlelight movement's actions of 2016 and 2017, even if the KCTU and the Korean Peasants League (*chŏn'guk nongmin ch'ongyŏnmaeng*) were distanced organizationally from the new demonstrators, many activists from those organizations raised their voices in various sociopolitical fora, and played a significant role in actually organizing and leading the demonstrations. In this sense, democratic unionism continued to play a primary role in social movements on both the discursive and practical levels. However, tensions remained between the union organizations and the new citizen-demonstrators during the Candlelight movement. These were exemplified by the fact that democratic labor unionists could not openly intermingle with the public on the streets.

This tension, as already noted, flows from the gradual change in the general public's perception of democratic labor unionism. This perception, in turn, arises from the labor unions' failure to effectively respond to the phenomenon described above – the expansion of the class of irregular workers – and to the enlarged body of low-income self-employed (Y. Lee 2015). In its infancy, the claim of democratic labor unionism to support the broader working class was facilitated by the fact that, at that time, workers evinced more homogeneous economic, social, and political features, compared with subsequent years (Koo 2001). During the decades preceding the financial crisis and the subsequent years of economic restructuring, workers more readily experienced "collectiveness," which was both a cause and effect of improvements in working conditions, enforcement of workers' rights, and building of democratic labor unionism. And, with still broader consequences for Korean society, the "collectiveness" of the workers contributed to both the establishment of workers' solidarity and the Korean transition to democracy.

However, the meaning of the "collectiveness" of labor unionism has more recently been critiqued in two ways. First, the "representativeness" of labor unions has been put into doubt by the rapid decrease of union density as a whole, concurrent with the diversification of labor unions. For instance, in 1989, in the immediate wake of the transition to democracy, union density stood at 19.8 percent as a whole. By 2017, it had dropped to 10.7 percent. Along with the decline in actual representation by unions (i.e. the decline in union density), unions have become less "representative" of the variegated interests of Korean workers. In particular, trade unions have perpetuated the norm of regular male worker-centeredness that characterized the Great Workers' Struggle of 1987. The victory of middle-class regular workers in this period normalized the regular male-centeredness in labor unionism, in part reflecting the realities in the labor market at the time (Kwon 2018). The persistence of that normalized pattern is reflected in the later composition of union membership; in 2012, 92 percent of unionized workers were regular workers, and about 8 percent were irregular workers (Y. Lee 2015). As a result, the agendas of regular workers in the large conglomerates have remained at the center of labor unionism.

K. Lee (2018) describes the contemporary Korean mode of collective bargaining as "confrontational cooperation," connoting that labor unions successfully deploy militant power to improve their share of earnings as labor-market "minorities" which consist mainly of regular workers of the large chaebol enterprises. At the same time, labor unions have been either cooperative with management or silent as to the interests of the labor-market "majorities" which comprise the growing irregular workforce.

Second, the unions' mode of collective action also raises questions about their "collectiveness." "Along with the institutionalization of industrial relations, strike action, which became the most effective means for unions to pressure employers, has been regarded as the typical form of union militancy" (B. Lee 2016: 4–5). Hence, in large enterprises, unions have continued to conduct "aggressive collective bargaining based on workplace collectivism, with frequent strikes in the process" (Yoo 2012: 179). This conventional mode of collective action could not be easily adapted by irregular workers facing vulnerable employment conditions. This difference in capacity for collective action was clearly reflected in the Candlelight movement. While middle-class regular workers participated in the demonstrations on-site, with their union members protected by the standardized five-day working week system, irregular workers, fearing discharge, were deterred from taking days off and could participate in the demonstrations only by sending supportive messages (Kwoen 2018).

Therefore, Korean workers increasingly faced a stark, fundamental question: is "collectiveness" of unionism possible, given the explosive growth in heterogeneity within the Korean workforce that flowed from the Asian financial crisis and the subsequent privileging of neoliberal employment policies and practices? Many other industrialized economies have witnessed a similar contraction of labor unions, along with the rise of neoliberalism and the growing heterogeneity of the working class (B. Lee 2015; Marginson et al. 2003). Like the labor movements in those countries, democratic labor unionism in Korea faces the dilemma of channeling "collectivism" without entrenching the "collective egoism" of a minority of the national workforce.

THE SCOPE OF "DEMOCRATIC VALUES" IN KOREA'S DEMOCRATIC LABOR UNIONISM

A poster, produced in 1999 by the KCTU to celebrate the 109th May Day, depicts a close-up of a male worker wearing a red vest jacket, on which is written "stabilization of employment." His clenched right fist expresses militant unionism and the will to fight for workers' rights. A woman with a baby in her arms stands dimly in the background, looking at the back of her husband, uttering "you are the only hope for us."

This poster was a focal point for female activists' critique of what "democracy" meant to democratic labor unions, and about the relation of that particular understanding of democracy to the women's movement. They maintained that the poster implicitly portrayed the skewed democratic values of democratic labor unionism, which they described as heterosexual, married, and male-centered. Seven years later, in the newly produced poster by the KCTU for the commemoration of the 116th May Day, male worker figures were presented with a slogan, "Workers, show your struggle power." The KCTU's self-identified "brotherhood" (Ledwith 2012: 192) further demonstrated the union's lack of consciousness regarding marginalized laborers such as homosexual, single, and female workers. More specifically, these two posters were also gendered in their depiction of women not as workers, but either as mothers or wives who are materially dependent on the income of their husbands. Therefore, female activists critiqued the posters on the ground that they were expressive attempts to legitimate the patriarchal order within democratic labor unions.

The timing of these posters is also significant. These images of the male breadwinner were published during the economic restructuring process after the Asian financial crisis. During that time, middle-aged irregular female laborers who worked in the cafeteria of the Hyundai heavy industries supported the male regular workers' struggles by providing food during the protests against the restructuring, but the women were subsequently laid-off in retaliation for their support of the protest, based upon a deal between the government, the labor union, and the employer. Ironically, this tripartite compromise was trumpeted as the first "peaceful" agreement without a police raid, and as "a new creation of the protest culture of the labor unionism." The agreement was patently motivated by the idea that married working women need not worry about job losses since they would presumably be supported by their male spouses. In truth, over 95 percent of the laid-off married female workers were the breadwinners of their households (Cho 1998).

The story of the female cafeteria workers was documented in a film released in 2001 with the apt title "Cooked Rice, Flowers, and Goats" (*pap, kkot, yang*). The cafeteria workers supported the workers' struggles by providing warmly "cooked rice" (*pap*) to the male workers three times a day, during the entire period of the protests. The male labor unionists praised the female workers as "flowers" (*kkot*) for their crucial on-site support of the male regular workers' interests. In the end, however, they were the "scapegoat" (*yang*) for the protests they had made a success.

This series of gender-biased imagery and events led women workers to interrogate the scope and representation of "democratic" labor unionism. Indeed, the challenge to the unions' cramped definition of democracy was led primarily by female labor movement activists and the broader women's movements, including female activists who had fought for democratization in the lead-up to the transition to democracy and the founding of democratic labor unionism. Female labor activists were, predictably, part of the women's movements that blossomed after the transition to democracy and were influenced by those movements' feminist ideas. In this conjuncture, women-only unions, such as the Korean Women Workers Association (KWWA) and the Korean Women's Trade Union (KWTU), were established in 1999.

The constricted democratic norm of the male-dominated unions has come under pressure to broaden still further in order to match the contemporary diversification of the labor market. In this context, democratic ideals were challenged to incorporate more than the principle of gender equality in unions and in the labor market. The unions face a difficult dilemma in re-defining labor's democratic norm in a way that adheres to "class-consciousness" but at the same time goes "beyond class-consciousness" in the sense of recognizing diversity within unity. On the one hand, the "democratic norm" must revitalize "class-conscious" unionism by embracing the massively emerging "precariat" (Standing 2011) of workers in marginalized, unstable jobs. Yet on the other hand, the complicated and ambiguous boundaries of employment practices under the neoliberalized labor market have "produced a fragmentation of the working class, eroding the sense of solidarity among workers" (Shin 2010: 213).

Under these circumstances, non-regular workers have emerged as potentially important agents in workers' struggles (B. Lee & S. Lee 2017). As "new actors" in Korean labor movements, they have defined new conceptions of workers' solidarity, shifting democratic norms from the attainment of narrowly defined self-interests of union members to the promotion of broader social justice and defense of the rights of the weak against the neoliberal labor regime. While mainstream Korean labor unions have been criticized for turning away from "social movement unionism," non-regular workers are situated as potential renovators of such unionism through their alliances with social movements (Shin 2010).

The contingent workers have endeavored to "utilize a diverse repertoire of collective action, such as staged hunger strikes, sit-in protests and street rallies" (2010: 225) with the cooperation of social movement activists, rather than by seeking support from conventional unions. Social movement actors that had previously shown less interest in labor issues have begun to cooperate with, and amplify the voices of, irregular workers. Members of the general public, seeing the rise of the precariat and the degradation of work all around them, have also begun to rally to the cause of irregular workers.

The perception of the multiple chasms between female and male, young and old, indigenous and foreign, heterosexual and homosexual, and married and single workers, along with the emergence of the "class-unspecific postmodern citizen," is now salient in the public sphere (B. Lee 2015: 212). The lag in unions' response to the multi-faceted new labor market is vividly conveyed by the Candlelight movement's very composition and organization. In particular, although labor activists have collaborated in building those movements with women's, immigrants', and same-sex organizations, the movements have remained independent of the mainstream union organizations themselves. B. Lee and Yoo (2013: 238) conclude that the ambiguous stance of the conventional trade unions – on the one hand, propounding transnational working-class solidarity, while, on the other, demonstrating "friendly indifference" to immigrant workers' needs – left immigrant workers no choice but to organize an independent immigrant workers union movement. Precarious youth workers also organized their own independent unions, such as the Youth Community Union (YCU) and the Arbeit Workers' Union (AWU) (Yoo 2015).

A CRITICAL ASSESSMENT OF DEMOCRATIC LABOR UNIONISM IN SOUTH KOREA FROM A FEMINIST STANDPOINT

As discussed previously, the ongoing debate about the role of mainstream unionism in the democratization process – not just in the unions' central role in achieving the nation's initial democratization, but in carrying forward democratic norms that resonate with contemporary social actors – demonstrates that those unions must adapt to the growing diversity of demands of an increasingly heterogenous workforce. First, those demands are variegated across a range of issues, such as trade unions' organizational culture, the content and scope of collective bargaining, forms of collective action, and the definition of democratic values. Second, the "core" members of the trade unions – who are mainly comprised of native-born, regular, chaebol-based, middle-class, heterosexual male employees – are encircled by a vast periphery of marginalized women and social minorities, reflecting the core workers' politics and strategies of closure and exclusion.

Women's movements insistently raise deep and difficult questions about the exclusion of women from powerful positions within trade unions, despite the feminization of the labor market. Accordingly, a significant body of research has been developed, from a gender perspective, regarding women's representation (Cockburn 1996), union leadership (Cooper 2012), masculinized labor union culture (Willis 2004), and collective bargaining structures and strategies (Dawson 2014). Women's increasing participation in both the labor market and trade unions – which has heightened awareness of the problems of gender rights and social justice within unions – has concurrently strengthened a vision and practical goal of building structures of social differentiation without exclusion (Young 1990).

In the Korean context, two feminist scholars, Hyesook Kim and Sunkyung Cho, pioneered these debates in 1995. They launched an academic critique of patriarchal order within the national democracy movements and the democratic labor unions that continued to lead the movements after the transition to democracy (Kim & Cho 1995). Other feminist scholars elaborated and broadened the critique, focusing on the militarism of union culture (Kwon 2005), the unions' masculinized and patriarchal organization (Seo Jeong 2001), and the unions' gendered modes of collectivism (Broadbent 2007). Kwon (2013: 220) maintains that the reason why feminists began to call these elements into question is that "they, *as a minority*, were in a better position to become critical toward the movement's patriarchy and nationalistic collectivism" [italics added]. In this sense, feminist ideology has contributed to the transformation of the overall politics of exclusion in trade unions – not just the exclusion of women – by addressing the necessity of including women *and* other marginalized minority workers' groups. In doing so, it has shone a light on the existence of minority workers' groups, starting with women, but expanding to many others, among whom are immigrant, disabled, same-sex, and precarious workers. Women's exposure of difference and exclusion can be continuously extended to more and more categories of vulnerable workers, as the contemporary labor market becomes ever more heterogeneous.

At the same time, a feminist vision of trade union democracy delivers a strong message of not merely including women and minority workers in the membership and leadership of trade unions as they currently exist, but rather fundamentally transforming the unions' structures, culture, and hierarchies (Briskin 1993). As Colgan and Ledwith (2002) maintain, trade union democracy should develop in two ways: first, by recognizing the "women" who are paradigmatic of all marginalized workers, and second, by acknowledging the differences among women and among all minority workers, in order to enable a politics of coalitions and solidarity, without submerging the interests of any sub-group of workers.

CONCLUSIONS

The labor movement's struggle in 1987 was indeed a historic turning point for the achievement of democracy in Korea. A well-organized, militant, and male-centered labor unionism in Korea not only achieved a milestone of working-class solidarity, but also became the symbol of political resistance against militant authoritarianism and the symbolic and material guardian of democracy in Korea. However, as the heterogeneity of the workforce broadened after the Asian financial crisis and implementation of neoliberal employment policies and practices, democratic labor unionism took on the features of "elite unionism" and a "labor aristocracy," primarily pursuing the interests of its own members – namely, regular middle-class male workers.

With the emergence of the Candlelight movement which, among other achievements, led to a corrupt President's resignation, women and a younger generation – who bore the brunt of neoliberal restructuring in Korea – have raised fundamental questions about labor's understanding of democracy. This chapter has argued that the "democratic norm" in Korean labor unionism should be assessed critically, interrogating the unions' "militant culture," their particular modes of "collectivism," and labor's concept of democratic values. These critical contemporary debates about the (dis)continuity and sustainability of democratic labor unionism are enriched by feminist concepts and practice, and correspond with the continuing diversification in the Korean labor market. To sum up, although I have highlighted democratic unionism from a feminist perspective in this chapter, it is worth mentioning that the segmentation of the Korean labor market and the mainstream labor unions' general insensitivity to emerging diversity are the results of complex interactions between the state, employer associations, trade unions, and civil society in a broader context (Cooke & Jiang 2017). We therefore need to conduct further systematic and extensive examination of the impediments to the development of democratic unionism under the current multiplex and diversifying labor environments.

REFERENCES

Briskin, Linda. 1993. "Union Women and Separate Organizing," in Briskin, Linda and Patricia McDermott, eds. *Women Challenging Unions*. Toronto: University of Toronto Press, pp. 89–108.
Broadbent, Kaye. 2007. "Sisters Organizing in Japan and Korea: The Development of Women-Only Unions," *Industrial Relations Journal* 38, 3: 229–251.
Cho, Hyorae. 2005. "daegieop nosagwangyewa nodongjohapui jeontuseong" [Industrial Relations and Militancy of Labor Union in Large Firms in South Korea], *saneopnodongyeongu* [Korean Journal of Labor Studies] 11, 2: 229–260.
Cho, Sunkyung. 1998. "kyŏngje wigi wa yŏsŏng koyong chŏngch'i" [Economic Crisis, Women's Work, and Employment Politics], *han'guk yŏsŏnghak* [Journal of Korean Women's Studies] 14, 2: 5–33.
Choi, Jang Chip. 2013. *nodong ŏmnŭn minjujuŭi ŭi in'ganjŏk sangch'ŏdŭl* [The Wounds of the Democratization without Labor]. Seoul: Humanitas.
Colgan, Fiona, and Sue Ledwith. 2002. "Gender and Diversity: Reshaping Union Democracy," *Employee Relations* 24, 2: 167–189.
Chun, Jennifer Jihye. 2005. "Public Dramas and the Politics of Justice: Comparison of Janitors' Union Struggles in South Korea and the United States," *Work and Occupations* 32, 2: 486–503.
  2009. *Organizing at the Margins: The Symbolic Politics of Labor in South Korea and the United States*. Ithaca, NY: Cornell University Press.
Chun, Jinnifer Jihye. 2012. "The Power of the Powerless: New Schemas and Resources for Organizing Workers in Neoliberal Times," in Akira Suzuki, ed. *Cross-National Perspectives on Social Movement Unionism: Diversities of Labour Movement Revitalization in Japan, Korea, and the United States*. Oxford: Peter Lang, pp. 37–60.
Cockburn, Cynthia. 1996. "Strategies for Gender Democracy: Strengthening the Representation of Trade Union Women in the European Social Dialogue," *European Journal of Women's Studies* 3, 2: 7–26.
Cooke, Fang Lee, and Yumei Jiang. 2017. "The Growth of Non-Standard Employment in Japan and South Korea: The Role of Institutional Actors and Impact on Workers and the Labour Market," *Asia Pacific Journal of Human Resources* 55: 155–176.

Cooper, Rae. 2012. "The Gender Gap in Union Leadership in Australia: A Qualitative Study," *Journal of Industrial Relations* 54, 2: 131–146.

Dawson, Tricia. 2014. "Collective Bargaining and the Gender Gap in the Printing Industry," *Gender, Work, and Organization* 2, 5: 381–394.

Dubin, Robert. 1973. "Attachment to Work and Union Militancy," *Industrial Relations: A Journal of Economy and Society* 12, 1: 51–64.

Hong, Chan-Sook. 2018. "2016–17 nyŏnŭi kwanghwamun kwangjang: yugyo kongnonjang esŏ shimin kongnonjang ŭro" [Kwanghwamun Plaza in 2016–2017: From a Confucian Public Space to Citizen-Led Public Space], *minjujuŭi wa in'gwŏn* [Journal of Democracy and Human Rights] 18, 2: 147–179.

Kim, Chul-Kyoo, and Hae-Jin Lee. 2010. "Teenage Participants of the 2008 Candlelight Vigil: Their Social Characteristics and Changes in Political Views," *Korea Journal (Autumn)*: 14–37.

Kim, Hyesook, and Sunkyung Cho. 1995. "minjok minju undong kwa kabujangje" [National Democracy Movement and Patriarchy], *sahoe p'yŏngnon kil* [Social Critics Way] 95, 8: 142–150.

Kim, Sungmoon. 2018. "Candlelight for Our Country's Right Name: A Confucian Interpretation of South Korea's Candlelight Revolution," *Religions* 9, 3: 1–20.

Koo, Hagen. 2001. *Korean Workers: The Culture and Politics of Class Formation*. Ithaca, NY and London: Cornell University Press.

Kwoen, Young-Sook. 2018. "ch'otpul ŭi undong chŏngch'i wa 87nyŏn ch'eje ŭi ijung chŏnhwan" [Candlelight Movement Politics and the Dual Transformation of Korean Democracy], *kyŏngje wa sahoe* [Economy and Society] 3: 62–103.

Kwon, Insook. 2005. *taehanmin'guk ŭn kundaeda* [Korea Is an Army]. Seoul: ch'ŏngnyŏnsa.

2013. "Gender, Feminism, and Masculinity in Anti-Militarism," *International Feminist Journal of Politics* 15, 2: 213–233.

Kwon, Jaok. 2018. "Forging Feminism within Labor Unions and the Legacy of Democracy Movements in South Korea," *Labor History* 59, 5: 639–655.

Ledwith, Sue. 2012. "Gender Politics in Trade Unions: The Representation of Women between Exclusion and Inclusion," *Transfer* 18, 2: 185–199.

Lee, Byong-Hoon. 2015. "Changing Cross-Movement Coalitions between Labor Unions and Civil Society Organizations in South Korea," *Development and Society* 44, 2: 199–218.

2016. "Worker Militancy at the Margins: Struggles of Non-regular Workers in South Korea," *Development and Society* 45, 1: 1–37.

Lee, Byong-Hoon, and Sophia Seung-Yoon Lee. 2017. "Winning Conditions of Precarious Workers' Struggles: A Reflection Based on Case Studies from South Korea," *Relations Industrielles* 72, 2: 524–550.

Lee, Byong-Hoon, and Hyung-Geun Yoo. 2013. "The Rise and Fall of Independent Immigrant Worker Unionism: A Case Study of the Migrants Trade Union in South Korea," *Journal of Industrial Relations* 55, 2: 227–242.

Lee, Gira. 2018. "68undongŭl t'onghae para pon 2016-2017nyŏn ch'otpul undong ŭi sŏnggyŏk kwa ŭimi" [Characteristics and Implications of the Candlelight Rallies in Comparison with 68 Movement], *yŏksa wa segye* [History and the World] 54: 527–554.

Lee, Kyung. 2014. "Fighting in the Shadow of the Past: The Mobilizing Role of Vernacular Memories of the 1987 Pro-Democracy Movement in the 2008 Candlelight Protests in Korea," *Memory Studies* 7, 1: 61–75.

Lee, Kwangil. 2018. "nodong undong ŭi panghyang chŏnhwan kwa saeroun chuch'e hyŏngsŏngŭi munje" [The Transformation and the New Subjectivity of the Labor Unionism], *chinbo p'yŏngnon* [The Radical Review] 75: 59–80.

Lee, Seung-Ook, Sook-Jin Kim, and Joel Wainwright. 2010. "Mad Cow Militancy: Neoliberal Hegemony and Social Resistance in South Korea," *Political Geography* 29: 359–369.

Lee, Yoonkyung. 2009. "Divergent Outcomes of Labor Reform Politics in Democratized Korea and Taiwan," *Comparative International Development* 44: 47–70.

2011. *Militants or Partisans: Labor Unions and Democratic Politics in Korea and Taiwan*. Stanford, CA: Stanford University Press.

2015. "Labor after Neoliberalism: The Birth of the Insecure Class in South Korea," *Globalizations* 12, 2: 184–202.

2016. "Sky Protest: New Forms of Labour Resistance in Neo-Liberal Korea," *Journal of Contemporary Asia* 45, 3: 443–464.

Marginson, Paul, Keith Sisson, and James Arrowsmith. 2003. "Between Decentralization and Europeanisation: Sectoral Bargaining in Four Countries and Two Sectors," *European Journal of Industrial Relations* 9, 2: 163–187.

Moody, Kim. 1997. *Workers in a Lean World: Unions in the International Economy*. New York: Verso.

Park, Mi. 2007. "South Korean Trade Union Movement at the Crossroads: A Critique of 'Social-Movement' Unionism," *Critical Sociology* 33: 311–344.

Park, Tae Joo. 2001. yŏsŏnggwa nojominjujuǔi [Women and Labor Democracy]. Statistics Korea. http://kostat.go.kr

Roh, Jung-Gi. 2010. "minjuhwa 20nyŏn kwa nodong sahoe ǔi minjuhwa" [20 Years of Democratization and Democratization of the Labor], *kiŏkkwa chŏnmang* [Memory and Prospect] 22: 37–62.

Seidman, Gay. 1994. *Manufacturing Militance: Workers' Movements in Brazil and South Africa, 1970–1985*. Berkeley: University of California Press.

Seo Jeong, Youngju. 2001. "chukkŏna hokŏn nappǔgŏna: nodongundong sogesŏ yŏsŏngǔro saranamgi [Surviving as a Woman in Labor Unionism: Either Being Dead or Being Bad], *yŏsŏng gwa sahoe* [Women and Society] 12: 20/39.

Shin, Kwang-Yeong. 2010. "Globalization and the Working Class in South Korea: Contestation, Fragmentation, and Renewal," *Journal of Contemporary Asia* 40, 2: 211–229.

Standing, Guy. 2011. *The Precariat: The Dangerous New Class*. London: Bloomsbury.

Wajcman, Judy. 2000. "Feminism Facing Industrial Relations in Britain," *British Journal of Industrial Relations* 38, 2: 183–201.

Waterman, Peter. 1993. "Social-Movement Unionism: A New Union Model for a New World Order?," *Review* 16, 3: 245–278.

Willis, Paul. 2004. "Shop Floor Culture, Masculinity, and the Wage Form," in Peter Murphy, ed. *Feminism and Masculinities*. Oxford: Oxford University Press, pp. 108–120.

Yoo, Hyung-Geun. 2012. "Militant Labor Unionism and the Decline of Solidarity: A Case Study of Hyundai Auto Workers in South Korea," *Development and Society* (December): 177–199.

Yoo, Hyung-Guen. 2015. "ch'ŏngnyŏn puranjŏng nodongja ihae taebyŏn undong ǔi ch'urhyŏn kwa sŏngjang" [The Advent and Growth of the Labor Rights Movements of Youth Precarious Workers in Contemporary Korea], *asea yŏn'gu* [Asia Research] 160: 38–77.

Young, Iris Marion. 1990. *Justice and the Politics of Difference*. Princeton, NJ: Princeton University Press.

PART V

Labor and Democracy Sectoral Case Studies: Platform Workers, Higher Education, and the Care Industry

19

Pursuing Democratic Depth in an Age of Multinational Power and Soft Labor Law

The Case of Platform Worker Protests

Julia López López

LABOR LAW AS A DEMOCRATIC INSTITUTION AND MULTINATIONALS AS POLITICAL ACTORS

The last decade has been a highly challenging period for labor law – especially in its role as a crucial democratic institution. The challenges faced by labor law include a set of interrelated external circumstances. As Adelle Blackett has argued, the external environment influencing labor law comprises global interdependency, technological innovation, labor migration, the increasing informality of work, and persistent poverty, inequality, and discrimination (2019). Globalized markets and the increasing value of technologies in production have contributed to the rise of new actors, new forms of regulation, and new labor institutions that have changed fundamental processes, substantive rights, and outcomes of labor law. The combination of powerful multinational firms and sophisticated technologies – many of them involving online platforms – has challenged the role of workers' representation in setting the agenda of labor rights and in configuring economic outcomes. In this context, labor law as a democratic institution has been transformed by an industrial relations ecosystem in which multinational firms are more than simply employers. Firms of global scale are significant political actors that often challenge the power of nation-states and unions, influencing existing domestic laws such as those that govern workers' representation (Verzaro 2019).

The increasing power of multinationals, under the model of neo-feudalism (Kuttner & Stone 2020) has rested in part on their ability to move production internationally, providing them with the capacity to negotiate the location of their operations – and of the employment they provide. This, in turn, has generated incentives for public authorities to establish export processing zones "free" of collective labor rights and to reduce the statutory protection of labor standards. The political leverage of multinationals has tended to increase with application of new technologies that enable employers to escape their labor responsibilities by contracting out to other entities or misclassifying workers as independent contractors. This development has challenged labor law to revise the definitions of employee and employer in order to assign legal responsibility to the corporation that actually determines the terms and conditions of the workers in question. The case of platform workers is one of the most emblematic of this challenge (Prassl & Risak 2019). Labor laws have been adapting to, but have not fully met the challenge of, these new forms of employment and similar impairments of worker protections resulting, in great part, from the political power of multinationals (Lyon-Caen 2018).

Crucially, the evolution of transnational and national labor law has generated a change from hard law regulations of labor markets and workplaces to soft law instruments. The shift to soft law is one of the most important features of the current transformations in the regulation of labor. This trend has important consequences for the role of labor law as a democratic institution because it reduces both the import of the state as sovereign and the opportunities for the meaningful participation of workers in outcome-determining processes of representation in both the workplace and in government. The defense of labor rights through the hard-law institutions of collective bargaining rights and legally binding collective agreements has been weakened by individualization of worker grievances against liberalization of labor markets and against inequality (Rueschemeyer et al. 1992). Inequality has further increased in the aftermath of economic crises, when technocratic or authoritarian governments pursue hard-law austerity policies that disserve the interests of ordinary people who comprise a majority of citizens (Salverda et al. 2014).

As a result of multinationals' political influence, the hard-law mechanisms of labor law and democratic policy-making are increasingly replaced by soft law instruments, such as codes of conduct, supplanting worker organizations', and individual workers' roles as regulatory actors. In this process, the multinational firm has, in effect, become the law-maker, formulating law while simultaneously softening its nature. At the same time, the firms' new rule-making power has been obscured by the lack of transparency generated by outsourcing and misclassification mentioned above.

Deliberation and regulation are two fundamental democratic features of labor law and collective bargaining. An immense literature in democratic theory foregrounds deliberation for its promotion of conversational interchange, reflection, and the joint setting of objectives by democratic actors. Regulation is central to democratic decisions that are binding – even against economically powerful actors – and that construct institutions embodying the principle of political equality, an axiomatic principle of democracy (Dahl 2006). Of course, regulation may not always serve the cause of political equality, but in the absence of regulation the asymmetries of power and resources generated by markets and corporations would remain unaltered by the democratic process.

Thus collective bargaining is of great importance not only for the shaping of material outcomes but also for enabling labor's contribution to democracy – through the deliberative component of bargaining and the regulatory effects of bargaining agreements. The promotion by neoliberal legal systems of social dialogue, with different forms of conversation or deliberation often in place of collective bargaining, has effectively reduced workers' capacity to participate robustly in the democratic process of labor regulation at the level of the workplace where the institutionalization of workers' voice through binding agreements is crucial.

I argue that neoliberal labor law has tended to weaken labor's ability to contribute to what democratic theorists call "democratic depth" (Fishman 2016; Roberts 1999). Democratic depth refers to the ability of the poor and disadvantaged to participate fully in democracy's political life to jointly set public policies and outcomes. The evisceration of institutions that incorporated a robust political role for organized labor's defense of workers' interests has diminished democracy's depth, understood in this way. Attempts to reduce the scope and impact of collective bargaining and to diminish labor-empowering regulation have undercut the capacity of unions to shape collective outcomes in ways that reflect the concerns and interests of economically disadvantaged actors. Reinforcing this trend is the development discussed above: the increasing power of resource-rich private actors, such as multinational corporations, has pushed labor law away from the primacy of sovereign law and regulation toward a hybrid model in which multinationals have gained new abilities to rule through corporate-responsibility instruments that reduce the level of participation for workers, undercutting the latter's earlier role in the regulation of labor conditions and political process.

Thus I argue that the institutional basis for labor's contribution to democratic depth has been undermined by new tendencies in the legal basis for regulation, bargaining, and workers' representation. However, I argue that, at the same time, another avenue leading to labor-based democratic depth has been reinvigorated, albeit in new ways: workers and their representatives have responded to the institutional shift – unfavorable to their agency – with novel or amplified strategies for constructing spaces for the defense of labor rights in a multilevel context through new forms of mobilization and negotiation. The goal of unions in these efforts is to defend a space for workers' agency to improve labor rights as citizens and workers – the space that has otherwise been constricted in the avenue of law and regulation. The case of platform workers illustrates both the contextual pressures of global markets, new technologies, and legal alterations, and the renewed and novel forms of mobilization that have emerged in that broader environment.

DECONSTRUCTING DEMOCRACY AS PARTICIPATION IN THE DESIGN OF PUBLIC POLICIES: FROM HARD LAW TO SOFT LAW LABOR REGULATION

International labor law has been one of the main building blocks in the evolution of labor rights globally. Since its founding in 1919, the International Labor Organization (ILO) has approved 190 Conventions, legal instruments that upon ratification by countries enter into their national legal order. The Conventions have created a robust international labor law that establishes a floor of worker rights within national labor law regimes. Thanks to the legally binding character of ILO Conventions once they are ratified, international labor law has been applied by national judges as national labor law. However, since 2000 only seven ILO Conventions have been approved, while the ILO has instead turned its energies to numerous new soft law initiatives and documents. And the shift from hard law to soft law has reduced the role of judges in applying and enforcing workers' rights.

Among the Conventions that have been approved in this period, an especially important one, due to its connection with inequality and democracy, is Convention 190.[1] This Convention addresses the elimination of workplace violence and harassment through a human rights approach. The commitment to protect workers is very clear and broad, covering workers in private and public services and in both the formal and informal economy. The protections against violence and harassment include provisions that would require hard law regulation in national legislation.

In contrast with hard law initiatives – such as this and other Conventions – since 1998 the ILO has increasingly generated soft law instruments intended to simply reorient labor regulation, general policy, or corporations' managerial behavior. This evolution from hard law and clear labor rights to soft law as governance has weakened labor rights and the capacity of unions to exercise agency as participants in democratic rule.

The point of departure of this new soft law approach was the 1998 Declaration on Fundamental Principles and Rights at Work (Declaration). The Declaration commits member states to respect and promote principles and rights in four categories (freedom of association and collective bargaining, the elimination of forced labor, the abolition of child labor, and the

---

[1] ILO, Violence and Harassment Convention. No. 190. 2019.

elimination of employment discrimination), whether or not they have ratified the relevant Conventions. While at first glance this appears to be an extension of the ILO's body of hard law – since it makes certain ILO law applicable even to states that have firmly resisted incorporation of international labor law into domestic law – on closer inspection the Declaration requires member states to adhere only to unspecified, vague soft law "principles" and not to the binding rights contained in the Conventions addressing the four categories just mentioned.

The policy of governance as an ILO strategy – which is to say the institution's elaboration of general soft law documents offering orientation rather than hard law binding regulations – has a main point of reference in the holistic approach of the Decent Work Agenda of 2008. This document sets out as strategic policies and objectives employment, social protection, social dialogue, and rights at work understood as labor standards, not rights. In 2008 the Declaration on Social Justice for a Fair Globalization completed the Decent Work Agenda. In the first period of this soft law approach, the Tripartite Declaration of Principles concerning Multinational Enterprises and Social Policy, later revised in 2017, applied principles (but not rights) built into ILO Conventions and Recommendations specifically to the operations of multinational enterprises (MNEs), in areas such as employment, training, and labor conditions. The shift from regulation to governance has been felt in centrally important areas, such as the promotion of participation and equality.

The new strategy has been consolidated in the ILO Centenary Declaration for the Future of Work of 2019 (Centenary Declaration).[2] Adopted by the ILO's International Labor Conference – the Organization's plenary governing body – this soft law document presents three pillars of human-centered action, which in combination are intended to drive growth, equity, and sustainability. The stated goal is to reinvigorate the social contract through a new path that requires committed action on the part of governments, as well as employers' and workers' organizations. In the ILO's new vision, social dialogue (that is, dialogue between representatives of workers, employers, and, in some instances, governments) can play a key role in ensuring the ongoing relevance of this contract to workplaces transformed by greater inclusivity, including the many millions of workers who are currently unemployed. Collective bargaining is mentioned only by way of reference to workers' rights in the Universal Labor Guarantee, which protects fundamental workers' rights, an adequate living wage, limits on hours of work, and safe and healthy workplaces. The Centenary Declaration's model of participation explicitly inserts social dialogue at the transnational level, combined with collective bargaining at the national level: "Our recommendations seek to strengthen and revitalize the institutions of work. Ensuring collective representation of workers and employers through social dialogue is a public good, actively promoted through public policies. All workers and employers must enjoy freedom of association and the right to collective bargaining, with the State as the guarantor of those rights."

These policies have been further elaborated on in the United Nations 2030 Agenda for Sustainable Development and in the ILO's Integrated Strategy on Fundamental Principles and Rights at Work 2017–2023, which underscore limitations on the impact of ILO Conventions. Those limitations are reflected in the fact that, first, more than 40 percent of the world's population lives in countries that have ratified neither ILO Convention No. 87 on freedom of association nor Convention No. 98 on collective bargaining, and, second, in many countries that have ratified them, violations of these rights persist in law and practice. It is important to recognize the crucial role of the ILO in the defense of labor rights, but at the same time acknowledge that the new institutional strategy of focusing on soft law strategies has

---

[2] Adopted by the Conference at its 108th session, 21 June 2019.

increased the power of employers relative to workers within the firm, including in multinational corporations.

As in the case of the ILO, the European Union has been moving toward soft law regulation in the labor field. As with the ILO, this transformation has diminished the depth of democracy in the EU member states, undercutting established avenues for the participation and empowerment of vulnerable people in the political arena.

The EU Treaty[3] envisions shared labor regulation between the regional body and the member states. Article 4 of the Treaty establishes that principle, along with the complementary notions of subsidiarity and the coordination of economic policies. Articles 5.1, 6, and 151 of the Treaty apply those principles to a wide range of labor-related subjects, including working conditions, information, and consultation for workers; representation and collective defense of the interests of workers and employers, including co-determination; equality between men and women with regard to labor market opportunities and treatment at work; and the combating of social exclusion.

Two documents that played a crucial role in the shift of the EU model from hard to soft law deserve mention: the transition from the hard law Charter of Fundamental Rights of 2000 (Charter) to the soft law Pillar of Social Rights of 2017. On its approval in 2000, the Charter encoded an ambitious model of constitutionalizing labor rights in the European Union. The Charter's model is applied by national judges and the European Court of Justice in interpreting European Union law. The Charter reaffirms an approach based on human rights, on constitutional traditions, and on international obligations common to EU countries and the European Convention for the Protection of Human Rights and Fundamental Freedoms.

The constitutionalization of labor rights in the Charter was a major step not only in the protection of workers' interests, but also in deepening the conceptualization of workers' rights to include citizenship rights. The broad content of the Charter is organized in four chapters: Chapter 1 develops a conception of human dignity that includes a group of rights;[4] Chapter 2 on freedoms includes, among others, the protection of personal data, freedom of thought, conscience, and religion, freedom of expression and information, and freedom of assembly and association;[5] Chapter 3 on equality before the law covers non-discrimination, cultural, religious, and linguistic diversity, equality between men and women, the rights of the child, the rights of the elderly, and integration of persons with disabilities; Chapter 4 on solidarity constitutionalizes workers' right to information and consultation, and the right of collective bargaining and action.[6] Finally, Chapter 5 covers citizens' rights,[7] and Chapter 6 focuses on justice.[8] Through the Charter of Fundamental Rights, the European Union set out a democratic model

---

[3] Treaty on the Functioning of the European Union, OJ C 326, 47–390 (Sept. 2012).

[4] Including the right to life, the right to the integrity of the person, prohibition of torture and inhuman or degrading treatment or punishment, and prohibition of slavery and forced labor.

[5] Chapter 2 also includes the right to education, freedom to choose an occupation and the right to engage in work, the right to asylum, and protection in the event of removal, expulsion, or extradition.

[6] Chapter 4 also includes the right of access to placement services, protection in the event of unjustified dismissal, the right to fair and just working conditions, the prohibition of child labor, the protection of young people at work and of family and professional life, and the rights to social security, social assistance, healthcare, access to services of general economic interest environmental protection, and consumer protection.

[7] These include the right to vote and stand as a candidate in elections to the European Parliament and municipal elections, the right to good administration, the right to access documents, and the establishment of the European Ombudsman.

[8] Chapter 6 includes the right to an effective remedy and a fair trial, the presumption of innocence and the right of defense, principles of legality and proportionality of criminal offences and penalties, and the right not to be tried or punished twice in criminal proceedings for the same criminal offense.

of labor law not only in a formal sense, but also crucially in a way that promotes democratic depth. However, the evolution of European labor law and of EU strategies for the future are quite complex, requiring a diachronic analysis.

An important soft law regulation approved by the European Commission is the Green Paper of 2006 (Green Paper) entitled "Modernizing Labor Law to Meet the Challenges of the 21st Century."[9] In this document the Commission stipulates the existence of several main challenges posed by the gap between existing legal frameworks and the realities of the labor market. The policy implemented by the Green Paper reaffirms a model of labor law based on an individualization of rights and the segmentation of workers' legal status, together with the promotion of self-employment. Collective labor rights are not part of the discourse in this model. The principle of participation as a fundamental component of labor law as a democratic institution is absent in the Green Paper's model of soft law regulation. The Paper encourages the use of atypical forms of contract, such as fixed-term, part-time, on-call, zero-hour, and temporary-agency contracts – notwithstanding the Green Paper's acknowledgement that "a greater diversity of contracts has certain negative effects. A succession of short-term, low-quality jobs with insufficient social protection can lead some people into a vulnerable position." This soft law approach to regulation is a strategic alternative to the democratic model elaborated on by the Charter of Fundamental Rights.

Yet another step in codifying the soft law approach to regulation is the 2017 Pillar of Social Rights (Pillar). Although the Pillar declares its commitment to delivering new and more effective rights for citizens in twenty key principles or objectives, among them are the transition towards non-collective, labor-market-liberalizing policies of open-ended forms of employment, the flexibility for employers to adapt quickly to changes in the economic context, and innovative forms of work that ensure quality working conditions. Likewise, the Pillar declares its commitment to encouraging entrepreneurship and self-employment. On the themes of social dialogue and the involvement of workers, the Pillar stipulates that "the social partners shall be consulted on the design and implementation of economic, employment and social policies according to national practices." The Pillar merely "encourage[s]" the partners to negotiate collective agreements. In practice, the social dialogue promoted by the 2017 Pillar typically yields general accords that seek to orient collective outcomes but which lack a legally binding character of the sort guaranteed by the Charter of 2000. Furthermore, the Charter's fundamental rights of both mobilizations and strikes are absent from the Pillar. The Pillar does recognize some rights – for example, workers or their representatives have the right to be informed and consulted in good time on matters relevant to them, in particular on the transfer of work, on restructuring and merger of undertakings, and on mass layoffs – but these had been previously explicitly guaranteed by the hard law stipulations of EU Directives.

The weakening of labor's institutional guarantees and instruments renders even more important than before labor's other main avenue to pursue equality and democratic depth: namely, direct mobilization, such as collective action, collective bargaining, strikes, demonstrations, and judicial actions. In this context it is crucial to examine worker mobilizations and their potential to foster outcomes beneficial to democracy's depth. We will focus on the protest of platform workers, such as independent drivers and riders, emblematic of workers' reactions to the liberalization of markets and the use of technology to segment production systems through the emergence of a new category of precarious work.

---

[9] COM(2006) 708 final (November 2006) (not published in the Official Journal).

PROTEST AND MOBILIZATION OF PLATFORM WORKERS: LOCAL STRATEGIES
TO CONFRONT GLOBAL LIBERALIZATION AND TO RECOVER UNIONS' AND
WORKERS' AGENCY

Social conflict in the form of mobilization, including strikes and protests, is a fundamental avenue to demonstrate the discontent of ordinary citizens and is therefore a way to increase the spaces for participation in the setting and implementation of public policies – for example, protests that result in the withdrawal of a proposed law or the elimination of an existing law (López López et al. 2011). The increasing power of multinationals and of other private actors in the regulation or governance of labor relations has contributed to constructing precarious labor markets, heightening inequality, and increasing the number of working poor. The line between formal and informal work has become more and more diffuse, and the segmentation of labor status is now a fundamental characteristic of labor markets (López López 2015). The definition of certain types of participants in the formal labor market as dependent or autonomous workers has opened new possibilities for categories of hybrid legal status with mixed consequences for labor and social rights. The specification of these largely new categories is contingent on forms of regulation that shape the interpretation and definition of these workers' legal status. In the case of the European Union and its national member states, the tendency has been to reduce the use of the labor contract in favor of the status of autonomous work. The legal status of workers also has important consequences for firms' responsibility as the case of transport workers has clearly shown.

The transport sector is a useful case study of the segmentation of workers and employees' legal status that has generated negative consequences for labor rights. And, as mentioned above, platform workers in the transport sector stand out as an especially interesting case to study new forms of protest against the liberalization of markets and precarious work. The use of multiple and multilevel strategies by unions and other workers' organizations – including negotiation, protest, and litigation – has emerged in response to multinationals' global strategy of liberalization for these workers (López López 2015).

Monopolistic strategies of multinational platform firms attempt to occupy the space of labor market regulation, displacing the state and workers' representatives, thereby weakening democratic institutions of participation. In direct contrast, riders, taxi drivers, and independent drivers who operate as platform workers constitute elements of a common frame in the geographies of mobilization – mobilization that seeks to increase areas of participation for workers, giving more voice to the most vulnerable people. This represents the first common element of platform worker protests. The second common element is the territorial focus of protest, initially on the local level. While mobilization is local, the goals are global (Rodrik 2011). Relations between levels of protest are crucial (Tarrow 2005).

The third common element is the important role played by the unions – with different intensity and levels of implication. Mobilization and protest by transport sector workers has involved unions and worker organizations mobilizing locally against the liberalization of markets, trying to give greater political voice to the state, judges, and workers relative to corporations.

The fourth common element is the multilevel and multimodality strategy of mobilization, acting at the local, national, and supranational levels through protest, demonstrations, negotiation, and judicial action (López López 2017). This assertion of a multilevel and multimodality strategy is in part a response to the exclusionary treatment of protest within many countries, such as Spain (Fishman 2019).

Outside transport, multinational firms with digital platforms are also hiring workers as independent contractors or self-employed workers, including in communication, healthcare services, and many other sectors. In many cases the legally dubious classification of workers as self-employees effectively shifts the entrepreneurial risk from the firm to the workers. Current debates on digital platforms concern not only the technologies involved, but also how multinational firms are increasing the use of these mechanisms to construct contractual networks and chains of enterprises in ways that evade national law.

Categorizing the employment status of platform workers as dependent, autonomous, or hybrid has provoked much debate not only over the legal definition of employee and employer – but also over the appropriate role of legislation and jurisprudence for workers in the gig economy. Mark Freedland and Nicola Kountoris have addressed the legal definition of workers as subjects of labor rights, underlining the contradictions posed by defining workers in the gig economy as self-employed autonomous workers or independent contractors, and the tensions that this creates for labor law, especially with regard to collective labor rights (2019). Due in part to their legal status, formally self-employed digital-platform workers are, in many countries, deprived of rights such as collective bargaining, fair salaries, guarantees against dismissal, social security benefits, and unemployment insurance (Stone 2019). At the same time, the employers retain control over workers' terms and conditions of employment within these systems (Prassl 2016, 2018).

Platform workers have mobilized at different levels and globally to achieve a more favorable labor status. They have submitted claims to labor departments or inspectorates at the administrative level, and to labor courts or courts of general jurisdiction at the judicial level. These efforts have yielded important results. In the European Union a great number of judicial decisions have recognized drivers in companies such as Glovo or Deliveroo as dependent workers rather than autonomous self-employees. The combination of worker mobilizations and responses by labor institutions such as labor courts and inspectors of labor has been crucial. Legal decisions defining platform workers as employees – rejecting the argument of the multinationals that they are self-employed autonomous workers – have greatly improved their circumstances not only in terms of labor conditions, but also with regard to healthcare and social security benefits (López López & de le Court 2020).

In the cases of non-platform taxi drivers and independent drivers, the courts have also played an important role. In a 2019 decision, the German Federal Court of Justice, Germany's supreme court for civil and criminal cases, addressed employers' requirement that professional drivers of cars for hire use the app Uber Black. The Court stated that the requirement violates section 49 of the German Passenger Transport Act, which provides that drivers for chauffeur services may accept only those assignments received at the chauffeur company's place of business. With this decision, and its focus on the practical nature of the relationship between the online platform and drivers, the German Court undermined the company's assertion that the drivers are autonomous workers.

In 2017, the European Court of Justice (ECJ) issued an important decision in the case of *Asociación Profesional Elite Taxi v Uber Systems Spain, SL*, initially adjudicated in Spain.[10] The ECJ decision held that Uber activities were, in fact, a transportation service and therefore subject to EU Directives dealing with firms and workers in that sector. Placing Uber in the legal category of transport sector firms carried with it greater regulation within the EU system than would have been the case if instead the Court had placed Uber legally in the "information

---

[10] 2017 ECR 981.

society service" sector. The Spanish case focused on the identification of the EU Directives that apply to Uber, and in that sense the case was a thoroughly multilevel legal determination.

Prior to the European Court of Justice's resolution of the question, massive taxi driver protests in front of the headquarters of the conservative Partido Popular, in power in the regional government of Madrid, pressed for regulation of platform driver services. Mobilizations of taxi drivers have included protests or strikes against multinationals. The principal demand of the taxi drivers is for regulation to avoid social dumping through the sector's growing reliance on formally independent drivers with precarious labor conditions.

As mentioned above, taxi driver protests are pressuring local governments for regulation of driver-for-hire platforms. In a number of ways, the protests of taxi drivers in Madrid and Barcelona are an unusual but interesting form of labor protest. The taxi drivers have emphasized the goal of stopping the social dumping of the digital platform companies; the protests were not focused only on claims about working conditions. Some of the protesters are owners of more than one taxi, whereas others are simply owner-drivers and others are employees of taxi owners. In addition, taxi employers and drivers are protesting and striking together in support of the demand for stricter regulation of Uber and Cabify. Theirs is a protest about unregulated, or weakly regulated, liberalized markets, not only working conditions. In the Catalan case, the municipal government of Barcelona and the Catalan Parliament approved regulation of Uber and Cabify with support from *Esquerra Republicana de Cataunya* (ERC), *Comuns-Podem* (a left coalition allied with Podemos), the CUP (a pro-independence left coalition) and the *Partit dels Socialistes de Catalunya* (PSC). The left-oriented political parties that supported this measure differ with one another on the question of Catalan independence, but they were able to stand together on this important matter.

A crucial point in these mobilizations is the major role played by solidarity among multiple unions and other associations. The taxi drivers' associations and the riders' unions have received support from major unions such as the Global Transport Union and, in the case of Spain, the predominant union confederations. When formally independent drivers who work as autonomous employees of multinational platforms demanded that local governments guarantee their right to work, they garnered the support of major Spanish unions, such as the *Unión General de Trabajadores* (UGT). In a mobilization in front of the Catalan government, Cabify workers protested the conditions they face and demanded the right to work. The Transport Union (UGT) supported their protest and *Comisiones Obreras* (CCOO) defended the Cabify workers against the multinational. This support helped achieve crucial regulatory actions – for example, the Catalan Government's implementation of certain limitations on the activity of Uber and Cabify.

DEEPENING DEMOCRACY AND MOBILIZATION: RECOVERING SPACES OF WORKER'S PARTICIPATION

In recent decades the contribution of collective labor law as a core element of social democracy has been questioned. Labor's institutional contribution to democracy's depth through regulatory institutions, collective rights, and the binding character of collective bargaining agreements has been restrained and redirected. The turn toward soft law and the individualization of dominant conceptions of labor rights have undercut the capacity of long pre-existing institutional mechanisms for labor to secure rights, recognition of workers' interests, and favorable outcomes for workers within political democracies. The existing institutional pathways that deepen democracy have eroded, for labor organizations and the workers represented by them. However, this challenging context has not in any sense eliminated labor's contribution to democratic depth. Instead, it has redirected it.

Unions and workers have reoriented their strategies in order to recover spaces of participation and influence – deeply shaping democratic outcomes through new types of mobilization. The multilevel strategies of these actors make use of a combination of negotiation and conflict, directed toward a carefully identified set of democratic institutions, including inspectors of labor, courts, and governmental authorities at multiple levels. The case of platform workers' mobilization is emblematic of local strategies in the face of global problems. The local strategies of the platform workers have creatively designed new types of mobilization focusing on new institutional targets of their demands. This innovative approach is the basis for multiple participatory endeavors to successfully secure social rights. New types of mobilization by new actors have reaffirmed labor's ability to foster democracy's depth despite the erosion of older institutional channels supportive of that same end.

REFERENCES

Blackett, Adelle. 2019. *Everyday Transgressions: Domestic Workers' Transnational Challenge to International Labor Law*. Ithaca, NY: Cornell University Press.

Dahl, Robert. 2006. *On Political Equality*. New Haven, CT: Yale University Press.

Fishman, Robert. 2016. "Rethinking Dimensions of Democracy for Empirical Analysis: Authenticity, Quality, Depth, and Consolidation," *Annual Review of Political Science* 19: 289–309.

2019. *Democratic Practice: Origins of the Iberian Divide in Political Inclusion*. Oxford: Oxford University Press.

Freedland, Mark, and Nicola Kountoris. 2019. "The 'Autonomous Worker' and the Personal Scope of Collective Labour Law," *Journal of the Ministry of Employment and Social Security* 144: 15–30.

Kuttner, R., and Stone, KV. The Rise of Neo-Feudalisms, *The American Prospect* (April 8, 2020).

López López, Julia. 2015. "Segmentation and the Debate on Labor Laws," *Comparative Labor Law and Policy Journal* 36, 2: 177–180.

2017. "Diminishing Unions' Agency: Weakening Collective Bargaining and Criminalizing Picketing in the Spanish Case," *Comparative Labor Law and Policy Journal* 28, 2: 169–186.

2019. "Introduction" and "Modes of Collective Action: Judicialization as a Form of Protest," in Julia López López, ed. *Collective Bargaining and Collective Action: Labour Agency and Governance in the Twenty-First Century*. Oxford: Hart Publishing, pp. 41–56.

López López, Julia, Consuelo Chacartegui, and César Gonzalez Cantón. 2011. "From Conflict to Regulation: The Transformative Function of Labour Law," in Guy Davidov and Brian Langille, eds. *The Idea of Labour Law*. Oxford: Oxford University Press, pp. 344–362.

López López, Julia, and Alexandre de le Court. 2020. "When the Corporate Veil Is Lifted: Synergies of Public Labour Institutions and Platform Workers," *King's Law Journal* 31, 2: 324–335.

Lyon-Caen, Antoine. 2018. "Sustainable Development, Social Rights, and International Trade," in Adalberto Perulli and Tiziano Treu, eds. *Sustainable Development, Global Trade and Social Rights*. Philadelphia: Wolters Kluwer, pp. 33–39.

Prassl, Jeremias. 2016. *The Concept of the Employer*. Oxford: Oxford University Press.

2018. *Humans as a Service*. Oxford: Oxford University Press.

Prassl, Jeremias, and Martin Risak. 2019. "Legal Responsibility in the Gig Economy: The Employer Perspective," *Journal of the Ministry of Employment and Social Security* 144: 31–44.

Roberts, Kenneth. 1999. *Deepening Democracy: The Modern Left and Social Movements in Chile and Peru*. Redwood City, CA: Stanford University Press.

Rodrik, Dani. 2011. *The Globalization Paradox: Democracy and the Future of the World Economy*. New York: W. W. Norton & Company.

Rueschemeyer, Dietrich, Evelyne Huber Stephens, and John D. Stephens. 1992. *Capitalist Development and Democracy*. Chicago: University of Chicago Press.

Salverda,Wiemer, Brian Nolan, Daniele Checchi, Ive Marx, Abigail Mcknight, István György Tóth, and Herman van de Werfhorst. 2014. *Changing Inequalities in Rich Countries: Analytical and Comparative Perspectives*. Oxford: Oxford University Press.

Stone, Katherine. 2019. "Unions and On-Demand Work in the United States," in Julia López López, ed. *Collective Bargaining and Collective Action: Labour Agency and Governance in the Twenty-First Century?* Oxford: Hart Publishing, pp. 101–119.

Tarrow, Sidney. 2005. *The New Transnational Activism*. Ithaca, NY: Cornell University Press.

Tilly, Charles. 2004. *Contention and Democracy in Europe, 1650–2000*. Cambridge: Cambridge University Press.

Verzaro, Matteo. 2019. "State's Absence: Is It a Draw for Labour Law?" in Perulli Adalberto and Stefano Bellomo, eds. *New Industrial Relations in the Era of Globalization*. Milan: Wolters Kluwer, pp. 51–86.

20

Corporatization of Higher Education

A Crisis of Labor and Democracy

Risa L. Lieberwitz

INTRODUCTION

Concepts of labor and democracy have infused the theory and practice of higher education in the USA since the development of the modern university[1] in the late 1800s and the early 1900s. Higher education's place in democratic life has been contested in two interrelated realms: (1) the social role of higher education, which concerns the public mission of the university and its relationship to other social institutions, including the government and industry; and (2) the internal labor model for university faculty. This chapter explores the ongoing push-pull between private economic interests, on the one hand, and higher education's contribution to wider democratic political culture and its correlative internal commitment to its faculties' academic freedom, tenure, due process protections, and rights to govern jointly with administrators, on the other.

The first section sets out the modes of interaction between the university's public democratic mission and its internal labor regime, and summarizes the changing historical forces that tilted universities toward either public democratic or private corporate interests in the nineteenth and twentieth centuries. That section then recounts the faculties' achievement of robust professional norms of democratic university governance, and describes the threat to universities' democratic public mission and to faculties' professional norms posed by concentrated economic power outside the university.

The second section examines more closely the specific ways in which higher education's democratic public mission is grounded in the university's internal labor regime protecting the faculty's autonomy and security. It then analyzes legal and ideological dimensions of higher education's location along the blurred boundary between the public and private sphere, and the post-World War II strengthening of the universities' public mission through increases in public funding and student movements' demands for curricular reform and greater transparency in university governance.

That examination leads to the third section, which analyzes the impact of neoliberal privatization policies – launched by the Reagan administration and continuing to this day – on higher education. In this period, the government reduced public funding of higher education, and universities commercialized academic research and tightened their relationship with corporate interests. Concurrently, the universities adopted an internal labor model that increased administrators' unilateral power by cutting back on tenure-track positions and resisting unionization,

---

[1] In this chapter, "university" refers to both colleges and universities.

with negative impacts on faculty independence inside the university and on the democratic polity outside campus gates.

The chapter concludes, in the fourth section, with a brief reflection on the potential for restoring both the democratic function of higher education and the faculties' central place in university governance through coalitions of faculty, student, staff, and community-based organizations.

HIGHER EDUCATION BETWEEN THE PUBLIC/DEMOCRATIC AND PRIVATE/CAPITALIST SPHERES

Creating the Modern University: Countervailing Social and Economic Forces

Throughout the nineteenth century, the evolution of the institutions of higher education from religious to secular and the acceptance of the scientific method in research and teaching created conditions favorable for faculty to demand academic freedom and collective autonomy from their university employers. As their expertise grew across specialized fields of science, faculty called for a system that placed evaluations of academic competence into faculty hands through peer review (Hofstadter & Metzger 1955: 350–351, 363–366). Such collective autonomy was a democratizing influence in the university structure by shifting power from university governing boards to the faculty to assess the merits of their colleagues' work, reflected in peer review of promotion decisions and publication content in the natural sciences and the rapidly growing social sciences (Byrne 1989; Hofstadter & Metzger 1955). In both subject areas, faculty were engaged in controversial teaching and research, from Darwin's theory of evolution to the growing labor movement and critiques of capitalism.

The further development of universities in the latter part of the nineteenth century occurred against the backdrop of the intensified clash between industrial capitalism and political democracy. The inequalities of wealth and political power in the Gilded Age were met by collective resistance of a growing labor movement and Progressive reformers (Metzger 1964: Ch. 4; Tiede 2014: 6). The importance of faculty independence was brought into bold relief as major industrialists' influence grew in universities along with their increasingly large financial donations, from thousands of dollars prior to the industrial era to millions of dollars in the late 1880s (Hofstadter & Metzger 1955: 413). This set the stage for a conflict with social scientists who criticized capitalism and specific industry practices. In several well-publicized cases, faculty were discharged because of their critiques and calls for social reform, including the forced resignation of economist E. A. Ross from Stanford University and the dismissal of economist Edward W. Bemis from the University of Chicago (Hofstadter & Metzger 1955: 426–427, 439; Schrecker 1986: 417).

The federal Morrill Act of 1862 gave overt university support to industry by creating land grant colleges to provide education and training needed by managers and employees in growing industries, such as manufacturing and commercial agricultural ventures. Faculty in new departments of the land grant colleges provided applied research to commercial interests in agriculture, mechanical arts, distribution, and business administration (Goldin & Katz 1999: 49–52; Hofstadter & Metzger 1955: 380).

These early stages of the modern university vividly exposed the gravitational pull of the two strongest competing forces in higher education: capitalism and democracy. Faculty asserted their interests in 1915 by creating a new organization, the American Association of University Professors (AAUP). Its founders included faculty who had been involved in the conflicts over disciplinary actions against social scientists by university governing boards (Hofstadter & Metzger 1955: 407; Schrecker 1983: 25–27). The AAUP's 1915 Declaration of Principles on Academic Freedom and Tenure (1915 Declaration) described the general conflict between capital and academic freedom, and the "special dangers" to the social sciences, in which "almost every question . . . is more or less affected with private or class interests; and, as the governing body of a university is naturally made up of men who through their standing and ability are personally interested in great private enterprises, the points of possible conflict are numberless" (AAUP 2015b: 8).

The 1915 Declaration and the AAUP's 1940 Statement of Principles on Academic Freedom and Tenure (1940 Statement) embody fundamental visions of the appropriate position of higher education in the broader society, and of faculty in universities. The 1915 Declaration distinguishes between universities with a public mission and those of a proprietary nature, explaining that only the former legitimately belong to the community of higher education (AAUP 2015b: 5). As the 1940 Statement recognized, this is a democratic vision of higher education that is "conducted for the common good and not to further the interest of either the individual teacher or the institution as a whole" (AAUP 2015c: 14). The 1915 Declaration and the 1940 Statement both describe the employment conditions required for faculty to fulfill the university's public democratic mission: academic freedom, the job security of tenure, due process prior to discipline or dismissal, and faculty self-governance, including faculty peer review (AAUP 2015b: 6, 9–12; AAUP 2015c: 16). These faculty rights are democratic in nature, indeed so democratic that labor advocates could only dream of their robust application to other categories of employees. The broad scope of academic freedom remains a striking model for workplace democracy, traversing the full range of interests of university faculty, including their teaching, research, and extramural speech.

The 1915 Declaration's and 1940 Statement's radical potential was tempered by several factors. First, the delegates to the founding meeting of the AAUP were primarily from elite colleges and universities, including Harvard, Yale, Columbia, Cornell, Princeton, and Johns Hopkins (Tiede 2014: 11). Although they organized the AAUP in 1915, at a time when the broader labor movement was forming, the AAUP founders did not envision themselves as creating a union or even as "employees." Emphasizing that individual professors' primary responsibility is to the public, the Declaration describes faculty as being more like "appointees" of the trustees, analogous to judicial appointees (AAUP 2015b: 6). It was not until 1971, after years of internal debate, that the AAUP voted to engage in union organizing and collective bargaining as a means to achieve its organizational goals, including in university governance (AAUP 2015h: 323; Gerber 2014: 108–116).

Moreover, in defining the AAUP's goals, the early leadership reached a compromise that limited the potential for internal democratic governance of universities, notwithstanding their embrace of the general principle of university democracy (Tiede 2014: 3–5). The AAUP opted not to propose democratic restructuring of the university that would have increased faculty collective power, including through faculty participation in electing the university president and governing board (Tiede 2014: 3–5). In the 1915 Declaration, the AAUP made a more limited challenge to the power of trustees and administrators by implanting the peer review system within the existing institutional structure (Hofstadter & Metzger 1955: 473; Metzger 1988: 1276–1278; Schrecker 1983: 25–27; Tiede 2015: 179–180). The 1940 Statement, issued jointly with the Association of American Colleges, adhered to the same template. Later critics described the peer review process as "self-policing" rather than self-governance, since peer review may be constrained by standards acceptable to the administration and trustees (Schrecker 1983: 25–27).

The AAUP's 1966 Statement on Government of Colleges and Universities also reflects the compromise of collective faculty autonomy within shared governance. The 1966 Statement was again formulated jointly with associations of university authorities, the Association of Governing Boards of Universities and Colleges and the American Council on Education. True, the Statement stipulated the faculty's primary responsibility, through their governing bodies, over academic matters such as curriculum, teaching, research, and faculty appointments and promotions (AAUP 2015i: 120–121); in these matters, faculty actions should be respected by the administration or governing boards in their final decision-making authority (AAUP 2015i: 120; Gerber 2014: 95–98; Tiede 2015: 179–180). But "final institutional authority" was firmly vested in the universities' governing boards (AAUP 2015i: 119).

The Public Mission of the University and Democratic Professional Academic Norms

The AAUP's demands for faculty academic freedom, tenure, and shared governance were largely successful. Those three principles have endured as a body of "extra-legal" rights demanded by the academic profession, internalized by faculty, and adopted over the decades in public and private universities throughout the USA (Lieberwitz 2002: 89–90; Olivas 2003: 4, 6–34). The 1940 Statement has been endorsed by over 250 scholarly and educational organizations (AAUP 2015c: 13, 16–19). These professional norms are central to the university's democratic purpose of serving the "common good, [which] depends upon the free search for truth and its free exposition. Academic freedom is essential to these purposes and applies to both teaching and research" (AAUP 2015c). The role of faculty to use their academic freedom to question the status quo, challenge students, and push beyond the confines of accepted "truths" is implicit in the 1946 President's Commission on Higher Education, which justified federal funding of public universities as "an investment in social welfare, better living standards, better health, and less crime. It is an investment in a bulwark against garbled information, half-truths and untruths, against ignorance and intolerance. It is an investment in human talent, better human relationships, democracy, and peace" (Brown 2015: 187). With this statement, the Commission captures the intrinsic and instrumental value of higher education in a democratic society, supporting both self-actualization and well-informed political decision-making (Brown 2015).

Academic professional norms resonate with the democratic constitutional rights of free speech, association, and due process, and with democratic self-governance. However, these norms, developed by the academic profession for itself, have a different reach than constitutional rights. Although the US Supreme Court has recognized academic freedom as "a special concern" of the First Amendment, academic freedom has limited scope and depth as a constitutional protection for faculty.[2] The threshold requirement of governmental or "state action" to trigger First Amendment freedoms and due process rights makes constitutional academic freedom inapplicable to private universities (Lieberwitz 2002: 89–90; 1987: 25–30, 38–39). Even in public universities, constitutional protection is limited by Supreme Court decisions that narrow the scope of First Amendment protection for public employees vis-à-vis their government employers (Fugate 1998: 205; Hiers 1993: 61; Lieberwitz 2002: 89–90).

In contrast, non-constitutional rights of academic freedom and due process – implemented through university contracts and professional norms – apply equally to faculty in public and private universities (Metzger 1988: 1291). Universities have widely adopted the AAUP's broad coverage of academic freedom to include teaching, research, and extramural speech and

[2] *Keyishian v. Board of Regents*, 385 US 589, 603 (1967).

association (AAUP 2015c: 14–15; AAUP 2015d: 31). Many AAUP investigations of alleged violations of academic freedom relate to extramural speech, including recent cases concerning
faculty speech on social media (AAUP 2015a). Academic freedom is strengthened by faculty
participation in shared governance, which provides additional protection for faculty ability to
dissent and to act independently from the university administration (AAUP 2015f: 123–125).

Unlike the First Amendment, the contours of professional academic freedom are defined and
applied through the peer review process (Post 2012). Although subjective factors play a part in
peer review, the legitimacy of faculty self-governance requires that colleagues apply academic
standards in good faith. In addition, "academic due process" typically provides faculty members
with rights to appeal from negative promotion decisions, as a safeguard against censorship or
retaliation by either their colleagues or the administration (AAUP 2015a: 16, 27). Under AAUP
principles, due process is applicable to investigations of faculty misconduct that may result in
severe sanctions, such as suspension or dismissal (AAUP 2015g: 79–90). Such due process
protections, together with the broad scope of academic freedom, aim to deter administrators
from bringing or sanctioning non-meritorious charges against faculty.

HIGHER EDUCATION AND THE PUBLIC/PRIVATE DISTINCTION: BETWEEN DEMOCRATIC AND CAPITALIST INSTITUTIONS

Higher education stands between the public/democratic and private/capitalist spheres,
belonging wholly to neither but serving both. Yet, the institutional and faculty independence
achieved in the development of the modern university tilted the balance toward the public
democratic sphere. Grounded in academic freedom, university democracy is a seedbed of wider
democratic culture and politics. The latter constitute the core of the universities' public mission.
As Supreme Court Justice Oliver Wendell Holmes stated, "Every idea is an incitement."[3]
Academic freedom to pursue controversial, and even subversive, ideas holds the potential to
inspire – indeed, to incite – students and the public to engage in social change and to infuse the
public sphere with the robust debate that is the lifeblood of a democratic society.

The extension of professional academic norms to faculty in both public and private universities is therefore radical in its departure from the "public/private distinction" that pervades US
ideology and law. The public/private distinction asserts that the public sphere of democratic
politics is inherently different, and separated, from the private sphere of the capitalist market and
workplace. The constitutional doctrine of "state action" embodies the public/private distinction
– or at least the myth of such a distinction – by obligating only the state to respect constitutional
rights, while also denying that the state has any obligation to provide genuine economic
autonomy to individuals (Fineman 2004). Critical theorists, at least as far back as the legal
realists of the 1920s, exposed the myth of the conceptual distinction between public and private,
in light of the law's manifest role in constructing the private market and the modern business
corporation and, conversely, the active intervention of concentrated private power in public
political institutions (Cohen 1927; Hale 1923). Critics have also traced the ideological power of
the public/private distinction, which is invoked to deflect political deviations from the common
law and corporate law rules that underpin the mythical "unregulated" market (Freeman &
Mensch 1987: 247–257; Kennedy 1982; Klare 1982; Shamir 2014: 1–18).

By bridging a democratizing public mission and professional norms of academic freedom,
tenure, due process, and shared governance, higher education institutions bring to life the

[3] *Gitlow v. NY*, 268 US 652 (1925).

theoretical critiques of the public/private distinction. Protections of those norms were unheard of for employees in 1915 and are quite rare outside the faculty's workplace to this day. The strength of those protections, as noted above, lies not just in their contractual enforceability, but also in their long-time acceptance as "extra-legal" academic professional norms. In contrast, most employees in the USA are subject to the common law doctrine of "employment-at-will," which is the legal embodiment of the public/private distinction in the workplace, giving private employers unilateral power to hire and fire for any reason, limited only in recent decades by legislation prohibiting employment discrimination based on defined categories such as race, sex, national origin, age, and disability (Summers 2000). Non-university employees gain protections of free speech, due process, job security, and workplace participation, akin to the protections enjoyed by university faculty, through collective bargaining in unionized workplaces, but the percentage of the national workforce that is unionized has declined steeply since the 1970s (Lieberwitz 2002: 89).

This description of professional academic norms is not intended to be an idealized, romanticized, or nostalgic depiction of the democratic nature of higher education in the USA. Higher education has always been a deeply flawed system. As recounted earlier, trustees and administrators retain final authority over many faculty decisions even if they typically defer to those decisions under the pressure of contractual and extra-legal academic norms. And until the last half century, nearly all universities were open almost exclusively to wealthy white male students taught by white male professors. Even as the academic profession gained academic freedom, tenure, and shared governance, hiring and promotion processes have maintained the disproportionate power of white men in tenure-track and tenured positions. The tenure process remains secretive in most universities, enabling tenured faculty to use seemingly an objective standard – or even explicitly biased standards – to exclude women, people of color, and political mavericks (Fisk 1972; Halewood & Young 2017: 256; Hartman 1989).

Despite their promotion of a wider democratic culture, universities, situated in a capitalist economy, aim to educate students mostly for corporate employment and remain subject to influence by individual donors and corporate funders. Thus, the challenge for democracy in politics and higher education is how not only to retain, expand, and enforce the professional norms of academic freedom, tenure, and shared governance, but also to protect university life from colonization by concentrated economic power outside the university.

The democratic potential of professional academic norms is enhanced where the government supports higher education as a public good. In the post-World War II period, the federal and state governments took actions that significantly expanded access to higher education for a wider range of students. The GI Bill created opportunities for returning members of the armed forces to attend universities, although the benefits went primarily to white male GIs (Kim & Rury 2007: 305, 324). The states expanded the number and size of two-year and four-year public universities in the so-called massification of higher education from 1960 through the mid-1970s, with state and federal funds helping maintain low tuition levels (Gumport et al. 1997: 2–12; Kim & Rury 2007: 302–313). Wendy Brown describes the post-war expansion of public higher education as "importantly articulat[ing] equality as an ideal … [and] the value of an American public educated for the individual and collective capacity for self-governance" (2015: 186–187).

The 1960s marked a period of increased enrollment of students who were working-class, women, and people of color, creating a more diverse student body (Brown 2015: 185–186); Gumport et al. 1997: 4–6; Kim & Rury 2007: 322–325). Coming out of the repressive period of the 1950s, student activists launched the Free Speech Movement; and mass campus protests addressed the urgent political issues of the times, including civil rights, Black Power, women's rights, and resistance to the Vietnam War (Halewood & Young 2017: 253–255; Kim & Rury 2007: 309–310). Students also demanded democratic participation in university decisions over curriculum, academic programs, and transparency and ethical accountability in university research. This activism transformed students and the university, with far reaching influences in the broader society. New academic programs in gender, race, and ethnic studies challenged the status quo of dominant pedagogical methods and content across the curriculum. Students inspired by campus activism pursued careers in social justice, public service, and academia. Thus, a more democratic university enhanced democracy more broadly with knowledge, ideas, and perspectives that informed the electorate in their personal, professional, and political choices (Brown 2015: 188–189).

After World War II, the federal government also expanded public funding for academic research, particularly in science and engineering. After 1960, federal funding constituted about 60 to 70 percent of university research support (AAAS 2018; Lieberwitz 2014: 252), although between 2000 and 2017, federal funding declined from 57 percent to 51 percent (Khan et al. 2020). Federal agencies award grants based on peer review processes. Although a federal agency shapes research agendas through its descriptions of research interests and award of grants, the public-interest ethos of some agencies and the peer review process place constraints on the use of agency power or personal financial interests to skew research grants in an unchecked capitalist, anti-democratic direction (Krimsky 2003: 204–207; Lieberwitz 2005: 118–120).

CORPORATIZATION TRENDS SINCE THE 1980S: IN CONFLICT WITH THE UNIVERSITY'S DEMOCRATIC MISSION AND FACULTY LABOR RIGHTS

Central to the intensification of neoliberalism in the post-Soviet era is the ideological position that capitalism has been proven the best system for creating wealth and addressing individual needs and desires. The 1980s Reagan administration was marked by a drumbeat against "big government" and for privatizing and decreasing public services. Since then, public functions have been privatized at a growing rate, from primary and secondary schools, to prison administration, to rebuilding cities after natural disasters, to firefighting services, to US military functions (Freeman & Minow 2009). While privatization rearranges the relationship between political and economic institutions, the public/private distinction is no less contradictory and incoherent than it was prior to the resurgence of neoliberalism. Even as the state reduces its role in providing for the public welfare, the state increases its role in supporting and subsidizing corporate power and wealth in the private market (Drucker & Tankersley 2019).

At the core of privatization in higher education is the steep decline in public funding, which has a particularly harsh effect on public universities (Mitchell et al. 2019; Newfield 2016). Reversing the 1960s expansion of public funding retreats from the view of higher education as a public good (Brown 2015: 182–183). Public and private universities have raised tuition, which increases the commodification of education and the financial obstacles to middle-class and working-class students, with particularly negative impacts on students of color (Gumport et al. 1997: 22–26; Mitchell et al. 2019: 9–15; Newfield 2016: 278–282). In the competition for student applicants, university administrators have turned to public relations firms to develop the university's "brand" in a way that will appeal to students as "customers" purchasing education as a product (Aldridge 2010; Thacker 2005). At the same time, students are taught the ideological lesson that it is their individual responsibility to pay high tuition fees by taking on debt, extra jobs, or both (Newfield 2016: 190–222). This changes the students' educational experience, as they feel pressured to take an instrumental and "safe" approach by pursuing business or STEM-related majors that will lead to lucrative and reliable employment opportunities in fields such as finance and engineering (Brown 2015: 182–183). The liberal arts have suffered as a result, undermining the democratic function of universities to provide a broad education that expands personal and professional choices, improves the quality of life, and creates a well informed electorate (Brown 2015: 190–191).

Privatization has had major impacts on the faculty. "Corporatization" is pervasive throughout the university, shifting the institutional social role of the university from serving a democratic public mission to serving private economic interests (Lieberwitz 2007; Schrecker 2010; Slaughter & Leslie 1999; Washburn 2005). The "entrepreneurial" university seeks to commercialize teaching and research and to expand university-industry relations. Universities have applied a corporate labor model that is at odds with professional academic norms, strengthening the top-down decision-making power of the administration, while undermining the faculty tenure system. As Andrew Meyer, the chairman of Suffolk University's Board of Trustees has stated, "This is a new chapter in the history of the university. We need people who understand that running an institution of higher education today means running a business" (Carmichael 2011).

Corporatization of Academic Research in the "Entrepreneurial" University

The application of the corporate business model to universities creates a strong incentive to commercialize academic research, and Congress amplified that incentive still further. Prior to 1980, research generated by publicly funding typically became part of the public domain (Eisenberg 1996: 1675–1676). The 1980 Bayh-Dole Act, however, permits and encourages universities and other federal fund recipients to patent and license research resulting from the use of federal funds, including exclusive licenses to for-profit corporations. In response, universities created technology transfer offices to promote the patenting and licensing of their research. In 1979, before the Bayh-Dole Act, US universities obtained 264 patents (Rai & Eisenberg 2003: 53). From 1991 to 2000, the patents granted to US universities increased by 131 percent, and licenses granted by the universities increased by 158 percent (Blumenthal 2003: 2454–2455). Between 1988 and 2003, US patents awarded to academic institutions quadrupled, from about 800 to more than 3,200 per year (Johnston 2007: 162) and by 2016 had more than doubled again (Marcus 2020: 5). Despite the fact that patents and licenses have not been lucrative for most universities, higher education institutions continue to increase their efforts to engage in these commercial activities (Marcus 2020; Valdivia 2013). This seeming contradiction reveals that universities may be motivated not only by profit-seeking, but also by an ideological belief in the market and the benefits of alignments with industry. As Lita Nelson, Director of MIT's technology licensing office observed about "strategic corporate alliances," their greatest significance is in strengthening relationships between businesses and the university (Lawler 2003: 331).

Corporate funding of academic research in public and private universities has also grown, from 2.3 percent of total academic research funds in the early 1970s to almost 8 percent by 2000 (Bok 2003: 12). One estimate is that between 1985 to 2005, corporate funding for university research increased by 250 percent, from $950 million to $2.4 billion (Palomino 2013). Corporate funding levels are difficult to state with accuracy, however, since much of it is not disclosed (McCluskey 2017: 4–5). Corporate funding includes the "strategic corporate alliances" extolled above by MIT's Lita Nelson, through which a for-profit corporation provides large-scale funding to a university program in exchange for the right to exclusively license patents on resulting academic research (AAUP 2014; Lieberwitz 2007: 310–318). Many individual faculty members also have relationships with industry, either through university research contracts or faculty consulting. In 1994, 90 percent of life science companies had some relationship with academia, either through faculty consulting or through corporate support of faculty research (Blumenthal et al. 1996: 371–372; Blumenthal 2002: 379). Corporate funding has also been influential outside of the sciences; for example, the Koch Foundation, funded by family wealth from the profits of energy-sector corporations, has made multi-million dollar donations to public universities to create academic institutes that promote the Foundation's conservative economic philosophy (Levinthal 2015).

Faculty members have also become directly involved in corporate ownership. During the 1980s and 1990s, faculty participated in founding twenty-four Fortune 500 companies and over 600 other companies in the life sciences (Blumenthal 2002: 385). Between 1996 and 2015, universities supported the formation of 11,000 start-up companies (Marcus 2020: 5; Valdivia 2013). A 1992 study found that about one-third of the lead academic authors of 789 articles in leading scientific journals had financial interests in their research, including patents, equity ownerships, or a position on corporate advisory boards or boards of directors (Bekelman 2003: 456; Krimsky et al. 1996: 395).

Commercializing academic research changes the relationship of the university to the public, the relationship of faculty to their research, faculty collegial relationships, and faculty-industry relations. These private market activities create conflicts of interest that take various forms. University patenting and licensing remove academic research from the public domain. Further, these commercial activities shift the university mission from serving professional intellectual norms – and the democratic public sphere encouraged by those norms – to instead serving the private economic interests of universities and for-profit corporations. This is the case whether universities profit from patents and licenses that result from publicly funded or from corporately funded research. In both cases, the profit motive and university-industry relations undermine the university's institutional independence, faculty impartiality in choosing and carrying out a research agenda, and the norms of the academic profession. Academic freedom, research integrity, and public trust in academic research depends on faculty researchers' independence, expressed in the AAUP statements as faculty "disinterestedness" (AAUP 2015b: 7). Studies show that corporately financed researchers are significantly more likely than researchers not funded by the corporation to reach favorable results concerning a corporation's product (AAUP 2014: 88–91; Krimsky 2003: 142–149). Corporations sometimes directly pressure faculty researchers to change research reports to eliminate negative results or not to publish them (AAUP 2014: 60–76). Privatizing academic research undermines academic communal values of sharing research methods and results with colleagues in informal settings and publishing research results in the public domain (Eisenberg 1987: 181–84; Merton 1973; Rai 1999–2000: 88–94). Increased patenting and licensing and closer university-industry relations have led to greater secrecy in research and delays in publishing research results (Kenney 1986: 108–111, 121–131; King & Stabinsky 1999).

The Entrepreneurial University's Corporate Labor Model

University corporatization imports a corporate labor model that expands the ranks of university administrators, while replacing tenure-track positions with non-tenure-track jobs and graduate-student teachers. These changes stratify university teaching, undermine tenure protections for academic freedom, and weaken employment status and standards.

Between the years of 1976 and 2015, the number of full-time university executives and managers grew by 140 percent, while full-time faculty grew by 86 percent (AAUP 2013–2014; Snyder & Hoffman 2002; Snyder et al. 2018). The national percentage of tenure-track/tenured faculty positions has plummeted from 78 percent in 1969 to the current level of 30 percent (AAUP 2016–2017; Benjamin 2010: 4). The proliferation of high-level administrators creates a larger class of managers with an incentive to sustain or increase their power to make unilateral decisions on academic-related matters, overriding or ignoring faculty academic freedom over issues traditionally within the purview of collective faculty governance (Duncan 1999; Gumport et al. 1997: 34–36; Lieberwitz 2007: 301–304; 2002: 96–99).

At the same time, the growth of second-class, non-tenure-track faculty positions breaks the link between academic freedom and the protections of job security. This employment model also has serious gender and racial impacts, as the shrinking percentage of tenure-track lines creates institutional obstacles to hiring and promoting women and people of color into faculty positions with the security of tenure (Benjamin 2010: 6–7; Halewood & Young 2017: 255–256). Non-tenure-track faculty positions range from low-wage teaching on a course-by-course basis to renewable one-year or multi-year contracts (Duncan 1999: 524–528). Such adjunct appointees are usually restricted to either teaching or research, with little or no part in shared governance (AAUP 2013–2014; Coalition for the Academic Workforce 2012). This harms the university's democratic mission, as non-tenure-track faculty members' insecure employment status and substandard working conditions undermine their freedom to voice intellectual views that are unpopular or that threaten the university's corporate connections. Further, the stratification in the labor force sows divisions among the faculty based on tenure status, making it more difficult to organize against incursions on shared governance.

The expanded ranks of low-wage non-tenure-track teachers also directly support universities' commercial ventures in education. Since the 1990s, many universities have created profit-driven, online distance-learning programs, often taught by adjunct instructors. Consisting of either degree-granting or non-credit courses, the programs may be lodged in the university's existing structure, in for-profit subsidiaries of a public or private nonprofit university, or in partnerships with for-profit corporations (Lieberwitz 2002: 104–105). By standardizing the courses, which are often owned by the university, distance learning programs can enable universities to increase the share of student-hours taught by a low-wage non-tenure-track faculty workforce (Lieberwitz 2002: 121–122; Straumsheim 2015).

As one response to universities' weakening of the tenure system and shared governance, faculty have unionized. This has been particularly successful in public universities under state collective bargaining laws. As of 2012, unionization rates were 42 percent of all public two-year college faculty members and 25 percent of faculty in four-year public institutions, but only 7 percent of faculty in private colleges and universities (Sproul et al. 2014: 8). On unionized campuses, shared governance bodies, such as faculty senates, continue to function within the faculty's collectively empowered rights and protections. Collective bargaining has an advantage over non-unionized forms of shared governance, since employers are legally required to bargain in good faith with the union over terms and conditions of employment. The lower percentage of unionization among faculty in private universities is not due to a lack of faculty interest. After the National Labor Relations Board (NLRB) asserted jurisdiction over private non-profit universities in 1970, faculty unionization was on the rise.[4] However, in 1980, the US Supreme Court erected an obstacle to private faculty unionization in its *Yeshiva University* decision, finding that tenure-track and tenured faculty with substantial governance roles are not "employees" under the

---

[4] *National Labor Relations Board v. Yeshiva University*, 444 US 672, 704 (1980) (Brennan, J., dissenting).

National Labor Relations Act (NLRA). In its 5–4 decision, the Court concluded that individual professors' autonomy in deciding academic policies, such as curriculum, teaching methods, and grading, makes them managerial employees without statutory rights to unionize and collectively bargain. The Court, which failed to acknowledge or even use the term "academic freedom," reasoned that the faculty's authority in shared governance is conditioned on the alignment of the faculty's interests with management's.[5] The dissenting opinion highlighted that, to the contrary, academic freedom and professional norms about the substantive quality of research and teaching give faculty the independence from the administration that undergirds shared governance.[6]

In 2014, the NLRB, with a liberal majority appointed by President Obama, interpreted _Yeshiva_ in a decision that takes into account the increasing corporatization of universities.[7] The Board held that the burden is on university employers to prove "managerial" status with evidence that faculty collectively exercise "actual – rather than mere paper – authority" in shared governance.[8] Unionization in private universities remains an uphill battle, though, as university administrations claim that even the growing ranks of non-tenure-track faculty are managerial (Flaherty 2019a).

Like tenure-track/tenured faculty in public universities, graduate student teaching and research assistants (TAs and RAs) have unionized under state collective bargaining laws. This has been a significant development to address their concerns with low wages and benefits, as well as poor working conditions (Herbert & Apkarian 2017: 31–32). In the private sector, TAs and RAs have had a difficult road to unionization, as the NLRB has oscillated on the question whether they are "employees" under the NLRA. In August 2016, the liberal NLRB answered that question in the affirmative.[9] While the conservative NLRB under the Trump administration proposed reversing that position through federal rulemaking processes, the Board ultimately withdrew its proposed rule (Flaherty 2019b; Flaherty 2021).

CONCLUSION: THE CRISIS OF LABOR AND DEMOCRACY IN HIGHER EDUCATION, AND PROSPECTS FOR CHANGE

This chapter has surveyed the deep interconnections among democracy in the wider culture and polity, the labor regime within universities, and concentrated economic powers. The university's public-facing democratic mission is interdependent with a labor model for faculty that is based on democratic professional norms of academic freedom, tenure, due process, and collective shared governance. Without democratic faculty labor rights, the university cannot fulfill its public mission. Conversely, the university's public mission is the foundation for faculty democracy. However, the corporatization of the university is so pervasive that it has severely weakened these relationships. Running the university like a business undermines the democratic character of the university's mission, faculty labor rights, and students' educational access and experiences. This is a crisis in democracy so deep as to be an existential crisis for the institution of higher education, the academic profession, individual faculty members, students, and the wider public.

At this moment in US history, the real costs of the corporatized university are shown in stark relief. In a society in which many of those in power pose a threat to democracy by rejecting the legitimacy of science, freedom of thought, and due process, universities should play a crucial

---

[5] 444 US 672, 689–690.
[6] 444 US 672, 799–700.
[7] Pacific Lutheran University, 361 NLRB 1404, 1422 (2014).
[8] 361 NLRB 1404, 1421.
[9] Columbia University, 364 NLRB No. 90 (2016).

role in providing countervailing information, analysis, and critique that serve the public interest in democratic revitalization.

As dismal as the current state of affairs may seem, it may be hopeful to remember that university faculty organized successfully at the height of industrial power in the early twentieth century to demand academic freedom to fulfill the democratic mission of higher education. Now, as then, it is essential to organize for institutional change in higher education. In the current crisis of democracy, the goals must be broad and inclusive, to demand universities with a public mission and democratic rights for faculty, students, and staff. The goals should include restoration of a labor model of faculty with full rights of academic freedom, tenure, and shared governance, and federal and state funding that enable universities to lower tuition rates, increase class and racial diversity of students and faculty, support publicly funded research for the public domain, and raise the percentage of faculty who are full-time tenured and tenure-track.

A broad vision for universities in the democratic interest requires broad-based tactics. This entails organizing and building alliances among faculty, students, staff, and community members in unions, shared governance bodies, student organizations, and community-based organizations. This is difficult under any conditions, but is particularly difficult in the current political context of extreme privatization and anti-union actions by legislatures, the courts, and federal agencies. However, by joining in campaigns on specific issues of common interest, coalitions among the groups just mentioned can build strength and take meaningful action toward a long-term goal of education in the interest of a democratic culture and government. The unprecedented convergence of a once-in-a-century public-health crisis, an economic depression, mass ferment over systemic racial injustice, and deep hardships in working-class life has created a fluid political environment that may open unforeseen opportunities for social change. Campaigns to revitalize the democratic role of universities should seize those opportunities.

REFERENCES

Aldridge, Susan C. 2010. "Strategy Matters More than Budget in Student Recruiting," *Chronicle of Higher Education* (Oct. 31, 2010).

American Association for the Advancement of Science. 2018. "R&D at Colleges and Universities." www.aaas.org/programs/r-d-budget-and-policy/rd-colleges-and-universities

American Association of University Professors (AAUP). 2013–2014. *The Annual Report on the Economic Status of the Profession, 2013–14.* www.aaup.org/our-work/research/annual-report-economic-status-profession

American Association of University Professors (AAUP). 2014. *AAUP Recommended Principles & Practices to Guide Academic-Industry Relationships.* AAUP Foundation. www.aaup.org/report/recommended-principles-practices-guide-academy-industry-relationships

2015a. "Academic Freedom and Tenure: The University of Illinois at Urbana-Champaign" (April 2015), pp. 1–21. www.aaup.org/report/UIUC

2015b. "1915 Declaration of Principles on Academic Freedom and Academic Tenure," Policy Documents and Reports, 11th *ed.* Baltimore: Johns Hopkins University Press, pp. 3–12.

2015c. "1940 Statement of Principles on Academic Freedom and Tenure with 1970 Interpretive Comments," *Policy Documents and Reports, 11th ed.* Baltimore: Johns Hopkins University Press, pp. 13–19.

2015d. "Committee A Statement on Extramural Utterances," *Policy Documents and Reports, 11th ed.* Baltimore: Johns Hopkins University Press, p. 31.

2015e. "On Collegiality as a Criterion for Faculty Evaluation," *Policy Documents and Reports, 11th ed.* Baltimore: Johns Hopkins University Press, pp. 227–228.

2015f. "On the Relationship of Faculty Governance to Academic Freedom," *Policy Documents and Reports, 11th ed.* Baltimore: Johns Hopkins University Press, pp. 123–125.

2015g. "Recommended Institutional Regulations on Academic Freedom and Tenure," *Policy Documents and Reports, 11th ed*. Baltimore: Johns Hopkins University Press, pp. 79–90.

2015h. "Statement on Collective Bargaining," *Policy Documents and Reports 11th ed*. Baltimore: Johns Hopkins University Press, pp. 323–324.

2015i. "Statement on Government of Colleges and Universities," *Policy Documents and Reports, 11th ed*. Baltimore: Johns Hopkins University Press, pp. 117–122.

2015j. "The Inclusion in Governance of Faculty Members Holding Contingent Appointments," *Policy Documents and Reports 11th ed*. Baltimore: Johns Hopkins University Press, pp. 197–209.

2016–2017. *Visualizing Change: The Annual Report on the Economic Status of the Profession, 2016–17*. www.aaup.org/sites/default/files/FCS_2016-17_nc.pdf

Bekelman, Justin E. Yan Li, and Cary P Gross. 2003. "Scope and Impact of Financial Conflicts of Interest in Biomedical Research," *Journal of the American Medical Association* 289, 4: 454–465.

Benjamin, Ernst. 2010. "The Eroding Foundations of Academic Freedom and Professional Integrity: Implications of the Diminishing Proportion of Tenured Faculty for Organizational Effectiveness in Higher Education," *AAUP Journal of Academic Freedom* 1. www.aaup.org/reports-publications/journal-academic-freedom/volume-1

Bok, Derek. 2003. *Universities in the Marketplace: The Commercialization of Higher Education*. Princeton, NJ: Princeton University Press.

Blumenthal, David. 2002. "Biotech in Northeast Ohio Conference: Conflict of Interest in Biomedical Research," *Health Matrix* 12: 377–392.

2003. "Academic-Industrial Relationships in the Life Sciences," *New England Journal of Medicine* 349: 2452–2459.

Blumenthal, David, Nancyanne Caucino, Eric Campbell, and Karen Seashore Louis. 1996. "Relationships between Academic Institutions and Industry in the Life Sciences – An Industry Survey," *New England Journal of Medicine* 334: 368–374.

Brown, Wendy. 2015. *Undoing the Demos*. Brooklyn: Zone Books.

Byrne, J. Peter. 1989. "Academic Freedom: A 'Special Concern' of the First Amendment," *Yale Law Journal* 99: 251–340.

Carmichael, Mary. 2011. "New Guiding Hands at Suffolk: School Set to Add 12 Trustees with Business Focus," *Boston.com* (Oct. 4, 2011). http://articles.boston.com/2011-10-04/news/30243289_1_board-members-higher-education-pappas-consulting-group

Coalition for the Academic Workforce. 2012. *A Portrait of Part-Time Faculty Members: A Summary of Findings on Part-Time Faculty Respondents to the Coalition on the Academic Workforce Survey of Contingent Faculty Members and Instructors*. www.academicworkforce.org/survey.html

Cohen, Felix. 1927. "Property and Sovereignty," *Cornell Law Quarterly* 13, 1: 8–30.

Drucker, Jesse, and Jim Tankersley. 2019. "How Big Companies Won New Tax Breaks From the Trump Administration," *The New York Times* (Dec. 30, 2019). www.nytimes.com/2019/12/30/business/trump-tax-cuts-beat-gilti.html

Duncan, Jr., John C. 1999. "The Indentured Servants of Academia: The Adjunct Faculty Dilemma and Their Limited Legal Remedies," *Indiana Law Journal* 74: 513–586.

Eisenberg, Rebecca S. 1987. "Proprietary Rights and the Norms of Science in Biotechnology Research," *Yale Law Journal* 97: 177–231.

1996. "Public Research and Private Development: Patents and Technology Transfer in Government-Sponsored Research," *Virginia Law Review* 82: 1663–1727.

Fineman, Martha Albertson. 2004. *The Autonomy Myth*. New York: New Press.

Fisk, Milton. 1972. "Academic Freedom in Class Society," in Edmund L. Pincoffs, ed. *The Concept of Academic Freedom*. Austin: University of Texas Press, pp. 5–26.

Flaherty, Colleen. 2019a. "Uncertainty for Non-Tenure-Track Unions," *Inside Higher Education* (Mar. 14, 2019). www.insidehighered.com/news/2019/03/14/federal-appellate-court-decision-could-make-it-harder-adjuncts-form-unions

2019b. "Ruling Out Grad Unions," *Inside Higher Education* (Sept. 23, 2019). www.insidehighered.com/news/2019/09/23/trump-labor-board-proposes-new-rule-against-grad-unions

2021. "Green Light for Student Employee Unions," *Inside Higher Education* (Mar. 15, 2021). www.insidehighered.com/news/2021/03/15/labor-board-withdraws-planned-rule-against-student-employee-unions

Freeman, Alan, and Elizabeth Mensch. 1987. "The Public-Private Distinction in American Law and Life," *Buffalo Law Review* 36: 237–257.

Freeman, Jody, and Martha Minow, eds. 2009. *Government by Contract: Outsourcing and American Democracy*. Cambridge, MA: Harvard University Press.

Fugate, Rachel E. 1998. "Choppy Waters are Forecast for Academic Free Speech," *Florida State University Law Review* 26: 187–259.

Gerber, Larry G. 2014. *The Rise and Decline of Faculty Governance: Professionalization and the Modern American University*. Baltimore: Johns Hopkins University Press.

Goldin, Claudia, and Lawrence F. Katz. 1999. "The Shaping of Higher Education: The Formative Years in the United States, 1890 to 1940," *The Journal of Economic Perspectives* 13, 1: 37–62.

Gumport, Patricia J., Maria Iannozzi, Susan Shaman, and Robert Zemsky. 1997. "Trends in United States Higher Education from Massification to Post Massification," *National Center for Postsecondary Improvement, School of Education, Stanford University*.

Hale, Robert. 1923. "Coercion and Distribution in a Supposedly Non-Coercive State," *Political Science Quarterly* 38, 3: 470–494.

Halewood, Peter, and Donna Young. 2017. "Rule of Law, Activism, and Equality: Growing Antisubordination Norms within the Neoliberal University," *John Marshall Law Review* 50, 2: 249–270.

Hartman, Chester. 1989. "Uppity and Out: A Case Study in the Politics of Faculty Reappointments (and the Limitations of Grievance Procedures)," in John Trumpbour, ed. *How Harvard Rules*. Boston: South End Press, pp. 287–302.

Herbert, William A., and Jacob Apkarian. 2017. "Everything Passes, Everything Changes: Unionization and Collective Bargaining in Higher Education," *Perspectives on Work*, pp. 30–35.

Hiers, Richard H. 1993. "Academic Freedom in Public Colleges and Universities: O Say, Does that Star-Spangled First Amendment Banner Yet Wave?" *Wayne Law Review* 40: 1–107.

Hirsch, Barry, and David Macpherson. 2017. "Union Membership and Coverage Database from the CPS" [Data from Unionstat]. http://unionstats.gsu.edu/CPS

Hofstadter, Richard, and Walter P. Metzger. 1955. *The Development of Academic Freedom in the United States*. New York: Columbia University Press.

Johnston, Josephine. 2007. "Health Related Academic Technology Transfer: Rethinking Patenting and Licensing Practices," *International Journal of Biotechnology* 9, 2: 156–171.

Khan, Beethika, Carol Robbins, and Abigail Okrent. 2020. "The State of US Science and Engineering 2020," *National Science Foundation* (Jan. 15, 2020). https://ncses.nsf.gov/pubs/nsb20201/u-s-r-d-perform ance-and-funding

Kennedy, Duncan. 1982. "The Stages of the Decline of the Public/Private Distinction," *University of Pennsylvania Law Review* 130: 1349–1357.

Kenney, Martin. 1986. *Biotechnology: The University-Industrial Complex*. New Haven, CT: Yale University Press.

Kim, Dongbin, and John L. Rury. 2007. "The Changing Profile of College Access: The Truman Commission and Enrollment Patterns in the Post-War Era," *History of Education Quarterly* 47, 3: 302–327.

King, Jonathan, and Doreen Stabinsky. 1999. "Patents on Cells, Genes, and Organisms Undermine the Exchange of Scientific Ideas," *Chronicle of Higher Education* (Feb. 5, 1999). www.chronicle.com/article/patents-on-cells-genes-and-organisms-undermine-the-exchange-of-scientific-ideas/

Klare, Karl. 1982. "The Public/Private Distinction in Labor Law," *University of Pennsylvania Law Review* 130: 1358–1422.

Krimsky, Sheldon. 2003. *Science In the Private Interest: Has the Lure of Profits Corrupted Biomedical Research?* Washington DC: Rowman & Littlefield Publishers.

Krimsky, Sheldon, L. S. Rothenberg, P. Stott, and G. Kyle. 1996. "Financial Interests of Authors in Scientific Journals: A Pilot Study of 14 Publications," *Science & Engineering Ethics* 2: 395.

Lawler, Andrew. 2003. "Last of the Big Time Spenders," *Science* 299, 5605: 330–333.

Levinthal, Dave. 2015. "Spreading the Free-Market Gospel," *The Atlantic* (Oct. 20, 2015).

Lieberwitz, Risa L. 1987. "Due Process and the LMRDA: An Analysis of Democratic Rights in the Union and at the Workplace," *Boston College Law Review* 29: 21–64.

2002. "The Corporatization of the University: Distance Learning at the Cost of Academic Freedom?" *Boston University Public Interest Law Journal* 12: 73–135.

2005. "Confronting the Privatization and Commercialization of Academic Research: An Analysis of Social Implications at the Local, National, and Global Levels," *Indiana Journal of Global Legal Studies* 12: 109–152.

2007. "Faculty in the Corporate University: Professional Identity, Law, and Collective Action," *Cornell Journal of Law and Public Policy* 16: 263–330.

2014. "University-Industry Relations in the United States: Serving Private Interests," in James L. Turk, ed. *Academic Freedom in Conflict: The Struggle Over Free Speech Rights In The University*. Toronto: James Lorimer & Company, Ltd., pp. 250–271.

Marcus, Jon. 2020. "Think Universities Are Making Lots of Money from Inventions? Think Again," *The Hechinger Report* (Jan. 17, 2020).https://hechingerreport.org/think-universities-are-making-lots-of-money-from-inventions-think-again/

McCluskey, Molly. 2017. "Public Universities Get an Education in Private Industry," *The Atlantic* (Apr. 3, 2017). www.theatlantic.com/education/archive/2017/04/public-universities-get-an-education-in-private-industry/521379/

Merton, Robert K. 1973. *The Sociology of Science*. Chicago: University of Chicago Press.

Metzger, Walter P. 1964. *Academic Freedom in the Age of the University*. New York: Columbia University Press.

1988. "Profession and Constitution: Two Definitions of Academic Freedom in America," *Texas Law Review* 66: 1265–1322.

Mitchell, Michael, Michael Leachman, and Matt Saenz. 2019. "State Higher Education Funding Cuts Have Pushed Costs to Students, Worsened Inequality," *Center on Budget and Policy Priorities* (Oct. 24, 2019). www.cbpp.org/research/state-budget-and-tax/state-higher-education-funding-cuts-have-pushed-costs-to-students

Newfield, Christopher. 2016. *The Great Mistake*. Baltimore: Johns Hopkins University Press.

Olivas, Michael A. 2003. "The Rise of Non-Legal Legal Influences Upon Higher Education." www.ilr.cornell.edu/depts/cheri

Palomino, Joachin. 2013. "Billions of Corporate Dollars are Hijacking University Research to Help Make Profits," *Alternet* (Apr. 22, 2013). www.alternet.org/2013/04/billions-corporate-dollars-are-hijacking-university-research-help-make-profits

Post, Robert C. 2012. *Democracy, Expertise, and Academic Freedom: A First Amendment Jurisprudence for the Modern State*. New Haven, CT: Yale University Press.

Rai, Arti Kaur. 1999-2000. "Regulating Scientific Research: Intellectual Property Rights and the Norms of Science," *Northwestern University Law Review* 94: 77–152.

Rai, Arti K., and Rebecca S. Eisenberg. 2003. "Bayh-Dole Reform and the Progress of Biomedicine," *American Scientist* 91, 1: 52–59.

Schrecker, Ellen. 1983. "Academic Freedom: The Historical View, in Regulating the Intellectuals," in Craig Kaplan and Ellen Schrecker, eds. *Regulating the Intellectuals: Perspectives on Academic Freedoms in the 1980s*. New York: Praeger, pp. 25–43.

1986. *No Ivory Tower: McCarthyism and the Universities*. New York: Oxford University Press.

2010. *The Lost Soul of Higher Education: Corporatization, the Assault on Academic Freedom, and the End of the American University*. New York: New Press.

Shamir, Hila. 2014. "The Public/Private Distinction Now: The Challenges of Privatization and of the Regulatory State," *Theoretical Inquiries in Law* 15, 1: 1–26.

Slaughter, Sheila, and Larry L. Leslie. 1999. *Academic Capitalism: Politics, Policies, and the Entrepreneurial University*. Baltimore: Johns Hopkins University Press.

Snyder, Thomas D., and Charlene M. Hoffman. 2002. *Digest of Education Statistics 2001. table 224*. National Center for Education Statistics.

Snyder, Thomas D., Cristobal de Brey, and Sally A. Dillow. 2018. *Digest of Education Statistics, 52nd Ed. 2016. tables 314.20, 314.30*. National Center for Education Statistics.

Sproul, Curtis R., Neil Bucklew, and Jeffery D. Houghton. 2014. "Academic Collective Bargaining: Patterns and Trends," *Journal of Collective Bargaining in the Academy* 6, 1: 1–10.

Straumsheim, Carl. 2015. "Supporting Online Adjuncts," *Inside Higher Education* (Nov. 12. 2015). www
.insidehighered.com/news/2015/11/12/study-explores-hiring-and-managing-practices-online-adjunct-fac
ulty-members

Summers, Clyde W. 2000. "Employment at Will in the United States: The Divine Right of Employers,"
University of Pennsylvania Journal of Labor & Employment Law 3, 1: 65–86.

Thacker, Lloyd. 2005. "Confronting the Commercialization of Admissions," *Chronicle of Higher Education*
(Feb. 25, 2015). www.chronicle.com/article/confronting-the-commercialization-of-admissions/

Tiede, Hans-Joerg. 2014. "'To Make Collective Action Possible': The Founding of the AAUP," *AAUP
Journal of Academic Freedom* 5: 1–29.

2015. *University Reform: The Founding of the American Association of University Professors.* Baltimore:
Johns Hopkins University Press.

Tuchman, Gaye. 2009. *Wannabe U: Inside the Corporate University.* Chicago: University of Chicago Press.

Valdivia, Walter D. 2013. "University Start-Ups: Critical for Improving Technology Transfer," *The
Brookings Institute* (Nov. 2013). www.brookings.edu/wp-content/uploads/2016/06/Valdivia_Tech-
Transfer_v29_No-Embargo.pdf

Washburn, Jennifer. 2005. *University Inc.: The Corruption of Higher Education.* New York: Basic Books.

21

The Fissured Welfare State

Care Work, Democracy, and Public-Private Governance

Gabriel Winant

INTRODUCTION

How did it come to pass that so many American workers do not fall within the protections and economic security of the regulated employment relationship established and elaborated under the New Deal state? Recent accounts of this phenomenon trace it to the legal innovations of employers in the late twentieth and early twenty-first centuries. The rise of the "fissured workplace" or the "gig economy" gets the blame in this account of destabilized employment (Kalleberg 2009; Rosenblat 2018; Weil 2014). Here the category of analysis is corporate organizational structure: subcontracting, franchising, and misclassification loom as the major culprits. In a distinct but related account, one might point to the employer offensive against unions of the 1970s and 1980s (which weakened collective bargaining fatally), the corporate defeat of labor law reform in the political conflict of the late 1970s, and critical strikes such as those at Phelps-Dodge, Hormel, and, of course, in air traffic control (McCartin 2011; Rachleff 1993; Rosenblum 1995; Windham 2017).

These accounts have the strength of pointing to specific institutional changes with immediate consequences for workers' collective power and voice. It is possible to arrive from these diagnoses at prescriptions for reform: joint-employer rules to hold companies accountable for the employment practices of their franchisees, subsidiaries, and suppliers; rethinking antitrust law to support the organization of misclassified and subcontracted workers and disempowered small businesses; legislative reclassification of workers, as California recently attempted; enabling unionization by means of card-signing rather than government-supervised elections, or speedier election processes; strengthened enforcement against unfair labor practices; treatment of labor rights as civil rights enforceable through judicial actions; more workers' power to determine bargaining units; restriction of the use of permanent replacements of strikers; and sectoral bargaining (Andrias 2019; Dubal 2017; Friedman et al. 1994; Kahlenberg & Marvit 2013; Morris 2005; Paul 2016). All these ideas and more have come to the fore in response to the emerging diagnosis of America's broken labor relations system in the last thirty years or so, which attributes the problem to the breakdown of the New Deal system. In its practical fruitfulness, this line of inquiry has proven itself already to some degree: reforms that emerge from this analysis now dot the programs of Democratic presidential contenders and form part of the PRO Act, passed by the House of Representatives in two subsequent Congresses.[1]

---

[1] *Protecting the right to organize (PRO) Act* of 2019, HR 2474, 116th Cong.

Yet for all the practical usefulness of this institutionalist approach – which recommends it enormously – it contains a theory of the origin of labor market inequality that deserves more scrutiny. It seems to suggest that the problem in labor relations is primarily political and legal – that it derives from political choices caused by the triumph of conservatives, and could be rolled back and fixed by political choices of empowered progressives. Understandably, a practical, reformist method tends somewhat to exclude sociological and economic explanations of trans-formations in employment. If the reasons for the degradation of work are deeper than changing jurisprudence or corporate structure, after all, then they are also less amenable to reform in any proximate way. Then we would need to ask whether the issue is not the convolutions of labor relations, but the tectonics of social relations. After all, even unionized workers in the low-wage service economy lag far behind unionized industrial workers in previous generations. While there is no question that there exists a margin for immediate improvement in the quality of "new economy" jobs, it is far from clear that "bad jobs" can be made "good" through a limited set of regulatory changes rather than wholesale reconstruction of social institutions (Boris & Klein 2012; Budig et al. 2019; Carré & Tilly 2017).

This chapter queries an underlying matter: the social division of labor. Labor markets have changed not only in their organizational structure and institutional governance, but also in the composition of employment by sector – especially important in a context of intense economic sectoral unevenness. That is, beyond the additional power accruing to the employer thanks to legal and organizational innovations, there is also a political and economic effect that derives from profound transformation in the mix of tasks for which employers hire labor – a transform-ation that has brought sweeping changes to the experience of employment, the prospects for workers' power, and thereby the functioning of democracy itself. The origins of this transform-ation lie deeper than those identified by the labor law reformers, and they pose more difficult dilemmas. Resolving the problems that arise from the changing social division of labor would point not just toward labor law reform – important but insufficient – but toward larger-scale reinvention and deepening of democracy.

While discrete supply chains have increasingly fissured and misclassified workforces – separating employees from profits through reorganized corporations and reconfigured legal practice – employ-ment as a whole has undergone polarization and dualization: the sorting of workers into high and low poles of the labor market by "skill," and the separation of those poles increasingly not only into distinct firms (for example, a hospital chain) or even industries (hospitals in general) but to a large degree distinct economic sectors (healthcare as a whole) – or even whole areas or supersectors of the economy: here we may think of the so-called care economy, where services are provided for the creation and maintenance of human capacities, including care for the young, old, sick, and disabled, encompassing education, healthcare, and related industries; housekeeping; food service; and domestic work (Autor et al. 2006; Hartwig 2015; Nordhaus 2008; Storm 2018; Temin 2017).

Social science on labor market dualism often assumes that "outsiders" are consigned to "atypical" employment – indeed that this is what defines "outsider" status (Emmenegger et al. 2012). But there exists a vast growing workforce in the United States of low-wage, marginalized employees whose employment seals them at the bottom of the economic order for reasons not captured by the categories of "normal" and "atypical": an individual worker might circulate, for example, between nursing assistant work at a hospital or nursing home (fairly normal employ-ment, although it has not always been) and home care (still more informalized) while remaining economically marginal throughout. This is due to the low-productivity effect that shapes job growth in post-industrial economies. The resulting dilemma for a growing mass of low-wage workers is that, to increase income and improve working conditions, it is not enough simply to confront their employer – regardless of whether the law aids or hinders that confrontation, or finds them in formalized or informal employment. Such questions affect workers' power, but do not determine the whole of it.

It is true that the provision of low-productivity services is shaped fundamentally by state institutions. Policymakers effectively set service workers' wages as they attempt to manage the various aspects of the post-industrial economy. But the underlying tensions framing this choice cannot be resolved through labor market policy alone.

First, there is the labor market policy "trilemma" between unemployment, wages, and fiscal discipline. If productivity in service-sector jobs is low, then either wages will be low as well; or labor market regulation will drive up wages but also increase unemployment; or the state may socialize more of the service sector, increasing wages and employment through expansive public expenditure. To increase their own wages and improve their own working conditions, workers on the losing end of this new division of labor must find some way to wield social power on a larger basis – some ground on which they may stand with a group of people sharing common interests beyond themselves – to achieve this last outcome (Boris & Klein 2012; Iversen & Wren 1998; Lopez 2004; McAlevey 2016; Rosenfeld 2014).

Second, the experience of employment in the care economy, construed broadly, is intrinsically linked to the experience of being a client of social services for the citizenry. The terms of social citizenship – the quality of entitlements for welfare state "insiders" – set the terms of work for the outsiders. This relationship obtains because of the labor-intensive quality of service work: each increment of increase in extent or intensity of social services is largely an increment of increase in a wage bill.

Labor that is socially useful without contributing much directly to capital accumulation constitutes a peculiar category, where solidarity is possible but economic leverage is weak. While a gap exists in workplaces everywhere between the value of work and the wages that workers draw (the basic essence of exploitation), there is a vastly disproportionate exploitative phenomenon that clusters in one huge, growing area of economic activity: the care economy. The mechanism that social scientists call "the care penalty" is widely attested empirically, and deeply related to the polarization of the labor market overall (England et al. 2002). As sociologist Rachel Dwyer has shown, the care economy accounted for 56 percent of job growth in the bottom quintile of the structure in the 1980s, 62 percent in the 1990s, and 74 percent in the 2000s. Approximately one-quarter of all jobs in the USA are now in the supersector designated by the Census as "educational services and healthcare and social assistance" (Dwyer 2013). As the industries that compose the care economy have grown, they have not – contrary to common assumptions – been increasingly integrated into a gender- or race-blind common labor market; they retain their ghettoized features (Duffy 2011).

Low-wage job growth is most concentrated, in other words, in highly polarized economic activities where, although the institutional factors of misclassification, subcontracting, and anti-unionism often are in play, the forces holding down wages and driving exploitation for the lower-ranking occupations are older and deeper. They are to some degree built into the very nature of the human-service labor process in capitalism. In any case, they have been encoded long since in a set of institutions that well predate the current legal environment (Cobble 1996: 340–341).

HISTORICAL ORIGINS OF THE CARE PENALTY

The gendered and racialized valuation of economic activity is very old, and a continuous genealogy connects the degradation of service work to older forms of servitude within the institutions of marriage and slavery (Glenn 1992). While tasks had long been divided between men and women in the world of small-scale agricultural and handicraft production, the nineteenth century saw an evolution, as Jeanne Boydston puts it, from a "gendered division of labor" to a "gendered definition of labor" (Boydston 1990: 55). Women's work within the domestic sphere, once socially differentiated and subordinate but part of the socially recognized division of labor, increasingly became illegible as productive of value – instead dissolving into the decommodified sphere of intimate life. With this development emerged what we have come to know as "private life," which rested upon the sanctified domestic sphere's separation from the world of commerce (Coontz 1988: 161–329).

This configuration was always a bourgeois norm and failed to represent or dictate social reality for the working class. Women's waged work remained common throughout the nineteenth century, particularly in the forms of domestic work, laundry, sex work, and light, labor-intensive industrial production – brooms, textiles, garments, cigars, shoes, and so on (Blewett 1988; Boris 1994; Dublin 1979; Glenn 1990; Hunter 1997; Kessler-Harris 2001: 20–179; Rosen 1982). As working-class economic and political organization advanced in the late nineteenth and early twentieth centuries, however, and middle-class reformers grew more concerned with social stability, ideas about the need to "protect" women from various types of wage work grew stronger, and the male breadwinner ethos increasingly became ideological common sense. With the transition to mass production and the rise of internal labor markets in the first decades of the twentieth century, the family wage norm grew stronger still, although working-class households still often lacked sufficient or steady enough income to achieve it (Greenwald 1989; Kessler-Harris 2001: 180–214; May 1985; Woloch 2015).

It was only with the New Deal's ascendancy in the 1930s and 1940s that the breadwinner-housewife dyad became fully established as something approaching a general form of working-class intimate social organization (Kessler-Harris 2001). While the rising industrial union movement, welfare state, and wartime mobilization threatened in their most expansive versions to overspill and transform this inherited constraint, the conservative reaction of the late 1940s and 1950s forestalled any such possibility. Antiracist and feminist activists in labor and the state were largely purged, and a range of social policies to entrench the male-headed heterosexual nuclear family model resulted, synthesized with the labor movement and Keynesian state (Boris & Michel 2001; Canaday 2009: 137–254; Johnson 2004; Korstad & Lichtenstein 1988; McEnaney 2014; Milkman 1987; Stoltzfus 2003; Storrs 2013).

While background conditions long predated the 1940s, it was the political transformation of the 1940s that created the specific institutional context for the marginalized care economy: the simultaneous solidification and increasing conservatism of the New Deal state locked in the subordination of care work. First, as the advance of the labor movement slowed, collective bargaining calcified, ceasing to function as the vehicle of large-scale political transformation and instead becoming an unevenly available point of access to economic security for a working class whose divisions now became increasingly institutionalized (Cutler 2004; Lichtenstein 1995: 271–298). Increasingly politically isolated, unions gradually shed their more universalistic political ambitions – for peacetime price controls, for example, and a national health plan (Derickson 1994; Jacobs 2005; 221–261). They instead pursued the parochial economic interests of their members, becoming a pillar in a pluralistic coalition rather than the agents of a historical mission (Davis 1986; Lichtenstein 1989). Together with employers, incentivized by tax policy to substitute benefits for wages, organized labor constructed around itself a privatized monetary policy regime, with cost-of-living adjustments shielding members from the inflation that post-war Keynesianism inflicted on the unorganized sectors of the economy; and a privatized welfare

state, delivering the economic security to the industrial working class that the New Deal had
failed to win for all (Klein 2003; Stapleford 2009: 253–295).

In the late 1940s, unions began to extend contract negotiations to health and retirement
benefits, gains soon upheld in federal court as mandatory subjects of bargaining. Over the course
of the 1950s, with ambitions for universal healthcare now clearly in the rearview, the labor
movement constructed its huge private islands of health security. The United Steelworkers, for
example, enrolled all their members and their dependents covered by the basic steel master
contract in Blue Cross of Western Pennsylvania, constituting them into a massive single
actuarial pool with tremendous buying power in the healthcare market. The 1959 steel industry
contract directly affected 5 to 6 percent of all Blue Cross group enrollment nationwide ("Blue
Cross Enrollment Affected by Steel," 1959). As industrial workers won these kinds of gains,
hospitals in the areas where they were concentrated expanded to service this new market.
Utilization rose, and the health system grew. By the 1970s, well-covered, high-utilizing industrial
workers and their dependents constituted an enormous segment of healthcare recipients in
Northern urban areas (Paul-Shaheen & Carpenter 1982; Winant 2019).

The post-war welfare state was divided, uneven, and partially privatized –with private benefits
stimulating large secondary industries to service them, and publicly provided, lower-quality
services. This regime had a clear inside and outside. Insiders were the subjects of collective
bargaining, the largely (though not exclusively) white and overwhelmingly male workforce in
the areas of the economy involved in the mass production, maintenance, and distribution of
manufactured goods. Outsiders, on the other hand, who did not enjoy the security that flowed
through collective bargaining, were also largely relegated to second-tier social benefits. They
were generally compelled either to attach themselves by marriage or another dependency
relationship to an insider, or to organize collective social life in non-normative fashion –
frequently under penalty of stigmas associated with patriarchy, white supremacy, and
heteronormativity.

Yet the inside and outside were not divided into separate, parallel tracks – they were linked
and interwoven. The outsiders, in a variety of capacities, served the insiders: wives reproduced
the household and family; service workers brought about social reproduction on a larger scale, in
schools, hospitals, public employment, and domestic work. The late 1940s also strengthened the
categorization of these kinds of labor as outsider tasks, second-class quasi-labor: efforts to include
women's unwaged work in national income accounts were defeated, while feminists were
purged from the administrative state, social policy was rewritten to enforce single-breadwinner
heterosexual households, and women were pushed out of union jobs (Canaday 2009: 137–254;
Kessler-Harris 2001: 170–202; Milkman 1987: 99–160; Storrs 2013). Hospitals, reclassified by
Congress as outside the scope of commerce, became exempted from the National Labor
Relations Act – joining domestic and agricultural employment in this shadow zone
("Exemption of non-profit hospital employees," 1971). As historian Joseph Slater observes,
meanwhile, a "wave of statutes passed across the country barring public sector strikes" (2017:
169). All told, the solidification of the New Deal in its moderate post-war phase accompanied the
intensification of the precarity of care work.

These two phenomena – the solidification of the welfare state for some, exclusion for others –
were connected. The security that working-class insiders – steelworkers, auto workers, and so
on – enjoyed derived not just from the social benefits they accessed, but the labor that those
benefits procured for them. "Security," the key ideological term of this moment in welfare state
history, is something of an abstraction. In concrete form, security was not just money (as in, say,
unemployment insurance) but also labor – that is, care: the ability to organize a household

around decommodified domestic labor; the attention of nurses and caretakers in health settings accessed through private insurance and retirement benefits; the public school system for children in a country where secondary education became, for the first time, universal (thanks to the New Deal's decommodification of childhood).

We might draw a helpful analogy here to debates surrounding economic development in the Global South. Where mainstream economists and modernization theorists viewed the relative impoverishment of Latin America as a result of backwardness, dependency theorists argued that the real cause was exploitative terms of exchange with the Global North. The Third World, in this view, was created to serve the First, and its underdevelopment was an ongoing structural effect rather than a premodern holdover (Amin 1974). Similarly, the position of feminized and racially-marginalized labor in post-war American society was not simply an inherited legacy but rather a continuous path dependency – drawing on longer historical roots but generated anew for that moment, to meet a set of demands induced by the New Deal state to serve its core constituency.

INDUSTRIAL DECLINE AND THE CRISIS OF THE WELFARE STATE

The New Deal state's first two decades built up a system to provide security for the working class unevenly, mobilizing the excluded fractions both to depend upon and to care for the privileged groups. As a general rule, the distinction could be found in access to industrial employment, collective bargaining, and the private welfare state that prevailed in the organized sectors of the economy. Those who had access to employment there were secured by it, at least relatively; those who lacked it had to attach themselves to those who had it in relationships of economic and social dependency, and to provide care to those on whom they depended. It was a divided and uneven system, but it had a nucleus. What happened to this regime, then, when its socioeconomic center – industrial production – began to erode?

Deindustrialization was not an event, but a process. As soon as the interwar period, many American industries had shown signs of maturity and stagnation, from which the wars and social interventions between the 1930s and 1950s – and the ensuing bump in effective demand – had provided temporary relief. But a string of recessions in the 1950s and early 1960s suggested the challenge for American manufacturing in peacetime. As economic exclusion appeared on the margins of the industrial core of the economy initially, onlookers first interpreted the phenomenon as a residue of the past rather than an omen of the future. The social programs of the 1960s are best understood in this light: Medicare and Medicaid, for example, were extending the security of the New Deal to those whom it had not reached yet and making good, for all retirees, on the principle of seniority enshrined by internal labor markets and unionization. In retrospect, however, we can see that the early phases of deindustrialization caused the growth of surplus populations outside of the track of the private welfare state: the "other America" was not, as many assumed in the early 1960s, only a residual phenomenon – but equally an emergent one (Harrington 1962; Katznelson 1989; Offner 2019; Sugrue 1996). In the case of healthcare, the advent of collectively bargained insurance in the 1940s contributed to massive capacity expansion and price increases in the healthcare industry in the 1950s, pricing out of the market those not part of a powerful organized patient-consumer bloc – such as retirees and the unemployed. This was the structural source of the pressure to pass Medicare and Medicaid (Cohen et al. 2015; Marmor 1970: 14–38; Stevens & Stevens 1974).

Already in the late 1950s, in other words, signs of trouble had begun to appear. There was rising industrial conflict, as seen in a major employer offensive and a series of massive strikes in core industries. Simultaneously, there developed increasing consciousness of poverty in discrete pockets of American social geography. The impoverished hollows of Appalachia and the new ghettoes of the urban North were not yet understood to exist in any clear relation to a secular socioeconomic change underway. But in retrospect we can recognize them as forerunners of the more familiar crisis of the 1970s and 1980s. The "other America" and "urban crisis" of the 1960s became the blue-collar blues of the 1970s, then the all-out manufacturing collapse of the 1980s. Industrial job loss evolved, widening from a problem of the stigmatized urban black and rural white populations into a full-scale macroeconomic and social crisis: factory closures, mass layoffs, mass incarceration, financialization, and political realignment (Brenner 2006).

As this process unfolded, the systems of economic security in place for welfare state insiders came under increasing pressure (Iversen & Cusack 2000; Wren 2013). Industrial job loss left in its wake populations that were demographically older: seniority-based labor markets translated economic disturbance into a generational bias against the young in the pattern of employment, causing high rates of youthful outmigration. It left populations that were poorer, as income was lost and not replaced, with cascading negative effects for the level of business locally and the fiscal capacity of local government. And it left populations that were sicker, because they were both older and poorer. Through the 1960s and 1970s, health utilization among industrial workers and their dependents soared. They formed an aging group, as the cohort that entered the workforce at the high-point of industrial employment (1945–1955) got older and was not fully replaced. As factory work contracted, economic instability ate away at the edges of working-class communities. But these increasingly economically stressed populations enjoyed a quite secure and large, but earmarked, stream of income – it could only be spent in one way. Declining industrial centers developed increasingly gigantic healthcare markets (Paul-Shaheen & Carpenter 1982; Winant 2019). Economic stress thus became more and more medicalized, as it could translate into a form of heavily subsidized consumption if it could present as a medical symptom.

In these conditions, however, each access point to first-tier, private social benefits had to stretch to secure a larger group of people and a set of more acute needs, as the percentage of industrial workers in the working-class population diminished. As the public sector welfare state came under the pressure of deepening fiscal crisis in the 1970s, then monetary tightening and political austerity in the early 1980s, health insurance benefits – both public and private – proved to be the most durable. This was owed in part to their legal and institutional structure, and in part to the tremendous political power exerted on behalf of the cohort of aging industrial workers and retirees. Private-sector health benefits negotiated in collective bargaining proved untouchable in many cases through the 1980s, with the government stepping in to compel ongoing insurance coverage. After declaring bankruptcy in July 1986, for example, LTV Steel terminated retiree health coverage. Under pressure from the militancy of retirees and remaining workers and the elected representatives from Pennsylvania and Ohio, however, the company quickly reversed itself and extended benefits for six months. In 1987, the federal government assumed responsibility for LTV's liabilities. Then in 1988, the Retiree Benefits Protection Act passed Congress, strengthening the rights of retirees in the event of employer bankruptcy (Hartzell 1988; *Retiree Health Benefits* 1987; Torassa 1988). In the public sector, too, Medicare proved remarkably resilient against the turn to welfare state austerity through the 1970s and 1980s – even though it remained a second-class program of health insurance provision (Schwartz & Mendelson 1991). The veterans' welfare state, protecting the most normative heroic breadwinners, ran against the current as well, becoming increasingly entrenched as welfare state liberalism was in retreat across the board (Mittelstadt 2015). Even Medicaid, the poor sibling of the public healthcare programs, expanded its budgetary footprint by almost half from 1981 to 1988; in contrast, other poverty programs, such as food stamps, shrank outright over this period (Marmor et al. 1992: 41).

The result was the countercyclical behavior of the healthcare industry. As working-class buying power drained from the rest of the economy, it pooled up in healthcare markets. Capital fled factories in the late 1970s and early 1980s, but it poured into hospitals, for which the environment of monetary tightening after 1979 proved a boon, given that the economic downturn did not diminish healthcare utilization at all but increased demand for hospital bonds (Cohodes & Kinkead 1984). While the Sun Belt and huge areas of rural America were economic beneficiaries of right-wing Keynesian intervention against deindustrialization in the form of military procurement and prison construction, in the urban centers the most significant form of fiscal stabilization flowed through the channel of health insurance, secure compared to the turbulence all around, thanks to its anchoring in first-tier social citizenship (Gilmore 1999, 2007). For example, an Urban Institute study found that while public spending in Allegheny County, Pennsylvania (home of Pittsburgh) fell 4 percent just from 1982 to 1983, healthcare played the most significant role cushioning the fall. "The decline in government spending . . . in Allegheny County would have been much sharper had it not been for the growth in spending for the federal Medicare program. If Medicare is excluded, government spending in Allegheny County in these program areas dropped 8 percent" (Musselwhite et al. 1985: 17). A 1985 study of the Monongahela Valley, the depressed steel making district outside Pittsburgh, found that $123 million in income flowed into the area in 1985 alone from the US Steel retiree benefits program. "If those payments had not been there, the distress in the Mon Valley would have been infinitely worse than what it is now," reflected Lefty Palm, the Steelworkers' regional director (Montgomery & Davis 1990; "Researchers Examine Steelworkers' Benefits," 1985). As a whole, the region's hospitals saw their margins improve in the early 1980s, exactly when the economy around them collapsed (Health Policy Institute 1984).

Hospitals, nursing homes, and home care agencies boomed in the final three decades of the twentieth century, fed by this backdoor countercyclical effect. As they did so, they hired people – in particular the newly available labor pool of women entering the workforce as men lost manufacturing jobs (Winant 2019). The construction of the care economy thus happened as an event *internal* to the post-war welfare state: the new areas of employment were institutionally keyed to the service of the welfare state insiders, while structurally consigned to second-tier outsider status themselves. While large areas of care work finally became regulated through the FLSA, NLRA, and state-level public sector labor law over the course of the 1960s and 1970s, this was far too little and too late to yield a fundamental change in the nature of employment in the industry. As the next section explores, care labor was already locked into an institutionally-subordinate structural position: unionization faced increasingly hostile management, but even where it was achieved, the possibilities for economic leverage were limited. As sociologist Gøsta Esping-Andersen puts it, "'Postindustrial' transformation is institutionally path-dependent. This means that existing institutional arrangements heavily determine, maybe even overdetermine, national trajectories. More concretely, the divergent kinds of welfare regimes that nations built over the post-war decades, have a lasting and overpowering effect on which kind of adaptation strategies can and will be pursued" (Esping-Andersen 1999: 4).

THE CONSEQUENCES OF FRAGMENTATION AND THE POLITICS OF CARE

The dilemma that resulted for care work from this history is not hard to describe – it can be summed up in a single question: who does the care worker work for? It has proven quite challenging to reach a social consensus on the answer to this question, due to the presence of layers of organizations – often private-sector – mediating between social demand for care and social supply of care. For example, in the infamous decision in *Harris* v. *Quinn*, Justice Samuel Alito puzzlingly described home care workers as "partial-public" and "quasi-public" employees. "While customers exercise predominant control over their employment relationship with personal assistants, the State, subsidized by the federal Medicaid program, pays the personal assistants' salaries," writes Alito.

> Other than providing compensation, the State's role is comparatively small. The State sets some basic threshold qualifications for employment. (For example, a personal assistant must have a Social Security number, must possess basic communication skills, and must complete an employment agreement with the customer.) The State mandates an annual performance review *by the customer, helps the customer* conduct that review, and mediates disagreements between customers and their personal assistants. The State suggests certain duties that personal assistants should assume, such as performing "household tasks," "shopping," providing "personal care," performing "incidental healthcare tasks," and "monitoring to ensure the health and safety of the customer." (citation deleted) In addition, a state employee must "identify the appropriate level of service provider" *"based on the customer's approval of the initial Service Plan"* (emphasis added) and must sign each customer's Service Plan. (2014: 2–4, added emphasis in original)

The court's majority saw in the three-way relationship between the state, the client, and the worker a formal structure very similar to that connecting a firm, a subcontractor, and workers – say a building manager, a building services corporation, and custodians; or between Uber, a passenger, and a driver; or between McDonald's, a franchisee, and the workers in a given franchise store.

While home care points to this dilemma in very obvious ways, it extends throughout the care economy. As the previous section discussed, the hospital and nursing home industries too were shaped historically by a high degree of organizational fragmentation, which developed from the direct and indirect effects of private-sector collective bargaining in the post-war period. Institutional providers are typically organizationally separated from the insurer. This separation is another version of fissuring: the relationship between the worker, the hospital, or nursing home, and the regulators and payors that set the levels of staffing, the reimbursement rates from insurers that shape wages, the accreditation and safety regulations that determine working conditions – to together these are the way that the payor, the regulator, and especially the public when it functions in both these capacities, are in effect the franchisors of the provider institution (Campbell & Morgan 2011). Through Medicare and Medicaid reimbursement policy, federal and state government fix prices for a huge portion of health provider activities, while setting standards for the private market. Dependent on reimbursement, provider institutions functionally require public certification to operate. If disfavored by quality certification processes, institutions have little recourse: they have no right to turn to the courts until they have exhausted administrative channels of appeal while incurring the costs of remedy.[2] States may leverage reimbursement to regulate employment even more directly: nursing homes in Illinois, for example, are required to make a quarterly submission of detailed Medicaid payroll information to the state, with the state and federal government both budgeting additional revenue for staffing 2.5 person-hours per Medicaid patient per day, and threatening noncompliant institutions with fines ("Understaffed Nursing Homes Face Hefty Fines under Newly Passed Illinois Legislation," *The Chicago Tribune*, June 4, 2019).

---

[2] *Shalala* v. *Illinois Council on Long Term Care*, 529 US 1 (2000).

Collective bargaining in these industries is carried out with the franchisee – the administration of the provider institution. The determinants of the conditions of work, while fundamentally politically conditioned, are not easily within reach of workers. This fissured structure shapes working conditions *regardless of the presence of collective bargaining*, although collective bargaining mitigates some harm to workers. This problem emerged, however, as soon as hospitals became covered under the NLRA in 1974. At a 1975 symposium organized by the American Hospital Association with representatives from labor, government, and hospital management, this question became a central area of discussion. "There are all sorts of cost control and cost commission and rate review commission people who, whether visible or invisible, sit there with management. On the other side are union representatives, so the maneuvering room for a voluntary hospital is very limited," commented one administrator (American Hospital Association 1976: 10). Another administrator, from a New York hospital, complained that collective bargaining was "all a game staged for the public, and the governor and the mayor produced the plays. All the noise, the squabbling, the reported drama of negotiating sessions had nothing to do with what was really going on in a room three floors above us. That's where the governor's money man was sitting with the pocketbook" (American Hospital Association 1976: 46). From labor's side too, it immediately appeared as a dilemma. "It can be very frustrating to negotiate with management and realize what they are offering you is contingent on funding from another source, whether it be legislature or whether it be a third party. It is an out for management. In fact, when we negotiate contracts, management says, 'We would like to give it to you but it depends on the legislature'" (American Hospital Association 1976: 47).

Bargaining in healthcare is thus irretrievably politicized, because the industry is so heavily regulated and subsidized by the public sector that produced it – despite being mainly privately administered. But unlike the public sector proper, it is governed in indirect fashion. Workers do not face the real power – the state – directly in industrial relations. Moreover, attempts to transcend this pattern of industrial relations and bargain through the political process encounter the fierce political opposition of the intermediating franchisee layer: for example, when the Massachusetts Nurses Association tried to win a ballot initiative to raise hospital staffing levels in 2018, it was crushed by an enormous opposition campaign from the state hospital association (Brooks 2018).

While this pattern is highly pronounced and significant in healthcare and home care, it exists in other areas of the care economy as well. Childcare, for example, has worked in broadly similar ways to elder care and healthcare, considered from the perspective of employment. The possibility of broad social responsibility for childcare similarly emerged, and similarly was quashed, in the 1940s and again in the 1970s (Stoltzfus 2003; Swinth 2018). Here, too, responsibility for care subsequently was devolved where possible onto women's unwaged family labor, while the comfortable and some of the poor gained the possibility of access to waged care (of very different sorts) through their own spending on domestic help, or through the welfare state after the Great Society began to subsidize childcare (Michel 2000).

The fragmentary and tiered system that developed in this case did not have an identical structure to healthcare, with its two large public insurers, public subsidies, and public regulation of the whole market through both the contracts of the public insurers and the supervision of private collective bargaining. Nonetheless, childcare shares the basic pattern of public-private fragmentation with the healthcare system (Gustafsson & Stafford 1994). It is similarly, as Abby J. Cohen puts it, "really no system at all, but rather a collection of funding streams" (1996: 26). As regards employment, the insider-outsider dynamic of the post-war welfare state obtains here as well, with outsider care labor in increasing demand after the economic decline of manufacturing becoming sufficiently severe in the 1970s: as working-class women entered the workforce in growing numbers to supplement the lost or suppressed wages of their husbands, demand for childcare skyrocketed. Their status as outsiders – as producers of care and economic security rather than recipients of care and economic security – thus caused the increasingly large childcare workforce to be cemented at the racialized and feminized bottom of the labor market (Tuominen 1994).

Across the different lines of care work, the organizational fragmentation born out of the public-private structure of the welfare state has institutionalized the racial and gendered logics of second-tier citizenship into the employment experiences of care workers. There is, however, one exception, and it proves the rule: primary and secondary education. As an early and anomalous direct extension of state capacity (albeit at the state and local levels), the school system maintained very high rates of immediate public employment – and consequently unionization – in care work, only marginally diminished by attempted privatization in the last several decades (National Center for Education Statistics 2019). While there are still profound problems of underfunding, associated in turn with wage suppression and workload increase, it is nonetheless the case that teachers form a political force unparalleled elsewhere in the care economy – or arguably anywhere in the economy (Blanc 2019). While nurses' unions represent something of an equivalent in healthcare, RNs do not remotely approach teachers either in union density or in terms of success in shaping the institutional conditions of service provision. For example, their primary policy campaign nationwide – staffing regulation – has largely failed to take off (Clark & Clark 2006). This force is manifest in the militancy of teachers' collective action and their ability to maintain incomes and workplace control significantly in excess of the rank-and-file of the healthcare workforce. Indeed, healthcare's enormous bottom ranks, the product of downward pressure on margins, have no comparable equivalent in education: school paraprofessionals and "unskilled" labor (such as cafeteria workers, student safety staff, custodial workers, and so on), while underpaid and exploited – and a dynamic component of the labor movement – are dwarfed in number by teachers (Juravich 2014).

This disjuncture between public education and the rest of the care economy rests on the political power of organized teachers, and this in turn is based on the relatively compressed occupational hierarchy and the overwhelmingly public ownership and administration of the industry. Educational working conditions can be politicized directly, because schools are in the public sector and school workers can more easily speak with one voice (Ashby & Bruno 2016; Schirmer & Apple 2018). For decades, political candidates and ballot initiative campaigns – not to mention social movements – have demanded smaller classrooms, educational provision for different needs by language and ability, and much more. Teachers' unions have long participated in these conflicts, although such struggles generally took a more mediated form in recent history – playing out through electoral campaigns, lobbying, and so on – until the strike wave beginning in 2018. The recent historical phenomenon known as "Red for Ed," however, saw teachers mobilize their social power directly into political power, demanding and securing legislation through political strikes – precisely what has been impossible in the fragmented health and childcare industries, despite what in theory would appear to be the comparable social power of those equally socially necessary care workers (Blanc 2019; Dyke & Bates 2019; Hertel-Fernandez et al. 2021).

CONCLUSION

The care economy's paradox – socially necessary yet not valuable as organized within the United States capitalism – emerged historically from the status of care provision as relatively unamenable to capital accumulation in any direct fashion, regardless of how critical its indirect role in the social reproduction of labor-power and of capitalist society more broadly. Even once it became increasingly commodified in the late twentieth century, care provision – whether not-for-profit or for-profit in terms of its tax status – remained a low-margin undertaking heavily dependent on public subsidy. Even where it attracts major for-profit investors, as in private equity's infiltration of the long-term care industry, it remains essentially a game in which private capital seeks to absorb as much public subsidy as possible while depressing the wage bill and sweating the workforce to the maximum that will not provoke regulatory intervention (Harrington et al. 2011).

Precisely the qualities of care work that have made it relatively resistant – not immune – to commodification, and consequently assigned systematically to subordinated workers as degraded or valueless activity, are in turn fundamentally connected to the process by which the sector has come to occupy so much of the labor market (Benanav 2019). Economic activity more promising for investment, because it offered opportunities for increasing productivity or labor cost arbitrage, was increasingly automated or arbitraged right out of the American labor market – or, like finance, never generated much employment to begin with. What remained, in terms of job growth, were the sectors of employment that had been constructed in one way or another as adjuncts to industrial work, and which became profitable only if labor costs could be held down.[3]

This construction of care as a system surrounding and sustaining capital accumulation was itself political. It regulated race, gender, and sexuality, and it mediated class conflict. It was an undertaking carried out through the state. Ultimately this is the reason that care workers – with the notable exception of teachers – experience so much difficulty in the attempt to improve and control their own working conditions: because their workplaces have been produced by the state and franchised to the private sector to carry out state functions, separating the purpose of the work from its control and administration.

At the same time, as formalized care work has become increasingly central to the economy as a whole, a greater share of the population has become tied up in the problems created by the fissuring of care. In one form or another, almost all of us depend on the healthcare, home care, childcare, and education systems. There exists, mediated through the ever-expanding public-private hodgepodge of our care institutions, a growing degree of social interdependence. Yet this interdependence does not admit of democratic self-governance for the huge populations bound up with it, precisely because of the interposition of private institutional actors.

While one could conceive of democratic means by which care workers and those for whom they care to together determine the shape of the institutions of care provision that shape social life, instead both are caught up in the vicissitudes of private governance, which positions caregivers and those who depend on them as antagonists. When caregiving is fissured, care is rationed by market price (even with public regulation and subsidy), and this rationing device generates an implicit opposition of interests between workers and their patients, clients, or students. Privatized welfare provision, in other words, produces both weak democratic control over a vast area of social activity, and at the same time weak care workers' organization. At the same time, however, it engenders an enormous potential constituency based in the common interest of a system of care that works for the common good, operated by empowered care workers shaping their own conditions of work – and with them, humane conditions of survival for those who depend on them (Dwyer & Wright 2019; Givan 2016; Tronto 2013).

---

[3] On the transformation of labor markets, see Aaron Benanav, "Automation and the Future of Work – 1," *New Left Review* 119 (September-October 2019), 5–38.

REFERENCES

American Hospital Association. 1976. *Taft-Hartley Amendments: Implications for the Healthcare Field*. American Hospital Association.

Amin, Samir. 1974. *Accumulation on a World Scale: Critique of the Theory of Underdevelopment*. Translated by Brian Pearce. New York: Monthly Review Press.

Andrias, Kate. 2019. "An American Approach to Social Democracy: The Forgotten Promise of the Fair Labor Standards Act." *Yale Law Journal*, 128, 3: 616–709.

Ashby, Steven, and Robert Bruno. 2016. *A Fight for the Soul of Public Education: The Story of the Chicago Teachers Strike*. Ithaca, NY: ILR Press.

Autor, David H., Lawrence F. Katz, and Melissa S. Kearney. 2006. "The Polarization of the US Labor Market." *American Economic Review* 96, 2: 189–194.

Benanav, Aaron. 2019. "Automation and the Future of Work – 1." *New Left Review* 119: 5–38.

Blanc, Eric. 2019. *Red State Revolt: The Teachers' Strike Wave and Working-Class Politics*. Brooklyn: Verso.

Blewett, Mary H. 1988. *Men, Women, and Work: Class and Protest in the New England Shoe Industry*. Champaign: University of Illinois Press.

"Blue Cross Enrollment Affected by Steel: Collective Bargaining and Blue Cross." 1959. *Blue Cross Bulletin* 1(8). Isidore Sidney Falk Papers, Sterling Memorial Library. Yale University.

Boris, Eileen. 1994. *Home to Work: Motherhood and the Politics of Industrial Homework in the United States*. Cambridge: Cambridge University Press.

Boris, Eileen, and Jennifer Klein. 2012. *Caring for America: Home Health Workers in the Shadow of the Welfare State*. Oxford: Oxford University Press.

Boris, Eileen, and Sonya Michel. 2001. "Social Citizenship and Women's Right to Work in Post-war America." In *Women's Rights and Human Rights: International Historical Perspectives*, edited by Patricia Grimshaw, Katie Holmes, and Marilyn Lake, 199–219. New York: Palgrave Macmillan.

Boydston, Jeanne. 1990. *Home and Work: Housework, Wages, and the Ideology of Labor in the Early Republic*. Oxford: Oxford University Press

Brenner, Robert. 2006. *The Economics of Global Turbulence*. Brooklyn: Verso.

Brooks, Chris. 2018. "How Massachusetts Healthcare Companies Defeated Question 1." *Jacobin*. November 8, 2018. https://jacobinmag.com/2018/11/question-1-massachusetts-nurses-staffing-patient-ratios

Budig, Michelle J., Melissa J. Hodges, and Paula England. 2019. "Wages of Nurturant and Reproductive Care Workers: Individual and Job Characteristics, Occupational Closure, and Wage-Equalizing Institutions." *Social Problems* 66, 2: 294–319.

Campbell, Andrea Louise, and Kimberly J. Morgan. 2011. *The Delegated Welfare State: Medicare, Markets, and the Governance of Social Policy*. Oxford: Oxford University Press.

Canaday, Margot. 2009. *The Straight State: Sexuality and Citizenship in Twentieth-Century America*. Princeton, NJ: Princeton University Press.

Carré, Françoise, and Chris Tilly. 2017. *Where Bad Jobs Are Better: Retail Jobs across Countries and Companies*. New York: Russell Sage Foundation.

Clark, Paul F., and Darlene A. Clark. 2006. "Union Strategies for Improving Patient Care: The Key to Nurse Unionism." *Labor Studies* 31, 1: 1–19.

Cobble, Dorothy Sue. 1996. "The Prospects for Unionism in a Service Society." In *Working in the Service Society*, edited by Cameron Lynne MacDonald and Carmen Sirianni, 333–358. Philadelphia: Temple University Press.

Cohen, Alan B., David C. Colby, Keith A. Wailoo, and Julian E. Zelizer, eds. 2015. *Medicare and Medicaid at 50: America's Entitlement Programs in the Age of Affordable Care*. Oxford: Oxford University Press.

Cohen, Abby J. 1996. "A Brief History of Federal Financing for Childcare in the United States." *The Future of Children* 6, 2: 26–40.

Cohodes, Donald R., and Brian M. Kinkead. 1984. *Hospital Capital Formation in the 1980s*. Baltimore: Johns Hopkins University Press.

Coontz, Stephanie. 1988. *The Social Origins of Private Life: A History of American Families, 1600–1900*. Brooklyn: Verso.

Cutler, Jonathan. 2004. *Labor's Time: Shorter Hours, the UAW, and the Struggle for American Unionism*. Philadelphia: Temple University Press.

Davis, Mike. 1986. *Prisoners of the American Dream: Politics and Economy in the History of the US Working Class*. Brooklyn: Verso.

Derickson, Alan. 1994. "Health Security for All?: Social Unionism and Universal Health Insurance, 1935–1958." *Journal of American History* 80, 4: 1333–1356.

Dubal, V. B. 2017. "Wage Slave or Entrepreneur: Contesting the Dualism of Legal Worker Identities." *California Law Review* 105, 1: 65–124.

Dublin, Thomas. 1979. *Women at Work: The Transformation of Work and Community in Lowell, Massachusetts, 1826–1860*. New York: Columbia University Press.

Duffy, Mignon. 2011. *Making Care Count: A Century of Gender, Race, and Paid Care Work*. New Brunswick, NJ: Rutgers University Press.

Dwyer, Rachel E. 2013. "The Care Economy? Gender, Economic Restructuring, and Job Polarization in the US Labor Market." *American Sociological Review* 78, 3: 390–416.

Dwyer, Rachel E., and Erik Olin Wright. 2019. "Low-Wage Job Growth, Polarization, and the Limits and Opportunities of the Service Economy." *RSF: The Russell Sage Foundation Journal of the Social Sciences* 5, 4: 56–76.

Dyke, Erin, and Brendan Muckian Bates. 2019. "Educators Striking for a Better World: The Significance of Social Movement and Solidarity Unionisms." *Berkeley Review of Education* 9, 1.

Emmenegger, Patrick, Silja Hausermann, Bruno Palier, and Martin Seeleib-Kaiser, eds. 2012. *The Age of Dualization: The Changing Face of Inequality in Deindustrializing Societies*. Oxford: Oxford University Press.

England, Paula, Michelle Budig, and Nancy Folbre. 2002. "Wages of Virtue: The Relative Pay of Care Work." *Social Problems* 49, 4: 455–473.

Esping-Andersen, Gøsta. 1999. *Social Foundations of Postindustrial Economies*. Oxford: Oxford University Press.

"Exemption of Non-Profit Hospital Employees from the National Labor Relations Act: A Violation of Equal Protection." 1971. *Iowa Law Review* 57, 2: 412–450.

Ferguson, Susan. 2019. *Women and Work: Feminism, Labor, and Social Reproduction*. London: Pluto.

Friedman, Sheldon, Richard W. Hurd, Rudolph A. Oswald, and Ronald L. Seeber, eds. 1994. *Restoring the Promise of American Labor Law*. Ithaca, NY: Cornell University Press.

Gilmore, Ruth Wilson. 1999. "Globalization and US Prison Growth: From Military Keynesianism to Post-Keynesian Militarism." *Race & Class* 40, 2-3: 171–188.

2007. *Golden Gulag: Prisons, Surplus, Crisis, and Opposition in Globalizing California*. Berkeley: University of California Press.

Givan, Rebecca Kolins. 2016. *The Challenge to Change: Reforming Healthcare on the Front Line in the United States and the United Kingdom*. Ithaca, NY: Cornell University Press.

Glenn, Evelyn Nakano. 1992. "From Servitude to Service Work: Historical Continuities in the Racial Division of Paid Reproductive Labor." *Signs* 18, 1: 1–43.

Glenn, Susan A. 1990. *Daughters of the Shtetl: Life and Labor in the Immigrant Generation*. Ithaca, NY: Cornell University Press.

Greenwald, Maurine Weiner. 1989. "Working-Class Feminism and the Family Wage Ideal." *Journal of American History* 76, 1: 118–149.

Gustafsson, Siv., and Frank P. Stafford. 1994. "Three Regimes of Childcare: The United States, the Netherlands, and Sweden." In *Social Protection Versus Economic Flexibility: Is There a Trade-Off?* edited by Rebecca M. Blank, 333–362. Chicago: University of Chicago Press.

Harrington, Michael. 1962. *The Other America: Poverty in America*. New York: Simon & Schuster.

Harrington, Charlene, Brian Olney, Helen Carrillo, and Taewoon Kang. 2011. *Health Services Research* 47, 1: 106–128.

Hartwig, Jochen. 2015. "Structural Change, Aggregate Demand, and Employment Dynamics in the OECD, 1970–2010." *Structural Change and Economic Dynamics* 34: 36–45.

Hartzell, Dan. 1988. "Ritter Promises Help on Pensions." *Allentown Morning Call*, May 16, 1988.

Health Policy Institute. 1984. "The Implications of a Changing Economy for the Hospital System in Southwestern Pennsylvania." Records of the Health and Welfare Planning Association, 1908–1980, Library and Archives Division, Senator John Heinz History Center.

Hertel-Fernandez, Alex, Suresh Naidu, and Adam Reich. 2021. "Schooled by Strikes? The Effects of Large-Scale Labor Unrest on Mass Attitudes toward the Labor Movement." *Perspectives on Politics* 19, 1: 73–91.

Hunter, Tera W. 1997. *To 'Joy my Freedom: Southern Black Women's Lives and Labors after the Civil War*. Cambridge, MA: Harvard University Press.

Iversen, Torben, and Anne Wren. 1998. "Equality, Employment, and Budgetary Restraint: The Trilemma of the Service Economy." *World Politics* 50, 4: 507–546.

Iversen, Torben, and Thomas R. Cusack. 2000. "The Causes of Welfare State Expansion: Deindustrialization or Globalization?" *World Politics* 52, 3: 313–349.

Jacobs, Meg. 2005. *Pocketbook Politics: Economic Citizenship in Twentieth-Century America*. Princeton, NJ: Princeton University Press.

Johnson, David K. 2004. *The Lavender Scare: The Cold War Persecution of Gays and Lesbians in the Federal Government*. Chicago: University of Chicago Press.

Juravich, Nicholas Albert. 2017. "The Work of Education: Community-Based Educators in Schools, Freedom Struggles, and the Labor Movement, 1953–1983." PhD diss., Columbia University.

Kahlenberg, Richard D., and Moshe Z. Marvit. 2013. "Architects of Democracy: Labor Organizing as a Civil Right." *Stanford Journal of Civil Rights and Civil Liberties* 9, 2: 213–246.

Kalleberg, Arne L. 2009. "Precarious Work, Insecure Workers: Employment Relations in Transition." *American Sociological Review* 74, 1: 1–22.

Katznelson, Ira. 1989. "Was the Great Society a Lost Opportunity?" In *The Rise and Fall of the New Deal Order, 1930–1980*, edited by Steve Fraser and Gary Gerstle, 185–211. Princeton, NJ: Princeton University Press.

Kessler-Harris, Alice. 1983. *Out to Work: A History of Wage-Earning Women in the United States*. Oxford: Oxford University Press.

    2001. *In Pursuit of Equity: Women, Men, and the Quest for Economic Citizenship in the Twentieth Century*. Oxford: Oxford University Press.

Klein, Jennifer. 2003. *For All These Rights: Business, Labor, and the Shaping of America's Public-Private Welfare State*. Princeton, NJ: Princeton University Press.

Korstad, Robert, and Nelson Lichtenstein. 1988. "Opportunities Found and Lost: Labor, Radicals, and the Early Civil Rights Movement." *Journal of American History* 75, 1: 786–811.

Lichtenstein, Nelson. 1989. "From Corporatism to Collective Bargaining: Organized Labor and the Eclipse of Social Democracy in the Post-war era." In *The Rise and Fall of the New Deal Order, 1930–1980*, edited by Steve Fraser and Gary Gerstle, 122–152. Princeton, NJ: Princeton University Press.

    1995. *The Most Dangerous Man in Detroit: Walter Reuther and the Fate of American Labor*. New York: Basic Books.

Lopez, Steven Henry. 2004. *Reorganizing the Rust Belt: An Inside Study of the American Labor Movement*. Berkeley: University of California Press.

Marmor, Theodore R. 1970. *The Politics of Medicare*. Piscataway, NJ: Transaction Press.

Marmor, Theodore R., Jerry L. Mashaw, and Philip L. Harvey. 1990. *America's Misunderstood Welfare State: Persistent Myths, Enduring Realities*. New York: Basic Books.

May, Martha. 1985. "Bread before Roses: American Workingmen, Labor Unions, and the Family Wage." In *Women, Work, and Protest: A century of US Women's Labor History*, edited by Ruth Milkman, 1–21. New York: Routledge.

McAlevey, Jane. 2016. *No Shortcuts: Organizing for Power in the New Gilded Age*. Oxford: Oxford University Press.

McCartin, Joseph A. 2011. *Collision Course: Ronald Reagan, the Air Traffic Controllers, and the Strike That Changed America*. Oxford: Oxford University Press.

McEnaney, Laura. 2014. "A Women's Peace Dividend: Demobilization and Working Class Women in Chicago, 1945–1953." In *Gender and the Long Post-war: The United States and the Two Germanys, 1945–1989*, edited by Karen Hagemann and Sonya Michel, 73–94. Baltimore: Johns Hopkins University Press.

Michel, Sonya. 2000. *Children's Interests/Mother's Rights: The Shaping of America's Childcare Policy*. New Haven, CT: Yale University Press.

Milkman, Ruth. 1987. *Gender at Work: The Dynamics of Job Segregation by Sex during World War II*. Urbana: University of Illinois Press.

Mittelstadt, Jennifer. 2015. *The Rise of the Military Welfare State*. Cambridge, MA: Harvard University Press.

Montgomery, Edward A., and Otto A. Davis. 1990. "Private Income Security Schemes in Times of Crisis: A Case Study of US Steel." *Labor and Society* 15, 1: 75–88.

Morris, Charles J. 2005. *The Blue Eagle at Work: Reclaiming Democratic Rights in the American Workplace*. Ithaca, NY: ILR Press.

Musselwhite, James C. Jr., Rosalyn B. Katz, and Lester B. Salamon. 1985. *Government Spending and the Nonprofit Sector in Pittsburgh/Allegheny County*. The Urban Institute Press.

Nordhaus, William D. 2008. "Baumol's Diseases: A Macroeconomic Perspective." *The B.E. Journal of Macroeconomics* 8, 1. 1–39.

Offner, Amy C. 2019. *Sorting Out the Mixed Economy: The Rise and Fall of Welfare and Developmental States in the Americas*. Princeton, NJ: Princeton University Press.

Paul, Sanjukta M. 2016. "The Enduring Ambiguities of Antitrust Liability for Worker Collective Action." *Loyola University Chicago Law Journal*, 47, 3: 969–1048.

Paul-Shaheen, Pamela, and Eugenia S. Carpenter. 1982. "Legislating Hospital Bed Reduction: The Michigan Experience." *Journal of Health Policy, Politics, and Law* 6, 4: 653–675.

Rachleff, Peter. 1993. *Hard-Pressed in the Heartland: The Hormel Strike and the Future of the Labor Movement*. Boston: South End Press.

"Researchers Examine Steelworkers' Benefits." 1986. *Latrobe Bulletin*. May 9, 1986.

Retiree Health Benefits: The Fair-Weather Promise: Hearings before the Special Committee on Aging of the US Senate, 99th Congress, 2nd sess. (1987).

Rosen, Ruth. 1982. *The Lost Sisterhood: Prostitution in America*. Baltimore: Johns Hopkins University Press.

Rosenblat, Alex. 2018. *Uberland: How Algorithms Are Rewriting the Rules of Work*. Berkeley: University of California Press.

Rosenblum, Jonathan D. 1995. *Copper Crucible: How the Arizona Miners' Strike of 1983 Recast Labor-Management Relations in America*. Ithaca, NY: ILR Press.

Rosenfeld, Jake. 2014. *What Unions No Longer Do*. Cambridge, MA: Harvard University Press.

Schirmer, Eleni, and Michael W. Apple. 2018. "Struggling for the Local: Money, Power, and the Possibilities of Victories in the Politics of Education." In *The Struggle for Democracy in Education: Lessons from Social Realities*, edited by Michael W. Apple, 41–68. New York: Routledge.

Schwartz, William P., and Daniel N. Mendelson. 1991. "Hospital Cost Containment in the 1980s – Hard Lessons Learned and Prospects for the 1990s." *New England Journal of Medicine* 324, 15: 1037–1042.

Slater, Joseph E. 2017. *Public Workers: Government Employee Unions, the Law, and the State, 1900–1962*. Ithaca, NY: Cornell University Press.

Stapleford, Thomas A. 2009. *The Cost of Living in America: A Political History of Economic Statistics, 1880–2000*. Cambridge: Cambridge University Press.

Stevens, Robert, and Rosemary Stevens. 1974. *Welfare Medicine in America: A Case Study of Medicaid*. New York: The Free Press.

Stoltzfus, Emilie. 2003. *Citizen, Mother, Worker: Debating Public Responsibility for Childcare after the Second World War*. Chapel Hill: University of North Carolina Press.

Storm, Servaas. 2018. "The New Normal: Demand, Secular Stagnation, and the Vanishing Middle Class." *International Journal of Political Economy* 46, 4: 169–210

Storrs, Landon. 2013. *The Second Red Scare and the Unmaking of the New Deal Left*. Princeton, NJ: Princeton University Press.

Sugrue, Thomas J. 1996. *The Origins of the Urban Crisis: Race and Inequality in Post-war Detroit*. Princeton, NJ: Princeton University Press.

Swinth, Kirsten. 2018. *Feminism's Forgotten Fight: The Unfinished Struggle for Work and Family*. Cambridge, MA: Harvard University Press.

Temin, Peter. 2017. *The Vanishing Middle Class: Prejudice and Power in a Dual Economy*. Cambridge, MA: MIT Press.

Torassa, Ulysses. 1988. "Director of PBGC Turns Optimist." *Pittsburgh Post-Gazette*. January 23, 1988.

Tronto, Joan C. 2013. *Caring Democracy: Markets, Equality, and Justice*. New York: New York University Press.

Tuominen, Mary. 1994. "The Hidden Organization of Labor: Gender, Race/Ethnicity and Childcare Work in the Formal and Informal Economy." *Sociological Perspectives* 37, 2: 229–245.

Weil, David. 2014. *The Fissured Workplace: Why Work Became So Bad for So Many and What Can Be Done*. Cambridge, MA: Harvard University Press.

Winant, Gabriel. 2019. "'Hard Times Make for Hard Arteries and Hard Livers': Deindustrialization, Biopolitics, and the Making of a New Working Class." *Journal of Social History* 53, 1: 107–132.

Windham, Lane. 2017. *Knocking on Labor's Door: Union Organizing in the 1970s and the Roots of a New Economic Divide*. Chapel Hill: University of North Carolina Press.

Woloch, Nancy. 2015. *A Class by Herself: Protective Laws for Women Workers, 1890s–1990s*. Princeton, NJ. Princeton University Press.

Wren, Anne, ed. 2013. *The Political Economy of the Service Transition*. Oxford: Oxford University Press.

Index

Ingram Content Group UK Ltd.
Milton Keynes UK
UKHW031824040523
421036UK00014B/44